Auxiliary Verb Constructions

OXFORD STUDIES IN TYPOLOGY AND LINGUISTIC THEORY

SERIES EDITORS: Ronnie Cann, *University of Edinburgh*, William Croft, *University of New Mexico*, Scott DeLancey, *University of Oregon*, Martin Haspelmath, *Max Planck Institute Leipzig*, Nicholas Evans, *University of Melbourne*, Anna Siewierska, *University of Lancaster*

PUBLISHED

Classifiers: A Typology of Noun Categorization Devices
Alexandra Y. Aikhenvald

Auxiliary Verb Constructions
Gregory D. S. Anderson

Pronouns
D. N. S. Bhat

Subordination
Sonia Cristofaro

The Paradigmatic Structure of Person Marking
Michael Cysouw

Indefinite Pronouns
Martin Haspelmath

Anaphora
Yan Huang

Copulas
Regina Pustet

The Noun Phrase
Jan Rijkhoff

Intransitive Predication
Leon Stassen

Co-Compounds and Natural Coordination
Bernhard Wälchli

PUBLISHED IN ASSOCIATION WITH THE SERIES

The World Atlas of Language Structures
edited by Martin Haspelmath, Matthew Dryer, Bernard Comrie, and David Gil

IN PREPARATION
Reciprocals
Nicholas Evans

Applicative Constructions
David Peterson

Double Object Constructions
Maria Polinsky

Auxiliary Verb Constructions

GREGORY D. S. ANDERSON

OXFORD
UNIVERSITY PRESS

OXFORD
UNIVERSITY PRESS

Great Clarendon Street, Oxford OX2 6DP

Oxford University Press is a department of the University of Oxford.
It furthers the University's objective of excellence in research, scholarship,
and education by publishing worldwide in

Oxford New York

Auckland Cape Town Dar es Salaam Hong Kong Karachi
Kuala Lumpur Madrid Melbourne Mexico City Nairobi
New Delhi Shanghai Taipei Toronto

With offices in

Argentina Austria Brazil Chile Czech Republic France Greece
Guatemala Hungary Italy Japan Poland Portugal Singapore
South Korea Switzerland Thailand Turkey Ukraine Vietnam

Oxford is a registered trade mark of Oxford University Press
in the UK and in certain other countries

Published in the United States
by Oxford University Press Inc., New York

© Gregory D.S. Anderson 2006

The moral rights of the author have been asserted
Database right Oxford University Press (maker)

First published 2006

British Library Cataloguing in Publication Data

Data available

Library of Congress Cataloguing in Publication Data

Data available

Typeset by SPI Publisher Services, Pondicherry, India
Printed in Great Britain
on acid-free paper by
Biddles Ltd., King's Lynn

ISBN 978–019–928031–5

3 5 7 9 10 8 6 4 2

TO MARY

Contents

Acknowledgements

This study of auxiliary verb constructions was at different times funded by grants from the following organizations: Hans Rausing Fund for Endangered Language Preservation, Volkswagen Stiftung, IREX and the Wenner-Gren Foundation. This support is gratefully acknowledged. I would also like to thank audiences or participants at the following for sharing comments on earlier versions of parts of various chapters, including CLS 1999, WECOL 1999, University of Manchester Grammatical Change Seminar in 2002 and 2003, and the Departmental Seminar at Swarthmore College 2005 in particular. All errors of course remain my own.

Tables

List of Abbreviations

>	operating on	~	alternates with
†	extinct	1	1st person
1INB	1st inclusive series-B	1R	Relating to first person
2	2nd person	3	3rd person
3∧INC	3rd sg. Incompletive	3DIR	3rd person Directive
3NS	3rd Non-singular	3NSP	3rd Non-Sing. Perfective
3NM	3rd Non-masculine	9/10	Class-9/10
I	Class I	II	Class II
III	Class III	IV	Class IV
A	Agent	ABIL	Abilitive
ABL	Ablative	ABS	Absolutive
ACC	Accusative	ACT	Actor
ACTN:NMLZ	Action Nominalizer	ADESS	Adessive
ADJ	Adjective	ADV	Adverbial
AFF	Affected	AGT	Agent
ALL	Allative	ALLOC	Allocentric
ANA	Anaphora, Anaphoric	ANIM	Animate
ANT	Anterior	AOR	Aorist
AP	Aorist Participle	APPL	Applicative
ART	Article	ASSOC	Associative
ASP	Aspect[ual]	ASS	Assertive
ASSUM	Assumptive	ATT	Attemptive
ATTR	Attributive	AUG	Augment
AUGM	Augmented	AUX	Auxiliary (verb)
AV	Auxiliary verb	AVC	Auxiliary Verb Construction
BEN	Benefactive	BFR	Buffer
BITV	Bivalent Itive	BND	Bounded
BNDRY	Boundary	CA	Completed Action
CAP	Capabilitive	CAUS	Causative
CD	Compounding Suffix	CEL	Celerative
CERT	Certainty	CL	Classifier
CLOC	Cislocative	CLS	Class
CLS.5	Class-5	CLSFR	Classifier

CM	Concatenative Marker	CNJ	Conjunct
CNJCTV	Conjunctive	CNSTR	Construct
CNTRFACT	Counterfactual	COM	Comitative
COMP	Complementizer	COMPL	Completive
CON.ADV	Connective Adverbial	CONC	Concord
CON[D]	Conditional	CONJ	Conjunction
CONN	Connective	CONNEG	Connegative
CONSEC	Consecutive	CONT	Continuative
COORD	Coordinate	COP	Copula[r]
COREF	Coreferential	CTP	Contemporative
CURR	Current	CUST	Customary
CV	Converb	DAT	Dative
DC	Derivational Clitic	DEBIT	Debitative
DECL	Declarative	DEF	Definite
DEM	Demonstrative	DEONT	Deontic
DEP	Dependent	DES	Desiderative
DESCR	Descriptive	DETR	Detransitivizer
DIM	Diminutive	DIR	Directional
DISJ	Disjunct	DIST	Distal
DIST.PST	Distant Past	DISTR	Distributive
DL	Dual	DO	Direct Object
DS	Different Subject	DSOC	Dissociative
DUBIT	Dubitative	DUR	Durative
DVBL	Deverbalizer	EFF	Effected
EMB	Embedded	EMPH	Emphatic
EP	Epenthetic	EPIPAT	Epipatetic
ERG	Ergative	ES	Echo Subject
ESS	Essive	EVID	Evidential
EVNT	Event	EX	Exclusive
EXHORT	Exhortative	EXOC	Exocentric
EXT	Extent, Extension	EYWTNS	Eyewitness
F	Feminine	FACT	Factitive
FIN	Finite	FOC	Focus
FP.FV	Feminine Past Final Verb	FPN	Free Pronominal
FREQ	Frequentative	FUT	Future
FV	Final Vowel	GEN	Genitive
GIV	Given	GER	Gerund
GNRL	General	H	Honorific
HAB	Habitual	HMN.ARG	Human Argument
HON	Honorific	HORT	Hortative

HPL	Human Plural	HSY	Hearsay
HYP	Hypothetical	IE	Indo-European
ID	Identification Clitic	IFT	Infinite Complement
I.I	Independent Indicative	ILL	Illative
IM	Immediacy	IMC	Imperfective Converb
IMM	Immediate	IMP	Imperative
IMPF	Imperfect[ive]	IN	Inclusive
INAN	Inanimate	INC^MID	Incompletive Mid tone
INCEP	Inceptive	INCH	Inchoative
INCL	Inclusive	INCOMPL	Incompletive
IND	Indicative	INDEF	Indefinite
INDEP	Independent	INDMA	Indicative, male addressee
INF	Infinitive		
INFER	Inferential	INHAB	Inhabitant
INNER.REL	Inner relation	INS	Instrumental
INT	Intentional	INTNSF	Intensifier
INTNSV	Intensive	INV	Inverse
INVIS	Invisible	INVOL	Involuntary State
IPFV	Imperfective	IRF	Irrealis Future
IRR	Irrealis	ITER	Iterative
ITR	Intransitive	JUNC	Juncture
KY	*ky*-class	LEX	Lexical
LIG	Ligative	LIM	Limiter
LOC	Locative	LV	Lexical verb
M	Masculine	MAN	Manner
MDL	Middle	MF	Mono-focal
MIN	Minimal	MOD	Modal
MP	Medio-Passive	MR	Modified Root
MR 1	Modal Root 1	MRKR	Marker
MS	Masculine Singular	MULT.ACT	Multiple Action
NACT	Non-Actual	NAR	Narrative
NEG	Negative	NEUT	Neuter, Neutral
NF	Non-Final; Non-Finite	NFUT	Non-Future
NH	Non-Honorific	NMLZR	Nominalizer
NOM	Nominative; Nominal	NONACC	Non-Accomplished
NONSEQ	Non-Sequential	NONSPEC	Non-Specific
NONSPKR	Non-Speaker	NONWIT	Non-Witnessed
NPRS	Non-Present	NPST	Non-Past
NR.PST	Near Past	NSG	Non-Singular
NSP	Non-Specific	O	Object

OA	Orientation Auxiliary	OBJ	Object
OBLG	Obligative	OBLQ	Oblique
OBS.VWPT	Observer's Viewpoint	OBV	Obviative
OCC.WITH	Occupied with	OF	O[bj]-Focus
OPT	Optative	P	Patient
PASS	Passive	PAT	Patient
PAUC	Paucal	PAUS	Pausal
PBL	Possibilitive	PC	Progressive Clitic
P/E	Prosecutive/Equative	PERL	Perlative
PERM	Permissive	PF	Perfect[ive] (Babungo)
P/F	Present/Future	PI	Punctiliar Indicative
PL	Plural	PL.INC	Plural Inclusive
PLUP	Pluperfect	PM	Predicate marker (IMPRF)
POL	Polite	POLYFOC	Polyfocal
POSS	Possessive	POSTP	Postposition
POT	Potential	PP	Past participle
PREP	Prepostion	PREPRO	Pre-pronominal
PRES	Present	PRET	Preterite
PREV	Previous	PRF	Perfect
PRFV	Perfective	PRGPRC	Progressive Particle
PROB	Probabilitive	PROG	Progressive
PROHIB	Prohibitive	PROL	Prolative
PROSEC	Prosecutive	PROX	Proximate
PRPF	Present Perfective	PRS	Present
PRTCL	Particle	PRTCPL	Participle
PRX	Proximal	PSB	Possibilitive
PSSV	Passive	PST	Past
PSYCH	Psychological State Verbalizer	PUNC	Punctual
		PURP	Purposive
PV	Preverb	Q	Interrogative
QT	Quot, Quotative	RCPNT	Recipient
REC.INTERNAL	Recent Past Internal	RECIP	Reciprocal
REC.PST	Recent Past	REDPL	Reduplication
REF	Reference	REM	Remote
REPET	Repetitive	REPRT	Reportative
RES	Resumptive	RESTRCV	Restrictive
RF	Remote Future	RFLX	Reflexive
RLS	Realis	RP	Remote Past
RR	Reflexive/Reciprocal	RXP	Reflexive Pronoun
S	Subject	S=O	Subject = matrix object

SBJ	Subjunctive	SBNR	Subordinator
SBSC	Subsecutive	SER	Serialized
SF	Stem-Formant	SFX	Suffix
SG	Singular	SIM	Simultaneity
SIMULT	Simultaneous	SPC	Specifier
SPCF	Specificity	SS	Same Subject
ST.EXT	Stem Extension	SUB	Subordinate
SUBJ	Subject	SUBORD	Subordinator
SUBSEQ	Subsequential	SUFF	Suffix
SUP	Supine	SUPP	Support Verb
SVC	serial verb construction	SW	Switch Subject
T	Tense	T/A	Tense/Aspect
TAM	Tense Aspect Mood	TEMP	Temporal
TEMP.STAT	Temporary State	TH	Thematic
THM	Theme	TLOC	Translocative
TNS	Tense	TOP	Topic
TOP.CHGE	Topic Change	TP	Today's Past
TR	Transitive	TRANSIT	Transitional
TRNSTVZR	Transitivizer	UA	Unit Augmented
UNACMPL	Unaccomplished	UND	Undergoer
UNEXP	Unexpected	UNFIN	Unfinished
UNM	Unmarked	V, VB	Verb
VB.EXT	Verb Extension	VBLZR	Verbalizer
VC	Verb Class	VE	Verbal extension
VENT	Ven[i]tive	VERS	Version
VI	Verb Introducer	VISIB	Visible
VN	Verbal Noun	VPT	Viewpoint
X	Unidentified Morpheme		

1

Auxiliaries and Auxiliary Verb Constructions

Introduction and overview

The present volume constitutes a discussion of the inflectional patterns attested in auxiliary verb constructions among the languages of the world. It addresses, among other topics, formal patterns of inflection, the nature of heads and headedness (and, by association, dependency) in auxiliary verb constructions and generally, and historical developments in creating these patterns in auxiliary verb systems, including the relation of serial verb constructions to auxiliary verb constructions and shifts from bi-clausal complement or clause chained structures to auxiliary verb constructions.

The approach I am taking in this volume can be described as panchronic functional-constructional. It is functional in the sense that the object of study is defined as a particular continuum of verb–verb combinations occupying a large but restricted range of functional domains. The study is constructional in that the data observed and analysed are concerned with the formal means of encoding functional (morphosyntactic) categories projected across components of a construction. Lastly, the study is panchronic as its object of investigation considers synchronic (bipartite) auxiliary verb constructions, as well as variation and diachronic developments, including univerbation of former auxiliary verb constructions into complex verb-words.

1.1 Sampling methodology

The basis of the typology presented in this volume was first developed in a range of recent studies (Anderson 1999, 2000, 2004a). The database for the discussion throughout the book is a set of approximately 800 representative languages from across the world, sampled predominantly according to principles discussed in the typological literature (e.g. Bell 1978, Dryer 1989, Rijkhoff et al. 1993, Rijkhoff and Bakker 1998, Perkins 2001; cf. also Dryer

1992, Blake 2001, Song 2001), together with my own insights on general typological research on the one hand and auxiliary verbs on the other.

Admittedly, the various studies just mentioned differ considerably from one another in their individual approaches and recommendations. In the present volume, the sampling method that I use is based on insights gained from these sources and my own experience doing linguistic typology. Like many samples, I attempt to be as genetically and geographically representative of linguistic diversity globally as possible. This means not only large-level stocks like Indo-European but relevant large subdivisions, where possible. I thus have every major subgroup of Indo-European represented except for Tocharian (viz. Albanian, Anatolian, Armenian, Baltic, Celtic, Germanic, Greek, Indo-Aryan, Iranian, Italic/Romance, and Slavic). In addition, I have included as many language isolates and members of micro-families as possible and relevant as well. This includes Ket, Nivkh, Yukaghir, Zuni, Warembori, Sulka, Oksapmin, Chamacoco, Itonama, Movima, Pirahã, Warao, Mapudungun, Yagua, Huave, Seri, Haida, Wappo, and Burushaski.

However, it must be noted that the language samples used in all typological surveys are inherently convenience samples to some extent, that is, dependent on languages which have been described or which can be determined (based on what sources are available) to have (or not have) the feature under investigation—i.e. which languages have descriptions or experts that can be consulted. This is of, course, not strictly in accord with the principles of maximal genetic and geographical diversity.

Another characteristic of the sample used in this study stems from my interest in both macro-level and micro-level variation. Ignoring micro-level diversity in closely related languages is surely to be avoided when doing typology, and thus, where relevant, data from several closely related languages are included in the present volume. The selection of such language groups on which to focus this micro-variationist analysis is based mainly on insight gleaned from my personal experience with the languages in question or their traditions of analysis. Stated differently, having studied a large number of languages from a wide range of families, I have become acquainted with families and/or regions where the languages have particularly rich, developed, or otherwise interesting systems of auxiliary verb constructions. Often, there is considerable variation in formal types of auxiliary verb constructions from an inflectional standpoint within a language family, or even within a single language. This variation is sometimes systematic and explainable from a historical perspective. Such variation can only be examined if a sufficiently large number of related languages are included. Thus, language 'super-families' like Bantu and Oceanic each have a large number of entries not only because of the sheer size of the unit in question, and thus the need to include languages from as many subgroups as possible, but also because of the fact there are extensive, developed, and varied systems of auxiliary verb constructions found in a wide range of the languages. Other smaller families are also well represented in the sample because they happen to possess a large number of structurally (and functionally) varied auxiliary verb constructions, and these are discussed in some detail. For example, there are thirty-two Turkic languages represented among the languages of the database. For a complete list of the languages used in the database, see the Appendix.

The present investigation primarily, though not exclusively, includes languages showing some kind of bound or fused functional elements, in the guise of affixes or clitics, and the languages cited here also mainly exclude those with no auxiliary verb forms described in, or perceivable from, the relevant sources. This latter set includes both languages with extreme degrees of synthesis that have obscured the auxiliary origins of various pertinent functional categories within the verbal complex, as well as most but not all languages traditionally referred to as 'isolating'. To be sure, these latter languages often show auxiliary-like functional elements which occur in specific, designated positions relative to lexical verbal elements and which index/ encode functional categories of the predicate and which are of verbal origin. However, due to a variety of reasons, including both practical considerations of space, but most importantly, the fact that these verbal phenomena are sufficiently interesting and complex in these isolating languages to merit their own specialized investigation, such phenomena are only briefly touched upon herein, particularly in the discussion of verb serialization, doubled inflection, and the LEX-headed inflectional pattern, in Chapters 3, 4, and 7.[1]

Examples in the chapters are roughly presented in the order of the following four macro-areas: Eurasia, Africa, macro-Indo-Pacific, and New World. To the first category, include all Indo-European languages, Caucasian languages, all Sino-Tibetan languages, Dravidian, Burushaski, all Uralic, 'Altaic', and isolates and small families of Siberia, Austroasiatic and other Southeast Asian languages, and languages of the Middle East. To Africa belong the languages of the four super-stocks: Khoisan, Afroasiatic, Nilo-Saharan, and Niger-Congo. The languages of the widespread and large Bantu family are often treated separately from the (perhaps) genetically related languages of West Africa. To the macro-Indo-Pacific region belong the Australian

---

[1] Also, as pointed by Schiller (1990), in these so-called 'isolating' languages, it is sometimes difficult to distinguish 'finite' and 'non-finite' forms of verbs and more importantly between nouns and verbs on multiple levels.

TABLE 1.1. Macro-grouping for data presentation

Eurasia	Africa	Macro-Indo-Pacific	New World
Indo-European	Khoisan	Papuan phyla	North American phyla
Sino-Tibetan	Afroasiatic	Australian	South American phyla
Afroasiatic	Nilo-Saharan	Austronesian	Mesoamerican phyla
Uralic	Niger-Congo		
Caucasian languages			
Dravidian			
Austroasiatic			
'Altaic' families			
Eurasian isolates			
and other			
small families			
Southeast Asia			

Aboriginal languages, Oceanic, and other Austronesian languages, as well as the non-Austronesian 'Papuan' languages of New Guinea, Indonesia, and surrounding islands. Finally, New World languages are presented in the roughly geographical divisions of North America, South America, and Meso-America.[2]

1.2 Auxiliary verbs as understood in this volume

Before launching into the discussion, a brief definition is here given of how the terms used in the present work are understood. Overall it can be said that I am sympathetic with the understanding of auxiliaries and the process of auxiliation expressed in Heine (1993) and Kuteva (2001): that auxiliaries are not discrete entities *per se* but rather mono-clausal form–function combinations occupying a non-discrete space on several large form–function continua that include serial verb constructions, clause-chaining, and verb plus complement clause combinations on the one hand and tense-aspect-mood affixes on the other.

'Auxiliary verb' is here considered to be an item on the lexical verb–functional affix continuum, which tends to be at least somewhat semantically bleached, and grammaticalized to express one or more of a range of salient verbal categories, most typically aspectual and modal categories, but also not

---

[2] These should be understood only as a means of organizational convenience, not as indicative of large, macro-areal groupings in any linguistic sense.

infrequently temporal, negative polarity, or voice categories. Auxiliary verbs can thus be considered to be an element that in combination with a lexical verb forms a monoclausal verb phrase[3] with some degree of (lexical) semantic bleaching that performs some more or less definable grammatical function; see also the definition of 'auxiliary verb construction' below. An auxiliary verb has structural reality and therefore exists in representational form in the interlinear glosses as AUX in its default manifestation.[4] Although I use the term 'auxiliary verb' to refer to this entity so expressed in the glossing (which may have occasional Ø-(null) realizations in individual constructions in individual languages), it is worth mentioning that this term should be understood more in the context of the combinatorial matrices described below: auxiliary verb constructions.

This definition of auxiliary verb is admittedly somewhat vague. This is intentional. There is no, and probably cannot be, any specific, language-independent formal criteria that can be used to determine the characterization of any given element as a lexical verb or an auxiliary verb. As in all scalar, gradual, or gradient phenomena, clines of grammaticalization and semantic bleaching have 'grey areas', where the element in question has accrued some features generally associated with end-points or focal points on the continuum (i.e. canonical realization of the form–function cluster called auxiliary verb), but perhaps not other features. It seems likely that the degree of grammaticalization and semantic bleaching deemed sufficient to stop calling some particular verbal element X_V usages of lexical verb X_{LV} and start calling it auxiliary verb X_{AV} will vary from researcher to researcher, even when working on the same language. As Heine (1993: 66) notes, 'we are dealing with chains [of grammaticalization] and since chains are by definition continuous structures, setting up stages along these structures must remain an arbitrary and/or artificial endeavor'.

The grammaticalization path of L[exical] V[erb] > > A[uxiliary] V > AF[fi]X is a common one (for more on this see Chapter 7). According to Heine (1993: 48ff.), during the period of shift from full lexical verb to grammaticalized functional element, there is a certain amount of ambiguity associated with the use of the not-yet semantically bleached auxiliary element: think *I am going to work* in English with ambiguity between a literal motion

---

[3] Often from a historically biclausal complement, clause-chained formation, or monoclausal serialized structure, with potential for morphosyntactic residue in various instances where relevant.

[4] Note that, although highly interesting from both a historical developmental and functional perspective, the irregular or archaic allomorphy exhibited by inflected forms of auxiliary verbs in paradigms (as with forms of 'be' many in Indo-European languages, English 'have' etc.), merits independent in-depth analysis and thus remains beyond the scope of the present volume.

interpretation with a nominal complement and a functional interpretation (a variant of the future) with a verbal form in the infinitive complement of a new AVC in 'be going (to)'. Thus, a form may have lexical functions simultaneous with other uses of the same (or almost the same) string as a grammatical operator, the former usually restricted to particular context(s).

Indeed, a single element can be found as a lexical verb, in a variety of auxiliary verb constructions, and as a bound element within a single synchronic state in a single individual language. Take for example the verb stem *al*-in Xakas, a Turkic language of Siberia. As a main verb, it means simply 'take' or 'get'. This element has been grammaticalized from a quasi-serialized formation as a marker of subject version (1ii-ii) or self-benefactive voice (action benefiting the actor). It has been further grammaticalized as a marker of perfective aspect (1iv) and capabilitive mood (1iii), albeit in three separate, independent developments. Finally, for many speakers, with the verb 'find' *tap*-it has been fused in the subject version function into a verbal affix (1v); a similar phenomenon is encountered in certain people's speech with the lexical verb 'take' *al*-in the function of a capabilitive mood affix as well (1vi).

(1) Xakas (Turkic; Siberia)

  a. *pɪs köp aŋ-nar   at-ɪp al-ɣan-da,   köp axča al-ɣa-bɪs*
      we a lot animal-PL shoot-CV SUBJ.VERS-PST-LOC a lot money get-PST-1PL
      'when we shot ourselves a lot of animals, we got a lot of money'
      (Anderson 1998a: 69) [AVC$_i$, LVC]

  b. *min tay ɣa-da čör-čedɪp,   köp čistek teer-ɪp   al-ɣa-m*
      I   taiga-LOC   walk-PRES-CV a lot berry gather-CV SUBJ.VERS-PST-1
      'while walking in the taiga, I gathered up a lot of berries'
      (Anderson 1998a: 54) [AVC$_i$]

  c. *ol   pu   nime-nɪ   al-ɪp   al-ar*
      s/he this thing-ACC take-CV CAP-FUT
      'she will be able to take this'
      (Field notes) [AVC$_j$]

  d. *min anda öz-ɪp=teen-ɪp   al-ɣan-ja   pol-ɣa-bɪn*
      I   there grow-CV open-CV PRF-PST-P/E be-PST-1
      'I was there until it grew and opened'
      (Anderson 1998a: 79) [AVC$_k$]

e. *ɲu kniga-nɨ*   tab–il–za-m   min xayda   örɪn-e-m
   this book-ACC   find-SUBJ.VERS-CON-1   I   oh.boy   be.happy-FUT-1
   'if I find this book, boy will I be happy'
   (Field notes) [AFXᵢ]

f. *ol*   anɨ   al-(ɨ)b-al-ɣan
   s/he 3.ACC take -CV-CAP-PST
   'she could have taken it'
   (Field notes) [AFXⱼ]

1.3 Auxiliary verb constructions

The Auxiliary verb construction (AVC) is here defined as a mono-clausal structure minimally consisting of a lexical verb element that contributes lexical content to the construction and an auxiliary verb element that contributes some grammatical or functional content to the construction. AVCs thus represent a cluster of syntactic, semantic, and morphosyntactic features (and also prosodic/phonological ones), the analysis of the formal and functional structure of which is the basis of this volume.

Note that by definition AVCs, as here understood, require a particular auxiliary element in combination with a (class of) lexical predicate(s). The set of auxiliaries used in a particular language is always finite by definition, but auxiliation is a dynamic process, so the class is continually losing and acquiring new members at different rates, and is thus ever-reforming. Logically a language may possess from one to very many such constructions, and in some languages the elements that might be considered auxiliaries in the present work can constitute a very large number indeed. English offers examples of a number of auxiliary verb constructions. For example, the progressive AVC is not marked by *be* or the lexical verb in the *-ing* form, but rather, the combination *be* X-*ing*. Further, the auxiliary *be* has been grammaticalized in other AVCs as well in English (*be* + X-*ed* to mark passive (with other well-known morphosyntactic features (objects are promoted to subject, original semantic agent may optionally be expressed as the complement of the preposition *by*)).

The most common exceptions to the productive application of an auxiliary verb construction to the set of all verbs in a given language include restrictions on the valence or certain semantic features of the lexical element in the construction, for example, the semantic role of its arguments, or the general incompatibility of certain kinds of lexical and functional semantics, e.g. the unusualness of progressive semantics with statives. Thus, in English, the AVC in *be* X-*ing* generally applies to all lexical verbal predicates, but is semantically incompatible with stative verbs: compare *I am running, I am hitting Greg*, but **I am knowing (it)* (McDonald's current (2004) slogan (*I'm loving it*®) notwithstanding). An example of another type of restriction on AVCs comes from the selection of dummy auxiliaries in deriving verb stems based on the transitivity of the resulting predicate, seen in such phenomena as the distribution of *etmek* (transitive) and *olmak* (intransitive, reflexive, passive, detransitive) in standard Turkish (e.g. *teslim etmek* 'hand over, surrender sthg' vs. *teslim olmak* 'surrender self, capitulate').

A further kind of restriction on the applicability of a given AVC across the verbs of a particular language may be seen in the use of different transitive [*bo*] and intransitive [*læʔ*] forms of the progressive in the South Munda language Gtaʔ of the southeastern part of central India.

(2)   a.   Gtaʔ   b.   Gtaʔ
       coŋ n-læʔ-e   aʔcoŋ m-bo-ke
       eat-1-PROG. ITR-FUT   feed 1-PROG.TR-PST
       'I will be eating'   'I was feeding'
       (Mahapatra et al. 1989)

Another characteristic of the process of auxiliation is 'partial' semantic bleaching seen in certain AVCs where the auxiliary is restricted in its syntagmatic sense relations to actions etc. that show (some) semantic compatibility with the (original) lexical semantics of the auxiliary, for example, the incompatibility of 'sit' and 'lie' auxiliaries in continuative/progressive/durative > present functions with verbs meaning 'run', or the opposition of 'short' vs. 'tall' readings in progressive AVCs with certain predicates using 'sit' and 'stand', respectively, seen in the following formation from Tofa (Turkic, Siberia (Russia)).

(3)   a.   Tofa   b.   Tofa
       neš   ün-ü p   turu   neš   ün-üp   olïrï
       tree grow-CV AUX.PROG   tree grow-CV AUX.PROG
       'a tall tree is growing'   'a planted/dwarf tree is growing'
       (Rassadin 1978: 151)

To recap, as a form–function continuum, auxiliary verb constructions are necessarily vaguely definable, dynamic, ever-emergent and changing. These may constitute a closed class from a strict synchronic perspective but not when viewed diachronically in any sense, or, of course, in the panchronic approach adopted in the present work.

1.4 AVCs and other complex predicate types

In this section, I briefly present a typology of complex predicate types as discussed in the linguistic literature, making no claims about the validity of the possibility of discretely defining any individual predicate type *per se* cross-linguistically. This is not to say, however, that in the analysis of any individual language (or sets of languages), discrete categories cannot be defined formally, nor subtypes within a given category. Remember that auxiliary verb constructions are monoclausal, with the auxiliary serving as a functional operator on the semantic lexical head. That is, the auxiliary serves to aid in the expression of the particular realization of the event type encoded by the lexical verb as grounded in the larger context of the communicative discourse surrounding that event. However, this development of 'auxiliary functions' of certain verbs is not *ex nihilo*. Rather, auxiliary verb constructions appear to have their origins in a range of complex predicate types, some apparently mono-clausal, other bi-clausal. Such source constructions include a wide range of serial verb constructions (both core and nuclear juncture formations), verb plus clausal complement sequences, clause-chained or conjunctive sequences, and—not extensively discussed here (for which see Heine and Reh 1984, Heine 1993)—case-marked (locative, comitative, etc.) nominal predicate-plus-copula formations. Because the continuum of developments that yields auxiliary verb constructions from these heterogenous sources are by definition themselves indivisible into strict, discrete categories, but rather may show overlapping and ambiguous status in a wide range of domains (semantics, morphosyntax, etc.), there is considerable potential for varied residual archaisms to be preserved idiosyncratically in a given AVC. It thus is not possible to identify, for example, at which point verb–verb sequence $X_{[SVC/V+Compl]}$ becomes verb–verb sequence $X'_{[AVC]}$. This should be borne in mind in the discussion in Chapter 7, for example, in the presentation of the historical developments of AVCs.

I have already defined auxiliary verbs and auxiliary verb constructions as understood in the present work in 1.2 and 1.3 above. Heine (1993: 15ff.) discusses a wide range of views in the theoretical literature on the various formal and functional definitions of auxiliary verbs or auxiliary verb constructions, and has amply demonstrated the great discrepancies in these various understandings, to which the interested reader is referred.

The extent of the notional and functional domains of auxiliaries offered in the literature include (Heine 1993: 16) tense, aspect, and mood categories (Steele 1978; Ramat 1987), just tense and aspect (Conrad 1988, Bußmann

1990), only tense and mood (Akmajian et al. 1979, Steele et al. 1981, Langacker 1991), or aspect and mood alone (Pullum and Wilson 1977, Crystal 1980). As amply exemplified in Anderson (2004a), even restricting the functional domains of auxiliaries to TAM categories only is not maintainable for Turkic, so these hypotheses are untenable.

Another issue relating to the various understandings put forth in the literature regarding auxiliaries in traditional theoretical linguistics is the head/dependency relations exhibited between the auxiliary verb component and lexical verb component of the construction. This entire debate basically boils down to one complex meta-methodological or meta-theoretical issue: the conflation of syntactic, semantic, and morphosyntactic dependency relations into a single head-dependent notion. Heine (1993: 18ff.) summarizes various positions relating to this (although not in the terminology adopted in the present work), viz. (i) the auxiliary is the dependent and the lexical verb the head (Huddleston 1984, Langacker 1991), (ii) neither is head, i.e. there is no head, with auxiliaries occupying a functional projection of some sort (e.g. INFL) taking a VP complement, or sister to VP (Akmajian et al. 1979), or (iii) auxiliary is head (Zwicky 1993), etc. From a different terminological perspective and a slightly earlier investigative period, this variation in opinion on the head/dependent relationship between the auxiliary verb and the lexical verb is evocative of the debate between the main verb status (or lack thereof) of the auxiliary verb or the lexical verb in early generativist work (e.g. Ross 1969, Palmer 1974, 1979).

Heine (1993: 22–4) collates a number of such views that exist in the literature on what auxiliary verbs are and how these latter fit within an architecture of grammar to demonstrate this variety of opinions; such views may at times be contradictory. As a family resemblance relation holds between the various constructions that can be characterized as reflecting the form–function epiphenomena of AVCs, there are no necessary and sufficient formal or functional defining features for such formations, nor should such features be expected.[5] This dynamic nature of the continuum has led numerous researchers to finely divide such (semi-)functional elements found in the grammar of particular languages which deviate in some way from 'expected' ways of behaviour exhibited by 'good' or 'true' auxiliaries. Terms such as 'semi-auxiliary', 'quasi-auxiliary', etc. may be found in the works of individual linguists concerned with these categorizations. Given that various verb–verb concatenations occupy different points on the AVC continuum, and only certain ones occupy focal points with 'canonical' behaviour (predetermined

---

[5] As Kuteva (2001: 10) states, this kind of relation involves relevant properties, not necessary and sufficient ones.

by the linguist's meta-analytic assumptions), and that there is a common metatheory of investigation that requires a strict divide between synchronic and diachronic 'grammar' or states of languages, such categorization is inevitable. Further, categorization that is overly restrictive regarding possible functions of AVCs can also lead to overly narrow splitting of these—for example, the tradition of 'auxiliaries' vs. 'deficient' verbs found in the analysis of (mainly Southern) Bantu languages.[6]

1.4.1 *AVCs and serial verb constructions*

Despite being only sporadically mentioned in the literature on serial verb constructions (SVCs), or in the literature on the grammaticalization of auxiliaries, serial verb constructions are nevertheless one of the most common sources of auxiliary verb constructions.[7] Like auxiliary verb constructions, there has been no one opinion about the types of verb–verb formations that

---

[6] This is not to say, however, that 'deficient' verbs in a given Bantu language may not form a definable subset of functional verbal elements in opposition to auxiliaries. As discussed by Mkhwatsha (1991) and Heine (1993), all such stems appear to be derived from their corresponding lexical verb stem in Zulu (but they show the characteristic morphosyntax that distinguishes a class of auxiliaries in the language).

(i) Zulu

Deficient verb form/use		Lexical verb form/meaning	
-*buye*	'do again'	-*buya*	'return'
-*cishe*	'do almost, nearly'	-*cisha*	'extinguish'
-*dlule*	'do nevertheless'	-*dlula*	[sur]pass'
-*fike*	'do first'	-*fika*	'arrive'
-*hambe*	'do all the way along'	-*hamba*	'go'
-*mane*	'just do, merely'	-*mana*	'stop, halt'
-*phike*	'just do, merely'	-*phika*	'refuse, deny'
-*phinde*	'do again'	-*phinda*	'repeat'
-*qale*	'do first'	-*qala*	'begin'
-*qede*	'do as soon as'	-*qeda*	'finish'
-*sale*	'do afterwards'	-*sala*	'stay behind'
-*shaye*	'do completely'	-*shaya*	'hit'
-*sheshe*	'do quickly'	-*shesha*	'hurry'
-*suke*	'just do, merely'	-*suka*	'move away'

(Mkhatshwa 1991; Heine 1993: 60)

(ii)

Characteristic	Auxiliaries	Lexical verbs
TAM markers	+	+
NEG	+	+/−
Derivational extensions	+	−
Object prefixes	+	−

(Mkhatshwa 1991; Heine 1993: 62)

Basically, deficient or defective verbs in these languages are auxiliaries with adverbial semantics, and auxiliaries are considered to be those with aspectual or modal functions. For a summary of the various views in the Bantuist literature, see Setshedi (1974).

[7] Of course, there are mentions of this development, particularly in the discussion of SVCs in individual languages (e.g. DeLancey 1991 on modern Tibetan).

constitute a serial verb construction. Like AVCs, SVCs are thought to be mono-clausal concatenations of verbs that express a 'single event'. A further similarity between the understanding of AVCs in the present work and of SVCs in certain specialist literature on these latter formations is, as succinctly put by Lord (1993: 2), that 'rather than [being] a separate universal category, serialization is more accurately characterized as a syndrome of features and phenomena.'

As pointed out by Senft (2004) in a recent critical assessment of this issue (and earlier by Givón (1991a)), even the concept of a 'single event' in this characterization of serial verb formations is of dubious definability. Depending on the tradition, virtually any verb–verb combination may be considered a serial verb construction. For the purposes of the present volume, I consider any such sequence where there is a sequential and/or componential meaning that follows from the content semantics expressed by each verbal element to be a serial verb construction, even if construed only in tandem with a following lexically content-bearing expression, such as the 'classic' serializing combinations of (same-subject) 'take come' > 'bring' and (switch-subject) 'hit die' > (strike to death >) 'kill'.

Like auxiliary verb constructions, SVCs often consist of two elements (although strings of six or seven serialized verbs can be used in some Papuan languages, e.g. the oft-cited Kalam). One of these elements, usually referred to as V_1 or V_2 in the literature, may become specialized, and develop functional semantics through a process of grammaticalization. There are several common paths of development for (former) serial verbs that become functional elements, roughly characterizable as a 'nominal' and a 'verbal' channel. The nominal channel frequently yields adpositional-like formations, although these may preserve some of their verbal morphosyntax, e.g. subject inflection or negative marking, as in the following Akan forms (4). They also may take on adverbial-like subordinating functions, similar to converb forms of verbs in the 'adverbial' modification of actions, etc. (Bisang 1995).

(4)   a.   Akan
          Kofi n-ye adwuma m-ma Amma
          Kofi NEG-do work NEG-give Amma
          'Kofi does not work for Amma'
          (Seuren 1990: 18; Schachter 1974: 266)

      b.   Akan/Twi
          mi-guaree me-baa mpono
          1[:PST]-swim 1[:PST]-come shore
          'I swam to the shore'
          (Sebba 1987: 184; Christaller 1875: 131)

c. Akuapem Akan

ma-yɛ	*adwuma*	*ma-ma*	*Amma*
1.PRF-do	work	1.PRF-give	Amma

'I have worked for Amma'
(Schachter 1974: 260)

However, when V_1 or V_2 in a SVC becomes grammaticalized as a functional verbal element, commonly referred to as 'aspectual' or 'modal serialization', etc. in the description of various languages, these elements are considered to have entered into a process of auxiliation from the perspective of the present volume, and I often (re-)analyse these formations as AVCs in the presentation below. Thus, I am saying that the point at which a mono-clausal, mono-event verb–verb combination becomes an AVC and stops being an SVC cannot really be defined *per se*; but once functional semantics become the default interpretation (with obvious and indeed expected periods of ambiguity), I am likely to include these constructions in the database that forms the foundation for the present typological investigation. Indeed, in certain language families, there is a tendency for serialized or clause-chaining constructions and auxiliary constructions to show an overt formal similarity to each other. Take, for example, the distribution of the so-called 'proximate' element in languages of the Misumalpan family as described by Hale (1991, 1997).[8] It appears on the first element in a deictic serialized formation, in a clause-chained (or serialized) sequence with 'finish', and in auxiliary constructions in Miskitu and Ulwa.[9]

---

[8] Similar phenomena are seen in other languages as well. For example, in Kathmandu Newar (Shakya 1992), the so-called concatenative marker is found on the lexical verb in an AVC, and the nearly identical 'non-final' marker occurs in serialized formations (short vs. long vowels in a system where vowel length bears a minimal functional load). Compare the following examples in this regard:

(iii) Kathmandu Newar

Jon wan-æ con-a	*Jon wan-æ: con-a*
John go-CM AUX-PRF	John go-NF stay-PRF
'John was going'	'John went and stayed'

(Shakya 1992: 101)

It is possible that the opposition is really a false one and that the non-final marker had a now lost segment, which is a normal path of development for the long vowels attested in this Newari variety. It is also possible, of course, that the forms originally were identical and the vowel length a secondary development to differentiate these functionally different but formally similar/identical constructions. Note that this same functional element is called a 'participle' by Genetti (1986).

[9] In at least one formation in these languages, there is an infinitival complement sequence highly similar to English, similar enough in these languages to suspect a calqued formation. Note that the Miskitu form below even uses a borrowing from English in this construction, further supporting its probable calqued nature.

(iv) Miskitu
   yang Bilwi ra w-aia want s-na

(v) Ulwa
   yang Ulwah yul-naka walta-ya-ng

(5) a. Miskitu
    usus pal-i bal-an
    buzzard fly-PROX come-PST:3
    'the buzzard came flying'
    (Hale 1991: 7)

    b. Ulwa
    kusma limd-i waa-da
    buzzard fly-PROX come-PST:3
    'the buzzard came flying'

    c. Miskitu
    naha w-a-tla mak-i ta alk-ri
    this house-CNSTR build-PROX end reach-PST:3
    'he finished building this house'
    (Hale 1991: 6)

    d. Ulwa
    aaka uu-ka yamt-i angka wat-ikda
    this house-CNSTRbuild-PROX end reach-PST:3
    'he finished building this house'

    e. Ulwa
    bikiska isd-i bang-ka
    children play-PROX AUX-PL:3
    'the children are playing'
    (Hale 1991: 9)

    f. Ulwa
    yang bas-k-i kipt-i lau-yang
    I hair-CNSTR-1 comb-PROX AUX-1
    'I am combing my hair'

    g. Miskitu
    yang utla kum mak-i s-na
    I house one build-PROX AUX-1
    'I am building a house'

    h. Miskitu
    yang utla kum mak-i kap-ri
    I house one build-PROX AUX-1:PST
    'I was building a house'

In the specialist literature on serial verb constructions there has been a tacit or explicit acknowledgment of the insights of the Role and Reference Grammar (RRG) framework for distinguishing two kinds of broad types of SVCs, viz. nuclear and core juncture serialization. Without explicitly adopting the machinery or even necessarily the theoretical assumptions of RRG in the present analysis, I have adopted these designations both because of the preponderance of this terminological tradition in the post-generative analysis of SVCs (including other typologically oriented works in this very series explicitly not using the formal machinery of this particular syntactic framework, e.g. Crowley (2002e)), and to acknowledge that there are potential correlations between certain source SVC types and particular target AVC types, from the

I Puerto Cabazas to go-INF want AUX-1   I Ulwa speak-INF want-PRES-1
'I want to go to P.C.'   'I want to speak Ulwa'
(Hale 1991: 5)

point of view of the development of certain inflectional patterns, as discussed in Chapter 7.

The distinction between core juncture and nuclear juncture serialization goes back at least to Foley and Olson (1985). Originally it was thought that these different types were found with SVO and SOV languages respectively. Their insights have been refined and revised over the years so that finer-grain distinctions of subtypes may be recognized as well as the clausal constituent order restrictions weakened. Serial constructions may have the same subject across the elements or may have different subjects (typically, object of one verb is subject of other) in so-called 'switch-subject' serialization. Further, as recognized by Crowley (1987, 2002e), there may also be no argument sharing (a feature frequently cited as definitional for a SVC) in so-called 'ambient serialization' forms, in which case the second verb may have a 'general meaning' (rather loosely defined). It turns out that these different categorizations, as well as the nuclear juncture/core juncture serialization distinction, all have consequences for specific individual developments into various different patterns of inflection for auxiliary verb constructions as well. That is, the particular source SVC often correlates to the inflectional type of AVC resulting. These developments are outlined and exemplified in 7.1. Such patterns include doubled, split, LEX-headed and split doubled formations, as well as AUX-headed ones to a lesser degree.

1.4.2 *AVCs verb/complement structures*

As has been often discussed in the literature, another common source for auxiliary verb constructions—and thus another type of formation where individual exemplars may be ambiguous between an auxiliary target construction and the original source construction—is the verb–complement formation. There are broadly speaking two structural types of these verb/complement formations that give rise to AVCs, namely a monoclausal verb plus nominal complement, and a biclausal verb plus clausal complement structure. The verb in the clausal complement structure may bear an overt marker of nominalization or some other kind of formal (co-)subordination or pseudo-complementation. The union of an original biclausal formation into a synchronic auxiliary verb construction is a process that has been well discussed in the literature on the diachronic syntax of auxiliary formations from a range of different perspectives (e.g. Vincent 1982, Harris and Ramat 1987, Harris and Campbell 1995, Drinka 2003, Bentley and Eythórsson 2004, Lightfoot 1979). Given limitations of space and the relative frequency of such discussions in previous analyses of auxiliaries, I refer the interested reader to the relevant literature cited here and various other citations therein. In terms of the inflectional typology below, AVCs deriving from this type of formation most typically show the so-called AUX-headed inflectional pattern (see below), but may also yield various doubled split or split/doubled patterns.

1.4.3 *Coordinate formations and AVCs*

Another source for deriving AVCs, albeit one that occurs with significantly less frequency than the serialization or subordination strategies just mentioned, is the use of coordinate or conjoined structures. As is the case with the preservation of subordinating morphology in many of the auxiliary formations deriving from verb plus complement sequences, clause-linking morphology may also be found in AVCs deriving from a coordinative or chaining construction. Thus, same-subject morphology, converbal or conjunct-marked forms, or various medial/non-final verbal affixes may appear on lexical verbs (or, less commonly, auxiliaries) in AVCs deriving from such structures. Some examples of this type are discussed in Chapters 2, 4, and 5.

1.4.4 *Other AUX-like elements*

A variety of other complex predicate formations discussed in the literature that may overlap with or exhibit features similar to AVCs deserve mention in this section as well. Such complex predicate types include co-verb plus (generic) inflecting verb structures. Although best described in a range of non-Pama-Nyungan languages of Northern Australia (see Schultze-Berndt (2000) and McGregor (2002) for two recent and rather different views of these kinds of formations and why they consider them not to be specialized uses of AVCs in Australian languages), the generic verb plus inflecting verb structure may appear in various other languages as well, e.g. Tsafiki, a Barbacoan language of Colombia as described by Dickinson (2002). In such formations, the inflecting verbs contribute something to the content semantics (and argument structure) of the event in a less abstract way than the functional semantic contrasts found in auxiliary formations.[10] This is thus reminiscent of the relation between components of a serial verb formation, of which these constructions probably in fact represent a particular diachronic development.

Another construction that is also akin to AVCs but is generally distinguished from them is commonly referred to as a 'light verb' formation (also called

---

[10] As Dickinson (2002: 7, 11) puts it, 'coverbs are rich in specific lexical meaning and carr[y] semantic participants, but lacks information concerning event structure'; he adds that the 'semantic compatibility of coverb and generic verb determines [how widespread the] distribution of various individual coverbs is', noting that there is some 'productivity, but [also] semantically-based restrictions' on permissible combinations. Similar arguments are made for 'light verb' constructions by various researchers; see below.

'compound verb formation' in various linguistic traditions (Hook 1991)). In one recent presentation on such formations in Urdu, an Indo-Aryan language of Pakistan, Butt and Geuder (2003), light verbs are analysed as contributing partially lexical and partially functional semantics to the formation. That is, they are not fully 'grammaticalized', just semantically generalized. An example of this is ostensibly to be seen in examples such as the following:

(6)　Urdu
　　Yaasiin=nee keek k^{h}aa lii-yaa
　　Yassiin-ERG cake eat take-PRF.M.SG
　　'Yassin ate the cake, completely, for himself'
　　(Butt and Geuder 2003: 295)

Verbs used as light verbs in such formations are not like 'real' lexical verbs, as they do not assign theta-roles, for example. They show that they are not like 'real' auxiliaries in this language as these latter have different kinds of syntactic behaviour in Urdu from that of light verbs. The authors make various assumptions about the discreteness of such categories as auxiliaries and light verbs not just in Urdu but for all languages—an assertion that this volume maintains has no empirical validity and categorically rejects.[11] Light verb plus verb combinations, like the co-verb plus generic inflecting verb forms just mentioned, appear to be intermediate steps on the serial verb–auxiliary verb continuum, all such constructions being monoclausal formations, and no

---

[11] In fact, as Butt and Geuder (2003: 307ff.) discuss, there are different classes of auxiliaries in Urdu that exhibit different morphosyntactic behaviour betraying their different origins, e.g. person agreement or gender agreement with a subject.

(v)　Urdu
　　us=nee xat likh-aa (hæ/th-aa)
　　he=ERG letter write-PRF.M.SG AUX:3:PRS/AUX:PST-M.SG
　　'he wrote (has/had written) a letter'
　　(Butt and Geuder 2003: 310)

I agree with the authors that light verbs and the different classes of auxiliaries should be characterized differently in the analysis of Urdu grammar, if this must be treated in a purely synchronic way (an idea that I categorically reject as well, naturally); however, when viewed from the panchronic typology of complex predicates, such differences become less interesting. The authors specifically acknowledge the ambiguity in interpretation between clause-chaining interpretations and a complex predicate reading imposed by this synchronic view with respect to light verb formations in Urdu (Butt and Geuder 2003: 320). Auxiliaries, they maintain, derive from embedding constructions, while light verbs derive from clause-chaining formations (p. 343), adding the theory-internal reasoning that auxiliaries belong to functional projections of I and T, and are not dominated directly under a V-node, as are light verb plus main verb combinations. Although the formal machinery assumed belongs to a quasi-GB type of syntactic theory, this analysis is consistent with an a Role and Reference Grammar-style analysis that would consider the light verb plus main verb (and, for that matter, probably also the co-verb plus generic inflecting verb combinations as well in Australian languages and Tsafiki) likely to have derived from nuclear layer serialization formations.

discrete boundaries are possible between these, theoretically speaking. Rather, as the semantic generality of certain light or inflecting verbs in these constructions extends to new applicability for their use, and their contribution to the semantics of the clause grows more abstract/functional, the formations slide into auxiliation and become AVCs.

1.5 Inflection, dependency and headedness in AVCs

1.5.1 *Inflection*

'Inflection' is here defined as the obligatory encoding on the verb of a range of functional properties, including such categories as tense, mood, aspect, subject, and object.

Personal inflection in the verb can be triggered syntactically, semantically, or discourse-pragmatically, due to the fact that, for example, a given language may show agreement with only the right-or leftmost noun in a conjoined construction (including disjunctive formations) or juxtaposed phrase; may show plural agreement with a grammatically singular noun; or may show agreement with any animate referent in the discourse, regardless of its argument status (or lack thereof). For more, see Anderson (1997) and Anderson and Eggert (2001).

In the present work, agreement and inflection will be considered to be determined by the interaction of a complex set of syntactic, semantic, and discourse-pragmatic considerations, which vie with one another in order to determine the overt realization of person and number inflection in particular. Some examples are given below to demonstrate this, but the point will not be laboured much further in this study.

Perhaps it is not overstating the case to claim that in most languages, both syntactic and semantic factors are involved in determining verbal agreement. As Corbett (1991: 225–6) puts it: 'syntactic agreement (or agreement *ad formam*, or "grammatical" agreement) is agreement consistent with form' and that 'semantic agreement (or agreement *ad sensum*) is agreement consistent with the gender [or other agreement category] assigned by semantic assignment rules.'

It is a cross-linguistic tendency for simplex NPs to trigger syntactic agreement; however, when the agreement trigger is a coordinative phrase, agreement is often semantically determined (Wechsler 1999: 6). In the case of conjoined NPs, one usually speaks of a resolution rule, 'a rule which specifies the form of an agreeing element (or target) when the controller consists of conjoined noun phrases' (Corbett 1991: 261). Of course it is possible for a language to lack a resolution rule, in which case partial agreement results, i.e., agreement with only one of the conjoined NPs, often the closest in terms of linear structure, or according to the principles of some kind of agreement hierarchy (e.g. the well-known 'Animacy Hierarchy'). Partial agreement is generally seen as a special case of syntactic agreement (see Corbett 1991; Sadock 1998). Resolution rules, on the other hand, are usually semantically motivated, though they may be syntactically motivated if the semantics are inapplicable, as with purely arbitrary gender assignment (cf. Wechsler 1999).

As alluded to above, a not infrequent phenomenon found in a range of languages is to show agreement with only the closest, in terms of linear syntax, of a set of conjoined noun phrases.

For example, consider the facts on agreement in the verb with conjoined noun phrases in Yasin Burushaski, a variety of the enigmatic language isolate of northern Pakistan. Here, nouns belong to one of four classes, each with their own set of inflectional characteristics (see Anderson, (to appear, a) for details). However, when nouns of different classes are conjoined (and this includes personal pronouns with nouns as well), only the rightmost noun shows agreement. Note that this is true in both conjunctive and disjunctive structures. Note also that Burushaski is a so-called 'primary object' language (Dryer 1986) and that recipient arguments are encoded morphologically in the verb, as are patients (although the noun itself distinguishes overt dative case from Ø-marked absolutive). Data below are from Anderson and Eggert (2001) and the author's field notes on the Yasin variant of Burushaski, also known as Werchikwar.

(7) Yasin Burushaski (language isolate; northern Pakistan)

a. *ne bal ka on gu-del-i* vs.   b. *ne on ka bal del-i*
   he door and you 2-hit-1   he you and door hit-1
   'he hit the door and you'   'he hit you and the door'
   (Anderson and Eggert 2001)

c. *on kitap ja-ɣa ya hir-e e-či-a*
   you book I-DAT or man-1.OBLQ 1-give-2
   'you gave the book to me or the man'

vs.

d. *on kitap hir-e ya ja-ɣa a-či-a*
   you book man-1.OBLQ or I-DAT 1-give-2
   'you gave the book to the man or me'

Yasin Burushaski is in fact unusual in this regard, in that conjunctively conjoined noun phrases are treated in a manner identical to disjunctively conjoined ones, and strict linearity or syntactic agreement seems to override semantic agreement. With disjunctively conjoined noun phrases (Eggert

2002), linear agreement is found in a range of other languages, e.g. Ndebele, a Bantu language of southern Africa.

(8)   Ndebele (Bantu; southern Africa)

    a.   *u-mangoye*   *loba   i-nja*   *i-dle*   *inyama*
        1/2A.SG-cat   or   9/10SG-dog 9/10SG-eat steak
        'the cat or the dog ate the steak'
        (Moosally 1998: 103)

    b.   *i-nja*   *loba   u-mangoye*   *u-dle*   *inyama*
        9/10SG-dog or   1/2[ANIM].SG-cat 1/2[ANIM].SG-eat steak
        'the dog or the cat ate the steak'
        (Moosally 1998: 103)

Regarding semantic agreement, in such languages as English, especially dialects in the UK, collective or semantically plural nouns that are grammatically singular not infrequently appear, at least in colloquial spoken varieties, with plural agreement. That is, semantic agreement overrides syntactic.

(9)   English
    i.   *the committee are meeting in room 7* (not *is*)
    ii.   *Manchester United vow to bring the trophy home again this year* (not *vows*)

Local agreement, possibly in combination with semantic agreement, occurs frequently in English with quantified or pseudo-quantified expressions. Thus one hears and even sees written such things as the following.

(10)   English
    a wide range of products are (is) available

Discourse-triggered agreement is also attested in a range of languages where overt indexation may be of animate possessors of arguments rather than logical arguments themselves: so-called 'possessor raising'/'possessor ascension'/'external possession' (Anderson 1995). However, in some head-marking languages, verbs may encode a salient participant in the discourse, even if that participant has little—or nothing—to do with the argument structure of the verb. Such is the case, for example, in certain 'copying-to-object' formations in the Algonquian language Fox (Meskwaki).

(11) Fox (Meskawki) (Algonquian, Central US)
    ne-kehke:nem-ekw-a ni:na e:h=pwa:wi-ke:ko:hi-ašeno-niki
    1-know-INV-3/I.I.   1.TOP AOR=not-anything-disappear-INAN.OBV/AOR
    'he knows that as for me nothing is missing'   (liter. 'he knows me...')
    (Anderson 1997: 233)

Here the matrix verb inflects for a first singular 'object' but logically requires a clausal complement; however, if there was an argument of the lower clause that could be 'raised' to object, one might expect forms like *he knows you ate at the restaurant last night*, but this participant has no role in the lower clause at all, which means 'nothing is missing'. The sentence relates to how the incident described affects this highly salient participant, and this latter is indexed in the matrix verb, despite the fact that it is in no semantic sense an argument of the matrix or the embedded predicate. Thus, discourse considerations may also override both syntactic and semantic considerations when dealing with verbal inflection in a range of languages. For further discussion see Anderson (1997, 1998b).

1.5.2 *Heads*

The notion of 'head' occupies a central position in many theories of grammar currently in use. Indeed, both an entire major typological parameter, viz. 'head-marking vs. dependent-marking' (Nichols 1986), as well as a framework of syntactic analysis, e.g. Head-Driven Phrase Structure Grammar, contain the term 'head'. For the most part, the notion of 'lexical head' or 'phrasal head' itself seems to be non-controversial or at least intuitively definable, or describable in a manner generally acceptable to the majority of linguists working on this area of research. These heads tend to be the 'part of speech' that the phrase they belong to can be described as; thus, in traditional syntactic terms, the noun is the head of the noun phrase, the verb the head of the verb phrase, etc.

Among the definitions of (lexical) 'head' put forward by various researchers are included: 'the obligatory element in the phrase category' and 'the node which has no bars and is of the same category (N, V, etc.) as the phrase itself' (Cowper 1992: 20, 33); '(the) head word which determines the nature of the overall phrase' (Radford 1997: 18); 'the lexical item that contributes the PRED semantic form to a constituent's ↓ f-structure' (Kaplan and Bresnan 1995: 97); '[the] word which is centrally important in the sense that it determines many of the syntactic properties of the phrase as a whole' (Sag and Pollard 1989: 143); 'with respect to both its internal and its external syntax, the Head is the syntactic category determinant... the Head is the morphosyntactic locus... [it] exhibits the morphosyntactic properties... including those determined in agreement and government' (Zwicky 1993: 297–8). Croft (2001), working in his Radical Construction Grammar framework, departs somewhat from the modern structuralist and generativist notions of head which derive from Bloomfield (1933) and states rather that '[the] head is a symbolic relation between a syntactic role and a semantic component, [i.e.] the intersection of two semantic properties, profile equivalence and primary information bearing unit' (2001: 241–2), and further that '[the] (semantic) head is the profile equivalent that is the primary information-bearing unit, that is, the most contentful item that most closely profiles the same kind of thing that the whole constituent profiles' (2001: 259). This latter statement is at least in the spirit of most definitions of lexical head.[12]

The status of headedness in auxiliary verb constructions has been addressed at least obliquely by such researchers as Zwicky (1985, 1993), Mufwene (1991), and Croft (2001). Zwicky (1993: 303–4) states that auxiliaries are considered heads in generative frameworks but that they are also clearly semantic 'functors', i.e., they act like modifiers, not arguments. Ultimately Zwicky comes down in favour of considering morphosyntactic properties as primary in the determination of headedness in AVCs (in favour of the auxiliary verb). Mufwene (1991) likewise noted the inherent tension between the syntactic and semantic properties of auxiliary verbs vis-à-vis lexical verbs in AVCs. Croft, as is typical of his Radical Construction Grammar framework, takes a different stance, shifting the primary focus to the semantic properties of auxiliary verbs. As he puts it (Croft 2001: 259):

auxiliaries and verbs both profile the state of affairs denoted by the clause. The auxiliaries profile the process as very generally grounded in a mental space/possible world or discourse space (such as present vs. past time reference). The verb profiles a much more specific situation type and hence is the (semantic) head.

In the present study, 'head' is used in a way that is related to these but nevertheless differs slightly. Specifically, (at least) these three levels of headedness are identified here as relevant.

(12)

    a. 'Inflectional head' or morphosyntactic locus of inflection. This is where the primary verbal participants and functional categories are encoded in order for the construction to be grammatical. Inflectional head is a concept belonging to the domain of functional semantics and/or morphosyntax. Being the locus of encoding the obligatory temporal deictic and aspectuo-modal distinctions of the utterance and its referents, the inflectional head plays a significant role in communicative discourse.

---

[12] For an alternative view on these issues, see Hudson (1987).

b. 'Phrasal head'. This is proposed to account for the fact that in OV languages one predominantly finds the order Lexical verb–Auxiliary verb while in VO languages the order is Auxiliary verb–Lexical verb. Auxiliary verbs thus frequently have the same linear relation to the associated lexical verb as lexical verbs do with their objects, and correspondingly the auxiliary is thus considered to function as the (syntactic) phrasal head. Phrasal head is sometimes also referred to as 'structural head'. One overt manifestation of this is the often formally dependent or subordinate form in which the non-phrasal head lexical verb appears. However, in certain languages it is the lexical verb that determines the selection of a specific auxiliary verb used in the construction (e.g. the transitive vs. intransitive progressive auxiliary, determined by the valence of the lexical verb in Gta? mentioned above). In the present study, the notion of phrasal head is considered to be a relation of structural syntax and/or 'linearity'. Also, importantly, it is clear that a distinction between phrasal head and inflectional head must be kept separate in AVCs, but may be co-terminous; this is extensively exemplified in relevant chapters below.

c. 'Semantic head'. The 'semantic head' determines, among other features, the valence, the semantic role of the arguments associated with the predicate, etc. It is the lexical verb. The notion of semantic head belongs to the domains of lexical semantic and argument structure.

There are at least four logical possibilities with respect to the locus of inflection in auxiliary verb constructions. These are: (1) inflected auxiliary verb (AV), with the lexical verb (LV) in a constructionally determined unmarked or marked (non-finite, participial, gerundive, etc.) form; (2) neither AV nor LV inflected; (3) both inflected; or (4) unmarked or specially marked auxiliary verbs, with inflected lexical verbs. Split systems or mixings of the above are also attested.

In the following chapters, I present data from a wide variety of languages showing the range of inflectional phenomena found in auxiliary verb constructions. I label these the 'AUX-headed', 'doubled', 'LEX-headed', 'split' and 'split/doubled' macro-patterns. Each of these shows a considerable degree of variation within these broadly identified patterns.

For the present, the five inflectional patterns discussed here can be distinguished by the element of the construction that serves as the inflectional head:

(13)   → AUX-headed pattern

	LV	AV
→ 'syntactic' ('phrasal')	−	+ [often]
→ semantic ('semantic')	+	−
→ morphosyntactic ('inflectional')	−	+

→ Doubled pattern

	LV	AV
→ 'syntactic' ('phrasal')	−	+ [often]
→ semantic ('semantic')	+	−
→ morphosyntactic ('inflectional')	+	+

→ LEX-headed pattern

	LV	AV	
→ 'syntactic' ('phrasal')	−	+	[often]
→ semantic ('semantic')	+	−	
→ morphosyntactic ('inflectional')	+	−	

→ Split pattern

	LV	AV
→ 'syntactic' ('phrasal')	−	+ [often]
→ semantic ('semantic')	+	−
→ morphosyntactic ('inflectional')	$+_i/-_j$	$-_i/+_j$

→ Split/Doubled pattern

	LV	AV
→ 'syntactic' ('phrasal')	−	+ [often]
→ semantic ('semantic')	+	−
→ morphosyntactic ('inflectional')	$+_i/+_j, -_i/+_j$	$-_i/+_j, +_i/+_j$

To summarize, the only really significant variable within the inflectional systems of AVCs witnessed on a macro-typological scale is the inflectional head.[13] The syntactic, phrasal, or linear head is generally determined by the relative position of subject, object, and verb, and therefore is not indicative of any one class or subtype of auxiliary verb construction, but rather reflective of the typology of clausal syntax exhibited by a particular language; as

---

[13] In individual languages, different types of lexical predicate + auxiliary combinations show different (morpho)syntactic behaviour and can be identified as sub-classes of elements within all the different patterns, including AUX-headed and LEX-headed patterns. For example, various constructions in the language may require nominalized or adverbialized subordinate forms (participle, gerund, infinitive) of the lexical verb or marked vs. unmarked lexical verbs in various AVCs in that language.

mentioned above, the phrasal head is generally the auxiliary verb. This has no role in determining the inflectional head. The lexical verb is the semantic head, as it determines the valence of the predicate, the semantic role of its arguments, etc. Therefore, these play no major role in determining classes of AVCs cross-linguistically.[14]

In the AUX-headed type, the inflectional head is the auxiliary verb; in the LEX-headed type, the inflectional head is the lexical verb. In the doubled pattern, the auxiliary and lexical verbs are inflectional co-heads. In the split pattern, the assignment of any one element to the status of inflectional head is complicated by the fact that the very criteria for determining this (e.g. referent indexes, tense or polarity markers) are split, but there is no consistency with respect to the distribution of these functional categories across all languages showing split inflection. Finally, the last two patterns can mix and form the unusual split/doubled pattern. While these patterns and their multiple sub-types are discussed in detail in subsequent chapters, I exemplify each briefly here. Note that, with regard to the inflectional typology that constitutes the focus of this volume, languages tend to exhibit one pattern predominantly or exclusively, but many show more than one pattern as well.

⟶ AUX-*headed*

(14) Huallaga Quechua (Quechuan; Peru)
      Pillku-man   aywa-sha   ka-shaq
      P-GOAL   go-PRTCPL   AUX-1FUT
      'I will have gone to Pillku'
      (Weber 1989: 18)

(15) Iatmul [Papuan, Sepik-Ramu; Papua New Guinea]
      klə-kə   li-kə-win
      get-DEP   AUX-PRES-1SG
      'I am getting it'
      (Foley 1986: 144)

⟶ LEX-*headed*

(16) Doyayo (Adamawa-Eastern; Cameroon)
      gɔ² hi³ da³ hi³ e⁴li⁴mɔ⁴
      when 3PL REM 3PL call:2
      'when they would call you'
      (Wiering and Wiering 1994: 220)

---

[14] In certain languages, features of the original lexical semantics or sub-categorization frame of the auxiliary verb (e.g. licensing of specific case to a subject or object) may be reflected in the construction, reflecting 'partial' grammaticalization of the functional element and AVC.

Moi (West Papuan)
w-agi si   *w-isis se*
3-die PRF   3-done PRF
'he is dead'   'it is done'
(Menick 1995: 69)

Mödö (Nilo-Saharan, Central Sudanic, Bongo-Bagirmi; Sudan)
tí mókɔnyì yí
FUT 1:rescue you
'I will rescue you'
(Persson and Persson 1991: 19)

Kaulong (Austronesian; Papua New Guinea)
nga-ion-i koho
1R-know-TR PRF
'I already know it'
(Ross 2002: 401)

⟶ *Doubled*
(17) Gorum (Parengi) (Austroasiatic, South Munda; India)
miŋ   ne-gaʔ-ru   ne-laʔ-ru
I   1-eat-PST   1-AUX-PST
'I ate vigorously'
(Aze 1973:279)

(18) Sobei (Austronesian; Papua, Indonesia)
w-enon   yo-fi
1.REAL-AUX   1.REAL-make
'I was making'
(Sterner and Ross 2002: 181)

⟶ *Split*
(19) Jakaltek (Jacaltec) (Mayan, Kanjobalan; Guatemala)
šk-ach   w-ila
COMPL-ABS2   ERG1-see
'I saw you'
(Craig 1977: 60)

(20) Eleme (Cross-River, Niger-Congo; Nigeria)
ɛbai   rɛ-do-do-rõ   *né-e   ńsā*
1PL   1PL-REDPL-be.PRES-PRTCL   give-3SG   book
'We are still giving him books.'
(Anderson and Bond 2004-MS)

⟶ *Split/doubled*
(21)   Pipil (Uto-Aztecan; El Salvador)
       n-yu   ni-mitsin-ilwitia
       1-AUX   1-2PL-show
       'I'm going to show you'
       (Campbell 1985: 137)

(22)   Burushaski (isolate; northern Pakistan)
       ȷ́áa   a-yúgušanc   moó-y-a   bá-a
       I.GEN   1-daughter.PL   2PL-give-1   AUX-1
       'I herewith am giving you my daughters'
       (Berger 1998b: 161)

Why is the notion of inflectional head relevant? The basic assumption I am making is that verbs are the canonical realizations of predicates of propositions, and appear to constitute the core elements of clauses in both a semantic and syntactic sense cross-linguistically. Indeed in many (head-marking) languages, the verbal piece is the only obligatory element in a clause. The verb serves as the default locus of encoding functional categories (tense, arguments, etc.). Where/how these categories are realized, and therefore, what words in the sentence a hearer focuses on, are clearly important within a context of communicative discourse. Inflectional heads thus encode the junction of the semantic, syntactic and discourse features associated with the utterance and its components. Further, the various structures that these functional categories are realized in similarly present themselves an obvious concern for linguistic typology. Specific to the analysis of auxiliary verb constructions, verb/verb constructions and the history of complex verbal formations generally, this analysis of the formal indexation of functional semantic properties in AVCs across the world's languages in the present typology importantly captures generalizations observable about the development of complex verb structures cross-linguistically in a straightforward manner.

1.6 Brief history of the study of auxiliary verbs and AVCs

Monograph-length studies on auxiliary verbs and auxiliary verb constructions have been published on a large number of languages. The topics covered in these studies range from syntactically oriented phenomena to processes of grammaticalization and diachronic semantics. The list below is representative, and is not intended to be understood as exhaustive.

This set of monographs devoted primarily or exclusively to the analysis of some aspect of the system of auxiliary verbs, or even individual auxiliary verbs, includes a large number of studies on English, at the Old, Middle, Early Modern, and Modern stages (Ellesgård 1953, Twaddell 1963, Warner 1993). A considerable amount of research has also been devoted to the analysis of auxiliary verb constructions in German at the Old High, Middle High, and modern level over the past century and a half (Aron 1914, Bouma 1973, Öhlschläger 1989, Müller and Reis 2001). The system of auxiliary verbs in Dutch too, like those of its West Germanic sister languages, has also been the subject of dedicated investigations, although to a significantly lesser extent than German or English (Loubser 1961). Even the auxiliary system of Yiddish has been given a monograph length study (Eggensperger 1995).

Perhaps unsurprisingly, the major Romance languages have all enjoyed considerable specialist attention with regards to their systems of auxiliary verb constructions. This includes French at various historical periods (Castaréde 1962), Spanish (Klein 1968), Italian and related Italic-Romance languages of the region (La Fauci 1979). The auxiliary verb systems of various other Romance languages have also been the focus of specialist studies, including Portuguese (Pontes 1973) or Catalan (Espinal i Farré 1998).

To be sure, the varied and complex systems of auxiliary verbs from a wide range of other Indo-European languages have been the subject of specialist studies over the past century or so. These include studies of auxiliary verbs in such diverse and distantly related languages as modern Persian (Farrokhpey 1979), Cornish (Kenethlow 2002), Nepali (Sarma 1980), Hindi (Hacker 1958), and Greek (Basset 1979).

Basque has among the most complicated and diversified systems of auxiliary verb constructions found in Eurasian languages. Several volumes have been devoted to the analysis and origins of the Basque system of auxiliary verbs, including the standard language, as well as various Basque dialects (Etxebarria L. 2002; Yrizar 1991, 1992).

Dravidian languages make extensive use of auxiliary verbs, and a number of Dravidian languages have enjoyed an advanced and developed indigenous grammatical tradition. Several monographs on Dravidian auxiliaries have appeared in English, including Agesthialingom and Srinivasa Varma (1980) or Steever (1988), which operate on a comparative or pan-Dravidian level (see also Krishnamurti 2003: ch. 7), as have studies devoted to the analysis of auxiliary verbs in particular Dravidian languages, e.g. Tamil (Annamalai 1985) or Malayalam (Rajasekharan Nair 1990).

Turkic languages, like Dravidian, make extensive use of auxiliary verbs in their grammars. Accordingly, monographs on the system of AVCs have appeared on Turkish and western Turkic languages generally (Johanson 1971, Demir 1993; Sev 2001), on Siberian (Altai-Sayan) Turkic languages (Anderson 2004a), on Uzbek (Xožiev 1966) and Tatar in particular (Schönig 1984). A small number of studies devoted to the auxiliary verb systems of Mongolic languages have appeared as well, e.g. Ozawa (1965), on Middle Mongolian.

Of all the languages of eastern Asia, the system of auxiliary verbs in Japanese stands out as the best studied. There have been a large number of specialist studies devoted to the analysis of this salient feature of Japanese grammar, most written in Japanese, some in English (Sawada 1995, Kiagawa and Iguchi 1988). Chinese (Mayorga 1979, Alleton 1984) and Korean (Chung 1979, Suh 2000) too both have each had several lengthy investigations devoted to the analysis of their auxiliary verbs. Further, Park (1994) offered a comparative study of auxiliary verbs in three Tibeto-Burman languages.

Although predominantly isolating, the languages of southeastern Asia, which mainly stand outside the scope of the present volume, have likewise been the subjects of book-length analyses devoted to auxiliary verbs. This includes several languages of Thailand, including Bouyei (Burusphat 1998), Myang Lao (Mundhenk 1967), and Thai (Sookgasem 1990).

African languages have also enjoyed a small number of monographs or dissertations dedicated to auxiliary verbs. Thus, studies have appeared on such a diverse array of languages as the Bantu Zulu (Slattery 1981, Mkhatshwa 1991), Tswana (Setshedi 1974), and SeSotho (Chaphole 1988), the West African language Igbo (Emenanjo 1985), the Kru language family (Marchese 1986), and the Nilotic language Maasai of East Africa (Hamaya 1993).

Serial verbs and serial verb constructions, which play a significant role in the historical development of auxiliary verb constructions, have enjoyed less attention on the monograph-length scale than has the better-known auxiliary verb. Nevertheless, volumes have appeared on general historical trends in serial verb constructions (Lord 1993), Creole languages (Sebba 1987), and the Oceanic language family (Crowley 2002e, Bril and Ozanne-Rivierre 2004). In addition, over the past two decades collections of studies on serial verbs or complex predicates have offered papers from a range of perspectives and frameworks. These include Lefebvre (1991), Joseph and Zwicky (1990), and Alsina et al. (1997).

Monographs devoted to the cross-linguistic study of auxiliaries have been relatively few in number up to now. Such volumes include Heine (1993) and Kuteva (2001). Many volumes devoted to grammaticalization such as Hopper and Traugott (1993), Heine et al. (1991), Heine and Reh (1984), Heine and Kuteva (2002), and Traugott and Heine (1991) also devote considerable space to the analysis of auxiliary verbs. All grammaticalization-oriented studies of auxiliaries focus primarily on the historical processes of semantic bleaching (or combined bleaching and enrichment (Kuteva 2001)) and typologize event categorization from this perspective. In particular, morphosyntactic developments of AVCs have been largely ignored in these studies.

1.7 Functional typology of AVCs: an overview

Auxiliaries, as described above, are grammaticalized elements that perform a very large number of discourse and indexical functions across the languages of the world. Indeed, virtually every non-nominal (person, number, class) category described as 'inflectional' (see also 1.4 above) can or has been encoded through an (erstwhile or present) AVC.

1.7.1 *TAM categories*

The most basic and geographically and genetically widespread functions of AVCs cross-linguistically are to encode (or allow for the encoding of) tense, aspect (including inherent/lexical aspect and Aktionsart), and mood categories. Tense categories subdivide first into past (23–4), present (25–7), and future (28–9); then within each of these categories there are various fine-grained shades of remoteness and immediateness in particular for past (e.g. 'today', 'yesterday') and future (and often further in combination with some aspectual category in the present). Note that AVCs are by far the most common source for tense morphology cross-linguistically. I offer but a small portion of tense-encoding AVCs below.

(23)   Canela-Krahô (Macro-Jê; Brazil)
    i-te a-pupun
    1-PST 2-see
    'I saw you'
    (Popjes and Popjes 1986: 130)

(24)   Wambaya (Australia)
    gajbi ny-a
    eat 2-PST
    'you ate it'
    (Nordlinger 1998: 25)

(25)   Jingulu
    bukbali ya-ju
    blowing 3-AUX
    'the wind is blowing'
    (Pensalfini 2003: 210)

(26)   Tuvan
    sen-i sakt-ip tur men
    you-ACC remember-CV AUX 1
    'I remember you'
    (Anderson and Harrison 1999: 65)

(27)   Turkmen
    Ol men-den utan-ip dur
    He I-ABL be.ashamed-CV PROG/PRES
    'he is ashamed of me now'
    (Hansar 1977: 169)

(28) Tswana (Bantu; Botswana)   (29) Wambaya
      ba-tloga bá-goroga   *ganjim-a gun-u*
      3PL-AUX 3PL.DEP-arrive   finish-FUT 3M-FUT
      'they will soon arrive'   'he will finish it'
      (Setshedi 1974: 16)   (Nordlinger 1998: 51)

AVCs are frequently grammaticalized to encode a range of modal categories as
well. These include such diverse categories traditionally falling under the
super-heading 'Modal' as hearsay or evidentials of various types, (ir)realis,
desiderative, various deontic and epistemic notions of capability, likelihood,
possibility, obligation, etc. See examples (30–34).

(30) Mapudungun (Araucanian; Chile, Argentina)
      kim-la-n ülkantu-n
      AUX-NEG-1 sing-DEP
      'I cannot sing'
      (Zuñiga 2000: 27)

(31) Betta Kurumba (Dravidian; India)
      aḏəna ka:rə buḏʈ a:pəḏə
      aḏən-a ka:rə buḏ-əl a:g-pu-əḏə
      3SR-ACC car drive-INF AUX-IRF-SG
      'he can drive a car'
      (Coelho 2003:2)

(32) Xakas
      min nime-e   čobal-č atxan-im-ni   sɪrer   pil-če   polar-zar
      I what-DAT   be.sad-PRES.PRTCPL-1-ACC you.PL   know-PRES.I   PROB-2
      'you probably know what I am sad about'
      (Anderson 1998a: 60)

(33) a. Chepang (Tibeto-Burman; Nepal)
          ŋa waŋ-sa kheŋ-na(-ŋ)?
          I come-IRR:NMLZR AUX-NPST-1EX
          'I ought to come'
          (Bybee et al. 1994: 261; Caughley 1982: 94)

      b. Chepang
          ŋa waŋ-sa kheʔ-(ŋo)-to
          I come-IRR:NMLZR AUX-1EX-SECONDARY.LINK
          'I must come'
          (Bybee et al. 1994: 261; Caughley 1982: 94)

(34)   Tswana (Bantu; Botswana)
       ba-na ba-se-ka ba-robala
       PL-children 3PL-NEG-AUX3PL-sleep
       'the children must not sleep'
       (Setshedi 1974: 42)

Aspectual and Aktionsart categories are also among the most common functions encoded within an AVC across the languages of the world. Among the most frequently attested aspectual notions found in AVCs are perfective (35–6), imperfective (37), progressive (38), continuative (39), habitual (40), proximative (41), inchoative/inceptive (42), and terminative/completive (43).

(35)   Gta?   (36)   Rama (Chibchan; Nicaragua)
       c-coŋ (n)ḍi-ŋge   *siksik sut-aaps aaku-u*
       Rdpl-eat-1-PERF-PAST   chicken 1PL-lose AUX-TNS
       'I have eaten'   'we have lost the chicken'
       (Mahapatra et al. 1989)   (Young and Givón 1991: 223)

(37)   a.   Loniu (Austronesian; Papua   b.   Loniu
            New Guinea)
            yo u-tɔ min tan   *iy a i-sɔ čɛlu*
            I 1-AUX sit down   s/he still 3-AUX stand
            'I was sitting down'   'she was still standing there'
            (Hamel 1994: 105)   (Hamel 1994. 107)

(38)   a.   Gta?   b.   Gta?
            coŋ n-læ?-ge   *a?coŋ m-bo-e*
            eat-1-PROG.I-PST   feed 1-PROG.II-FUT
            'I was eating'   'I will be feeding'
            (Mahapatra et al. 1989)

(39)   Raga (Austronesian; Vanuatu)
       ra-m ban
       3PL-CONT go
       'they are going'
       (Lynch et al. 2002: 45)

(40)   Lavukaleve (East Papuan; Solomon Islands)
       homela-v koi deava sia me-v fiv koi fo'sal vo-kuru me-v fiv
       woman-PL also diving do HAB-PL 3PL:FOC also fish:PL 3PL:OBJ-hit
       HAB-PL 3PL:FOC
       'women also usually go diving and catching fish'
       (Terrill 2003: 385)

(41) a. Jaqaru (Aymaran; Peru)   b. Jaqaru
yatxi-nh sa-w-tʰa   *jaj-ntza-nh sa-w-ta*
learn-DEP AUX-COMPL-1   get-down-DEP AUX-COMPL-2
'I almost learned'   'you almost got down'
(Hardman 2000: 109)

(42) a. Tofa   b. Tofa
am uru:-nuŋ bèhe: ɯndɯɣ   *kir-e ver-gen men*
  bol-u ve-:r de:ʃ   *ɯna:rɯ*
child-3-GEN head: 3   enter-CV ASP-PST 1 to
  become-AUX INCH-P/F COMP   there
'(otherwise) the child's head would   'I went into there'
  become so'
(ASLEP Field Notes (MK623))

(43) Remo
baɖ-oʔ suŋ-oʔ-niŋ
slap-PST.II COMPL-PST.II-1
'I finished slapping'
(Fernandez 1968: 55)

1.7.2 Negative polarity

In a large number of languages, negative is expressed by means of a negative
auxiliary element. This, for example, is a family-level characteristic of Uralic
(although not attested as a synchronic AVC in every member of the family).
As discussed in Chapter 2, it is common for the lexical verb in these negative
auxiliary constructions in a range of Uralic languages to appear in a dependent negative form, the so-called 'co(n)negative' (44–8).

(44) Kamas   (45) Nganasan
e-m nere-ʔ   *ñi.-sɨ.ə kuə-ʔ*
NEG-1 be.frightened-CONNEG   NEG-PST die-CONNEG
'I am not, will not be frightened' 's/he did not die'
(Künnap 1999b: 25)   (Helimski 1998b: 508)

(46) Mari   (47) a. Komi   b. Komi
o-k kodo ə̂lje   *o-g mun*   *e-g mun*
NEG-3 leave:CONNEG   NEG:PRES-1 go   NEG:PST-1 go
  AUX:PST[:3]
's/he was not leaving'   'I don't go'   'I didn't go'
(Kangasmaa-Minn   (Hausenberg
  1998: 239)   1998: 315)

(48) a. Veps   b. Veps
          e-n luge   *e-n luge-nd*
          NEG-1 read   NEG-1 read-PST.PRTCPL
          'I don't read'   'I didn't read'
          (Payne 1985: 218–19; Laanest 1975: 91; Hämäläinen 1966: 96)

Other language families make use of negative auxiliaries as well. Thus, such constructions are found in the Tungusic languages (e.g. Udihe) of Siberia, the Eastern Kru language Neyo of Côte d'Ivoire, the Austronesian language Kokota, Papuan Kwerba, or the Yuman language Mesa Grande 'Iipay to name a few, within different inflectional patterns, viz. AUX-headed (Udihe, Neyo), split (Kokota), LEX-headed (Kwerba) or doubled ('Iipay).

(49) Udihe (Tungusic; Siberia)   (50) Kokota
      bi ei-mi sa: *o-ti dupa-i manei si-ago*
      I NEG-1 know   2-NEG punch-3 s/he FOC-2
      'I don't know'   'don't punch him'
      (Nikolaeva and Tolskaja 2001: 214)   (Palmer 2002: 513)

(51) a. Neyo (Kru; Côte d'Ivoire)   b. Neyo
          ma ne wa yo la   *e ne fe ka*
          But NEG.1 PAST child bring   I NEG.1 strength have
          'but I didn't bring the child'   'I don't have any strength'
          (Marchese 1986: 32)

(52) a. Kwerba   b. Kwerba
          co kwai kot-ri-m   *co kot-ri-m-o baye*
          I NEG:FUT cut-AUG-IRR   I cut-AUG-IRR-NEG NEG:PST
          'I will not cut it'   'I did not cut it'
          (de Vries and de Vries 1997: 12–13)

(53) a. Mesa Grande 'Iipay   b. Mesa Grande 'Iipay
          '-aa-x 'e-maaw   *me-saaw-x me-maaw*
          1-go-IRR 1-NEG.AUX   2-eat-IRR 2-NEG.AUX
          'I didn't go'   'you didn't eat it'
          (Couro and Langdon 1975: 71; Miller 2001: 302)

1.7.3 Voice

Voice categories are also among those that may be expressed through an auxiliary verb construction among the various languages of the world. Probably the most common of these are passive and causative, which are marked by periphrastic auxiliary formations in such languages as English (passive), and Korean or Slave Athapaskan (causative).

(54) English
      Alan was killed by Bill

(55) Slave (Athapaskan; Canada)
      bebí déh-w'a 'ah-lá
      baby 3-burp 1-CAUS
      'I burped the baby'
      (Rice 2000: 209; Rice 1989)

(56) Korean
      John-i Mary-lul us-ke ha-ss-ta
      John-NOMMary-ACC laugh-ADV AUX-PST-DECL
      'John made Mary laugh'
      (Li 1991: 129)

Benefactive voice marking is also a common function of AVCs, generally encoded by an auxiliary originally meaning 'give' (presumably itself derived from some kind of serialized formation). One example of the numerous languages that exhibit such a construction includes Telefol, a Papuan language of the Ok family.

(57) Telefol (Ok, Trans-New Guinea; Papua New Guinea)
      boko b-'neé-l-antém-a
      speak BEN:PUNCT-1OBJ-PUNCT-FUT-3[M]
      'he will tell me'
      (Heeschen 1998: 83)

1.7.4 *Version and orientation/directionality*

Among the lesser-known functions of auxiliary verb constructions is the expression of categories of version and orientation or directionality. The former category encodes a grammaticalized discourse function of 'affectedness' (or 'focus' in some traditions of analysis). Auxiliary verb constructions marking version categories constitute a family-level feature of Turkic (Anderson 2001), where two such formations are found, one marking subject version (42), i.e. action primarily affecting the subject (in either a positive or negative fashion), the other 'object' version, i.e. action primarily affecting a nonsubject (43). The former construction is sometimes called the 'self-benefactive' and the latter 'benefactive'. Examples of this kind of function

expressed by auxiliary verb constructions may be seen in the following
examples from Tofa, a moribund Turkic language of Siberia.

(58)   Tofa
        ɸɸren-ip al-dɯɯ-vɯɯs
        many word learn-GER SUBJ.VRS-REC.PST-1PL
        'we learned many words'
        (ASLEP Field Notes (MK623))

(59)   Tofa
        onu   sooda-p   beer   be
        s/he.ACC   say-GER   OBJ.VERS.P/F   Q
        'should I say it (again for you)'
        (ASLEP Field Notes (PVB))

Turkic languages also make use of AVCs to mark directionality or orientation.
These indicate motion toward or away from a deictic centre. Tofa again offers
clear examples of these kinds of formations. One, the cislocative formation
(also known as ven[i]tive, etc.), marks motion or orientation towards a
deictic centre, while the other, the translocative (or andative, itive), marks
motion or orientation away from a deictic centre.

(60)   Tofa
        onson vjertaljo:t-tar uh^j-up kel-gen
        then helicopter-PLfly-CV CLOC-PST
        'then the helicopters flew in'
        (ASLEP Field Notes (MK))

(61)   Tofa
        men ɲan-a ver-gen men
        I return-GER TLOC/INCH-PST 1
        'I set off for home'
        (ASLEP Field Notes (SDA117))

The previous two formations retain some of the original semantics of the
verbs involved and almost assuredly derive from original serial verb constructions, later grammaticalized in their current functions within these AVCs.
Although only partially semantically bleached, the formations are not new
ones in Tofa. In fact, both sets of constructions (the two version categories
and the two orientation/directionality ones) are quite old in the family, with
cognate forms found throughout the languages of the Turkic family, and
indeed even among the oldest attested Turkic language sources as well (albeit

with certain specific details of developments left out here: see Anderson (2004a)).

1.7.5 'Adverbial' functions

Adverbial notions may also be expressed through auxiliary verb formations. Take, for example, the following forms from Eleme, a Benue-Congo language of Nigeria, in which the auxiliary verb expresses the adverbial semantics 'very' ('to very X').

(62)　Eleme

　　i.　ɔ̀-ʔɔtɔ　tʃá-î　　ɛpɔ́　　　ii.　è-ʔɔtɔ-rî　tʃá　ɛpɔ́
　　　　2-AUX　run-2PL　afraid　　　　3-AUX-3PL　run　afraid
　　　　'you became very afraid'　　　　'they became very afraid'
　　　　(Field notes; Anderson and Bond: 2004-MS)

In Altai-Sayan Turkic languages, e.g. Xakas, a sudden action or 'to suddenly' is marked by an AUX-headed AVC.

(63)　Xakas

　　ib-deŋ　　sïγara　par-a　xon-γa-m
　　house-ABL　from　go-CV　UNEXP.II-PAST-1
　　'all of a sudden I left the house'
　　(Pritsak 1959: 621)

1.8 Structure of the volume

Chapter 2 presents what is dubbed the 'AUX-headed' pattern of inflection. This is the one that is statistically the most common and characteristic of the better-known languages of the world (as well as a large number of lesser-known languages). In the AUX-headed pattern, the auxiliary verb is the inflectional head of the construction, indexing all obligatory verbal inflectional categories, with the corresponding lexical verb appearing in a dependent, nominalized, infinitive, or unmarked form. For some researchers, the AUX-headed inflectional type is the only possible type for AVCs (Harris and Ramat 1987).

Chapter 3 addresses the LEX-headed inflectional pattern. In this construction, the lexical verb bears all the obligatory inflectional categories, and the auxiliary verb may appear in an uninflecting form, expressing only the category that it functions to encode. This construction is noteworthy insofar as the phrasal head is generally the auxiliary verb, but the inflectional head is the lexical verb. In many descriptions the auxiliary in the LEX-headed pattern is analysed as an uninflecting particle. However, when considering the functional semantics of the element, and the fact that these historically originate from verbal elements, the semantics of which are in accord with the semantic developments typical of the process of auxiliation, it seems clear that these in certain instances should rather be considered as reflecting an AVC of the LEX-headed inflectional pattern.

Chapter 4 discusses the 'doubled' inflectional pattern. In this pattern, both the lexical verb and the auxiliary verb bear the obligatory verbal inflectional categories, operating as co-heads. The Doubled inflectional pattern frequently arises from an original serialized verb construction (see Heine 1993), further discussed in Chapter 7.

Not all languages show obligatory verbal inflection on only the auxiliary verb, only the lexical verb, or simultaneously on both, as in the AUX-headed, LEX-headed, and Doubled (or co-headed) inflectional patterns, respectively. There are also languages which split the obligatory inflectional categories between the auxiliary verb element and the lexical verb element. Chapter 5 deals with this so-called 'split' pattern. Chapter 5 also addresses the striking split/doubled pattern. In this group are languages that split certain types of inflectional categories between the auxiliary verb part and/or the lexical verb of the construction, but other inflectional categories are realized on both the auxiliary verb and the lexical verb.

Chapter 6 examines and exemplifies various kinds of fusing of original bipartite auxiliary verb constructions into complex verb forms. This chapter addresses the historical (phonological) developments of integration etc. that typify the changes from AVC to complex verb forms of numerous types.

Chapter 7 discusses the historical syntax, morphosyntax, and semantics of the developments of auxiliary verb constructions under investigation. This chapter begins with an overview of the original structures that gave rise to the patterns themselves, specifically the constructions that give rise to the various inflectional subtypes of auxiliary verb constructions from the perspective of their diachronic relation to serial verb constructions, verb plus clausal complement structures, and clause-chaining formations. It also discusses in brief the historical semantic processes of grammaticalization reflected in the development of auxiliary verb constructions, classifying different typical paths of lexical to functional semantic specialization.

2

Aux-headed Constructions

Overview

In this chapter, I discuss what I call the AUX-headed pattern of inflection in auxiliary verb constructions. Statistically the most common pattern of inflection in auxiliary verb constructions in the world's languages is this AUX-headed construction, where the syntactic/phrasal and inflectional head coincide. Indeed, this is the pattern seen in various formal sub-patterns in most well-known languages, and the only pattern recognized by various researchers (e.g. the articles in Harris and Ramat (1987)); this has formerly been called the 'Basic' pattern of inflection in auxiliary verb constructions (AVCs) (Anderson 1999, 2000, 2004a). Broadly speaking, the AUX-headed pattern of inflection in AVCs is characterized by the following features: The auxiliary verb often simultaneously serves the dual purpose of indexing some functional category itself while serving as an anchor or locus for the encoding of obligatory verbal inflectional categories necessary to render the clause finite. These may include markers of tense, modality, aspect, argument properties, polarity, and finiteness. The lexical verb occurs in some predetermined 'dependent' form, which may also include a bare/uninflected stem or gender/number-marked 'nominal/adjectival' forms.

2.1 Formal subtypes of AUX-headed auxiliary verb constructions

Many languages contrast various AVCs by both different auxiliary verbs and/ or different forms required of the attendant lexical verb, particular combinations being individually grammaticalized to mark various functional categories. A given language may thus include many such subtypes of AVCs all

TABLE 2.1. Aux-headed inflectional pattern

Inflectional (functional) head	Auxiliary verb
Phrasal/syntactic head	Auxiliary verb
Semantic head	Lexical verb

falling under the general rubric of the AUX-headed inflectional pattern. In fact, English may serve as an excellent example to demonstrate this. As alluded to in Chapter 1, the auxiliary verb *be* 'be' in its various forms occurs in at least two very common AVCs in English: a progressive in *be* + *-ing* and a passive in *be* + '*-ed/-en*' (the latter with numerous allomorphs, including Ø). The auxiliary verb *have* 'have' occurs with the lexical verb in the '*-ed/-en*' form to form a perfect. The forms of the lexical verb in English AVCs have been described as present vs. past and/or passive or perfect participles, gerund(-ive/ial)s, etc. By definition they are non-finite without the accompanying auxiliary verbs (except in their clausal subordination functions suggested by the use of the term 'gerund', e.g. {while} *Going* to the store, I saw John).

Because AVCs occupy a continuum, it is not surprising that a large number of verb–verb constructions in a given language may possess 'sufficient' features for individual researchers to consider them to be 'proper' AVCs but not for others. Imagine the following hypothetical situation. Suppose a language has a verb–verb construction akin to the AVCs in English described above, which seem to represent, formally and functionally, canonical characteristics of AVCs as generally understood in linguistic theory. They encode perfect(ive) or progressive aspect or future tense in an AUX-headed configuration, with subject and tense where possible/relevant encoded on the auxiliary verb and with the lexical verb appearing in a fully dependent/predetermined shape. Lots of other verb–verb constructions may exist in this language that show varying degrees of similarity to this construction; that is, they show some but not all of the features that these AVCs show. For example, some ambiguity or opportunity to divide formal sub-patterns of verb–verb combinations may rest on issues of (morpho) phonology. Infinitive forms in English come to mind. Because modern English lacks a morphological infinitive, verb–verb combinations with the second verb in the infinitive are less likely to be considered AVCs than the canonical ones mentioned above, and may be given instead a term such as semi-auxiliary, quasi-auxiliary, or pseudo-auxiliary. Given the continuum-like and ever-emergent nature of AVCs, which is at odds with the rigid understanding of lexical categorization underpinning much of traditional grammatical analysis, such vacillation or uneasiness is hardly surprising. This is examined in slightly more detail below in the discussion of 'infinitive' forms of lexical verbs in AUX-headed AVCs.

Within the specific context of constructions exhibiting the AUX-headed inflectional pattern, the scalar quality or nature of AVCs may manifest itself through variation in the form of the lexical verb required by a particular AVC. Thus, some of these dependent 'combining' forms of lexical verbs in these constructions may be more grammaticalized than others in the context of the verb–verb combinations permissible in the language. In many languages, a range of such forms of verb may serve as the form of the lexical verb in AVCs. Many such forms share a 'nominal' or adverbial quality and are generally considered to be 'non-finite' (by definition so, being the forms of lexical verbs found with the 'finite' auxiliary verb in an AUX-headed AVC). These lexical verb formations are often marked as overtly nominal, possibly through morphophonological means (the form has the tonal/prosodic qualities of a noun), morphological means (the form possesses a nominalizing affix), or perhaps morphosyntactically (the form possesses a morphological index that exhibits nominal (morpho)syntax, e.g. gender agreement, number agreement (but not person)), or even syntactically (the element occupies a syntactic position otherwise licensed or privileged for nominal elements). Examples illustrating these follow. South Munda Remo shows reduplicated allomorphs of lexical stems in a number of AVCs.

(1) a. Remo (South Munda, Austroasiatic; India) b. Remo
        bəba ḍen-t-iŋ   *gəgay ḍen-t-iŋ*
        R:slap PROG-NPST-1   R:die PROG-NPST-1
        'I am slapping'   'I am dying'
        (Fernandez 1968: 35, 54)

In Yosundúa Mixtec and Ma'di, tonal alternation marks aspectuo-modal categories. For example, tone marks the following verb form as unambiguously completive in Yosondúa Mixtec.

(2) Yosondúa Mixtec (Mixtecan; Otomanguean; Mexico)
     ni yaxī dā ndīkā   *ni kā íkónúú dā*
     COMPL COMPL:eat he banana   COMPL PL CONT:walk.around he
     'he ate bananas'   'they were traveling around'
     (Farris 1992: 55)

In Ma'di, the category NON-PAST is marked by low tone doubly in the following example. Note that this tonal tense-marking is lacking in the 'Burulo dialect (Blackings and Fabb 2003: 215).

(3) Ma'di (Central Sudanic; Nilo-Saharan; Uganda, Sudan)
     ma`tɔ ̀m̩:ū
     I NPST-AUX NPST-go
     'I'm about to go'
     (Blackings and Fabb 2003: 165)

Nominalizations of the lexical verb in an AVC is common in languages from around the world, including Papuan Tairora and Ecuadorian Quechua.

(4) Tairora
     uba-ti-ba a-mi-ro
     talk-say-NMLZR 3OBJ-AUX-3
     'he told him'
     (Vincent 1973: 562)

(5) Ecuadorian Quechua
     puñu-k ri-ni
     sleep-NOM AUX-1
     'I am going to sleep'
     (Muysken 1977: 76; Marchese 1986: 111)

Those that show adjectival (nominal) agreement qualities, for example gender but not person, are common in many better-known Indo-European languages, but relatively uncommon elsewhere.

(6) French
     elle a été vue
     she AUX:3 been:PP seen:PP:F
     'she has been seen'
     (Bentley and Eythórsson 2004: 449)

Auxiliary verb constructions may be marked by word order as well. This is the case in German and Kru languages, where auxiliaries come second and the lexical verb is moved to final position; note that this is also the same order of elements in clauses that consist of a subject, verb and two nominal arguments (or adjuncts).

(7) German (Germanic, Indo-European; Germany, Switzerland, Austria)
     er hat das Buch genommen   *er gab mir das Buch*
     he AUX:3 the.NEUT book   he give.PSTI.DAT the.NEUTbook
         PRTCPL:take:PRTCPL
     'he has taken the book'   'he gave me the book'

(8) Kuwaa (Kru isolate)
     ɯɔ́ ó wá jī-yā
     he PST rice eat-PRF
     'he has eaten rice'
     (Marchese 1986: 38)

In addition to the range of forms in which the lexical verb may appear within an AUX-headed AVC, the range of categories encoded by, or within, the auxiliary verb varies considerably from language to language. Some auxiliary verbs mark tense and/or subject, while others encode a variety of aspectual or modal categories as well as properties of non-subject arguments. The range is considerable and as varied in realization as there are attested systems. This variation is not what matters *per se* in the context of this discussion. What matters from the perspective of the present volume is that the obligatory inflectional categories found in clauses that lack auxiliaries, and therefore are not embedded within an AVC (assuming the language has such formations[1]), are those found on the auxiliary verb, not the lexical verb. This is what defines the inflectional head, after all.

To summarize, auxiliary verb constructions of the AUX-headed inflectional pattern show considerable formal micro-variation. This has resulted from several conspiring but logically independent factors. A large number of auxiliary verbs are found which may combine with a large number of ('nominal(ized)' or 'adverbial(ized)') forms of lexical verbs. These latter may themselves show a range of formal sub-patterns, reflecting also such language-specific factors as degrees of dependency or bondedness, perhaps with various types of residual external syntax speaking to the originally independent nature of the lexical verb.

As alluded to in Chapter 1 above, an enormous range of terminology may be found to describe the forms in which lexical verbs appear in AVCs across the languages of the world, depending in part on other functions or origins of the elements concerned within the grammatical systems of relevant languages, as well as on the accepted terminological metalanguage of the tradition of grammatical analysis within which the presentation is situated. To be sure, various terminological gradations may well have significant structural or formal/functional consequences or reality for the analysis of a given language or group of languages, but maintaining these terminological distinctions in a non-*ad hoc* manner on a cross-linguistic/theoretical level is simply untenable. My treatment of certain constructions as similar, which might maintain salient differences on a language-specific basis, may cause concern for specialists in various domains, but the approach taken here views these distinctions as basically local cross-linguistic/typological micro-variation on a broader common meta-categorial theme. Further, and most importantly from the perspective of the present volume, the obligatory verbal inflectional categories for the particular system are encoded on the auxiliary, and thus the auxiliary verb serves as the inflectional head in these AVCs in all the languages examined below, regardless of the morphophonology or morphosyntactic

---

[1] This requirement for some (although perhaps very few) inflected lexical verbs does appear to be the case cross-linguistically. Even those Australian languages with virtually no clauses without auxiliaries usually have a small number of verbs that behave in this way, even if they are just (original) lexical functions of the very same verbs serving as auxiliaries in the system. It might be the case, however, in theory at least, that a language could have no inflecting verbs that can appear without a verbal complement.

categories of the specific dependent forms of the lexical verbs involved. Considering all of these admittedly disparate AVCs under the single heading of this chapter is thus justified.

That said, the data themselves are presented below organized by the term used to describe the forms of the lexical verbs in the AVCs themselves by the presenter from which the data is taken—a process that is admittedly potentially misleading except in the case of my own field notes, where I alone am to blame for all terminological infelicities. Thus, 'infinitives' are treated together, as are 'participles', 'converbs', etc., with the understanding that what constitutes an 'infinitive' or a 'participle' or a 'gerund' does not necessarily mean the same thing for each language, nor, perhaps unsurprisingly, even for different investigators researching one and the same or closely related languages, but also that from the perspective of the inflectional typology of AVCs, the particular dependent form of a lexical verb in an AUX-headed pattern is not that important *per se*.

2.2 Infinitive forms of lexical verbs in AVCs of the AUX-headed pattern

The most common term for the form of the lexical verb used in an AUX-headed AVC is 'infinitive', with admittedly a range of functions in different languages. It is the default assignation among the languages of the world of the non-finite form of a lexical verb accompanying the inflectional head auxiliary in languages with AUX-headed AVCs in my database. However, as mentioned above, while the opposition of an 'infinitive' marker to another formal marker as non-finite lexical components of AUX-headed AVCs may be a salient one morphosyntactically in a given language, one should not necessarily expect all elements so designated to share all or (when looking at the totality of phenomena described as such) perhaps *any* formal or functional properties. For example, take the formation that is called the 'infinitive' in Russian, English, and Xakas (9).

(9) a. Russian: *-at', -ut',-it', -ti,* etc.
              May take reflexive clitic.
              dvig-at' [=*sja*] 'move'

     b. Xakas: *-AryA, -iryA*
              Does not take subject marking.
              kıl-erge 'to come'

c.   English: *to X*
May fuse with preceding AUX in colloquial/rapid
speech in relatively recently grammaticalized AVCs.
Semi-/quasi-/pseudo-auxiliary formations:
gonna < going to *wanna* < want to

Here, there is even considerable non-identity in the formal and functional properties of these elements within the individual grammatical systems in which they are situated. As is well known, Russian and English belong to two subgroups of Indo-European, viz. Slavic and Germanic, while the last language belongs to the unrelated Turkic family. The infinitive is morphologically marked by a suffix in Russian and Xakas, but by a prepositional phrase in English.[2] The Xakas infinitive is morphologically segmentable (historically) into a participle + case form.[3] For the English and Russian data, the interested reader is referred to the relevant literature on the history of these well-investigated languages.

Russian infinitives may appear as the form of the lexical verb in the periphrastic/imperfective future construction (10). The emergent or semi-auxiliaries of English take infinitive complements (11). In Xakas (12), the infinitive occurs as the lexical complement in an AVC in an intentional construction (actually two separate AVCs, with the specific auxiliary verb used varying according to dialect). A similar construction occurs in the closely related Shor language (13), where its appearance within an AVC has been attributed to influence from Russian (Nevskaja 2000).

(10)   Russian   (11)   English
ja budu čitat'   *I have to go*
I FUT:1 read:INF   I AUX.PRES INF go
'I will read'   'I have to, must go'

(NB: contraction to *hafta* common in appropriate registers of English)

---

[2] English used to have a morphological infinitive suffix like German, but this was replaced with the present 'periphrastic' construction. Note that the *to* in the English infinitive, while etymologically a preposition, is not currently the same as this element. In at least two common constructions in colloquial spoken American English, informal register and/or rapid speech, the 'complementizer' or 'subordinator' element *to* coalesces with a preceding verbal element. These occur in the emergent AVCs in English marking intentional future ([be] *going to* > *gonna*) and desiderative (*want to* > *wanna*; cf. *I'm gonna tell him* vs. **I'm gonna France tonight*. One might imagine a register of English where these have become the norm and thus where the AVCs involved have been reanalysed from taking infinitival lexical complements to zero-marked ones (albeit still within the overall AUX-headed pattern).

[3] Note that the infinitive in Xakas and the etymologically identical construction consisting of the future participle plus the dative case may be distinguished in the language. The infinitive (at least in its function as the lexical complement of certain AVCs) only appears in same-subject constructs by definition. However, the participle plus case sequence may appear in both same-subject and different-subject constructions, and may additionally have an overt encoding (albeit at times redundant) of the person and number of the subject of the clause (Anderson 1998a).

(12) Xakas   cf. (13) Shor
      ol ïly-irya čör-dı   *men iš-ke par-arya čör-čä-m*
      he cry-INF INT-PST   I work-DAT go-INF INT-PRES-1
      'he intended to cry'   'I intend to go to work'
      (Anderson 1998a: 68)   (Nevskaja 1993: 87)

Despite the obvious non-similarities at multiple levels involved-for example, the degree of bondedness of the elements concerned, the transparent connection (or lack thereof) to other forms in the language, or potentially significant variation in their external morphosyntax (e.g. whether the case assigned to an accompanying nominal complement of semantically or syntactically transitive verbs is an accusative/objective-type case that is also characteristic of typical finite uses of the verb or a genitive, relational, or adnominal from typical of nominalizations)-one nevertheless feels confident-or at least specialist researchers in the analysis of the relevant languages do-in calling each of these forms 'infinitives'. Thus, the class of 'infinitives' outlined below is not really a discrete or coherent one, at least in the context of the form of a lexical verb found in an AUX-headed AVC, but rather one that is inherently heterogeneous and varied, and therefore similar to all categories that arise from a grammaticalization or conventionalization of a particular form/ construction in a specified function. In other words, categories such as these are constantly being re-formed, and thus inherently must consist of elements that depend on the particular grammatical system within which they are situated to be adequately defined. That is, 'infinitive' and all the categories of forms of lexical verbs in AUX-headed AVCs discussed in this chapter are construction-based and language-specifically manifested.

Further, 'syntactic' infinitives like the construction characteristic of English, or ones that consist of complementizers plus verbal complement, occupy points on a grammaticalization cline that includes morphological infinitival forms of lexical verbs. Unfortunately, the inherently dynamic or non-discrete nature of auxiliary verb constructions, occupying as they do multiple points on several form–function continua that may also include at other points a range of (i) verb/complement sequences[4] or (ii) serialized verb forms which have entered the verbal periphrasis channel (whether they be 'nuclear' or 'core' SVCs in origin), makes quantifying or qualifying these in discrete, categorial terms an inevitably flawed process.

---

[4] Sometimes 'sufficiently' grammaticalized to be considered as manifesting such enlightening typological categories as 'semi-', 'quasi-', or 'pseudo-auxiliary' constructions. All these terms result from an attempt to categorize discretely a set of phenomena that occupy a continuum, i.e. which are inherently non-discrete.

Leaving aside these meta-methodological caveats on what it means to be an infinitive within the context of the lexical complement of an AUX-headed AVC, I now briefly discuss a variety of languages that utilize infinitive forms of lexical verbs in constructions of this type showing the AUX-headed inflectional pattern.

Kharia (J. Peterson, to appear) is a South Munda language spoken in east-central India by over 200,000 people. It has an infinitive element in-*na* which is generally thought to be a loan element from local Indo-Aryan but might in part (or in whole) reflect an extension of the homophonous intransitive future marker (J. Peterson, personal communication). Most lexical verbs in AVCs in Kharia do not take the infinitive form, but rather appear in a Ø-stem form or a reduplicated stem allomorph, see below.

(14) Kharia
kol-ob-ño?-ḍom-dhab-na la?-ki-kiyar
RECIP-CAUS-eat-PASS-QUICK-INF AUX-PST-3DL
'they two were being fed by each other quickly'
(Malhotra 1982)

Note that there is some evidence that the use of the infinitive with the lexical verb in the infinitive form is of relatively recent historical origin. In earlier sources (Banerjee 1894) there are forms lacking the infinitive that are found in Kharia with it in later sources (Biligiri 1965).[5]

(15) a. Kharia   vs. b. Kharia
         iŋ ño?-cuki-k-iŋ   *ño?-na cuki-k-iŋ*
         I eat-COMPL-PST.1-1   eat-INF COMPL-PST.I-1
         'I have finished eating'   'I have finished eating'
         (Banerjee 1894)   (Biligiri 1965)

A number of other languages of the South Asian macro-region make use of infinitive lexical verbs in AUX-headed AVCs. This includes the Dravidian Betta Kurumba, the Indo-Aryan Maithili, and the Tibeto-Burman Garo in India, Dolakha and Kathmandu Newar, Chantyal, and Belhare all of Nepal and linguistically belonging to the Tibeto-Burman family, as well as in the Tibeto-Burman language Cogste Gyarong of China.

---

[5] This particular AVC is apparently not used in many modern Kharia varieties in any event (J. Peterson, pers. comm.).

(16) Betta Kurumba (Dravidian; India)
      aḍəna ka:rə buḍɽ a:g-pu-əḍə
      aḍən-a ka:rə buḍ-əl a:g-pu-əḍə
      3SR-ACC car drive-INF AUX-IRF-SG
      'he can drive a car'
      (Coelho 2003:2)

(17) a. Maithili   b. Maithili
          həm-ra ja-e-ke əich   *həm-ra jə-e-bak əich*
          I-ACC/DAT go-INF   I-ACC/DAT go-INF
            AUX:PRES:3NH+1H   AUX:PRES:3NH+1H
          'I have to go'
          (Yadav 1996: 230)

(18) Garo
      anʔching reʔang-na nang-a   *anga reʔang-na manʔ-ja*
      we.INCL go.away-INF AUX-PRES   I go.away-INF CAP-NEG
      'we need to go'   'I cannot go'
      (Burling 2003: 398–9)

(19) Dolakhā Newār
      na-i ten-agi   *na-i don-ju*
      eat-INF AUX-3.PRES   eat-INF AUX-3PST
      'about to eat'   'finish eating'
      (Genetti 2003: 361)

(20) Kathmandu Newar (Nepāl Bhāśā)
      jī: ja nɔ-e mɔ-phu:
      I.ERG rice eat-INF NEG-CAP/IMPF
      'I'm not able to eat rice'
      (Hargreaves 2003: 380)

(21) Chantyal
      thū-nu thū-nu la-gəy a-thū
      drink-INF drink-INF AUX-PROG NEG-drink
      'she was about to drink but didn't'
      (Noonan 2003a: 323)

(22) Belhare
      kitap-chi pi-ma ŋ-khe-yu
      book-NSG give-INF 3NSG-must-NPST
      'they must be given books'
      (Bickel 2003: 565)

(23) Cogste Gyarong
ŋa ĵuNĵak ka-pa khya-ŋ
I swimming INF-do CAP-1
'I can swim'
(Nakano 2003: 485)

Apart from Russian and English, a small number of other Indo-European languages of Europe in the sample are found with infinitive forms of lexical verbs in AUX-headed AVCs. This diverse group of IE languages includes the extinct forms of Slavic labelled Old Bulgarian and Old Macedonian, and the Celtic language Breton.

(24) Old Bulgarian
šteš pozna
FUT:2 recognize:SHORT.INF
'you will recognize'
(Tomić 2004: 535)

(25) Old Macedonian
xoščet pogovorěti
3:FUT speak:INF
'(s)he will speak out'
(Tomić 2004: 534)

(26) Breton
emaon o vont
be:PROG:1 PRGPRC go:INF
'I am going'
(Press 1986: 148)

As mentioned above, the Altai-Sayan Turkic languages Xakas and Shor make limited use of infinitive forms of lexical verbs in AUX-headed AVCs. Other Turkic languages of the region, and indeed further afield within the family, do not use such forms in auxiliary verb constructions (Anderson 2004a).

This is not to say that infinitive forms of lexical verbs in AUX-headed AVCs are otherwise unattested in Siberia. Indeed, such formations are found in a range of Uralic languages of western and central Siberia. Thus, such forms are found in Selkup and in a fused construction in the extinct Mator of the Samoyedic branch, in Khanty of the Ugric branch, and outside Siberia in the Finnic language Estonian.

(27) a. Selkup
ili-qo olap-s-ak
live-INF begin-PAST-1
'I began to live'
(Helimski 1998a: 575)

b. Selkup
utir-qo ɛsimp-ak
drink-INF AUX-1
'I am thirsty'

(28)   Mator[†]
      tčёk-sɨ-gan-em
      X-INF-AUX-1
      'I am mistake[n]'
      (Khelimskij 1993)

(29)   a.   Khanty   b.   Khanty
          man-ti pit-t-al   *man-ti pit-l-ə-m*
          go-INF AUX-NPST.EVID-3   go-INF AUX-NPST-EP-1
          'he will go (apparently)'   'I will go'
          (Nikolaeva 1999: 88)   (Nikolaeva 1999: 26)

(30)   Estonian
      tal   *'tuleb 'oodata*
      s/he:ADESS   AUX:3 wait:INF
      's/he has to wait'
      (Viitso 1998: 139)

A small number of Daghestanian (Northeast Caucasian) languages have auxiliary verb constructions that have been described as utilizing lexical verbs in an infinitive form. This includes the Lezgic language Lezgi[an] and the Avar-Andi-Dido[Tsez] language Hunzib.

(31)   Lezgian
      am juǧ-di jif-di ǧam č'ugwa-z šeˆ-iz ẋa-na
      she:ABS day-ADV night-ADV grief pull-IMC cry-INF AUX-AOR
      'she cried day and night in grief'
      (Haspelmath 1993: 146)

(32)   Hunzib
      mə kaǧár čax-á li
      you letter:CLS.5 write-INF AUX:CLS.5
      'you will (really) write a letter'
      (van den Berg 1995: 105)

Among the languages of Africa, infinitive forms of lexical verbs in AUX-headed AVCs are characteristic of Cushitic languages of eastern Africa, various Nilotic languages, as well as Koegu of the Surmic subgroup and the Kuliak language Ik within Nilo-Saharan, all primarily spoken in eastern Africa.

(33)   a.   Somali   b.   Somali
          waan héli doon-aa   *waydin karín doon-taan*

I find.INF AUX-1   you.PL cook.INF AUX-2PL
'I will find it'   'you (PL) will cook it'
(Orwin 1995: 109)

     c.   Somali   d.   Somali
        waan barán jir-ay   *waydin karín jir-teen*
        I learn.INF AUX-1.PST   you.PL cook.INF AUX-2PL.PST
        'I used to learn it'   'you (pl) used to cook it'
        (Orwin 1995: 110)

(34)   Lotuko (E. Nilotic)
      a-ttu nɪ lɛtɛn
      1-FUT I go:INF
      'I'll leave immediately'
      (Heine and Reh 1984: 132; Muratori 1938: 161ff.)

(35)   a.   Lango[6]   b.   Lango
        mitô cèm   *ámìttò cèm*
        3:AUX:HAB eat:INF   1:AUX:PROG eat:INF
        'he's about to eat'   'I want to eat'
        (Noonan 1992: 139)

(36)   Koegu
      a-ma-i mat-en
      1-NEG-i drink-INF
      'I don't/didn't drink coffee'
      (Hieda 1998: 369)

Fused forms with the lexical verb in the infinitive form, but with the seemingly reverse syntax of the periphrastic/syntactic construction, are also found in Koegu.

(37)   Koegu
      a-am-en-[i]-ken
      1-eat-INF-NEG:PROG
      'I'm not eating'
      (Hieda 1998: 368)

---

[6] Note that the same auxiliary element in Lango may have more than one function (and thus appear in more than one AVC) at the same time, here differentiated not by the form of the accompanying lexical verb (cf. the discussion below of Xakas AVCs using the same auxiliary verb but differentiated by the specific converb form of the lexical verb) but rather by the inflectional form of the auxiliary verb.

As mentioned above, infinitive lexical verbs are commonly found within AUX-headed AVCs in various Bantu languages.

(38) a. Kaguru   b. Kaguru
         ni-si ku-langa   *ch-isi ku-langa*
         1-NEG INF-see   1PL -NEG INF-see
         'I don't see'   'we don't see'
         (Torrend 1891: 233)

(39) Bukusu
      bà-lí xû:-bón-á
      3PL-AUX INF-see-FV
      'they see'
      (Aksenova 1997: 17)

(40) Nkore-Kiga
      ni-m-baasa ku-za-yo nyencakare   *ni-m-manya ku-vuga*
      PC-1-AUX INF -go-there tomorrow   PC -1-AUX INF-drive
      'I can go there tomorrow'   'I can drive'
      (Taylor 1985: 165)

Note that although infinitive forms are found relatively frequently in any number of different Bantu languages, there is considerable variation across the family as to which constructions require lexical verbs in the infinitive form, and which require other forms (e.g. a bare stem, or a (partially) inflected form).

Among West African languages in my database, only Diola Fogny possesses this constructional subtype (41).

(41) Diola Fogny (Niger-Congo, Atlantic, Northern; Senegal/Gambia)
      i-lakɔ   *fu-ri*
      1-AUX   INF-eat
      'I was eating'
      (Heine 1993: 46)

'Infinitive' is a term that is rarely used in relation to non-finite verb forms in the metalanguage that has become codified in the linguistic analysis of Papuan, Austronesian or Australian languages. As such, it is hardly surprising that an infinitive form of the lexical verb in an AUX-headed AVC is not found in the database for Austronesian languages, and is found in only four Papuan languages, Daga, Yale, Una and Korowai.

(42) a. Daga   b. Daga
          wa-pen ta-ian   *war-pen ta-in*
          say-INF AUX-1SG.PRES.DUR   get-INF AUX-1SG/FUT
          'I am still trying to speak'   'I will try to get it'
          'I am ready to speak'
          (Murane 1974: 126)

(43) a. Yale (Mek; Papua New Guinea) b. Yale
          le-do a-ok   *bunu-do ba-lam-ek*
          speak-INF AUX-3.REM.PST   swarm-INF AUX-DUR-3PL.
                                                REM.PST

          'he spoke (once)'   'they swarmed'
          (Heeschen 1998: 82, 88)

      c. Yale
          mede-do ba-lam-la
          run-INF AUX-DUR-3.PRES
          'he is running'
          (Heeschen 1998: 88)

(44) a. Una
          atam bu-na ukunyi kib-k-ow
          there sit-INFusually AUX -2:SC-3:3:PST
          'he usually seated you there'
          (Louwerse 1988: 23)

      b. Una
          otam ya-na ukunyi kib-s-ow
          over.there come-INFusually AUX -1PL:SC-3:3PST
          'he usually came to us from that place over there'
          (Louwerse 1988: 23)

(45) Korowai
      nu dépo-ngga wé-ma-lé
      I smoke-INF.CONN CONT-SUPP -1:REAL
      'I smoke continuously'
      (van Enk and de Vries 1997: 93)

With regards to Australian languages, as alluded to above, any kind of morphologically marked subordinate forms of lexical verbs are rare in AUX-headed AVCs, where bare-stem forms of the lexical verbs are the norm in these types of constructions; see below. However, in one Australian language,

Ndjébbana, a lexical verb does appear in an infinitive form, but only in
negative constructions in a split/doubled-looking pattern.[7]

(46) Ndjébbana
      kóma na-bbéngka ka-yangkayí-na
      NEG INF-float 3MIN.MASC-AUX-CNTRFACT
      'it did not float'
      (McKay 2000: 249)

Note that the infinitive is used in the moiety-lect/dialect/speech variety of the
riverside Yirriddjanga Ndjébbana, in combination with an irrealis and coun-
terfactual form of the inflected auxiliary; in the speech of the coastal Djowanga Ndjébbana, on the other hand, the lexical verb is found without the
infinitive prefix.

(47) Yirriddjanga Ndjébbana
      kóma na-rórrddja nga-ya-ngka-yína
      NEG INF-clean 1MIN >3MIN-IRR-AUX-CNTRFACT
      'I didn't clean it'
      (McKay 2000: 161)

(48) Djowanga Ndjébbana
      kóma nga-ya-rarraddja -ngóna
      NEG1 MIN>3MIN-IRR -clean-CNTRFACT
      'I didn't clean it'
      (McKay 2000: 160)

A similar distribution is seen in New World languages. 'Infinitive' forms rarely
appear to be in the terminological metalanguage used for analysis devoted to
the indigenous North American languages, and only one such language in the
database exhibits an AUX-headed AVC with the lexical verb in an infinitive
form, Central Hill Nisenan of the Maiduan family (Penutian).

(49) a. Central Hill Nisenan[†]   b. Central Hill Nisenan[†]
          uk'ojmeedyk-y bemi   *homope bemi peba-m*
          feel.like.going-INF AUX:2   which.one:ACC AUX:2 ask-PROG
          'do you feel like going'   'which one are you asking about'
          (Eatough 1999: 28)

---

[7] Given this distribution, a different terminological tradition may have considered these to represent 'connegative' forms (see below).

c. Central Hill Nisenan[†]
homo-na kani uk'oj-i
where-ALL AUX:2 go.away-INF
'where are you going'
(Eatough 1999: 29)

d. Central Hill Nisenan[†]
nik-ne-(i) dani e-(i)
1-mother-ACC AUX.1 see-INF
'I saw our mother'

Among South American languages, such a form is found in the present study only in the isolates Cayuvava and Leko of Bolivia, and the Zaparoan language Arabela.

(50) a. Arabela (Zaparoan; Peru)
hanija kia-ta kia-nu pani-ja-ni

I you-COM go-INF want-CONT-1R

'I want to go with you'
(Wise 1999: 333, 328; Rich 1999: 91)

b. Arabela
hanija kia pani-tia-a
kia-nu-ni

I you want-APPL-CONTgo-
INF-1R

'I want you to go'

(51) Cayuvava (isolate; Bolivia)
hir-ave ra-čoka
1PL.EXCL-CAP.AUX INF-come
'we can come'
(Key 1967: 38)

(52) Leko (isolate, Bolivia)
Pedru Maria paus-mo-ch puidis-in-aya-te
Pedro Maria forget-REC-INF AUX-NEG-PL-3
'Pedro and Maria cannot forget each other'
(van der Kerke 1998: 202)

~
(53) Leko (isolate, Bolivia)
P. M. paus-ich puidis-mo-in-aya-te
P. M. forget-INF AUX-REC-NEG-PL-3
'P. and M. cannot forget each other'
(van der Kerke 1998: 202)

Note that when comparing the second Leko example with the first, the quasi-inflectional reciprocal element shows variable distribution, seemingly attracted to the auxiliary verb. Similar 'attraction' occurs with quasi-inflectional voice suffixes, reciprocal among them, in Quechua varieties as well (van der Kerke 1998).

(54)   Quechua
       Pedru-wan Maria much'a-na-ku-y-ta muna-nku
       Pedru-COM Maria kiss-REC-RFLX-INF-ACCwant-3PL
       'Pedro and Maria want to kiss each other'
       (van der Kerke 1998: 202)

       ~

(55)   Quechua
       much'a-y-ta muna-na-ku-nku
       kiss-INF-ACC want-REC-RFLX-3PL
       'Pedro and Maria want to kiss each other'
       (van der Kerke 1998: 202)

In Meso-America, infinitival lexical verbs in AVCs are found in such languages as Jiliapan Pame (Otomanguean), and if one considers 'light', 'inflecting', 'dummy', or pro-verbs in combination with Spanish infinitives to represent an example of this subtype,[8] in Tequistlatec (Chontal of Oaxaca) as well.

(56)   a.   Jiliapan Pame (Otopamean; Mexico)   b.   Jiliapan Pame
            ka ma nsáhot   *hu ma nsáhot*
            1 AUX INF:dig   you AUX INF:dig
            'I will/am going to dig'   'you will/are going to dig'
            (Manrique C. 1967: 345)

(57)   a.   Tequistlatec (Tequistlatecan; Mexico)   b.   Tequistlatec
            pásed-úy mándár   *ʔée-m'a aɍépentír*
            AUX-DUR order   AUX-INCOMPL repent
            'order'   'repent'
            (Waterhouse 1967: 359)

2.3 Nominalized forms of lexical verbs in AVCs of the   AUX-headed pattern

While 'infinitive' appears to be the default designation for the (nominalized) lexical component of an AUX-headed AVC cross-linguistically, many other such forms may be encountered. Again, it is important to note that within a given grammatical system an infinitive complement may in fact stand in some

---

[8] Note that that it is common for verbs to be borrowed in infinitive forms when used with dummy/ inflecting stems like this in any number of languages. Xakas (Turkic, Siberia), for example, is riddled with constructions of this type, using Russian infinitives in combination with the inflecting stem *pol-* 'be' (Anderson 1998a).

morphosyntactic opposition with another nominalized form bearing a different designation with which it contrasts in some salient fashion (e.g. the case of
a nominal complement, degree of bondedness). In fact, it may be possible
and/or desirable (if premature) to speak of cross-linguistic or theoretically
relevant subcategories of non-finiteness that distinguish between infinitives,
nominalizations, and other elements discussed below; but in the present
context, such a distinction cannot be maintained as quantifiable, qualifiable,
or even definable in any non-*ad hoc*, or non-language-(or even construction-)
specific way, extrapolating on data from the 800 languages found in my
database.

Overtly nominalized lexical verbs in AUX-headed AVCs are found in only
about half as many languages as 'infinitives', but again show a genetic/areal
linguistic (and tradition-of-analysis) distribution that can be defined. What
constitutes a 'nominalized' form, and whether this element is to be considered
derivational (roughly, category-changing and/or with unpredictable semantic
consequences) or inflectional (with relatively more semantic regularity/pre-
dictably),[9] naturally might vary from language to language, and even among
researchers examining one and the same language or group of closely related
languages. The terms used may actually vary not inconsiderably across the
languages below, but include at least 'verbal noun', 'nominalizer', and the
notoriously nebulous 'supine'.

A small number of Tibeto-Burman languages make use of a nominalizing
element on lexical verbs in a range of AVCs of the AUX-headed type. Such
examples include the following from Lhasa Tibetan, Impal Meithei, and
Kham.

(58) a. Lhasa Tibetan   b. Lhasa Tibetan
          sä?payii^n   *sü?kiyii^n*
          bsad-pa yin   gsod-ki yin
          kill.PST-NMLZR AUX   kill.PRS-NMLZR AUX
          'killed'   'will kill'
          (DeLancey 2003: 277)

      c. Lhasa Tibetan
          nga-s kho-r bshad=rgyu khas=len byas-pa yin
          I-ERG he-LOC tell-NOM promise do-NMLZR AUX.PRF.CONJNCT
          'I promised to tell him
          (DeLancey 2003: 284)

---

[9] Admittedly this is a gross oversimplification of these complex issues, but I leave the subtleties of
this far from resolved controversy to the theoretical morphologists.

(59) Impal Meithei
    ə́y čak čá-bə həw-r-e
    I cooked.rice eat-NMLZR AUX-PRF-ASS
    'I have started eating cooked rice'
    (Chelliah 2003: 436)

(60) a. Kham
      ba-o dəi-ke-o
      go-NMLZR AUX-PFV-3
      's/he was allowed to go'
      (Watters 2003: 697)

    b. Kham
      ba-o e-ke-o
      go-NMLZR AUX-PFV-3
      'she allowed him to go'

    c. Kham
      no:-ye o-za-lai ba-o pərī:-ke-o
      she-ERG 3-child-po go-NMLZR AUX-PRF-3
      'she made her child go'
      (Watters 2003: 696)

These nominalized forms of lexical verbs do not even form a coherent group within these three genetically related (Tibeto-Burman) languages, despite in part reflecting cognate elements. All serve as one or several of a set of lexical verb forms that may combine with auxiliary verbs in AVCs, a system which differs not inconsiderably in both nature and make-up in each of these Tibeto-Burman languages. For example, the pan-Tibeto-Burman nominalizing element-*pa* in Lhasa Tibetan forms a multi-part paradigmatic set with another nominalizing suffix in-*ki*, both further embedded within a larger paradigmatic contrast known as 'conjunct' and 'disjunct' inflection in the specialist literature on Tibeto-Burman languages. The system of AVCs exhibited by Lhasa Tibetan reflects a complex set of grammaticalized constructions using a relatively restricted set of formal elements. However, there is neither a consistent meaning associated with the suffixal nominalizing element nor the auxiliary *per se* across all phonologically similar constructions; rather, individual constructions consisting of various combinations of a relatively limited set of elements have been grammaticalized in a range of different functions. A partial list of these (based on DeLancey 1991, 2003) may be seen in (61).

(61) Lhasa Tibetan
    -*pa* form of lexical verb   -*ki* form of lexical Verb
    -*pa yin* PRF CONJ   -*ki yod* IMPRF CONJ
    -*pa red* PRF DISJ   -*ki 'dug* IMPRF DISJ (or IMP)

In Kham, there are various quasi-nominal forms of lexical verbs appearing within AUX-headed AVCs. One is more nominal in 'feel' (and origin) and this contrasts with a more adverbial type formation (61) (the gerund/converb etc. style discussed in 2.4 below).

(62) a. Kham
        hu-də le
        come-NF AUX:IMPFV
        's/he has come'
        (Watters 2003: 697)

      b. Kham
          rəi-də nəi-wo
          bring-NF AUX-3:IPFV
          's/he has brought it'

In Burushaski, a language isolate of northern Pakistan, there are a small number of AVCs that require the verb to appear in a nominalized form called the 'supine' in the Western grammatical tradition of analysis for the language but an adverbial 'gerund' (*deepričastie*) in the Russian linguistic tradition of analysis of Burushaski.

(63) a. Burushaski
        et-iš ai-ya-mai-ya
        that do-GER NEG-1-AUX-1 AUX.1
        'I can't do that'
        (Klimov and Edel'man 1970: 52)

      b. Burushaski
          duwal-š a-mo-mʌn-ʊmo
          fly-SUP NEG-II-AUX-II.PST
          'she was not able to fly'
          (Lorimer 1935–8: 327)

      c. Burushaski
        bʌyum gʊtɛ tsil min-iš et-i
        mare this water drink-SUP AUX-IMP
        'let the mare drink this water'
        (Lorimer 1935–8: 328)

This underscores the lack of significance attached to the terminological variability associated with the particular form of the lexical verb that is required by various auxiliary verb constructions. This same kind of situation is encountered both within the analysis of individual languages and most strikingly when viewed cross-linguistically, as from the perspective of the present volume. This is because these 'dependent' forms of lexical verbs constitute a continuum that exhibits various characteristics of nominal, adverbial, or adjectival phrases or complements (or verbal as well), with the specific details and manifestations of these varying considerably across languages.

    In the dialect of Ket spoken in Kellog village, Krasnoyarsk Kray, Russia, a verbal noun may appear with a lexical verb to create an AVC. Note that the details of Ket verb structure are strikingly complex, and the interested reader is referred to the rather different analyses found in Werner (1997a, 1997b) and Vajda (2000, 2001, 2003) for details.

(64)   Kellog Ket
    at us'en daqaudin-di-t
    I sleep:VN it:DES:PST-1-SF
    'I wanted to sleep'
    (Werner 1997b: 249)

Further east, Kolyma Yukaghir is another language where the lexical verb in an AUX-headed AVC may appear in a nominalized 'supine' form.

(65)   Kolyma Yukaghir
    juku+joŋžā marqil' min-din l'e-mle
    small+goose girl take-SUP AUX-OF:3
    'the small goose girl is going to marry'
    (Maslova 2003b: 179)

In one tradition of analysis the extinct but important Indo-European language Hittite, once spoken in present-day Turkey, utilizes a so-called 'supine' form in one of its subtypes of auxiliary verb constructions. Other traditions of analysis for the same language consider the element in which the lexical verb appears in this language to be not a supine but rather a participle. Such terminological tension or variation underscores the suggestion made in this chapter that there is a lack of cross-linguistically meaningful distinctions in terminology used to designate the 'marked' form required of the lexical verb component that characterizes the AUX-headed pattern of inflection of AVCs.

(66)   Hittite[†]
    nu=mu[ID] *SIN.D U-aš* DUMU [I]*ZI-DA-A nam-ma-ya da-ma-a-uš*
    UKÚ. MEŠ
    and (against)-me Armadattas son of Zidas furthermore other men
    ù-wa-a-i ti-{iš-ki}-{u-wa-an} ti-i-e-ir
    ill.will stir.up-ITER-SUPINE begin-3PL.PRET
    (Held et al. 1988: 49)

Another group of Indo-European languages that utilizes a verbal noun or nominalized form of the lexical verb within the broader context of an AUX-headed AVC is the Celtic subgroup. Thus, such forms are found in Celtic languages like North Welsh and Manx.

(67)   North Welsh   (68)   Manx
       nawn ni weld John fory   *tami fa:kin ad*
       AUX:1PL we see:VN John tomorrow   INDEP:1 see:VN them
       'we will see John tomorrow'   'I see them, am seeing them'
       (Watkins 1993: 327)   (Broderick 1993: 258)

African languages do not commonly exhibit constructions of this formal
subtype. Such forms are, however, characteristic of a small number of
Niger–Congo languages of West Africa, isolated Chadic languages, and the
Nilo-Saharan language Ik.

(69)   Doyayo (Adamawa; Cameroon)
       a.   *wal²³ taa¹²-be¹ el¹ko³*
            man NEG-1 call∧INC∧MID
            'I'm not having an affair with anyone'
            (Wiering and Wiering 1994: 251)

       b.   *hi¹-taa¹²-wɛ¹seek¹ an¹ doo²³rɔ¹bo³*
            3PL-NEG-1PL look.at∧INC like person true
            'they don't consider us respectable people'
            (Wiering and Wiering 1994: 252)

(70)   Kwami (Chadic, Afroasiatic; Nigeria)
       yìn ɗə̀mángò mècè
       they AUX:PL:PST travel:VN
       'they could travel'
       (Leger 1994: 251)

(71)   Ik [Kuliak; Uganda][10]
       ńtá náɓ-uɗot-í-í fit-és^a
       NEG AUX-AND-1-NEG wash-INF . NOM
       'I did not finish washing'
       (König 2002: 126)

The lexical verb only infrequently appears in a nominal[ized] form in Papuan
and Austronesian languages, and not at all in the Australian languages of the
database. Note that the fully inflected auxiliary encodes object as well as
subject in this Tairora form.

---

[10] Strictly speaking, this appears to be a complex affix consisting of an infinitive and a nominalizing element.

(72)   Tairora
       uba-ti-ba a-mi-ro
       talk-say-NMLZR 3OBJ-AUX-3
       'he told him'
       (Vincent 1973: 562)

(73)   a.   Tutukeian Leti   b.   Tutukeian Leti
            mu̧-èla ni̧ a-mmali   *t-èla k-ni̧ -akri*
            2-AUX NMLZ-laugh   1PL-AUX cry..-NMLZ-..cry
            'you are laughing'   'we are crying'
            (van Engelenhoven 1995: 172)

       c.   Tutukeian Leti
            mu̧ -èla t-ni̧ -oli
            2-AUX see..-NMLZ-..see
            'you are seeing it'

(74)   a.   Kwamera (Austronesian; Vanuatu) b.   Kwamera
            r-am-apwah   *iak-apwah n-arai-ien nei*
               n-en-ien ti nife   *ia takwir*
            3-CONT-NEG   1-NEG NOM-cut-NOM wood
               NOM-go-NOM cause what   LOC mountain
            'why isn't he going?'   'I don't cut wood on the
                                                  mountain'

       (Lindstrom and Lynch 1992: 28)

Unlike infinitives, nominalized lexical verbs are generally speaking not that
uncommon in AUX-headed AVCs among the indigenous languages of the Americas. They are found in a number of families, mainly in the macro-Andean region,
e.g. Tucanoan, Mura-Pirahã, Quechua, Paezan, Puquinan, and Huarpean.

(75)   a.   Cubeo (Tucanoan; Colombia)
            bue-be-kiji-bẽ ape-ixi ba-ki̧rõ
            study-NEG-FUT:MS:NMLZ-FUT:3 other-CLS:year AUX-FUT:INAN:SG:NMLZ
            'he won't study next year'
            (Morse and Maxwell 1999: 31)

       b.   Cubeo (Tucanoan; Colombia)
            Alberto kũĩ-wã-r̃ẽ tito-ji ba-te-ʹabẽ
            Alberto turtle-PL-OBJ shoot.with.arrow-NFUT:MS:NMLZ AUX-DYN-
               N√H:3M
            'Alberto was shooting turtles with an arrow'
            (Morse and Maxwell 1999: 61)

(76) Pirahã [Mura[n]; Brazil]
      hi ob-áaʔái kahaí kai-sai
      3sg AUX-INTNSFR arrow make-NMLZR
      'he really knows how to make arrows'
      (Aikhenvald and Dixon 1999: 356)

(77) Ecuadorian Quechua
      puñu-k ri-ni
      sleep-NOM AUX-1
      'I am going to sleep'
      (Marchese 1986: 111; Muysken 1977: 76)

(78) Pacaroas Quechua
      rika-pu-šqá-s(u) ka-nki
      see-LEX.SFX-STAT.NOM-Q AUX-2
      'have you ever seen it?' or 'did you ever get to see it?'
      (Adelaar 2004: 223)

(79) Puquina† (Puquinan Peru, Colombia)
      no hucha pampacha-sso asch-anta
      1.PAT sin forgive-STAT AUX-3.IMP
      'let my sins be forgiven'
      (Adelaar 2004: 355)

(80) a. Paez (Nasa Yuwe)
          nasa yuwe-aʔs piya-na ũs-tʰu
          Nasa Yuwe-ACC learn-NOM AUX-1
          'I am learning Nasa Yuwe'
          (Jung 1989: 74; Adelaar 2004: 136)

      b. Paez (Nasa Yuwe)
          yat-te ka:piya-ʔh-yaʔ takʰ-e-ʔ-tʸ
          house-LOC teach-TR-INF begin-IMPF-CUST-3PL.EVNT.DECL
          'they began teaching them in the house'
          (Jung 1989: 242; Adelaar 2004: 137)

(81) a. Guambiano (Barbacoan)
          unt yáu-wan má-p-ik ki-n
          child meat-ACC eat-NOM-ADJ be-NON.SPKR
          'the child is eating the meat'
          (Vásquez de Ruiz 1988: 69; Adelaar 2004: 146)

b. Guambiano (Barbacoan)
    nyi purá kʷac-ɨp wa-n
    you maize husk-NOM AUX/sit-NON.SPKR
    'you are (sitting and) husking maze'
    (Vásquez de Ruiz 1988: 69; Adelaar 2004: 146)

(82) Allentiac† (Huarpean)
      quillet-ec el-tichan m-a-npen
      love-VB.EXT PASS-NOM AUX-THM-2
      'you are loved'
      (Adelaar 2004: 547)

Note that as is apparent from the first Cubeo example, this language has nominalizing morphology on the auxiliary verb as well the lexical verb in some AVCs. That is, both appear to be co-dependent (co-headed or co-subordinate), and thus this is somewhat akin to the doubled inflectional pattern described in Chapter 4.

2.4 Gerund/converb forms of lexical verbs in AVCs of the AUX-headed pattern

Unmarked for certain genetic and areal subgroups of the languages of Eurasia and, unrelatedly, Khoisan as well, an adverbial form of the lexical verb may appear in AUX-headed AVCs. This form has been called gerund (gerundive, gerundial) or converb or sometimes just verbal adverb or adverbializer. Such a form is found across Eurasia, and is especially common in the Turkic languages, where there is a highly developed system of these forms. Such constructions also appear in Mongolic, Korean, Nivkh, and the Daghestanian language Hunzib in the Caucasus.[11]

(83) a. Hunzib
          ož-di-l ƛoq'ol guk'-un lo
          boy-OBLQ-ERG hat put-GER AUX
          'the boy has put on his hat'
          (van den Berg 1995: 101)

---

[11] Note that, depending on the particular resulting auxiliary verb construction, the converb element may have both adverbial subordinate and clause-chaining coordinate functions or origins: see Ch. 7.

b.   Hunzib
sɨd-i-i hə̃s kutakalda b-aat'-čo-s-sa zuq'un lo
On:OBLQ-OBLQ-DAT one very HPL-love:PL-PRES-GEN-*sa* AUX-GER
AUX:HPL
'they apparently loved each other very much'
(van den Berg 1995: 94)

(84)   Nivkh
jaŋ hup-ř hunv-nd
he sit-CV:MAN AUX-FIN
'he is sitting'
(Gruzdeva 1998: 30)

In certain highly Turkicized varieties of Uralic, e.g. the extinct Kamas or dialectal Mari (see below), gerund forms of lexical verbs are found in AVCs. In Kamas, these occur in mainly fused forms. In this regard, Kamas is highly reminiscent of the Altai-Sayan Turkic language Xakas, to which the Kamas speakers were assimilated linguistically during the nineteenth and twentieth centuries. Many aspects of the auxiliary verb system, including the selection/ grammaticalization of particular auxiliaries in particular functions, is also quite similar to Xakas, and likewise probably reflects interference from this latter language (G. Klumpf, personal communication, 2001).

(85)   a.   Kamas[†]   b.   Kamas
       *mənzə-lä iʔbe > mənzᵊlʲlɛßᵊ   *ətʲer-laa-walʲa-m*
       cook-GER AUX > cook.GER.AUX   tie.up-GER-AUX-1
       'is cooking'   'I have tied it up'
       (Donner 1944: 85, 101; Simoncsics   (Simoncsics 1998: 590)
       1998: 584)

       c.   Kamas[12]   d.   Kamas
       kuja dʲəmdə-laa-ʔbə   *kəm uʔ-la-ʔbə*
       sun shine-GER-AUX   blood flow.GER.AUX.PRES.3
       'the sun is shining'   'the blood is flowing'
       (Simoncsics 1998:590)   (Künnap 1999b:34)

(86)   Xakas
oyna-p-ča-m
play-CV-PRES-1
'I am playing'
(Field notes)

---

[12] The Kamas gerund may either be harmonic *la/lä laa/lää* or non-harmonic *-laa*.

Other agglutinating, SOV languages variously described as 'Altaic' exhibit this particular sub-pattern of marking on lexical verbs within an AUX-headed pattern of inflection in auxiliary verb constructions. This includes Korean and Mongolic languages.

(87) Korean
      che=ga   *mun=ul*   *chi-go*   *issayo*
      he=NOM   door=ACC   hit-GER   AUX.PROG.DECL.POL
      'he is hitting the door'

(88) [Khalkha] Mongolian (Mongolic; Mongolia, China)
      ta yuu sur-č wain
      you what study-CV AUX
      'what are you studying?'
      (Hangin 1968: 31)

(89) a. Buryat   b. Buryat
          nom unsha-zha bai-na   *unsh-aad bai-na*
          book read-CV:IMPRF AUX-DUR   book read-CV:PRF AUX-DUR
          'he is reading a book'   'he has read it'
          (Skribnik 2003: 117)

Outside Eurasia, only a handful of languages have been described with such forms, e.g. the Tacanan language Cavineña from Bolivia (where it is called the 'manner' suffix), the Jivaroan language Shuar of Ecuador, Karo of the Tupi-Guaraní family from Brazil, and the isolate language Urarina of Peru.

(90) Cavineña (Tacanan)
      had^{y}a hu-diru-e ya-ȼe hu-čine ya-ȼe-ha etare-hu
      thus go-return-MAN 1-DL:ABS AUX-PST 1-DL-GEN house-to
      'thus we returned home'
      (Camp 1985: 39)

(91) Urarina (isolate; Peru)
      kʉ ahtĩĩ raãsaʉre iɲaẽ ahkaʉrʉ heruri kahtaã ʉhʉaj̃ nia ahkaʉ haʉ
      kʉ ahtĩĩ raãsa-ʉre iɲaẽ ahkaʉrʉ heruri kahtaã
      there nevertheless dance-3PL already 3PL belt/waist middle

      ʉ-h-a-ĩ n-i-a ahkaʉ haʉ
      come-CONT-ST.EXT-GER AUX-ST.EXT-3 water as/because
      'nevertheless they (still) danced and the water (almost) reached the
          middle of their waists'
      (Olawsky 2002: 63)

(92)   Káro (Tupi; Brazil)
       aʔwero toba okay
       aʔ=wero top-a o=kap-t
       3=speech see-GER 1=AUX.FUT-IND₁
       'I will listen to him'
       (Gabas 1999: 60)

(93)   Shuar (Jivaroan)
       kanu nahána-sa puhá-hey
       canoe make-GER AUX-1
       'I am making a canoe'
       (Adelaar 2004: 443; Karsten 1935: 555)

In addition, a small number of Austronesian language, e.g. Adzera and Wampar, show gerundive forms of lexical verbs in AVCs. Elsewhere in the macro-Indo-Pacific region this sub-pattern is highly marked.

(94)   Wampar
       ji gi-su ha-ra gum
       I 1/SUBJ.MRKR-AUX go-GER garden
       'I will go to the garden'
       (Holzknecht 1989: 150)

(95)   Adzera
       ji gi-su fa-da gum
       I SUBJ.MRKR-AUX go-GER garden
       'I will go to the garden'
       (Holzknecht 1989: 150)

One notable exception to this comes from the Khoisan linguistic tradition. Many Khoisan languages have a quasi-adverbial form of the lexical verb used when appearing within (AUX-headed) AVCs (a gerund-like form ultimately perhaps derived from a copula verb: see Heine 1986; Vossen 1997). The elements concerned are called in the traditional terminology of the field of Khoisan studies 'juncture' forms.

(96)   Naro (Khoisan, Central; Botswana)
       ≠'ũ-á dá-hã
       eat-JNCT 1-PRF
       'I have eaten'
       (Heine 1986: 15)

Note that many complex verb forms in other Khoisan languages, as in the Xakas and Kamas examples above, show fused or slightly more phonologically cohesive/bonded forms with the juncture morpheme.

(97)   Buga-/Anda (Kxoe) (Central Khoisan; Angola, Namibia)
       (tí) ʔá-ná -hà-bé
       I know-JNCT-PST-NEG
       'I don't know (it)'
       (Vossen 1997: 192)

(98)   a.   Cara (Shua) (Central Khoisan; Botswana)   b.   Cara (Shua)
            khùì -à-tá   *khùì-à-há*
            lift-JNCT-PST   lift-JNCT-IMPF
            'lifted'   'was lifting'
            (Vossen 1997: 181)

For more on synthetic compounds of this type arising from fused AVCs of the AUX-headed type, see Chapter 6.

As alluded to above, one language group for which a converb or gerund form of the lexical verb used in AVCs is the default form is the Turkic language family. Virtually all Turkic languages from all historical periods use some converb or another on the lexical verb in these constructions. Note that the specific inventory of converbs varies considerably among the individual Turkic languages. Importantly however, even when elements in this function are lost from a given language, formally different but functionally similar elements renew this system. Compare in this regard the following forms from several Turkic languages. Each uses a cognate auxiliary verb in a functionally cognate construction; only the specific form of the converb used varies (or another specified non-finite form of the lexical verb, e.g. a participle, same subject marker, Ø, etc.). These are tabulated in Table 2.2.

Further, in some languages particular converb plus auxiliary combinations have been grammaticalized in specific functions in opposition to combinations with the same auxiliary verb and a lexical complement in a different converb form, e.g.-*Ip ber* vs.-*A/j ber* in Tuvan (99), marking benefactive/object version and inchoatives respectively.

(99)   a.   Tuvan   b.   Tuvan
            biži-(j) ber-di-m   *biž-ip   ber-di-m*
            read-CV INCH-PAST.II-1   write-CV BEN-PAST.II-1
            'I began to write'   'I wrote (it) for someone else'
            (Field Notes)

TABLE 22. Subject-version AVCs in selected Turkic languages

Language	LV form	AV stem	Citation	Gloss
Shor	-Ip	al	ta-p al-gan-nar	'they found for selves
Tofa	-GAʃ	al	tùt-kaʃ al-ɣan	'caught for himself'
Turkmen	-Iv	al	yïrti-ïv al-yaardï	'was tearing off for self'
Uighur	-iw-	-al-	yez-iw-al-di-m	'wrote down for self'
Yakut (Sakha)	-An	il	taay-an il-la	'he guessed for himself'
Xalaj	-Ø-	-al-	tut:-āl-du-m	'I seized it (for myself)'
Chuvash	-sA	il	kălarsa il	'steal for self'
Orkhon Turkic	−α*	al-α	ölür-tü-müz al-tï-miz	'we killed for selves'

*-α indicates the inflections found on the auxiliary are also found on the lexical verb: this represents the doubled inflectional pattern discussed in Ch. 4.

(Sources: Rassadin 1994: 198; Doerfer 1988: 169; von Gabain 1974: 279 l.3; Hahn 1991: 612; Hansar 1977: 90; Korkina et al. 1982: 289; Nevskaja 1993: 45; Skvorcov 1985: 111)

In other languages, a given auxiliary may appear in one and the same functional AVC with a lexical verb (optionally) in more than one converb form. This situation is found with the translocative (andative) formation in Tofa. See Anderson (2004a) for more details.

(100)   Tofa
       hün bàt-a bar-gan
       sun descend-CV TLOC-PST
       'the sun set'
       (Rassadin 1978: 155)

(101)   Tofa

ay-da-a	čil baɣa	ol ool-nï	al-ïp	bar-ɣan	ay-ɣa
moon-LOC-DC	demon	that boy-ACC	take-CV	TLOC-pst	moon-DAT

       'the moon-demon took this boy up to the moon'
       (Rassadin 1971)

Note that, given certain processes of erosion, it is sometimes the case that only the converb remains of an original (now fused) AVC in a given Turkic language, i.e. the original auxiliary itself has a Ø realization. Compare the following first and third person present forms in such Central Asian Turkic languages as Kyrgyz and Karakalpak. Similar forms are found in Bashkir (Bashqort) and dialectal forms of Chuvash as well.

(102) a. Kyrgyz   b. Kyrgyz
           jaz-a-m   *bol-ot*
           write-PRES/FUT-1   be[come]-PRES/FUT.3
           'I write'   'it becomes'
           (Junusaliev 1966: 496)

(103) a. Karakalpak   b. Karakalpak
           al-a-saŋ   *al-adï*
           take-PRES-2   take-PRES.3
           'you take'   's/he takes'
           (Baskakov 1966b: 311)

(104) Bashkir
       ukï-j-mïn
       read-PRES<CV-1
       'I read'
       (Juldašev 1966: 182)

(105) a. 'Dialectal' Chuvash   b. 'Dialectal' Chuvash
           Jul-a-p   *jul-a-n*
           remain-PRES(<CV)-1   remain-PRES(<CV)-2
           'I stay, remain'   'you stay, remain'
           (Johanson 1976: 58)

Similar phenomena can be seen in other languages. Compare the following two forms, one from the dialect forming the basis of standardized or literary Mari and one from one of its spoken dialects. The transparent AVC of the dialectal Mari form has been fused and has lost the original auxiliary element altogether.

(106) 'Dialectal' Mari   (107) Literary Mari
       nal-ən ul-na   *nal-ən-na*
       take-GER AUX-1PL.PRES   take-GER-1PL.PRES
       'we have taken'   'we have taken'
       (Kangasmaa-Minn 1998: 238)

2.5 Participle forms of lexical verbs in AVCs of the AUX-headed pattern

Verbal forms described as participles form an integral part of the auxiliary verb systems in a wide range of unrelated languages. These may appear in non-finite and/or subordinate clauses of various types. Depending on, of course, the system relevant to a particular language, participles generally encode some combination of tense and aspect categories ((im)perfect(ive), past, present, future), and possibly argument properties as well. Although a range of familiar Indo-European languages show adjectival or nominal morphosyntax associated with these, e.g. gender and number agreement, but not person, e.g. French, Spanish, Italian, Hindi/Urdu, this subtype of participle construction is actually fairly uncommon cross-linguistically. Note that number agreement does not even occur in all varieties of these languages, e.g. Genzano of Lazio, Italy.

(108) a. Hindi
          ghumta hũ
          take.walk:IMPF:M AUX:1
          'I take a walk'
          (Kachru 1990: 482)

     b. Hindi
          ghum rəhi hũ
          take.walk CONT:FEM AUX:1
          'I am taking a walk'

(109) Italian
     è stata vista
     be:3 been:PP:F seen:PP:F
     'she has been seen'
     (Bentley and Eythórsson 2004: 449)

(110) French
     elle a été vue
     she AUX:3 been:PP seen:PP:F
     'she has been seen'

Cf.

(111) Genzano (Italian, Romance, Indo-European; Lazio, Italy)
     hanno sbocciate
     AUX:3PL bloomed:PP:F
     'they (the roses) have bloomed'
     (Bentley and Eythórsson 2004: 466)

Similar phemomena are found, however, in a small number of other gender-dominant languages in my database, like the Omotic language Gimira (Benchnon) of Ethiopia or the Tucanoan language Desano of Colombia.

(112) a. Gimira (Benchnon) (Omotic)
          yi¹ si³ han³k̓i⁵ yis⁴ku ² e³
          he:SUBJ go.PST.PRTCPL:M AUX:PRES:3M
          'he is going'
          (Breeze 1990: 31)

     b. Gimira (Benchnon) (Omotic)
          wu¹sa³ han³k̓a⁴ yis³ten²e³
          she:SUBJ go:PST.PRTCPL:F AUX:PST:3F
          'she was going'
          (Breeze 1990: 31)

c. Gimira (Benchnon) (Omotic)
    wu¹sa ³ han³k̆ a⁴ yis⁴tar⁴ ge² ne³
    she:SUBJ go:PST.PRTCPL:F AUX:PST:NEG:3F
    'she was not going'
    (Breeze 1990: 31)

(113) a. Desano (Tucanoan; Colombia)
           su?ri koe-go ii-kū-bō pera-ge
           clothes wash-FEM AUX-ASSUM-3FEM port-LOC
           'she probably is washing clothes at the river landing'
           (Miller 1999: 67)

       b. Desano
           pisadā wai-re ba-di-gɨ arī-bī
           cat fish-SPC eat-PST-M AUX-3M
           'the cat must have eaten the fish'
           (Miller 1999: 68)

       c. Desano
           Boo ɨ̄tābū-ge wa?a wa-di-rā arī-bā
           Boo rapids-LOC go AUX-PST-AN:PL AUX-3PL
           'They must have gone to the Boo rapids'
           (Miller 1999: 68)

Note that in some languages, lexical verbs in AVCs may show only number agreement, e.g. Kolyma Yukaghir (here with the subordinator suffix -*jōn*-):

(114) Kolyma Yukaghir
       tāt irk-in puge-ge tāt ejre-jōn-pe ō-d'īl'ī
       CON.ADV one-ATTR summer-LOC CON.ADV walk-SBNR-PL AUX-ITR:1PL
       'so, one summer, we went roaming'
       (Maslova 2003b: 180)

The reverse situation is encountered in Arabic varieties, where auxiliaries may have only partial agreement (e.g. number) but the lexical verb marks subject person (and number). This is thus a kind of split or LEX-headed formation, possibly derived from a doubled formation through the loss of the original person inflection on the auxiliary. In a recent article on this kind of 'semi-agreement' in Chadian Arabic, Kihm (2003) sets out an inflectional morphosyntactic operator set of the type: *T[impf, Number, Person] @...@ V[impf, Number, Person]*, embedded within a theory of syntax of the verb phrase dating back to Pollock (1989). Kihm claims that in such forms as in the following from Chadian Arabic (115), person is not realized, i.e. 'no substring of the form links to that subset in the feature set, which is normal for participles' (Kihm 2003: 340–1), but may in fact be realized in other constructions in Standard Arabic (116). That is, 'person is latent in T and is only realized in ... V' in Chadian Arabic progressive presents, but not in Standard Arabic pluperfects, where doubled inflection occurs (see Chapter 4).

(115) Chadian Arabic (Afroasiatic, Semitic; Chad)
       aniina gaa'idiin naakulu
       we AUX:ACT.PRTCPL:PL 1PL:eat:PL
       'we are eating'
       (Kihm 2003: 340)

(116) Standard Arabic
       kun-tu katab-tu
       AUX.PRF-1 read.PRF-1
       'I had written'
       (Kihm 2003: 341)

These adjectival or nominal agreement properties are in no sense necessary or even typical properties of elements called participles functioning as forms of lexical complements in AUX-headed AVCs. A variety of Tibeto-Burman languages, as well as various local varieties of Indo-Aryan languages, including extinct ones, make use of participle forms of lexical verbs in AVCs showing no such properties. Examples include the following:

(117) a. Kinnauri   b. Kinnauri
           bə-sid du-k   *tuŋ-o nito-k*
           come-PST.PSSV AUX-1   drink-PRS.PRTCPL AUX-1
           'I have come'   'I shall be drinking'
           (Sharma 1988: 139)   (Sharma 1988: 146)

(118) Maithili [Indo-Aryan]
       kha-it ch-əl-ah
       eat-IMPF AUX-PST-3H
       'he was eating'/'he used to eat'
       (Yadav 1996: 235)

(119) Dolakhā Newār
       musukka ŋil-en coŋ-gu
       smiling smile-PRTCPL AUX-3.PST.HAB.REM
       '(they) were smiling prettily'
       (Genetti 2003: 365)

(120)   Koṭgaṛhi Himachali (Indo-Aryan; India)
        tɛb:ɛ gɔ sɔ rakš ʻudːzʻuɪ
        then AUX:PRET that ogre rise.up:PRTCPL[13]
        'then those ogres rose up'
        (Hendriksen 1990: 162)

European Indo-European languages frequently show formations of this type
with the lexical verb in a participle form. Such formations are found for
example in Tosk Albanian and Icelandic.

(121)   Tosk Albanian
        të mos kishe ardur, do ta kishim kryer projektin
        SBJ.COMP NEG AUX:2PL.SBJ come:PRTCPL FUT SBJ.COMP+3:ACC AUX:
        PST:1.IMP finished:PRTCPL project:DEF.M.ACC
        'if you had not come, we would have finished the project'
        (Tomić 2004: 539)

(122)   Icelandic
        hún hefur farið til Lundúna
        she AUX:3 go:PP to London
        'she has been (gone) to London (and has come back)
        (Bentley and Eythórsson 2004: 451)

Non-Indo-European languages of Europe (Northeast Caucasian, Basque,
Finnic) show similar constructions as well, with lexical verbs in a so-called
participle form in an AUX-headed AVC.

(123)   a. Basque (isolate; Spain, France)
            kale-an   ikus-i   z-a-it-u-t gaur
            street-LOC   see-PRF   2-PRS-PL-TR-1 today
            'I have seen you in the street today'
            (Saltarelli 1988: 223)

        b. Basque
            atzo   Peru   ikusi   nuen
            yesterday Peru   see:PRF 1:AUX:PST:3OBJ
            'yesterday I saw Peru'
            (Hualde and Ortiz de Urbina 2003: 265)

---

[13] Note the German/Dutch-like syntactic pattern found in the last example, with the participle
found in clause-final position. This is in fact probably the archaic position for this element, reflecting
the observable cross-linguistic tendency that (originally) subordinate formations preserve older syntax
even when main-clause syntax has innovated a new structure. Auxiliary verb constructions, some of
which originally come from biclausal formations, may likewise reflect this archaic syntax, albeit in a
frozen or grammaticalized manner, depending on the language.

(124) Tsez (Northeast Caucasian; Russia)
t'ek t'et'er-xo joł
boy book read-PRS.PRT is
'the boy is reading the book'
(Polinsky 1995: 3)

(125) Godoberi
Rumi-bú bú=ka
fall.asleep:PST-PART NEUT=AUX:PST
'I fell asleep'
(Kibrik 1996: 63)

(126) North Saami   (127) Finnish
le-áje-n boahtá-n   *ol-i-n tul-lut*
AUX-PST-1 come-PP   AUX-PST-1 come-PRTCPL
'I had come'   'I had come'
(Abondolo 1998b: 28)

(128) a. Estonian   b. Estonian
'ol-en `sööt-nud*                *'ol-in `sööt-nud
AUX-PRES:1 feed-PST.PRTCPL   AUX-PST:1 feed-PST.PRTCPL
'I have fed'   'I had fed'
(Viitso 1998: 140)

Constructions with the lexical verb in a participle form play an integral part of
Burushaski verbal inflection (Anderson, to appear, a). At least one complex
verb form involves a participle form of the lexical verb followed by an
inflected form of the auxiliary. Note that the participle may optionally encode
a first person subject yielding formations that reflect either an AUX-headed
construction or a doubled construction, but with the lexical verb in either
instance appearing in a participle form.

(129) a. Burushaski   b. Burushaski
ǰe á-yan-um bay-a-m ~   *ǰe á-yan-a-m báy-a-m*
I 1-sleep-AP AUX-1-AP   I 1-sleep-1-AP AUX-1-AP
'I fell asleep'
(Berger 1998b: 133)

Note that Burushaski also exhibits a further subtype of AVC involving a case-
marked participle form of the LV in combination with a particular auxiliary
verb. For more on case forms of lexical verbs and AVCs see below.

A range of Turkic languages belonging to various historical strata show
participles of lexical verbs in certain AVCs. Various AVCs in Tuvan take a

lexical verb in a participle form. This tendency may be found even in Old Turkic sources. Most commonly, participle forms of lexical verbs occur in the formation of compound TAM forms using a copular verb stem (*pol/bol, tur,* etc.) seen in most Turkic languages of Siberia, e.g. Xakas. Further, in Tofa and Ös (Middle Chulym), there appear to be newly emergent forms using lexical verbs in participle forms. These may in part possibly be reinforced by the advanced moribund state of these latter two languages, and the concomitant narrowing of some, and expansion of other, functions of various elements in the grammar that this sociohistorical linguistic process frequently entails (Harrison and Anderson 2003, Anderson 2001, Anderson and Harrison, to appear).

(130)   Tuvan
    nomu-m   *čedir-ip*   *al-ïr*   *čas-tï-m*
    book-1   lose-CV   SUBJ.VERS-P/F AUX-REC.PST-1
    'I nearly lost my book'
    (Anderson and Harrison 1999: 45)

(131)   Old Turkic
    Yay-lïγ   *taγ-ïm-a*   *aγ-ïpan,*   *yaylay-ur*   *tur-ur män*
    Summer-ADJ mountain-1-DAT go.up-CV pass.summer-AOR AUX-AOR 1
    'I go up to my summer mountain and pass the summer (there)'
    (von Gabain 1941 [1974]: 121)

(132)   Xakas
    anaŋ   *tipsï-de-gï it-ter-nI*   *kör-er*
    then   hollow.wooden.meat.storehouse-LOC-DC
              meat-PL-ACC   see-FUT

    pol-za,   *pulan*   *sün*   *it-ter-ï*   *pizir-γan*
    AUX-CON   elk   maral.deer meat-PL-3   cook-PAST
    pol-tïr-lar
    AUX-EVID.PAST-PL
    'then when he would look at the meat in the hollow wooden
    storehouse, it (had) turned out that they had cooked meat (there)
    of elk and maral deer'
    (Anderson 1998a: 58)

(133)   Tofa
    dört   *arta-r*   *ber-di-vis*
    four   remain-P/F ASP-REC.PST-1PL
    'there are four of us left'
    (ASLEP Field Notes)

Participles are found on lexical verbs in a number of Afroasiatic languages but are otherwise highly marked in the African macro-region. Other examples are attested, albeit rarely, with lexical verbs in participle forms in such languages as Beja, Afar, and Oromo of Wellegga, all of the macro-Ethiopian linguistic area.

(134) Oromo of Wellegga   (135) Oromo of Wellegga
    adeemaa(n) jira   *adeemaa hin-jiru*
    go-PRTCPL AUX:PRES   go-PRTCPL NEG-AUX:PRES
    'he is going'   'he isn't going'
    (Gragg 1976: 189)   (Gragg 1976: 189)

(136) Beja (Cushitic, Afro-Asiatic; Eritrea, Sudan)
    tam-èe ʔee-fè
    eat-PRTCPL 1.AUX
    'I shall be eating'
    (Hudson 1976b: 105)

(137) Afar
    d' kam-uk sug-'t-e
    eat-IMPRF.PRTCPL AUX-2-PST/PRF
    'you were eating'
    (Bliese 1976: 147)

Diyari is among the few languages of the macro-Indo-Pacific region that has been described as having participle forms of lexical verbs in AUX-headed AVCs.

(138) Diyari (Australian, Pama-Nyungan; Australia)
    ŋathu   *jukurru*   *wayi-rna*   *wanhthi-yi*
    1sg.Agent kangaroo cook-PRTCPL DISTANT.PAST-PRES
    'I cooked a kangaroo (a long time ago)'
    (Dixon 1980: 430)

Primarily lacking in both the languages themselves and the linguistic meta-language of the study of indigenous languages of North America, participles *qua* participles appear in such South American languages as Huallaga Quechua, Kaxuyana, and a range of other Cariban languages.

(139)   a. Huallaga Quechua (Quechuan; Peru)
       away-sha ka-ra-n
       go-PRTCPL AUX-PAST-3
       'he had gone'
       (Weber 1989: 24)

b.   Huallaga Quechua
     allcha-ka:-chi-sha ka-shka-:
     fix-PASS-CAUS-PRTCPL AUX-PERF-1
     'I have been healed'
     (Weber 1989: 246)

(140)   Waiwai (Cariban, Brazil, Guyana)
        ti-kah-so nasɨ
        ADV-slip-PRTCPL 3.AUX
        's/he slipped'
        (Gildea 1998: 220)

(141)   Kaxuyana (Cariban, Brazil)
        suriana wɨya sesu t-emo'ka-ʃe nast
        Juliana ERG Sérgio ADV-teach-PRTCPL 3AUX
        'Juliana taught Sérgio'
        (Gildea 1998: 231)

Participle forms of lexical verbs also may be found in AUX-headed AVCs in the isolate language Purépecha (Tarascan) of Mexico. Note that the order of the auxiliary and lexical verb component of AVCs is variable in this language.

(142)   a.   Purépecha (Tarascan)
             'i táɽeta xúKs-kata xáɽa-š-ti
             DEM field sow-PRTCPL be-AOR-3
             'the field was sown (by my son)'
             (Chamereau 2000: 143)

        b.   Purépecha
             'i tʰirerakua xáɽa-š-ti kuáᵃɽata-tini
             DEM table AUX-AOR-3 break-PRTCPL
             'this table is broken'

2.6 Tense-aspect-mood forms of lexical verbs in AUX-headed AVCs

Various languages are described as possessing AVCs of the AUX-headed inflectional pattern where the form of the lexical verb appears to be a tense-aspect-mood (TAM) marker. While split patterns of inflection exist (see Chapter 5)—and in some of the cases below, this may well be the better analysis—lexical verbs appear in various participle-like forms encoding a range of tense, aspect, and mood categories.

In the South Munda language Remo, transitive verbs appear in the PST.II form while intransitives appear in a bare stem (or Ø-marked) form with the same auxiliary verb in functionally identical AVCs.

(143) a. Remo   b. Remo
           baḍ-oʔ suŋ-oʔ-niŋ   *gay suŋ-oʔ-niŋ*
           slap-PST.II COMPL-PST.II-1   die COMPL-PST.II-1
           'I finished slapping'   'I finished dying'
           (Fernandez 1968: 55)

       c. Remo   d. Remo
           baḍ-o ʔ suŋ-suŋ ḍen-ta   *gay suŋ-suŋ ḍen-ta*
           slap-PST.II RDPL-COMPL   die RDPL-COMPL
              PROG-NPST   PROG-NPST
           's/he is finishing slapping'   's/he is finishing dying'

In the closely related Gutob language, both transitive (PST.II) and intransitive (PST.I) take their respective past tense suffixes. Gutob may have innovated this from the curious Remo-like pattern.

(144) Gutob
       naik-barik sobu su-sun-nen ḍu-tu pigs-oʔ suŋ-tu-niŋ
       headman-et al. all REDPL:say-PL AUX-FUT.II break-PST.II INTNSV-
          FUT.II-1
       'the headman et al. are all saying that I broke (it)'
       (Zide, n.d.)

(145) Gutob
       simra-gu ḍu-loŋ-nen
       enjoy-PST.I AUX-FUT.I-PL
       'they will have enjoyed it'
       (n Zide, n.d.)

Several of the forms in which lexical verbs appear in Basque function as tense-cum-participles, e.g. the future participle:

(146) Basque
       bai, eingo zenduzen bai
       yes do:FUT 2:AUX:PST:3PL:OBJ yes
       'yes, perhaps you did them'
       (Hualde and Ortiz de Urbina 2003: 267)

As mentioned previously, the 'connegative' element in Amanab requires a past tense form of the verb (here an auxiliary), even if the form is present tense in meaning:

(147) a. Amanab (Waris, Trans-New Guinea)
           ka mas anwana-fe-g-mo
           I NEG know-AUX-PST-NEG
           'I don't know'
           (Minch 1992: 147)

       b. Amanab
           mas ka anwana-fe-g-mo
           NEG I know-AUX-PST-NEG
           'I'm not the one who knows'

A handful of Australian languages mark lexical verbs in AVCs with a participle suffix. Note that, as in many languages, e.g. Turkic, participles and tense markers are often historically related, and thus in some instances the construction may actually be a doubled or split pattern, or become one, rather than an AUX-headed pattern. Australian languages showing this type of AUX-headed AVC pattern include Yuwaalaraay, Panyjima, and the very small number of auxiliary constructions in non-Pama-Nyungan Jaminjung.

(148) Yuwaalaraay
       gi:r ŋaya gi-ya:ṇa wi: garalday
       PRTCL I AUX-PROG:PRES wood:ABS cut:PROG:FUT
       'I will cut wood'
       (Williams 1980: 71)

(149) a. Panyjima
           ngaliyakuru panti-wuru nyarru-wayi-ku juju-ngarli-la
           1PL.EXCL AUX-HAB dance-INCH-PRES old.man-PL-LOC
           'we used to dance with the old people'
           (Dench 1991: 140)

       b. Panyjima
           ngunha marlpa panti-ku witi-pi-lku palya-ntharri-ngarli-ku
               yarnta-warntura-la
           that man AUX-PRES play-PROG-PRES woman-PL-PL-ACC
               day-DISTR-LOC
           'that man is flirting with (groups of) women each day'
           (Dench 1991: 150)

(150)   a.   Jaminjung (Australia)
            bulug-mayan=biya yurr-yu ngiyina minyga gugu ti:
            drink-CONT=now 1PL.INCL-be.PRS DIST what's.it.called water tea
            'let's be drinking now, that, what's it called, tea'
            (Schultze-Berndt 2000: 129)

        b.   Jaminjung
            gurrany=biya nga-ngga burlug-mayan marring
            NEG=now 1SG-go.PRS drink-CONT bad
            'I don't drink [alcohol], it's bad'
            (Schultze-Berndt 2000: 129)

In Nez Perce, a lexical verb may appear with a stative suffix within an AUX-headed construction.

(151)   a.   Nez Perce
            wáapci'yaw-ni'n hi-wc'ée-yu'
            kill-STAT 3NOM-AUX-ASP
            'she will become killed'
            (Rude 1986: 131; Phinney 1934: 343:5; 453: 10)

        b.   Nez Perce
            mét'u 'óykalo síiw-yi'n hi-w-s-íix
            but all paint-STAT 3NOM-AUX-ASP-PL.NOM
            'but all are painted'
            (Rude 1986: 131; Phinney 1934: 343:5; 453: 10)

Cariban languages offer further examples of TAM-marked lexical verbs, embedded within a different formal system. Here auxiliaries variably appear as free-standing elements or within fused auxiliary plus subject complexes: see Chapter 6.

(152)   Wayana (Cariban, French Guiana, Surinam)
        kuraši t-panaŋma-y man i-ya
        rooster COMPL-hear-COMPL 3.AUX 1-AGT
        'I heard the rooster'
        (Gildea 1998: 24)

(153)   a.   Apalaí (Cariban, Brazil)   b.   Apalaí
            oe'-ñõõko ase   *otu'-ñõõko akene*
            come-IMPRF 1AUX   eat-CONT 1.AUX.PAST
            'I'm coming'   'I was eating'
            (Gildea 1998: 211)

(154) Pemón (Cariban, Brazil, Guyana, Venezuela)
manuun-nəpək pərətuukuu   u-po-n koka-pə' esi-'pa
eechii-pə
dance-PROG frog AUX-PAST   1-clothes-POSS wash-CONT AUX-PAST
'Frog was dancing'   'I was washing/washed my clothes'
(Gildea 1998: 23)

Similar tense-marked lexical verbs are found in the negative past in the unrelated Epena Pedee (Saija), a Chocó language of Colombia.

(155) a. Epena Pedee   b. Epena Pedee
           Jose-pa pʰáta kʰo.ʔé pa-hí   *wā-itʰée pa-hí*
           Jose-ERG plantain eat:NEG AUX-PST   go-FUT AUX-PST
           'Jose did not eat the plantain'   'I was going to go'
           (Harms 1994: 15-16)

       c. Epena Pedee   d. Epena Pedee
           kʰui-máa pʰaní   *kʰui-máa pʰana-hi-dá*
           swim-PROG AUX:PL   swim-PROG AUX-PST-PL
           'they are swimming'   'they were swimming'
           (Harms 1994: 103)

Other isolated phenomena couched within an AUX-headed AVC may be locally common. For example, in various languages of Vanuatu the lexical verb appears in a so-called 'modified root' form with a complex morpho-phonological relation to the basic stem (see Crowley 2002e for more details). An example of this is given for Raga in (171) in the section on reduplication below.

2.7 Other forms of lexical verbs in AVCs of the AUX-headed pattern

In addition to the highly functionally varied set of forms in which lexical verbs may be required to appear within AUX-headed AVCs from numerous languages across the world described above, a range of other terms have been offered to describe the form of the lexical verb in AUX-headed AVCs. In the following sections, I outline a few of these that have appeared in at least six entries in my database. A further nearly fifty elements have been described for individual languages or highly restricted sets of languages.

2.7.1 *Subordinate/dependent forms of lexical verbs in AVCs of the* AUX-*headed pattern*

One restricted sub-pattern of lexical verb forms found in an AUX-headed AVC is a general 'subordinate' or 'dependent' form. For example, such a neutral dependent or subordinate marker on the lexical verb has been described in a small number of Papuan languages, a handful of African languages, and a scattering of New World languages.

A considerable range of Papuan languages make use of a general dependency or subordination marker on the lexical verb in an AUX-headed AVC. Examples of this type may be found in the Angan language Baruya, the East-Central/Southeastern language Koiari, and Central/Southern New Guinea Asmat, all ostensibly of the Trans-New Guinea Phylum, as well as the TNG isolate language Oksapmin.

(156)   Baruya (Angan)
  paihɨr-ya yɨwano *paihɨ'-ná yɨwano*
  tread-EMB I:AUX:PST tread-REF I:AUX:PST
  'I trod'   'I trod'
  (Lloyd 1997: 301–2)

(157)   Oksapmin
  timon pati
  timo-ndi p-Ø-pti
  lie.down-PUNCT:SUBORD AUX-CONT-PRES.PL
  'they are lying down'
  (Lawrence 1972: 62)

(158)   Koiari
  tatire da vima
  laugh:DEP I AUX-PRS:1
  'I'm laughing'
  (Dutton 1996: 30)

(159)   a.   Asmat   b.   Asmat
   mó-por pák em-ce · mí *mó-por pák em-í*
   DEP-see NEG AUX-1:FUT DEP-see NEG AUX-1:PRS
   'I shall not see it'   'I don't see it'
   (Voorhoeve 1965: 127)

Such formations are restricted in African languages, but occur in at least three: Bantu Dzalamo, Chadic Ngizim, and the Cross-River language Eleme.

(160)   Dzalamo
    sikhala ni-lond-a
    1:NEG:AUX DEP-love-ASP
    'ich liebte gerade nicht'
    (Meinhof 1948: 113)

(161)   Ngizim (Chadic, Afroasiatic; Nigeria)

ná tá'-w	*kwá tá'-w*	*nàa tá-w*	*kwàa ta-w*
1:PRF eat-DEP	2PL:PERF eat-DEP	1:IMPRF eat-DEP	2PL:IMPERF
			eat-DEP

    (Schuh 1976: 5)   [+√traight tone]

(162)   Eleme
    è-bo-rî-ru   *e-ma:*   *àdádʒi ɔɔnɛnɛ*
    3-should-3PL-PRTCL DEP-bring Adaji   gift
    'they should bring Adaji a gift'
    (Anderson and Bond 2004)

Among South American languages, the Arawakan language Lokono stands out as offering a particularly clear instantiation of this sub-pattern. Similar formations occur in Jaqaru and Mapudungun. Note that, as these three examples demonstrate, the relative order of the auxiliary and the dependent marked lexical verb is irrelevant cross-linguistically (although obviously not so in the grammar of a given individual language).

(163)   Lokono (Arawakan; northern South America)
    abare l-a simaky-n
    suddenly 3SGMASC-AUX yell-SUBORD
    'suddenly he yelled'
    (Aikhenvald 1999b: 98)

(164)   a.   Jaqaru (Aymaran; Peru)   b.   Jaqaru
        yatxi-nh sa-w-tʰ a   *jaj-ntza-nh sa-w-ta*
        learn-DEP AUX-COMPL-1   get-down-DEP AUX-COMPL-2
        'I almost learned'   'you almost got down'
        (Hardman 2000: 109)

(165)   Mapudungun (Araucanian; Chile, Argentina)
    kim-la-n ülkantu-n
    AUX-NEG-1 sing-DEP
    'I cannot sing'
    (Zuñiga 2000: 27)

Finally, the Salish language Klallam offers another example of an AVC with the lexical verb appearing in an overtly dependent form. Strictly speaking, the subject clitics in these Klallam forms suggest a 'pseudo-AUX-headed structure' (see Chapter 3), but the important observation for the present purposes is that some auxiliaries require lexical verbs to be in a dependent marked form while others do not.

(166) a. Klallam   b. Klallam
         x̣'áy=cn ʔuʔ=t'íym   húy=cn t'íym
         AUX=1 DEP=sing   finish=1 sing
         'I'll sing too'   'I finished singing'
         (Montler 2003: 119–20)

2.7.2 Reduplicated forms of lexical verbs in AVCs of the AUX-headed pattern

In a range of unrelated languages, a lexical verb may be obligatorily reduplicated in an AUX-headed AVC. Such a formation may be found in such a diverse array of languages as Candoshi, Ngangkikurungkurr, Sinaugoro, Siane, Harar Oromo, and especially the South Munda language family.

In Harar Oromo, reduplication in combination with a verbal noun suffix may appear as a lexical verb component to an AVC. This reduplication probably reflects more the semantic nature of the event (distributed, repeated action) rather than just a grammaticalized feature of certain auxiliary verb constructions.

(167) Harar Oromo
      muxá c'ac-c'áps-úu jir-a
      tree REDPL-break-VN AUX-PRES
      'he is breaking the tree in places'
      (Owens 1985: 85)

Candoshi has reduplication associated with an AVC but, as is commonly the case (and mentioned just above with regards to Harar Oromo), the reduplication does not appear as a synchronically opaque result of a grammaticalized AVC (as it does in Munda languages discussed below), but rather reflects the repetitive semantics of the sentence itself. This encoding of event semantics is, of course, the main source for the origin of reduplicated lexical verbs in AUX-headed AVCs in any event, whatever the language (and probably true of South Munda as well, historically speaking). Forms like these in Candoshi and Harar Oromo therefore merely reflect an earlier, less opaque historical stage in this grammaticalization process.

(168)   Candoshi (isolate; Peru)
tpots kos kos kos aſira-g-ana
people to.arrive REDPL REDPL AUX-CURR.PST-3PL
'a group of people arrived, then another, then another'
(Wise 1999: 325; Tuggy 1982: 41)

With this in mind, have a look at the following sentences from the Australian
language Ngankikurungkurr.

(169)   a.   Ngankikurungkurr
falmi fagarri w-errme wirrki batybity w-itinge-gu tye mempirr
woman two 3NSP-VC13:PST 3DO hold:REDPL 3NS-AUX-PST-DL PST
       child
'the two women were holding their babies'
(Hodinnott and Kofod 1988: 92)

   b.   Ngankikurungkurr
minta nimbi werrme patpit waddi epe
NEG ABL 3NSP:VC13:PST rise:REDPL OA:3NS-AUX-PST but
werrim patpit wannim detyengi
3NDP-VC13-PRES rise:REDPL OA:3NSP-go-PRES today
'they used not to fly before but they do today'
(Hodinnott and Kofod 1988: 129)

   c.   Ngankikurungkurr
minta ngebi gerrgirr ngini
NEG 1-VC16-FUT cut.REDPL FUT
'I will not cut it'

Each one of the examples could be interpreted as reflecting the real-world-
event semantics described by the proposition, but in an increasingly less
obvious manner. The ongoing or durative nature of the event may have
triggered the reduplication in the first example (169a), while the repetitive
or habitual nature of the flying may likewise have merited the reduplication of
the lexical verb stem (169b). Both of these are well within the bounds of
'typical' functions of reduplication of verbal predicates cross-linguistically.
The third example, on the other hand, could also be interpreted as involving a
repeated action of cutting, but the connection is less clear. In this particular
instance the reduplication has less motivation, and appears to be more an
instance of a grammaticalization or conventionalization of this process, in
conjunction with the use of a particular auxiliary element in particular functions.

Variable motivation for a reduplicated verbal form of a lexical verb in an AUX-headed AVC structure also emerges when one examines data from languages of the Austronesian family. In Raga, reduplication appears with a durative connotation, and thus reflects rather transparently its event-semantic motivation. In Sinaugoro, on the other hand, while the act of eating is perhaps canonically durative or repetitive in nature, it is motivated in these particular examples at least as much by a grammaticalization of the reduplication process on a lexical verb stem in combination with the particular auxiliary verb to mark together a particular function as it is by this connection to the event semantics, if not more so. This is seen by the fact, among others, that reduplication is required even if the event is unrealized.

(170) a. Sinaugoro

      b-a-na ḡani-ḡani

      REM-1-INT/IMP eat-REDPL

      'I'd like to eat, I have to/must eat'

      (Tauberschmidt 1999: 24)

     b. Sinaugoro

      b-a-ra ḡani-ḡani senaḡi asi ḡa-gu

      REM-1-IRR eat-REDPL but NEG EDIBLE.POSS-1

      'I would [have] eat[en], but I don't have anything'

(171) a. Raga   b. Raga

      na-n van-vano   *na-m ban-vano*

      1-PST REDPL-go   1-PRS REDPL-go

      'I used to keep on going'   'I keep on going'

      (Crowley 1991: 217)

Note the process of 'root modification' operative in these Raga forms that is a further formal option for lexical stem modification in auxiliary verb constructions in certain Oceanic languages, especially those of Vanuatu. Tense markers in Oceanic were probably originally auxiliaries that required their lexical verb to either appear in a basic or modified form. For details see Crowley (2002e) and the discussion and references therein. It is clear that stem reduplication and root modification are separate and orthogonal (interacting) processes in Oceanic languages like Raga.

The Papuan language Siane offers a further example of reduplication of a lexical verb in an AVC in my database. Again, the semantics of the event, partially encoded by the auxiliary itself, marking habitual action, is responsible for the conventionalization of this process of modification characteristic of this AVC. Note that in this Siane form, the lexical verb is reduplicated but the stem of the auxiliary is realized as Ø by morphophonological rule.

(172)   Siane
    etí-tí nó-no [o]-á-mó n-ê
    thus-COORD.POLYFOC eat-REDPL AUX-3PL-FOC.GIV exist-IND
    'it's a fact that they habitually eat like that'
    (James 1983: 34)

As alluded to above, the South Munda languages perhaps present the canonical instantiation of AUX-headed AVCs requiring reduplicated stem forms of lexical verbs. Virtually all members of the South Munda language family of east central India make some use of reduplicated lexical verbs in AVCs. It may thus be considered reasonably likely to be an old feature in the South Munda family. However, the details and nature of the phenomenon varies considerably among the languages as outlined below.

The simplest systems are those of Sora and Kharia, where an old auxiliary requiring a lexical verb in a reduplicated form appears in (variably) fused complex, marking continuous action in Kharia and frequentative action in Sora:

(173)   Sora   (174)   Kharia
    gugu-lo:-te-n   *ño?ño?-lo-ta*
    RDPL:call-FREQ-NPST-ITR   RDPL:eat-CONT-PRES.I
    'he calls (me) frequently'   'he is continuously eating'
    (Ramamurti 1931)   (Biligiri 1965)

Note that in Sora, the reduplicated form primarily occurs with intransitive roots. In the Juang progressive, only monosyllabic roots are reduplicated; polysyllabic roots are not, i.e. it is morphophonologically triggered.[14]

(175)   a. Juang   b. Juang
        aiñ jɔjɔ-nɔm-an   *arɔ-ki uru-nɔm-an-ki*
        I RDPL.eat-PROG-PST.I   they RDPL.drink-PROG-PST.I-PL
        'I was eating'   'they were weeping'
        (Pinnow 1960)

---

[14] Note that not only reduplication but also other morphologically realized dependent markers/forms of lexical verbs in fused AVCs may be determined by similar morphotactic features, such as the distribution of the infinitive with certain tenses (e.g. present) in Swahili.

(i)   Swahili
    ni-na-ku-ja   *ni-na-taka*
    1-PRES-INF-eat   1-PRES-want
    'I eat'   'I want'

In Remo, certain auxiliaries always require the reduplicated form of the lexical verb. This includes (quasi-/semi-)fused auxiliary forms as well.

(176) a. Remo
          bɔ-ba ḍen-t-iŋ
          Rᴅᴘʟ-slap ᴘʀᴏɢ-ɴᴘsᴛ-1
          'I am slapping'
          (Fernandez 1968: 35, 54)

     b. Remo
          gɔ-gay ḍen-t-iŋ
          Rᴅᴘʟ-die ᴘʀᴏɢ-ɴᴘsᴛ-1
          'I am dying'

In Gta?, some auxiliaries require the reduplicated form of the lexical verb, while others do not. Interestingly, the Gta? perfective auxiliary form is one that is cognate with the Remo progressive, which similarly requires the reduplicated form of the lexical verb suggesting that this association of reduplication in combination with this auxiliary verb, regardless of the operational or functional semantics of the resulting construction, dates back to the period of the Gutob-Remo-Gta? continuum (Anderson 2001).

(177) Gta?
       c-coŋ (n)-ḍiŋ-ge
       Rdpl-eat 1-PERF-PAST
       'I have eaten'
       (Mahapatra et al. 1989)

(178) Gta?
       coŋ n-læʔ-e
       eat 1-PROG.I-FUT
       'I will be eating'

2.7.3 *Switch reference forms of lexical verbs in AVCs of the* ᴀᴜx-*headed pattern*

Because auxiliary verbs and lexical verbs in the ᴀᴜx-headed pattern (almost always) obligatorily have the same subject, it may not be surprising that the dependent form in which the lexical verb appears within a given AVC in particular languages is identical with a same-subject marker used in narrative discourse. Such a form is found in such diverse languages as those of the tree-dwelling Korowai of Papua, Indonesia, Gokana of Nigeria, Walapai of the American Southwest, and the Altai-Sayan Turkic languages Tofa and Tuvan.

With regards to Turkic, the only languages that have a dedicated same-subject marker are Tuvan and Tofa. There is some fluctuation of the function of the element in Tuvan (Anderson and Harrison 1999), but in certain registers the association of the element -*GAʃ* with same subject functions is quite clear (Bergel'son and Kibrik 1987a, b). It is cognate with a purposive converb in Xakas (Anderson 1998a). In Tofa, on the other hand (Anderson and Harrison, in preparation), possibly in part as a result of the general collapsing of functional categories stemming from the advanced moribund state of the language, there are a range of AVCs where the lexical verb may appear in a same-subject marked form, instead of the expected converb form.[15]

(179) Tofa
    dilyi oluk   bar-ip broœ üšpül   tùt-kaš al-ɣan.
    fox right.away go-CV one hazel.grouse catch-SS SUBJ.VERS-PST
    'right away the fox caught himself a hazel grouse'
    (Rassadin 1994: 198)

In Korowai, the same element used in clause-linking as well as certain serialized constructions appears on the lexical verb in certain AVCs. As auxiliary verb constructions (at least of the AUX-headed type) by definition share a subject across the lexical and auxiliary verb components, the occasional, perhaps residual, presence of a same-subject marker within an AVC that derives historically from a biclausal structure should not be overly surprising.

(180) a. Korowai (Awyu-Ndumut; Indonesia)
        i-nè khami-bo
        see-SS AUX-AUX:3:REAL
        'he was looking'
        (van Enk and de Vries 1997: 88)

     b. Korowai
        i-nè khami-ba-lè
        look-SS AUX-AUX-1PL:REAL
        'we are looking'
        (van Enk and de Vries 1997: 93)

Cf.

     c. Korowai
        mébol damil-no le-nè lu-ba-lé
        grave open-SUPP:SS come-SS ascend-PRF-1:REAL
        'I opened up the grave, and came up (the stairs)'
        (van Enk and de Vries 1997: 88)

---

[15] In other Turkic languages, the same subject functions seen in Tuvan and Tofa are marked by the default converb element in -*p*, which also happens to be the most common form for lexical verbs in AVCs in these languages. For more see Anderson and Harrison (to appear).

2.7.4 *Connegative forms of lexical verbs in AVCs of the* AUX-*headed pattern*

In a range of languages, lexical verbs in AVCs bear a marker of negative subordination. This is called the 'co(n)negative' form in Uralic languages where the construction is common, and this is the terminology mainly used in the present work. There are at least two common ways that this construction seems to have developed: a specialization of some kind of irrealis marking (which is semantically compatible with negative) or a fusing of a reinforcing particle; this latter formation I call the '*pas* construction' after the well-known formation in French. Thus one finds connegative forms in a small but diverse range of languages from the sample that includes the Nilo-Saharan Majang, various southern Bantu languages (e.g. Mbalanhu, where the connegative form only occurs in perfective or non-present constructions), Papuan Amanab, Burmese, the Salish language Klallam, and many languages of the Uralic family and Tungusic Evenki.

Examples of connegative AVCs from the languages of Africa include ones in Surmic languages of the Nilo-Saharan phylum and various Bantu speech varieties, e.g. Mbalanhu or Herero. Note that the reduplication of the lexical verb serves to mark reciprocal action in the following Majang form.

(181) Majang
  ku-ɛr-ko wo-<no>-noy-it
  NEG-3PL-PST exchange<REDPL>-NEG
  'they did not exchange with each other'
  (Unseth 1991: 245)

(182) a. Mbalanhu (Bantu; Namibia)
      ándí longó   *íhándí longó*
      NPST:1 work   NEG:NPST:1 work
      'I [am] work[ing]'   'I'm not working'
      (Fourie 1993: 22–5)

    b. Mbalanhu
      ándí ká longó   *íhándí ká longá*
      NPST:1 FUT work   NEG:NPST:1 FUT work:NEG.NPRS
      'I will work'   'I won't work'

    c. Mbalanhu
      óndá longó   *ínándí longá*
      PST:1 work   NEG:PST:1 work:NEG:NPRS
      'I worked'   'I did not work'
      (Fourie 1993: 26–7)

(183) a. Herero[16]   b. Herero
           tu-a tuŋg-a   *ka-tu[-]tuŋg-ire*
           1PL-AUX build-PRF   NEG-1PL[-]build-NEG.PRF
           'we have built'   'we have not built'
           (Meinhof 1948: 104)

       c. Herero   d. Herero
           ka-tu w-ire   *ka-tu-a w-ire*
           NEG-1PL fall-NEG:PRF   NEG-1PL-AUX fall-NEG:PRF
           'we haven't fallen'   'we hadn't fallen'
           (Meinhof 1948: 105)

Outside of Uralic and Bantu, this pattern is highly marked. Take, for example, the Papuan language Amanab. There is a negative element *mas* which requires a negative form of the verb: an enclitic or suffix *-mo* which always attaches to a past form of the verb. This latter may in turn reflect a fused auxiliary (or light verb or pro-verb, etc.) and may itself reflect a univerbation of something akin to the reinforced negative '*pas* construction' familiar from French.

(184) a. Amanab (Waris, Papua New Guinea)
           ka mas anwana-fe-g-mo
           I NEG know-AUX-PST-NEG
           'I don't know'
           (Minch 1992: 147)

       b. Amanab
           mas ka anwana-fe-g-mo
           NEG I know-AUX-PST-NEG
           'I'm not the one who knows'

       c. Amanab   d. Amanab
           ka mas ika-g-mo   *ka mas ika-i*
           I NEG go-PST-NEG   I NEG go-SBJ
           'I did not go'   'I will not go'
           (Minch 1992: 113)

---

[16] Note that in Herero, not all perfect constructions with auxiliaries show the connegative (negative perfect) form of the lexical verb.
(ii) Herero
      ha-tu-ja muna
      NEG-1PL-AUX see
      'we have not yet seen'
      (Meinhof 1948: 114).

Without question, the language family for which the connegative formation is best described is the Uralic language family. Negatives in Uralic languages are predominantly formed with a negative auxiliary element followed by the lexical verb, which is in turn followed by a so-called 'connegative' suffix. Such negative formations as the following may be found in languages across the Uralic language family.

(185) a. Mari
         o-k kodo ə̂l^{j}e
         NEG-3 leave:CONNEG AUX:PST[:3]
         's/he was not leaving'
         (Kangasmaa-Minn 1998: 239)

      b. Mari
         nal=ə̂n o-na-l ul=maš
         take-GER AUX:NEG-1PL-PST.II AUX-VN
         'we had not been taking'

(186) Udmurt   (187) Erzya
      u-g miniš^{j}ki   *ez-iñ kunda(k)*
      NEG:NPST-1go:CONNEG:1/2   NEG-1PST catch(:CONNEG)
      'I don't go'   'I didn't catch'
      (Csúcs 1998: 292)   (Payne 1985: 217; Feoktisov 1966: 187)

(188) a. Nenets   b. Nenets
         ni-n xane"   *ni-naś xaju"*
         NEG-2PRS trade:CONNEG   NEG-2PST stay:CONNEG
         'you don't trade'   'you didn't stay'
         (Payne 1985: Shcherbakova 1954: 199–200)

(189) Enets
      obuhʊru teðaru neð? modə?
      nothing so.far NEG.1AOR see.CNEG
      'so far I see nothing'
      (Künnap 1999a: 22)

(190) a. Nganasan   b. Nganasan
         kuə-d^{j}üə   *ñi-sïə kuə-ʔ*
         Die-PST   NEG-PST die-CONNEG
         's/he died'   's/he did not die"
         (Helimski 1998a: 508)

(191)   Kamas
     e-m šo-ʔ
     NEG-1 come-CONNEG
     'I'm not coming'
     (Simoncsics 1998: 595)

Evenki shows a similar pattern, likewise using a negative auxiliary that encodes subject and tense followed by a special 'connegative' form (the *-ra* form) of the lexical verb. Uralic influence in this development may be at least partly responsible for (maintaining?) this construction in Evenki (Anderson 2004b).

(192)   a.   Evenki
          bəjə a:čin-ma:-n ə-čə:-ß sa:-ra
          man NEG-ACC-3 NEG-PST-1 know-RA
          'I didn't know about the man's absence.'
          (Bulatova and Grenoble 1999: 16)

      b.   Evenki   c.   Evenki
          ə-kəl ŋəne-rə   *atirka:n ə-či-n sukə-ßə ga-mu:-ra*
          NEG-IMP2SG go-RA   old.man NEG-AOR-3 axe-ACC take-DESID-RA
          'Don't go!'   'The old man did not want to take the axe.'
          (Bulatova and Grenoble 1999: 46–7)

Other Tungusic languages also make use of the connegative construction, for example, Orok and Orochi. Certain Udihe forms may reflect this as well.

(193)   a.   Udihe (Tungusic; Siberia)   b.   Udihe
          bi ei-mi sa: *sin-tigi e-zeŋe-i dian-a*
          I NEG-1 know   you-LAT NEG-FUT-1 say-O
          'I don't know'   'I won't tell you'
          (Nikolaeva and Tolskaja 2001: 214)

      c.   Udihe
          ine'i e-ini ŋene
          dog NEG-3 go
          'the dog is not walking'
          (Nikolaeva and Tolskaja 2001: 214)

(194)   a.   Orok
          si ə-tci-si bū-ra   ~
          you NEG-PST-2 give-PRT(CONNEG]
          'you didn't go'
          (Payne 1985: 214; Petrova 1967, 1968)

b. Orok
    si ə-tci-l bū-rə-si
    you NEG-PST-PRTCPL give-PRT(CONNEG)]-2

(195) a. Oroch[i]   b. Oroch[i]
           ə-ʒi gun-ə   *ə-ʒi gun-ə-su*
           NEG-IMP speak-PRTCPL   NEG-IMP speak-PRTCPL-2PL
           'Don't speak!'   'Don't speak (pl)!'
           (Payne 1985: 215; Avrorin and Lebedeva 1968)

Note, however, that Even, a close sister language to Evenki (much closer than Udihe, Orok, or Orochi), has no such connegative forms.

(196) Even (Tungusic, Northern; Siberia)
       bi: eh-ĕm hukler
       I   NEG-1 sleep
       'I'm not sleeping'
       (Dutkin 1995: 48)

2.7.5 *Case-marked forms of lexical verbs in AVCs of the* AUX-*headed pattern*

A small number of languages make use of case morphology either alone or in connection with some other nominalizing/non-finite marking on the lexical verb in an AUX-headed AVC. This includes various Mande languages (e.g. Mende, Bobo-Fing), a smattering of other African languages, Australian Yanyuwa, Burushaski, and Estonian. Case-marked verbs are commonly used to mark subordinate or dependent clauses in a wide range of languages, e.g. Burushaski (Anderson 2002) and languages of central Siberia (Anderson 2004b), so the appearance of case-marking on a dependent lexical verb in an AUX-headed AVC, although not overly common in the languages of the world, should not be surprising. The other common source for case-marked lexical verbs in an AUX-headed AVC is a lexical verb in a nominalized form followed by a locative element (sometimes comitative) and a copular verb. This so-called 'nominal' or 'locative' adpositional periphrasis channel of AVC development typically forms AVCs which mark progressive or durative aspect, present tense, etc., and has been well discussed in the literature on the grammaticalization of auxiliaries (e.g. Heine and Reh 1984, Heine 1993).

In Burushaski, a lexical verb may appear in a durative participial form with a genitive case-marker followed by an inflected auxiliary verb. This marks durative, progressive, or continuative action.

(197)   a.   Burushaski
             hiŋ yakal baréime bam
             door at look:DUR:AP:GEN I.AUX:AP
             'he was looking at the door'
             (Berger 1998: 172)

        b.   Burushaski
             sihát qʰaráap maíme díya
             health worsen AUX:DUR:AP:GEN AUX:IV
             'the health grew ever worse'
             (Berger 1998: 172)

(198)   a.   Burushaski
             in yáguču̇me hurútu̇mo
             s/he search:DUR:AP:GEN AUX:II.PST
             'she kept searching for him'
             (Berger 1998: 172)

        b.   Burushaski
             harált diáaršume hurútimi
             rain *d:*precipitate:DUR:AP:GEN AUX:IV.PST
             'it kept raining'
             (Berger 1998: 172)

The use of a case-subordinator on a lexical verb in an AUX-headed AVC is also found in Estonian, here realized in the form of the so-called 'illative supine'.

(199)   Estonian
        ta 'peab 'ootama
        he AUX:3 wait:ILL.SUP
        'he must wait'
        (Viitso 1998: 139)

Note that Kolyma Yukaghir uses a case-marked lexical verb as a complement of an emergently grammaticalized (serialized) purposive form.

(200)   Kolyma Yukaghir
        tami-l-ŋin qon-d'e
        help-ACTN.NMLZ-DAT go-INTR:1SG
        'I went to help'
        (Maslova 2003b: 152)

Among African languages, the languages of the Mande group of Niger-Congo deserve special mention in this regard. As is well known (cf. Heine and Reh

1984, Heine 1993, Kuteva 2001, Heine and Kuteva 2002), one of the most common origins of progressive constructions cross-linguistically, and in West African languages in particular, is a nominalized verb form in combination with a locative expression (case, adposition, etc.). These constructions may require a copular verb of some sort to allow for finite verb inflection. Copular verbs in this type of formation frequently constitute a subtype of auxiliary, and thus the pattern may become generalized.

(201) a. Mende   b. Mende   c. Mende
           nya lo tewe-ma   *ngi ye tewe-ma*   *nga ye tewe-ma*
           1:PRES AUX cut-LOC   1:PST AUX cut-LOC   1:FUT AUX cut-LOC
           'I am cutting'   'I was cutting'   'I will be cutting'
           (Heine and Reh 1984: 123; Migeod 1908; Innes 1969)

(202) Bobo-Fing (East Mande; Burkina Faso, Mali)
       ma ti ya-hû Sya
       I AUX go-LOC Bobo
       'I am going to Bobo'
       (Heine and Reh 1984: 123)

Note that the Mende example is in fact a complex AVC with the first element actually a fused subject/TAM form that is common both in West Africa and a range of other regions of the world. For more on this construction, see Chapter 6.

In other African languages, the presence of case morphology as a dependent marker of lexical verbs in an AUX-headed AVC occur only in a handful of constructions in various individual languages in the database. Such examples include an AVC made up of an inflected auxiliary verb followed by an oblique case preposition in combination with a nominalized form of the lexical verb in the Nilo-Saharan language Anywa, and the use of a verbal noun plus dative case form in the negative future (here feminine singular) in Harar Oromo.

(203) Anywa
       wā-cóggó kī mɛ̀ɛ́ŋ
       1PL.EXCL-AUX OBLQ dance:VN
       'we started to dance'
       (Reh 1996: 266)

(204) Harar Oromo (Cushitic, Afroasiatic; Ethiopia)
       isíi-n déem-úu-f hin-jírat-t-u
       she-NOM go-VN-DAT NEG-AUX.PRES.PROG-FEM-DEP
       'she will not be going'
       (Owens 1985: 73)

Case morphology on lexical verbs in AUX-headed AVCs is highly marked in the macro-Indo-Pacific region, even in languages with developed systems of case marking, e.g. certain Australian languages. One such language does exhibit a construction of this type, however, the Pama-Nyungan language Yanyuwa.

(205)   Yanyuwa (Warluwaric, Pama-Nyungan)
        li-ardu-birri jal-ini lhurra-ngka
        PL.NOM-child-DIM.PL 3PL-PRES play-ABL
        'the children are playing'
        (Kirton and Charlie 1996: 15)

Case morphology on verbal predicates in subordinate or complement clauses is relatively common in the indigenous languages of Australia, seen for example in the following Dharumbal form.[17]

(206)   Dharumbal
        nhula wu-thayu yigi-nh
        he.NOM give-PURP=DAT want-NPST
        'he wants to give'
        (Terrill 2002: 41)

Postpositional and prepositional elements may also appear in the function of marking dependency or non-finiteness on the lexical verb in an AUX-headed AVC. This is of course just one step earlier in the grammaticalization process described for case above, as such adpositional constructions are the default sources for case constructions cross-linguistically. Such languages with dependent verbs marked by an adposition in AVCs include English (*to*), Scots Gaelic, Umbundu, Ngambay-Moundou, and Lezgian.

(207)   Scots Gaelic
        bha mi a' tighinn
        AUX:PST I PREP coming
        'I was coming'
        (Gillies 1993: 203)

---

[17] As will be discussed in Ch. 7, it would be understandable if a given researcher were to consider such forms as this Dharumbal formation not to be AVCs *per se* but rather something on the form–function continuum of verb–verb structures that stretches between biclausal verb complement structures and emergent monoclausal AVCs.

(208)   a.   Ngambay-Moundou (C. Sudanic; Chad)
            m-îsî mbā k-ùsà dā
            1-AUX for NOM-eat meat
            'I am eating meat'
            (Heine and Reh 1984: 126; Vandame 1963: 94–6)

        b.   Ngambay-Moundou
            m-ár mbā k-ùsà dā
            1-AUX for NOM-eat meat
            'I am eating meat'

(209)   a.   Umbundu (Bantu, Niger-Congo; Angola)
            tu-li l' oku-lya
            1PL-AUX with INF-eat
            'we are eating'
            (Heine and Reh 1984: 125; Valente 1964: 281)

        b.   Umbundu
            wa-kala l' oku-papala
            3-AUX with INF-play
            'he was playing'
            (Heine and Reh 1984: 126)

(210)   Lezgian
        aburu hada-z ewer gu-da-j-wal x̂a-na
        they:ERG that-DAT call-FUT-PRTCPL-PURP AUX-AOR
        'they were going to call him'
        (Haspelmath 1993: 147)

Note that in Umbundu the constructions consist of an originally copular
(now auxiliary) verb (meaning 'be' and 'sit', respectively, in the examples
above) combined with a clitic preposition and the infinitive form of
the lexical verb. In Ngambay-Moundou, there are likewise two auxiliaries
('sit' and 'stand') coming from a copular construction combined with a
PP complement of a lexical verb. Heine and Reh (1984) label this development
the 'PP-periphrasis' subtype of development or grammaticalization chain of
AVCs. The Lezgian form shows an enclitic purposive postposition or case
suffix on the lexical verb. The original purposive semantics in this kind of
complement is straightforward and requires little further comment.

2.7.6 *Connective/conjunctive forms of lexical verbs in AVCs of the* AUX-*headed pattern*

A small number of languages have grammaticalized an original conjunctive or connective construction using a morpheme/particle that conjoins the two verbs. This is a frozen construction, reflecting the originally bi-clausal nature of AVCs, and, although infrequently attested in AVCs of the AUX-headed pattern, nevertheless constitutes a minor sub-class. The connection of this kind of marking to residual uses of same-subject marking in AVCs should be obvious, less so perhaps to adverbial 'converb' or gerund markers in such formations.

If it is not yet clear, let it be stated categorically here that all of the forms of lexical verbs discussed in the present chapter are considered to occupy points in a form–function continuum of elements marking the (in)dependence and cohesiveness of the lexical verb with the auxiliary verb in the AUX-headed AVC (where the auxiliary encodes all obligatory verbal inflections). The opposition of any two or more forms may have significant structural or functional consequences within the grammars of specific languages, but there are no coherent factors for splitting any of these into discrete, individuated, and precisely defined groups from a cross-linguistic perspective. AVCs emerge when particular verbs are conventionalized in their use with another verb that appears in any number of possible forms, depending on the language and its resources. AVCs often therefore result from grammaticalized combinations of clausal coordination and subordination, and the inclusion of various elements that reflect these origins in a small number (statistically speaking) of these AVC systems should come as no surprise.

Among the languages showing this minor inflectional pattern of originally conjunctive chained or conjoined clauses developing into AVCs are the Afroasiatic languages Tigrinya and Burji, Muskogean Koasati, and Coast Tsimshian.

(211)   Burji (Cushitic, Afro-Asiatic; Ethiopia)
    duk'as-ina ee gagar-i yeDa [gagareDa]
    cold-FOC me catch-CONJ AUX:1 [catch:AUX:1]
    'I have a cold'
    (Hudson 1976a: 264)

(212)   Tigrinya
    kəbällə' 'əyyu
    CONJ-eat 3:AUX
    'he will eat'
    (Leslau 1968: 69)

(213) a. Koasati
im-awí:ci-t á:ta-li-t
3DAT-help-CONN AUX.SG-1-CONN
'I kept on helping them...'
(Kimball 1991: 94)

b. Koasati
im-alíkci-t fáyli-l-á:hi-k óm
3DAT-cure-CONN AUX.SG.TRANS-1-intent-SS AUX
'it is the case that I am about to quit curing him'
(Kimball 1991: 95)

(214) a. Coast Tsimshian
nah-łá-'al dzáb-m̓ ha²liq'éexł
PRF-PROX-SUBSEQ make-1PL sleds
'we used to make sleds'
(Dunn 1979: 229)

b. Coast Tsimshian
łá-n-wila dzáb-a ha²liq'éexł
PROX-1-SUBSEQ make-CNNCTV sleds
'and then right away I make sleds'

2.7.7 *Irrealis/subjunctive forms of lexical verbs in AVCs of the* AUX-*headed pattern*

Irrealis or subjunctive forms of lexical verbs in AUX-headed AVCs are also found in a small but disparate group of languages in the sample. This includes the Afroasiatic language Karekare, the Australian language Warlpiri, and Nisenan and North Embera from North and South America, respectively. Generally speaking, forms of this type appear in formations with unrealized or hypothetical semantics, for example conditional, counterfactuals, negatives, and futures. In later chapters, where lexical verbs appear in dependent forms in other inflectional patterns, this 'modal' type of subordination is commonly the form used. As Bisang (2001: 1401) notes, irrealis modality is less finite than realis marking.

(215) a. Karekare   b. Karekare
nà tài   *kú tài*
1SBJNCT eat:SBJNCT   2PL:SBJNCT eat:SBJNCT
(Schuh 1976: 5)

(216)   a.   Warlpiri
             ngarrka-ngku kaji-lpa makiti marda-karla kala-ka marlu luwa-rni
             man-ERG AUX-AUX gun have-IRR AUX-PRES kangaroo shoot-NPST
             'if the man has a gun, he is likely to shoot a kangaroo'
             (Granites and Laughren 2001: 157)

        b.   Warlpiri
             ngarrka-ngku kaji makiti marda-karla kapu marlu luwa-karla
             man-ERG AUX gun have-IRR AUX:FUT kangaroo shoot-IRR
             'if the man had a gun, he would have shot the kangaroo'
             (Granites and Laughren 2001: 157)

(217)   Nisenan (Maiduan (Penutian), USA)
        pii-jee-wis da-ni
        swim-go.along-IRR AUX-1
        'I'll go swimming'
        (Mithun 1999: 457)

(218)   N. Embera (Chocó; Colombia, Panama)
        tama-pa kʰá-puɾu akʰupari b-u-ma wā-i-ta b-u-a
        snake-ABL bite-COND doctor be-PRES-LOC go-IRR-ABS∧FOC
        AUX-PRES-DECL
        'if you are bitten by a snake, you have to go to the doctor'
        (Mortensen 1999: 10)

2.8 Bare or unmarkd forms of the lexical verb ∅

By far the most common form of the lexical verb forms found in AUX-headed
AVCs in the languages of the database is a zero-marked form or bare stem.
This occurs in language families from across the globe. It is the unmarked
form for Australian languages, common in Papuan languages and found in
most West African languages, and occurs relatively commonly in various
Afroasiatic and Bantu languages as well as in a wide scattering of indigenous
North, Meso-, and South American languages, and in various languages of
South Asia, Tungusic languages, Sumerian, etc.

    Among Eurasian languages, ∅-marked or bare-stem forms of lexical verbs
in an AVC may be found in the Mon-Khmer language Khasi (and other
isolating languages like Hmong Njua) and various Tibeto-Burman languages
(Tamang, Bokar, Hayu, Kinnauri).

(219) a. Khasi   b. Khasi
         u nang trei   ~   *u nang ba'n trei*
         3M AUX work   3M AUX INF work
         'he can work'
         (Roberts (1995)[1891]: 54)

(220) a. Khasi   b. Khasi
         nga'n ioh leit   *nga'm ioh wan*
         I:FUT AUX go   1:NEG AUX come
         'I will be able/permitted to go' 'I cannot come'
         (Roberts (1995)[1891]: 54)

(221) a. Hmong Njua (Hmong-Mien) b. Hmong Njua
         nwg tau moog   *nwg tsi tau moog*
         3 PST go   3 NEG PST go
         'he went'   'he didn't go'
         (Harriehausen 1990: 54)

(222) Tamang
       ¹ŋa-ta sarpa-se ¹sat ⁴tam-pa
       I-DAT snake-ERG kill AUX-IMPFV
       'a snake was about to kill me'
       (Mazaudon 2003: 304)

(223) Qiang
       the:-dʐoqu-le dagɜ̃-wu piʈʂ sei ma-lɜ̃-jy
       3-foot-DEF break-INST-now walk NEG-CAP-ASP
       'his/her foot is broken so s/he can't walk'
       (La Polla 2003: 585)

(224) Bokar
       iʃi tɯɯŋ-ja-me aruŋ du-nam mi:-ha-m mitpen moŋ-bo
       water drink-WHEN-OBJ well dig-NMLZR:OBJ person-DEF-OBJ forget
          NEG.AUX-FUT
       'when drinking water, (we) will not forget those who dug the well'
       (Sun 2003: 465)

(225) Hayu
       ā:ki gā̃ũ-mʊ tso-khata jamma dza cuxtomem bumi pixpi-ha
       1PL.OBLQ village-of child-PL all eat AUX:3>3P:ASS Bumi
          grandmother-ERG
       'Grandmother Bumi had already eaten up all the children of our village'
       (Michailovsky 2003: 529)

(226) a. Kinnauri   b. Kinnauri
           nic du-ñ   *tuŋc du-k*
           live AUX-2   drink AUX-1
           'you live'   'I drink'
           (Sharma 1988: 138)

Similar constructions may be found in the extinct isolate language Sumerian, and (as mentioned above in the discussion of connegative forms in Evenki) in Tungusic Udihe of Eastern Siberia.

(227) Sumerian[†] (isolate; Ancient Mesopotamia (Iraq))
       É.ninnu me-bi an ki-a pa=è mu-ak-ke₄ {mu-ak-e}
       Eninnu *me*-INAN.POSS heaven earth-LOC make.resplendent PRF-AUX-3
       'he makes the *me* of Eninnu resplendent in heaven and earth'
       (Gudea cyl. AI 11)
       (Thomsen 1984: 271)

(228) a. Udihe (Tungusic; Siberia)   b. Udihe
           bi ei-mi sa: *ine'i e-ini ŋene*
           I NEG-1 know   dog NEG-3 go
           'I don't know'   'the dog is not walking'
           (Nikolaeva and Tolskaja 2001: 214)

The Siberian Turkic language Xakas offers an interesting example of a phonological conditioning of a bare stem form of a lexical verb in an AVC. Whether or not a lexical verb will appear with the *-p* converb form in Xakas is determined by whether or not the stem ends in a consonant or the auxiliary begins with one. If the lexical verb ends in a consonant and the auxiliary is consonant-initial, there is no *-p*, i.e. the lexical verb appears in a Ø-marked or bare-stem form; otherwise the *-p* surfaces. Note that this is true both of synchronically bipartite (or periphrastic) AVCs in Xakas and of complex verb forms deriving from fused AVCs of this type.

       fused:
(229) a. Xakas   b. Xakas
           kil-če-m   *oyna-pča-m*
           'I come'   'I play'
           first singular present: $-(p)čA-m <$ *-p čat*
           $< kil-$ $< oyna-$

       (Field Notes)

periphrastic:

(230) a. Xakas   b. Xakas
           at-ɨp al-ɣa-m   *at pir-ge-m*
           'I shot (for me)' 'I shot (for s.o. else)'
           first singular past: -*GA-m*
           < *at-al*   *at-pir*

Unmarked or bare-stem forms of lexical verbs in AUX-headed AVCs are found
in a number of Papuan languages as well, e.g. the isolate Sulka, putatively of
the East Papuan Phylum, Orya of the Tor Lake Plains Stock, Binanderean
Suena, and Gahuku, Agarabi, and Kewapi of the East New Guinea Highlands
Family of the Trans-New Guinea Phylum.

(231) a. Orya (Tor Lake Plains Stock)
           otol dan-na mawa dwen gwi-bi-rin
           banyan nuts-DEF birds ACT:PL:eat REPET-DAT:F-REC
           'banyan nuts are often eaten by birds'
           (Fields 1997: 245)

       b. Orya
           Habel walas tol-a in-sa lek tya-k-a in zep ase-k-a
           Abel child small-DEF that-UND hit ACT:SG:CAUSE:UND:
               M-PST-ACT:M that then disappear-PST-ACT:M
           'Abel hit that small boy and that is why (he) disappeared'
           (Fields 1997: 247)

(232) Sulka (family-level isolate)
       ngara mo-turang mar-mruo
       3PL:FUT RECIP-help 3PL:FPN-RECIP
       'they will help each other'
       (Tharp 1996: 86)

(233) a. Gahuku   b. Gahuku
           gosavaʔ noune   *asuʔ Ø-ne-t-at-ive*
           sharpen 1PL:AUX:PRES   finish AUX-1-BEN-FUT-3
           'we sharpen it'   'I will be finished with it'
           (Deibler 1976: 10)   (Deibler 1976: 19)

(234) a. Agarabi   b. Agarabi
           náh y-e-m-íh   *naa-rén e-m-íh*
           eat AUX-NEUT-IND-3   eat-ABIL AUX-IND-3
           'he ate'   'he is able to eat'
           (Goddard 1980: 61–2)

(235) a. Kewapi   b. Kewapi
           yada pi-mi   *yada pea-ateme*
           fight AUX-3PL:PRES:EXOC   fight AUX-3PL:PRES:ALLOC
           'they are fighting among   'they are fighting on
              themselves'   someone's behalf'
           (Yarapea 1993: 100)

(236) a. Suena
           ma uri susau-wa
           taro plant AUX:PST-3PL
           'they planted taro for a long time'
           (Wilson 1974: 40)

       b. Suena
           ma uri susaw-iso-wa
           taro plant AUX:PST-CONT-3PL
           'they used to continuously plant taro for a long time'

(237) a. Imonda   b. Imonda
           ka uagl auaia fe-f-t   *ka maim uagl fe-f*
           I go no AUX-PRES-CNTRFACT   I anyway go AUX-PRES
           'I would not go'   'I will go anyway'
           (Seiler 1983/4: 165–6)

Austronesian languages also show forms with Ø-marked lexical verbs in
AUX-headed AVCs. Note that the Ø-pattern for the lexical verb appears only
in past in Halia, elsewhere a LEX-headed pattern may be seen.

(238) a. Halia   b. Halia
           alia u la   *alia e la-g*
           I AUX.PST.1 go   I AUX.NPST go-1
           'I went'   'I go'
           (Allen 1971: 65)

(239) Solos
       no hen no-ma a tsi pos mahu
       you eat AUX-2-FUT ART bit taro tomorrow
       'you will be eating taro tomorrow'
       (Ross 1982b: 23)

(240) a. Hoava (Austronesian; Solomon Islands)
      o-da piala
      OPT-1PL.INCL smoke
      'we want to smoke'
      (Davis 2003: 151)

     b. Hoava
      o-di ṇani
      OPT-3PL eat
      'they want to eat'

(241) Madak
di-ba-lok kaka len-mani atdi melemu
3PL-REM.FUT-AUX get N.MRKR:PL-money their later
'they will get their money later'
(Lee 1989: 71)

(242) a. Atayal
      musaʔ-sakuʔ m-imaʔ hiyaʔ
      ASP-1S INTR-wash 3:FN
      'I'm going to wash him'
      (Huang 1994: 132)

     b. Atayal
      musaʔ-makuʔ pma-n hiyaʔ
      ASP-1GEN wash-TR 3:FN
      'I'm going to wash him (all over)'
      (Huang 1994: 133)

(243) a. Loniu (Austronesian)
      yo u-tɔ min tan
      I 1-AUX sit down
      'I was sitting down'
      (Hamel 1994: 105)

     b. Loniu
      iy a i-sɔ čɛlu
      s/he still 3-AUX stand
      'she was still standing there'

Note that modified root mutation alone (or its absence) may mark the lexical verb element in AVCs in Austronesian languages like Apma of Vanuatu.

(244) a. Apma
      na-t van
      1-PST go
      'I went'
      (Crowley 1991: 217)

     b. Apma
      na-m ban
      1-PRES go
      'I go'

Members of all major languages stocks of Africa show auxiliary verb constructions in which the lexical verb appears in a bare stem form. This includes such languages as !Ora (Khoisan), Mamvu (Nilo-Saharan), Kana (Niger-Congo), and Pero (Afroasiatic).

(245) !Ora (Khoe-Khoe) (Central Khoisan, Namibia, Botswana)
≠ʔan tama-r hã
know NEG-1 DUR
'I don't know'
(Vossen 1997: 190)

(246) a. Dinka
 yin acaa kony apɛi
 you IND:PST:1OBJ help very
 'you have helped me very much'
 (Hieda 1991: 102–3; Nebel 1948: 21)

b. Dinka
 wamuth aca tiŋ
 your.brother IND:PST:1 see
 'I saw your brother

(247) a. Mamvu
 ɔɔbɛ mu-taju
 dance 1-AUX
 'I was dancing'
 (Heine and Reh 1984: 126; Vorbichler 1971: 248–50)

b. Mamvu
 mu-tajɪɓɔ ɛ
 1-AUX dance
 'I was dancing'

(248) Kana
 m̀-wēè   *bʉ̀ʉ̀*
 1-PAST   read book
 'I read a book/books'
 (Ikoro 1996: 89)

(249) Mbodomo (Gbaya, Adamwa-Ubangi; Cameroon)
 ɛ́lɛ́ dúŋ-ú wɔr m̀ɔ̀ Odile mà ɓɔ̀-à
 1pl AUX-PST talk something Odile SIM arrive-PST
 'we were talking when Odile arrived'
 (Boyd 2003: 46)

(250) Godié
 ɔ yi-ɛ-a zɪka lɨ
 he FUT-it-REC.PST yesterday eat
 'he was going to eat it yesterday'
 (Marchese 1986: 79)

(251) Pero (West Chadic, Nigeria)
 nì-íkkà có mín
 1-PROG drink beer
 'I am drinking beer'
 (Frajzyngier 1989: 104)

(252) Sidamo (Cushitic; Ethiopia)
 harʔa caleemmo
 go AUX:1
 'I can go'
 (Hudson 1976a: 273)

(253) a. Nkonya
 bo-ɖe obu yi
 3PL-AUX house build
 'they are building a house'
 (Reineke 1972: 53)

b. Nkonya
 ɔ-ɖe mboe mɔ
 3-AUX animal kill
 'he is killing animals'

(254) Swahili
ni-na-taka cheza
1-PRES-AUX play
'I am about to play'
(Givón 1971: 149)

(255) Kikongo
y-a-kala kanga   ~   *y-a-ka kanga*
1-PST-PROG bind
'I was binding'
(Heine and Reh 1984: 88)

Australian languages have figured in the discussion relatively little so far. This is because the majority of Australian languages exhibiting an AUX-headed AVC structure use a bare-stem or Ø-marked form of the lexical verb. This is the default pattern for this group of languages, occurring in Pama-Nyungan and non-Pama-Nyungan languages alike.

There are several different subtypes of AUX-headed auxiliary verb constructions attested across the range of Australian languages. Certain languages possess only a handful of inflecting verbs and these often include a small set of auxiliaries, or most commonly a set of inflecting verbs that includes auxiliary and lexical uses of individual items, all other verbs requiring an inflectable 'auxiliary' verb. While it is beyond the scope of the present study to make a detailed presentation of all AVCs of the AUX-headed type in Australian languages, even those in which the lexical verb appears in a Ø-marked form, I make a few general comments here . Some 'auxiliaries' appear to be second-position clitic sequences. This type may yield 'pseudo-AUX-headed' forms (see below) given appropriate conditions. The set of non-inflecting lexical verbs may include 'regular' verbal stems as well as elements that are ideophonic, etc., in origin. I will not enter into this contentious and ongoing debate on the nature of non-inflecting lexical verbs in various individual Australian languages (or indeed as a whole): the interested reader is referred to such works as Schultze-Berndt (2000) and MacGregor (2002).

The simplest system of AVCs in Australian languages with a bare stem of the lexical verb occurs in the following Wambaya sentence. Here the auxiliary consists of just a past tense and a subject marker. Synchronically this is probably best analysed as a zero allomorph of an auxiliary verb with tense and subject morphology; diachronically it is most likely a subject-marked auxiliary verb grammaticalized in a past tense function. A slightly more complex but similar form is seen in the Daly language Yunggor as well; here auxiliary and tense marker are separate morphemes.

(256) Wambaya
gajbi ny-a
eat 2-PST
'you ate it'
(Nordlinger 1998: 25)

(257) Yunggor
yakayu yak ya-yaŋka-k
NEG eat 1-AUX-NON.FUT
'I did not eat it'
(Tryon 1974e: 60)

As languages with an often highly developed morphological apparatus, it is perhaps not surprising to find AUX-headed AVCs in various Australian languages with object indexed as well as subject within the auxiliary word. Such a formation may be found, for example, in Mullukmulluk.

(258)   Mullukmulluk
muyin^y-man^y ali taR yi-min^y-arin^y
dog-from leg bit 3M-AUX-1.OBJ
'the dog bit my leg'
(Tryon 1974b: 15)

Similar forms are found in a range of Australian languages, e.g. Ami or Mangarrayi.

(259)   Maŋarrayi
mir? ga-ŋa-wuyan-ɲa-n
know NON3.NPST-1-3PL-AUX-PRES
'I know them'
(Merlan 1979: 45)

(260)   Ami
mit^yirim ka-ya-ŋan^y karat ayi
dog NONFUT-AUX:NONFUT-1OBJ bite CA
'the dog bit me'
(Tryon 1974l: 171)

Yukulta presents an entirely different situation. Here the form looks to be an AUX-headed construction similar to the Mullukmulluk form just given. However, the entire AUX-complex functions as a Wackernagel (second-position) clitic, attaching to the first element in the sentence, here an overt subject pronoun. Given that this is a clitic sequence with a phonologically determined realization (albeit with a morphemically ordered sequence), it is not strictly speaking possible to categorize this formation as an AUX-headed AVC; rather, it is an instance of what I call a 'pseudo-AUX-headed' form.

(261)   Yukulta
ŋata-ŋa-npu-ŋa-nti kurit^ya
I.NOM-1-2/3PL-TR-FUT see.IND
'I'll see them/you (pl)'
(Keen 1983: 222)

The following Wardaman form shows another feature that is not particularly uncommon in Australian language, but less common in languages from other regions of the world. This is the relative flexibility in linear order between an auxiliary verb and a lexical verb in an auxiliary verb construction. Note that this linear order is irrelevant for determining where to place the inflectional morphology, which, as expected in an AUX-headed construction, is always the auxiliary verb.

(262)   Wardaman
        yarrimanbu-yi birrg gerne-rri yirlorloban gerne-rri birrg mawuya
        Taipan-ERG take AUX-PST King.Brown.ABS AUX-PST take poison.ABS
        'Taipan took it away, he took the poison away from King Brown'
        (Merlan 1994: 66)

Some North American Indian languages exhibit AVCs with lexical verbs in unmarked forms as well. This includes such western languages as Nez Perce or the Uto-Aztecan Tübatulabal and Serrano.

(263)   Nez Perce (Sahaptian; USA)
        . . . *ka koná likíp pée-ku-ye*
        subord there touch 3>3-AUX-ASP
        '[quickly the girl cut her shirt] where he had touched her'
        (Mithun 1999: 480; Rude 1985)

(264)   a. Tübatulabal (Uto-Aztecan; USA)   b. Tübatulabal
            ta'naha''-gilu''ts ti'' ti'k   *ih-ma'-ts ti'k*
            OPT-1PL PRTCL eat   here-HORT-3 eat
            'would we were eating'   'let him eat here'
            (Voegelin 1935: 128)   (Voegelin 1935: 129)

(265)   Serrano (Uto-Aztecan, USA)
        k^{w}i'=n k^{w}a'a
        POT-1 eat
        'could I eat it'
        (Langacker 1977: 36)

A number of South American languages have AUX-headed AVCs in which the lexical verb appears in an unmarked, bare form. In some languages this is a minor or rare alternative to morphologically marked lexical verbs found in other AVCs in the language. Such a situation is found, for example, in the Chibchan Ika and Tucanoan Desano, both indigenous languages of Colombia.

(266)   Ika   (267)   Desano
        a-seʔ-ri du tšua u-na   *bõhõtõ yẽã ii-bã gɨa-re*
        3-ERG-TOP well see AUX-DIST   hand grasp AUX-3PL 1X-SPC
        'he looked it over well'   'they shook our hand'
        (Frank 1990: 21)   (Miller 1999: 6)

It occurs as the default form for lexical verbs in AVCs in other languages, however, e.g. the Chocó language Northern Embera of Colombia and Panama, Chibchan Chimila of Colombia, as well as the Panoan Chacobo of Bolivia.

(267)   Northern Embera
        Ariel-ta huers'a ipʰida b-a-sʰi-a
        Ariel-ABS∧FOC force laugh AUX-IMPF-PST-DECL
        'Ariel was laughing so hard'
        (Mortensen 1999: 12)

(268)   Chacobo (Panoan; Bolivia)
        wɨ̌ʒa ʔi-kiʔa
        scratch AUX-REPRT
        'scratches'
        (Prost 1967: 313)

(269)   a. Chimila (Chibchan)   b. Chimila
            hoggʷa ŋa-tte   *hoggʷa dᶻa-tte*
            bathe AUX-DECL   bathe AUX-DECL
            'he bathes'   'he will bathe'
            (Trillos Amaya 1997: 157; Adelaar 2004: 76–7)

        c. Chimila
            kenne ka-uka-ra-tte
            eat AUX-2-DL-DECL
            'the two of you ate'
            (Trillos Amaya 1997: 124; Adelaar 2004: 78)

In addition, Cocama of the Tupi-Guaraní family and Paumarí of the small Arawá family of Brazil show similar formations in which the lexical verb in an AUX-headed AVC appears in an unmarked bare-stem form.[18]

---

[18] As will be discussed in Ch. 5, this is actually probably a pseudo-AUX-headed split pattern, with a Ø subject-marking on the lexical verb for third singular.

(270) Cocama
úri yumîra cúpü rána-cúri
he is.angry to 3PL-FAR.PST
'he scolded them'
(Faust 1971: 79)

(271) a. Paumarí (Arawá, Brazil)
Maria-ra vara o-ni-'a-ki-ho
Maria-OBJ speak 1-AUX-TRNSTVZR-NONTHEME-1
'I will speak to Mary'
(Chapman and Derbyshire 1991: 332)

b. Paumarí
vara i-ra o-ni-'a-ki-ho
speak 2-OBJ 1-AUX-TRNSTVZR-NONTHEME-1
'I will speak to you'

Summary

There are a number of verb–verb constructions in the languages of the world where one verb which itself (optionally) encodes some functional category, also serves as the locus for indexing all obligatory inflectional verbal categories necessary to render the clause finite, and which generally adds only (or almost only) functional/operational semantics to the construction, combines with another verb that contributes lexical or content semantics to the construction. The lexical verb in this verb–verb concatenation may appear in any number of different 'non-finite', 'dependent', or 'conjunctive' (etc.) forms when viewing such constructions cross-linguistically. Such non-finite forms are given a range of designations, depending in part on such factors as other functions of the same element within the grammatical system of the language concerned and the form and function of other elements with which it may contrast, as well as the tradition of analysis that defines the appropriate metalanguage suitable for presentation of data for particular languages, language families, or regions. Terms such as infinitive, nominalizer, gerund, participle, etc. are common and often motivated language-specifically. A lack of terminological order or even compatibility unfortunately permeates various such traditions of analyses, and this has rendered the situation difficult to say the least when it comes to attempting a coherent cross-linguistic comparison and categorization of possible formal subtypes of AUX-headed AVCs. Fortunately, the details of possible meaningful oppositions or lack thereof in

TABLE 23. Sample non-finite forms of lexical verbs in AUX-headed AVCs

INF	NOMLZR	GER	PRTCPL	TAM
Garo Sel'kup	Impal Meithei	Nivkh	Hindi French	Remo
Somali Kaguru	Burushaski	Xakas	Diyari Gimira	Basque
Yale Ndjébbana	Manx Tairora	Shuar Naro	Desano	Amanab
Leko	P. Quechua	Adzera	Godoberi	Apalaí
			Chad. Arabic	Panyjima

SUB/DEP	REDPL	SS	CONNEG	Case
Koiari	Harar Oromo	Korowai	Majang	Burushaski
Ngizim	Candoshi	Tofa	Mbalanhu	Estonian
Lokono	Sinaugoro		Amanab	Kolyma Yukaghir
	Gta?		Nganasan	Bobo Fing
	Ngankikurungkurr	Evenki	Yanyuwa	

CONJ	IRR/SBJ	Bare Stem (Ø)		
Burji	Karekare	Tamang	Pero	Sumerian
Koasati	Walpiri	Udihe	Yunggor	Kikongo
	Nisenan	Sulka	Apma	Madak
		!Ora	Mamvu	Kana
		Tübatulabal	Chacobo	

various individual languages among the uses of various forms of lexical verbs in AVCs is not a major hurdle from the perspective of the present volume; such details are seen as merely minor kinds of local variation on the AUX-headed pattern, and do not in any way obscure the overall general picture. That is to say, whether an object is demoted to genitive/oblique status with certain non-finite constructions and not others, when both may fill the slot of the specific realization of the lexical verb in an AVC in the language, is not relevant typologically speaking, although it may have significant consequences for the grammar of the language concerned. In any event, it is better to conceive of all the forms that lexical verbs might appear in to occupy some kind of continuum–or more accurately several intersecting and inter-connected continua–from more to less 'dependent'/ '(non-)finite', 'verbal'/'nominal', 'bound'/'free-standing', etc. These continua represent the ever-emergent and dynamic processes that constitute the grammaticalization epiphenomena of AVCs as here conceived.

The boundaries between various types of category of 'non-finite' forms of lexical verbs in AVCs may or may not be rigidly definable structurally, etc., but in any case they are porous enough to allow new members. Thus, as mentioned above, both infinitives and certain converb forms in Xakas are derived from the combination of a participle and a case-marker. These very few elements could fit into the discussion under four different headings above. Some languages allow variation between different forms of the lexical verb with the same auxiliary in the same function, while others show paradigms or semi-paradigms with more than one form obligatory in different forms (sometimes in a suppletively construed paradigm). An example of both types can be found in English. Compare the suppletively construed capabilitive paradigm (272) with lexical forms in either a bare-stem or an infinitive form, or the various forms of the lexical verb found with *start* (273).

(272)   *can go*   could go   *will be able to go*

(273)   *started to dance   started dancing*

One can force a contrast to the forms in (273) in English, but these two variants may also be used in the same context.

It is important to remember, and to state here explicitly, that although a wide range of languages show auxiliary verb constructions of the AUX-headed type—and indeed this is the default understanding of the concept of AVC found in most theories of grammar and covered fairly extensively here—all of the subtypes described above combined form only one type of macro-pattern found among the languages of the world. Other macro-patterns are the topic of Chapters 3 to 5.

3

LEX-headed Auxiliary Verb Constructions

Introduction

Possibly the most controversial of the categories discussed in this volume, the LEX-headed pattern of inflection in auxiliary verb constructions consists of an uninflecting or fixed form of an auxiliary verb and a lexical verb with all obligatory tense, subject, etc. inflectional morphology characteristic of finite clauses lacking auxiliaries. The auxiliary verb elements in LEX-headed AVCs are often considered particles rather than verbs, but their verbal origin is clear in lexical origin, syntactic position, function, etc. While the inflectional head is the lexical verb, the auxiliary verb may be the phrasal or syntactic head, which in some languages necessitates some kind of dependent verb morphology on the inflectional head lexical verb. In a small number of instances, the auxiliary verb itself may be in a marked dependent form (see below).

The LEX-headed pattern of inflection in AVCs can be roughly schematized as in Table 3.1, excluding individual exceptions of course.

3.1 Subtypes of LEX-headed AVCs

The auxiliary verb in a LEX-headed AVC appears in a phrasal head position like an auxiliary of the AUX-headed type, thus canonically after the lexical verb in most OV languages and before the lexical verb in many VO languages (with notable exceptions). By definition it encodes some sort of functional semantics, usually tense, mood, or aspect (see below for a list of the

TABLE 3.1. Lex-headed inflectional pattern of AVCs

Inflectional (functional) head	Lexical verb
Phrasal/syntactic head	Auxiliary verb
Semantic head	Lexical verb

auxiliary verb functions in LEX-headed forms in the database). The lexical
verb, on the other hand, bears markers for subject, tense, etc., depending on
the verb structure of a particular construction. Note that, as with all the
patterns described in this volume, LEX-headed AVCs also appear in fused
forms in complex verb forms in a range of unrelated languages from across
the world (e.g. Shambala and Chamula Tzotzil: see Chapter 6).

Unlike AUX-headed AVCs, where one can attempt to categorize the forms
that lexical verbs appear in, this is obviously not the case with LEX-headed
formations, where virtually all verbal inflectional categories may be indexed
by a lexical verb in some language possessing LEX-headed AVCs; so it is not
really meaningful to discuss this. A subset of these languages exists in which
the lexical verb encodes the finite inflectional categories of the verb but may
bear an overt marker of dependency, presumably triggered by the (unmarked
or dummy third singular/clausal subject-marked) auxiliary verb. This represents the mismatch between the inflectional head (the lexical verb) and the
structural head (the auxiliary verb) characteristic of LEX-headed AVCs. I have
collected the categories marked by auxiliaries found in LEX-headed AVCs, but
this is a diverse group and yields little insight into the nature of which kinds of
functional categories are most likely to be encoded in this manner, or even
into whether that question is a valid one to ask in the first place. There is a
descending order of frequency of the functional category that auxiliaries have
in LEX-headed AVCs of the following type: FUT > PRF > PROG > PST > NEG >
CAP > COMPL > PRS/CONT/NEG.PST/OPT.

A simple and straightforward example of a LEX-headed pattern of inflection is seen in Enets, a Samoyedic language of northern central Siberia, where
the auxiliary is unchanging and occurs before the lexical verb, which appears
in a tense-marked form.

(1)   Enets
      oŋat̂ pə-bi
      AUX eat-PST
      'he began to eat'
      (Künnap 1999a: 29)

Similarly simple LEX-headed AVC forms are found in the South Slavic languages Bulgarian and Macedonian. Here the clipped auxiliary, historically a
third singular form of the auxiliary verb (see below), precedes a subject-
marked lexical verb. Note that almost all other verb–verb constructions in
Bulgarian require the complementizer/subordinator *da* and thus appear to
more transparently reflect, or in some cases actually remain in, a biclausal
stage on the grammaticalization continuum.

(2) a. Bulgarian   b. Bulgarian
         ti šte izpusne-š vlaka   vs.   *ti trjabva da otide-š*
         you FUT miss-2 train:the   you must COMP go-2
         'you will miss the train'   'you must go'
         (Rudin 1983: 10)

     c. Bulgarian
         nie šte pristign-em utre
         we FUT arrive:1PL.PRF.PRS tomorrow
         'we will arrive tomorrow'
         (Tomić 2004: p. 524)

(3) Macedonian
     studenti-te k'e dojd-at utre
     student-DEF.PL.FUT come:3PL.PRF.PRS tomorrow
     'the students will come tomorrow'
     (Tomić 2004: 523)

The Austroasiatic language Temiar belonging to the Aslian subgroup spoken
in Malaysia offers another example of a LEX-headed AVC. The perfect auxiliary occurs before a subject-marked lexical verb.

(4) Temiar (Aslian, Austroasiatic; Malaysia)
     hɔj na-cīb
     PRF 3-go
     'he has gone'
     (Benjamin 1976: 166)

A similar construction is found in Ainu, but here the auxiliary follows rather
than precedes the lexical verb, showing that the linear order or phrasal head
status has nothing to do with inflectional head patterns. Completives are
formed in the same way in this fascinating and enigmatic isolate language of
Japan (and Russia).

(5) a. Ainu, Itadori dialect (isolate; Japan) b. Ainu, Ishikari
         nep   kamuye i-turen   rok   kus   *kampi   a-nukar   okere*
         what   god   1-bless   PRF   perhaps   letter   1-see   COMPL
         'perhaps some god has blessed me'   'I finished reading the letter'
         (Shibatani 1990: 79)

Numerous unrelated languages across the world show AVCs of the LEX-
headed type in which the auxiliary verb appears in an unchanging form.
This is the most common subtype of AVC showing the LEX-headed

inflectional pattern. Auxiliary verbs of this type may appear either preverbally or postverbally with respect to inflected lexical verb, depending on the syntax of the language in question. Thus, such African languages as the Niger-Congo language Obolo and Mödö of the Nilo-Saharan stock show preverbal auxiliaries (befitting the characteristic SVO and VS orders typical of these languages, respectively).

(6) Obolo (Andoni)   (7) Mödö
     kè ò-sî   *tí móɓɔ̀nyì yí*
     SBJNCTV 3-go   FUT 1:rescue you
     'he should go'   'I will rescue you'
     (Aaron 1999: 172)   (Persson and Persson 1991: 19)

The Omotic language Hamer of Ethiopia shows a similarly simple system to Obolo and Mödö, but here the auxiliary follows the lexical verb in perfect constructions but precedes it in imperfect forms, with the lexical verb encoding aspect or mood.

(8) a. Hamer
         nokom-bar i də niʔ-e
         water.hole.in.use-ABL I AUX come-IMPRF
         'I am coming from the water'
         (Lydall 1976: 411)

     b. Hamer
         sʌxʌ wo də yeʔ-ɛ
         tomorrow we AUX go-IMPRF
         'tomorrow we are going'
         (Lydall 1976: 422)

(9) Hamer (Omotic; Ethiopia)   b. Hamer
     kum-o i de
     eat-PURP I AUX   yesterday he come-PRF AUX
     'I should [be] eat[ing]'   'he came yesterday'
     (Lydall 1976: 423)   (Lydall 1976: 422)

Other African languages show LEX-headed AVCs where the lexical verb may appear in a wide range of inflected forms, for example the Northern Khoisan language Ju/'hoan, Tarafit Berber, and the Chadic language Hdi, where auxiliaries precede their accompanying lexical verb; in Central Khoisan !Ora where auxiliaries follow lexical verbs; and in the Kuliak language Ik, where auxiliaries may either precede or follow lexical verbs in LEX-headed AVCs.

(10) Ju|'hoan (Khoisan)
      ha kú ú-á |ám-à hè
      CL.I IPFV.AUX go-VE day-REL this
      'he will be going today'
      (Güldemann and Vossen 2000: 109)

(11) Hdi (Chadic; Cameroon, Nigeria)
      dzà'á gùy-éy-mú tá vghá màxtsím
      FUT meet-POT:OBJ-1PL OBJ body tomorrow
      'will we meet tomorrow?'
      (Frajzyngier and Shay 2002: 197)

(12) Tarifit Berber
      tuʕya iwðə-ɣ
      AUX arrive-1S.SG.M.F
      'I had (already) arrived'
      (McClelland 2000: 24)

(13) a. !Ora (Khoe-Khoe) (C. Khoisan, Namibia, Botswana)
          ≠ʔan tama-r hã
          know NEG-1 DUR
          'I don't know'
          (Vossen 1997: 190)

      b. !Ora
          mũ-tama da hã
          see-NEG 1PL DUR
          'we have not seen'

(14) Ik [Kuliak; Uganda]   b. Ik
      Ƙó-iá ak bié-é ho   *Itámááná zɛɠw-íd-o awa-ɔ*
      go-1 PRF outside-DAT house   must stay-2-NAR home-ABL
      'I have gone outside the house'   'I must stay at home'
      (König 2002: 26)   (König 2002: 277)

The Adamawa language Doyayo of Cameroon shows a more complex system of marking on the lexical verb and indeed the auxiliary as well. The auxiliary partially encodes person of the subject through the tone associated with the auxiliary, and the lexical verb may index a range of tense/mood/aspect and argument property categories.

(15) a. Doyayo (Adamawa, Niger-Congo; Cameroon)
          mi¹ (gi²) kpel¹-ko¹
          I AUX pour-PROX
          'I'm going to pour'
          (Wiering and Wiering 1994: 55)

      b. Doyayo
          gi¹ wɔl¹-s-i¹-wi³-ge³
          [3.]AUX take.by.force-BEN-EP-1PL-3
          'he will catch him for us'
          (Wiering and Wiering 1994: 77)

The simplest LEX-headed systems in Papuan languages can be seen in Hatam and Koiari. In Hatam, auxiliaries follow subject-marked lexical verbs and in Koiari, an African type structure of Subj Aux O Verb is found, with portmanteau subject/tense markers on the lexical verb.

(16) Hatam   (17) Koiari
      di-ttei kep biei   *da ma oko oti-ma*
      1-carry AUX wood   I MOD here go-PRS: 1/3
      'I kept carrying wood'   'I'm off right now'
      (Reesink 1999: 74)   (Dutton 1996: 24)

Kwerba of the Dani-Kwerba stock of the putative Trans-New Guinea phylum is a language where the LEX-headed pattern of inflection in AVCs is quite common. Auxiliaries mark such categories as progressive, perfective, intentionality, etc. and appear in an unmarked, preverbal form. The lexical verbs may be either fully finite and appear with realis marking, or may appear in a semi-dependent irrealis form (more common), in either instance serving as the locus for encoding tense and argument properties in the clause.

(18) a. Kwerba
          co cara [a-]kot-ri-s
          I PRF SG-cut-AUG-RLS
          'I have cut it'
          (de Vries and de Vries 1997: 8, 14)

      b. Kwerba
          co kaita b-a-kot-ri-s
          I UNFIN PRES-SG-cut-AUG-RLS
          'I have not yet cut it (but I intend to)'

c. Kwerba (Dani-Kwerba; Trans-New Guinea)
co ic-abo wïre b-a-kot-ara-ri-an-mas
I wood-OBJ PROG PRS-SG-cut-MULT.ACT-AUG-DIST-IRR
'I am cutting a piece of wood over there'
(de Vries and de Vries 1997: 6)

d. Kwerba
nino bo kwa ec-e-nan
we that PRF REC.PST-1PL-eat
'we ate them'
(de Vries and de Vries 1997: 8–9)

e. Kwerba
co kwa [a-]-ku-m
I PRF SG-go-IRR
'I shall go'

f. Kwerba
Came-bo mara b-a-kot-ri-s
Came-OBJ PRPF PRES-SG-cut-AUG-RLS
'straight away he cut Came'
(de Vries and de Vries 1997: 9)

g. Kwerba
com tat bïre b-a-mon-am
my father STAT PRES-SG-sit-IRR
'my father is still alive'

h. Kwerba
co bo (a-)kot-ri-m
I CAP SG-cut-AUG-IRR
'I can cut it'
(de Vries and de Vries 1997: 14)

i. Kwerba
nano wïre b-ang-ku-m
WE.DL PROG PRES-DL-go-IRR
'we two are going'
(de Vries and de Vries 1997: 22)

Other languages of greater New Guinea with LEX-headed AVCs include Moi of the West Papuan phylum, where auxiliaries follow lexical verbs and Bukiyip of the Torricelli Phylum, where auxiliaries precede inflected lexical verbs.

(19) a. Moi (W. Papuan)
w-agi si
3-die PRF
'he is dead'
(Menick 1995: 69)

b. Moi
w-isis se
3-done PRF
'it is done'

c. Moi
n-asili se'
2-bathe PRF:Q
'have you bathed yet?'

(20) Bukiyip (Torricelli; Papua New Guinea)
pwe m-e-yotu
AUX 1PL-RLS-stand
'we kept on standing'
(Conrad and Wogiga 1991: 55)

A wide range of Austronesian (AN) languages exhibit AVCs of the LEX-headed inflectional pattern. This includes such a diverse range of Austronesian languages as Micronesian Ulithian, Oceanic Kele, Kaulong, Sudest, Kairiru and Iwal of New Guinea, and Buma of the Solomons, Central Malayo-Polynesian Kola of Indonesia, and Formosan Paiwan of Taiwan.

(21) a. Ulithian (AN; Micronesia)   b. Ulithian
          ye βʷe fawu-xili-ya   cf.   *re xafaŋa-xo loxo*
          he FUT row-TR-3   they send-2 thither
          'he will row for him'   'they sent you there'
          (Lynch 2002c: 799–800)

(22) a. Kele (AN)   b. Kele
          su ha-sa hare um   *i i-le kah*
          they 3PL-come CONT house   he 3-go COMPL
          'they are coming'   'he has gone'
          (Ross 2002a: 137–8)

(23) Kairiru (AN; Papua New Guinea)
      tuyieq̣ wot ti-lieq piyei
      we.DL.INCL AUX 1PL-go where
      'where do we 2 (incl) intend to go?'
      (Wivell 1981: 127)

(24) a. Sudest (AN; Papua New Guinea)
          na ya-wa
          IMM.FUT 1-go
          'I will go (today)'
          (Anderson and Ross 2002: 336, 337)

      b. Sudest   c. Sudest
          ne thï-kaiwo   *mbala i-wa*
          fut 3PL-work   OPT 3-go
          'they will work (after today)' 'he should go'

(25) Kaulong (AN; Papua New Guinea) (26) Buma (AN)
      nga-ion-i koho   *dapa kape le-le mobo*
      1R-know-TR PRF   they FUT 3PL-go tomorrow
      'I already know it'   'they will go tomorrow'
      (Ross 2002b: 401)   (Tryon 2002: 579)

(27) Iwal (AN)
     kabut etenik ande gi-ble
     stick DEM AUX 3-break
     'this stick is already broken'
     (Bradshaw 2001: 67)

(28) a. Kola (AN)   b. Kola
         ni bisa a-dom boka tuybay   *maw ku-bana aka Dobo*
         he CAP 3-make canoe new   PRF 1-go to Dobo
         'he can make a new canoe'   'I already went to Dobo'
         (Takata and Takata 1991: 91–2)

(29) a. Paiwan (AN; Taiwan)   b. Paiwan
         urhi pura˙pura˙ven   *urhi vaik ti˙maju*
         FUT REDPL-make.drunk   FUT go he
         'we will make him drunk'   'he will go'
         (Egli 1990: 38)   (Egli 1990: 113)

Note the lexical verb may appear in a dependent form in some of these Austronesian forms (e.g. reduplicated, as in the first Paiwan example). Note also that except for Kele, where non-Austronesian influence may explain the post-verbal position of the auxiliary, all examples above show the auxiliary verb preceding the lexical verb in these Austronesian languages.

Kimaragang (Dusun) of Indonesia uses two LEX-headed AVCs (where the auxiliary verbs come from grammaticalized past and present forms of 'do') in which the auxiliary verb appears clause-initially and the lexical verb appears in the appropriate 'focus' form and with non-finite marking. This is similar to the dependent form of the lexical verb found in AVCs in such indigenous New World languages as Classical Yucatec, Toba-Maskoy, and Coahuilteco (see below).

(30) a. Kimaragang
         nan okuh tinduk-o do wulanut
         AUX.PST I (PAT) bite-ACC.FOC/NON-FIN NON.PAT/INDEF snake
         'I was bitten by a snake'
         (Kroeger 1988: 236)

     b. Kimaragang
         man tekau [kuh-ikau] jarum-ai
         AUX I-you needle-DAT.FOC-NON-FIN
         'I will give you a shot'

Only a handful of Australian languages utilize the LEX-headed inflectional pattern for AVCs. These include the Pama-Nyungan language Djapu Yolngu, and the non-Pama Nyungan language Jingulu.

(31) Djapu Yolngu
dhuwal-ny bitja-n ŋayi yurru wuyupthu-n yulŋuny
this.ABS-PRO do.thus-UNM 3SG.NOM FUT continue-UNM for.some.time
'this [the language] will continue in this way for some time to come'
(Morphy 1983: 70)

(32) Jingulu
angkula ngaja-nga-ju
NEG[.CAP] see-1-PRES
'I can't see'
(Pensalfini 2003: 229)

It is possible that the past tense element *tye* in the Daly language Ngankikurungkurr should be analyzed historically as a verb; if so, the following formation would constitute an instance of an AVC of the LEX-headed pattern.

(33) Ngankikurungkurr
minta kana tye wirrnyeregu tye mi-bebi tye warrane
NEG PUNC PST 3NSG:see:RFLXV:FUT PST CAUS-SELF PST OA:3NSP:AUX:
    PST:D
'they never saw each other again'
(Hoddinott and Kofod 1988: 129)

A wide range of indigenous languages of North, Central, and South America make use of auxiliary verb constructions of the LEX-headed inflectional pattern. The Salish language Tillamook exhibits an example of this type. The uninflecting auxiliary precedes the subject- and object- (and other TAM-) marked lexical verb. Its distant relative, the Interior Salish language Lillooet (St'at'imets/Sƛ'áƛmxc), shows a similar construction with the progressive. Both languages are typically verb-initial in structure.

(34) Tillamook[†] [Salish; USA]
gʷə qʼkʷ-ə́s-wə-s
FUT bite-PURP-2OBJ-3SUBJ
'he will bite you'
(Egesdal and Thompson 1998: 241)

(35)   Lillooet (St'at'imets/Sƛ'áƛmxc)
       wá? cú-n-as
       PROG tell-TRANS-3.TRANS.SUBJ
       's/he is telling him/her'
       (van Eijk 1997: 154)

In other North American languages there are LEX-headed AVCs found with lexical verbs either following or preceding the auxiliary. Examples of the former type include Pochutla and Yuchi, and of the latter Chickasaw. For Chickasaw, Munro (2003) acknowledged the verb-like qualities of these elements but considered the structures they are embedded within to be 'less verbal' than ones that take same subject (−ss) suffixes on the lexical verb. It seems better rather to consider them both to be grammaticalized AVCs, one with the lexical verb in a dependent (ss) form and an inflected auxiliary in an AUX-headed AVC and the other with an inflected lexical verb in a LEX-headed AVC; the 'less verbal' nature of the unmarked complements may reflect their more recent origin or their stage of development on the grammaticalization continuum.

(36)   a.   Yuchi (Euchee)
            kede nẽ-k'ala yo-chwœ̃ te ne-tsa te
            now NEG-thing 2.ACT.PLUS-hear AUX 2.ACT-sleep AUX
            'now you can't hear anything so you can sleep'
            (Linn 2001: 293)

       b.   Yuchi (Euchee)
            di dze-ne-to te
            I 1.PAT-2.ACT-go.with AUX
            'you can go with me'
            (Linn 2001: 296)

(37)   Pochutla   (38)   Chickasaw (Muskogean; USA)
       as wel n-o-kca-n   *sa-sipokni ki'yo*
       NEG CAP 1-REFL-get.up-SBJ   1-be.old NEG
       'I can't get up'   'I'm not old'
       (Langacker 1977: 36)   (Munro 2003: 8)

Consider briefly the following form from Coahuilteco, an isolate language sometimes thought to be distantly related to Hokan languages (assuming this latter grouping exists in anything but a fairly narrow sense). This sentence has a LEX-headed AVC marking future tense that is subordinate to a clausal complement taking semi-auxiliary 'want'. Note that the lexical verb appears in an overtly dependent form in this LEX-headed AVC.

(39)   Coahuilteco[†] (isolate; USA)
       cin uxʷaʼ l̓ tu-kʷeʼn na-k-pa-ma ś san pa-n na-ka ʼwa pam
       I sky NEUTRAL-PLACE-1 1-2-SUBORD-see FUT SUBORD-1 1-want INTSV
       'I very much want to see you in Heaven'
       (Mithun 1999: 394; Troike 1996)

It is these overtly dependent marked lexical verb forms in LEX-headed AVCs that represent the easiest subtype of the LEX-headed AVC pattern to understand in terms of the familiar AUX-headed pattern. These dependent yet head-looking forms possibly reflect the inherent tension in the status of the element present due to the mismatch in headedness of the lexical verb: although the lexical verb is the inflectional head in the AVC it is a phrasal/structural dependent on the auxiliary, and may therefore be overtly marked as such. Forms like the Coahuilteco one above manifest this dependent status by appearing in a dependent form.

Siouan languages show an old auxiliary construction that appears as a bound element in some of the languages and, relevant to the topic of the present chapter, a LEX-headed AVC as well. Such a situation is found, for example, in the Siouan language Lakhota. Here the future auxiliary appears following the inflected lexical verb.

(40)   a.   Lakhota (Siouan; USA)   b.   Lakhota
            úpi kte   *ūkaśtakapi kte*
            come-PL FUT   1PL-strike-PL FUT
            'they will come'   'we shall strike'
            (Buechel 1939: 31)   (Buechel 1939: 35)

This element—historically the verb 'want'—has a range of realizations and functions across the members of the Siouan language family. It has been grammaticalized to mark such categories as desiderative, future, potential, and intentional, also retaining its original lexical verb 'want'. It seems likely that the element *kte* in Lakota was originally a lexical verb meaning 'want' that, via a similar series of semantic changes that gave rise to the English future auxiliary *will* (probably via a modal desiderative > potential mood path of development), became a marker of future tense. The range of functions of cognate elements in other Siouan languages is strongly suggestive of such a development (Rankin et al. 2002: 197).

(41)   Cognate forms in Siouan < 'want'

Crow	*išši*	'want to'
Hidatsa	*hte*	desiderative
Mandan	*-kt-*	future
Dakota	*kta*	'potential'
Winnebago	*ke*	'intentive'
Omaha	*tte*	'potential mode'
Kansa	*tte*	'potential mode'
Osage	*hte*	'potential mode'
Quapaw	*tte*	'potential mode'
Lakota	*kte*	potential; future
Biloxi	*te*	'want'
Tutelo	*ta*	future
Proto-Siouan	**kte*	

(Rankin et al. 2002: 197)

Given the relative frequency with which future formations are marked by LEX-headed constructions, from a typological perspective this Lakota construction appears to be perfectly normal. See Rankin et al. (2002: 197–8) for more on this from a Siouanist and theoretical perspective.

Various South American languages show LEX-headed auxiliary verb constructions. The relative order of the auxiliary and the lexical verb is of course irrelevant and may vary in related languages: e.g. the auxiliary appears after the lexical verb in Kipeá (Kariri) but before it in Canela Timbíra, both indigenous languages of Brazil.

(42)   a.   Kapón(g) (Carib; Guyana)
            wi-enji weyrika-tza man
            1-daughter die-PERF AUX
            'my daughter died'
            (Gildea 1998: 175, 178)

       b.   Kapón(g)
            uurə endakna-pɨ mang
            1SG eat-PAST AUX
            'I had eaten'

(43)   Kipeá (Kariri) (isolate; Brazil)
       ku-te di
       1PL.INCL-come FUT
       'we will come'
       (Rodrigues 1999b: 186)

(44)   Canela Timbíra (Macro-Jê; Brazil)
       kapi tɛ pɔ kuran nɛ ke ha ku-kʰu
       Capi ERG.PAST deer kill AND 3.SS FUT 3-eat
       'Capi killed a deer and will eat it'
       (Rodrigues 1999b: 197)

Other South American languages with LEX-headed AVCs include Sanuma of
the small Yanomami family of Brazil and Venezuela, Mapudungun of the
Araucanian family of Chile and Argentina, Toba-Maskoy of Paraguay, and
Cuiba-Wamonae, a Guahiban language of Venezuela and Colombia. In
Sanuma and Toba-Maskoy the auxiliary follows the lexical verb and marks
the future, which is statistically speaking the most common category marked
by auxiliaries in LEX-headed AVCs. In Cuiba-Wamonae, the auxiliary precedes
the lexical verb.

(45)   a.   Sanuma (Yanomami; Brazil, Venezuela)
            sa hama a-su-lö kite
            I visit leave-FOC-DIR FUT
            'I will go away on a visit'
            (Borgman 1990: 208–9)

       b.   Sanuma
            hi sa walo-a ko-ta-ki kite
            here I arrive-DUR return-EXT-FOC FUT
            '... I will arrive here'

(46)   Toba-Maskoy (Mascoian; Paraguay)   (47)   Mapudungun (Mapuche)
       šing-aašin-ïk s"āt   *pepí küθaw-la-n*
       1PL:OBJ:FUT:KY-CLASS-√-DEP FUT   AUX work-NEG-IND.1SG
       'nos darán noticias, nos comunicarán'   'I am not able to work'
       (Susnik 1977: 101)   (Smeets 1989: 219)

(48)   a.   Cuiba-Wamonae (Guahiban; Venezuela, Columbia)
            ba xane nawita
            AUX eat a.lot
            'be accustomed to eating a lot'
            (Kerr 1995: 203)

       b.   Cuiba-Wamonae
            be poná-e-n
            AUX go-FUT-1
            'I want to go'

Note that in Toba-Maskoy, as in Coahuiliteco, the lexical verb appears in an overtly dependent form, marking its syntactic/structural/phrasal dependent status, despite its inflectional head status. Also, in the second Cuiba-Wamonae form, the lexical verb is obligatorily in the future in this construction and thus in a sense is in a predictable, construction-dependent form.

Auxiliaries in Meso-American languages generally come in a position preceding the lexical verb, and this is also true of those Meso-American languages with LEX-headed AVCs. This includes Pipil of the Uto-Aztecan family, Chamula Tzotzil of the Mayan group, various Totonac varieties, Huautla de Jimenez Mazatec, and—further outside the traditional understanding of Meso-America linguistically and culturally—in Tol (Jicaque) of Honduras.

(49) Pipil
     weli ni-nehnemi wehka
     CAP1-walk far
     'I can walk far'
     (Campbell 1985: 139)

(50) a. Chamula Tzotzil   b. Chamula Tzotzil
        muk ta x-kolta- oʃ uk bal   *muk bu tʃ -a-x-max-ik*
        NEG INCMPL 1-help-2PL going   NEG RESTRCTV INCMPL-2-1-hit-2PL
        'I will not help you go'   'I will not hit you'
        (Suarez 1983b: 120)

(51) Misantla Totonac (Totonacan; Mexico)
     kináṇ náh ʔ̱íkčúulayáa
     kináṇ na(ł) ik-čuula-yaa-wa
     we FUT 1SUB-make.X-IMPF-1SUB.PL
     'we will make X'
     (MacKay 1999: 117)

(52) San Marcos Atexquilapan (Totonacan)
     ʔ̀ṵt tą́n púu-łkáa   *ʔ̀ṵt tą́n š-púu-łkáa*
     s/he PROG INNER.REL-measure.X   s/he PROG PST-INNER.REL-measure.X
     's/he is weighing X'   's/he was weighing X'
     (MacKay 1999: 134)   (MacKay 1999: 137)

(53) a. Yecuatla (Totonacan)
        ʔ̀ṵt ʔą́n púu-łkáa   ∼ *ʔ̀ṵt tą́n púu-łkáa*
        s/he PROG INNER.REL-measure.X
        's/he is weighing X'
        (MacKay 1999: 134)

b. Yecuatla (Totonacan)
    ʔụ̀t ʔą̣n púu-ɬkáa-štạn   ~   *ʔụ̀t tą́n púu-ɬkáa-štạn*
    s/he PROG INNER.REL-measure.X-PST
    's/he is weighing X'
    (MacKay 1999: 137)

(54) a. Tol (Jicaque)[1] (isolate? Honduras)
    kʰul kelél lya
    fish AUX eat:1:PRES
    'I want to eat fish'
    (Holt 1999a: 32)

    b. Tol
    ma kelél wa móʔo hák-cʰa
    NEG AUX house LOC 3: come: PRES-IMPF
    's/he didn't want to come into the house'
    (Holt 1999a: 32)

(55) Huautla de Jimenez Mazatec (Mazatecan; Mexico)
    he³ ki³-so³ko³-na³
    AUX COMPL-find-3>1
    'it has been found by me' (I found it)'
    (Pike 1967: 323)

In the Mayan language Classical Yucatec, the preverbal auxiliary may be followed by an inflected lexical verb with a dependent 'conjunct' inflectional marker. This is thus like the constructions in Coahuilteco and Toba-Maskoy above, and likewise overtly manifests the inflectional head but structural dependent features of the lexical verb commonly found in the LEX-headed pattern of inflection of AVCs.

(56) Classical Yukatek[†] (Mayan; Mexico)
    tan ʔin-lúb'-ul   *tan ʔa-b'is-ik teloʔ*
    PROG 1:TR-fall-INCOMPL   PROG 2:TR-take-CNJ there
    'I am falling'   'you are taking it there'
    (McQuown 1967: 235)

3.2 Reanalysed 'clausal' subject forms as LEX-headed AVCs

Among the common sources for a LEX-headed AVC is a biclausal structure in which the clause containing the lexical verb functions as a third singular/

---

[1] Note that Tol *kelel* 'want' < Spanish *querer*.

default subject of a certain class of predicates that permit clausal complements. After a gradual process of grammaticalization and clausal union has
taken place, the formation now functions as a LEX-headed AVC. Take the
example of Acholi, a Western Nilotic language. One modal formation in
Acholi is marked by a LEX-headed AVC using the auxiliary *omyero*. Historically, this is a third singular past form of a verb meaning 'be suitable',
grammaticalized into this modal form, i.e. *omyero* < *o-myero* 3-be.suitable/
fit.PAST.

(57)   Acholi (Nilo-Saharan; Western Nilotic; Uganda, Sudan)
        in   omyero   i-cam   mot
        you   should   2-eat   slowly
        'you should eat slowly'
        (Heine 1993: 41)

A range of other Nilotic languages of the Nilo-Saharan family in the east
African region show AVCs of this type. For example, the Eastern Nilotic
Maasai or Turkana of Kenya and Tanzania. Note that in Maasai, certain classes
of auxiliaries take a finite, subject-marked lexical verb (58a) while others (58b)
take a marked dependent form of the lexical verb (see also 3.4 below).

(58) a. Maasai (East Nilotic; Kenya, Tanzania) b. Maasai
          ɛ-tɔn a-irrag   *ɛ-ɲ r n-a-lɔ*
          3-AUX1-lie. down   3-AUX COMP-1-go
          'I am still lying down'   'I ought to go'
          (Tucker and Mpaayei 1955: 101; Hamaya 1993: 8)

(59) a. Turkana   b. Turkana
          è-id-u-kin-ò ɛ̀-twàn-ɪ̀   *ɛ̀ -à-pɔtʊ̀ tɔ-tɔ-k-a̒*
          3-AUX-EPIPAT-DAT-VB 3-dead-ASP   3-PST-AUX 3-dead-PL-PL
          'he almost died'   'then they died'
          (Dimmendaal 1983: 162)   (Dimmendaal 1983: 175) <come>

      c. Turkana
          è-item-o-kin-ò i-yoŋ̒ i-los-i-o tɔ̀kɔ̀na̒
          3-AUX-EPIPAT-DAT-VB you 2-go-ASP-VB now
          'you must go now'
          (Dimmendaal 1983: 162)

African and Eurasian languages are far from unique in showing LEX-headed
AVCs originating from clausal-subject formations. Thus, a range of such forms is
found in the Papuan language Gahuku. Unlike the Nilotic forms above, where,

in line with the overal clausal typology of these languages, the LEX-headed AVCs have the auxiliary preceding the lexical verb (these are VSO languages largely), the predominantly SOV languages of New Guinea show the phrase structure typical of their AVCs, with the auxiliary indexing a clausal subject following the inflected lexical verb. Note that illocutionary force markers (indicative, interrogative) appear on the auxiliary, so perhaps these constructions should be considered to represent the split pattern not the LEX-headed pattern (see further Chapter 5); alternatively, these may be phrase-final clitics (at least in origin this seems likely) and therefore may have originally been LEX-headed AVCs and now are split, or are 'pseudo-split' LEX-headed formations.

(60) a. Gahuku
          v-it-ani-moʔ n-e-he
          ɡo-FUT-2-TOP AUX-3-Q
          'will you be able to go'
          (Deibler 1976: 44)

      b. Gahuku   c. Gahuku
          v-am-it-o-moʔ n-e-ve   *nanamuʔ v-am-it-ani-moʔ n-e-ve*
          ɡo-NEG-FUT-1-TOP AUX-3-IND   why ɡo-NEG-FUT-2-TOP AUX-3-IND
          'I will not be able to go'   'why won't you be able to go'
          (Deibler 1976: 44)

Tobelo shows a similar pattern, but with the auxiliary indexing a clausal subject appearing initially, not finally as in Gahuku.

(61) Tobelo
      i-boto ho-ma-kete-ade-ade
      3-AUX 1IN-RFLXV-CONT-REDPL-tell.story
      'we've finished telling stories'
      (Holton 2003: 64)

Note that Tobelo shows split/doubled forms that are similar in form to these LEX-headed forms, but the object of the lower clause appears redundantly as the subject of the higher clause, and thus these may arise from raising constructions or switch subject serialization formations, unlike the LEX-headed forms, where the LEX-headed auxiliary seems to bear a dummy, expletive, or 'clausal' third person marker (i.e the element encodes an argument that is filled by the inflected lexical verb (historically speaking)). These seem to derive from a switch subject serialization formation as discussed in Chapter 7, and may also be alternatively analysed or have passed through an intermediate stage of split/doubled structure.

(62)   Tobelo
    t-a-diai i-boto-oka
    1-3-do 3-AUX-PRF
    'I have done it'
    (Holton 2003: 63)

Austronesian languages have LEX-headed AVCs as well in which the auxiliary indexes a third person singular clausal subject, not any of the arguments of the lexical verb. Examples include Manam and Eastern Mekeo.

(63)   Manam
    lása ne-mín-to ʔa-resabar-idi-a-la-na-tó-be i-éno
    enemy POSS-2PL-PAUC 2PL-provoke-3PL.OBJ-BEN-LIM-BFR-PAUC-and
       3-AUX
    'you kept provoking your enemies'
    (Lichtenberk 1983: 201)

(64)   Eastern Mekeo
    e-mia fa-ʔua-lai
    3-AUX OBLG:1-drop-away
    'I nearly fell'
    (Jones 1998: 423)

Some LEX-headed AVCs appear to be grammaticalizations of a construction known as 'ambient serialization' (Crowley 1987, 2002e). In this type of serial verb construction, there is no argument sharing (see Chapter 1 for more on SVCs and AVCs) between the components, with the element that becomes the auxiliary bearing a third person subject marker.

One common subtype of ambient serialization construction that has developed into this kind of LEX-headed AVC comes from the use of a verb meaning 'finish' as a perfective, completive, terminative, etc. marker.[2] This generally—and iconically—follows the lexical verb over which it has functional scope. In Papuan Daga the verb marks a third singular subject regardless of the subject encoded in the lexical verb.

---

   [2] One language that shows a nuclear serialization construction with this same function and origin, developing into an AVC, is the Edoid language Engenni of Nigeria. The 'finish' element appears in a nuclear or root-serialization-looking construction following the lexical verb.
(i)   Engenni
    ò kpei dhe me
    he wash finish me
    'he finished washing me'
    (Lord 1993: 227; Thomas 1978: 171)

(65) Daga

in-en uon=ta-n   *ong-en uon=ta-ia*
sleep-3SG/PST finish-3SG/PST   come: 1-1SG/PST finish-3SG/PRES
'he finished sleeping'   'I finished coming', 'I have just come'
(Murane 1974: 124–5)

While 'finish' iconically comes after elements it has functional scope over generally, there are languages in which LEX-headed AVCs which mark the perfective by using an auxiliary meaning 'finish' have the auxiliary preceding the lexical verb, as in the Australian Paman language Kugu Nganhcara.

(66) Kugu Nganhcara
ngaya kana munje-ng
I.NOM PRF bathe-1
'I've already had a bath'
(Smith and Johnson 2000: 439)

A similar but different origin may be seen for other LEX-headed structures, which arise from switch subject serialization of the type *{Subj Xed Obj>Subj be.finished}$_{[SVC]}$ {Subj (has) [finish](ed) Xing Obj}$_{[AVC]}$. For more on this see the discussion on the split/doubled inflection in 5.2 and 7.1.

3.3 Other patterns

A peculiarity of certain African languages, among them languages with LEX-headed AVCs, is the use of a 'cognate accusative' construction involving either a reduplication-like doubling of the verb stem or a verbal noun of the verb in a zero (or perhaps prosodically) marked form with both transitive and intransitive verbs. These may be grammaticalized as components of AVCs in individual instances, e.g. the Omotic language Hamer.

(67) a. Hamer   b. Hamer
          kʊm-ʌ o də kʊm-ɛ   *kisi kʊmʌ dɛ kʊm*
          eat-PRF we AUX eat-IMPRF   he eat-PRF AUX eat
          'we shall eat' 'we shall have eaten'   'he is eating'
          (Lydall 1976: 423)   (Lydall 1976: 422)

Note that in the isolate language Tol (Jicaque) of Honduras, a member of the far-flung and tenuous Hokan stock, the future auxiliary occurs with a future form of the verb (marked by a non-cognate prefix) in a kind of quasi-LEX-headed cum split/doubled form.

(68)   Tol (Jicaque) (isolate (Hokan); Honduras)
    pɨlɨ́l kaßayú ka kasá la-n-cʰiʔná-s
    blanket horse FUT over ITER-FUT-spread-3
    'he is going to spread the blanket over the horse'
    (Holt 1999a: 25)

In Baale, a Surmic language of Ethiopia, perfective forms are also in a kind of complex pseudo-split/doubled construction which really consists of an auxiliary occurring before a lexical verb that itself may bear a subject prefix and a perfective and subject suffix, all fused together.

(69)   a.   Baale   b.   Baale
        wá kɨ̄ɡ ´d-ā   *wá ūgúd-ū*
        PRF 1:drunk:PRF-1   PRF 2:drunk:PRF-2
        'I drank'   'you drank'
        (Yigezu and Dimmendaal 1998: 286)

Copula formations may also develop into LEX-headed AVCs in various languages, e.g. the Cariban language Panare.

(70)   a.   Panare
        y-u-ña-n kəh e'ñapa
        3-INTRANS-fall-T/A COP.ANIM.PROX Panare
        'The Panare man falls/is going to fall'
        (Gildea 1998: 157)

       b.   Panare
        yi-pa-npəh nəh mitʃi
        3-feed-PROG COP.ANIM.DIST cat
        'the cat is feeding them'

Covert LEX-headed constructions are found in the Mayan language Acatec of Guatemala. Here various clitics, e.g. the Wackernagel clitic=*oj*, seem to produce a range of pseudo-split constructions:

(71)   a.   Acatec (Mayan; Guatemala)
        man=oj (j)in-lo' ixim pan=an
        NEG=FUT ERG:1-eat CL/the bread-1
        'I won't eat the bread'
        (Peñalosa 1987: 300)

       b.   Acatec
        man lalan=oj ja-wey-i
        NEG PROG=SUFF ERG: 2-sleep-AUG
        'you are not sleeping'

Seri, another language of Mesoamerica, shows similar covert LEX-headed AVCs only in an auxiliary final clause structure, and involving not a Wackernagel-type second-position clitic, but rather a clause-final enclitic. This yields a 'pseudo-split' pattern, i.e. what looks like a split pattern but is really a LEX-headed one.

(72)   a.   Seri
            mé ʔé ʔim-ís-ał ka=ʔa
            you I 1OBJ-SUBJ.NMLZ-accompany AUX=DECL
            'you will accompany him'
            (Marlett 1990: 525)

       b.   Seri
            ma-ʔ-s-níp ʔa=ʔa
            2OBJ-1-IRR-hit AUX=DECL
            'I will hit you'

       c.   Seri
            i-ʔ-á:pł kiʔ ko-ʔp-s-óXi ʔa=ʔa
            3POSS-ACT:NMLZ-cold the 3OBJ-1-IRR-die AUX=DECL
            'I'm going to die from the cold weather'
            (Marlett 1990: 529)

The probabilitive construction in the Altai-Sayan Turkic language is historically a future form of the auxiliary *pol-*'be[come]'. It follows a tense- and subject-marked form of the lexical verb. Note that in the closely related Xakas language, this construction shows split inflection (see Chapter 5), with tense on the lexical verb as in Shor, but subject on the auxiliary.

(73)   Shor
       üš   *kün*   *ert-ip,*   *aylan-maan*   *pol-za-m*
       3   day   pass-CV   return-NEG.CV   aux-con-1
       men   *až-ïp* *öl-ge-m polar*
       I   'already' die-PST-1 PROB
       'if three days pass and I don't return, I am probably dead'
       (Nevskaja 1993: 35)

A similar construction is seen with pluperfect tense forms in Chulym Turkic. Here the lexical verb appears in a tense- and subject-marked form followed by the past auxiliary *boln* (here also followed by the evidential particle, itself a split- or LEX-headed AVC in origin).

(74) a. Chulym Turkic
          Men   ol   dzen-de   kel-ga:-m   boln   emže:di
          I   that time-LOC come-PST-1 AUX:PST EVID
          'I had already come apparently at that time'
          (Dul'zon 1960: 142)

      b. Chulym Turkic
          Sän   kel-ge-ŋ   boln
          You   come-PST-2 AUX:PST
          'you had come'
          (Dul'zon 1960: 142)

3.4 Dependency relations in LEX-headed AVCs

Languages which mark lexical verbs as dependent although they function as
inflectional heads within a LEX-headed AVC include the Papuan Kwerba and
Austronesian Kele. In both of these languages, the lexical verb is marked as
dependent via irrealis marking.

(75) a. Kwerba (Dani-Kwerba; Trans-New Guinea)
          co ic-abo wïre b-a-kot-ara-ri-an-am
          I wood-OBJ PROG PRS-SG-cut-MULT.ACT-AUG-DIST-IRR
          'I am cutting a piece of wood over there'
          (de Vries and de Vries 1997: 6, 9)

      b. Kwerba
          co kwa [a-] -ku-m
          I PRF SG-go-IRR
          'I shall go'

      c. Kwerba
          com tat bïre b-a-mon-am
          my father STAT PRES-SG-sit-IRR
          'my father is still alive'
          (de Vries and de Vries 1997: 9)

(76) Kele (Austronesian; Manus Province, Papua New Guinea)
      yu ka k-u-le
      I INCEP IRR-1-go
      'I am about to go'
      (Ross 2002a: 138)

Paumarí, an Arawá language, offers a further example of the subtype of
LEX-headed AVC with a dependent-marked lexical verb. Here the non-

thematic auxiliary *hiki* appears with an inflected lexical verb. Note, however, that as in various other languages discussed, Coahuilteco, Kwerba, etc., the lexical verb may also bear overt markers of dependency in this LEX-headed AVC.

(77)　a.　Paumarí
　　　　ho-ra no'a-vini hiki ihai-a
　　　　1-OBJ give-DEP.TRANS AUX:NONTHEME medicine-OBLQ
　　　　'she gives me medicine'
　　　　(Chapman and Derbyshire 1991: 332)

　　　b.　Paumarí
　　　　i-ra o-ka-mona-hi-vini hiki hida o-athi ka-papira-ni
　　　　you-OBJ 1-BEN-tell-BEN-DEP.TRANS AUX:NONTHEME DEM 1-message
　　　　　GEN-paper-F
　　　　'I will tell you my written message'
　　　　(Chapman and Derbyshire 1991: 332–3)

In a small number of instances, it is instead an *auxiliary* verb that appears in a marked dependent form. This is the case in Kombai. The negative verb in this language of Papua, Indonesia, appears with a same subject marker before lexical verbs in various negative formations.

(78)　Kombai
　　　do-mo ade-n-i
　　　NEG-SS eat-TRANSIT-IMP
　　　'don't eat'
　　　(de Vries 1993: 18)

Consider now the following data from the Papuan language Umbungu Kaugel of the East New Guinea Highlands stock.

(79)　Umbungu Kaugel
　　　akena nambe te-ko pu-nu-ye
　　　Hagen what AUX-2.DEP go-2[.PST]-Q
　　　'how did you go to Hagen?'
　　　(Head 1990: 105)

　　　kako nambe te-pa te-ri-mu-ye
　　　belt what AUX-3.DEP make-DIST.PST-3.PST-Q
　　　'how did he make his belt?'

These are especially intriguing, as well as typical of a certain kind of Papuan language (e.g. some of those belonging to the large East New Guinea Highlands family), and thus they merit some specific comment here. If one were limited to the interlinear glossing alone, the first form suggests a possible interpretation as a doubled or split/doubled construction rather than an AUX-headed construction (e.g. the second singular subject is doubly encoded), which it is. In general, I refer to such forms as exhibiting a 'pseudo-pattern', in this specific instance a pseudo-doubled or pseudo-split/doubled one. Indeed, as I have alluded to where relevant, there are forms which properly should be analysed as belonging to some other inflectional pattern, but seem to have the surface or 'first-glance' appearance of an AUX-headed construction (cf. also the so-called 'pseudo-AUX-headed' forms). Given reanalysis, these formations can become the patterns that they mimic, of course.

Let me first situate this Umbungu Kaugel construction within the broader Papuan context. Among the most salient typological features of certain so-called 'non-Austronesian' languages of New Guinea is a system of both medial verb forms—forms that occur in non-final sentence position—and forms that indicate what the subject of the next clause is, so-called 'anticipatory subject' forms. These are not to be considered examples of a switch reference system *per se*, although they are functionally similar, relating as they do to clausal participant tracking and continuity. Switch reference systems are in fact relevant to the formation of certain AVCs in particular languages (as discussed already in Chapter 2), and are highly developed in numerous Papuan languages as well (see Roberts (1997) for a overview).

In these anticipatory subject forms, the specific person/number of the subject of a clause following another may be encoded on the verb in the first clause, as well as in the second clause—hence the designation 'pseudo-doubled'. The most striking fact about this construction, and one that may have jumped out to the reader, is that it is the *auxiliary verb* that appears in a dependent form, not the lexical verb, due to the medial position of the auxiliary.

What is necessitated by the construction itself in these two instances is the presence of a dependency marker on the verb; the anticipatory subject, on the other hand, is motivated by the embedding of the AVC within a larger clause structure.

In Papuan Ono, an auxiliary appears in an unmarked form in a LEX-headed AVC, except when the clause it appears in is embedded in larger sentences and the auxiliary must, as the phrasal (structural) head of the first clause, bear some marker of same or different subject status (different subject in the example below). This would be an example of pseudo-dependent marking on an auxiliary in a LEX-headed AVC embedded in a larger complex sentence, from which the apparent instance of dependent marking derives.

(80) Ono
    ŋei weku eŋe sitog-e sari met-ki mogat-ka sari-ke
    man one he run-ss come.ss AUX-3.DS run.after-him come-3FP.FV
    'one man was running away and she ran after him'
    (Phinnemore 1988: 116)

3.5 Alternations between LEX-headed and other patterns

The negative 'particle' found in certain formations in Samoyedic Kamas is historically a third singular form of the negative verb. This is but one of several variant negative constructions attested in this language that was virtually extinct at its time of documentation.

(81) Kamas
    man ej šo-bija-m
    I NEG come-PST-1
    'I didn't come'
    (Künnap 1999b: 25)

As mentioned in Chapter 2, Uralic languages generally and Samoyedic languages in particular typically make use of an AUX-headed construction with a negative auxiliary and connegative marked lexical verb. Kamas originally apparently had a cognate formation, with an inflected negative auxiliary preceding a connegative-marked lexical verb. At the period of documentation when Kamas was a moribund language, this structure was either undergoing a shift to a LEX-headed formation or ultimately becoming a fused split construction as discussed in Chapter 5.

(82) a. Kamas
        man e-m šo-ʔ
        I NEG-1 come-CONNEG
        'I don't come'
        (Simoncsics 1998: 594)

    b. Kamas
        tan e-l-lə šü-ʔ
        you NEG-PRES-2 enter-CONNEG
        'you don't enter'

    c. Kamas
        e-m nere-ʔ
        NEG-1 be.frightened-CONNEG
        'I am not, will not be frightened'
        (Künnap 1999b: 25)

The LEX-headed pattern of inflection of auxiliary verb constructions may alternate with another pattern within a given language. Thus, for example, in the Central Sudanic language Mbay the progressive may appear in a LEX-headed or doubled construction.

(83) a. Mbay (C. Sudanic, Chad)

     ndì m̄-sá yáa̰   or *m̄-ndì m̄-sá yáa̰*

     AUX 1-eat food   1-AUX 1-eat food

     'I am/was eating'

     (Keegan 1997: 69)

    b. Mbay (C. Sudanic, Chad)

     ndì kə̀-sà-ñ yáa̰   or *kə̀-ndì kə̀-sà-ñ yáa̰*

     AUX 1PL-eat-PL food   1PL-AUX 1PL-eat-PL food

     'we are/were eating'

     (Keegan 1997: 69)

In Western Mekeo, a clausal-subject construction with 'finish' is found, while the formation in Eastern Mekeo appears with doubled inflection.

(84) Eastern Mekeo   (85) Western Mekeo

    la-iva la-fua   *a-oabi e-pua*

    1-speak 1-finish   1-speak 3-finish

    'I have finished speaking'   'I have spoken'

    (Jones 1998: 425)

In the Bantu language Tonga, the negative *ta* may appear with subject marking in an AUX-headed AVC in a relative construction, or with subject marking on the lexical verb in LEX-headed construction in finite clauses.

(86) Tonga

    ta ba-boni   *aba mbantu ba-ta boni*

    NEG 3PL-see   they people 3PL-NEG see

    'they do not see'   'they are the people who do not see'

    (Torrend 1891: 232–3)

Summary

A number of languages possess constructions that consist of an inflected lexical verb and a (mainly) uninflected functional element. When these elements are historically verbs and appear in the structural position occupied by auxiliaries, such elements are considered to be auxiliaries embedded in a LEX-headed AVC. Lexical verbs, although bearing obligatory inflectional categories for the clause (other than those embodied or encoded by the auxiliary itself), may also bear an overt marker of dependency, further underscoring their presence in a grammaticalized AVC, albeit one in which the auxiliary itself bears no inflection. The LEX-headed pattern here also (perhaps idiosyncratically) includes situations in which there is a dummy third singular 'clausal' subject marker found with the auxiliary, sometimes reflecting the construction's origin in a reanalysed biclausal verb plus complement structure or in an ambient serialization construction.

4

Doubled Inflection

Introduction

In this chapter I discuss auxiliary verb constructions showing the doubled pattern of inflection. This means that both the lexical verb and the auxiliary verb are the inflectional co-heads. True doubled constructions, where every obligatory inflectional category is encoded on both the lexical verb and the auxiliary verb, are actually not that common in languages that possess rich morphological systems. Instead, one commonly finds a so-called 'split/ doubled' pattern, where some of the inflectional categories are encoded on the lexical verb or the auxiliary verb, while others appear on both; these are discussed in 5.2. With systems that are only partially developed morphologically, a true doubled pattern is more frequently encountered. That said, there are a number of languages where doubled inflection is found in auxiliary verb constructions, and these are outlined below.

In terms of the inflectional typology in the present framework, the auxiliary verb and lexical verb serve as inflectional co-heads. These are schematized in Table 4.1.

4.1 Doubled subject (and object) inflection

4.1.1 Doubled subject inflection

In terms of categories that are doubly marked in the co-headed AVCs discussed below, by far the most common belong to the domain of referent

TABLE 4.1. Inflectional heads in AVCs (discussed so far)

	Auxiliary verb	Lexical verb
Aux-headed	+	−
Lex-headed	−	+
Co-headed	+	+

properties, in particular the person/number features of the subject. TAM categories may also be found encoded on both the lexical verb and the auxiliary verb in co-headed AVCs, but less commonly than subject features.

Although more is said about the historical development of AVCs in Chapter 7, it is worth noting in passing here that the doubled pattern is sometimes labeled a serial verb construction and, as with LEX-headed (and to a lesser extent AUX-headed) forms, co-headed AVCs frequently derive from SVCs, in particular so-called core-juncture or core-layer serial verb constructions (Foley and Olson 1985, Crowley 1987, 2002e, Sebba 1987, Lord 1993). Further, doubled constructions may sometimes be derived from so-called 'echo formations', where certain lexical elements obligatorily appear in connection with another, both with the same categorial status (noun, verb) and identical or very similar semantics, as in the following form from Gutob, a South Munda language of India. (*buron-. . .aʔso-*)

(1) Gutob
    maj-nen rone+bone ḍeŋ-gu buron-gu-nen+aʔso-gu-nen
    3-PL happy+ECHO AUX-PAST.I live-PAST.I-PL+ECHO-PAST.I-PL
    'they became happy and lived (on that way)'
    (Zide, n.d.)

Note that similar echo or lexical doublet formations are common in Old Turkic, and may have given rise to a doubled inflectional pattern in certain AVCs (see below).

Core serialization forms, as mentioned previously, are also frequently grammaticalized as AVCs (see Heine and Reh 1984). Heine (1993) dubs this the 'Serial[ization] Schema' for auxiliation. One of the most common of such formations has been called the 'deictic' serial verb construction (Schiller 1990). This involves the directional-deictic verbs 'go' and 'come' in tandem with another verb, both bearing relevant inflections (e.g. subject, tense). Formations of this type are found in such languages as the West Papuan Tobelo and Oceanic Numbami.

(2) Tobelo
    tanu h-oíki   ho-ma-ohiki
    should 1IN-go 1IN-RFLXV-bathe
    'we should go bathe'
    (Holton 2003: 26)

(3) Numbami
    muna-wasa   muna-yonggo
    2PL:IRR-go   2PL:IRR-see
    'go have a look'
    (Bradshaw 1993: 148)

Note that such constructions can occur in nuclear-juncture serialization formations as well, e.g. in South Munda Gtaʔ.

(4)   Gta?
       n-weʔ-gag-ce
       1-swing-tie-ss
       'after I swung and tied...'
       (Mahapatra and Zide, n.d.)

(5)   a.   Gta?   b.   Gta?
             e-tur-n-ke-e   *næŋ ḍugḍi e-ko-n-lœʔ-e*
             go-look.for 1-see-FUT   I garden go-sit-1-stay-FUT
             'I will go look for and find (her)'   'I will go sit and rest in the garden'
             (Mahapatra and Zide, n.d.)

An extreme example of core serialization with a deictic verb may be found in
the Oceanic language Maleu, where even five inflected verbs, including the
deictic verb *-la* 'go', which appears twice, are attested:

(6)   Maleu
       em-molmol em-pot em-la em-molmol em-la
       1PL.EX-walk 1PL.EX-down 1PL.EX-go 1PL.EX-walk 1PL.EX-go
       'we walk down'
       (Haywood 1996: 162)

Core serialization forms with subject doubly marked may in individual
languages alternate with forms that bear only a single marker of subject on
the leftmost verb in a nuclear serialization construction, e.g. Larike.

(7)   Larike
                   au-'eu au-'anu   ~   *au-'eu anu*
                   1-go 1-eat   1-go eat
                   'I'm going to eat'
                   (Laidig and Laidig 1991:28)

Note the similarity of this construction with the AUX-headed pattern alternating with co-headed forms in individual AVCs, such as the Diola Fogny
forms mentioned in Chapter 2 above, repeated here.

(8)   Diola Fogny (Atlantic; Senegal, Gambia)   b.   Diola Fogny
             i-lakɔ   *fu-ri*   or   *i-lakɔ   i-ri*
             1-AUX   INF-eat   1-AUX   1-eat
             'I was eating'   'I was eating'
             (Heine 1993: 46)

I stress this connection between the doubled inflectional pattern of AVCs and the core serialization pattern because, as I have argued throughout this volume, AVCs occupy formal and functional continua, similarly occupied by certain kinds of serial verb constructions, and that there is significant functional and formal overlap between these two. Within individual languages, however, there may be formal properties that distinguish points on this continuum, such as phrasal prosody and morphosyntactic features, and AVCs and SVCs (or other complex predicate types) may be formally different from one another within a given grammatical system.

For example, in the Oceanic language Taba, SVCs are intonationally distinct from biclausal verb sequences. Taba, like many languages, utilizes the deictic/motion serial construction.

(9)   Taba
     t-han t-ronda po-pe Ploili
     1PL.INCL-go 1PL.INCL-stroll down-ESS Peleri
     'we went strolling in Peleri'
     (Bowden 2001: 304)

However, the functional domain of verbal structures with this prosodic characteristic in Taba include some functions canonically associated with AVCs cross-linguistically. Thus, Bowden (2001: 316ff.) talks of modal (and aspectual) serialization seen in such constructions as the following:

(10) a. Taba   b. Taba
        k-pe k-ahate   *n-pe n-ahan*
        1-make 1-AUX   3-make 3-AUX
        'I can't make them'   'he can do it'
        (Bowden 2001: 316)

      c. Taba   d. Taba
        m-yoa m-han   *n-curat n-ulang*
        2-AUX 2-go   3-write 3-AUX
        'you've almost gone'   'she wrote it again'
        (Bowden 2001: 318)   (Bowden 2001: 295)

I have glossed these elements AUX as they have undergone relatively pronounced semantic bleaching and function to mark modal and aspectual categories typical of AVCs. The fact that they are intonationally similar to SVCs present in the language simply reflects their origin in a (core) serialized structure, indicated both by the prosodic unity of the elements and by the doubled inflectional pattern. Note that these emergent AUX formations may have the auxiliary grammaticalized in a position either preceding the lexical verb or after this element. This latter fact further suggests considering these to be AVCs not SVCs (insofar as such a distinction is really meaningful in a cross-linguistic or theoretical light—a fact that has yet to be demonstrated adequately).[1]

A similar example is found in the Central Sudanic language Ngiti. The formation consists of a doubled subject construction that marks a kind of Aktionsart or aspect indicating action on the verge of happening.[2] This is glossed here as an AVC but is called a SVC by Kutsch Lojenga (1994). This underscores the nebulous nature of what qualifies as one or the other of these constructions, which in any event are often historically related, via a unidirectional *functional* path of SVC > AVC. Given the continuum of verb constructions that constitutes the focus of this study, this indeterminate nature of certain formations should come as no surprise.

(11)   Ngiti[3]

  nyɨ ny-àtsū ny-ikpe

  you 2SUBJ.CONC-AUX:PRF:PRS 2-cough:PRF:PRS

  'you were on the point of coughing'

  (Kutsch Lojenga 1994: 191)

The Torricelli Phylum language Bukiyip offers another example of the connection between core serialized constructions and AVCs of the doubled inflectional pattern. As in Taba, SVCs are prosodically distinct from verb–complement sequences in Bukiyip. Some of these, however, are being grammaticalized as AVCs and others have already been so grammaticalized. Thus, from an original deictic SVC in Bukiyip a kind of future construction is developing.

---

[1] While it ultimately may be possible to differentiate AVCs and/or SVCs from verb–verb (or verb–complement) sequences cross-linguistically, and certainly is on a language-specific basis, it is my belief that it is fairly unlikely that AVCs and SVCs could ever be formally (or maybe even functionally) differentiable from each other. Functionally, SVCs show more transparent semantics of the sequenced verbs; but as they gradually slide into functional specialization in various contexts or combinations, they veer off into the domain of AVCs.

[2] Kutsch Lojenga analyses the element on the lexical verb as a 'subject pronominal' but the identical element on the auxiliary verb as a 'subject concord' marker, despite the presence of an overt subject pronoun (to which these bound elements are obviously related). This has to do with various theoretical assumptions made by her that have no bearing on the present discussion.

[3] Note that the *u* marks a low-mid contour tone in this Ngiti example.

(12) Bukiyip (Torricelli; Papua New Guinea)
biyebih m-u-nak m-u-lu lowas
day.after.tomorrow 1PL-IRR-go 1PL-IRR-cut trees
'the day after tomorrow we will (go) cut trees'
(Conrad and Wogiga 1991: 3)

As in the English *I am going to work,* there is some ambiguity between the deictic serialized construction and the emergent grammaticalized AVC. However, from an inflectional typology standpoint, it is clear that this belongs to the core serialization > doubled inflection pattern of the SVC-to-AVC continuum. Slightly more grammaticalized in terms of functional semantics is the following Bukiyip AVC that likewise clearly derives from the core serialization SVC.

(13) Bukiyip (Torricelli; Papua New Guinea)
y-e-ne y-a-pwe
1-RLS-do 1-RLS-be
'I remained resting'
(Conrad and Wogiga 1991: 55)

Indeed, ambiguity is found in a number of languages. Given that doubly marked AVCs may develop out of core serialized SVCs, perhaps it should be expected that a given formation may have serialized or auxiliary interpretations—basically, a more literal/sequential connection between the two verbs or one in which one of the two verbs has taken on a greater degree of functional semantics and lost some of its content semantics. Consider in this regard the following forms from the Australian language Djapu Yolngu. This Paman language possesses both SVCs and AVCs where inflectional categories are marked on both, here showing either the so-called 'unmarked' tense forms or a 'potential' mood. Note that Pama-Nyungan languages frequently possess several conjugations where the tense/aspect markers are formally different but encode the same inflectional category. Like many languages, the verb meaning 'sit' may appear in serialized formations and in auxiliary functions. In some instances both interpretations are possible, i.e. 'sit' may either be interpreted in a serialized understanding, e.g 'sit and X' or 'X and sit', or it may have a durative or continuative aspectual function. Note the following example in this light.

(14) Djapu Yolngu
mukthu-rr nhini
be.quite-POT sit/AUX.POT
'keep quiet' or 'sit quietly'
(Morphy 1983: 90)

Either interpretation is possible and, out of context, it is impossible to predict which is likely to be preferred; in any event, the connection between the two is so close in this particular instance that the distinction might not really matter in normal discourse. The following is another example of this ambiguity in Djapu Yolngu. As in the previous example, it can mean either of the possible interpretations.

(15)   Djapu Yolngu
        naŋʔ-naŋdhu-n nhina bala dhukarr-kurr
        /Redpl/-run-UNM sit.UNM TLOC road-PERL
        '(it) ran and sat over there in the road (and then ran on again in fits and starts)'

or

        '(it) kept running away along the road'
        (Morphy 1983: 91)

In this case the second interpretation is the semantically more normal interpretation, but *not* the one that was apparently the intended one when this sentence was uttered.

Similar to the significant grey area between SVCs and AVCs, there is likewise a cline of verbs in verb–verb combinations ranging from complement-taking verbs to auxiliary verbs (and thus from non-AVCs to AVCs) in various languages, for example, in Fehan Tetun of East Timor. This in part has to do with ability to take or not take subject marking, among other features. Thus, the Fehan Tetun form *ho'i* 'currently' always takes subject marking, the forms *lalika* and *musti* (< Malay) never do, while many other potential auxiliary elements do under optional or as yet unclear conditions. Some of these forms thus appear in co-headed AVCs.

(16)   Fehan Tetun (Austronesian)
        lale ha'u k-o'i k-ola ó
        else I 1-NEG.DES 1-take you
        'otherwise I refuse to take you back'
        (van Klinken 1999: 215)

For more on the cline of auxiliary-like elements in Fehan Tetun, see van Klinken (1999: 217).

4.1.2 *Doubled subject and object inflection*

As mentioned at the beginning of this chapter, person/number features of discourse referents or verbal arguments are by far the most frequently attested category marked in a doubled inflectional pattern in AVCs among the languages of the sample. Most commonly this pattern reflects 'just' the subject alone. Other options include both subject and object (very rarely object alone, as this is a relatively marked pattern cross-linguistically, although not unattested as once believed), or other arguments or referents. A range of minor sub-patterns occurs within this overall pattern, as outlined below.

While for the most part I have limited myself to a discussion of languages exhibiting some amount of bound inflectional morphology, leaving a systematic analysis of potentially similar formations in (predominantly) isolating languages to a subsequent study, it is worth noting that doubled inflection does in fact occur with AVCs in languages favouring an isolating structure. It is important to remember that grammaticalization paths as understood encompass at least two separate but often interconnected clines or continua, one roughly speaking functional, the other prosodic. These operate together but independently. Thus, a construction may be more grammaticalized functionally than prosodically; this is reflected in unbound morphology. In fact, this actually becomes clearer and more easily demonstrated when examining languages of the 'isolating' type.

Doubled constructions with unbound subject agreement may be found, of course, not only in grammaticalized AVCs but also in SVCs and in complement-taking verbs (below, but not obligatorily with Ø complementizers), i.e. the structures that typically give rise to AVCs of the doubled inflectional pattern.

Sticking for the time being with Oceanic languages, examine the following forms from Nalik of New Ireland and Namakir of Vanuatu. In the former, a complement-taking verb (*zaxot* 'want') appears with a marker for its subject and with a subject-marked clause and no raising or co-referential subject deletion.

(17)   Nalik (Austronesian; New Ireland, Papua New Guinea)
    ga zaxot ga na bag-bak
    I want I FUT share/shave
    'I want to share/shave'
    (Volker 1998: 53)

In Namakir, a core-serialized construction is found, with the doubled subject marker appearing in an unbound form. Both a complement-taking verb and a serialized construction, with all relevant verbs taking appropriate (unbound) subject inflection, may be found in the same sentence in Namakir, yielding structures with three markers of subject in a single sentence.

(18) a. Namakir
          na-polis ri devan ri daliw
          ART-police 3PL be.in.line 3PL walk
          'the police marched in line'
          (Sperlich 1993: 100)

      b. Namakir
          ni marisa ni devan ni daliw
          1 cannot 1 be.in.line 1 walk
          'I cannot walk in line'
          (Sperlich 1993: 102)

Constructions of this type with bound agreement markers are found in various other Oceanic languages as well, e.g. Sougb of the Papua district of Indonesia. Thus, both verb–complement and serialized forms are found in Sougb, both with subject marking on all relevant verbs. Note also the deictic nuclear serialization/compound form seen in the second Sougb example.

(19) a. Sougb (Austronesian; Papua, Indonesia)
          dan d-ouwan d-ec d-eiya cinogo
          I 1-want 1-walk 1-see land
          'I want to walk around to see the place'
          (Reesink 2002: 250)

      b. Sougb
          dan d-ec d-ed-eiya camat
          I 1-walk 1-go-see administrator
          'I am going to visit the administrator'

To be sure, these 'pseudo-auxiliary' constructions, i.e. forms somewhere on the SVC or verb/complement-to-AVC continuum, are found in languages across the world, not just Oceanic or Austronesian languages. Thus, for example, one finds constructions of this type with bound subject morphology in the Mataco-Guaykuruan language Toba.

(20) Toba
      sa-wotayke s-taqayapegeʔ namqom
      1-DES 1-talk.with Toba
      'I want to speak with a Toba'
      (Manelis Klein 2001: 42)

Given the formal/functional continuum that these 'doubly' inflected forms occupy, with large 'fuzzy' areas along it between one construction and another, in some cases it is unclear whether one is dealing with a verb–complement structure or an AVC. Such is the case, for example, in the following form from Palaung, an Austroasiatic language of Myanmar and southern China.

(21) Palaung (Austroasiatic, Palaung-Wa; Myanmar, South China)
yɛ:	ka	bɛ:	yɛ:	rɛ̌
we	NEG	AUX	1PL	wait

'we could not wait'
(Milne 1921: 19)

Other languages have a formally similar structure, but within a grammaticalized AVC. Constructions like these show a greater degree of functional grammaticalization than prosodic integration. Auxiliary verb constructions of this type, i.e. with a grammaticalized auxiliary verb but unbound inflectional morphology, are typical of certain West African languages. Take, for example, the Gur (Niger-Congo) languages Kirma and Tyurama. Progressive AVCs are marked in both languages with doubly inflected AVC but without bound subject morphology. Note that in Kirma, the progressive has two variants, though both appear with subject inflection before the auxiliary and before the lexical verb.

(22) a. Kirma (Gur)   b.   Kirma

mi ta mi wo	mi di ta mi wo
1 AUX 1 eat	1 AUX 1 eat
'I am eating'	'I am eating'

(Heine and Reh 1984: 117; Prost 1964: 56–9)

(23) Tyurama (Gur)

me na me wu
I AUX I eat

'I am eating'
(Heine and Reh 1984: 117; Prost 1964: 103, 105)

Of course, it is not a priori clear what actually constitutes a bound element in a given language in every instance. There are instances when, perhaps because of the tradition of analysis or some other metatheoretical concern, a researcher analyses something as unbound, when another researcher might well consider the element as not entirely free-standing or independent prosodically. A relatively clear example of this comes from Nawuri, a Guang Kwa language of Ghana. This language uses a range of AVCs of varying inflectional patterns. I first give an example of a seemingly unbound AUX-headed AVC in

Nawuri. The subject and auxiliary vary along an ATR harmonic pattern triggered by the vowel feature of the lexical verb.

(24) a. Nawuri   b. Nawuri
          o tee dʒi   *ɔ tɛɛ ba*
          s/he ASP eat   s/he ASP come
          's/he already ate'   's/he already came'
          (Casali 1995: 77)

In this case, the auxiliary as well as the subject marker might have been analysed differently by another researcher as bound elements or at least clitic, rather than free-standing prosodically independent words. In any event, Nawuri also shows doubled inflection, regardless of whether one wants to consider these subject markers as bound or free-standing.

(25) a. Nawuri   b. Nawuri
          ɔ maŋ bɪla ɛ taalɪ ɛ waa gusuŋ   *ɛ daŋ ɛ sawʊ*
          3 NEG again 3^INC CAP 3^INC do work   3^INC PROG 3^INC cry
          'he is no longer able to work'   'he is crying'
          (Casali 1995: 77)   (Casali 1995: 78)

Although there is prosodic (and indeed phonological) unity among these elements, Casali (1995) rejects these formations as possibly being one word in Nawuri in large part because, as he believes, a language may not have two subject markers in one word. As is amply demonstrated in Chapter 6 (and indeed in a range of other works: Anderson (1993, 1999, 2000)), this is certainly not the case cross-linguistically and therefore is not a strong argument against this alternative analysis.

Other African languages show similar formations with ambiguously bound elements but embedded within a different formal system from that of Nawuri. Such is the case in the Cameroonian Bantu languages Duala (26) and Babungo (27).

(26) a. Duala
          a mabé á nyɔ́ mao búnya tɛ́
          he AUX:PRES he drink palmwine every day
          'he drinks palmwine every day'
          (Heine and Reh 1984: 118; Ittmann 1939: 96)

      b. Duala   c. Duala
          ná ta nǎ pɔ   *o tá ǒ pɔ*

I AUX:PST I come   you AUX:PST you come
'I came'   'you came'
(Heine and Reh 1984: 118; Ittmann 1939: 97)

(27) Babungo (Grassfields Bantu; Cameroon)
      ŋwə́ dù tə́ ŋwə́ kû
      he AUX he die:PF
      'he has already died'
      (Schaub 1985: 219)

The Babungo form appears to be a straightforward case of a semi-isolating doubled agreement pattern, here in a co-headed AVC with an 'adverbial' aspectual auxiliary meaning 'already'. On the other hand, it is possible that the tonal characteristics of the second subject marker in Duala indicate that these are dependent forms; such a formation is found in numerous other Bantu languages (see below). Thus, this Duala formation would properly belong to the sub-pattern of doubly inflected AVCs where the lexical verb appears in a dependent form, which reflects (as was argued in the preceding chapter regarding the LEX-headed construction—where perhaps this pattern is even more surprising) the syntactic, phrasal, or structural headedness of the auxiliary in these AVCs, despite the fact that *inflectionally* the auxiliary verb and the lexical verb are co-heads. This formal mismatch between various morphosyntactic features further underscores the non-identity between structural/phrasal heads and inflectional heads in AVCs. Doubly inflected AVCs with the lexical verb (or the auxiliary verb) in a dependent form are further discussed in 4.4.

In the Panoan language Capanawa of Peru, yet another type of quasi-isolating (or semi-isolating) system of doubled subject inflection is encountered. Here, subject proclitics or prefixes attach to a subject case inflection and precede an auxiliary that has been grammaticalized as a declarative marker as well as the tense-marked lexical verb. This is thus a combination of an isolating doubled subject pattern with a LEX-headed formation with respect to tense.

(28) a. Capanawa (Panoan; Peru)   b. Capanawa
          ʔɨ-n taʔ ʔɨ-n ka-ʔi   ʔɨ-n taʔ ʔɨ-n pi-ʔi
          1-SUBJ DECL 1-SUBJ go-PRES   1-SUBJ DECL 1-SUBJ eat-PRES
          'I am going'   'I am eating [it]'
          (Loos 1999: 242)

As mentioned at the beginning of this chapter, doubled subject-marking in AVCs is found in a range of unrelated languages from across the world. A fairly straightforward example of this comes from the isolate language Ainu, in particular the dialect formally spoken on Sakhalin Island in Russia.[4]

(29)   Ainu, Sakhalin dialect (isolate; Russia/Japan; possibly extinct)
      ku-maa ku-'e'askay
      1-swim 1-CAP
      'I can swim'
      (Hattori 1967: 77)

Although a true doubled formation is relatively marked in the Bantu language Kinyarwanda, it is possible that a few such AVCs of this pattern are found in this language. Note that, as in the Duala form above, the subject marker on the lexical verb in this Kinyarwanda construction may indicate prosodically that this element is a dependent form, not a free-standing one.

(30)   a.   Kinyarwanda   b.   Kinyarwanda
        ba-hor-a bâ-som-a   *ba-raar-a bâ-som-a*
        3PL-AUX-ASP 3PL-read-ASP   3PL-AUX-ASP 3PL-read-ASP
        'they might be reading'   'they are always reading'
        (Kimenyi 1980: 9)

Note, as a further complicating issue, that this AVC might actually be a pseudo-doubled form that in actuality reflects a split/doubled pattern that is common in Bantu languages (more on this below).

---

[4] Note that in Sakhalin Ainu there was variability in the inflectional pattern of AVCs that corresponded to different registers, with the doubled pattern found in the prestige register. This 'prestige' factor may have to do with the construction being older. Of course, the reverse could also be true, with the Sakhalin Ainu forms representing an innovation from the original LEX-headed pattern form, which was preserved in the most informal style in Sakhalin Ainu and was typically found as such in other Ainu dialects. Were this the case, the doubled pattern originated from the LEX-headed pattern (via redundant use of subject-marking on the auxiliary), with an AUX-headed pattern constituting a further secondary (or really tertiary) development from the doubled pattern within the history of Sakhalin Ainu. This variation may be seen in the following forms:

(i)   Ainu[†], Sakhalin dialect (isolate; Russia, Japan)

    ku-maa ku-'e'aykah   *maa ku-'e'aykah*   *ku-maa 'e'aykah*
    1-swim 1-cannot   swim 1-cannot   1-swim cannot
    'I can't swim'   'I can't swim' ('Informal')   'I can't swim' ('quite informal')
    (Hattori 1967: 77)   (Hattori 1967: 78)   (Hattori 1967: 78)
    maa 'an 'an-e'aykah   *maa 'an-e'aykah*   *maa-'an 'e'aykah*
    swim-1(PL) 1(PL)-cannot   swim 1(PL)-cannot   'we/I can't swim'
    (Hattori 1967: 77)   (Hattori 1967: 78)   (Hattori 1967: 78)

A variety of other African languages show AVCs of the doubled inflectional pattern, including the future formation in the Atlantic language Dyola, as well as certain AVCs in Harar Oromo.

(31)   Dyola (West Atlantic)
       u-ja u-waloa di e-kolo-ŋ
       1PL-AUX 1PL-enter LOC PREP-well-the
       'we will enter the well'
       (Marchese 1986: 111; Givón 1973)

(32)   Harar Oromo (Cushitic, Afroasiatic; Ethiopia)
       d'agay-aní jir-an
       hear-PL AUX-PL
       'they *have* heard'
       (Owens 1985: 74)

Indeed, such a pattern with doubled subject-marking in an AVC is found in a number of languages from across the world, e.g. the Austronesian languages Kaliai-Kove or Motu.

(33)   a.   Kaliai-Kove (Austronesian)
            ti-la ti-taro puo ɣaia aia
            3PL-AUX 3PL-throw net pig for
            'they throw pig-hunting nets'
            (Coates 1969: 89)

       b.   Kaliai-Kove
            ŋa-reɣa tařua ta-la ta-moro ɣane
            1-want we.two 1PL-AUX 1PL-remain here
            'I want us to stay here'
            (Coates 1969: 84–5)

(34)   Motu (Austronesian; Papua New Guinea)
       lau na-abia na-to
       I 1-take 1-AUX
       'I was about to take
       (Lawes [1896]: 14)

Such constructions are also attested in various North American languages such as the Siouan Biloxi and Yuman language Jamul Tiipay, the Tupi-Guaraní language Urubu-Kaapor of Brazil, or the nearly extinct Uto-Aztecan language Pipil of El Salvador.

(35) Biloxi   (36) Jamul Tiipay
      n-de ni n-kande   *nyaach a'-shay '-aa*
      1-go NEG 1-AUX   I:SUBJ 1-be.fat 1-AUX
      'I am not going'   'I'm getting fat'
      (Einaudi 1976: 153)   (Miller 2001: 271)

(37) Urubu-Kaapor (Tupi-Guaraní, Brazil)
      taramõ: te u-hyk u-wyr
      recent.time INTNSF 3-arrive 3-AUX
      'he just arrived'
      (Kakamasu 1986: 396)

(38) Pipil
      ti-yu-t ti-yawi-t ti-pa:xa:lua-t ne:pa ka ku:htan
      1PL-AUX-PL 1PL-go-PL 1PL-walk-PL there in woods
      'we are going to go take a walk there in the woods'
      (Campbell 1985: 138)

Note that in Jamul Tiipay, Miller (2001) distinguishes between auxiliary verbs
and auxiliary clauses. It is auxiliary clauses that show the doubled subject
inflectional pattern. In the extinct Kamas language of Siberia, negative third
singular imperatives occur in which the third singular imperative suffix
appears doubly marked on both the lexical verb and the auxiliary, which in
this particular instance encodes negative polarity.

(39) Kamas[†]
      i-gə xaŋ-ga
      NEG.IMP-3.IMP go-3.IMP
      'let him not go'
      (Künnap 1999b: 25)

Finally, a doubly marked subject construction is also found in the 'tribal'
Dravidian language Parji. Here the lexical verb appears in a (quasi-)participial
form with a subject suffix followed by an inflected auxiliary.

(40) Parji
      nil-t-en mē-d-an
      stand-PAST-1 AUX-NPAST-1
      'I am standing, have stood up'
      (Steever 1988: 89)

As these examples demonstrate, doubly inflected AVC forms can have the
auxiliary verb either preceding or following the lexical verb, depending on the

clausal syntax of the relevant language. Furthermore, the Pipil form cited above has both a doubly inflected AVC and a core serialized formation using a deictic/motion verb. In both cases, full doubled inflection is found, here consisting of a circumfix marking first plural subject (prefix) and general plural subject (suffix).

This type of doubled subject-marking in an AVC can also be embedded within a formal system where the auxiliary consists of a portmanteau subject-cum-auxiliary form. This combines with a lexical verb bearing a marker of subject and thereby constitutes a type of doubled inflectional pattern. Such a formation is found for example in the Tupi-Guaraní language Gavião and perhaps the Central Sudanic (Mangbetu) language Meje of the Democratic Republic of Congo and Uganda.

(41) a. Gavião (Tupi-Guarani)
        dʒaá paa-gà-á
        1PL.INCL-AUX 1PL.INCL-go-BNDRY.MRKR
        'let's go'
        (Rodrigues 1999a: 118)

     b. Gavião
        a-tsap kotʃ dzãno mága aa-kaà
        3SGCOREF-house to 1SG.brother 3SG.AUX 3SG-go
        'my brother goes to his own house'
        (Rodrigues 1999a: 118)

(42) Meje
     má ʋhó ú méku-a
     1:AUX already there 1:come-NPST
     'I'm already (in the process of) coming'
     (McKee 1991: 167)

Of course, as the lexical verb bears a tense marker and the auxiliary does not (apparently—or perhaps it does covertly, but is realized as Ø due to (morpho)phonological conditioning), this Meje formation may be more properly analysed as a split/doubled pattern of AVC akin to the doubled pattern seen in Gavião with a fused subject + auxiliary.

While doubled subject-marking appears to be relatively frequent in AVCs among the languages of the world, doubled object formations are less common. Such formations are attested, however, in the South Munda language Gorum, which also has doubled subject inflection attested in AVCs. Note that in addition to subcategorized patients and recipients (showing a so-called 'primary' object pattern: Dryer (1986)), use of the doubled 'object' formation can also mark a possessor of a logical argument in Gorum as well, even if the verb is semantically intransitive.

(43) a. Gorum
          e-niŋ bam-(m)-iʔŋ duk-iʔŋ
          1 OBJ-1 hit-1OBJ AUX-1OBJ
          'it (an arrow) has hit me'
          (Aze 1973: 298)

      b. Gorum
          putiputi-nom ir-om luʔr-om
          heart-2 beat-2 AUX-2
          'your heart is beating'
          (Aze 1973: 284)

Doubled object formations can also be found in languages lacking bound inflectional morphology, for example in Palaung, a language distantly related to Gorum within the Austroasiatic stock.

(44) Palaung (Austroasiatic, Palaung-Wa; Myanmar, south China)
      bi: ra:t   e:h   yɛ: kɪ:n   yɛ:
      man   steal   curse   we   curse   we
      'the thieves cursed us'
      (Milne 1921: 21)

In the form cited above (44), the verb does not actually occur within an AVC but rather in a lexical doublet or serialized 'echo' formation, with each of the verbal components taking an object pronominal.

In a small number of languages, e.g. Maasai, portmanteau subject + object forms may appear on both auxiliary verbs and lexical verbs, for example, in the passive-like unspecified agent construction. Note that, as with the Kinyarwanda form, it is possible that the tonal/prosodic/phonological qualities of the subject + object marker on the lexical verb reflects a dependent form in Maasai.

(45) Maasai (East Sudanic, Nilo-Saharan; Kenya/Tanzania)
      áá-púó-í áà-ìdòŋ
      3-1-come-VERB 3-1-beat
      'I shall be beaten'
      (Dimmendaal 1983: 137; Tucker and Mpaayei 1955: 188)

Another relatively minor pattern found in a small number of languages shows a structure in which a subject of an auxiliary is co-referential with an object form of a lexical verb, and is marked on each component accordingly. In other instances, the second marker is not an object but rather a suffixal marker of subject. Schematically structures of this type take the following shape:

(46) Subj-AV LV-Obj(=/Subj)

This kind of disjoint doubled inflection, or non-structurally similar means of encoding subject on the auxiliary and the lexical verb in a doubly inflected AVC, is found in a number of Eastern Jebel languages from the Eastern Sudanic branch of the Nilo-Saharan phylum. An instance of this pattern is seen in Gaam. Here the subject is marked by a prefix on the auxiliary but internally on the lexical verb.

(47) a. Gaam (Eastern Jebel; Sudan, Ethiopia) b. Gaam
   āā-lā māɫ ʄɛg   *ūū-lū mūɫ ʄɛg*
   1-FUT drink:1 water   2-FUT drink:2 water
   'I will drink water'   'you will drink water'
   (Bender 1989: 164)

In its sister language Aka, auxiliaries again appear with a subject prefix, while the lexical verb appears in a dependent form with varied formal means of encoding the subject, through a combination of ablaut-like alternations and suffixation.

(48) a. Aka (Eastern Jebel, Eastern Sudanic; Sudan) b. Aka
   e-wál bɔ́gei   *ɪn-wɔ́l bìgáa sai*
   1-AUX go:DEP:1   2-AUX go:DEP:2
   I am going'   'you are going'
   (Bender 1989: 165)

A similar pattern is found in Kelo, only here the auxiliary is a fused subject/auxiliary formation historically. (See Chapter 6)

(49) a. Kelo (East Jebel, East Sudanic; Sudan) b. Kelo
   ɔ́ŋ béɔ̀   *ín bɔ́ì*
   I:NPRS go:FUT(:1)   you:NPRS go:FUT:2
   'I will go'   'you will go'
   (Bender 1989: 166)

A fourth formal option for Eastern Jebel languages is seen in Molo of Sudan. Here the subject 'pronoun' is not a fused auxiliary, but the lexical verb consists of a subject/auxiliary fused with a lexical verb itself fused with a subject marker (so-called 'fused/fused' forms: see Chapter 6). Note that the person/number of the former auxiliary/subject marker (now tense/subject marker) may be indicated in Molo through tonal alternation.

(50) a. Molo   b. Molo
          ɔŋ tìi:-bé   *ìn tɔ́-bɔ́i*
          I PRS:1:go:1   you PRS:2:go:2/3
          'I go'   'you go'
          (Bender 1989: 166)

      c. Molo   d. Molo
          ɔy tɔ̀-sá   *uu tɔ̀-só*
          we PRS:PL-go:1PL   you(PL) PRS:PL-go:2PL
          'we go'   'you (PL) go'

Note that this Eastern Jebel pattern contrasts with the Nilotic pattern in which the lexical verb appears in a dependent subject marked form in a subject (prefix) slot in the verb, for example in Teso.

(51) Teso
      a-bu ke-ner
      1-AUX.PST 1SBJ-say
      'I said'
      (Heine and Reh 1984: 104; Hilders and Lawrance 1956: 14)

Note that this 'disjoint' doubled inflectional pattern is not limited to members of the Eastern Jebel subgroup of the Nilo-Saharan language family, where diffusion may account for its presence in several languages in different formal guises. A pattern of the type currently under consideration is also found in the Austronesian language Tawala. According to Ezard (1997), multiple marking of persons is the main cohesive element of Tawala discourse.

TABLE 4.2. Doubled subject and/or object patterns in AVCs

Doubled subject and/or object pattern		Language(s)
S-LEX	AUX-S	Tawala, Aka, Gaam
LEX-S	AUX-S	Parji, Kamas, Harar Oromo
S-AUX	S-LEX	Pipil, Dyola, Songye
S-LEX	S-AUX	Urubu-Kaapor, Biloxi, Motu, Jamul Tipay, Kaliai-Kove, Sakhalin Ainu
S-AUX	S.DEP-LEX	Teso
S:AUX	S-LEX	Meje, Gaviaõ
AUX:S	LEX:S	Molo, Kelo
LEX-Obj	AUX-Obj	Gorum
S-Obj-AUX	S-Obj-LEX	Maasai

(52) Tawala
      ta-hilage pahi-ta
      1PL.INC-die completely-1PL.INC
      '... we might be destroyed'
      (Ezard 1997: 23)

In addition to referent properties being doubly marked in a co-headed AVC pattern, a range of other categories may be encoded on both the lexical verb component and the auxiliary verb component. Most commonly the categories indexed belong to the general domain of tense, aspect, and mood. Further, there is a range of languages that have TAM and referent properties doubly encoded in an AVC, or indeed forms with two uses of a portmanteau subject/TAM affix, one each on a lexical verb and on an auxiliary verb. Each of these sub-patterns of doubled inflection in AVCs is briefly exemplified below.

4.2 Doubled TAM inflection

The formal means of encoding the tense, aspect, and mood categories that appear in doubly inflected AVCs varies considerably depending on the language in question. Of course, as is the case for all morphological processes, suffixation is the most common formal process for encoding these TAM categories in co-headed auxiliary verb constructions. A relatively simple and straightforward example of this may be found in the Tibeto-Burman language Tamang. Here the future suffix appears on both the lexical verb and the auxiliary verb.

(53) Tamang
      ¹ni-la ¹ta-la
      go-FUT AUX-FUT
      'he might go'
      (Mazaudon 2003: 303)

Older Turkic sources also show doubled TAM inflection in various AVCs. Auxiliary verb constructions with TAM categories marked on the lexical verb and the auxiliary verb can be found in some of the earliest attested Turkic sources in the indigenous Runic script (in a range of local varieties). This includes possibly the most famous of all early Turkic inscriptional sources, the Kül Tegin stele found in the Orkhon river valley of northern Mongolia, as well as relatively poorly known lesser inscriptions in the so-called 'Yenisei' variant of the Runic Turkic script found in southern Siberia.

(54)   Orkhon Turkic (Kuxl Tegin)
        Türgiš bodun-uγ ölür-miš al-miš
        Türgiš people-ACC kill-PST.II SUBJ.VERS-PST.II
        'killed the Türgiš people (to our benefit)'
        (von Gabain 1974: 278)

(55)   Yenisei Runic Turkic
        yügür-ti bar-di
        run-REC.PST TLOC-REC.PST
        '(he) ran away'
        [M I7, 17: Yen]
        (Clauson 1972: 354)

In the Central Sudanic language Ma'di, NON-PAST appears doubly marked in certain AVCs. Rather than a tense suffix as is found in the Tamang form above, a preposed low tone serves as the formal index of this temporal category appearing before both the auxiliary verb and the lexical verb.

(56)   Ma'di (Central Sudanic; Nilo-Saharan; Uganda, Sudan)
        má `kɔ `mū
        I NPST:AUX NPST:go
        'I'm about to go'
        (Blackings and Fabb 2003: 165)

According to Blackings and Fabb (2003: 215), this system of doubled NON-PAST marking via tone is not found in the 'Burulo dialect of Ma'di. Such variation in inflectional pattern in AVCs is relatively common in closely related languages from across the world.

While doubled TAM marking (i.e. without doubled subject marking as well) is relatively marked as a pattern cross-linguistically, it does occur with some frequency in Australian languages. Note that this pattern is found primarily in Pama-Nyungan languages like Gumbaynggir, Nyawaygi, Djapu Yolngu, or Wargamay. Non-Pama-Nyungan languages tend to be more inflectionally rich, encoding argument properties in the verbal form as well, and thus languages of this type with doubly inflected AVCs tend to belong to the fully inflected (referent properties plus TAM) subtype, discussed below.

In Gumbaynggir, a range of such doubly marked TAM formations can be found in various AVCs. For example, future, present, or past may be doubly marked. Note that, as is common in Pama-Nyungan languages, the formal means of encoding this tense category show several conjugational/allomorphic patterns, and thus may not be formally shared across the auxiliary verb and lexical verb in a given AVC. What is doubled is the category, not necessarily its means of formal encoding. Identical or formally related markers for a single category may be found in Gumbaynggir AVCs, however, as in the final two forms below using the incapabilitive auxiliary.

(57) a. Gumbaynggir
    gumbaynggir gurubiliw ŋi:nda ŋara:ŋgu
    Gumbaynggir AUX:TRANS:FUT you:ERG learn:FUT
    'you will learn Gumbaynggir quickly'
    (Eades 1979: 308)

    b. Gumbaynggir
    ŋaya gurubi birmadi
    I AUX:PRES run:PRES
    'I run fast'

    c. Gumbaynggir
    ŋa:ɟa muday biyambay yaraŋ nuŋu:
    I:ERG AUX:PRES eat:PRES DEM kangaroo:OBJ
    'I can't eat that kangaroo'

    d. Gumbaynggir
    gula:na mudaŋ da:lgaŋ
    he AUX:PST sing:PST
    'he couldn't sing'

As the first two forms demonstrate, what I am labeling AUX may have adverbial functions not typically associated with auxiliaries in better-known languages, but found in AVCs in a range of unrelated languages, as mentioned and further exemplified in 1.7.

In Nyawaygi, one finds serialized/emergent auxiliary constructions of this doubly inflected TAM pattern, here with the characteristically Australian tense/aspect category 'unmarked'. The form below has progressive semantics that are commonly associated with the verb 'lie' in its function as an auxiliary (Heine 1993; Kuteva 2001; Heine and Kuteva 2002), but retains its lexical meaning as well. This is a classic example of how difficult it can be to differentiate discrete constructional category types on the formal–functional continuum of verb–verb combinations or complex predicate types.

(58) Nyawaygi
    ɲaŋga wiriliɲa yu:ɲa
    3SG.s asleep-UNM lie-UNM
    'he's (lying down) sleeping'
    (Dixon 1983: 498)

Similarly double marked AVCs with the unmarked tense category realized on both the lexical verb and the auxiliary verb are found in other Pama-Nyungan languages as well, e.g. Wargamay or Djapu Yolngu.

(59) Wargamay
ŋaɟa ɟalguɽu gargiɽimay gunbay
I(ERG) meat(ABS) finished.CAUS.UNM cut.UNM
'I finished cutting the meat up'
(Dixon 1981: 81)ʄ

(60) Djapu Yolngu
Ba:niyala-puyŋu-w Ga:ngan-puyŋu-w warrpamʔ-thu-n-a
dhawarʔyu-n-a bitrul
B-INHAB-DAT G-INHAB-DAT all-AUX-UNM-IM finish-UNM-IM petrol
'the Baniyala &Gangan people's petrol was all   finished'
(Morphy 1983: 88)

As alluded to above with regards to dialects of Ma'di, variation in the inflectional pattern of a given formation is attested within a single construction in a single language. Again, in this particular instance, it is not clear whether one should consider the following formation to be an AVC showing variably AUX-headed or co-headed patterning, or a verb plus complement formation where the second (lexical) verb is optionally inflected or dependent on the first (would-be auxiliary) verb. Such a situation is found in the extinct Australian language Dharumbal.

(61) a. Dharumbal[†]   b. Dharumbal[†]
nhula wu-thayu yigi-nh   nhula yigi-nh yanggari-nh
he.NOM give-PURP want-NPST   he.NOM want-NPST run-NPST
'he wants to give'   'he wants to run'
(Terrill 2002: 41)   (Terrill 2002: 49)

TABLE 4.3. Doubled TAM patterns in AVCs

Doubled TAM inflectional pattern		Language(s)
LEX-TAM	AUX-TAM	Tamang, Old Turkic, Nyawaygi
AUX-TAM	LEX-TAM	Gumbaynggir, Dharumbal, Wargamay, Djapu Yolngu
TAM:AUX	TAM:LEX	Ma'di

4.3 Doubled subject and TAM inflection

A range of inflectionally rich languages which possess AVCs with a fully doubly inflected structure may be found across the world. All relevant inflectional categories are realized on both the lexical verb and the auxiliary verb in these constructions. A relatively straightforward example of this comes from Orkhon Turkic, where this pattern is seen (in certain tense/aspect forms) with the AVC encoding subject version or self-benefactive action (Anderson 2001, 2004a).

(62)   Orkhon Turkic (Kül Tegin)
    ölür-tü-müz al-tɨ-miz
    kill-PST-1PL SUBJ.VERS-PST-1PL
    'we killed them (to our benefit, for us)'
    (von Gabain 1974: 279 l.3)

Another clear example of this fully inflectionally co-headed formation may be seen in the South Munda language Gorum (a.k.a. Parenga or Parengi). In this language there are a range of sub-types of patterns of AVCs exhibiting doubled, split, and split/doubled formations. A variety of such doubly marked AVCs are found in Gorum, as in the following three examples.

(63) a. Gorum
      kula ne-giʔ-sun miŋ ne-butoŋ-tuʔ ne-i-tuʔ
      tiger 1-see-when I 1-fear-NPST:AFF 1-AUX-NPST:AFF
      'when I see the tiger, I'll be afraid'
      (Aze 1973)

    b. Gorum
      miŋ ne-gaʔ-ru ne-laʔ-ru
      I 1-eat-PST 1-AUX-PST
      'I ate vigorously'
      (Aze 1973:279)

    c. Gorum
      indi basa-n le-reŋ-u le-kuʔn-u
      this base-LOC 1PL-leave-TR 1PL-AUX-TR
      'we temporarily leave (our stuff) at this base'

In all the above forms subject is doubly marked. In the first form, both verbs are marked for non-past tense, as well as the characteristically Gorum category of 'affectedness', the term used to describe the system of 'version' found in this language. Version is a category that comes out of the Kartvelian

(Georgian) linguistic tradition but is actually found in numerous other languages of the world (Anderson and Gurevich 2005). It is notionally related to and often confused with categories of voice, and encodes a discourse-based notion of 'primary affectedness' formally, here marking subject version, i.e. action primarily affecting a subject argument (or actor). Also, the final form above shows another characteristically Gorum feature (also found in its sister language Sora), inflectional (in)transitivity. As an inflectional category, this also appears doubly marked on both the lexical verb and the auxiliary verb in this AVC.

As mentioned above, in Gorum's more distant sister language Gutob, so-called 'echo' formations show a fully doubly marked formation, with both tense and subject encoded on both components of the echo construction.

A doubled inflectional pattern in AVCs as in Gorum (but not the quasi-serialized echo formation) is relatively marked in Munda, where the AUX-headed structure dominates, but it is found in a range of Dravidian languages in South Asia. This is especially common in tribal Dravidian languages of central India where the South Munda languages are spoken (Anderson 2003); but doubled AVCs of this type are also found in such divergent and remote Dravidian languages as Kurukh and Brahui, suggesting that this doubled inflectional formation may in fact be an old one in Dravidian (see Steever (1988) for more on this formation, which, in part because of the doubled inflectional pattern, is there called a serial verb construction, not an AVC as here).

(64) Brahui
      num xalkure hināre
      you thrash-PST-2PL AUX-PST-2PL
      'you have thrashed'
      (Steever 1988: 105)

(65) Kurukh
      bas-c-ar ker-c-ar
      inhabit-PST-3PL AUX-PST-3PL
      'they settled in'
      (Steever 1988: 98)

(66) Konda
      tōṛis-n-a sī-n-a
      show-NPST-1 AUX-NPST-1
      'I will show (you)'
      (Steever 1988: 73)

On the periphery of South Asia in Northern Pakistan, the isolate language Burushaski makes use of a limited amount of doubled inflection in auxiliary verb constructions as well. In certain compound tense formations consisting of a lexical verb and an auxiliary verb with first singular subjects, both the lexical verb and the auxiliary verb may appear in a first person marked form indicated by -*a*-in position class +3 in the verb template (Anderson forthcoming). Note that this alternates in certain people's speech with an AUX-headed construction, subject appearing only on the auxiliary verb.

(67) Burushaski
    jĕ áyanum báyam   ~*jĕ áyanam báyam*
    I sleep:PRTCPL AUX:1:PRTCPL   I sleep:1:PRTCPL AUX:1:PRTCPL
    'I fell asleep'
    (Berger 1998b: 133)

The pluperfect formation in Standard Arabic shows a pattern with doubled subject plus tense/aspect marking. Of course the means of encoding the non-referent information is not affixal *per se* but rather templatic/non-concatenative in the manner characteristic of Semitic languages.

(68) Standard Arabic
    kun-tu katab-tu
    AUX.PRF-1 read.PRF-1
    'I had written'
    (Kihm 2003: 341)

Although occurring in a relatively large number of Bantu languages, a fully doubly inflected AVC forms a somewhat minor pattern within the grammars of the languages of this family. Such formations are found, for example, in Kirundi, Songye, and Siswati, belonging to three separate regional (cum genetic) subgroups within the family, viz. J, L, and S.

(69) Kirundi (J61)
    niya azaná ubwǎ:tsi bw'inzu tu-zo:-ba tú-zo:-sáka:ra inzu
    if 3-bring thatch of.house 1PL-FUT-AUX 1PL-FUT-thatch house
    'if they would bring the thatch (tomorrow), we will thatch the house
       (after tomorrow)'
    (Botne 1986: 307)

(70) Kirundi
    ní wazá mukwe:zi kuúza tu-zo:ba tw-â:-saka:-ye inzu
    if 2:come month to.come 1PL-FUT-AUX 1PL-PST-thatch-COMPL house
    'if you come next month, we will have thatched the house'
    (Botne 1986: 309)

(71)   Songye (L.23)
       tu-funíné tu-yaa ka-kuná
       3PL-AUX 3PL-go *ka*-plant
       'we were going to plant'
       (Botne 1999: 485; Stappers 1964: 179)

(72)   Siswati (S.43)
       ba-tawu-be ba-tawu-cala nakuvakala kukhala inkwela
       3PL-FUT-AUX 3PL-FUT-start when.to.be audible to.produce.sound whistle
       'they will be about to start when the whistle sounds'
       (Botne 1986: 307; Ziervogel and Mabuza 1976: 187)

The Nilotic language Lango also possesses a single construction of this type. In other words, this constitutes a fairly marked pattern for this language.

(73)   Lango
       án àbín àkwálò gwènò
       I 1:AUX:PERF 1:steal:PERF chicken
       'I did steal the chicken'
       (Noonan 1992: 139)

In Oromo of Wellega, suffixes encode person/number/gender and tense in a single portmanteau form. These categories are marked on both lexical verb and the auxiliary verb. However, similar to the varied tense conjugations of Pama-Nyungan languages like Gumbaynggir, there is a non-identity between the formal means of encoding these categories on the two components of the AVC. Thus, this entails a functional/categorial doubling, not a formal one, but nevertheless must be considered as exemplifying the co-headed auxiliary verb construction.

(74)   Oromo of Wellega
       k'ab-a tur-e   *k'ab-di tur-te*
       have-3M.PST AUX-3M.PST   have-3F.PST AUX-3F.PST
       'he had'   'she had'
       (Gragg 1976: 185)

The Kuliak language Ik exhibits variation between a fully inflected deictic (core-) serial-like construction, and one that is overtly similar to an AUX-headed AVC, with a dependent marked lexical verb and no double marking.

(75)   a.   Ik (Kuliak; Uganda)
            ɡó-no saɓá-no loŋóta
            go-1PL.IMP kill-1PL.IMP enemies:OBL
            'let's go kill enemies'
            (König 2002: 313)

b. Ik
   ǵó-no saɓ-ési loŋóta-i
   go-1PL.IMP kill-INF:OBL enemies-GEN

Of all the over 2,000 languages of the macro-Indo-Pacific region, encompassing the Austronesian and Australian languages families as well as the multiplicity of phyla and families of greater New Guinea conventionally called Papuan, the language that perhaps makes the most extensive use of doubly inflected AVCs is Daga of the purported Trans-New Guinea phylum. As in the doubled AVCs of Oromo of Wellega, there is not always an identity in the formal means of encoding the doubled categories; rather, the functional categories are encoded twice through non-identical formal means. The doubled structures in this language utilize portmanteau subject cum tense(/aspect) suffixes, all fused into a synthetic complex. For more on fused formations of this type, see Chapter 6.

(76) a. Daga
        war-ingi-n
        get-1:T/A-1:T/A
        'I was getting it'
        (Murane 1974: 48)

     b. Daga
        war-in-ton
        get-1PL:T/A-1PL:T/A
        'we were getting it'

     c. Daga
        war-iangin-a
        get-1:T/A-1:T/A
        'I just got it'
        (Murane 1974: 52)

     d. Daga
        war-ianit-oni
        get-1PL:T/A-1PL:T/A
        'we just got it'

A similar situation is also seen in the Austronesian language Sobei of Papua district, Indonesia (formerly Irian Jaya). Here the portmanteau subject-mood elements are likewise non-identical between the lexical verb and the auxiliary, and appear as prefixes, not suffixes.

(77) Sobei (Austronesian; Papua, Indonesia)
     w-enon yo-fi
     1.REAL-AUX 1.REAL-make
     'I was making'
     (Sterner and Ross 2002: 181)

The Australian language Ndjébbana has certain AVCs that likewise reflect a doubled inflectional pattern. A relatively simple example of this with an intransitive verb is seen in (78).

(78) Ndjébbana
       bi-rri-ngidjí-na bá-rri-na
       3UA-RE(UA)-TALK-REM 3UA-RE(UA)-AUX
       'the two of them talked'
       (McKay 2000: 218)

More complex AVCs with doubled inflection are also found in this Burarran
(non-Pama-Nyungan) language with transitive verbs, including portmanteau
subject-acting-on-object prefixes (S>O), as well as the opaque augment *ka*
[*kó*], which may originally have been a fused AUX in an original Aux V
configuration.

(79) Ndjébbana
       kanja ngaba-yú-ka-ya-bba ngaba-yú-ka-na
       well 1/2.AUGM>3MIN-IRR-kó-drink-EXT 1/2AUGM>3MIN-IRR-kó-AUX
       'well we'll always drink (here/this water)
       (McKay 2000: 200)

A fully doubled pattern of inflection in AVCs is highly marked among
languages of the Americas in my sample. One such example is found however
in the Mayan language Tzutujil.

(80) Tzutujil (Mayan; Guatemala)
       n-oq-taxin-i   *n-oq-ki(ʔ)-kot-i*
       CONT-1PL-AUX-CLASS   CONT-1PL-sweet-VBLZR-CLASS
       'we are in the process of enjoying ourselves'
       (Butler and Butler 1977: 70)

TABLE 4.4. Subject + TAM doubled patterns

Doubled inflectional pattern		Language(s)
S-AUX-TAM	S-LEX-TAM	Lango, Kinyarwanda
S-LEX-TAM	S-AUX-TAM	Gorum
S-TAM-AUX	S-TAM-LEX	Kirundi, Siswati
S-TAM-LEX	S-TAM-AUX	Ndjébbana
LEX-TAM-S	AUX-TAM-S	Old Turkic, Brahui, KonÚdÚa
TAM-S-AUX	TAM-S-LEX	Tzutujil
LEX-S/T	AUX-S/T	Oromo of Wellegga
S/T-AUX	S/T-LEX	Sobei
LEX-S/T:AUX:S/T		Daga

4.4 Doubled negation

Perhaps it comes as no surprise that doubled negative formations in AVCs are quite uncommon in the languages of the database. In fact, the only clear example I have of a doubled negative formation where an identical negative element appears twice comes from the Papuan language Auyana, and here it is formally realized not through a process of negative affixation but rather by doubling of the negative particle *imbo*. Strictly speaking, this appears to be an AUX-headed construction, insofar as the auxiliary bears the tense morphology in this example.

(81) Auyana
    imbo piko?o imbo foyana
    NEG copulate NEG AUX:PST
    'they could not copulate'
    (McKaughan 1973b: 358)

More commonly attested is a pattern that has a single marker of negation on the auxiliary verb, while the lexical verb appears in a dependent negative combining form, called the 'connegative' in the Uralic linguistic tradition. These formations were mainly discussed in Chapter 2, as the constructions appear to belong to the domain of AUX-headed AVCs. One might call such a construction a 'pseudo-doubled' formation. Such formations are found for example in the Bantu language Herero and the Australian language Yukulta. Note that the connegative element on the lexical verb is often called the negative perfect(ive) in the description of various Bantu languages, and may appear within a larger fused or univerbated structure.

(82) a. Herero
        tu-a tuŋg-a
        1PL-AUX build-PRF
        'we have built'
        (Meinhof 1948: 104)

    b. Herero
        ka-tu[-]tuŋg-ire
        NEG-1PL[-]build-NEG.PRF
        'we have not built'

    c. Herero
        ka-tu w-ire
        neg-1PL fall-NEG:PRF
        'we haven't fallen'
        (Meinhof 1948: 105)

    d. Herero
        ka-tu-a w-ire
        NEG-1PL-AUX fall-NEG:PRF
        'we hadn't fallen'

(83) a. Yukulta
          walira-kati ʈiyaɽari wuḻanin'ɽa
          NEG-1.PRES eat.IND.NEG food.DAT
          'I'm not eating any tucker'
          (Keen 1983: 230, 237)

      b. Yukulta
          walira-ŋka puʈiyaɽari
          NEG-3.PRES sleep.IND.NEG
          'he isn't sleeping'

Note that not all negative formations are marked in this manner in Herero, where classic AUX-headed formations may also be found.

(84) Herero
      ha-tu-ja muna
      NEG-1PL-AUX see
      'we have not yet seen'
      (Meinhof 1948: 114)

4.5 Structural dependency and inflectional co-headedness in AVCs

While auxiliary verb constructions of the 'doubled' inflectional type have been optionally called 'co-headed' formations in this chapter, it is worth reiterating that this concept of headedness pertains only to inflectional headedness, not syntactic phrasal or structural headedness. Within this latter domain, there may in fact be an overt head–dependent relation existing between the lexical verb and the auxiliary verb. As was found in both the AUX-headed and LEX-headed constructions discussed above, the auxiliary verb appears to be most frequently considered the structural head, with the lexical verb appearing in a 'predetermined' dependent form. This is most obvious in languages exhibiting the doubled subject inflectional sub-pattern. The auxiliary verb may also appear in a dependent marked form in the doubled pattern, although this is not at all common. The dependent form in which the lexical (or auxiliary) verb may appear in these AVCs covers virtually the full range of dependent forms found in AUX-headed constructions. Thus there are subtypes of this dependent marked construction variously encoded by so-called 'modal' dependency (optative, irrealis, subjunctive), generalized dependent or subordinate markers, dependent forms of inflectional categories, same-subject marking, converbs or adverbial dependency, infinitives, participles, etc.

In the following sections I exemplify these subtypes of the doubly inflected AVC pattern where either the lexical verb (4.5.1) or the auxiliary verb (4.5.2) appears in an overtly dependent form, despite bearing doubled inflection as well.

Note that, as mentioned above, it is possible that certain formations in particular languages (e.g. Austronesian Sobei) that have doubled category inflection but a non-identity among the various formal means of encoding these categories actually reflect the sub-pattern in question, i.e. where either the lexical verb or the auxiliary verb appears in an overtly dependent form. It is also possible, of course, that this disjoint marking of categories merely constitutes the historical origin for a synchronically opaque system of this type.

4.5.1 *Doubled inflection with 'dependent' marked lexical verb*

Cross-linguistically, the most common pattern in which the lexical verb bears some overtly dependent form but nevertheless bears doubled subject inflection belongs to the broad category of 'modal subordination' or 'modal dependency'. Most likely this derives from a verb–complement structure where the dependent lexical verb derives from a clause marked as unrealized, etc. Unsurprisingly, this is most common with forms indicating volition, desire, potentiality, etc. as well as future forms, which (as is well known) frequently derive from a grammaticalization of a volitional verb (cf. Heine's 1993 'Volitional' event schema) and involve an event semantic sense of unrealizedness, potentiality, etc.

Doubly inflected AVCs where the lexical verb appears in a modal dependent/subordinate form are found in such African languages as Kana of Nigeria and the Bantu language Hemba, Austronesian Kele of Papua New Guinea, and in at least one AVC in the Yuman language Jamul Tipay.

(85) a. Kana   b. Kana

        ṁ-sá   *ṁ-dʒīgē*   *Legbo* *é-sá*   *à-lú*

        1DEF-AUX 1OPT-snatch   L.   3DEF-AUX 3.OPT-come

        'I may snatch her'   'Legbo may join us later'

        (Ikoro 1996: 196)

(86) Hemba   (87) Kele (Austronesian)

     tu-sw-a tu-tal-e   *yu u-pe k-u-le*

     1PL-AUX-IND 1PL-see-SBJCT   I 1-DES (say) IRR-1-go

     'we will see'   'I wish[ed] to go'

     (Aksenova 1997: 34)   (Ross 2002a: 139)

(88) Jamul Tiipay

     maach me-wi-x me-tuuyaw

     you.SUBJ 2-do-IRR 2-AUX.CNTRFACT

     'you could have done it (but didn't)'

     (Miller 2001: 294)

In the Cushitic language Afar, subject on the lexical verb may be either prefixal or suffixal, but the lexical verb appears in a subjunctive form. Again, an unrealized action is expressed by the AVC, and thus this kind of modal dependency makes sense semantically speaking.

(89) a. Afar   b. Afar
          t-d̪kam-u way-ˈt-a   *ˈgen-n-u way-ˈn-a*
          2-eat-SBJ AUX-2-IMPRF   go-1PL-SBJ AUX-1PL-IMPRF
          'you are about to eat'   'we are about to go'
          (Bliese 1976: 147)

Related to these modal subordinate formations, a variety of Nilotic languages possess AVCs in which subject is doubly encoded, once each on the auxiliary verb and the lexical verb, but the formal markers indexing these categories are non-identical. The lexical verb element bears a 'subjunctive' subject prefix form. While in certain languages the semantics associated with the construction make the use of a non-realized marker straightforward (future, negative, etc.), it is clear that in various Nilotic languages this pattern has simply been generalized within AVCs; such is the case, for example, in Teso, where this form is found in past tense constructions as well.

(90) a. Turkana (Eastern Nilotic; Kenya)
          kì-pon-iˋa-tɔ-mat-à
          1PL-go-A 1PL.SBSC-drink-PL
          'we shall drink'
          (Dimmendaal 1983: 136)

      b. Turkana
          à-ìlr-aˋ k-ɪ-pɔtuₒ eèsi tà-ar-aˋ erisiₐˋ
          1-hear-IT CON-2-come you(N) 2PL-kill-PL cheetah
          'I heard you came to kill a cheetah'

(91) a. Teso   b.   Teso
          a-bu ke-ner   *e-roko ke-buno*
          1-AUX.PST 1SBJ-say   3-NEG 3SBJ-come
          'I said'   'he has not yet come'
          (Heine and Reh 1984: 104–5; Hilders and Lawrance 1956: 14; 46)

      c. Teso   d. Teso   e. Teso
          a-bu ka-duk   *i-bu ko-duk*   *a-bu ko-duk*
          1-PST 1SBJ-build   2-PST 2SBJ-build   3-PST 3SBJ-build
          'I built'   'you built'   'he built'
          (Heine and Reh 1984: 185; Hilders and Lawrance 1956: 29–30)

f. Teso
   a-bu etelepat ko-lot ore bian
   he-AUX.PST boy 3SBJ-go home yesterday
   'the boy went home yesterday'
   (Heine and Reh 1984: 185; Hilders and Lawrance 1956)

Note that the auxiliary in the first Teso form *bu* derives historically from the lexical verb in the second example ('come'). The last Teso forms derives from a structure of the type V S Complement > Aux S V—a common source for doubly inflected AVCs with the lexical verb in a dependent form.

In the Nupoid language Gade of Nigeria, there are constructions that appear to have pure doubled inflection (albeit within a system where the prosodic independence of the agreement elements has been maintained, i.e. these show an isolating structure), while others use a dependent marked form of the agreement marker with the lexical verb, here indicated by tonal contrasts, not affixally.

(92) a. Gade   b. Gade
         m̀bà ba nị̀ ba gẹ   *baa cícị̀ bàà sị́ gízẹ̀*
         and 3PL AUX 3PL go   3PL AUX 3PL.DEP buy yam
         'and they happened to go'   'they should still be buying yams'
         (Sterk 1994: 18)

In various auxiliary constructions in the Papuan language Umbungu Kaugel, lexical verbs appear with a dependent form of a subject in an anticipatory subject form. Although embedded within an entirely different formal system, these constructions are similar to both the Nilotic dependent subject-cum-modal forms and the tense-marked dependent subject forms in Gade.

(93) a. Umbungu Kaugel
         ulke molo-pa te-ke-mo
         house be-3.DEP AUX-PRES-3.PRES
         'she is probably in the house'
         (Head 1990: 106)

      b. Umbungu Kaugel
         oleanga pu-ku te-ngi
         yesterday go-2.DEP AUX-2/3.PL[NR.PST]
         'they probably went yesterday'

c. Umbungu Kaugel
    akena nambe te-ko pu-nu-ye
    Hagen what AUX-2.DEP go-2[.PST]-Q
    'how did you go to Hagen?'
    (Head 1990: 105)

d. Umbungu Kaugel
    kako nambe te-pa te-ri-mu-ye
    belt what AUX-3.DEP make-DIST.PST-3.PST-Q
    'how did he make his belt?'

Same-subject marking on a lexical verb in a doubled subject inflected AVC is found in a range of Yuman languages, for example Mojave, Tolkapaya, Paipai, or Jamul Tiipay.

(94) a. Mojave (Yuman; USA)
          hatčoq ʔ-kaʔa:-k ʔ-aʔwi:-m
          dog 1-kick-SS 1-AUX-REALIS
          'I kicked the dog'
          (Mithun 1999: 581; Langdon 1978; Langacker 1998: 41)

      b. Mojave
          k-itwei-k k-aʔwit-m
          IMP-AUX.DO.SELF-SS IMP-do-TNS
          'do it yourself!'
          (Munro 1976a/b; Miller 2001: 326)

(95) Tolkapaya (Yavapai) (Yuman; USA)   (96) Paipai (Yuman; USA)
      m-yaam-θ-k m-yum   *ʼ-sik-k ʼ-yak-k ʼ-yu-m*
      2-go-θ-SS 2-AUX   1-drink-SS 1-lie-SS 1-AUX-PRED
      'you should only be going'   'I am drinking (lying down)'
      (Hardy 1998: 20)   (Langacker 1998: 41)

(97) Jamul Tiipay
      puu-ch we-saaw-ch we-chaw
      that.one-SUBJ 3-eat-SS 3-AUX.COMPL
      'he finished eating'
      (Miller 2001: 315)

Fused forms historically deriving from structures of this type are found in their sister language Walapai as well.

(98) a. Walapai (Hualapai)   b. Walapai
      nya-ch ʔ-sma:-ʔ-yu   *ma-ch mi-sma:-ng-yu*   (∼ -k-m-)
      I-SUBJ 1-sleep-SS.1-AUX   you-SUBJ 2-sleep-SS.2-AUX
      'I am sleeping'   'you are sleeping'
      (Watahomigie et al. 1982: 84)

Auxiliary verb constructions in which the lexical verb appears in a gerund-marked dependent form, despite showing a doubled inflectional pattern, are found in Karo of the Tupi-Guaraní family. Note that doubled subject inflection is only seen with intransitives in this construction; with transitives, a split pattern is attested (see Chapter 5, and Gabas (1999: 178)).

(99) a. Káro (Tupi; Brazil)
          tenaʔwara reʔkay
          teʔ=naʔwat-a teʔ=kap-t
          1PL.EXCL=leave-GER 1PL.EXCL-AUX.FUT-IND$_1$
          'we will leave'
          (Gabas 1999: 61)

      b. Káro
          nān mihmān ekab eyaʔwara
          nān pihmān e=kap-ap e=yaʔwat-a
          who COM 2=AUX-IND$_2$ 2-leave-GER
          'with who will you leave'
          (Gabas 1999: 61)

General dependent or subordinate markers are found on lexical verbs in AVCs of this type as well. This is relatively uncommon but does occur in AVCs in the isolate language Cayuvava, in Barbareño Chumash in a quasi-serialized AVC, and in the Bantu language Venda, where it alternates with a straight doubled formation lacking the dependency marker on the lexical verb, varying according to the auxiliary used in the construction; that is, certain AVCs have a dependent marked lexical verb and others do not, even when both bear doubled subject inflection in Venda.

(100) Cayuvava
       me-h-ãhēre ki-hi-vevere
       MOD-1-AUX DEP/SUBORD-1-run
       'I am running'
       (Key 1967: 35)

(101)   Barbareño Chumash[†] (Chumashan; USA)
    kímkasiynówòn hisiyanšìn
    kim+ka=s-iy-nowon hi=s-iy-anšin
    and+then=3-PL-AUX DEP=3-PL-eat.meal
    'and then they stopped eating'
    (Ono 1996: 30)

(102)   a.   Venda (Bantu; South Africa, Zimbabwe)
          ndo-vha   *ndo-vhona*
          1.PRF-AUX   1.PRF-see
          'I had seen'
          (Heine 1993: 38)

       b.   Venda
          vha-dzula   *vha-tshi-vhala*
          3PL-CONT   3PL-DEP-read
          'they always/continuously read'

Note the following forms from Gade in this regard. The first form appears to be a straightforward AUX-headed formation, with the characteristically African syntax of Subject Auxiliary Object Verb (Gensler and Güldemann 2003). This may also occur in a doubled subject inflection form (with the same characteristic syntax); but in this latter instance, the lexical verb in final position appears in a dependent form.

(103)   a.   Gade   b.   Gade
       ñ nị ìkù gwụ̀   *ñ nị ìkù ñ nị gwụ̂*
       1 AUX money receive   I AUX money 1 AUX receive:DEP/ASP
       'I have received money'   'I have received money'
       (Sterk 1994: 18–19)

Lexical verbs in a dependent infinitive form but in a doubly subject-marked construction are found in a small number of languages, for example the Bantu languages Chichewa or the Beya dialect of Lega.

(104)   Chichewa
    a-khala a-ku-gwir-a ntchito kuchokera chaka chatha
    3-AUX 3-INF-work-FV since year last
    'they have been working since last year'
    (Bentley and Kulemeka 2001: 33)

(105)   Beya Lega
    tu-li tu-ku-kangúlá i̧ swá
    1PL-AUX 1PL-INF-clear field
    'we are clearing the field (now)'
    (Botne 2003: 441)

In the Caddoan language Pawnee a pseudo-auxiliary verb complement construction is found with doubled subject marking and the second or 'lexical' verb in an infinitival subordinate form. This type of construction is one common source for dependent marked lexical verbs in doubly inflected AVCs.

(106)   Pawnee (Caddoan; USA)
    rawa taticka ratkura:ʔi:wa:ti

rawa	*ta-t-icka*	*ra-t-ku-ur-ra:-i:-wati-i*
now	IND-1-'AUX'	INF-1-INF-PREV-way-x-dig-SUBORD

    'now I want to talk about...'
    (Mithun 1999: 373; Parks 1976)

4.5.2 *Doubled inflection with 'dependent' marked auxiliary verb*

As mentioned above, in addition to dependent marked lexical verbs in a doubly subject-inflected AVC, which speak to a head–dependent relation between the auxiliary (head) and lexical (dependent) verb in terms of structural syntax, there are also a very small number of languages with dependent marked *auxiliary* verbs in doubly inflected AVCs. Thus, although rarer than the reverse situation, lexical verbs can also be the phrasal or structural head in an inflectionally co-headed AVC.

One such language exhibiting a construction of this type is Mbyá Guaraní. Here the auxiliary verb appears with a marker of dependent serialization. Note that the plural subject is encoded through the use of a specifically plural auxiliary element in the first Mbyá Guaraní example below.

(107)   a.   Mbyá Guaraní (Tupi-Guarani; Paraguay, Brazil)

ha'e	*rire*	*je*	*o-arõ*	*o-kua-py*
3.ANA after	HSY	3-wait	3-AUX.PL-SER

       'after that they all waited for him'
       (Dooley 1990: 479)

     b.   Mbyá Guaraní

ha'e	*vy*	*je*	*o-juka=ta*	*o-iko-vy*	*javy*	*je*
3.ANA	SS	HSY	3-kill=about to	3-AUX-SER	when	HSY

       'and so, just as he was about to kill them...'
       (Dooley 1990: 480)

A doubled future construction with a dependent marked auxiliary verb is found in the Khoisan language Kua, which distinguishes this formation from the present and past constructions in this language. A special future cum juncture form appears before a future-marked lexical verb. As mentioned in Chapter 2, juncture elements in Khoisan languages appear to be a subtype of the adverbial (gerund, converb, etc.) dependency formation.

(108)   Kua

tá kye' kṹ	*tá ku'a' kṹ.nà*	*tá kṹ.á.ha'*
I PRES go	I FUT.JNCT go-FUT	I go.JNCT.PRF
'I go'	'I will go'	'I went'

(Heine 1986: 18)

Summary

Unlike the previous two patterns of inflection where the auxiliary verb (AUX-headed) or the lexical verb (LEX-headed) serves as the inflectional head, there are also a number of languages with AVCs where both the lexical verb and auxiliary verb serve as inflectional co-heads. With respect to the categories doubly marked in this doubled macro-pattern of inflection of auxiliary verb constructions, by far the most common doubled category is subject, occurring in around 80 per cent of the examples. Doubled tense/aspect marking or fully doubly inflected forms (all TAM and referent categories, etc.) are much less common cross-linguistically speaking, but nevertheless occur in a range of unrelated languages.

Although AVCs of the doubled pattern show a co-head relation between the lexical verb and the auxiliary verb inflectionally speaking, the auxiliary verb, as in the other patterns, is often the structural head, with the lexical verb bearing some overt index of dependency. On rare occasions, it is instead the auxiliary that is dependent-marked in doubled inflectional forms.

5

Split and Split/Doubled Inflectional Patterns

Overview

Up to this point in the discussion of the various types of heads relevant to the typological analysis of inflection in auxiliary verb constructions, I have been making an acknowledged oversimplification of the facts for ease of explication. In each of the three preceding macro-patterns of inflection in auxiliary verb constructions, I have taken it as uncontroversial that the categories of syntactic heads, semantic heads, and inflectional heads should be considered separate, individuated, and uniquely identifiable discrete categories, when in fact this is not the case. In particular, there are AVCs that show obligatory inflectional categories, and therefore the means of determining the inflectional head, scattered across the lexical verb and auxiliary verb components. I call these the 'split-pattern' forms. In addition, AVCs in certain languages show what I am calling the 'split/doubled' pattern: in these AVCs, some categories are marked on either the auxiliary verb and/or the lexical verb alone, while others are marked on both, i.e. they show both split and co-headed characteristics.

5.1 Split patterns

5.1.1 *Lexical verb in a negative form; auxiliary verb marks subject and TAM*

One of the most common splits found in auxiliary verb constructions cross-linguistically is one in which the lexical verb encodes negative polarity, while argument properties and TAM categories are found on the auxiliary verb. This kind of split pattern is somewhat like a subtype of the AUX-headed pattern, with a negative dependent lexical verb. It is clear that this is overtly the case in certain languages, where negative forms of such dependent verb markers function as gerunds/converbs or participles. This might also arise from a connegative form, with the original negative particle or auxiliary completely eroded or with a zero allomorph.

This particular split sub-pattern of inflection with negative marked lexical verb and TAM/subject-marked auxiliary verb is found across a wide range of unrelated languages of Eurasia. This includes a large number of Native Siberian languages, including Khanty, Kamas, the Altai-Sayan Turkic languages, Palana Koryak, Chukchi, and Buryat.

(1)   Khanty
     ma je:rnas-e:m o:nt-li u:-l
     I dress-1 sew-NEG.PRTCPL AUX-NPST:3
     'my dress is not sewn yet'
     (Nikolaeva 1999: 41)

(2)   Tuvan
     men   ol   nom-nu   nomču-vastay ber-di-m
     I   that book-ACC read-NEG.CV   inch-past.ii -1
     'I stopped reading that book'
     (Anderson and Harrison 1999: 46)

(3)   a. Palana Koryak (Chukotko-Kamchatkan; Siberia)
        gəmme el   e-l'lep-ke t-itə-tkən   el
        I   not   NEG-look-NEG 1-AUX-PRES   not
        'I'm not looking'
        (Žukova 1980: 114–115)

      b. Palana Koryak
        e-l'lep-ke   *mət-ella-tkən*
        NEG-look-NEG   1PL-AUX-PRES
        'we are not looking'

      c. Palana Koryak
        el   e-l'lep-ke   ella-tkən-etək
        not   NEG-look-NEG AUX-PRES-2PL
        'you (PL) are not looking'
        (Žukova 1980: 115, 114)

      d. Palana Koryak
        gəmme el e-l'lep-ke   tə-tit-əŋ
        I   not NEG-look-NEG 1-AUX-FUT
        'I won't look'

(4)   Chukchi (Chukotko-Kamchatkan; Russia (Siberia))
      ənkʔam remk-ə-n-ʔm qəmel
      and folk-EPEN-ABS=EMPH then
      loŋ-ə-cʸe-qaanmat-a n-it-qin=ʔm
      NEG=EP-INTNS-slaughter.reindeer-NEG HAB-AUX-3=EMPH
      '...and the people hardly slaughtered reindeer...'
      (Dunn 1999: 75, 320)

(5)   Buryat (Mongolic; Russia (Siberia))
      bi eneenyiiyi xe-zhe shada-xa-güi xa-b
      I maybe do-CV:IMPRF AUX-FUT.PRTCPL-NEG AUX-1
      'maybe I will not be able to do it'
      (Skribnik 2003: 119)

In the particular case of Kamas, it is interesting to note that the form cited
below was probably a relatively recent innovation from a different pattern,
possibly calqued on the pattern pervasive in Xakas, the language to which
most Kamas shifted (in addition to Russian), and the pattern common in all
the Turkic languages spoken in the region.

(6)   Kamas
      oʔb-l   =*ej*   *moo-ᶢ́a-m*
      collect-GER   =NEG   AUX-PRES-1
      'I can't collect'
      (Simoncsics 1998: 594)

Now one clause, this construction has three verbs in it, historically speaking.
The negative formation in a stage of Kamas immediately preceding the
moribund state of its documentation consisted of a negative verb and a lexical
verb, here in a gerund (or 'converb') form, previously (perhaps) in a 'connegative' dependent form. This negative verb fused in a third person singular
form with the (now) preceding lexical verb complement, yielding a negative
form associated with a following inflected auxiliary verb formation in a split
pattern. Thus it went from an AUX-headed pattern to a split pattern, to
conform to the norms of the language(s) that Kamas speakers were shifting
to (mainly Xakas but other Altai-Sayan Turkic languages as well). As mentioned above, other Kamas speakers (who shifted directly to Russian?) appear
to have innovated an unchanging negative particle-like formation based on
Russian models using the original third singular form of the negative auxiliary
ej. The fused split construction, on the other hand, looks identical to the

structure found in the Altai-Sayan Turkic languages, and this can hardly be coincidence. The hyper-variation found in moribund Kamas probably reflects the complex sociolinguistic milieu in which the terminal Kamas speakers existed, with different contact sources yielding different variant structures. The Khanty form in (1) above may be similarly the result of the diffusion of a pattern common in the area (Anderson 2004b).

(7)   Variation in Kamas negative formations
       [NEGV LV:NEG.DEP]$_{AH}$ > [LV:DEP NEGV:3]$_{AH}$ >
       [LV:DEP:NEG AV+S:TMA]$_{split}$

Other Eurasian languages with this type of negative split AVC include various South Asian languages, e.g. individual Kiranti (Tibeto-Burman) languages of Nepal or the South Munda language Remo of India.

(8)   Thulung   (9)   Dumi (Rai)
       mi-pe-thiŋa bu-ŋa   *ma-lit mɨt-t-a*
       NEG-eat-CV AUX-1   NEG:PRF:GER-cut AUX-NPST-2/3
       'I have not eaten'   'he has not cut it (yet)'
       (Ebert 2003a: 513)   (van Driem 1993: 240)

(10)   a.   Remo   b.   Remo
             a-sum ḍen-gi-ti-ŋ   *a-sap ḍen-gi-ti-ŋ*
             NEG-eat PROG-PAST.I-NPAST-1   NEG-come PROG-PAST.I-NPAST-1
             'I have not been eating'   'I have not been coming'
             (Fernandez 1968: 54, 58)

       c.   Remo   d.   Remo
             a-sum ḍen-gə-ta   *a-sap ḍen-gə-ta*
             NEG-eat PROG-PAST.I-NPAST   NEG-come PROG-PAST.I-NPAST
             's/he has not been eating'   's/he has not been coming'

A small number of Papuan languages show a similar pattern, with a negative lexical verb and argument- and TAM-inflected auxiliary. This includes the Angan languages Baruya and Menya, as well as Yareba and Bena Bena.

(11)   a.   Baruya   b.   Baruya
             ma-vaihɨ̂r-ya yɨ̂wano   *ma-vaihɨ̂r-i yɨ̂wano*
             NEG-tread-EMB AUX:1:PST   NEG-tread-do AUX:1:PST
             'I did not tread'   'I did not tread'
             (Lloyd 1997: 302)

(12) a. Menya
      iqu woŋuä manyiyäqä imiŋqe
      i-qu woŋuä ma-n-i-i-qä i-miŋ-qäqä-i
      that-3 work NEG-1-do-BEN-NMLZR AUX-PST/IFPV-3.DSOC-IND
      'he didn't work for me'
      (Whitehead 1991: 258)

     b. Menya
      nyi hiŋuä maqeqäŋqä imäqänä
      nyi hiŋuä ma-qe-q-n-qä i-m-ŋqä-ä-nä
      I eye NEG-2DL-rub-DETR-NMLZR AUX-1/IRR-GOAL-1/ASOC-QT
      'I must not see you two'
      (Whitehead 1991: 285)

(13) a. Yareba
      u-t-awa u-s-i-nu
      do-CLS.MRKR-NEG AUX-CM-NR.PST-3
      'he didn't do it'
      (Weimer 1972: 65)

     b. Yareba
      i-t-awa u-f-e-i-si
      eat-CLS.MRKR-NEG AUX-FUT-1PL-N.SG-1PL
      'we can't eat it'

(14) Bena Bena
     me-molo netoʔehibe
     NEG-put 1:AUX:PST:3
     'he did not put it for me'
     (Young 1964: 77)

It is possible that the negative prefixes in the Angan languages and Bena Bena are (i) cognate and (ii) a fusing of a pro-clitic negative, and that these were, like the Kamas forms discussed above, perhaps originally AUX-headed forms, with the lexical verb variably in an overtly dependent form or a zero-marked stem (cf. the Menya forms above)—two common forms for lexical verbs in the AUX-headed pattern.

In the Sepik-Ramu language Ambulas of the Ndu family, the negative probably belongs to a class of modal-type elements that appear as suffixes on the lexical verb in split configurations.

(15)   a.   Ambulas
            kéraa-kaapuk (~kéraa-marék) lé ya-k
            get-NEG she AUX-PST
            'she did not get it'
            (Wilson 1980: 71)

       b.   Ambulas
            kéraa-katik lé ya-k
            get-HYP she AUX-PST
            'she would have received it'

This particular split paradigm of lexical verb with negative, auxiliary verb
with argument and TAM categories appears to be highly marked in Africa,
occuring in only a small number of African languages in my database,
including the Omotic Gimira (Benchnon) and Western Nilotic Dhó-Alûr,
both from northeastern Africa.

(16)   a.   Dhó-Alûr   b.   Dhó-Alûr
            é-cópó bìn-òŋgó   *íbí-còpò cìdh-òŋgó*
            3-CAP:3 come-NEG   2-CAP:2 go-NEG
            'he cannot come'   'you will not be able to go'
            (Knappert 1963: 126)

(17)   a.   Gimira(Benchnon) (Omotic)   b.   Gimira(Benchnon)
            ta¹na³ ha⁴mar⁴gu³ yis³tu²e³   *ha⁴mar⁴gu³ šî³du²e³*
            I go:NEG.PRTCPL AUX:PST:1   go:NEG.PRTPCL AUX:PST:3M
            'I had not gone'   'he did not go'
            (Breeze 1990: 32)

A number of unrelated languages of northern South America occur where the
type of inflectional split may be found with negative-marked lexical verbs and
argument-and TAM-inflected auxiliaries. This group includes Arawakan
Lokono, Waiwai of the Cariban family, Tacanan Cavineña, Tucanoan Tuyuca,
the isolate Waorani (Auca), and Chibchan Ika and, in the negative potential,
in the isolate Warao as well.

(18)   Wai Wai   (19)   Lokono
       to-hr es-ko   *ma-siki-n th-a no*
       go-NEG AUX-2.IMP   NEG-give-SUBORD 3SGFEM-AUX it
       'don't go'   'she did not give it'
       (Hawkins 1998: 124)   (Aikhenvald 1999: 98)

(20) Cavineña
dut'a apuna-tu kʷa-haka-ma hu-kʷare meta babi-ra
all night-3:ABS go-stop-NEG AUX-REM.PST night hunt-to
'every night he always went to hunt'
(Camp 1985: 41)

(21) a. Waorani (Auca) (isolate, Ecuador)
apǽde-dābāĩ ĩ-kæ-bo-ĩ-pa
speak-NEG AUX-INCEP-1-INFER-ASSRTV
'I shall not speak'
(Peeke 1994: 273)

    b. Waorani
ēyē-dãbāĩ ĩ-bīdi-ta-wo
hear-NEG AUX-2PL-PST-DUBIT
'did you not hear'

(22) a. Ika (Chibchan; Colombia)
ɜima kusari an-a-g-uʔ nʌn-na ni
that deer REF-1/2PL-eat-NEG AUX-DIST CERT
'we did not eat that deer'
(Frank 1990: 6)

    b. Ika   c. Ika
    č-uʔ nar-w-in   *čwa a-uʔ nar-w-in*
    see-NEG AUX-1-DECL   see AUX-NEG AUX-1-DECL
    'I do not see'   'I have not seen'
    (Landaburu 2000: 743)

(23) Tuyuca (Tucanoan; Colombia, Brazil)
kĩã-rē yaa-ré eka-rí kĩã-rē
3PL-SPCF eat-NMLZ:INAN give.food-NEG 3PL-SPCF
tĩã-ri tii-hǎ-yira
serve.drink-NEG AUX-EMPH-EVID
'they did not give them anything to eat or drink'
(Barnes 1994: 332)

(24) Warao
masi hata-komoni ta-n-a-e
deer spear-NEG.POT AUX-SG-PUNC-PST
'he could not spear the deer'
(Romero-Figeroa 1997: 104)

In North America, the only language in the database with this pattern is Aleut. Here, if not an independent innovation, it might reflect diffusional pressure from northeastern Russia, where it is not uncommon (see Palana Koryak and Chukchi cited above).

(25)   Aleut (Eskimo-Aleut; North Pacific (Alaska/Russia))
  anaĝi-x̂   *hamang*   *uku-lakan* *a-na-q*
  anything-SG   (behind).there see-NEG.CONJ AUX-REM-1
  'I did not see anything there'
  (Bergsland 1997: 199)

A slightly different split is found in the Eastern Cushitic language Dasenech of Kenya. In this language the lexical verb marks negative and tense (tonally), but subject is encoded through a subject-fused auxiliary.

(26)   a.   Dasenech (Cushitic; Ethiopia, Kenya)   b.   Dasenech
    yáá má-laalan   *yáá ma-láálan*
    AUX:1 NEG-sing:PRES   AUX:1 NEG-sing:PST
    'I do not sing'   'I did not sing'
    (Sasse 1976: 200)

A somewhat similar patterning is found in Andamanese varieties as well (e.g. Aka-Jeru), although the subject marker and auxiliary have not been univerbated as in Dasenech.

(27)   a.   'Andamanese' (Andamanese; India)   b.   'Andamanese'
    ʈɔ-[w]atta ʈɔːp-ɸolɔ   *ʈɔ-[w]atta ʈɔːp-ɸoɸelɔ*
    1-AUX bathe-NEG:PST   1-AUX bathe-NEG:PST
    'I did not bathe him'   'I did not bathe him'
    (Manohoran 1989: 102)

5.1.2 *Lexical verb marks object, Auxiliary verb marks subject*

Another common split found in auxiliary verb constructions cross-linguistically consists of an object encoded in the lexical verb and subject encoded in the auxiliary verb component. The object, subcategorized for by the lexical verb stem, is found with it, while the subject is encoded at the clause level and is 'raised' to the auxiliary.

This particular split inflectional pattern is not common in Eurasian languages. It is found among the languages of my database only in Northeast Caucasian (Nakh) Ingush, as well as Tibeto-Burman Kinnauri.

(28) Ingush (Northeast Caucasian, Nakh; Russia)

yz	*cynna*	*bii*	*b-iett-azh*	*v-a*
3ᵢ	3.DAT	fistⱼ	Bⱼ-hit-CV.SIM	Vᵢ-AUX

'He hits him'

(Peterson 1999)

(29) a. Kinnauri

khya-ci-du-k

see-2-AUX-1

'I am seeing you'

(Sharma 1988: 140)

b. Kinnauri

khya-ci du-k

see-2 AUX-1

Note the variation between a split pattern and fused split pattern seen in the Kinnauri form above.

Among the roughly 180 African languages in my database, this split of lexical verb encoding object, auxiliary verb encoding subject occurs in only Ewe and some Ogonoid languages of West Africa. Note that split/doubled patterns of this type (object on the lexical verb, subject on both) are relatively common in African languages, however.

(30) a. Ewe

mì-le kpó-m

2PL-AUX see-1

'you see me'

(Allen 1993: 39)

b. Anexo-Ewe

mu-la sɔ-e

1-AUX carry-it

'I am carrying it'

(Heine and Reh 1984: 122)

(31) a. Kana

m-wèè   ā-kūē

1-PAST   2-call

'I called you'

(Ikoro 1996: 207, 212)

b. Kana

m̀-dāàb   ā-mùè

1-MOD:FACT   2-see

'I can see you'

c. Kana

m-wèè ā-dáb mùè

1-PAST 2-MOD see

'I was able to see you'

As the last Kana form demonstrates, the rule in Kana actually appears to be S-AUX O-VB regardless of whether this latter verb is an actual lexical verb, or another verb functioning as an auxiliary. This distribution may reflect the (original) clitic nature of the agreement elements.

Kana's sister language Eleme also shows a lexical verb plus object, auxiliary verb plus subject configuration.

(32) Eleme

èbai rɛ-do-do-rõ	*nɛ́-e*	*ǹsā*
1PL 1PL-REDPL-be.PRES-PRTCL	give-him3SG	book

'we are still giving him books'

(Field Notes; Anderson and Bond 2004-MS)

That this derives from a serial construction seems likely, as the exact structure
is found in the following serialized verb plus auxiliary formation:

(33) Eleme

    àbà   *ba-bere*   *tʃú*   *ńsā*   *no*   *nɛ́-e*

    3PL   3PL.DEF-PRF take book DEM give-3SG

    'they have picked up the book and given it to him'

    (Field notes; Anderson and Bond 2004)

The only group of languages that of the database in which this pattern might
be said to occur relatively commonly is Oceanic languages. Thus AVCs where
object is encoded on the lexical verb but subject on the auxiliary may be found
in such Oceanic languages as Anejoñ, Gela, Kokota, Kwaio, Raga, Simbo,
Sinaugoro, and Torau.

(34) Gela

    k(-)u riɣi-ra na kau

    FUT./-1 see-3PL ART dog

    'I will see the dogs'

    (Crowley 2002b: 532)

(35) a. Sinaugoro

       mai numa bi-si-ni rovo-a

       this house REM-1PL.INCL-INTENT/IMP pull.down-3SG

       'let's pull down this house'

       (Tauberschmidt 1999: 22)

    b. Sinaugoro

       ḡata-gu n-a ḡita-ia

       friend-1 INTENT/IMP-1 see-3

       'I must/want to see my friend now'

       (Tauberschmidt 1999: 28)

(36) a. Kwaio (Austronesian; Solomon Islands) b. Kwaio

       gila ta-la leka   *'oo to-'o age-a*

       they FUT-3PL go   you FUT-2 do-3

       'they will go'   'you will do it'

       (Keesing 1985: 119)

(37) a. Raga (Austronesian; Vanuatu) b. Raga

       ramuru ḡita-ra   *ra-n ḡita-ḡo*

       3DL.CONT see-3PL   3PL-PRF see-2

       'they are looking at them'   'they saw you'

       (Crowley 2002a: 631-2)

(38) a. Simbo
        na peso ɣu ma-na tabara-niyo
        the land EMPH 1:AUX:IRR-DEF:IRR pay-2OBJ
        'my ground I will give you as my price'
        (Palmer 1996: 252)

      b. Simbo
        ara ma-na pi-pito-nia na ve-vea-na na boroyo
        I 1:AUX:IRL-DEF:IRR REDPL-tell-3OBJ the REDPL-resemble-3:POSS
          the pig
        'I'm going to tell the story of the pig'
        (Palmer 1996: 254)

(39) Torau   (40) Anejom̃ (Anstronesian; Vanuatu)
      pa-e alo-dia   *Ek atce-n añak jai et atam̃añ aan*
      FUT-3 make-3PL.OBJ   1.AOR fight-3 I but 3.AOR man/strong he
      'he will make them'   'I fought him but he was too strong'
      (Ross 1982b: 15)   (Lynch 2002a: 749)

(41) a. Kokota (Anstronesian; Solomon Islands)
        ara n-a fakae-di keha huğru nakoni
        I REAL-1 see-3PL NSP all person
        'I saw all (of a group of) people'
        (Palmer 2002: 505)

      b. Kokota
        o-ti dupa-i manei si-ago
        2-NEG punch-3 s/he FOC-2
        'don't punch him'
        (Palmer 2002: 513)

It is possible that the original trigger or source for the development of this
pattern was a Wackernagel-type second position subject clitic that fused with
the preceding clause initial auxiliary, that is from an original LEX-headed
pseudo-split structure.

 With fused Subject/TAM auxiliaries, a similar pattern is seen in the Austronesian languages Niuean and Tigak.

(42) Niuean
      tai wane, kere fale-a fanga qi a-da
      some:PL man 3PL:NFUT give-3OBJ food to REC-3PL
      tai wane qe aqi kesi fale qa-da

some:PL man 3:NFUT NEG.AUX 3PL:NEG give REC-3PL
'some of the men they did give food to, some of them they did not
    give to'
(Haji-Abdolhosseini et al. 2002: 455)

(43)   Tigak
    naga kalum-i
    1.PST see-3
    'I saw him'
    (Beaumont 1989: 40)

Various Papuan languages show this split inflectional pattern in certain
AVCs, including constructions in Upper Asaro.

(44)   Upper Asaro
    ni-vile' og-ave
    1-surpass 3-AUX
    'he has surpassed me'
    (Strange 1973: 89)

In Papuan Gahuku of the East Central Highlands cluster, a split pattern is
found in compound verb stems where subject and TAM are on the second
element and object on the first. The Gahuku split forms are structurally
similar, therefore, to the inflection of 'compound' stems of the type <-N V->
with a 'light', 'dummy', or inflecting verb in Burushaski.

(45) a. Gahuku   b. Gahuku
          a-helele no-viz-ive   *ke-helele viz-it-ive*
          3-afraid ... PROG- ... afraid-3 3PL-afr-..-aid-FUT-3
          'it is making him afraid'   'it will make them afraid
          (Deibler 1976: 36)

(46)   Burushaski
    gu-mʌntsa maiyam
    2-help AUX:FUT:1
    'I shall help thee'
    (Lorimer 1935–8: 233)

These constructions alternate in Gahuku with ones with AUX-headed structure. These latter show object encoding on the auxiliary as well, the lexical
verb appearing in a dependent 'compounding' form. Mixed forms are also
found, with the object and the compounding marker on the lexical verb.

(47) a. Gahuku   b. Gahuku
          l-o ni-m-it-ive   *l-i ki-m-it-ave*
          say-CD 1.OBJ-AUX-FUT-3   say-CD 3PL.OBJ-AUX-FUT-3PL
          'he will tell me'   'they will tell them
          (Deibler 1976: 38)

Note that this pattern is found with a curious serialized construction in Gahuku as well, with the subject marked on the second verb but the object on the first. This is probably the type of construction that gave rise to the kind of split AVC under discussion here.

(48) Gahuku
      ni-p̣il-i hil-it-ave
      1OBJ-smite-CD die-FUT-3PL
      'they will murder me'
      (Deibler 1976: 39)

Only one language in the database from Australia has a split inflectional structure where the lexical verb encodes object and the auxiliary subject; this is Kamor, of the Daly family.

(49) Kamor
      pukunuŋ nuŋkur tat̮ʸ-nint̮ʸi ka-wu-y
      soon you hit-2OBJ 1-AUX-FUT
      'I am going to hit you soon'
      (Tryon 1974f: 66)

Note that Kamor shows variation in this respect too, with alternative AUX-headed structure (with the object encoded on the auxiliary) when there is a compound verb stem.

(50) a. Kamor   b. Kamor
          t̮ʸamaR kerer ler-ŋu pö-mö   *tal pö-mö-ŋu*
          dog leg bite-1OBJ 3M-AUX   spear 3M-AUX-1OBJ
          'the dog bit my leg'   'he speared me'
          (Tryon 1974f: 66)   (Tryon 1974f: 67)

Among North American languages in my database, only the Muskogean languages Koasati and Apalachee have this pattern. Note that in these examples in these languages, the object may (Apalachee) or does (Koasati) belong to the dative series, and that the verbs preceding the auxiliaries, whether they be lexical verbs in AVCs or auxiliaries dominated by another auxiliary, appear in a marked same subject or connective form.

(51) a. Koasati
          im-awí:ci-t á:ta-li-t
          3DAT-help-CONN AUX.SG-1-CONN
          'I kept on helping them...'
          (Kimball 1991: 94)

      b. Koasati
          im-alíkci-t fáyli-l-á:hi-k óm
          3DAT-cure-CONN AUX.SG.TR-1-intent-SS AUX
          'It is the case that I'm about to quit curing him'
          (Kimball 1991: 95)

(52) a. Apalachee[†] (Muskogean; USA)
          holahta onhiya hacin-coɫɫi-t il-ka ihka
          cacique every 2PL:DAT-write-SS 1PL:SUBJ-AUX PROG
          'we, all the caciques, are writing to you'
          (Kimball 1987: 139)

      b. Apalachee
          i-fa-t ot haci-pila-t onka-li ka nok to:lo onka-li ka inahuba-t naliki
          3:STAT-have-SS PART 2PL:OBJ-help-SS AUX-1SS AUX thing two
              AUX-1SS AUX be.prepared-SS ???
          'I will help you with armaments and all that is necessary'
          (Kimball 1987: 144)

      c. Apalachee
          pin-holahta coba pin-rey in-nota-t in-kasamina-t siki-t il-ka-hi-n
          1PL:POSS-cacique great 1PL-king 3:DAT-speak-SS 3:DAT-respect-SS
              NEG:AUX-SS 1PL-AUX-FUT-SW
          'we would not respect or speak to out great cacique, and our king'
          (Kimball 1987: 146)

A scattering of Amazonian languages possess auxiliary verb constructions where the lexical verb marks objects of transitive verbs and the auxiliary verb marks the shared subject. Such forms are found in Cariban Chayma of Venezuela and the Macro-Jê language Canela-Krahô.

(53) Chayma (Cariban; Venezuela)
      tʃ-ara-r-puek w-a-ʒ
      3-carry-NMLZR-OCC.WITH 1-AUX-TAM
      'I'm carrying it, I carry it'
      (Gildea 1998: 216)

(54) a. Canela-Krahô (Macro-Jê; Brazil]   b. Canela-Krahô
      i-te a-pupun   *i-mã a-kĩn*
      1-PST 2-see   1-TEMP:STAT 2-like
      'I saw you'   'I like you'
      (Popjes and Popjes 1986: 130–131)

This split pattern of object on lexical verb, subject on auxiliary verb may also be found in languages that have a fused subject/TAM auxiliary formations. Such languages include Cariban Carijona and Apalaí.

(55) a. Carijona (Cariban; Colombia)   b. Carijona
      əyi-ene-neme wae   *yi-ene-neme manai*
      2-see-CAP 1.AUX   1-see-CAP 2.AUX
      'I can see you'   'you can see me'
      (Gildea 1998: 187)

(56) Apalaí
      o-ere'-ñõōko ase
      2-startle-IMPRF 1.AUX
      'I'm gonna startle you'
      (Gildea 1998: 211)

A similar pattern is found in certain (original) Yukatek Maya AVCs.

(57) a. Yukatek Maya   b. Yukatek Maya
      k-in tàa-s-k-o'b   *t-in tàa-s-h-o'b*
      IMPF-1 come-CAUS-TR.IMPF-3PL   PFV-1 come-CAUS-TR.PFV-3PL
      'I (will) bring them'   'I [have] brought them'
      (Lehmann 1990: 41)

Similar in origin but different in realization is the following form from Yukatek's sister language Mam of Guatemala. Here the 'subject' marker occurs on the auxiliary verb as a suffix/enclitic, while the 'object' marker appears as prefix/proclitic on the lexical verb in contrast with Yukatek where this element is rather realized as a suffix/enclitic like subject marking.[1]

---

[1] Note that K'ekchi Mayan has a formation similar to the Mam one but realized as fused or univerbated complex in this language.
(i) K'ekchi (Mayan; Guatemala)
    x-at-ka-ch'aj   *x-o-a-ch'aj*
    TNS-B2-A1PL-wash   TNS-B1PL-A2-wash
    'we washed you'   'you washed us'
    (Berinstein 1998: 214)

(58)   Mam (Mayan; Guatemala)
    n-chi tzaj t-limo'n Pegr
    PROG-3PL.ABS DIR.come 3SG.ERG-push Peter
    'Peter is pushing them'
    (Collins 1994: 366)

A different and entirely unrelated system of fused subject/TAM auxiliaries and object marked lexical verbs comes from San Idefonso Otomí, an Otomanguean language of Mexico.

(59)   San Ildefonso Otomi
    ja gá tōn-kagi but gà pengi gà tsiš-ʔi
    COMPL 2:PST win:FUSIONED-1OBJ but 1:FUT return 1:FUT take:ANIM:
        FUSIONED-2:OBJ
    'you beat me, but I will come back to get you'
    (Palancar 2004: 57)

The Bantu language Northern Sotho shows complex structures (probably bound phonologically, although this is not represented orthographically) with tense-marking auxiliaries to which subject markers were attached, followed by lexical verbs with prefixes encoding object.

(60)   Northern Sotho (Bantu, Niger-Congo; South Africa)
    bá tló e tlíʃa   < **bá tlá go e tlíʃa*
    they FUT it bring   they come INF it bring
    'they will bring it'
    (Lombard 1978: 319)

According to Lombard (1978), this derived from a structure in which the lexical verb was overtly marked as dependent by the infinitive marker *go-*, but nevertheless reflected this subject/object split inflectional pattern

5.1.3 *Lexical verb marks TAM categories, Auxiliary verb marks subject (object)*

A small number of languages show a split between an auxiliary verb with a subject marker and lexical verb encoding various TAM categories. In Doyayo, an Adamawa language of Cameroon, tense is marked on lexical verbs and all argument properties on the auxiliary. This includes subcategorized object arguments as well as benefactives, etc.

(61)   a.   Doyayo (Adamawa; Cameroon)
        hí¹ gí²-s-í¹-mí³-ge-³   *wãã́-ko³*
        they AUX-BEN-EP-1-3 catch-PROX
        'they will be catching him for me'
        (Wiering and Wiering 1994: 75)

b. Doyayo
   mí³ gí²-s-i-g kaa¹-ko¹
   I AUX-BEN-EP-3 weep-PRES
   'I'm crying to him'

Note that TAM categories as conceived here include illocutionary force categories as well (interrogative, indicative/declarative, etc.); such a system is found, for example, in Tairora, a Papuan language. Note the variation between the split pattern and an AUX-headed construction in these Tairora forms (62a/b).

(62) a. Tairora   b. Tairora
        aru-e ke-ro   *~ aru ke-ro-e*
        hit-Q AUX-he   hitAUX-he-Q
        'did he hit it?'
        (Vincent 1973: 563)

     c. Tairora   d. Tairora
        aiho bi bai-ro   *baite-ma bai-ro*
        air go AUX-3   sleep-IND AUX-3
        'the air is going'   'he is sleeping'
        (Vincent 1973: 581)

     e. Tairora   f. Tairora
        ne-e bai-ra   *oʔubi bai-rera*
        eat-Q AUX-2   sit AUX-1:FUT
        'are you eating'   'I will continue to sit'
        (Vincent 1973: 581)

The Australian language Gurindji also marks subject in auxiliaries and tense in lexical verbs. Unlike Tairora, where auxiliaries follow their accompanying lexical verbs, in Gurindji the order is rather variably Aux V or V Aux.

(63) a. Gurindji (Australia)
        nangala kutij karri-nya
        Nangala stand AUX-PST
        'Nangala (subsection) stood up'
        (McGregor 2001: 5)

     b. Gurindji
        (ngayu) ngu-rna karnti karrap nya-nya
        I AUX-1 tree see see-PST
        'I saw a tree'

The Australian language Walmatjarri shows a split pattern, with a cliticized modal auxiliary root with a subject marker appearing in second position and a lexical verb marking TAM categories.

(64) a.   Walmatjarri
           ngajirta=ma-rna lapany-ja-rla
           NEG=MR₁-1 run-IRR-PST
           'I didn't run'
           (Hudson 1978: 40)

      b.   Walmatjarri   c.   Walmatjarri
           yan-ta-rla=ma-rna   *kayan=nga-lu kang-ka-rla*
           go-IRR-PST AUX.MR₁-1   neg=aux.mr₂-3PL carry-IRR-PST
           'I intended to go'   'they couldn't carry it'
           (Hudson 1978: 41)

Nisenan, an extinct member of the Maiduan family of California, marks irrealis on the lexical verb but subject on the auxiliary verb that occurs in phrase-final position.

(65) Nisenan[†] (Maiduan (Penutian); USA)
      pii-jee-wis da-ni
      swim-go.along-IRR AUX-1
      'I'll go swimming'
      (Mithun 1999: 457)

Lastly, Tucanoan Desano of Colombia shows a construction with a perfect marked lexical verb and subject marked auxiliary.

(66) Desano (Tucanoan; Colombia)
      waʔa-a wa-bã
      go-PRF AUX-3PL
      'they have gone'
      (Miller 1999: 78)

5.1.4 *Lexical verb marks subject, Auxiliary verb marks TAM categories*

A relatively uncommon pattern is found in which the lexical verb marks the subject, but TAM categories are marked on the auxiliary verb. Note that this is the reverse of the split sub-pattern presented in 5.1.3.

The Central Sudanic Ma'di offers a first example of a language with an AVC exhibiting split inflection of this particular subtype. Subject appears on the lexical verb and the negative auxiliary appears with tense marking.

(67) Ma'di (Central Sudanic; Nilo-Saharan; Uganda, Sudan]
    a. *ópî ɔ̄-rǐ vùrú kʊrʊ̀*   b. *ópî kɔ̄-rǐ vùrú kū*
       Opi 3-sit down NEG:PST   Opi 3DIR-sit NEG:NPST
       'Opi did not sit down'   'Opi shouldn't sit down'
       (Blackings and Fabb 2003: 145)

Rotuman of Fiji shows a similar split pattern, only the tense-marked auxiliaries precede subject-marked lexical verbs, rather than follow them as in Ma'di.[2]

(68) Rotuman (Anstronesian; Fiji)
    gou tä-la laʔa-tou
    I DEM/AUX??-FUT go-1
    'I'll be going now'
    (Schmidt 2002: 827)

In present formations in its distant sister language Halia, subject appears on the lexical verb and the auxiliary encodes an obligatory tense specification. In the past, the auxiliary encodes subject and the lexical verb appears in an unmarked (or Ø-marked) form, i.e. in an AUX-headed pattern.

(69) a. Halia   b. Halia
       alia u la   *alia e la-g*
       I AUX.PST.1 go   I AUX.NPST go-1
       'I went'   'I go'
       (Allen 1971: 65)

Coast Tsimshian shows a split pattern of inflection in the proximative construction. Subject appears on the lexical verb and various TAM forms appear on the auxiliary verb, which may itself optionally appear in an overtly dependent form.

(70) a. Coast Tsimshian   b. Coast Tsimshian
       nah-łá-'al dzáb-m̥ ha'liq'éexł   *łá-dm̥ dzáb-u ha'liq'éexł*
       PRF-PROX-SUBSEQ make-1PL sleds PROX-FUT make-1 sleds
       'we used to make sleds'   'I'm about to start making sleds'
       (Dunn 1979: 229)

A range of South American languages possess typologically similar forms. For example, Makushi of the Cariban family marks tense on auxiliaries and subject on lexical verbs, just as the languages adduced above do.

---

[2] Note that the 'auxiliary' in this construction may derive historically from a demonstrative element.

(71) a. Makushi   b. Makushi
          i-karau ko'man-nîpî-'pî   *mîikîrî yarima-sa-i'-ya wanî-'pî*
          3-cry AUX-TRNSTVZR-PAST   3 send-COMPL-3-ERG AUX-PAST
          'he kept crying'   'he has/had sent him'
          (Abbott 1991: 127–8)

The Central Tucanoan language Retuarã of Colombia shows an interesting
formal distinction between a split-inflected AVC with subject marked on the
lexical verb (which appears in an overtly dependent purposive form) and a
tense-marked auxiliary verb.

(72) a. Retuarã(Central Tucanoan; Colombia)
          bãharoka yi-oʔo-ẽrã baa-yu bãẽ
          story 1-write-PURP AUX-PRES now
          'I am going to write a story now'
          (Strom 1992: 72)

      b. Retuarã
          ki-re sa-yîʔã-ẽrã baa-reʔka potohĩ
          3M-HMN.ARG 3M-capture-PURP AUX-PST when
          'when it was going to capture him'

This contrasts with a deictic SVC in a quasi-AUX-headed construction in
Retuarã with a purpose-marked lexical verb and a subject and tense marked
auxiliary.

(73) Retuarã
      bãẽ uʔya-rĩ yi-aʔ-yu
      now bathe-PURP 1-go-PRES
      'now I am going to bathe'
      (Strom 1992: 73)

In Amuesha, a Pre-Andine Arawakan language of Peru, reportative is marked
on the auxiliary and (subject and) object on the lexical verb

(74) Amuesha (Preandine Arawakan; Peru)
      aw-oʔ ot-a·n-eht
      AUX-REPRT say -OBJ-3PL
      'he said to them'
      (Wise 1986: 608)

In Sierra Popoluca, auxiliaries are marked for aspect but not person, while
lexical verbs take person marking but no aspectual marking.

(75)   Sierra Popoluca (Mixe-Zoquean; Mexico)
       nɨk-pa ta-moːŋ-i
       go-ɪɴᴄ 1ɪɴB-sleep-ɪᴛʀ?
       'we are going to sleep'
       (Marlett 1986: 382)

In certain AVCs in Pipil, a nearly extinct Uto-Aztecan language of El Salvador, auxiliaries mark tense, while subject and object are encoded on lexical verbs.

(76)   a.   Pipil (Uto-Aztecan; El Salvador)
            te: weli-k ni-k-namaka ne uchpa:nwas ne k-al-wi:ka-ke-t
            ɴᴇɢ ᴄᴀᴘ-ᴘʀᴇᴛ 1-it-sell the broom that it-ᴅɪʀ-take-ᴘʀᴇᴛ-ᴘʟ
            'I could not sell the broom which they brought'
            (Campbell 1985: 139)

       b.   Pipil
            pe:h-ki kin-mu:tia
            begin-ᴘʀᴇᴛ 3ᴘʟ-scare
            it started scaring them'
            (Campbell 1985: 140)

The Northeast Caucasian language Hunzib exhibits a pattern where the class marker of the absolutive argument is found on the lexical verb (whether you want to call this subject or object is actually irrelevant here), which may appear in a tense/participle or gerundive form followed by a tense-marked lexical verb.

(77)   a.   Hunzib
            iyu-l xankʼal r-uwo-č zəǧ-ár
            mother-ᴇʀɢ khinkal ᴄʟs.ᴍʀᴋʀ-make-ᴘʀᴇs ᴀᴜx-ꜰᴜᴛ
            'mother will probably make khinkal'
            (van den Berg 1995: 101)

       b.   Hunzib
            αbu-l baba b-ox-on zəǧ-ár
            father-ᴇʀɢ bread ᴄʟs.ᴍʀᴋʀ-buy-ɢᴇʀ ᴀᴜx-ꜰᴜᴛ
            'father has probably bought bread'

5.1.5 *Lexical verb marks subject, TAM categories, Auxiliary verb marks negative*

The reverse of the pattern in 5.1.1 is also found in a small number of languages. Here the auxiliary verb encodes negative and the lexical verb encodes TAM categories as well as subject. This rare pattern is found in such Australian languages as Jingulu and in Ayoquesco Zapotec of Mexico.

In Jingulu, the negative modal *angkula* appears with a finite lexical verb. This construction is actually a pseudo-split formation with a (lexicalized) negative auxiliary.

(78) Jingulu
      angkula ngaja-nga-ju
      NEG(.CAP) see-1-PRES
      'I can't see'
      (Pensalfini 2003: 229)

In Ayoquesco Zapotec a formally quite different but structurally similar pattern is attested in which negative appears in a circumfixal form around the auxiliary verb followed by a mood-and subject-marked lexical verb.

(79) Ayoquesco Zapotec
      lo yo na-r-ak-deʔe Ø-zob-na
      face soil NEG-HAB-AUX-NEG POT-sit-1
      'on the ground I cannot sit'
      (MacLaury 1989: 138)

Finally, in the Australian language Ngengomeri, the negative auxiliary takes tense suffixes but subject prefixes occur with lexical verbs (which may themselves have fused auxiliary functional elements attached to them as in the following example).

(80) Ngengomeri
      kulťʸi nimpi ŋayi mimpe-ťʸe ŋa-rim-pawal ťawuku
      yesterday I NEG-PST 1-AUX:CONT-spear kangaroo
      'yesterday I did not spear any kangaroos'
      (Tryon 1974p: 261)

Insofar as the adverbial element -*GnaGa* operates as an auxiliary element and takes the negative prefix in Toba, a Mataco-Guaykuruan language, this language can also be said to have AVCs showing this marked inflectional pattern.

(81) Toba (Mataco-Guaykuruan; Argentina, Bolivia, Paraguay)
      sa-GnaGa r-keʔe
      NEG-AUX 3-eat
      'he did not yet eat'
      (Manelis Klein 2001: 38)

In Komi, a partially similar system is found with a negative element marking person but not number of the subject preceding a lexical verb marking the number of the subject.

(82)   Komi (Zyrian)
       oz mun-nï
       NEG:3 go-PL
       'they do not go'
       (Riese 1998: 272)

The Chibchan language Ika of Colombia has at least one AVC in which the auxiliaries mark distal time and lexical verbs mark subject and negative.

(83)   a.   Ika   b.   Ika
            nʌ-zei-ʔ nʌn-na   *kaʔtšon-uʔ-nʌn u-na*
            2-go-NEG AUX-DIST   find-NEG-AUX AUX-DIST
            'you did not go'   'he did not find it'
            (Frank 1990: 49)

5.1.6 *Lexical verb marks Subject, Auxiliary verb marks object*

The reverse of the pattern presented in 5.1.2 above is also found. Here the object is encoded on the auxiliary verb and the subject on the lexical verb. Such a marked construction is found in Bantu Akwa, Kugu Nganhcara, Tupi-Guaraní Cocama, and Mayan Jakaltek.

Auxiliaries precede lexical verbs and appear with object prefixes in Akwa; subject prefixes are found on the lexical verb.

(84)   a.   Akwa (Bantu, Niger-Congo; Congo)   b.   Akwa
            i-di ni-bo   *i-di ni-le*
            CLS.MRKR-AUX 1-see   CLS.MRKR-AUX I-say
            'I am seeing'   'I am saying'
            (Aksenova 1997: 26)

In Kugu Nganhcara, a curious 'possessor-raising' type of construction is found with an ablative/objective form on the negative 'auxiliary' and the accompanying lexical verb marked by a subject suffix.

(85)   Kugu Nganhcara
       ngaya kuʔan hingkurum kaʔim-ngkurum kala-ng
       1.NOM dog 2.ABL NEG-2ABL take-1
       'I didn't take your dog'
       (Smith and Johnson 2000: 400)

Tense auxiliaries with object prefixes are found following subject marked lexical verbs in the Tupi-Guaraní language Cocama.

(86) a. Cocama
      ái yúmi y-úi inú-cu
      he give it-IMM.PST them-to
      'he gave it to them'
      (Faust 1971: 78)

     b. Cocama
      Rafael-ári t-ikuáta n-úcu
      Rafael-ABOUT 1-advise 2-FUT
      'I will tell you about Rafael'
      (Faust 1971: 87)

In Jakaltek, a Mayan language of Guatemala, absolutive arguments are marked on aspectual auxiliaries which precede ergative marked lexical verbs. Semantically, these reflect an AVC with an inflectional pattern of the Cocama type, with lexical verbs encoding 'subject' and auxiliaries encoding 'object'. This pattern also occurs in imperatives, prohibitives, and exhortatives.

(87) a. Jakaltek (Jacaltec) (Mayan; Guatemala)[3]
      šk-ach   *w-ila*
      COMPL-ABS2   ERG1-see
      'I saw you'
      (Craig 1977: 60)

     b. Jakaltek
      tzet yuxin ch-in ha-teye
      why ASP-1ABS ERG2-laugh
      'why are you laughing at me'

     c. Jakaltek
      mach ch-in   ha-maka   cf.
      not   INCOMPL-ABS1 ERG2-hit
      'don't hit me'
      (Craig 1977: 71)

     d. Jakaltek
      mach   ch-ach   pisi
      not   INCOMPL-ABS2 sit
      'don't sit down'

---

[3] Note that the modal auxiliary stem-*u* ' may, can' either appears as the form taking the aspectual prefix *ch*-, in a construction with a dummy third person subject, with the person and number of the actual subject appearing on the lexical verb, or it appears in an unmarked form in a LEX-headed AVC, with the aspectual marker appearing with the absolutive suffix, and the lexical verb in an infinitive form, i.e. in a construction similar to the AUX-headed pattern.

(ii) Jakaltek
   a. *ch-u ha-kan beti'*
      ASP-(3)-MOD 2-stay here
      'you can/may stay here'
      (Craig 1977: 88)

   b. cf. *ch-ach u kan-oj beti'*   but c. **ch-ach u ha-kan beti'*
      ASP-ABS2 MOD stay-SFX here   ASP-ABS2 MOD 2-stay here
      'you can/may stay here'
      (Craig 1977: 88)

e.   Jakaltek
maj-ab ch-ach s-mak naj
NEG-EXHORT ASP-ABS2 ERG3-hit he
'would that he not hit you'
(Craig 1977: 73)

5.1.7 *Some other split patterns*

In a range of individual languages in my database there are various instances of unusual or anomalous split inflectional patterns attested in particular AVCs. For example, in the Tungusic language Evenki of Siberia, aspect and mood are usually marked on the lexical verb, but subject and tense are marked on the auxiliary. However, in some forms tense may be found on the lexical verb but evidentiality/status and subject on the auxiliary.

(88)   a.   Evenki
bu:-βki: bi-si-m
give-HAB AUX-PRES-1
'I give'
(Bulatova and Grenoble 1998: 35)

b.   Evenki
bu:-βki: bi-čə:-β
give-HAB AUX-PST-1
'I used to give'

c.   Evenki
si: əmə-məči:n bi-si-nni
you come-DEBIT AUX-PRES-2
'you should come'
(Bulatova and Grenoble 1998: 37)

d.   Evenki
nuŋan ti:ni-βə əmə-čə bi-rkə-n
s/he yesterday-ACC come-PST AUX-EVID-3
'he probably came yesterday'
(Bulatova and Grenoble 1999: 38)

Plurality may also be marked on the lexical verb in Evenki, as in the following example. This is thus reminiscent of agreement in gender/number with participles in AVCs in such well-known Indo-European languages as French and standard Italian. More relevantly, similar patterning is seen in Kolyma Yukaghir as well (Maslova 2003b).

(89) Evenki
      su: əmə-čə:-l bi-rkə-sun
      you.PL come-PST-PL AUX-EVID-2PL
      'you probably came'
      (Bulatova and Grenoble 1998: 39)

Other AVCs in Evenki also show noteworthy inflectional patterning. Examine in this regard the following two examples. Both consist of a subject-marked (and, where relevant, tense-marked) auxiliary verb and a lexical verb in the so-called conditional converb form. This latter element marks a subtype of adverbial subordination of a lexical verb (showing that the auxiliary should probably be considered the syntactic or phrasal head). It is difficult to classify this construction as AUX-headed as the (imperfective marking and) conditional marking appears to be an obligatory component in clauses of this type, or as split. I am perhaps arbitrarily assigning this to the split pattern. Note that a subject-marked auxiliary may appear in a position either preceding or following the lexical verb in this Evenki AVC.

(90) a. Evenki
          bi: toki:-βa ta:la-du: alba-m ala:t-ča-mi:
          I moose-ACC salt.lick-DAT AUX-1 wait-IMPF-CVI.COND
          'I couldn't wait for the moose at the salt lick'
          (Bulatova and Grenoble 1999: 39)

      b. Evenki
          huna:t ñami:-βa sir-mi: mulli-rə-n
          girl lead.deer-ACC milk-CVI.COND AUX-AOR-3
          'the girl was unable to milk the lead deer'
          (Bulatova and Grenoble 1999: 39)

In the probabilitive mood in the Turkic language Xakas, the tense is marked on the lexical verb, but person on the auxiliary.

(91) a. Xakas
          sin it-ken polar-ziŋ
          you do-PAST.I PROB-2
          'you probably did it'
          (Anderson 1998a: 60)

      b. Xakas
          min nime-e čobal-čatxan-im-ni sɪrer pil-če polar-zar
          I what-DAT be.sad-PRES.PRTCPL-1-ACC y'all know-PRES.I PROB-2
          'you probably know what I am sad about'
          (Anderson 1998a: 60)

Another modal construction in Turkic encoded through a split inflectional auxiliary verb construction is the archaic conditional formation in the nearly extinct Tofa language of east-central Siberia. In this moribund language, with currently fewer than forty speakers, a structurally old periphrastic conditional is marked by a lexical verb in the recent past (the -*DI*-past) for subject, followed by the archaic auxiliary *er*-with the conditional suffix. Note that this may occur in both realis and irrealis/counterfactual conditional clauses in Tofa.

(92) a. Tofa
    inda bol-di-m er-se sooda-ar men
    there be-REC.PST-1 AUX$_2$-COND say-FUT 1
    'when I will be there, I will say'
    (Rassadin 1978: 228)

    b. Tofa
    men al-di-m erse
    I take-REC.PST-1 AUX$_2$-COND
    'if I take'
    (Rassadin 1997: 379)

A small number of African languages possess split inflectional AVCs not discussed under the previous subheadings. One language, the Western Nilotic language Anywa, shows just such a formation. In Anywa, there is a range of auxiliaries expressing a wide variety of categories, including some specific Aktionsart functions as in the following example. The auxiliary marks tense, and the accompanying lexical verb is inflected for what is called the 'bi-valent itive', a directional- cum- valence marker characteristic of this language's grammatical system.

(93) Anywa (Western Nilotic, Nilo-Saharan; Sudan, Ethiopia)
    ŋùú ā-pút rèŋŋɔ́ báŋ ōjʌ̄k
    lion PST-AUX run:BITV to Ojak
    'the lion ran immediately to Ojak'
    (Reh 1996: 265)

In the isolate language Oksapmin of Papua New Guinea, subject is encoded within the lexical verb, while the auxiliary encodes both tense and the highly unusual but characteristically Oksapmin category of observer's viewpoint, related to notions of version and status/evidentiality. For more on this system, see Lawrence (1972).

(94)   Oksapmin
ko-ri-yaach haan yot pati hayaa-he
arrive-C-NONSEQ.DS.PL man two be.PRES.PL AUX-OBS.VWPT.IMM.PST
'. . . on arrival, two men were there'
(Lawrence 1972: 57)

Note the following multiply split formation in Ika, a Chibchan language of Colombia. Here the lexical verb occurs in the negative, the auxiliary encodes imperfective, and the future auxiliary takes an object prefix to mark subject. This is like a combination of certain patterns discussed above. More complex combinations of this sort are discussed below in section 5.2, in the context of split-doubled patterns of inflection in AVCs.

(95)   Ika
nik-uʔ nan-ʌn nʌ-ngua
work-NEG AUX-IMPF 1OBJ-FUT
'I will not work'
(Frank 1990: 48)

5.1.8   *TAM splits*

A last kind of split inflectional pattern in auxiliary verbs to be examined here is really more an issue of paradigmatic variation. In this, some TAM categories are marked on the lexical verb and some on the auxiliary verb.

One sub-pattern of this type consists of aspectual categories marked on the lexical verb and tense on the auxiliary. Such a pattern is characteristic of Chulym Turkic, for example, and is in line with GB-sympathetic views of the functional layering of the clause, with aspect closer to the V, and T as a high level operator (see Pollock 1989), a tendency embodied also in the placement of aspect categories in the nuclear layer of the clause but tense operators in the periphery in RRG models of grammar (Foley and Olson 1985, van Valin and La Polla 2000).

(96)   Chulym Turkic
män   kel-gelek   pol-ya-m
I   come-UNACMPL   AUX-PST-1
'I hadn't yet come'
(Dul'zon 1960:142)

All of the examples of this pattern in African languages in my database have a fused subject/TAM auxiliary form. This is found in Dagaare, a Gur language of Ghana and Burkina Faso, and probably independently in its distant sister language Dogon, of Mali and Burkina Faso.[4] Tense and subject are encoded within the auxiliary word and aspectual categories are encoded on the lexical verb in the following Dagaare and Dogon examples.

(97) a. Dagaare
          nangkpaana da teɛn-ɛ   la o gmɔrfɔ
          hunter PAST.AUX load-IMP fact his gun
          'Hunter was loading his gun'
          (Bodomo 1997: 80)

      b. Dagaare
          o da kul-ee la
          s/he PAST.AUX go.home-PRF.ITR FACT
          'she went home'
          (Bodomo 1997: 88)

      c. Dagaare
          o da kul-o la
          s/he PAST.AUX go.home-IMP FACT
          'she was going home'

      d. Dagaare
          o kul-o la
          s/he go.home-IMP FACT
          'she is going home'

(98) Dogon
      wo yanna jɛ-a wɔ
      he woman take-ANT AUX.PRES
      'he is married' (lit. 'has taken a wife')
      (Plungian 1995: 11)

In Papuan languages, split inflectional patterns between various TAM categories are also found. One such construction is found in Ambulas of the Ndu family of the Sepik-Ramu phylum. In Ambulas, future is found on the lexical verb and present on the auxiliary verb.

(99) Ambulas
      kéraa-n-o yé-ké dé y-o
      get-1PL-DS.FUT go-FUT 3SG AUX-PRES
      'we will get (it) and he will go'
      (Roberts 1997; Wilson 1980: 73–4)

TAM splits in auxiliary verb constructions in Australian languages are also attested. In Kugu Nganhcara, lexical verbs may encode subject and tense in portmanteau suffixes while auxiliary verbs mark future.

---

[4] Some diffusional or previous contact explanation is of course logically possible, but seems unlikely in this particular case.

(100)   Kugu Nganhcara
        thana puyu kana-pa uwa-yin
        3PL.NOM away PRF-FUT go-3PL.PRES
        'they are about to go away'
        (Smith and Johnson 2000: 440)

Auxiliaries in Arawakan Amuesha of Peru mark reportative, a clause-level operator, but subject, object and TAM categories are encoded in the lexical verb in a pseudo-split LEX-headed formation.

(101)   a.   Amuesha (Yanesha) (Preandine Arawakan; Peru)
             aw-oʔ aw-an-mʷ-e·t ent-o
             AUX-REPRT go-ABL-COMPL-3PL:RFLXV sky-LOC
             'then they went up to the sky'
             (Wise 1986: 605)

        b.   Amuesha
             aw-oʔ ot-a·n-eht
             AUX-REPRT say-OBJ-3PL
             'he said to them'
             (Wise 1986: 608)

Split inflection is also found in Mandan, a nearly extinct Siouan language. Here subject appears on the auxiliary and future and the adverbial 'celerative' ('quickly') on the lexical verb (102). In other Mandan formations, subjects appear on the lexical verb, and potential mood on the auxiliary (103).

(102)   Mandan (Siouan; USA)
        o-rut-rī:te ahka-kræ-oʔš
        FUT-eat-CEL CAP-PL-INDMA
        'they can eat it quickly'
        (Mixco 1997: 30)

(103)   a.   Mandan
             o-wa-ræ:h-ahka-kt-oʔš
             FUT-1ASG-go CAP-POT-INDMA
             'I might be able to go'
             (Mixco 1997: 33–4)

        b.   Mandan
             o-wa-ræ:h-ahka-rīk=oʔ-kt-oʔš
             FUT-1ASG-go CAP-MOD=AUX-POT-INDMA
             'I might be able to go'

5.1.9 *Pseudo-split patterns*

As has been alluded to both throughout this chapter and the volume generally, there are also instances of constructions in particular languages that have
the outward appearance of a split inflectional pattern, but which, owing to the
peculiarities of the morphophonology of the language, should properly be
classified as a different pattern. These I generally refer to as 'pseudo-split'
patterns. Such a pattern may arise from the use of a clitic, for example, that
happens to appear on an element in an AVC when its host could be any word
filling that structural position, rather than the element targeting the exact
verbal element. This is an important distinction to remember, because I have
argued that the degrees of bondedness between grammaticalized inflectional
markers and the elements they are realized on or within is orthogonal to the
grammaticalization of a particular construction. That is, clitic inflection
counts the same as a prefixal or suffixal realization of that functional element
to the overall grammaticalization of a construction; only the degree of
prosodic integrity of the elements involved is different. Pseudo-split patterns,
of course, can be reanalysed and yield true split patterns.

   One common pseudo-split pattern is the pseudo-split LEX-headed pattern.
Here an element appears to be found on the auxiliary, but it is not the
auxiliary *per se* that the element targets, just its structural (or functional)
position. Because, as I have asserted throughout this volume, auxiliary verb
constructions often derive from serial verb constructions, it should come as
no surprise that serialized constructions can give rise to pseudo-split patterns.

   Take a hypothetical example such as the following: a language has a
serialized construction consisting of an intransitive verb and transitive verb,
e.g. in a deictic serialized construction like 'go find' or something similar. The
two verbs probably share a subject argument and only the second (transitive)
verb takes object morphology. Subjects appear as second-position clitics and
appear after the first verb. This yields something similar to a common split
pattern in which the first (auxiliary) verb marks subject and the second
(lexical) verb marks object, assuming this is embedded within a system with
Aux V order. Just such a scenario is found in certain deictic serialized
constructions in the Salish language Klallam.

(104)   Klallam
        ʔənʔá=yaʔ=cn kʷʷənn-úŋə
        come=PST=1 see-2OBJ
        'I came to see you'
        (Montler 2003: 127)

It is easy to imagine situations where a pattern of this type would either be grammaticalized into a split AVC, not a SVC, or where the pattern became grammaticalized as a true split AVC, not a pseudo-pattern, as it currently is.

5.1.10 *Summary of split forms*

Split forms of inflection in auxiliary verb constructions consist of certain inflectional categories found only on the lexical verb and other ones only on the auxiliary. At least six such patterns are found across several unrelated languages from across the diffferent macro-regions. These are shown in Table 5.1, in roughly the relative order of frequency of their occurrence in the languages of the database.

Note that AUX-headed and split constructions can be similar to or develop into one another through the grammaticalization of a particular element from the AUX-headed construction on the lexical verb and extending its domain of application outside the original construction of which it was a member.

If the lexical verb belongs to the nuclear level of the phrase and the auxiliary to its core (or perhaps periphery), at least in origin, then one might consider the forms that encode the subject, negative/polarity, and tense categories of the construction in the auxiliary to mark agreement with the event described in the clause, not the inherent (argument, Aktionsart) properties of the verbal lexical element itself. As is often the case, the auxiliary verb appears to be the syntactic or phrasal/structural head in split inflectional auxiliary construction, marked by the auxiliary verb's tendency to appear in the structural position occupied by the predicate head and by the tendency for the lexical verb to appear in one of the marked forms of subordination discussed in Chapter 2.

TABLE 5.1. Summary of split inflection in AVCs

Lexical verb	Auxiliary verb	Languages
NEG	S/O, TAM	Buryat, Chukchi, Thulung, Remo, Baruya, Gimira, Lokono, etc.
OBJ	SUBJ	Kinnauri, Eleme, Gela, Kamor, Koasati, Canela-Krahô, etc.
TAM	S/O	Doyayo, Gurindji, Tairora, etc.
TAM_α	TAM_β	Chulym Turkic, Dagaare, Ambulas, Mandan, Amuesha, etc.
S/O	TAM	Ma'di, Halia, Coast Tsimshian, Retuarã, etc.
SUBJ	OBJ	Kugu Nganhcara, Cocama, Jakaltek, etc.
S/O, TAM	NEG	Ngengomeri, Ayoquesco Zapotec, Komi, Ika etc.

5.2 Split/doubled patterns

In addition to the split patterns discussed above, there is also a range of split/ doubled patterns found in the auxiliary verb constructions in the languages of the world in my database. There are three different formal subtypes of split/ doubled inflectional patterns, each with their own sub-patterns of varying frequency. This includes patterns that consist of certain categories marked on the auxiliary verb while others are found doubled on both the lexical verb and the auxiliary verb (5.2.1), patterns where lexical verbs occur with certain categories while other categories are marked on both components of the AVC (5.2.2), and lastly, patterns where some categories are marked on the lexical verb, some on the auxiliary verb, and some on both (5.2.3). As is the case with doubled inflection, by far the most common doubled category is subject in split/doubled patterns: languages with doubled subject inflection occur more than all other doubled inflectional categories combined.

5.2.1 *Categories marked on the Auxiliary verb plus doubled categories*

The first subtype of split/doubled pattern under investigation is the least common subtype. This is the pattern where certain categories are marked on the auxiliary verb and others are doubly-marked. This itself comes in a variety of subtypes, none found in that many total languages. One of the most frequently attested of such patterns (although in absolute terms still of relatively restricted occurrence) consists of TAM categories indexed on the auxiliary verb as well as subject, but subject alone on the lexical verb. That is, TAM categories are restricted to the auxiliary verb but subject is doubly marked.

In the Bantu language Hemba, there are several split/doubled inflectional patterns seen in AVCs. One such construction (105) consists of doubly marked subject, and tense on the auxiliary. The lexical verb appears in an indicative/ finite form with the final vowel -*a*.

(105) Hemba
    tw-a-li tu-tib-a muti
    1PL-TNS-AUX 1PL-cut-FV/IND tree
    'we were cutting the tree'
    (Aksenova 1997: 27)

This contrasts with another Hemba construction in which the lexical verb appears in a dependent modal formation, and the auxiliary verb appears in the indicative -*a* form. Thus, as with many sub-patterns of inflection seen in auxiliary verb constructions cross-linguistically, the lexical verb may be overtly marked as dependent (as the syntactic non-head) even when it has or shares inflectional head status.

(106)   Hemba
  tu-sw-a tu-tal-e
  1PL-AUX-IND 1PL-see-SBJ
  'we will see'
  (Aksenova 1997: 34)

Other Bantu languages show similar kinds of constructions. For example, in the Beya dialect of Lega and in Kimbu, the persistive/durative marker appears on the auxiliary, while subject is doubly marked. Note that in this formation in Kimbu but not Lega the lexical verb appears in a dependent (infinitive) form, despite bearing a marker of subject (however, as mentioned above in Chapter 4, Lega does have subject-encoding-yet-infinitive-marked lexical verbs in AVCs as well).

(107)   Kimbu (Bantu, F20; Tanzania)
  xʊ-xa≠h## xʊ-xʊ≠gula
  1PL-STILL-AUX 1PL-INF-buy
  'we are still buying'
  (Nurse 2003: 91)

(108)   Beya Lega (Bantu, D20; Democratic Republic of Congo)
  tu-kí[-li] tw-a-kangula ị swá
  1PL-PRSTV-AUX 1PL-ASP-clear field
  'we are still clearing the field'
  (Botne 2003: 442)

A slightly more complex AVC of this broad structural type is found in their sister language Sukuma. Here a tripartite formation is encountered in which the first auxiliary encodes past tense, the second auxiliary itself embodies the category persistive/durative ('still X-ing'), and all three components bear a subject marker.

(109)   Sukuma
  d-àà≠li dʊ́-tààlı dʊ̀-líí≠gʊ́là
  1PL-PST-AUX 1PL-STILL 1PL-DEP-buy
  'we were still buying'
  (Nurse 2003: 91)

The Siouan language Mandan shows a form similar to the first Hemba form above. In the following Mandan example, subject is doubly marked through the 'agentive' or 'A' series of agreement affixes, and the verb functioning as an auxiliary appears with various aspectual suffixes.

(110)　Mandan
　　　　i=ra-kxā ra-sīh-rīt-ka-oʔš
　　　　PV-A2-laugh A2-AUX-2PL-HAB-INDMA
　　　　'you are always laughing'
　　　　(Mixco 1997: 52)

The Tibeto-Burman language Dumi (Rai) of Nepal shows this same construction but within a univerbated complex.

(111)　Dumi (Rai)
　　　　roʔdi boʔo tsen-n-thə-n-t-a
　　　　Rai language teach-1>2-CONT-1>2-NPST-2/3
　　　　'I am teaching you Dumi'
　　　　(van Driem 1993: 200)

In the Australian languages Limilngan and Larrakia, lexical verbs appear in a future form with the desiderative auxiliary in a doubled-subject formation, with the TAM categories required by the specific semantics of the event encoded on the auxiliary verb. This is much like the modal subordination pattern of the lexical verb with doubled subject inflection just mentioned for Hemba. Note that in Larrakia there is a single marker of future, while this is doubled within the lexical verb form in Limilngan. In this particular instance, the split/doubled pattern probably arose from a verb/complement sequence.

(112)　Limilngan
　　　　i dak lambangi nga-n-a-yi nga-nami-ny
　　　　yes town 1-FUT-go-FUT 1-AUX-PST.RLS.PRF
　　　　'yes I wanted to go to town'
　　　　(Harvey 2001: 7)

(113)　Larrakia
　　　　ngana bordaan nga-gi-rri nga-gam gudlaa-gwa
　　　　I(MASC) town 1-FUT-go 1-AUX-PST.RLS.PRF yesterday-IV
　　　　'I wanted to go to town yesterday'
　　　　(Harvey 2001: 7)

In a very small number of cases the reverse of the Hemba pattern is found, with doubled TAM marking and a single marker of subject on the lexical verb. Such a pattern is found, for example, with the continuative in the Mayan language Tzutujil of Guatemala.

(114)   Tzutujil
        n-in-taxin-i   *n-bän*   *nuxäč'*
        CONT-1-AUX-CLASS   CONT-do   my.corn.harvest
        'I was in the process of harvesting my corn'
        (Butler and Butler 1977: 70)

An even more rare situation is seen in Tlapanec. Here subject is doubly encoded, once in the form of an affix on the lexical verb, once through a portmanteau subject acting on object affix (A>B) on the auxiliary. Subject is thus doubly marked, but object appears encoded only on the auxiliary verb (and then in the form of a portmanteau morph). The use of the auxiliary itself is triggered by the need to encode a 'dative' series argument (here 'me') that would not otherwise be morphologically realizable (Søen Wichmann, personal communication).

(115)   Tlapanec
        ni²mbo²ma:² ʃta³j-oʔ²
        2.forgot AUX-2>1
        'you forgot me'
        (Suarez 1983b: 124)

The near reverse of this situation is found in Ayacucho Quechua. Here the lexical verb occurs with a portmanteau subject>object morpheme (with the habitual nominalizer, i.e. a dependent marker), while the auxiliary marks object alone.

(116)   Ayacucho Quechua
        riku-su-q ka-nki
        see-3>2-HAB AUX-2
        'he used to see you'
        (Adelaar and Muysken 2004: 223)

In the Niger-Congo languages Ibibio and Ogbronuagom from Nigeria, auxiliaries mark negative and TAM categories (where relevant) and subject is doubly marked. These look like typical AUX-headed patterns but with doubled subject inflection.

(117)   a.   Ibibio
            Ùdèmé ítóoñóké ítáñ íkǫ̀ ǹté ábooñ
            Udeme CONCORD-start-NEG CONCORD-talk word like chief
            'Udeme has not started to talk like a chief'
            (Essien 1987: 154)

b. Ibibio
 Ùdèmé íkítóoñóké ítáñ íkɔ̀ ǹté áboöñ
 Udeme CONCORD-PST-start-NEG CONCORD-talk word like chief
 'Udeme did not start to talk like a chief'
 (Essien 1987: 154)

(118)   a. Ogbronuagum (Bukuma)   b. Ogbronuagum
      n-ń-née o-γíle   *ojí-ne ojí-kíle*
      1-FUT.NEG-AUX:1:NEG 1:NEG:ABIL-do   1PL:FUT.NEG-AUX 1PL-do
      'I can't do (it)   'we can't do it'
      (Kari 2000: 40–1) .

Note that according to Kari (2000: 27), the proclitic variant *o*-occurs as the
marker of first singular subject in only this specific AVC. It should thus either
be considered as marking a type of dependent subject, as in certain Nilotic
languages discussed in Chapter 4, or perhaps as not really a subject marker at
all but as some kind of dependent marker, the exact nature of which has yet to
be determined. All other first singular proclitics are homorganic syllabic
nasals, as seen in the first Ogbronuagom example above.

 The Siberian isolate language Nivkh has another rare pattern exhibited in
the inflection of certain AVCs. In capabilitive forms, the object is encoded via
a prefix on the auxiliary, while the finitizer is found on both the lexical verb
and the auxiliary verb.

(119)   Nivkh
    n'i kʰe ai-d j-ajm-d
    I sweep.net make-FIN OBJ-AUX-FIN
    'I can make a sweep net'
    (Gruzdeva 1998: 43)

In the Papuan language Ekari, also known as Kapauku, lexical verbs appear in
a nominalized (dependent) form with arguments encoded through possessive
morphology. The auxiliary verb in this construction also encodes the object,
as well as TAM categories. This thus has the appearance of split/doubled
construction, but a very rare type in which objects are doubly encoded.[5]

(120)   Ekari (Kapauku)
    okeiya ineebu nitipai
    they loss:1PL AUX:PST:1PL.OBJ
    'they defeated us'
    (Doble 1987: 66)

---

[5] It is also possible that this should be considered to be a variant of an AUX-headed formation.

In the Australian language Wambaya, as is typically the case in Australian languages, TAM categories are doubly encoded, while arguments are encoded in the auxiliary verb. Note that future comes in two allomorphs in the auxiliary in Wambaya *(-i/-u)* based on the person/number of the subject.

(121) a. Wambaya   b. Wambaya
           ngaj-ba nguyu-ny-u   *ngajbi ngiyi-ny-a*
           see-FUT 3[F]-2OBJ-FUT   see:NON.FUT 3[F]-2-NON.FUT
           'she will see you'   'she saw you' or 'she is looking at you'
           (Nordlinger 1998: 145)

The Daly (Australian) languages Maranunggu and Ami show yet another type of split/doubled pattern with unmarked lexical verbs. Subject person (and object where relevant) appears encoded only on the auxiliary, while subject number may be found both on the auxiliary and doubled in a (quasi-) free standing 'isolating' morph (see the first Ami form below in (123)). Future behaves in a similar fashion (122).

(122) Maranunggu
       tawar ŋa-wa-ni kalkal atu
       tree FUT-1-AUX climb FUT
       'I shall climb the tree'
       (Tryon 1974k: 145)

(123) a. Ami
           waŋka ka-ni-n'a pur nen'e yi
           corroboree NONFUT-AUX-3PL dance PL CA
           'they danced a corroboree'
           (Tryon 1974l: 165)

       b. Ami
           mit'irim ka-ya-ŋan' karat ayi
           dog NONFUT-AUX:NONFUT-1OBJ bite CA
           'the dog bit me'
           (Tryon 1974l: 171)

In some instances it is possible that the split/doubled pattern arose from a split inflectional pattern with split subject-marking, and innovated subject-marking on the component that was formerly lacking it, whether it was the auxiliary or the lexical verb, i.e. shifting to a doubled inflectional pattern with respect to subject-marking. Therefore, when dealing with doubled subject inflection, it is possible that split/doubled patterns could thus logically arise from both AUX-headed and split inflectional AVCs. LEX-headed formations can also derive from split/doubled formations through loss of the doubled category on the auxiliary.[6]

5.2.2 *Some categories on lexical verb, others doubled*

Also relatively infrequent but still attested in a range of unrelated languages, split/doubled patterns of inflection in AVCs are found in which certain categories are marked on the lexical verb and others appear on both the lexical verb and the auxiliary verb. As is typically the case, the doubled category marked on the auxiliary verb and the lexical verb in these types of construction is most commonly the relevant inflectional features of the subject.

A pattern familiar from the discussion of split inflection above is one in which the lexical verb encodes the object and both the lexical verb and the auxiliary verb encode the subject. Such a split/doubled inflectional pattern is found in such a diverse array of languages as Limbu, Manam, Kuot, Doyayo, Mbay, Lamba, and Pipil.

In Limbu the auxiliary follows the lexical verb and has portmanteau subject/tense suffixes. The lexical verb in some constructions appears in an adverbially subordinate gerund form, but encodes object and subject (at times in a portmanteau affix) as well.

(124) a. Limbu

sapt-u-ŋ-lɔ wa·-ʔɛ

write-3-1-GER   AUX-1

'I am writing (it)'

(van Driem 1987: 159)

b. Limbu

khɛnɛʔ i·t-nɛ-rɔ way-aŋ

you think-1>2-GER.PRES   AUX-1.PT

'I was thinking of you'

In Manam, subject prefixes appear on both the auxiliary and the lexical verb component of AVCs. Auxiliaries may either precede or follow lexical verbs in Manam, but with the same inflectional pattern. The lexical verb appears in a dependent or conjunctive form in some Manam AVCs of the split/doubled object/subject pattern.

---

[6] For example, in the Pipil progressive, there is variation between a LEX-headed and a split/doubled formation. Compare the following forms in this regard.

(iii) Pipil (Uto-Aztecan; El Salvador)

nemi ni-ta-kwa   *ni-nemi ni-k-chiwa luchár*

PROG 1-OBJ-eat   1-AUX 1-it-do fight

'I am eating'   'I am fighting'

(Campbell 1987: 272)   (Campbell 1985: 137)

(125)   a.   Manam
             tágo di-bóadu da-éneʔ-i
             NEG 3PL-CAP 3PL-climb-3OBJ
             'they can't climb it'
             (Lichtenberk 1983: 99)

        b.   Manam
             raʔána ʔu-em=emaʔ-i-be ʔu-sóaʔi
             what 2-REDPL=do-3OBJ-and 2-AUX
             'what are you doing?'
             (Lichtenberk 1983: 198)

Not all AVCs in Manam show this split/doubled inflectional pattern. For example, in the following form, there is a clausal subject form on the auxiliary, subject and object encoded on the lexical verb, and no subject agreement on the auxiliary. This probably reflects a grammaticalized form of an ambient serial construction to a split/doubled AVC.

(126)   Manam
        lása ne-mín-to ʔa-resabar-idi-a-la-na-tó-be i-éno
        enemy POSS-2PL-PAUC 2PL-provoke-3PL.OBJ-BEN-LIM-BF-PAUC-and
             3-AUX
        'you kept provoking your enemies'
        (Lichtenberk 1983: 201)

In Southeast Ambrym, a pattern is found in which subject is doubly marked and the lexical verb appears with a marker of transitivity indicating it requires an object. This is formally a diffferent system but reminiscent of the split/doubled patterning found in its sister language Manam.

(127)   Southeast Ambrym (Austronesian; Vanuatu)
        o-di o-lele-ni nœh
        2-AUX 2.have.premonition-TR what
        'what are you having a premonition of'
        (Crowley 2002d: 667)

Doyayo demonstrates relatively clearly how such split/doubled inflectional patterns develop from a serialized construction consisting of an intransitive V_1 verb that becomes an auxiliary and a V_2 verb that is transitive. In fact, in the following, the first AVC derives from a deictic serialized construction grammaticalized via the Motion event schema (see Chapter 7) to mark a TAM category and host a subject prefix, and this now functions as an auxiliary verb.

This pattern, consisting of an object found on the lexical verb with doubled subject inflection, is common in Doyayo.

(128) a. Doyayo
           be¹-re³ be¹-tɔ⁴-mɔ¹ gɔ ya⁴
           1-AUX 1-devour-2 ANA Q
           'would I then eat you up'
           (Wiering and Wiering 1994: 217)

      b. Doyayo
           hi¹-da³ hi¹-taa³-be¹
           3PL-POT 3PL-shoot-1
           'they might shoot me' or 'I might get shot'
           (Wiering and Wiering 1994: 222)

In example (129), the development of an {Intransitive Transitive} deictic serialized construction to a split/doubled (object/subject) AVC is clear, and the grammaticalization path is seen in multiple historical phases. The potential auxiliary derives from the lexical verb meaning 'come', which is used in deictic serialized constructions as well. Of course, these are intransitive verbs and only bear markers of subject, while the transitive lexical verb/second verb in the construction(s) bears markers of both the subject and its subcategorized object. A complex quasi-split/doubled AVC-cum-deictic SVC is the result.

(129) Doyayo
       hi¹-za¹ hi¹-zaa13 hi¹-lɔ-mɔ
       3PL-POT 3PL-come 3PL-bite-2
       'they might come bite you'
       (Wiering and Wiering 1994: 221)

In Barupu of the Skou phylum spoken in central coastal Papua, a similar formation is seen although here it remains in a deictic core-layer serialized construction.

(130) Barupu
       k-en-ute k-e-no-n-ya-mu
       R-1FEM-walk R-<1FEM>-go.along-ABOVE-2FEM
       'I walked past you (while you were lying down)'
       (Donohue 2003a: 122)

In Kuot, subject suffixes are found on both auxiliaries and the following lexical verb components in AVCs, object being encoded on the lexical verb. This yields the split/doubled object/subject pattern under discussion.

(131)   Kuot
   puo-ruŋ o-βas-tuŋ babam nuŋ
   AUX-1 3F.OBJ-read-1 leaf 2:GEN
   'I can read your book'
   (Chung and Chung 1996: 29)

The Central Sudanic language Mbay shows a typologically very similar formation. Subjects occur as prefixes and objects as suffixes in this language,
showing that neither relative order of auxiliary verb and lexical verb nor the
formal means of encoding the categories have any relevance to the distribution of these sub-patterns.

(132)   Mbay (Central Sudanic; Chad)
   m-ā m-él-á tàa lò-í
   1-AUX 1-tell-3 words of-2
   'I'll tell him what you said'
   (Keegan 1997: 116)

Pipil shows a similar pattern to the one found in Kuot, Mbay, and Doyayo.
Subjects are doubly marked (and this includes the prefixal and suffixal person
and number markers), while objects occur only on lexical verbs.

(133)   a.   Pipil   b.   Pipil
            n-yu ni-k-mana   *n-yu ni-mitsin-ilwitia*
            1-AUX 1-it-cook   1-AUX 1-2PL-show
            'I am going to cook it'   'I'm going to show you'
            (Campbell 1985: 137)

        c.   Pipil
            ti-yawi-t ti-k-ita-t
            1PL-AUX-PL 1PL-it-see-PL
            'let's see'
            (Campbell 1985: 138)

In a number of Bantu languages, a pattern is found where various TAM splits
or doubling occurs but subject is doubly marked and object only appears on
the lexical verb. One such language is Lamba, where past tense and subject are
both doubled, but object is found only on the lexical verb.

(134)   Lamba (M54)
   n-ā-li n-ā-mu-wona lēlo
   1-PST-AUX 1-PST-3-see today
   'I have seen him today'
   (Botne 1986: 307; Doke 1938: 305)

Split/doubled constructions are also attested where subject appears doubly marked on the auxiliary and lexical verb while the lexical verb alone encodes TAM categories. Such a pattern occurs in AVCs in Ciyao and Monumbo.[7]

(135) Ciyao
       ngá-li juvávééceeté soon! pélé-po tu-li tw-a-más-ilé góná
       not-AUX REL-3-speak-ASP again that.time 1PL-AUX 1PL-PST-finish-ASP
       sleep
       'no one spoke again, that was after we had gone to sleep'
       (Botne 1986: 305; Whiteley 1966: 214)

(136) a. Monumbo (Torricelli; Papua New Guinea)
           atap-ó ni
           bath:PRF-PRTCPL AUX
           'I have bathed'
           (Vormann and Scharfenberger 1914: 65)

       b. Monumbo
           mbotan[g]-etsé tsi
           cry:prf-PRTCPL:PL AUX:PL
           'they have cried'

In a small number of languages, there are individual auxiliary verb constructions where the lexical verb appears with markers of negation and TAM categories, while subjects are doubly marked. Such a formation is found in at least one AVC in the Colloquial Persian variety described by Ghomeshi (1999).[8]

(137) a. Colloquial Persian   b. Colloquial Persian
           man dâr-am mi-xun-am   *?man dâr-am ne-mi-xun-am*
           I AUX-1 CONT-sing-1   I AUX-1 NEG-CONT-sing-1
           'I am singing'   'right now I am not singing'
           (Ghomeshi 1999)

---

[7] In his study on complex verb forms in Bantu languages, Botne makes the assertion that the tense markers in the two different components of auxiliary verb constructions relate to internal event and external speech act temporal deixis, respectively. This argument, while interesting, and indeed maintained for certain Papuan languages as well by various researchers, does not appear to hold even for the data presented in Botne's study. For example, if the lexical verb takes tense, the auxiliary *-li* does not in Ciyao, at least on the basis of the examples given. Botne questions the motivation for two tense markers within a single construction anyway, but this is in part motivated by a lack of typological breadth available to him that the present investigation affords, and the consequent erroneous assumption that these types of constructions in Bantu can be motivated with the same formal apparatus and assumptions relevant for processes like English '*do*-support'.

[8] According to Ghomeshi (1999), the third example above is acceptable to some speakers in some contexts 'with constituent negation reading'.

Note that the negative form with negative on the auxiliary is apparently not acceptable for the speakers of Colloquial Persian who were the subject of her study.

(138)   Colloquial Persian
*man na-dâr-am mi-xun-am
I NEG-AUX-1 CONT-sing-1
'right now I am not singing'
(Ghomeshi 1999)

In the following Swahili form, the negative occurs in a circumfixal form (or a negative prefix and connegative suffix), and the auxiliary verb -*wa*, as a monosyllabic stem, takes the infinitive prefix as a meaningless prosodically motivated filler, or possibly is motivated as a residue of a formerly dependent form of the complement of the auxiliary verb *li-* in this complex AVC, now grammaticalized as a tense morpheme.

(139)   Swahili
tu-li-ku-wa ha-tu-fany-i
1PL-AUX>T/A-INF-AUX NEG-1PL-do-NEG
'we weren't doing anything'
(Aksenova 1997: 21)

In rare instances, one TAM category may only appear on the lexical verb while others may appear on both. One such language is Panyjima, an Australian language. Here present is doubly marked and progressive appears only on the lexical verb.[9]

(140)   Panyjima
ngunha marlpa panti-ku witi-pi-lku palya-ntharri-ngarli-ku yarnta-warntura-la
that man AUX-PRES play-PROG-PRES woman-PL-PL-ACC day-DISTRIB-LOC
'that man is flirting with (groups of) women each day'
(Dench 1991: 150)

A few other minor patterns of this broad structural type (where some categories are limited to the lexical verb while others appear on both lexical

---

[9] In Panyjima, as in Tofa (described in Ch. 2) and not infrequently attested in the languages of the world, *panti* 'sit', *karri* 'stand', and *ngarri* 'lie' all function as copula and/or auxiliary verbs (see Kuteva 2001). Of these in Panyjima, *panti* is the unmarked one, the other two being only partially semantically bleached. However, in the Paathapathu avoidance language *karri* is the unmarked auxiliary (Dench 1991: 184).

verbs and auxiliary verbs) deserve comment here. One such pattern comes from the Cushitic language Oromo of Wellega. Here lexical verbs mark negative but subject and tense are found in a doubled inflectional pattern. Fused forms derived from this pattern are characteristic of certain registers (141b), and these are usually realized as univerbated wholes (141b).

(141) a. Oromo of Wellegga   b. Oromo of Wellegga
           adeemte jirta   *adeemteerta* ~ *adeemteetta*
           GO.PRTCPL.2. AUX.2.PRES   GO.PRTCPL.2. AUX.2.PRES
           'you have gone'   'you have gone'
           (Gragg 1976: 189)

As categories are not encoded on the auxiliary verb exclusively on this subtype of the split/doubled inflectional pattern, they are unlikely to derive from purely AUX-headed formations if the AVC can be demonstrated to have arisen from another AVC directly, rather than a serialized or verb–complement construction. Split/doubled patterns of this particular type (some categories marked on the lexical verb, some on both the lexical verb and auxiliary verb) could, however, logically arise from both LEX-headed and split inflectional AVCs through the extension of the doubled category from the lexical verb to the auxiliary. Variation described in Chapter 7 may reflect this development.

5.2.3 *Some categories on Auxiliary verb, some on Lexical verb, some doubled*

The last subgroup of split/doubled AVC forms typically show TAM or negative categories marked on the auxiliary, subject doubly marked, and a range of different categories on the lexical verb. Such a pattern occurs in a variety of languages including Ös (Middle Chulym), a nearly extinct Turkic language of Siberia, Kemantney, an endangered Cushitic language of Ethiopia, various Bantu languages, Oceanic Vinmavis of Vanuatu, and Nambiquara of Brazil.

   One common realization of this subtype of the split/doubled inflectional pattern has subject doubly marked, while certain TAM categories appear only on the lexical verb and others only on the auxiliary. While these examples are mostly in line with a theory of a layered clause that has aspect as an inner operator (on the lexical verb) and tense as an outer operator (realized on the auxiliary), this is not always the case (cf. Oshikwanyama or Vinmavis).

(142) *Auxiliary Verb* = TAM_α *Lexical Verb* = TAM_β
       Doubled = Subj

Some forms of the past conditional in Ös exhibit a split-doubled inflectional pattern: Past tense is marked only on the lexical verb, conditional is found only on the auxiliary verb, while a second person subject is marked on both the lexical verb and the auxiliary verb.

(143)   Ös (Middle Chulym)
    Seŋ sur-ɣa-ŋ   *bol-za-ŋ,*   *men* *ayt-ɨr* *e:-di-m*
    you: GEN ask-PST-2 AUX-CON-2 I   say-FUT AUX/SBJ-REC.PST-1
    'if you had asked, I would have said'
    (Dul'zon 1960: 139)

In Kemantney, terminal generation speakers use constructions like the following, where subject is doubly marked, auxiliary verbs mark tense, and lexical verbs mark aspectual categories.

(144)   a. Kemantney (Qemant)
        ïntï was-y-ä-sab sïmb-ïy-eɣ^w
        you hear-2-IMPF-PROG AUX-2-PST
        'you were hearing'
        (Leyew 2003: 196)

     b. Kemantney
        annew was-ïn-ä-sab sïmb-ïn-eɣ^w
        we hear-PL-IMPF-PROG AUX-PL-PST
        'we were hearing'

In Bantu languages like Oshikwanyama of Namibia, auxiliaries and lexical verbs take subject markers, but lexical verbs and auxiliaries take different kinds of tense (or tense/aspect) markers.

(145)   Oshikwanyama (Bantu, Niger-Congo; Namibia)
    onda li nda kongele
    1:PST AUX 1 hunt:REM.PST
    'I had been hunting'
    (Zimmermann and Hasheela 1998: 123)

In its sister language Shambala of Tanzania, verbs appear with subject markers but lexical verbs appear in the modal-dependent 'subjunctive' form.

(146)   Shambala
    ní-zah-ti ni-kund-e
    1-TNS-AUX 1-hope-SBJ
    'I already hoped'
    (Aksenova 1997: 34)

Forms similar to this Shambala construction are found in the Bantu language Xhosa. Here the pluperfect formation alternates between a split/doubled inflectional AVC and a fused complex historically derived from this, but in which the auxiliary has been eroded to zero in the univerbation process, leaving only the tense and (doubled) subject prefix.

(147)   Xhosa (Bantu; South Africa)

    i.   *nd-a-ye*   *ndi-theth-ile*   ii.   *nd-a-ndi-theth-ile*

       1SG-PLUP-AUX   1SG-speak-PRF   1SG-PLUP-1SG-speak-PRF

      'I had spoken (long ago)'   'I had spoken (long ago)'

      (Heine 1993: 108)

In Vinmavis, subject is doubly marked, but the means of encoding this varies among different constructions in the language. This may reflect their degree of grammaticalization or may simply reflect their origin in different constructions, viz. a verb–complement vs. serialized construction. Both constructions would then be equally grammaticalized insofar as they both express functional categories or operational semantics and constitute split/doubled AVCs, just in two slightly formally different ways, one with a dependent subject marker, one without it.   It is unknown at present whether any residual syntactic properties may be associated with this residual formal contrast.

(148)   a.   Vinmavis (Austronesian; Vanuatu)   b.   Vinmavis

        no-rogulel nib^w i-yel   *i-tox i-matur*

        1.NONFUT-AUX 1FUT-sing   3NON.FUT-HAB 3-sleep

        'I can sing'   'he sleeps'

        (Crowley 2002c: 645)

Nambiquara, a group of dialects or closely related languages not demonstrably related to any other language group spoken in Mato Grosso and Rondônia states in Brazil, shows another interesting twist on this type of split/doubled inflectional formation. Note that coordinated lexical verbs appear only with subject marking on the rightmost conjunct, suggesting a kind of phrasal target for the subject required of the lexical verb component in a split/doubled inflectional AVC.

(149)   Nambiquara (isolate (Nambiquaran); Brazil)

    wã²-la² wa²hĩ³l-ĩ² wã²-ho³ʔ-ĩ²-na¹-tũ¹-ʔã¹

    clothes wash-COORD bathe-COORD-1-FUT-IMPRFV.THOUGHT 1-REC.

    INTERNAL-PRFV

    'I intend to wash my clothes and to take a bath'

    (Lowe 1999: 288)

Another split/doubled inflectional pattern found in a small number of unrelated languages is one in which auxiliary verbs encode TAM categories, lexical verbs mark object, and subject is doubly marked. A formation of this type is found in the 'quasi-auxiliary' verb–complement sequence in Arawakan Baure, offering an example of one typical path of development for a verb/verb complement sequence that has become grammaticalized as a split/doubled AVC.

(150)   Baure (Arawakan; Bolivia)
        íta-ro-kíʔinow ro-nikó-ni
        PROG-3M-want 3M-cut.with-1
        'he is wanting to eat me'
        (Baptista and Wallin 1967: 41)

Within an auxiliary verb construction, a similar formation is found in Luganda, a Bantu language of Uganda. In the following formation, the verb in the first clause has both a subject and an object prefix, while the second clause consists of two verbs and has two subject-markers, but only the class-marker for the object on the lexical verb. Note also that the subject of the auxiliary may have originally been the clause of the lexical verb itself.

(151)   Luganda
        bwe n-na-mu-laba y-a-li a-lu-soggo-ze
        when 1-PST-HER-see 3-PST-AUX 3-CLS.MRKR-dig.up-COMPL
        'when I saw her, she had dug them up'
        (Botne 1986: 310)

Similar to the pattern discussed in 5.1.1 with negative marked lexical verbs and TAM and subject categories on the auxiliary verb, an analogous pattern with doubled subject marking is found in the Papuan language Nasioi. This is schematized in (152) and exemplified in (153).

(152)   *Auxiliary Verb* = TAM *Lexical Verb* = NEG *Doubled* = Subj

(153)   a. Nasioi   b. Nasioi
            oo-amp-id-i oʔno-di-n   *oo-amp-aʔ oʔno-n*
            see-1-PL-while/neutral AUX.1-PL-PST   see-1-NEG AUX.1-TEMP
            'we were watching it'   'I don't see it'
            (Hurd and Hurd 1970: 73)   (Hurd and Hurd 1970: 74)

A similar pattern was found in the extinct isolate language Betoi, formerly spoken in Venezuela.

(154) a. Betoi[†] (isolate)   b. Betoi[†]
      r-u-omé ma-rr-ú   *r-u-omé ma-rr-u-mai*
      1-be-NEG PST-1-AUX   1-be-NEG PST-1-AUX-1PL
      'I was not'   'we were not'
      (Zamponi 2003: 34)

    c. Betoi[†]
      r-ij-omé r-u-cá
      1-die-NEG 1-AUX-IND
      'I do not die'

    d. Betoi[†]   e. Betoi[†]
      j-u-omé j-u-jui-daódda   *u-omé u-bi-daódda*
      2-be-NEG 2-AUX-2PL-COND be-NEG AUX-3PL-COND
      'if you were not'   'if they were not'

In at least one AVC in Betoi, on the other hand, a quasi-doubled pattern was seen, with subject doubly marked and a negative auxiliary. Note that the lexical verb in this Betoi form shows adjectival or nominal gender/number agreement as well.

(155) Betoi[†]
      r-iju-oi-(rrú) ref-oi-rru
      1-be.dead-SG:M-1 NEG:AUX-SG-1SG
      'I am not dead'
      (Zamponi 2003: 34)

The reverse situation is found in one Evenki construction, where the 'auxiliary' is the negative copula and the lexical verb 'be' takes the past tense suffix, both encoding the number of the subject as well.

(156) Evenki
      bira-du: kuŋaka:-r a:či-r bi-čə:-tin
      river-DAT child-PL NEG-PL be-PST-PL
      the children were not at the river' (?? "no children were at the river")
      (Bulatova and Grenoble 1999: 17)

In a small number of Bantu languages, some negatives are found only on the auxiliary verb, some only on the lexical verb, while subject remains doubly marked. Setswana and Kinyarwanda are two such languages displaying this pattern; however, two formally different systems are involved. In Setswana, the negative *ga-* occurs before subject prefixes and on the auxiliary, while negative *-sa-* occurs after the subject prefix on the lexical verb.[10]

---

[10] It seems that Setswana *-sa-*may have been a negative (copular) verb of some kind originally.

(157) a. Setswana (Bantu; Botswana)   b.   Setswana
           ga-ke-aka ka-rêka   *ga-o-aka wa-rêka*
           NEG-1-AUX 1-buy   NEG-2-AUX 2-buy
           'I did not buy'   'you did not buy'
           (Cole 1955: 250)

       c. Setswana
           ke-nê ke-sa-rêke
           1-AUX 1-NEG-buy
           'I was not buying'
           (Cole 1955: 251)

In Kinyarwanda, the same meaning can be conveyed either by an initial *nti-*on the auxiliary before subject prefixes or a subordinate/dependent negative *-da-* appearing in post-subject position on the lexical verb. This is typologically similar to the variation seen in different Setswana paradigms, but here manifested as constructional variation in one and the same functional formation.

(158) a. Kinyarwanda
           abagabo nti-bá-záa-ba bâ-som-a
           men NEG-3PL-FUT-AUX 3PL-read-ASP
           'the men won't be reading'
           (Kimenyi 1980:10)

       b. Kinyarwanda
           abagabo ba-zaa-ba bâ-da-som-a
           men 3PL-FUT-AUX 3PL-NEG.SUBORD-read-ASP
           (Kimenyi 1980:10)

Other patterns are also found in which the doubled category is not the subject, but mainly only in isolated instances in individual languages in my database. These include the following form from Makushí, where iterative is marked twice, tense on the auxiliary, and subject on the lexical verb.

(159) Makushí
       atti-piti e'-piti-'pi
       3.go-ITER AUX-ITER-PAST
       'he used to go (repeatedly)'
       (Abbott 1991: 129)

Ainu has an unusual pattern where the number of the object is doubly-marked, while the lexical verb alone encodes the subject and the auxiliary aspect.

(160)   Ainu, Sakhalin dialect (isolate; Russia/Japan; possibly extinct)
        ku-konte-hci hemaka-hci
        1-give-PL PERF-PL
        'I have given them'
        (Hattori 1967: 78)

Another atypical pattern of split/doubled inflection is seen in the following
AVC in Tobelo, a West Papuan language of the Northern Halmahera group
spoken in Indonesia. Here, subject appears on the lexical verb and object is
doubled, with perfective marked only on the auxiliary. Most probably this
arose from a switch subject serialized construction in which the object of V_1 is
the subject of V_2 (meaning something like 'I did it; it is finished'). When
grammaticalized as an AVC, this constituted a split/doubled inflectional
pattern. It may also reflect an ambient serialization form as well—a structure
not infrequently underlying formations marking completed action.

(161)   Tobelo
        t-a-diai i-boto-oka
        1-3-do 3-AUX-PRF
        'I have done it'
        (Holton 2003: 63)

Note also that there is a similar pattern in Warembori, a member of the
tiny Lower Mamberamo stock, perhaps genetically isolated or a divergent
member of the West Papuan phylum spoken in the Papua region of Indonesia.
According to the analysis of Donohue (1999), periphrastic causative AVCs
have subject (causer) and object (causee) marking on the causativizing
verb, the latter of which is marked as the subject of the causativized verb.
The subject of the causativized verb in the complement clause is copied
into the causativizing verb as its object. This is like a switch subject serialization construction yielding an AVC with a transitive auxiliary and, in this
structure, an intransitive lexical verb, as well as an indicative marker on the
lexical verb.

   Because in Tobelo the first (=lexical) verb is the transitive form and in
Warembori it is the auxiliary, this yields the various attested split/doubled
situations, with the location of the object marker varying according to which
verb in the structure was (originally) transitive, whether the auxiliary or the
lexical verb, in the resulting AVC.

(162) a. Warembori   b. Warembori
           e-van-i y-ande-o   *w-or-i i-nan-do*
           1-make-3 3-laugh-IND   2-give-3 3-sleep-IND
           'I made her laugh'   'you put her to sleep'
           (Donohue 1999: 35)   (Donohue 1999: 36)

In Lango, a Nilotic language of Uganda, another unusual split/doubled pattern is seen. In one AVC, auxiliary verbs mark habitual and progressive aspect and lexical verbs encode perfect as well as subject. Like the above two formations, object appears to be doubly encoded due to the residual serialized structure of the AVC, but of an entirely different sort. Here the auxiliary verb subject is the same as the lexical verb object, perhaps reflecting a switch subject serialization construction. It is possible that rather than a split/doubled formation, these should be considered dummy clausal subject markers, and that these Lango forms are actually pseudo-split LEX-headed formations.

(163) a. Lango   b. Lango
           ònwòŋò lócɔ̀ àcɛ̀m   *án ònwòŋò àbwôtɛ́*
           3:AUX:PERF man 3:eat:PROG   I 3:AUX:PERF 1:deceive:PERF:3
           'a man was eating'   'I had deceived him'
           (Noonan 1992: 138)

In the Bantu language Nkore-Kiga a number of interesting split/doubled inflectional AVCs are found. None of them are similar to Lango's, however, but merely individual realizations of common Bantu tendencies in inflection in AVCs. Many TAM categories are marked on the auxiliary verb (e.g. remote past, future), while lexical verbs encode object person/number/class as well as the present continuous. Subject inflection appears doubly marked.

(164) a. Nkore-Kiga (Bantu; Uganda) b. Nkore-Kiga
           a-ka-banza y-aa-rw-igura   *a-rya-banza n-aa-yeshongora*
           3M-RP-AUX 3M-TP-it-open   3M-RF-AUX PC-3M-sing.PRTCPL
           'he first opened it'   'first he will sing'
           (Taylor 1985: 36)

       c. Nkore-Kiga   d. Nkore-Kiga
           n-ka-ba n-teera enanga   *n-ka-ba ni-n-teera enanga*
           1-RP-AUX 1-play organ   1-RP-AUX PC-1-play organ
           'I used to play the organ'   'I was playing the organ'
           (Taylor 1985: 157)

e. Nkore-Kiga
m-baire ni-n-shoma
1-AUX.M PC-1-read
'I have been reading'
(Taylor 1985: 161–2)

f. Nkore-Kiga
ku o-raa-be n-oo-za-yo ki-mu-gambire
if 2-FUT-AUX PC-2-go-there it-him-tell
'when you go there, tell him so'

g. Nkore-Kiga
n-tuura ni-n-za-yo
1-AUX PC-1-go-there
'I always go there'
(Taylor 1985: 186)

h. Nkore-Kiga
a-guma n-aa-sheka
3M-AUX PC-3M-laugh
'he is constantly laughing'

Note that in the various split/doubled constructions in Nkore Kiga either the auxiliary verb or the lexical verb may appear in a marked dependent form, for example the -LOC on the auxiliary in (165a) and the participial form of the lexical verb in (165c).

(165) a. Nkore-Kiga
n-aa-ruga-ho n-aa-mu-shanga
1-TP-AUX-LOC 1-TP-3M.OBJ-find
'I eventually found him'
(Taylor 1985: 186)

b. Nkore-Kiga
a-ka-banza y-aa-rw-igura
3M-RP-AUX 3M-TP-it-open
'he first opened it'
(Taylor 1985: 36)

c. Nkore-Kiga
a-rya-banza n-aa-yeshongora
3M-RF-AUX PC-3M-sing.PRTCPL
'first he will sing'

Micro-variation in split/doubled marking in a small number of related languages may be seen in Dravidian. At least three different patterns of split/doubled inflection may be seen in various AVCs across the family. One pattern, found in such central Dravidian languages as Old Telugu, Gondi, and Muria Gondi, consists of a negative and subject marked lexical verb followed by a subject and TAM-marked auxiliary verb.

(166) Old Telugu
ceppanu aytini
say-NEG-1 AUX-PAST-1
'I did not say'
(Steever 1988: 60)

(167) Muria Gondi
punnon atan
know-NEG-1 AUX-PFV-1
'I didn't know'
(Steever 1997: 290–1)

(168)   Gondi
    nanna panj'on ay'enan
    I be.satiated-NEG-1 AUX-SBJ-1
    'I would not get satiated'

In the Parji language, some TAM categories are found on the lexical verb and others on the auxiliary verb, but both bear subject suffixes.

(169)   Parji
    nil-t-en mē-d-an
    stand-PST-1 AUX-NPST-1
    'I am standing, have stood up'
    (Steever 1988: 89)

In Old Tamil, the negative future was marked through the combination of a lexical verb in the future followed by a negative auxiliary verb, each with their own marker of subject.

(170)   Old Tamil
    cel-v-ēm all-ēm
    go-FUT-1PL NEG-1PL
    'we will not go'
    (Steever 1988: 42)

All of these are considered to be historically serial verb constructions by Steever (1988). This core-level serialization is overtly manifested through the doubled subject inflection seen across these examples. However, it is clear that these formations are in no way analogous, despite covering closely related languages and roughly similar verbal categories. The central Dravidian forms above are very similar to the split inflectional pattern presented in 5.1.1, only with doubled subject-marking on the lexical verb in addition to the auxiliary verb. The Parji form exhibits the pattern presented in 5.2.3 found in a number of unrelated languages. Old Tamil, on the other hand, shows a negative auxiliary verb and the uncommon pattern of doubled subject-marking and TAM categories on the lexical verb also seen in the Torricelli-phylum language Monumbo and in Bantu Ciyao.

One language that deserves special mention with respect to the split/ doubled pattern of inflection is the Arawakan language Warekena. There are multiple splits and multiple patterns of inflection seen in verb–verb combinations in Warekena. These constructions occupy various stages on the serial verb construction to auxiliary verb construction continuum, but are all labelled 'serial' by Aikhenvald in her (1998) description of the language from which the following forms are taken.

Warekena makes use of a negative circumfix or two-part negative construction. It is possible that this arose through either a *pas* construction of the French type (given its mobile nature described partially below) or a connegative formation characteristic of the Uralic languages among others; for more on Warekena see Aikhenvald (1998).

One set of split/doubled patterns seen in Warekena consists of a negative auxiliary verb, a lexical verb encoding object, and doubly marked subject. In examples (a) and (b), the negative circumfix *ya-...-pia* surrounds the auxiliary verb.

(171)   a.   Warekena (Arawakan; Venezuela, Brazil)
             ya-wa-ʃa-pia wa-pala
             NEG-1PL-AUX-NEG 1PL-run
             'we will not run (now)'
             (Aikhenvald 1998: 388)

        b.   Warekena
             ya-pi-be-pia pi-da-yu
             NEG-2-CAP-NEG 2-see-3SG.FEM
             'you cannot see her'

Complications arise when other auxiliary-type elements in Warekena are considered. The perfective element *-mia* may appear as a suffix or root serialized formation with *-inapa* 'finish', but in negative formations with *-be-*, the *ya*-prefix of the negative occurs before *-mia*, unmarked for subject, followed by subject-marked *-be* (and subject-marked lexical verb), but the suffixal element *-pia* appears after the second auxiliary element. The lexical verb appears with the non-accomplished suffix, which in this example marks a kind of irrealis state common with negatives.

(172)   a.   Warekena
             n-inapa-mia-hã   ni-buʃuka-hã
             3PL-FINISH-PERF-PAUS 3PL-cut-PAUS
             'they finished cutting (wood)'
             (Aikhenvald 1998: 387)

        b.   Warekena
             ya-mia wa-be-pia wa-wenita-wa
             NEG-PERF 1PL-CAP.AUX-NEG 1PL-buy-NONACC
             'we cannot buy anything'
             (Aikhenvald 1998: 388)

A further subset of patterns all show perfect marked on the auxiliary (although this element has 'quasi-auxiliary' status itself, already briefly alluded to above) but with subject doubly marked, albeit with different kinds of patterns seen with the lexical verb and other additional categories on the auxiliary. Object encoding seems to only occur with lexical verbs—a pattern attested numerous times throughout this chapter in split and split/doubled inflectional patterns from a wide range of languages. The special non-accomplished suffix and the pausal form may appear on either the lexical verb or the auxiliary verb. The pausal form appears doubly marked in at least one form, but the NON-ACC seems to never occur on both the lexical verb and the auxiliary verb in the same AVC in Warekena. However, it may be the case that the formation with doubled pausal marking reflects its status somewhere earlier in the SVC > AVC continuum in Warekena, as its serialized nature/origin is obvious.[11]

(173) a. Warekena
       yaliwa p-inapa-mia p-e-ni pi-ʃiani-pe
       now 2-finish-PERF 2-eat-3PL 2-child-PL
       'now you have completely finished eating your kids'
       (Aikhenvald 1998: 392) SVC>AVC

       b. Warekena
       wa ni-tʃia-mia-wa n-e-hē
       then 3PL-AUX-PERF-NONACC 3PL-eat-PAUS
       'then they were eating . . .'
       AVC

       c. Warekena
       wa-ʃa wa-dabana-ta wa-tʃina-li
       1PL-AUX 1PL-start-CAUS 1PL-tell-REL
       'let's start our story'
       (Aikhenvald 1998: 390) AVC

       d. Warekena
       n-inapa-mia ni-yeluta-wa
       3PL-FINISH-PERF 3PL-clear-NONACC
       'they finished making a clearing'
       SVC>AVC

Prohibitives with auxiliaries show at least two split/doubled inflectional patterns in Warekena. In the first such formation, the lexical verb occurs

---

[11] Similar forms are seen in Oceanic Paamese (Crowley 1987, 2002e).

with the negative suffix *-pia* and both lexical verb and auxiliary verb occur with subject prefixes. In the second form, negative appears split between the two components, the prefix *ya-*appearing on the auxiliary and the suffix on the lexical verb. Both verbal components encode subject while object suffixes appear only with the lexical verb.

(174) a. Warekena   b. Warekena
       pi-da pi-kulua-pia   *ya-pi-da p-e-pia-na*
       2-AUX 2-drink-NEG   NEG-2-AUX 2-eat-NEG-1
       'don't drink (it)'   'don't eat me'
       (Aikhenvald 1998: 394) AVC   AVC

The Niger-Congo language Eleme also deserves special mention in any discussion of split and split/doubled inflectional patterns in AVCs. Eleme possesses a rich and diverse range of inflectional sub-patterns and paradigmatic splits, seen both in synchronically simplex verb forms and in AVCs (cf. also Bond 2006). I briefly summarize some of these here. As alluded to above, there are also fused forms resulting from these AVCs in the Eleme TAM system as well as variation among different patterns with the same construction, which are discussed more in Chapters 6 and 7.

     In two split/doubled paradigms in Eleme, the auxiliary verb appears with a subject person prefix and a suffix marking person and number, followed by an enclitic particle that is obligatory in these formations. The lexical verb appears with a person/number suffix but with the dependent prefix.

(175) Eleme
       ò-do-î -rû   *e-gbòi-î*   *etʃû*
       2-AUX.PRES-2PL-PRTCL   DEP-stitch-2PL   clothes
       'you are stitching clothes'
       (Anderson and Bond 2004-ms)

(176) Eleme
       ò-bo-î-rû   *e-ma:-î*   *àdádʒi*   *ɔnɛnɛ*
       2-AUX-2PL-PRTCL   DEP-bring-2PL   Adaji   gift
       'you should bring Adaji a gift'
       (Anderson and Bond 2004-MS)

Other AVCs in Eleme show variation between the AUX-headed and the split/doubled inflectional pattern. Specifically, third plural is marked on the auxiliary verb alone, while second plural is marked on both the lexical verb and the auxiliary verb.

(177) a. Eleme
    ò-bo-î-rú   e-ma:-î   àdádʒi   ɔnɛnɛ
    2-AUX-2PL-PRTCL DEP-bring-2PL Adaji   gift
    'you should bring Adaji a gift'
    (Anderson and Bond, to appear)

    b. Eleme
    è-bo-rî -rú   e-ma: àdádʒi   ɔnɛnɛ
    3-AUX-3PL-PRTCL DEP-bring Adaji   gift
    'they should bring Adaji a gift'
    (Anderson and Bond, to appear)

In Eleme, a split/doubled pattern is also found in serial constructions where second plural subject appears on both elements but object only on the latter verb. Note that doubled subject-marking does not apply to other persons, e.g. third plural. This is without question structurally analogous to the source for the auxiliary constructions of a formally similar type in Eleme; only the cause of the original split between singly marked third plural and doubly marked second plural remains opaque. Data from related languages shed no light on this development.

(178) a. Eleme
    òbàù   tʃú-î   ńsã   no   ne-i-e
    2PL   take-2PL book DEM give-2PL-3SG
    'you delivered the books to him'
    (Anderson and Bond, to appear)

    b. Eleme
    àbà   tʃú-rĩ   ńsã   no   ne:
    3PL   take-3PL book DEM give.3SG
    'they delivered the books to him'
    (Anderson and Bond, to appear)

As mentioned above, the intransitive + transitive serialization channel is the most common source of subject/object split and split/doubled inflectional patterns in AVCs.

One final example of a split/doubled inflectional pattern in Eleme AVCs comes from the following form, where the negative verb appears initially and gets the third plural suffix, which is in turn followed by a subject-marked form of the copula, itself followed by a dependent marked form of the lexical verb bearing the second plural suffix. Curiously, subject is doubly marked for third and second plural in this Eleme formation. Only the locus of inflection differs for each: for second plural, it is found (in different allomorphs) in the copular auxiliary and the lexical verb (which appears in an overtly dependent marked form), while third plural appears with the clause-initial negative auxiliary and the copular auxiliary, but not on the lexical verb.

(179) a. Eleme

    ndʒɛsɛ   *b-òbà*   *e-bò-e-î*   *odʒîdʒî* *ɲo*
    must.NEG   COP-2PL   DEP-tie-PRTCL-2PL rope   DEM
    'you must not tie the rope'
    (Anderson and Bond 2004)

    b. Eleme

    ndʒɛsɛ-rî   *b-àbà*   *e-bò-e*   *odʒîdʒî* *ɲo*
    must.NEG-3PL COP-3PL   DEP-tie-PRTCL   rope   DEM
    'they must not tie the rope'
    (Anderson and Bond 2004-ms)

A number of Bantu languages seem to exhibit doubled forms in certain AVCs, and perhaps must be considered as such when the lexical verb is intransitive, but are actually and clearly split/doubled in nature when object agreement is a factor, as with transitive lexical verbs. This is also true of detransitivized transitives as well. In fact, many Bantu languages exhibit variation of this type.

A split/doubled pattern with tense on the auxiliary, subject doubly marked, and lexical verb with or lacking an object prefix in detransitivized vs. fully transitive formations is seen in the following examples from Luganda.

(180) a. Luganda (Bantu, Niger-Congo; Uganda)

    bwe n-na-mu-laba y-a-li a-soggo-la lumonde
    when 1-PST-HER-see 3-PST-AUX 3-dig.up-ST.EXT:FV potatoes
    'when I saw her, she was digging up potatoes'
    (Botne 1986: 310)

    b. Luganda

    bwe n-na-mu-laba y-a-li a-lu-soggo-ze
    when 1-PST-HER-see 3-PST-AUX 3-CLS.MRKR-dig.up-COMPL
    'when I saw her, she had dug them up'

Cf. true intransitive:

    c. Luganda

    tu-ba-ye tu-kol-a
    1PL-TNS-AUX 1PL-work-FV
    'we were working'
    (Aksenova 1997: 19)

Lastly, portmanteau morphs may yield unusual split/doubled constructions in the East New Guinea Highlands language Bena-Bena. The lexical verb occurs with the object and the subject is encoded by the auxiliary in portmanteau subject > object form; tense is also marked on the auxiliary. Negative appears on the auxiliary verb in the examples below, but may also appear on the lexical verb in other Bena Bena AVCs.

(181) a. Bena Bena   b. Bena Bena
           ko-loka me-halube   *nu-nu me-kibo*
           2-ask NEG-1[>2]:FUT:AUX   1-hug NEG-2:AUX:PROHIB
           'I will not ask you'   'don't hug me'
           (Young 1964: 82)

       c. Bena Bena   d. Bena Bena   e. Bena Bena
           ko-loka halube   *no-loka halane*   *ke-be galube*
           2-ask 1[>2]:FUT:AUX 1-ask 2>1:FUT:AUX   2-see 1>2:FUT:AUX
           'I will ask you'   'you will ask me'   'I will see you'
           (Young 1964: 81–2)

5.2.4 *Summary of split/doubled patterns*

Within the different super-templates for sub-patterns of split/doubled paradigms, the three-way split occurs in nearly half the examples of the languages in the database, with the remaining half divided roughly 30/20 between the lexical verb + doubled and the auxiliary verb + doubled super-templates for split/doubled inflectional patterns in AVCs. Some common sub-patterns of these super-templates are offered in Table 5.2.

5.3 Dependency within split and split/doubled patterns

As with the other patterns described in previous chapters, split and split/doubled patterns of inflection also occur with overt markers of dependency on the lexical verb. This manifests itself in virtually the full range of marked dependency formations presented in Chapter 2. Specifically, adverbial (converb, gerund) or generalized dependent/subordinate marking is common in Eurasian languages showing these inflectional patterns in auxiliary verb constructions (Turkic, Tibeto-Burman) as well as in Angan languages of Papua New Guinea, while same-subject marking is found in certain North American and Papuan languages and languages with participles of varying properties scattered throughout the world.

Gerundive or converb markers are characteristic of languages of Eurasia with AVCs, and are particularly common in such language families as Turkic

TABLE 5.2. Split/doubled inflectional patterns

Sub-patterns	Language(s)
AV = TAM 2× = SUBJ	Hemba, Kimbu, Mandan, Limilngan
AV = SUBJ 2× = TAM	Tzutujil
AV = S/O 2× = TAM	Wambaya
AV = OBJ 2× = SUBJ	Tlapanec
AV = SUBJ 2× = OBJ	Ayacucho Quechua
AV = NEG, TAM 2× = SUBJ	Ibibio, Obronuagom
LV = OBJ 2× = SUBJ	Limbu, Manam, Doyayo, Kuot, Pipil
LV = TAM 2× = SUBJ	Ciyao, Monumbo
LV = NEG 2× = SUBJ	Colloquial Persian, Swahili
LV = TAM$_\alpha$ 2× = TAM$_\beta$	Panyjima
LV = SUBJ 2× = OBJ	Sakhalin Ainu
LV = TAM$_\alpha$AV = TAM$_\beta$ 2× = SUBJ	Ös, Kemantney, Vinmavis, Nambiquara, Xhosa, Parji
AV = TAM LV = Obj 2× = SUBJ	Baure, Luganda
AV = TAM LV = Neg 2× = SUBJ	Nasioi, Betoi, Old Telugu, Gondi
AV = Tense LV = SUBJ 2× = ITER	Makushí
AV = Prf LV = SUBJ 2× = OBJ	Tobelo
AV = SUBJ LV = IND 2× = OBJ	Warembori
AV = HAB/PROG LV = PRF, SUBJ 2× = OBJ	Lango

and Kiranti (Tibeto-Burman) among others. In numerous Turkic languages of the Altai-Sayan region of south central Siberia, negative converb forms are found in the majority of AVCs, as well as within synchronic tense suffixes in numerous languages. Take for example the pairs of forms in Xakas, where negative -*Bin* replaces -*p* and -*A/i* in most AVCs and tenses (or TAM forms) derived from these historically, such as the present, the imperfect, evidential past, etc. (Anderson 1998a, 2004a). The Kiranti languages Dumi and Thulung of Nepal also use a negative gerund in certain negative AVCs. In addition, a so-called 'negative conjunctive' form is found in Aleut on the lexical verb in AVCs.

(182) Dumi (Rai)
       ma-lit mit-t-a
       NEG:PRF:GER-cut AUX-NPST-2/3
       'he has not cut it yet'
       (van Driem 1993: 240)

(183)   Thulung
      mi-pe-thiŋa bu-ŋa
      NEG-eat-CONV AUX-1
      'I have not eaten'
      (Ebert 2003a: 513)

(184)   Aleut (Eskimo-Aleut; North Pacific (Alaska/Russia))
      anaĝi-x̂   *hamang*   *uku-lakan*   *a-na-q*
      anything-SG   (behind).there see-NEG.CONJ AUX-REM-1
      'I did not see anything there'
      (Bergsland 1997: 199)

In extinct Samoyedic Kamas as well Mari, a Markham language of Papua New Guinea, gerunds or converbs are found on lexical verbs in split inflectional AVCs. As mentioned above, this particular development may reflect a structural 'Turkicization' of Kamas, based on locally dominant models for such constructions.

(185)   Kamas†
      oʔb-l   *=ej*   *moo-lʲa-m*
      collect-GER   =NEG   AUX-PRES-1
      'I can't collect'
      (Simoncsics 1998: 594)

(186)   a.   Mari [Austronesian]   b.   Mari
          zi ya-ha-gaiaŋ   *agua gi-ni ya-mpai-aiaŋ*
          I FUT-go-GER   you SUBJ.MRKR-want FUT-stay-GER
          'I will go'   'do you want to stay'
          (Holzknecht 1989: 150)   (Holzknecht 1989: 151)

A similar construction is seen with transitive verbs in the Tupi-Guaraní language Káro of Brazil.

(187)   Káro
      kanãy iʔkap aʔwĩa
      kanãy iʔ=kap-ap aʔ=wĩ-a
      then 1PL.INCL=AUX.FUT-IND$_2$ 3-kill-GER
      'then we will kill it'
      (Gabas 1999: 61)

General dependent/subordinate markers are found on lexical verbs in split inflectional AVCs in the Angan language Baruya of Papua New Guinea and in Arawakan Lokono and Guajiro of northern South America.

(188) a. Baruya   b. Baruya
       ma-vaihír-ya yíwano   *ma-vaihír-i yíwano*
       NEG-tread-EMB AUX:1:PST   NEG-tread-do AUX:1:PST
       'I did not tread'   'I did not tread'
       (Lloyd 1997: 302)

(189) Lokono
       ma-siki-n th-a no
       NEG-give-SUBORD 3SGFEM-AUX it
       'she did not give it'
       (Aikhenvald 1999b: 98)

(190) Guajiro
       nnoho-l-e:-či ta-sa-kɨ-in kami:rɨ
       NEG-M-FUT-OBJ.M 1-greet-them-SUBORD Camilo
       'I shall not greet Camilo'
       (Alvarez 1994: 98; Adelaar 2004: 119)

A lexical verb appearing in a marked dependent form realized through a same
subject marker is characteristic of Muskogean Apalachee.

(191) Apalachee[†] (Muskogean; USA)
       holahta onhiya hacin-coɬli-t il-ka ihka
       cacique every 2PL:DAT-write-SS 1PL:SUBJ-AUX PROG
       'we, all the caciques, are writing to you'
       (Kimball 1987: 139)

In Retuarã, another type of subordination found in AUX-headed AVCs is also
found in split inflectional AVCs, and that is case-marking (a pattern which
may itself have developed in some instances into an adverbial subordination
type, as discussed in Chapter 2). The purposive case marks lexical verbs in
some split inflectional AVCs in this Central Tucanoan language of Colombia.

(192) a. Retuarã
       bāharoka yi-oʔo-ērā baa-yu bãẽ
       story 1-write-PURP AUX-PRES now
       'I am going to write a story now'
       (Strom 1992: 72)

     b. Retuarã
       ki-re sa-yĩʔā-ērā baa-reʔka potohĩ
       3M-HMN.ARG 3M-capture-PURP AUX-PST when
       'when it was going to capture him'
       (Strom 1992: 72)

In its sister language Desano, lexical verbs may show gender/number agreement similar to French or Italian of a participle-like lexical verb in split inflected AVCs.

(193)　Desano
　　　suʔri koe-go ii-kū-bõ pera-ge
　　　clothes wash-FEM AUX-ASSUM-3FEM port-LOC
　　　'she probably is washing clothes at the river landing'
　　　(Miller 1999: 67)

Participial forms of lexical verbs in a split construction are found in Karo of the Tupi-Guaraní stock.

(194)　Káro
　　　iyɨt w-e-t a-ma-wiy-a
　　　squeeze 1-AUX-T/A 3SG-CAUS-go.out-PRTCPL
　　　'I squeezed it out'
　　　(Rodrigues 1999a: 120; Moore 1994: 154)

In a small number of cases of split or split/doubled inflectional AVCs, it is not the lexical verb but rather the *auxiliary* that appears in a marked 'dependent' form. One such example comes from Coast Tsimshian. In Coast Tsimshian, the quasi-subordinating (or conjunctive) SUBSEQ affix appears on auxiliaries in certain AVCs and may be an example of a dependent form of an auxiliary verb in a split/inflected AVC, albeit one probably derived from a clause-chained, serialized, or coordinative formation.

(195)　Coast Tsimshian
　　　nah-łá-'al dzáb-m̩ haʔliq'éexł
　　　PRF-PROX-SUBSEQ make-1PL sleds
　　　'we used to make sleds'
　　　(Dunn 1979: 229)

In the isolate language Cholon of Peru, auxiliaries in certain AVCs occur in post-verbal position in a nominalized form.

(196)　Cholón
　　　a-kt-i pokot-o-ke
　　　1-be-PRF AUX-FUT.NOMLZR-NOMINAL.PST(OPT)
　　　'I could have been'
　　　(Adelaar 2004: 473)

Within split/doubled formations, lexical verbs appear in modally dependent forms in such languages as Bantu Shambala, or with a general dependent 'adverbial' subordination marker in Eleme.

(197) Shambala
ní-zah-ti ni-kund-e
1-TNS-AUX 1-hope-SBJ
'I already hoped'
(Aksenova 1997: 34)

(198) Eleme
a. *ò-do-î-rǘ e-gbòi-î etʃǜ*
2-AUX.PRES-2PL-PRTCL DEP-stitch-2PL clothes
'you are stitching clothes'
(Anderson and Bond 2004-MS)

b. *ò-bo-î-rú   e-ma:-î àdádʒi   ɔ̀nɛnɛ*
2-AUX-2PL-PRTCL DEP-bring-2PL Adaji gift
'you should bring Adaji a gift'

Lexical verbs may also appear in a converb or gerund marked form in a split/doubled inflectional AVC. Such is the case in the following formation in the Daghestanian language Archi, where both lexical verb and auxiliary bear markers of the class of the absolutive (here logical object) argument, and the auxiliary bears the conditional morpheme as well.

(199) Archi
un ručka b-ešde-li bo-xo-nč'iš
you pen CLS-buy:PFV-CONV CLS-AUX:PFV:PBL-COND
'if you have bought a pen (which is very probable)...'
(Podlesskaja 2001: 1006)

Auxiliary verbs too may be dependent-marked in a split/doubled AVC. In Yuman Kiliwa, auxiliaries bear markers of same subject in the following split/doubled formations.

(200) a. Kiliwa   b. Kiliwa
p-m-ʔnyii-t m-ma+ʔ-iʔ   *p-m-uuy-t m-ma+ʔ-uʔ*
MP-2-AUX-SS 2-eat-RES   INDEF-2-AUX-SS 2-eat-Q
'you ate again'   'how did you eat it'
(Mixco 1985: 508)

Summary

A wide range of split and split/doubled inflectional patterns is attested in auxiliary verb constructions from around the world. These show a number of different sub-patterns, but all entail splits in which both the lexical verb and the auxiliary verb allow a different (sub)set of inflectional categories to be encoded on them, sometimes overlapping in the case of split/doubled patterns, or not in the case of true split patterns. Also, lexical verbs may be marked as syntactic, phrasal, or structural dependents on the auxiliary head, despite the inflectional head properties being distributed between the lexical verb and the auxiliary. In a small number of cases it is instead the auxiliary that is marked as dependent in a split or split/doubled AVC.

6

Complex Verb Forms from Fused Auxiliary Verb Constructions

Overview

Throughout the preceding chapters, I have alluded to the fact that all the macro-patterns and many of the sub-patterns discussed occur not only in synchronic bipartite auxiliary verb constructions but also in a range of complex verb forms that originated as AVCs. Of course, at times the morphosyntactic history of an individual construction is opaque, but it is commonly the case that the particular original inflectional pattern of the AVC is rather transparently realized in the structure of a complex verb form. In the sections below I present data on a wide range of such complex verb forms from all the macro-patterns of inflection detailed in the chapters above: the AUX-headed pattern, the LEX-headed pattern, and doubled, split and split/doubled patterns. Finally I present another common development of AVCs: the use of TAM encoded pronouns that derive from fused TAM auxiliary/subject formations.

6.1 Fused AUX-headed AVCs

As discussed in Chapter 2, there is a wide range of formal subtypes of the AUX-headed pattern of inflection in AVCs, relating mainly to the particular dependent form (including Ø-marked forms) that the lexical verb is required to be in by the construction, itself determined in a number of instances by the type of construction they originated in (see Chapter 7). These forms of lexical verbs in AVCs include adverbial subordination types (commonly referred to as gerunds, converbs, juncture, or general dependent/subordinate forms, depending on the grammatical tradition of analysis relevant to the language, language family, or region), participial or nominal/adjectival subordination types (including participles, infinitives, supines, etc.), modal subordination types, same-subject forms, and even coordinative/conjunctive formations. Virtually all the subtypes of AUX-headed AVCs may be found in a complex, fused, or univerbated structure across the languages of the world. In the paragraphs below, I outline a number of such subtypes of fused AUX-headed AVCs found in complex verb forms.

One language family where it is particularly easy to see complex verb forms clearly derived from AUX-headed AVCs in which the lexical verb appears in an adverbially dependent form is Turkic. One of the characteristic features of AVCs in Turkic languages is that the same construction may be grammaticalized in more than one function in one and the same language, and may appear in multiple functions when viewing the languages comparatively. Take, for example, the AUX-headed construction in *-p tur* in Xakas, a Turkic language of south-central Siberia. It is found in a synchronic AVC as one of four variant constructions marking a progressive present and in a fused or univerbated form, in which case the vowel of the former auxiliary shifts from round to unround, as dictated by the rules of vowel harmony operative in most Xakas dialects which disallow rounded vowels in post-initial (or post-stem) syllables. It is found in the function of an evidential past in this fused formation.

(1) Xakas
    ol   oyna-ptïr
    S/he   play-CV-EVID.PAST
    'he played apparently'
    (Field Notes)

(2) Xakas
    ol   oyna-p tur
    s/he   play-CV PRES.PROG
    'he is playing'

Cognates to both constructions in mainly fused formations are found throughout the complex continuum of Turkic languages and dialects found in the Altai-Sayan region of Siberia (Anderson 2004a). Thus, fused progressive presents deriving from the same sequence attested in the Xakas form above are seen in complex verb forms in such languages as Tuba-kiži, Lower Chulym, and Ös (Middle Chulym).

(3) Tuba-kiži
    Men čanak yaza-p-tï-m
    I ski make-CV-PRS-1
    'I am making skis'
    (Baskakov 1966a: 73)

(4) Lower Chulym
    ol oyna-p-tïr
    he play-CV-PRES
    'he is playing'
    (Dul'zon 1966: 454)

(5) Ös (Middle Chulym)
    kajdïn   kee-p-tir sæŋ
    from.where   come-CV-PRES.III-2
    'where do you come from'
    (Field Notes)

In highly eroded forms, indeed, even those in which the source construction may be realized by a single sound originally belonging either to the converb or to the auxiliary, semi-cognate formations, are found throughout the Turkic language family, especially those of the Kypchak group. These seem to derive not from an AVC in *-p tur* but stem from a similar AUX-headed structure in *-A tur* with a different converb form of the lexical verb but a cognate auxiliary element.

(6) a. Kyrgyz
     ǰaz-a-m
     write-PRES/FUT-1
     'I write'
     (Junusaliev 1966: 496)

    b. Kyrgyz
     bol-ot
     be[come]-PRES/FUT.3
     'it becomes'

(7) a. Nogay
     bar-a-man
     go-PRES-1
     'I go'
     (Baskakov 1966c: 292)

    b. Nogay
     *bar-**adï***
     go-PRES.3
     's/he goes'

(8) a. Karakalpak
     al-a-saŋ
     take-PRES-2
     'you take'
     (Baskakov 1966b: 311)

    b. Karakalpak
     *al-**adï***
     take-PRES.3
     's/he takes'

Even the divergent Chuvash shows a cognate formation, attesting to the extreme age of an AVC w/*tur* and an adverbially dependent lexical verb in Turkic.

(9) a. Chuvash
     Pul:-a=t-ăp
     be[come]-PRES-1
     'I become'
     (Doerfer 1988: 163)

    b. Chuvash
     Jul-at-ăp
     Remain-PRES-1
     'I stay, remain'

    c. Chuvash
     jul-at-ăn
     remain-PRES-2
     'you stay, remain'
     (Johanson 1976: 58)

    d. Chuvash
     jul-at'
     remain-PRES
     'he stays, remains'

Cognates with the evidential past formation of Xakas are found in the closely related Shor, as well as more distantly related Turkic languages like Tuba-kiži, Quu-kiži, Tuvan, and Teleut.

(10) a. Shor
          oyna-ptïr-zïŋ
          Play-EVID.PST-2
          'it seems you played'
          (Babuškin and Donidze 1966: 475)

      b. Shor[1]
          oyna-baandïr-(b)ïm
          play-NEG-EVID.PST-1
          'it seems I didn't play'

(11) Tuba-kiži
      Kara-Küreŋ-di öltür-üp sal-tïr
      Kara-Küreñ-ACC kill-CV PRFV-EVID.PST
      'he killed Kara-Küreŋdi (it seems)'
      (Baskakov 1966a: 82)

(12) Quu-kiži
      ..sari it-ke it-iŋ karïd-ïn-a ur-up ežik kïyn-ïn-a sal per-ten bo-ptïr
      yellow dog-DAT dog-GEN bowl-3-DAT pour-CV door edge-3-DAT put
      OBJ.VERS-IMPERF AUX-EVID.PST
      'she poured out food for the yellow dog into the bowl and put it by
      the threshold'
      (Baskakov 1985: 91)

(13) a. Tuvan
          söölgü üye-de öskelen-i ber-iptir sen
          last time-LOC change-CV INCH-EVID.PAST 2
          'it seems you changed recently'
          (Sat 1966: 395)

      b. Tuvan
          men kör-üptür men
          I see-EVID.PAST 1
          'I saw (it would appear)'
          (Anderson and Harrison 1999: 50)

(14) Teleut
      Suu-dïŋ üst-i d'akšï toŋ-golok bol-tïr
      Water-GEN top-3 good freeze-UNACMPL AUX-EVID.PST
      'it seems the water surface hasn't frozen up yet'
      (Baskakov 1958: 90)

---

[1] This is of course actually a fused split formation, the source of negative AVCs of this type throughout the Altai-Sayan Turkic languages.

As is apparent from the examples above, these evidential past suffixes may themselves appear on an auxiliary verb embedded within an AVC. Furthermore, as the Teleut example demonstrates, the converb element itself may have eroded to zero in the history of the development of this construction in a given individual Turkic language.

The category of converb has many formal realizations among the Turkic languages (and even within one and the same language), both within synchronic AVCs and within fused/univerbated forms. In the majority of Turkic languages, there are two basic converbs found with lexical verbs in AVCs, the -*[I]p* converb and the -*A* converb; originally there were others, the -*I* converb, the -*U* converb, and the -*IpAn* converb of Old Turkic (see Anderson, to appear). Divergent Turkic languages lack one or another (or both) of the common ones, and have replaced these functional elements with formally different but functionally similar converb forms, e.g. the -*An* converb of Yakut (Sakha), possibly clipped from -*IpAn*, or the -*sA* converb of Chuvash. Additionally, converbs may have Ø allomorphs in individual Turkic languages, as in various Xakas varieties, when both the lexical verb ends in a consonant and the auxiliary verb begins with one as described in Chapter 2.[2] The zero-allomorph forms might thus be considered in the terminology of the present volume as pseudo-zero converb-marked lexical verbs in AUX-headed AVCs.

A fusing of AUX-headed AVCs with the lexical verb appearing in a converb form is also found in Republican Turkish.

---

[2] Zero-converb are forms in fused AVCs are characteristic of both Xakas (Saɣai) and all Xakasoid (Xyzyl) varieties. A sampling of these are offered here:

(i) Saɣai
    min   *paᴣ-če-m*   *ol*   *at-naŋ*
    I   go-PRES.I-1   that   horse-INS
    'I am going on that horse'
    (Patačakova 1973: 40)
    vs.

(ii) Saɣai
    men   *Paza*   *suɣ-nuŋ*   *oŋ*   *qol-in-da*   *čurtta-pčadir-bin*
    I   P   water-GEN   right   hand-3-LOC   live-PRES.II-1
    'I live on the right bank of the Paza river'
    (Pritsak 1959: 619)

(iii)
    a. Xyzyl   b. Xyzyl
        par-šadi-m   *šölä-pšädı-m*
        go-PRES.III-1   speak-PRES.III-1
        'I am going'   'I am speaking'
        (Domožhakov 1948: 83)

(15) Turkish
    gel-iyor-um   <   **gel-e*   yoru-m
    come-PROG-1   come-CV   AUX-1
    'I am coming'

Fused forms may have a highly restricted distribution in a given language. As mentioned in Chapter 1, in Xakas, the auxiliary verb *al* in two different functions (different AVCs) have been fused in certain people's speech with exactly one verb each. This same AVC has been fully univerbated in its subject version function in Uighur, and shows no synchronic lexical restriction. It has thus been more phonologically integrated in Uighur than in Xakas, though functionally they appear to be nearly identical.

(16) Xakas
    pu kniga-nɨ tab-ɨl-za-m   *min   xayda örɪn-e-m*
    this book-ACC find.CV-SUBJ.VERS-COND-1   I   oh.boy be.happy-FUT-1
    'if I find this book, boy will I be happy'
    (Field notes)

(17) Xakas
    ol   *anɨ*   *al-(i)b-al-ɣan*
    s/he   3.ACC   take-CV-CAP-PAST.I
    'she could have taken it'
    (Field notes)

(18) a.   Uighur/Uyɣur
          adris-i-ni yez-iw-al-di-m
          address-3-ACC write-CV-SUBJ.VERS-PST-1
          'I wrote down her address'
          (Hahn 1991: 612)

       b.   Uighur/Uyɣur
          qol-um-ni kes-iw-al-di-m
          hand-1-ACC cut-CV-SUBJ.VERS-PST-1
          'I got cut on my hand'
          (Hahn 1991: 612)

Materials from the extinct Samoyedic language Kamas of south central Siberia have registered complex verb forms that appear to be fused auxiliary verb constructions. As described above, the fusing of auxiliary verb constructions is also characteristic of most Xakas varieties, to which Kamas speakers ultimately shifted. The auxiliaries used are also the most common ones in the Altai-Sayan area. For example, from the auxiliary 'to lie' comes the progressive, from the auxiliary 'to leave' comes the perfective. The perfective was clearly an AUX-headed construction originally. As for the progressive, it is mainly attested in the third person singular in these fused forms, and one cannot tell whether it was originally AUX-headed or LEX-headed; but it appears likely that it was also the type of formation which had a lexical verb in a gerund form and an auxiliary as the inflectional head.

(19) a. Kamas†
    mənzə -lä iʔbe > mənzᵊl ʲlɛ βᵊ
    cook-GER AUX > cook.GER.AUX
    'is cooking'
    (Donner 1944:85, 101; Simoncsics 1998: 584)

    b. Kamas†³
      kuja dʲəmdə -laa-ʔbə
      sun shine-GER-AUX
      'the sun is shining'
      (Simoncsics 1998: 586)

    c. Kamas†
      kəm uʔ-la-ʔbə
      blood flow-GER-AUX.PRES
      'the blood is flowing'
      (Künnap 1999b: 34)

    d. Kamas†
      ətʲ er-laa-walʲa-m
      tie.up-GER-AUX-1
      'I have tied it up'
      (Simoncsics 1998: 590)

Other fused auxiliary verb constructions of the AUX-headed inflectional type in Kamas, with the lexical verb appearing in the gerund form, include the following:

(20) Other fused AVCs in Kamas
    a. Kamas†
      məl-la-andə -ɣa-m
      wander-GER-GO. AUX-PART-1
      I go (wandering, i.e. nomadizing)'
      (Simoncsics 1998: 591)

    b. Kamas†
      ne kunōlamnə   < kunō-la am-nə
      wife sleep-GER-AUX-PRES
      'the wife sleeps'
      (Künnap 1999b: 23)

    c. Kamas†
      šaʔlāmbi < šaʔ-la xam-bi
      hide-GER-AUX-PRET
      'he hid himself'

---

³ The Kamas gerund may either be harmonic-*la/lä-laa/lää* or may be non-harmonic-*laa*.

Data on the other Sayan Samoyedic language, Mator, suggests that fused forms of the AUX-headed inflectional type also were common.

(21)   Mator[†]
    tček-sɨ -gan-em
    mistake[n]-INF-AUX-1
    'I am mistaken'
    (Xelimskij 1993)

Mari (Uralic) varieties (including literary Mari) show variation between gerund-marked lexical verbs in AUX-headed constructions and fused formations deriving from these with Ø-stem auxiliaries.

(22)   Dialectal Mari   (23)   Literary Mari
    nal-ǝn ul-na   *nal-ǝn-na*
    take-GER AUX-1PL.PRES   take-GER-1 PL.PRES
    'we have taken'   'we have taken'
    (Kangasmaa-Minn 1998: 238)

Fused AUX-headed AVCs with the lexical verb in a converb/gerund form is also found in modern Tamil, a member of the Dravidian language family spoken in southern India and Sri Lanka. For more on fused auxiliaries and AVCs more generally in Dravidian languages, see Krishnamurti (2003: 373ff.)

(24)   Tamil
    vaḍai cuṭ-a-ppo:-kir-en   <   *cuṭa   *po:kiren*
    vadai fry-CV-AUX-P/F-1   fry-ADV/PRTCPL go-P/F-1
    'I am going to fry (some)*vadai*'
    (Paramasivam and Lindholm 1980: 79)

As the various Eurasian grammatical traditions recognize adverbial verb forms in a range of functions (as discussed in Chapter 2 above), it is not surprising to find Eurasian languages dominating the early discussion of fused AUX-headed AVCs with 'adverbial' lexical verbs. Other such formations are found in a number of other languages from across the globe, several of which are briefly presented below.

    In a range of languages from the Markham group of Oceanic spoken in Papua New Guinea, gerund-marked lexical verbs have been fused into complex wholes with auxiliaries. Such forms are found in Sarasira, Mari, and Sukurum. Note that in Mari and Sukurum, the lexical verb appears in a gerund-marked form in synchronic bipartite verb plus complement clauses that give rise to AVCs as well.

(25) Sarasira
      ci si-ha-ca gum i
      I FUT-go-GER garden IRR
      'I will go to the garden'
      (Holzknecht 1989: 150)

(26) Mari (AN)
      zi ya-ha-gaiaŋ
      I FUT-go-GER
      'I will go'

(27) Sukurum
      si su-fa-ia gum e
      I FUT-go-GER garden IRR
      'I will go to the garden'

(28) Mari
      agua gi-ni ya-mpai-aiaŋ
      you SUBJ.MRKR-want FUT-stay-GER
      'do you want to stay'
      (Holzknecht 1989: 151)

(29) Sukurum
      si gi-su fa-ia Sarasira e
      I SUBJ.MRKR-AUX go-GER Sarasira IRR
      'I intend to go to Sarasira'

A lexical verb in a dependent form fused within an AUX-headed AVC into a larger complex is found in the Dani language of Indonesia, a member of the Dani-Kwerba stock.[4]

(30) Dani (Papuan, Trans-New Guinea, Dani-Kwerba; Papua, Indonesia)
      wat-h-y-lak-ytyk
      hit-REAL-DEP-AUX-1PAST
      'I was hitting him'
      (Foley 1986: 144)

As mentioned in Chapter 2, various Khoisan languages use a so-called juncture element functionally similar to converbs or infinitives in more familiar languages. Lexical verbs appear in these forms in a range of AVCs, some of which have been univerbated into larger complexes. Such fused forms occur (mainly in past and perfective formations) in the Central Khoisan languages Buga-|Anda, ||ani, and Kua of Angola/Nambia and Botswana.[5]

(31) Buga-|Anda (Kxoe)
      (tí) ʔ̂a-ná-hà-bé
      I know-JNCT-PST-NEG
      'I don't/didn't know'
      (Vossen 1997: 192)

---

⁴ Note that this has been called a fused serial construction as well.

⁵ It is difficult to tell whether these Khoisan constructions should be considered fused AUX-headed forms with an uninflected auxiliary, or fused LEX-headed forms with a dependent marked lexical verb.

(32) ‖ani   (33) Kua
      tí hì-á-hǎ   *tá kǔ.á.ha'*
      I work-JNCT-PERF   I go.JNCT.PRF
      'I have worked'   'I went'
      (Heine 1986: 18)   (Heine 1986: 18)

Participial marked forms (including markers of TAM-type categories) are found in fused formations in a range of languages. In the rapid-speech register of the Omotic language Gimira, lexical verbs in a participle form fuse with subject marked auxiliaries. Only the tonal features of the construction speak to its original nature.

(34) a. Gimira (Benchnon) (Omotic)
          wu'sa³ han³k'is⁴ku²e³
          she:SUBJ go:PST.PRTCPL:AUX:PRS:3
          'she is going'
          (Breeze 1990: 32)

      b. Gimira
          yi'sì³ han³k'is⁵ku²e³
          he:SUBJ go:PST.PRTCPL:AUX:PRS:3
          'he is going'

In Gadsup and Usarufa, two East New Guinea Highlands languages, a narrative and perfective form of the lexical verb, respectively, is found in a fused complex.

(35) Gadsup (Kainantu)
      kùm-èq-[mók]-ú
      go.down-NARR-AUX:COMPL-1
      'I had come down'
      (Frantz and McKaughan 1964: 88) [NB: optional Ø-auxiliary]

(36) a. Usarufa   b. Usarufa
          u-ma-sua-um   *u-ma-su-ka-um*
          make-PRF-COMPL-1   make-PRF-COMPL-PST-1
          'I have made'   'I had made'
          (Bee 1973)

      c. Usarufa
          u-ma-sua-na-um
          make-PRF-COMPL-FUT-1
          'I will have made'

In Arandic languages such as Alyawarra and Aranda, fused complexes deriving from AUX-headed AVCs are found. The lexical verb in these constructions appears in a so-called 'ligative' form, of possible participial origin. In Alyawarra, ligatives are morpho-lexically specified but mainly opaque in function.

(37)   a.   Alyawarra
            an-il-ani-yanga
            sit-LIG-AUX-NEG
            'don't keep sitting'
            or 'don't just sit there'
            (Yallop 1977: 64)

       b.   Alyawarra
            ayirn-iy-aynti-ka ilikithika
            ask-LIG-AUX-PST from.what
            'they kept asking what the matter was'

       c.   Alyawarra
            ayinha unta ingkurn-in-aynt-a
            I.ACC you.ERG paint-LIG-AUX-IMP
            'paint me all over'
            or '(you) keep painting me'
            (Yallop 1977: 64)

       d.   Alyawarra
            ayinga alp-an-iya aynt-an-itjika
            I.NOM go-AUX-PERM lie-AUX-PURP
            'I'm going for a while to camp'
            or 'I'll go away and stay for a while'
            (Yallop 1977: 65)

In Aranda, ligatives retain some of their probable original function, e.g. *-tji* punctiliar or *-l* continuous.

(38)   a.   Aranda
            tu-tj-alpuma
            hit-LIG-AUX
            'hit upon/after arrival'
            (Strehlow 1943–4: 172–3; Yallop 1977: 63)

       b.   Aranda
            tu-l-alpuma
            hit-LIG-AUX
            'hit while coming back'

Fused complexes are also found in the South American isolate language Kamsá. Here the progressive prefix was found on the original lexical verb, preceded by an auxiliary that encodes argument properties. This has been fused into a large univerbated whole.

(39) Kamsá (isolate)
    k-bo-č-c-obá
    2OBJ-1(DL)-FUT-PROG-kill
    'I shall kill you'
    (Howard 1977: 58)

Infinitive forms of lexical verbs are also found in fused constructions deriving from AUX-headed AVCs. One such language to show a construction of this type is the South African Bantu language Zulu. Here the infinitive prefix *uku-* is fused within this large complex, following an original auxiliary verb now grammaticalized as future marker (< 'come').

(40) Zulu
    ŋgi-za-ukuthand
    1-FUT-INF:love
    'I will love'
    (Meinhof 1948: 114)

Zulu's sister language, Swahili, shows another interesting pattern involving an infinitive marked lexical verb. However, rather than the infinitive being triggered by the construction *per se*, the form in the first verb in the historically complex AVC below is required to be in the infinitive form (-*kuwa*, not -*wa*) because it is a monosyllabic stem. Thus the infinitive form of the lexical verb may be triggered prosodically as well in AVCs, which like any AVC may be phonologically fused into a complex word (cf. reduplication of monosyllabic lexical verb stems in South Munda languages discussed in Chapter 2 and also below). The following two examples show the use of a monosyllabic stem and bisyllabic stem with the original auxiliary -*li* in Swahili, and the subsequent presence and absence correspondingly of the infinitive.

(41) a. Swahili
      wa-li-kuwa wa-ki-temba
      3PL.ANIM-PAST-AUX 3PL.ANIM-PRTCPL-walk
      'they were walking'

    b. Swahili
      ni-li-wa-ona ha-wa-fanyi kazi
      1-PAST-3PL.ANIM-see NEG-3PL.ANIM-do.NEG work
      'I saw them not working'

Bantu languages are far from alone in showing infinitive forms of lexical verbs in fused AUX-headed AVCs. Even well-known European languages such as

French show such formations. For example, the future in French *chanterai* is rather transparently related to a lexical verb in an infinitive form followed by a person/tense-inflected auxiliary, fused into a univerbated complex, i.e. *chanterai* < *chanter ai* [sing:INF AUX<have>:1].

Variation between a fused and a non-fused AVC with the lexical verb in an infinitive form is seen in Afar. In this Cushitic language of northeastern Africa, the future may be expressed periphrastically through an AUX-headed AVC in which the lexical verb appears in an infinitive form, or fused with a reduced and altered form of the subject inflected auxiliary.

(42) Afar
    ha:'d-e-tto   ~   *ha:'d-e li'to*
    fly-INF-AUX:2   fly-INF AUX:FUT:2
    'you will fly'
    (Bliese 1976: 147)

Various Bantu languages make use of fused AUX-headed formations in which the lexical verb appears in an independent form. Zulu again provides an example of such a construction. This differs from the above Zulu formation in the presence of the final (indicative) vowel-*a* and the lack of the infinitive prefix on the lexical verb.[6]

(43) Zulu
    ŋgi-ŋha-thand-a
    1-AUX-love-ASP
    'I can love'
    (Meinhof 1948: 112)

In South Munda languages, lexical verbs may be reduplicated in fused AUX-headed AVCs. Such is the case with monosyllabic stems in the progressive in Juang, and the frequentative and habitual in Sora. Polysyllabic stems are not reduplicated in these same environments.

(44) a. Juang   b. Juang
         aiñ jɔjɔ-nɔm-an   *aiñ je'gje'g-nɔm-an*
         I R:eat-PROG-PST.I   I R:.cry-PROG-PST.I
         'I was eating'   'I was weeping'
         (Pinnow 1960)

---

[6] Perhaps it is worth noting here that the segment –*a* that occurs at the end of the lexical verb in a large number of auxiliary (and non-auxiliary) constructions in Bantu languages is one of a set of morphemes (really the default one) in this position class in the verbal template and has a wide range of functions in Bantu grammatical systems. This –*a* has been given almost as many names as there have been analyses. These include such terms of convenience as 'final vowel', 'indicative' suffix, 'aspect' marker, etc.

(45) a. Sora   -*laŋ*   b. Sora
          kañkañ-laŋ-te-n   *guər-ləŋ-te-n*
          R:abuse-HAB-NPST-ITR   sacrifice-HAB-NPST-ITR
          'he abuses (all people)'   'he sacrifices'
          (Ramamurti 1931)

Zero-marked stems are the norm in Kherwarian North Munda fused AVCs. A number of aspectual or Aktionsart formations are found in fused construc-tions of this type in Santali.

(46) a. Santali (North Munda, Austroasiatic; India)
          hɛc-gɔd-ɔk-me
          come-AUX-ITR/PASS-2
          'come quickly'
          (Bodding 1929)

      b. Santali
          jɔm-si'd-ke-d-a-ko
          eat-AUX-ASP-TR-FIN-PL
          'they ate it all up'

Note that historically the entire complex 'perfective' tense/aspect system itself in these Kherwarian languages is also likely to reflect an earlier fusing of AUX-headed AVCs.[7]

(47) a. Santali   b. Santali   c. Santali
          dal-ke-d-a-e   *dal-le-d-e-a-e*   *dal-e-n-a-e*
          beat-AOR-TR-FIN-3   beat-AOR-TR-3-FIN-3   beat-AOR-INTR-FIN-3
          'he beat'   'he beat him'   'he was beaten'
          (Ghosh 1994: 100)

      d. Santali   e. Santali
          dal-aka-d-e-a-e   *dal-aka-n-a-e*
          beat-PERF-TR-3-FIN-3   beat-PERF-INTR-FIN-3
          'he has beaten him'   'he has been beaten'
          (Ghosh 1994: 102)   (Ghosh 1994: 103)

The so-called minor Kherwarian languages make use of these fused AUX-headed constructions as well.

---

⁷ On the inflection of auxiliaries in the 'imperfective' system in Kherwarian, see the section on split-headed fused AVCs below.

(48) Karmali   (49) Turi
    jo:m-chaba-ke-d-e   *go:t-cha:ba:-ta:-n-a:-ku:*
    eat-COMPL-ASP-TR-3   gather-COMPL-ASP-ITR-FIN-PL
    'he finished eating'   'they finished gathering'
    (Grierson 1906: 73)   (Grierson 1906: 131)

(50) Asuri
    goj-doho-le-n-a:
    die-AUX-ASP-ITR-FIN
    'had been dead'
    (Grierson 1906: 141)

A wide range of other languages possess complex verb forms deriving directly from either nuclear serialized constructions or AUX-headed AVCs in which the lexical verb appears in a zero-marked form (or in a zero allomorph of another dependent marking category as in the Ø converb forms of Xakas mentioned above). For example, among the languages of Africa, constructions of this type are found in Ewe of West Africa and Somali varieties of Eastern Africa.

In Standard Somali and in Jiddu, fused AUX-headed AVCs with a (seemingly) Ø-marked lexical verb are found. As mentioned in Chapter 2, cognate forms of these are found in other Somali varieties in AUX-headed AVCs in which the lexical verb appears in an infinitive form. Thus, it may be the case that the infinitive has eroded to Ø in these formations or appeared in a Ø-allomorph in the constructions that gave rise to these formations in Standard and Jiddu Somali.

(51) Standard Somali   (52) Jiddu Somali
    keen-ay-a(a)   *jeel-aas-ta*
    bring-AUX-IMPF:1?   beat-AUX-2PL
    'I bring'   'you (PL) are beating'
    (Heine and Reh 1984: 124)

In Ewe varieties, fused auxiliary verb constructions of various types are found. Note that lexical verb appears in a Ø form in certain of these constructions, as evidenced by the following form, in which the auxiliary has undergone partial erosion (loss of initial consonant, but the lexical verb it derives from stays in its expected, unmarked form).

(53) a. Ewe   b. Ewe
    ye-á-vá   *m-á-yi*
    3-FUT-come   1-FUT-go
    'he will come'   'I will go'
    (Heine and Reh 1984: 38)   (Heine and Reh 1984: 131;
              Westermann 1907: 63)

Note that not all fused forms in Ewe are from the LEX-headed structure, at least in the standard dialect. Compare the following forms in this regard. In Standard Ewe, the habitual formation appears to be derived from a LEX-headed construction (or a fused adverbial particle), perhaps ultimately from some kind of serial formation. In the Anexo Ewe variety, on the other hand, the habitual appears to have the form of a fused AUX-headed AVC, much like the future in Standard Ewe.

(54)   Standard Ewe   (55)   Anexo Ewe
        me-yí-na   *m-nɔ-sa*
        1-go-HAB   1-HAB-sell
        'I habitually go'   'I habitually sell'
        (Heine and Reh 1984: 128)

In the Papuan language Amanab of the Waris stock, fused AUX-headed AVCs appear with synchronically bipartite AVCs where the lexical verb appears in a zero-marked form. This suggests that the fused formation probably derived from a structure similar to that otherwise attested in this language.

(56)   a.   Amanab (Waris; Trans-New Guinea)
              er tata-m tigi-fi-g
              men pig-DAT hit-AUX-PST
              'the men have shot the pig'
              (Minch 1992: 111)

        b.   Amanab
              afa bro-nam pipa fian fe-na
              CONJ come-PST.PRTCPL trap make AUX-REM.PST
              'then having come, he had made a trap'
              (Minch 1992: 112)

In Binandere, the past form is a fused AVC of the AUX-headed type (< 'do') with the lexical verb in an unmarked form.

(57)   Binandere
        pitena
        give:PST.1
        'I gave'
        (Capell 1969: 17)

In Tauya, the stative marker appears to be derived from an auxiliary originally meaning 'stay' in a fused AUX-headed construction. This is a relatively common development cross-linguistically.

(58) a. Tauya   b.   Tauya
      nen epi-mene-i-ʔa   *ʔini-mene-pope-i-ʔa*
      they stand-STAT-3PL-IND   sleep-STAT-HAB-3PL-IND
      'they stand'   'they always slept
      (MacDonald 1990: 192–3)

A formally cognate element commonly occurs as a progressive marker in a number of languages of the region. Most also seem to occur, insofar as the data allow for such conclusions, in fused AUX-headed formations, suggesting that this construction may be an old (and probably also diffused) one in the region.

Benefactive formations frequently come from fused AVCs (these mainly derived from (nuclear) serialized formations involving 'give') in a number of different Papuan languages, e.g. Eipo (cf. Telefol, where it remains synchronically bipartite).

(59)   Eipo (Mek; Papua New Guinea)
      leb-areb-nama-ki-n
      speak-BEN-FUT-2-1
      'I will speak for/to you'
      (Heeschen 1998: 83)

(60)   Telefol (Ok; Papua New Guinea)
      boko b-'neé-l-antém-a
      speak BEN:PUNC-1OBJ-PUNC-FUT-3[M]
      'he will tell me'

The Oceanic language Taiof also has a fused AUX-headed AVC in which the lexical verb appears in a Ø-marked form.

(61)   Taiof
      aye to mat-e-n
      he VI die-AUX-3
      'he has died, is dead'
      (Ross 1982b: 27)

TABLE 6.1. Progressive forms in selected languages of Papua New Guinea

Hua	Fore	Gimi	Siane	More	Gahuku
-bai-	-mi-	-mri-	-mino-	no'/ne'	no ~ ni

(MacDonald 1990: 194)

A number of northern and western Native North American languages show
complex verb forms that appear to derive from a fused AVC of the AUX-headed
type in which the lexical verb appeared in a Ø-marked form. Thus, in Haida
(Enrico 1983, 2003), the enigmatic and possibly isolated language of the islands
off British Columbia and southeastern Alaska, there are fused AVCs of this type.

(62) a. Haida
          7la tiidaa<-s/-yaa-n>-k'uhl-$uu 7la 7ii.uwaan -da-gaang-aa-n-ii
          3 lying-NON.WIT-PST near-NEW.INFO 3 piled.here.and.there-AUX-
          FREQ-NONWIT-PST-TOP.CHGE
          'he kept them lying here and there near where he lay'
          (Enrico 1983: 150)

      b. Haida
          tlagu 7laa dang 7isdaa-$asii-s dan hl sk'ada -daa-$asaa-ng
          how 3 you do.to-FUT-DEP.TNS you I learn -AUX-FUT-PRS
          'I will teach you what you will do to her'
          (Enrico 1983: 153)

A number of complex forms in Washo also appear to be fused AVCs where the
lexical verb appears in an unmarked form. Such formations may derive from
nuclear serializion constructions, as in Engenni, mentioned above.

(63) Washo (isolate (Hokan); USA)
      émlu-ŋaŋa   *émlu-máma?*
      eat-AUX   eat-AUX
      'to pretend to eat'   'to finish eating'
      (Jacobsen 1964: 559)

Among South American languages, Ø-marked lexical verbs within the context
of a larger fused formation deriving from an AUX-headed AVC are found in
complex verbs in such languages as Northern Embera and Amahuaca. Note
that in Amahuaca, the auxiliary itself appears to have been fused originally
within a fused subject/TAM form; this then fused into a larger complex.

(64) N. Embera (Chocó; Colombia)
      īyāpa tʰa-b-ʉ-a
      breathe lie-AUX-PRES-DECL
      'he is lying down breathing'
      (Mortensen 1999: 10)

(65) Amahuaca (Panoan; Peru)
moha-mun hun jo-ha-nu
now-TH I come-1:IMM.PST-DECL
'Now I have just/actually arrived'
(Sparing-Chávez 1998: 447)

6.2 Fused LEX-headed AVCs

In addition to fused AUX-headed formations, all other macro-patterns discussed in Chapters 3–5, viz. the LEX-headed pattern, doubled inflection, and split and split/doubled patterns, have realizations in fused forms in complex verbs from languages across the world. Fused LEX-headed patterns are not widely discussed for the same reasons that synchronically bipartite auxiliary verb constructions of the LEX-headed type are not and this argument is not repeated here. However, it should be mentioned that it may at times be difficult to determine a LEX-headed from an AUX-headed (or some other) origin of a fused construction in certain instances—for example, if the form only occurs in third singular forms, which is morphologically and/or prosodically unmarked in the language. This is especially true if the lexical verb is fused in a LEX-headed construction in which the auxiliary verb is still the syntactic head and the lexical verb appears in a dependent form. This latter scenario could be argued in the case of certain formations in Khoisan languages discussed above.

Among the parameters along which fused auxiliary verb constructions of the LEX-headed type show variation is the relative position of the auxiliary verb and the lexical verb to one another. In languages showing AUX V structure, the fused complex appears with the former auxiliary in leftmost position. Complex verb forms originating from the univerbation of a LEX-headed AVC with AUX V order may be found in such a diverse array of languages as the extinct Athabaskan language Tututni, the Nilotic language Nandi, and Jilu Aramaic.

(66) Tututni[†] (Athabaskan; USA)
γə-š-ł-mas	*γ-i-ł-mas*
PROG-1-CLSFR-roll.along	PROG-2-CLSFR-roll.along
'I am rolling it along'	'you are rolling along'

(Golla 1976: 223)

(67) a. Nandi   b. Nandi   c. Nandi
     mâ-a:-kas   *mâ-a:-kás-é*   *tà-a:-kás-é*
     FUT-1-hear   FUT-1-hear-é   AUX-1-listen-ASP
     'I will hear it'   'I will be listening'   'I'm still listening'
     (Creider 1989: 111–12)

    d. Nandi   e. Nandi
       íp-a:-cám-é   *mâ:p-a:-cam*
       FUT-1-like-é   FUT-1-like
       'I'm going to like it'

(68) Jilu (Neo-Aramaic)
     bt-gárɪš-na
     FUT-pull-1
     'I will pull'
     (Fox 1991: 43)

Of course, LEX-headed AVCs also occur where the auxiliary follows the lexical verb, and these formations may be univerbated as well within large fused complexes. In these fused LEX-headed forms, the auxiliary occurs at the right edge of the word, which in certain grammatical forms require clause level affixes like the indicative in the first Önge (Andamanese) form below. Otherwise, the auxiliary occurs in final (right-edge) position.

(69) a. Önge (Andamanese; India)   b. Önge
     ekw-akobela-te-lle-be-gi   *antekë-lakwe*
     3PL-run-DIR-PL-COMPL-IND   sit-AUX
     'they came running'   'remain sitting'
     (Das Gupta and Sharma 1982: 22, 23)

    c. Önge
     tɔŋkita gaiboralea ijejidda kue-le eti gaikwa-be
     yesterday in.the.forest three pig-PL we kill-COMPL
     'yesterday we killed three pigs in the forest'
     (Das Gupta and Sharma 1982: 52)

A similar structure is found in a complex verb form in Namia, a Yellow River language of the Sepik-Ramu phylum, where the fused auxiliary appears in final position.

(70) Namia (Yellow River, Sepik-Ramu; Papua New Guinea)
on takwe p-la-ni-j-warir-le
1 tobacco PRF-south-sit-EP-wrap-AUX
'I began to sit down and wrap tobacco'
(Feldpausch and Feldpausch 1992: 43)

Other languages with fused formations deriving from auxiliary verb constructions of the LEX-headed type include Tacana, Camling, and Kunama.

(71) a. Tacana   b. Tacana   c. Tacana
y-ani-ani   *e-pu-ani*   *e-neti-ani*
INCOMPL-sit-AUX   INCOMPL-say-AUX   INCOMPL-stand-AUX
'is sitting'   'says'   'is standing'
(Ottaviano and Ottaviano 1967: 185–6, 188)

(72) Camling
mi-pera-khata
3PL-fly-AUX
'they flew away'
(Ebert 2003b: 542)

(73) a. Kunama (Nilo-Saharan; Sudan)   b. Kunama
a'ba olle na-ŋa-na-ŋa   *a'ba olle na-ŋ-ke*
I there 1-eat-FUT-OPT   I there 1-eat-AOR
'I will eat there'   'I ate there (once)'
(Bender 1996: 45)

In Aari, one stage in the phonological/prosodic integration of the original components in an AVC preceding the one found in Kunama and Tacana is attested. Here the uninflecting auxiliary appears as an enclitic to the inflected lexical verb. Such a stage may be a common one in the integration of lexical and auxiliary verb elements into univerbated complexes that characterizes the fused LEX-headed AVC formations under consideration. Strictly speaking, the lexical verb element is itself here properly a fused AUX-headed (or possibly split-inflected) AVC with which a later, now clitic, auxiliary combined to form the attested formation under consideration.

(74) a. Aari (South Omotic)   b. Aari
báʔseqit= ąąq(e)   *baʔtít=ąąq(e)*
bring:PLUP:1=AUX   bring:PLUP:1=AUX
'I had brought'   'I had brought'
(Hayward 1990: 476)

    c. Aari
        baʔkít-ääq(e)
        bring:NEG:PLUP:1=AUX
        'I had not brought'

In the negative progressive in Koegu, the auxiliary is uninflecting and in a LEX-headed structure, but nevertheless reflects its original syntactic head status by requiring the lexical verb to appear in an infinitive form, despite the fact that this form has undergone univerbation and now functions as a synchronic whole.

(75)   Koegu (Surmic, Nilo-Saharan; Ethiopa)
        a-am-en-[i]-ken
        1-eat-INF-NEG:PROG
        'I'm not eating'
        (Hieda 1998: 368)

6.3 Fused doubled inflection in AVCs

In a small number of languages, fused AVCs of the doubled inflectional pattern are found. As is the case with doubly inflected AVCs themselves, the most common pattern seen in fused doubled formations is doubled subject-marking.

    Auxiliary constructions in the Northern Yeniseic languages of Siberia are generally fused into single words synchronically. However, it is clear that many of the complex verbs, with their discontinuous stems, and probably also the past tense markers in Ket and Yugh, are fused auxiliary forms of the basic or doubled inflectional type. Although space does not permit an elaboration of this point here, there are at least two layers of fusing of auxiliaries in northern Yeniseic, one operating at a point when there was apparently AUX V structure (e.g. the tense/aspect markers which are in an AUX V configuration), and another fusing which speaks rather to a V AUX structure (to which belongs common stem-forming elements such as *-bet*, *-get*, *-tet*, in marking certain kinds of iteratives for example; see (77c, d)). The following Ket forms suggest a fused form of the doubled subject inflectional type, where the tense marker functioned originally as an auxiliary in an AUX V structure.[8]

---

[8] Note that the stem 'come' in Ket appears to be a compound historically, sometimes appearing bipartite, but otherwise as a disyllabic whole. Presumably one part is the Ur-ur-lexical element, and the other a lexicalized auxiliary, echo, or serial element.

(76) a. Ket (Yeniseic; Siberia) b. Ket
    d-i-lʲ-di-ʁa'   *k-i-lʲ-gu-ʁa*
    1-PV-PST-1sell   2-PV-PST-2-sell
    'I traded/dealt'   'you traded/dealt'
    (Verner 1997: 184)

    c. Ket   d. Ket
        d-o-lʲ-di-ʁa   *k-o-lʲ-gu-ʁa*
        1-PV-PST-1-sell   2-PV-PST-2-sell
        'I sold'   'you sold'

(77) a. Ket   b. Ket
    d-ik-s' i-ves'   *di᷄m-bes'*
    1-come-T/A-come   1:come:PST-come
    'I am coming'   'I came'
    (Werner 1997b: 229)

    c. Ket   d. Ket
        d-igbes'-a-vet   *d-igbes-ɔl'-bet*
        1-come-PST-AUX   1-come-PRS-AUX
        'I come'   'I used to come'
        [NB: not w/2ⁿᵈ person in standard Amharic]

Non-standard dialectal varieties of Amharic show a formation with a relatively straightforward doubled-subject AVC fused into a large complex.

(78) a. Amharic (Semitic, Afroasiatic; Ethiopia) b. Amharic
    sämt-äh-all-äh   *sämt-äš -all-äš*
    hear-2M-AUX-2M   hear-2F-AUX-2F
    'you (m) have heard'   'you (f) have heard'
    (Leyew 2003: 194)
    [NB. Not w/2nd person in standard Amharic]

The Papuan language Daga shows a similar formation. Here, however, the formation varies between a synchronic bi-partite AVC and a fused construction.

(79) a. Daga   b. Daga
    onam-iwanum   *onam wanum*
    come:3PL-3PL:CONT   COME:3PL 3PL:CONT
    'they are coming'   'they are coming'
    (Murane 1974: 64)

A complex range of doubly inflected formations that derive historically from auxiliary verb constructions are found in a number of different Tibeto-Burman languages. Most of these, properly speaking, should be considered as reflecting fused forms of the split/doubled pattern, and are discussed accordingly below. One Tibeto-Burman language with a straightforward fused doubled subject construction is Cogste Gyarong.

(80)   Cogste Gyarong (Tibeto-Burman; China)
   ñi-gyo tə-rgyap nə-t-sar-ñ mo ŋos
   2PL-HON marriage PFT-2PL-marry-2PL Q AUX.AFF
   'have you got married?'
   (Nakano 2003: 476)

In two unrelated groups of African languages, there is a curious AVC pattern, fused into a larger complex that has two agreement markers referring to the same argument, the semantic subject. However, one appears in the structural position of an auxiliary verb subject, the other in the position of a lexical verb object. One group of languages belongs to the Surmic sub-group of Nilo-Saharan, the other to the Chadic language family. This formation is thus reminiscent of a switch subject serial construction.

   One such language with fused complexes of this type is the Surmic language Tennet. Note that this same unusual configuration occurs in synchronic bi-partite AVCs in various related languages of the Nilotic family as well (see Chapter 4).

(81)   a.   Tennet
         k-a-kát-a ạnnạ́ tạạng íllạ́-w-a
         1-PRF-spear-1 I cow spear-EP-OBLQ
         'I speared the cow with a spear'
         (Dimmendaal 1998: 49)

       b.   Tennet
         k-á-múdâ atin ngáá immá ngá
         1-IMPF-find:1 FUT woman another where
         'where will I get another wife?'
         (Dimmendaal 1998: 52)

Note that some Tennet formations instead suggest a fused AUX-headed construction. Whether this is phonologically or morpho-semantically conditioned requires further research.

(82)   Tennet
   k-a-tángû
   1-PRF-sleep
   'I slept'
   (Dimmendaal 1998: 48)

Koegu also shows a fused formation of this type. However, unlike Tennet, which appears to derive from a structure like s-AUX LEX-OBJ⇐s>, Koegu shows a different original syntax, and rather looks like something of the shape s-LEX AUX:s. Note that in Koegu, the lexical verb may optionally appear in a dependent form in this fused doubly inflected construction.

(83) a. Koegu   b. Koegu
          a-am-iyaa   *a-am-en-iyaa*
          1-eat-T/A:1   1-eat-INF-T/A:1
          'I eat'   'I am eating'
          (Hieda 1998: 365)

In Chadic Pero of Nigeria, a similar formation appears to be attested. As the first example shows, in verb/complement structures, subject appears as a prefix on the matrix verb and a suffix on the complement. Fused structures that were originally biclausal may also appear in this formal guise. Compare examples (a) and (b–d) below.

(84) a. Pero (West Chadic; Nigeria) b. Pero
          nì-mén-jì di-ee-nò dǐjì̃   *nì-kóp-kó -ée-nò*
          1-want-HAB seat-AUGM-1   1-leave-COMPL-AUGM-1
          'I want to sit down'   'I left'
          (Frajzyngier 1989: 114)

      c. Pero   d. Pero
          ɲì-n-di-ée-nò   *nì-mé-nà -ée-nò*
          1-CONSEC-settle-AUGM-1   1-return-COMPL-AUGM-1
          '... and I settled'   'I returned'
          (Frajzyngier 1989: 114)   (Frajzyngier 1989: 115)

In fused complexes involving a transitive verb, the suffixal position is occupied by an apparent object marker. This suffix appears to redundantly refer to the subject with intransitives. Working out the historical origin of these curious doubly marked constructions remains a task for future research.

(85) a. Pero   b. Pero
          mà-lékkéd-ée-mà   *nì-tà-mè-tù-ée-nò*
          2PL-disperse-AUGM-1   1-FUT-return-VENT-AUGM-1
          'disperse for me!'   'I will return'
          (Frajzyngier 1989: 115)   (Frajzyngier 1989: 118)

c. Pero
    tà-píl-tù-ée-nò
    fut-buy-VENT-AUGM-1
    's/he will buy for me'
    [tábílléenò]
    (Frajzyngier 1989: 111)

d. Pero
    cì-tà-wát-tù-ée-nò
    2F-FUT-come-VENT-AUGM-1
    'you should bring for me'
    [cèRàwáttéenò]

e. Pero
    nì-mún-(í)nà-ée-cù
    1-give.COMPL.VENT-PREPRO-3PL
    'I gave them'
    [nìmúnnéjù]
    (Frajzyngier 1989: 112)

In so-called Eastern Jebel languages of the Nilo-Saharan phylum, complex fusings within a system of ablaut and tonal alternation yield an intricate and multiply subject-encoded formation. Such a complex of factors are found interacting in languages like Molo, seen in the following set of forms. The vowel quality and tone of the subject/tense prefixes varies as do those of the vowels of the lexical verb stem.

(86) a. Molo
          ɔ̀ŋ tìi:-bé
          I PRS:1:go:1
          'I go'
          (Bender 1989: 166)

      b. Molo
          in tə̀-bə̂i
          you PRS:2:go:2/3
          'you go'

      c. Molo
          ɔ̀y tə̀-sá
          we PRS:PL-go:1PL
          'we go'

      d. Molo
          uu tə̀-só
          you(PL) PRS:PL-go:2PL
          'you (PL) go'

Doubled subject formations may also be found in various Native North American languages. For example, there are constructions of this broad structural type in certain Yuman languages. In second person forms in both Walapai (Hualapai) and Jamul Tipay, subject prefixes appear both before lexical verbs and before auxiliary verbs in fused AVCs. Note that in both of these languages, the lexical verb appears in a dependent, same-subject form. Note also that in Walapai, first singular does not appear in such formations, although in this instance this gap may have been originally motivated by phonological factors, not morpho-semantic ones.

(87) a. Walapai (Hualapai)
   nya-ch Hwalbáy-ʔ-gwa:w-i
   I-subj Hualapai 1-speak-aux
   'I am speaking Hualaapai'
   (Watahomigie et al. 1982: 86–7)

   b. Walapai
   ma-ch Hwalbáy-saʔám- mi-gwa:w-ng-i
   you-subj Hualapai 2-speak-ss.2-aux
   'you are speaking Hualapai'

   c. Walapai
   nya-ch wa:-h ʔ-saʔám-wi
   I-subj door-dem 1-close-aux
   'I am closing the door'

   d. Walapai
   ma-ch wa:-h mi-saʔám-ng-wi
   you-subj door-dem 2-close-ss.2-aux
   'you are closing the door'

(88) Jamul Tiipay
   me-xnu-ch-me-yu
   2-be.sick-ss-2-aux.q
   'are you sick?'
   (Miller 2001: 273)

Fused doubly inflected AVCs in which the doubled category is some kind of TAM category are quite rare in the languages of my database. There are really only two clear examples of this. One comes from the Omotic language Hamer, where the so-called 'descriptive' aspect marker appears twice in a fused doubly inflected AVC.

(89) Hamer
   ena kum-i-d-i
   people eat-descr-aux-descr
   'the people have eaten'
   (Lydall 1976: 422)

The only other example comes from the Australian language Martuthunira. Here a formerly periphrastic causative construction has been fused into a large complex, with both the original lexical verb element and the original auxiliary marked for past tense.

(90) Martuthunira
   kartu-lwa nganaju kuyil-nguli-lha-ma-lalha yimpala-rri-waa drunka-
      npa-waa

2SG:NOM-ID 1SG:ACC bad-PSYCH-PST-CAUS-PST like.that-INVOL-
PURP.S=o drunk-INCH-PURP.S=o
'you're the one who made me feel bad, to become like that, to get
drunk'
(Dench 1995: 145)

6.4 Fused split and fused split/doubled inflection in AVCs

Fused complex verb forms that clearly derive from an auxiliary verb construction with split inflection are not particularly common in the languages of
my database. They are attested, however, in relatively restricted instances in
languages from around the globe.

For example, in North Munda Santali, the so-called imperfective series of
forms represents for some speakers a historical univerbation of an auxiliary
verb construction of the split inflectional type; for others these remain
synchronically bipartite formations.[9] Object and valence (an inflectionally
marked category in Santali) appeared suffixed to the original lexical verb
element and subject (and the finitizer) on the lexical verb.

(91) a. Santali   b. Santali
         uni dal-iñ-kan-a-e   *dal-et'-me-tahēkan-a-e*
         s/he beat-1-PROG-FIN -3   beat-PRES(.TR)-2-IMPERF-FIN-3
         'he is beating me'   'he was beating you'
         (Ghosh 1994: 95)   (Ghosh 1994: 106)

The Tibeto-Burman language Kinnauri shows a similar, albeit morphologically
much simpler construction. Lexical verbs appear with object suffixes, and
auxiliaries with subject suffixes. This appears either as a synchronic bipartite
AVC or as a univerbated complex, both reflecting this split inflectional structure.

(92) a. Kinnauri   b. Kinnauri
         khya-ci-du-k   *khya-ci du-k*
         see-2-AUX-1   see-2 AUX-1
         'I am seeing you'
         (Sharma 1988: 140)

[9] This is an unusual case in a number of respects. In Santali subject clitics appear enclitic to the
word immediately preceding the verb, or if the verb is the only word of the sentence, then enclitic to
that form (Bodding 1929, Ghosh 1994). In these imperfective series formations in Santali, however, the
subject marker does not attach to the object (and T/A) marked lexical verb, but rather always appears at
the end of the complex. Thus, these forms are targeted as unitary complexes for the purpose of the
placement of the subject clitic, but for phrasal prosody and stress placement, etc. appear to be two
separate words (J. Peterson, pc). More research is required on Santali to help elucidate these
complicated issues.

The conditional construction in the extinct Samoyedic language Kamas presents an interesting picture with regards to the historical univerbation of an auxiliary verb construction of the split type. The Kamas conditional appears to be a fused form of the verb *izä* [AUX:PST] a past form of an auxiliary < 'be' > with the lexical verb in the -*na* form, variably labelled conjunctive, conditional, or optative, and the auxiliary eroded to Ø. It could be the result of a fused split form, with subject and mood on the former lexical verb and tense on the former auxiliary.

(93) Kamas
      i?be-nä-m-zä
      lie-CNJCTV-1-AUX.PST
      'if I lie/lay'
      (Simoncsics 1998: 591)

It is also possible (although perhaps not wholly likely) that the final -*zä* in the Kamas conditional is at least in part influenced or reinforced by neighbouring Turkic conditional formations that are marked by a formally similar construction, e.g. Tuvan.

(94) Tuvan   cf. (95) Xakas
      kel-zi-m-ze   *kil-ze-m*
      come-COND-1-COND   come-COND-1
      'if I come'   'if I come'
      (Field notes)   (Field notes)

The Tuvan form appears to be reconstituted from a split construction in **X-di-m i/e[r]-se* < Old Turkic AUX *er-/är-*(to appear). As mentioned in Chapter 5 above, the nearly extinct Tofa has preserved something close to the original construction.

In Yeniseic Yugh of north central Siberia, object was marked on the original auxiliary verb component (< 'take'?), but subject was marked on both the original lexical component and the original auxiliary component,—i.e. these arose from a fusing of an original auxiliary verb construction of the split/doubled pattern.

(96) Yugh
      t-ku-g-di-χɨ·p
      1–2-SUBJ.VERS-1-sell
      'I sell you'
      (Werner 1997a: 138)

One group of languages where complex verb structures historically derived from AVCs of the split inflectional type are relatively commonly attested is found in a range of Oceanic languages of the Bougainville region of New Guinea. In Petats and Haku, an original structure of [Lexical Verb-Object Auxiliary Verb-Subject] is relatively transparently maintained in the fused verb form.

(97) Petats
      elia e nin-e-no-g u korits
      I VI eat-3OBJ-AUX-1 ART taro
      'I am eating taro'
      (Ross 1982b: 17)

(98) Haku
      aku e nan-e-nu-gu potutu
      I VI eat-OBJ-AUX-1 taro
      'I am eating taro'
      (Ross 1982b: 22)

In the related Selau language, on the other hand, the original auxiliary has been eroded to zero yielding a synchronically opaque formation.

(99) Selau
      ala e nu-ya-gu osono
      I VI eat-OBJ-1 taro
      'I am eating taro'
      (Ross 1982b: 22) <∅-AUX or [OBJ-]AUX-SUBJ fused?

In their sister language Mono, which belongs rather to the Western Bougainville sub-family and is spoken in the Solomon Islands, a similar structure is encountered, only here the relative order of the auxiliary element and the lexical verb element of the AVC is reversed, i.e. it comes from a structure of the type [Subject-Auxiliary Verb Lexical Verb-Object].

(100) Mono
       ha-na-nuhu-i
       1-FUT-dive-3OBJ
       'I will dive for it'
       (Ross 1982b: 14)

Other languages with similar structures include Ewe, a Kwa language of West Africa, which shows a formation formally identical to Mono.

(101) Ewe
       wò-la-vó-é
       2-FUT-fear-it
       'you will be afraid'
       (Allen 1993: 39)

Maramanandji reflects a rather different formal structure. In this Australian language of the Daly group, the large complex consists of an auxiliary fused to mark subject and a lexical verb that marks object and tense.

(102)   Maramanandji
    yitin kili-ŋ-tutur-a tʲurŋantʲi
    dog 3M:AUX:NONFUT-1OBJ-bite-PST yesterday
    'the dog bit me yesterday'
    (Tryon 1974i: 115)

The Northwest Caucasian language Kabardian offers a final example of a fused split pattern showing the subject with the original auxiliary element and the object with the original lexical element. Thus, in the following fused form, the original capabilitive auxiliary with its subject appears fused within a larger complex with a lexical verb bearing multiple grammatical affixes.

(103)   Kabardian (Northwest Caucasian; Russia)
    sx̂ʷɛpx̂ʷɛśá·q'ɛm
    s-x̂ʷə-w-x̂ʷa-ś'ə-ay-q'm
    1-CAP-2-BEN-do-PST-NEG
    'I was not able to do it for you'
    (Colarusso 1992: 110)

In a number of Australian languages, fused forms of a different type are encountered. In the form below, the auxiliary encodes tense and the lexical verb marks subject and object. Such a formation can be seen, for example, even in complex place names in Jawoyn that derive from fused AVCs of the split type.

(104)   a.   Jawoyn (Gunwinyguan)
        nyanbu-bi-borna-yal-wu-m
        3NSG>1NSG-APPL-liquid-cook-AUX-PST.PUNC
        'they brewed tea for us'
        (Merlan 2001: 368)

    b.   Jawoyn
        ga-wutjwutj-mar/mang
        3-bubble-AUX.PRES
        'it bubbles, it boils'
        (Merlan 2001: 371)

Note that in the second Jawoyn example, the 'lexical verb' is properly speaking likely to be an ideophone, and that different dialect forms are also reflected in the auxiliary at the end of the complex.

Another Australian language with somewhat similar formations is Mangarrayi, as described by Merlan (1979). In this language there are two broad formal types of auxiliary-like constructions. The first pattern is a massively fused auxiliary encoding all subject and object and relevant TAM categories which follows an unmarked lexical verb (105). This Merlan refers to as the particle plus auxiliary formation. The Mangarrayi AUX element itself is internally complex, consisting of the following structure AUX → PREFIX-AUX-SUFFIX. Roughly speaking, tense is marked suffixally and argument properties prefixally, with other categories spread among the various affix types. The second class Merlan calls compound verbs, which consist of an inflecting verb as a bound initial element (106). These are restricted and mainly lexicalized in the language, but likewise probably reflect an original auxiliary verb construction.

(105)   Mangarrayi
        mir? ga-ŋa-wuyan-n̪a-n
        know NON3.NPST-1-3PL-AUX-PRES
        'I know them'
        (Merlan 1979: 45)

(106)   Mangarrayi
        ŋa-wuyan-yiri+wa-b
        1-3PL-see+AUX-PST.PUNCT
        'I saw them'
        (Merlan 1979: 46)

Indeed, the latter forms look very much like a fused split AVC similar to the one encountered in Jawoyn, with subject and object marked on the lexical verb and tense on the (original) auxiliary. This formal pattern also subsumes original 'light verb' or 'dummy verb' or 'inflecting verb' structures, where the lexical element is not a verb stem but rather a nominal, and the auxiliary is the inflectable or copular verb stem. Note that according to Merlan (1979), many Australian languages utilize both of these patterns, but others lack one or the other, e.g. Ngalakan lacks the first pattern, as do some other Arnhem Land languages.

A non-Australian language showing a fused split pattern of this type is the endangered Cushitic language Kemantney (Qemant) of Ethiopia. Here, in certain complex verb forms deriving from a historical fusing of a split AVC, lexical verbs appear with subject suffixes, but TAM suffixes appear on the original auxiliary element.

(107) Kemantney (Qemant) (Cushitic; Ethiopia)
       ïntï ti-aɣʷäy-ïz bägä-s xašänt-ïy-an-ekʷ
       you 2-head-by sheep-ACC steal-2-AUX-IMPRF
       'you have stolen the sheep by yourself'
       (Leyew 2003: 181)

Further, in the Southern Nilotic language Nandi of Kenya, most fused AVCs
are apparently of the LEX-headed type, but at least one appears to be a split
inflectional form similar to that of Kemantney and Jawoyn, where the original
auxiliary encodes tense while subject was restricted to the original lexical verb
element. These were then fused into a complex verb form.

(108) Nandi
       ká-tâ-a:-kás-é
       PST-AUX-1-listen-ASP
       'I have just listened'
       (Creider and Tapsubei Creider 1989: 111)

Another fused split pattern comes from the negative present in Dhurga. If one
considers the negative to be a lexical verb in Dhurga, then the negative present
appears to be a construction in which the lexical verb marked tense and the
auxiliary-marked subject fused into a larger univerbated complex. Note that
in the closely related Dharawal, the negative appears as a preverbal particle
(although perhaps this is really a LEX-headed formation, as LEX-headed
constructions often appear to be covert particle formations).

(109) Dharawal   (110) Dhurga
       ŋambana dʸam-i-ŋal   *dʸam-a-ŋamba-ga*
       NEG talk-PRES-1DL.INCL   talk-PRES-NEG-1
       'we two are not speaking'   'I talk not'
       (Eades 1976: 65)

Some languages also appear to have complex verb forms that might be
referred to as 'fused pseudo-split' or 'pseudo-fused pseudo-split'. In this
Bunuba form, a tense-marked lexical verb serves as host for an auxiliary
element that encodes subject and object properties (remember the first
type of Mangarrayi construction discussed above). Clitic forms of this type
are often a stage in the process leading to full prosodic/phonological univerbation, and as such perhaps should be considered a semi-fused split
formation.

(111) a. Bunuba (Australian)   b. Bunuba
           wug'-bila   *mila'-wila*
           cook-FUT.1>3.AUX   see-FUT 1>3.AUX
           'I'll cook it'   'I'll see him/her/it'
           (Rumsey 2000: 78)

Complex verb forms that represent a historical univerbation of an auxiliary verb construction exhibiting the split/doubled inflectional pattern are also found in a small number of languages. One such language is the Kartvelian (South Caucasian) language Georgian. The perfective form of a certain conjugational class in Georgian appears to be a univerbated split/doubled auxiliary verb construction. In the first person singular (and originally in older sources in the second person singular as well (which has become opaque due to phonological change (Shanidze 1976)), the verb consists of a subject-marked auxiliary in an original V AUX configuration preceded by a lexical verb that marks subject, appearing in a dependent participle form.

(112) a. Georgian (Kartvelian; Georgia) b. Georgian
           da-v-č'er-il-var   *mo-v-k'lu-l-var*
           PV-1-catch-PRF.PRTCPL-1:AUX   PV-1-kill-PRF.PRTCPL-1:AUX
           'I have caught'   'I have killed'
           (Aronson 1982: 301)

       c. Georgian
           mo-k'lu-l-xar
           PV-kill-PRF.PRTCPL-2:AUX
           'you have killed'
           (Aronson 1982: 301)

With certain transitive verbs, the fused auxiliary indexes the semantic object although the form suggests rather a syntactic (and morphosyntactic) subject, with the semantic subject appearing as a syntactic object fused into the same kind of complex as the forms above.

(113) Georgian
       v-u-k-i-var
       1-3-praise-PRF-1:AUX
       'he praised me'
       (Aronson 1982: 272)

As alluded to above, a number of Tibeto-Burman languages of the Kiranti subgroup show a wide range of fused auxiliary verb constructions of the split/doubled type. One such formation is found in Athpare. Here a telic auxiliary

marking object and past tense appears fused (in the V AUX structure typical of
Kiranti languages) to an object-marked lexical verb. Various other complex
structures in a range Kiranti languages are briefly discussed by Ebert (2003a).

(114)   Athpare
        lept-u-des-u-e
        throw-3PAT-AUX:TELIC-3PAT-PST
        'he threw it away'
        (Ebert 2003a: 512)

In its sister language Dumi (Rai), like Athpare also spoken in Nepal, there is
another split/doubled inflection pattern seen in a complex fused verb form,
historically deriving from an auxiliary verb construction, itself likely derived
from a deictic serialization formation. Thus the so-called 'allative aspect'
marker in Dumi appears with a non-past tense marker and a subject fused
into a large complex following a subject-marked lexical verb.

(115)   Dumi (Rai) (Tibeto-Burman; Nepal)
        aŋ dza: dza-ŋ-pət-t-ə
        I rice eat-1-ALL-NPST-1
        'I'm going to eat'
        (van Driem 1993: 199)

In the following Dumi complex construction, the present progressive formation, both the lexical verb and the original progressive or continuous aspect
auxiliary bear portmanteau subject > object suffixes, the original auxiliary in
this first AVC bearing a non-past marker.

(116)   Dumi (Rai)
        roʔdi boʔo tsen-n-thə-n-t-a
        Rai language teach-1>2-CONT-1>2-NPST-*a*
        'I am teaching you Dumi'
        (van Driem 1993: 200)

In the Pakistani language isolate Burushaski, there is a somewhat opaque
element, the so-called *d*-prefix, that appears in a range of verbs. This appears
to be an original auxiliary element meaning 'come'. In forms with speech act
participant and class II (female human) nouns as subjects, there may be
doubled subject marking in a fused complex, but only a single marker that
encodes object or negation. These thus appear to be (albeit synchronically
lexicalized) reflexes of univerbated AVCs showing a split/doubled inflectional
pattern.

(117) a. Burushaski   b. Burushaski
           du-kú-man-um-a   *a-tú-ku-man-um-a*
           d-2-be.born-PST-2   NEG-d-2-be.born-PST-2
           'you were born'   'you weren't born'
           (Berger 1998b: 91)

Note that synchronically Burushaski is rigidly SOV, but that this original
auxiliary element appears to be fused from a preverbal position. Its ultimate
origin in a deictic serialized formation seems likely (e.g. 'come be' > 'be
born'). As all that remains of this verb for 'come' is the *d*-prefix in Burushaski,
perhaps it is unsurprising that some inflected forms of this verb include
(semi-) fused AVCs (showing V AUX order) with doubled subject inflection
in a split/doubled form.

(118) Burushaski
       d-áaya=wá-yam
       come-1-AUX-1: PST
       'I have come'
       (Berger 1998: 140)

The Dravidian languages Pengo and Kolami both show fused complex verb
forms that appear to derive from AVCs of the split/doubled inflectional
pattern. Both languages show doubled subject inflection, with negative in
Kolami on the original lexical verb and tense on an original auxiliary with a
synchronic Ø realization. In Pengo, the original lexical verb component
marked tense.

(119) Pengo (Kolami Dravidian; India)   (120) Kolami
           huṛ-t-aŋ-n-aŋ   *sī-e-t-an*
           see-PAST-1-AUX-1   give-NEG.1(AUX)-PAST-1
           'I have seen'   'I didn't give'
           (Steever 1988: 79)   (Steever 1988: 91)

In certain fused complex verb forms in Kemantney that originally derive from
split/doubled AVCs, subjects appear on both the original lexical verb and the
original auxiliary, but TAM categories on the auxiliary only.

(121) a. Kemantney (Qemant) (Cushitic, Afroasiatic; Ethiopia)
           ïntï was-y-an-y-äk^w
           you hear-2-AUX-2-IMPF
           'you have heard'
           (Leyew 2003: 193)

b. Kemantney
    ïntändew was-y-ïn-wan-y-äk^w-ïn
    you.PL hear-2-PL-AUX-2-IMPF-PL
    'you (PL) have heard'
    (Leyew 2003: 193)

c. Kemantney
    naydew was-nï-wan-äk^w-ïn
    they hear-PL-AUX-IMPF-PL
    'they have heard'
    (Leyew 2003: 193)

In the Western Nilotic language Dhó-Alúř, fused auxiliary verb constructions of a complex type are found. Some fused original AVCs show doubled subject-marking, others do not. The lexical verb in these constructions appears in the so-called independent forms, while the fused subject/tense auxiliary prefix, as well as tense-marked lexical verb, are formally encoded not through segmental addition but through tonal alternation. Compare the following three forms that differ in function but formally are distinguished only tonally, the segmental features of the forms being otherwise identical. Such a system may have arisen from the use of segmentally minimal or reduced elements (auxiliary, tense suffixes, etc.) whose only synchronic realization is the tonal alternation.

(122) a. Dhó-Alúř   b. Dhó-Alúř   c. Dhó-Alúř
           á-lwóŋ-ò   *álwòŋò*   *â-lwóŋ-o'*
           1:NPRS-call-INDEP   1:NPRS-call:FUT-INDEP   1:PRS-call-INDEP
           'I (have) called'   'I shall call'   'I call'
           (Knappert 1963: 104–6)

In the fused progressive construction, non-present forms of the subject markers combine with the original progressive auxiliary (tonally marked for tense) followed by the lexical verb in the independent form. In the present progressive there is a single marker of subject; in the tonally different past progressive, subject is doubly encoded in the univerbated complex.

(123) a. Dhó-Alúř   b. Dhó-Alúř
           á-bè-lwóŋ-o'   *á-bé[ɖ]-á-lwóŋ-ò*
           1-PRS.PROG-call-INDEP   1-PST.PROG-1-call-INDEP
           'I am calling'   'I was calling'
           (Knappert 1963: 111)

Relatively straightforward examples of a univerbated complex verb form deriving from an auxiliary verb construction of the split/doubled type come from various Australian languages of the Daly family. In Marithiel, Marityabin, and Marengar an array of split/doubled formations have been fused into large complexes.

(124) a. Marithiel
ŋawu-kutluk-wa nitʸiŋani
1:AUX:FUT-cough-FUT tomorrow
'I shall cough tomorrow'
(Tryon 1974g: 81)

b. Marithiel
kaŋi-kutluk-a tʸuwuŋanan
1:AUX:PST-cough-PST yesterday
'I coughed yesterday'

c. Marithiel
kiny-iŋ-kur-a tʸuwuŋanan
3M:AUX:PST-1OBJ-hit-PST yesterday
'he hit me yesterday'
(Tryon 1974g: 85)

(125) a. Marityabin
tʸipaki ki-mpi-pup-ta-ya
tobacco 3AUX-2OBJ-give-EMPH-PST
'he gave you some tobacco'
(Tryon 1974h: 98)

b. Marityabin
kil-iŋ-titip-a
3M:AUX:PST-1OBJ-bite-PST
'he bit me'

(126) a. Marengar
nitʸiŋani kur-inʸ-pet-ni
tomorrow 3M:AUX:FUT-2OBJ-wash-FUT
'he will wash you tomorrow'
(Tryon 1974j: 127)

b. Marengar
watʸan pali-ŋ-titip-a
dog 3M:AUX:PST-1OBJ-bite-PST
'the dog bit me'
(Tryon 1974j: 131)

Some of the forms above involve the characteristically Australian system of doubled tense marking, others do not. Also, if an object is present, it will appear on the original lexical verb element, while subject appears only on the original auxiliary verb element, with which the subject marker has fused, optionally with tense specification yielding the doubled tense construction just alluded to. This combination of separate developments yields a uniquely and characteristically Daly-family configuration: a split between the lexical verb with object markers but the auxiliary verb with subject markers, tense encoded on either just the lexical verb or both, and the subject-tense-auxiliary itself fused and subsequently fused into a larger complex.

Although functionally somewhat unusual, the element that means 'non-singular actants performing the action specified' in the Papuan language Yareba appears originally to have been an auxiliary verb. This seems to have been embedded within a split/doubled inflectional configuration in which the lexical verb marks tense but both the lexical verb and the original auxiliary mark the subject.

(127)   a.   Yareba
            i-f-e-i-si
            eat-FUT-1PL-NON.SG-1PL
            'we will eat'
            (Weimer 1972: 64)

   b.   Yareba
        ani-b-o-i-ta
        go-FUT-2PL-NON.SG-2PL
        'you will go'

One of the most complicated systems of fused AVCs found in any language belongs to the Papuan language Yele. In this language, auxiliaries appear both preverbally and postverbally in an often quasi-circumfixal manner. The auxiliaries themselves are opaque fused elements that encode a range of subject/object and TAM categories. Often these categories are expressed in both the preverbal and the postverbal elements, while other categories are restricted to one or the other. In such cases, one may find structures where split/doubled inflectional patterning is found in these fused auxiliary elements in Yele (with unmarked lexical verbs).

(128)   a.   Yele
            Kaawa ngê dê m:uu té
            Kaawa SG.ERG PI:IMM.PST:3SBJ see TR:PI:PRX:3PL:O.MF
            'Kaawa saw them'
            (Henderson 1995: 15)

   b.   Yele
        saw nt:u ngmê-nî ńuwo
        saw body INDEF-PI:REM:1SBJ took:REM
        'I took a saw blade'
        (Henderson 1995: 16)

For an extensive list and discussion of these forms with many examples, see Henderson (1995: 20 ff., esp. 35–8).

In Warembori, a complex verb form seemingly derived from yet another split pattern is found. Presumably this construction derived from a serialized construction of the type Subject-Transitive Verb-Object + Verb-Subject = Object. This marks a type of applicative formation and is inflectionally a split/doubled pattern, synchronically univerbated into a large complex verb.

(129)   Warembori (Lower Mamberamo; Papua New Guinea)
  e-per-i-ta-e
  1-throw-3-APPL-3
  'I threw it into it' (i.e. fish into water)
  (Donohue 2003a: 139)

Fused deictic SVCs are found in other Papuan languages as well, for example in Sentani. Here both the initial deictic motion verb and the second verb, i.e. the verb that in AVCs fills the functional slot of the lexical verb component, are inflected for tense, with object and subject marked only on the latter verb. This therefore yields something that in structure (given appropriate but really only minimal functional adjustment of the semantics of the construction) could give rise to AVCs showing split/doubled inflectional patterns. In any event, the Sentani forms demonstrate that it is not necessary for fused complexes of this type to derive from AVCs; they may come directly from deictic SVCs as well.

(130)   Sentani
  ə-j-mokoj-j-an-ɛ
  go-HAB-do.to-HAB-3OBJ-2:IND
  'you always go and do to him'
  (Cowan 1965: 39)

Other morphologically complex verb forms deriving from split/doubled auxiliary verb constructions are found in such North American languages as Siouan Crow and the extinct isolate Timucua. In Crow, subject is doubly marked, but TAM categories and the declarative suffix appear on the original auxiliary verb element only. This yields long complex verbs such as the following:

(131) a. Crow (Siouan; Montana) b. Crow
   b-eelax-b-isshi-k   *da-saax-daa-hku-i-k*
   1-urinate-1-MOD-DECL   2-snore-2-AUX-HAB-DECL
   'I need to urinate'   'you always snore'
   (Graczyk 1991)

In Timucua, the proximate tense appears doubly marked in the original AVC on both the former auxiliary and the lexical verb stem, but subject appears only on the original lexical verb component.

(132) a. Timucua[†] (isolate; Southeast Georgia/Florida)
   chi-huba-so-le-ha-be-la
   2-love-TRANS-PROX-FUT-BND-PROX
   'you will love him'
   (Granberry 1993: 100)

b. Timucua[†]
chi-huba-so-le-he-la
2-love-TRANS-PROX-CAP-PROX
'you can love him'
(Granberry 1993: 101)

6.5 Fusing of subject/pronoun, TAM, polarity, and auxiliary in AVCs

In many different languages, although concentrated in certain geographical areas, one finds a range of seemingly tense-marked (or TAM, polarity, etc.) pronouns. In many instances what these forms are actually (at least historically) are fused auxiliary verb plus subject formations. Such forms occur in the position of auxiliaries in the relevant languages with such formations, e.g. clause-finally in the Chimbu language Salt-Yui of Papua New Guinea, or initially in Niuean.

(133)   a.   Salt-Yui   b.   Salt-Yui
             heba i ne mongwi   *ne i ongwi*
             sweet.potato this eat 3:AUX:PST   eat this 3:AUX:EFF
             'he was eating this sweet potato' 'he was eating'
             (Irwin 1974: 49)

(134)   Niuean (Polynesian, Austronesian; Niue)
        kwai fale qa-mu ta qai
        1:FUT give RCPNT-2 some:SG tree
        'I'll give you a tree'
        (Haji-Abdolhosseini et al. 2002: 455)

In Nissan (Nehan), it is clear that these are verbal forms, as they occur with subject pronouns and in an AUX-headed inflectional pattern (with Ø-marked lexical verb). In emergent auxiliary constructions, both verbs occur with the fused subject auxiliary forms.

(135)   a.   Nissan (Bougainville, Oceanic, Austronesian; Papua New Guinea)
             ingeg i turung ker
             we 1PL:AUX:PRES FUT sing
             'we will sing'
             (Todd 1982: 1198)

        b.   Nissan
             ingo ku nihing pokoso puk
             I 1:AUX:PST IMM.PST get home
             'I just got home'
             (Todd 1982: 1198)

c. Nissan
    ingo u malara u an
    I 1:PRES:AUX want 1:PRES:AUX eat
    'I want to eat'
    (Todd 1982: 1200)

One area where free-standing forms of fused auxiliary cum subject pronouns
(AUX/SUBJ) occur relatively commonly is Australia, where the auxiliary element is an integral part of the inflection in a number of languages. In Pitta-
Pitta, there is a series of 'future subject pronouns'. This is a lexicalized system
probably deriving from the fused AUX/SUBJ forms.

(136)   Pitta-Pitta
        1   *ŋan^yu*   3M.NR   *ɲuŋuyu*   3F.NR   *ŋanŋuyu*
        2   *inŋu*   3M.GNRL *ɲuŋuka*   3F.GNRL *ŋanŋuka*
                        3M.FAR   *ɲuŋua:rri*   3F.FAR   *ŋanŋua:rri*
        (Blake 1979: 195)

They occur either preceding or following future-marked lexical verbs in a
split/doubled pattern not uncommon in Australian languages.

(137)   a. Pitta-Pitta   b. Pitta-Pitta
            ŋan^yainu ŋan^yu kaɲʈa   *ʈaʈi-kainu ŋaɲa-ŋu*
            tomorrow 1:FUT go-FUT   eat-1:IMP we:FUT
            'tomorrow I'll go'   'let's eat'
            (Blake 1979: 202–3)

In Bāgandji, the forms encode case as well as tense and person categories and
generally occur postverbally.

(138)   a. Bāgandji   b. Bāgandji   c. Bāgandji
            baridjiri ḏaɳi gāba   *bami ŋaḏu*   *ḏaɳi wadi*
            far.away go FUT:1:NOM   see PAST:1:ERG   go PAST:3PL
            'I'll go a long way off' 'I can see'   'they've gone'
            (Hercus 1982: 123)

        d. Bāgandji   e. Bāgandji
            gila ḏiŋga-ri ŋaḏu   *bina-ri gimba*
            NEG rise-VBLZR/ASP PRES:3 climb-VBLZR/ASP FUT:2
            'he's not getting up'   'you'll climb'
            (Hercus 1982: 124)

Note that in Bārundji these have been optionally fused into larger complex
verb forms. These types of formations I refer to as 'fused/fused' constructions.

(139) a. Bārundji   b.   Bārundji
           balga-wuḏu   *balgu waḏu*
           hit-PRF:1:TR   hit:PRF PST:1:ERG
           'I have beaten'   'I have beaten'
           (Hercus 1982: 126; Wurm and Hercus 1976: 42)

Wambaya contrasts a present and a past for intransitives and a future/non-future series for portmanteau transitive subject > object forms.

(140) a. Wambaya   b.   Wambaya
           nyagajbi ngi   *gajbi ny-a*
           be.tired 1SG(.PRES)   eat 2-PST
           'I'm tired'   'you ate it'
           (Nordlinger 1998: 25)

(141) Wambaya

	present	past
1	*ngi*	*ng-a*
2	*nyi*	*ny-a*
3	*gi*	*g-a*
3M	*gini*	*gin-a*
3NM	*ngiyi*	*ngiya*
1DL.INCL	*mirndi*	*mirnd-a*

(Nordlinger 1998: 40–1)

(142) Wambaya

	non-future	future
1>2	*ngi-ny-a*	*ngu-ny-u*
2>1	*nyi-ng-a*	*nyu-ng-u*
3M>1	*gini-ng-a*	*gunu-ngg-u* (NB= 3m>RR)
3NM>2	*ngiyi-ny-a*	*nguyu-ny-u*

The system in Wambaya is actually extremely complex; it includes a range of specific fused formations of this type with directional, aspectual, etc. semantics, seen in examples such as the following:

(143) a. Wambaya   b.   Wambaya
           ngu-ny-uda   *murnd-uba*
           1-2OBJ-NACT.PST   1DL.INCL-NPST.TLOC
           (Nordlinger 1998: 41)

	c.	Wambaya	d.	Wambaya	e.	Wambaya
		ngay-ala		*gana-ng-ala*		*nga-ngg-ala*
		3NM-HAB.NPST		3M-1OBJ-HAB.NPST		1-RR-HAB.NPST

(Nordlinger 1998: 41)

This AUX element is obligatory in Wambaya and it encodes the tense/aspect features and argument properties of the clause. According to Nordlinger (1998: 50), V AUX is the most common order, but not the exclusive one in Wambaya.

Another part of the world where constructions of this type are relatively common is Africa. There are three separate clusters of African languages where constructions like this or related to this AUX/SUBJ fusing are encountered: a Mande and Kru series in West Africa, a Chadic series in Nigeria, and a Nilo-Saharan cluster in Sudan.

In Mande languages, such as Boko/Busa and Bokobaru, subject and auxiliary are fused into a single word.

(144)   Boko/Busa (Mande, Niger-Congo; Nigeria, Benin)
      mɛ́ gá-ò
      1:FUT go-COM
      'I will go with him'
      (Jones 1998: 133)

(145)   Bokobaru
      má gé aànɔ̀
      1:FUT go 3:COM
      'I will go with him'
      (Jones 1998: 133)

This word can also play host to clitic object pronouns.

(146)   Boko/Busa
      ñ-aà ʿè
      2:PRF-3OBJ see
      'you saw him'
      (Jones 1998: 131)

Mende proper has a more complex system encoding tense/aspect and polarity categories through an ablaut-like gradation of vowel quality and quantity.

(147)	a.	Mende	b.	Mende	c.	Mende	d.	Mende
		ng-a tewe		*ng-aa tewe*		*ng-i tewe*		*ng-ii tewe*
		1-PM cut		1-NEG:PM cut		1-AOR cut		1-NEG.AOR cut
		'I cut'		'I do not cut'		'I cut'		'I do/did not cut'

      (Heine and Reh 1984: 208; Migeod 1908: 84)

In Kru languages, a number of such formations are encountered. For example, in Neyo, tone and length contrasts make grammatical oppositions, reflecting an earlier fusing of a subject and an auxiliary element. The imperfective form in the closely related Klao shows a similar development, albeit with a different tonal realization.

(148) a. Neyo
      ɔ-ɓlī-ɛ̄
      he sing-IMPF
      'he sings, can sing'
      (Marchese 1982: 18)

     b. Neyo
      ɔ̄ɔ̄ ɓlī-ɛ̄
      he:IMPF sing:IMPF
      'he is singing'

(149) Klao (Kru)
    ɔ̄ɔ̄ blē
    3:IMPF sing
    'he is singing' he habitually sings'
    (Marchese 1982: 3)

In Vata and Neyo polarity may be encoded in these fused subject/auxiliary forms as well, in addition to tense/aspect.

(150) Vata (Kru; Côte d'Ivoire)
    ɔ́ɔ́ lá uá kɔ̄`
    3:NEG call T person
    'he wasn't calling anyone'
    (Marchese 1986: 198)

(151) Neyo
    né mla dili-no
    1:NEG:NPST drink raphia-wine
    'I don't drink raphia wine'
    (Marchese 1982: 6)

In Dewoin, another form is offered below, incorporating the AUX/SUBJ form into a doubly future marked complex AVC (i.e. from a former split/doubled pattern), with a dependent marked lexical verb.

(152) Dewoin (Western Kru, Niger-Congo; Liberia)
    ɔ́ɔ́ mū sāyɛ̀ pi-ì mǔ
    he:PRS FUT meat cook-NOM FUT
    'he's going to cook meat'
    (Marchese 1982: 17)

In Central Sudanic Meje, there is a fused AUX/SUBJ element followed by a subject-marked lexical verb in another kind of split/doubled pattern.

(153) Meje
    má bhó ú méku-a
    1:AUX already there 1:come-NPST
    'I'm already (in the process of) coming'
    (McKee 1991: 167)

A similar formation is seen in its sister language Kelo, of the Eastern Jebel group of Eastern Sudanic.

(154) a. Kelo
    ɔ́ŋ béɔ̀
    I:NPRS go:FUT[:1]
    'I will go'
    (Bender 1989: 166)

    b. Kelo
    ín bɔ́ì
    you:NPRS go:FUT:2
    'you will go'

Among Chadic languages, Ngizim and Karekare offer examples of related phenomena. In Ngizim, fused AUX/SUBJ forms appear with dependent marked lexical verbs in an AUX-headed AVC or in a dependent modal form.

(155) a. Ngizim
    ná ta'-w
    1:PRF eat-DEP
    'I ate'
    (Schuh 1976: 5)

    b. Ngizim
    kwá ta'-w
    2PL:PERF eat-DEP
    'you (PL) ate'
    [+√straight tone]

    c. Ngizim
    nàa tá-w
    1:IMPRF eat-DEP
    'I was eating'

    d. Ngizim
    kwàa tá-w
    2PL:IMPERF eat-DEP
    'you (PL) were eating'

    e. Ngizim
    nà cí
    1SBJ eat:SBJ
    'that I eat'
    (Schuh 1976: 5)

    f. Ngizim
    kwà cí
    2PL:SBJ eat:SBJ
    'that you (PL) eat'

In Karekare, which is closely related to Ngizim, lexical verbs may appear in a range of forms, with tense/aspect/mood in covertly doubly marked forms.

(156) a. Karekare
    nà tú-kòo
    1:PRF eat-PRF
    'I ate'
    (Schuh 1976: 5)

    b. Karekare
    kú t-án-kòo
    2PL:PRF eat-PRF
    'you (PL) ate'

    c. Karekare
    nàa tə́-nà
    1:IMPRF eat-IMPRF
    'I was eating'

    d. Karekare
    kwáa tə-nà
    2PL:IMPRF eat-IMPRF
    'you (PL) were eating'

    e. Karekare
    nà tài
    1SBJ eat:SBJ
    'that I eat'
    (Schuh 1976: 5)

    f. Karekare
    kú tài
    2PL:SBJ eat:SBJ
    'that you (PL) eat'

The Mon-Khmer language Khasi of eastern India and Bangladesh has an emergent system of TAM/polarity-marked fused SUBJ/AUX forms that themselves may appear in a larger analytic AVC.

(157) a. Khasi   b. Khasi
      nga'n ioh leit   *nga'm ioh wan*
      I:FUT AUX go   1:NEG AUX come
      'I will be able/permitted to go'   'I cannot come'
      (Roberts [1891]: 54)

Another area where fused AUX/SUBJ forms are found with some frequency is the
northern Amazon. In a range of Cariban languages AUX/SUBJ forms are used but
they are found in a number of different constructions. For example, in Waiwai
and Kaxuyana, they appear to require lexical complements in a participle form
in some AVCs. That is, as with many other auxiliary verb constructions, the
lexical verb appears in a dependent form in these fused AUX/SUBJ forms.

(158) Waiwai
      ti-kah-so nasi
      ADV-slip-PRTCPL 3.AUX
      's/he slipped'
      (Gildea 1998: 220)

(159) Kaxuyana
      suriana wiya sesu t-emo'ka-ʃe nast
      Juliana ERG Sérgio ADV-teach-PRTCPL 3AUX
      'Juliana taught Sérgio'
      (Gildea 1998: 231)

In Panare, first singular objects appear on the AUX/SUBJ from, and aspect on
the lexical verb in a curious split (or pseudo-split AUX-headed) formation.

(160) Panare
      petyúma-mpəh kəh-yu məh
      hit-PROG.TRANS 3AUX-1OBJ 3SG
      's/he is hitting me'
      (Gildea 1998: 205)

In Apalaí lexical verbs may appear in various aspectual forms in what appears
to be a split pattern with the AUX/SUBJ form. Note that object prefixes
appear on the lexical verb in Apalaí (162).

(161) a. Apalaí   b. Apalaí
      oe'-ñõõko ase   *topu arõ-õko ase*
      come-IMPRF 1AUX   stone take-IMPRF 1AUX
      I'm coming'   'I'm taking a stone'
      (Gildea 1998: 211)

  b. Apalaí
      otu'-ñōōko akene
      eat-CONT 1.AUX.PAST
      'I was eating'

(162) Apalaí
      o-ere'-ñōōko ase
      2-startle-IMPRF 1AUX
      'I'm gonna startle you'
      (Gildea 1998: 211)

In Tiriyó and Wayana, there is a circumfixal completive found on the lexical verb. In Tiriyó, the auxiliary may precede the lexical verb unlike in all the examples above (and also the Wayana form below) where it follows it, but the completive construction appears to be cognate in the two languages.

(163) Tiriyó
      wəri nai t-tə-e
      woman 3.AUX COMPL-go-COMPL
      'the woman went'
      (Gildea 1998: 24)

(164) Wayana
      kuraši t-panaŋma-y man i-ya
      rooster COMPL-hear-COMPL 3.AUX 1-AGT
      'I heard the rooster'
      (Gildea 1998: 24)

Similar fused AUX/SUBJ forms are found in Gavião of the Tupi-Guaraní family spoken by several hundred people in Brazil. These can be found embedded within either an AUX-headed (a) or doubled (b) formation (with both AVCs having lexical verbs in a dependent form).

(165) a. Gavião
          māā dza-βípi pogò-á
          1.AUX house-wall cover-BOUNDARY.MARKER
          'I covered the walls'
          (Rodrigues 1999a: 117; Moore 1984: 74)

      b. Gavião
          dʒaá paa-gà-á
          1PL.INCL-AUX 1PL.INCL-go-BOUNDARY.MARKER
          'let's go'
          (Rodrigues 1999a: 118; Moore 1994: 80)

In certain Oceanic languages, the fused AUX/SUBJ forms are embedded within 'classic' split inflectional AVCs, e.g. with object encoded on the lexical verb (and subject of course fused into the auxiliary). Such a formation is found in Tigak, Niuean, and Simbo.

(166) Tigak (New Ireland, Oceanic, Austronesian; Papua New Guinea)
    naga kalum-i
    1.PST see-3
    'I saw him'
    (Beaumont 1989: 40)

(167) Niuean
    tai wane, kere fale-a fanga qi a-da tai wane qe aqi kesi fale qa-da
    some:PL man 3PL:NFUT give-3OBJ food to RCPNT-3PL some:PL man
        3:NFUT NEG.AUX 3PL:NEG give RCPNT-3PL
    'some of the men they did give food to, some of them they did not give to'
    (Haji-Abdolhosseini et al. 2002: 455)

(168) a. Simbo (New Georgia, Oceanic, Austronesian; Solomon Islands)
       poi sa teku-a p-ia na koburu
       then 3:AUX:RLS take-3OBJ ERG-she the child
       'then she took the child...'
       (Palmer 1996: 251)

    b. Simbo
       eyo gari ton-ia ria na rereko
       OK 3PL: AUX:RLS lead-3OBJ they the female
       'all the women would lead her...'
       (Palmer 1996: 252)

TABLE 6.2. Kâte sentence-final fused TAM + subject forms

Realis Punctiliar

1.PRES	1.NR.PST	1.FAR.PST	1.NR.FUT	1.FAR.FUT
-kopa'	*-pa'*	*-po*	*-pemu*	*-tsokopa'*

Realis Habitual		Irrealis		Intentional	
1.PRES	1.PST	1.FUT	1.PST	1.PRES	1.FUT
-ekopa'	*-jupa'*	*-tsipo*	*-tsapo*	*-pe*	*-tsepa'*

(Johnson 1972)

TABLE 6.3. Kâte sentence-medial fused TAM + subject forms

Type I		
1.RESULT	1.SIMULT	1.DURATION
-*era*	-*hu̇'/-te'*	-*ku*
Type II		
1.RESULT	1.SIMULT	1.DURATION
-*pe*	-*hape*	-*kupe*

(Johnson 1972)

In addition to the formations above, where fused AUX/SUBJ forms appear within larger AVCs exhibiting any of the inflectional types where auxiliaries are inflected (i.e. AUX-headed, doubled, split, and split/doubled), these elements can of course *themselves* become fused into a larger verbal complex, much like any of the other constructions discussed in 6.1–6.4. As mentioned above, I call these 'fused/fused' formations.

One area where complex verb forms of fused complexes that themselves already involved fused AUX/SUBJ formations is in a number of languages of New Guinea. Some languages make use of enormous numbers of verb forms the origin of which is likely to be just such fused AUX/SUBJ forms. One such language is Kâte. Examine the sets of first person singular forms in Tables 6.2 and 6.3 from this language of the Eastern Huon branch of the Huon-Finisterre stock.

The grammar of Kâte is not unlike that of many Papuan languages. It contrasts a series of inflectional markers used on verbs that appear in final position, and those that appear medially. Within each set various subsets are recognized that contrast a range of TAM categories as well as person and number. Many other Papuan languages make use of fused complexes such as these in Kâte, for example, its sister languages the Western Huon languages Burum and Selepet, Mugil of the Madang-Adalbert Range stock, and Sulka, a family-level isolate of the East Papuan phylum.

(169) a. Burum
           dawinâŋi bau erâ-tsap
           when he pig shoot-he:IMM.PST
           'when did he shoot the pig'
           (McElhanon 1967: 25)

       b. Burum
           i uran bau erâ-yop
           he yesterday pig shoot-he:REM.PST
           'he shot the pig yesterday'

(170) a. Selepet
           gâi-nek-sap
           cut-1OBJ-he:IMM.PST
           'he cut me'
           (McElhanon 1967: 39)

      b. Selepet
           gâi-neh-op
           cut-1OBJ-he:REM.PST
           'he cut me'

(171) a. Mugil
           ya leh-day
           I go-FUT:1
           I will go'
           (Z'Graggen 1971: 150)

      b. Mugil
           ni/in/ne leh-da
           you/s/he go-FUT:2/3
           'you, s/he will go'

      c. Mugil
           iy leh-auʔ
           we go-FUT:1PL
           'we will go'

Sulka, while indeed showing fused AUX/SUBJ forms fused into larger complexes, had the auxiliary element originally preceding rather than following the lexical verb, as in the Huon and Madang/Adalbert Range languages. As such, the AUX/SUBJ form was grammaticalized as a prefix, not a suffix.

(172) a. Sulka (family-level isolate, linked to Yele-Solomons)
           dok-mruo ngora-kol
           1:FPN-RXP 1:FUT-get
           'I myself will get it'
           (Tharp 1996: 86)

      b. Sulka
           kua-ngoe
           1:PRS-go
           'I am going'
           (Tharp 1996: 91–2)
           <*[1-AUX √]

      c. Sulka
           ko-ngoe
           1-go
           'I left'

      d. Sulka
           koma-ngoe
           1:HAB-go
           'I always go'

      e. Sulka
           kom-ngoe
           1:PST:HAB-go
           'I usually went'
           (Tharp 1996: 91–2)

      f. Sulka
           kopa-ngoe
           1:PRS:COND-go
           'if I go' 'I should go'

      g. Sulka
           t-lua-sap
           3:PST-NEG:PRS-run
           'he is not running'
           (Tharp 1996: 94)

      h. Sulka
           ner-la-sap
           3:FUT-FUT:NEG-run
           'he will not run'

      i. Sulka
           t-lo-sap
           3:PST-PST.NEG-run
           'he did not run'
           (Tharp 1996: 94)

Within Eurasia, fused/fused complexes coming from fused AUX/SUBJ forms are relatively uncommonly attested. One language that has such formations is

Dolakhā Newār, a Tibeto-Burman language of Nepal, as well as certain other Newari varieties (Shakya 1992).

(173) a. Dolakhā Newār   b. Dolakhā Newār
           na-i ten-agi   *na-i don-ju*
           eat-INF AUX-3.PRES   eat-INF AUX-3PST
           'about to eat'   'finish eating'
           (Genetti 2003: 361)

In Somali, tense/subject suffixes may also derive from a fused AUX/SUBJ formation of the type under discussion.

(174) a. Somali (Cushitic, Afro-Asiatic; Somalia)
           waan tégi waa-yay
           I go NEG.AUX-1.PST
           'I didn't go'
           (Orwin 1995: 127)

       b. Somali
           waan cún-ay-ay
           I eat.INF-PROG-1.PST
           'I was eating it'
           (Orwin 1995: 120, 152)

       c. Somali   d. Somali
           waan karín-ay-ay   *waan imán-ay-aa*
           I cook.INF-PROG-1.PST   I come.INF-PROG-1.PRES
           'I was cooking it'   'I am coming'

In the Daly language Marithiel of northern Australia, a fused complex has arisen from a split inflected AVC in which the object and tense were marked on the lexical verb and the subject on the auxiliary verb with which it subsequently became fused, later all fused together into the attested form.

(175) a. Marithiel (Daly; Australia)   b. Marithiel
           kini-pi-ya tʸuwuŋanan   *ŋi-mpi-pup-a tʸuwuŋanan*
           2:AUX-smoke-PST yesterday   1:AUX-2OBJ-give-PST yesterday
           'you smoked yesterday'   'I gave it to you yesterday'
           (Tryon 1974g: 78)

Similar fused/fused AUX/SUBJ formations are found in the Oceanic language Nāti of Vanuatu. This set of forms involves a negative/connegative type formation as well, i.e. the lexical verb appears in a dependent negative form.

(176) a. Nāti
         ni-teŋ
         1:REAL-cry
         'I cried'
         (Crowley 1991: 215)

       b. Nāti
           ni-sa-nteŋ-ve
           1:REAL-NEG-cry-NEG
           'I didn't cry'

       c. Nāti
          na-nteŋ
          1:DIST-MR:cry
          'I will cry'

       d. Nāti
           na-sa-nteŋ-ve
           1:DIST-NEG-MR:cry-NEG
           'I won't cry'

Summary

Many languages possess complex verb forms whose origin lies in the fusing of some type of auxiliary verb construction. This includes the simple univerbation of AVCs of various inflectional types into complex verb forms, the origins of which may range from quite transparent to entirely opaque. A further such development is seen in the emergence, (attested in a range of unrelated languages) of what appear to be tense/aspect/mood encoding (usually subject) pronouns. In many such cases, these latter represent the fusing of a subject marker/pronoun and an auxiliary element.

7

The Origins of Patterns of Inflection in Auxiliary Verb Constructions

Overview

The various auxiliary verb constructions discussed in this volume, whether synchronically bi-partite as presented in Chapters 2–5 or univerbated as in Chapter 6, generally (although not exclusively) derive historically either from serial verb constructions or from verb complement sequences of various types. Conjunctive, clause-chained, or same-subject formations, as well as verb plus nominal complement/adjunct forms, may also give rise to auxiliary verb constructions of various inflectional types. In any case, AUX-headed, LEX-headed, doubled, split, and split/doubled inflectional patterns may be the result, depending on the morphosyntax (and predicate structure) of the input construction. In this chapter, I briefly outline and exemplify paths of development for each of the inflectional macro-patterns discussed above. In addition, I give an overview of the semantic paths of development that are typically associated with the grammaticalizing process of auxiliation.

As I mentioned in Chapter 1, two of the basic sources for AVCs cross-linguistically are verb complement sequences—in which case one speaks of clausal union, as these are originally biclausal structures and two events, two propositions, etc., and serial verb constructions—in which case (at least in certain SVCs) the component sequential elements are considered parts of a semantic event whole and unitary propositionally. In 7.1, I briefly give examples of serial verb constructions and formally similar auxiliary verb constructions for a range of different languages and, in 7.2, do the same for verb complement sequences, and clause-chained or conjunctively sequenced structures as well. In each instance, I give examples of source and target structures for the constructions involved for each of the macro-patterns of inflection discussed in this volume. In 7.3, I discuss diachronic semantic developments in the shift from lexical to functional elements undergone by the verbs that serve as the auxiliaries in AVCs. I finish the chapter with some examples of variation within a single language, or across related languages, that reflect the result and/or these processes of change.

7.1 Serial verb construction > AVCs

As mentioned throughout the discussion in the previous chapters, serial verb constructions (SVCs) are among the most common sources of auxiliary verb constructions in the languages of the world. I do not intend to say much here about whether in a non-theory-specific way the range of phenomena discussed under the heading of 'serial verb constructions' in the literature have any defining or even coherent cross-linguistic characteristics: the interested reader is referred to Bril (2004), Senft (2004), Crowley (2002e), Aikhenvald (1999c), among others.[1] However, I will assume, as many current researchers on this topic do, that there are several broadly definable patterns of verb serialization for which, at least for the sake of descriptive convenience and consistency, I will use the following terms primarily derived from the RRG-based literature on SVCs: nuclear serialization, core serialization, same-subject serialization, switch-subject serialization, and ambient serialization. It will turn out that these labels also show significant correlation to the various inflectional types of auxiliary verb constructions that result from this heterogeneous collection.

(1)

Nuclear serialization	Difficult to distinguish from verb compounding. Tight bond between V_1 and V_2. Aspectual categories belong to this layer (Foley and Olson 1985).
Core serialization	Elements may intervene between V_1 and V_2. Argument categories belong to core layer of clause.
Same-subject	When V_1 and V_2 share the same subject in a serialized formation.

---

[1] Many of the features of serial verb constructions discussed by authors such as Zwicky (1990) and Schiller (1990) are now mainly not used as definitional of these formations. A recent assessment of these criteria has been reduced to the following:
tight restrictions on the nominal arguments associated with each verb no contrast in the basic inflectional categories of serialized verbs no grammatical or intonational marking of clause boundaries between the verbs or generally and nebulously (although correctly) that SVCs are 'syntactic constructions involving what can be analysed at the surface level as single clauses, but which are nevertheless expressed by means of multiple predicates' (Crowley 2002e: 19).

Switch-subject   Usually involves an intransitive and transitive
                          verb, with subject of one being the object of the
                          other, but refers to any serialized formation in
                          which there is no subject co-reference.
Ambient-serialization   When no argument is shared between V_1 and V_2.
                          Expresses 'generalized states' (Crowley 2002e).
                          May have 'clausal' subject marking.

Before discussing these general trends in the development of serial verb
constructions to auxiliary constructions, a few issues should be kept in
mind. First, serial verb constructions, like auxiliary verb constructions, are
best considered a continuum of verb–verb concatenations, or as Lord (1993: 2)
puts it, 'a syndrome of features and phenomena', rather than a discrete
construct. Given the processes by which one verbal sequence slides into
another from a structural/functional perspective, a certain amount of ambiguity is possible with respect to any given formation or sets of formations, and
there is likely to be significant disagreement among investigators specializing
in these issues. Further, it is important to keep in mind in the discussion on
the development of serial constructions into auxiliary constructions that:

each link of the grammaticalization chain represents a stage of the auxiliation process,
where the preceding and the succeeding functions, and their respective linguistic
expressions, coexist side by side. Thus there is an intermediate stage of overlapping
marked by semantic ambiguity, formal ambiguity, or both. (Kuteva 2001: 138)

Thus, there is a continuum of monoclausal verb–verb combinations that
straddles the constructions generally known as AVCs and SVCs in the relevant
literature without there being any coherent rubrics for categorizing a given
sequence as representative of one or the other type of formation.[2] Nor should
there be such features expected, given the inherently continuous and ever re-
emergent nature of language and the form–function continua that these
constructions occupy. Thus, when such verb–verb combinations show particular kinds of functional specialization of one or the other component, then
it is proper to speak of 'auxiliary' functions of these combinations in serializing languages, 'auxiliary serialization' (Crowley 2002e: 77), or, in the terminology of the present work, AVCs that have developed from SVCs.

---

[2] The array of definitions and criteria for serial verb constructions offered in the literature is truly
staggering: see Crowley (2002e), Bril (2004), and Senft (2004) for a recent synopsis of opinions. Seuren
(1990: 20) departs from the classic definition of SVCs and considers serialization to reflect a relationship of pseudo-complementation between the components, much like English *John went fishing*, where
the relation between the two elements is 'one of concomitant, resultative or purposive circumstance'.

Although a common source of auxiliary constructions, it is perhaps surprising that the development of serial verb constructions to auxiliary verb constructions is not well discussed in the literature on serial verb formations, grammaticalization, diachronic syntax, or auxiliary verbs. This is not to say, however, that these types of development have been completely ignored: they are just not as commonly found as one might guess. Thus, for example, DeLancey (1991:15) explicitly recognizes the potential deictic serialization origin ('go and X', 'come and X') for certain kinds of AVCs.

In any language which regularly produces verb chains of the sort that we are claiming form the breeding ground for serialization constructions, there will regularly be formed chains of motion verbs for which no sequenced-event interpretation is pragmatically or even semantically available... it is the semantically unitary nature of sequences such as these which motivates the development of a uni-clausal syntactic construction.

Lord (1993: 9–30, 216–33) also acknowledges that verbal auxiliaries are possible outcomes of SVCs in both West African and Asian languages. Further cross-linguistic evidence from these regions and others briefly outlined below supports these assertions.

7.1.1 Verbal outcomes of SVCs

In the following sections, I give a cursory sampling of auxiliary constructions deriving from serialized constructions in a range of languages. There is also a range of other examples of phenomena pertaining to various AVCs, reflecting origins in serial verb constructions found throughout Chapters 3, 4, and 5 in particular.

Formations reflecting nuclear serialization may be found in a wide range of languages in the database exhibiting a range of different inflectional patterns, in particular, LEX-headed formations and certain split patterns as well (for examples of the latter, see the discussion of same subject serialized forms below).

For example, a formation originally showing nuclear serialization may be realized as a subtype of LEX-headed AVC if the original V$_2$ of the construction is specialized in an auxiliary function. Such a development appears to have occurred in the case of the durative auxiliary formation in the West Papuan language Hatam (2a). A similar pattern is seen in non-grammaticalized SVCs in Hatam as well (2b). That this belongs to a nuclear serialization formation and not a core one in Hatam is seen by the disallowing of doubled subject inflection (characteristic of core formations in the language) in this SVC, and by extension in the AVC derived from a structurally similar SVC.

(2) a. Hatam
         di-ttei kep biei
         1-carry AUX wood
         'I kept carrying wood'
         (Reesink 1999: 74)   **di-ttei di-kep*

     b. Hatam
         api ni-kwei kwen tut sop-nya-o munggwom-nya-o
         then 1EX-come cook with woman-PL-or child-PL-or
         'then we'd come and cook the meat with the women and children'
         (Reesink 1999: 98)   **ni-kwei ni-kwen*

Core serialized formations serve as the source for auxiliary verb constructions of a wide range of inflectional types. This is the source for many AVCs of the doubled inflectional pattern. There is a wide range of subtypes of doubly inflected AVCs originating from core-serialized constructions. These include doubled subject and TAM forms, forms with doubled subject and object, and forms with doubled TAM markers. To the first category belong various AVCs in such languages as Australian Ndjébbana and Yanyuwa or Oceanic Lewo.

(3) Lewo
     sisi kokan la a-su ṁa a-tagi ke-ga wa
     child small PL 3PLSUBJ-AUX DUR 3PLSUBJ-cry CONT-just yet
     'the small children are still crying'
     (Early 1993: 70)

(4) Ndjébbana
     nji-rri-rakarawé-ra nji-rri-bé-na namarnakkurrkka
     1UA-RE-move-REM 1UA-RE-AUX-REM creek
     'we went along the creek'
     (McKay 2000: 277)

(5) a. Yanyuwa
         nganth-inju kambala-wingka-la kambal-anma-la walkurr baji
         where-to 1PL.INCL-go-FUT 1PL.INCL-stay-FUT asleep there
         'where will we go sleep?'
         (Kirton and Charlie 1996: 29)

     b. Yanyuwa
         kal-inyamba-wukanyi-la namba-lu kal-anma-la ngayama-ntha-
         rra kulu bawuji

3pl-RFLXV-talk-FUT there-to 3PL-AUX-FUT agree-PRTCPL-PRES and
finished
'they will talk together until they reach agreement (and conclude)'
(Kirton and Charlie 1996: 48)

As the first Yanyuwa example shows, SVCs also exist in the language which show the source construction for the AVC attested in the second example. Other, subsequent developments, such as the fusing of an aspectual particle or LEX-headed auxiliary may yield a split/doubled pattern in individual constructions, for example the following one in Ndjébbana.

(6) Ndjébbana
     bá-rra-balo ba-rra-bala-yirrí-ya
     3AUGM-RE-come.hither 3AUGM-RE-hither-go-CTP
     'they were coming towards us'
     (McKay 2000: 267)

Bukiyip of the Torricelli Phylum, Papua New Guinea, offers another example of the connection between core serialized constructions and AVCs of the doubled inflectional pattern. SVCs are prosodically distinct from verb plus complement sequences in Bukiyip. Some of these, however, are being grammaticalized as AVCs and others have already been grammaticalized. Thus, from an original deictic SVC in Bukiyip a kind of future construction is developing.

(7) Bukiyip
     biyebıh m-u-nak m-u-lu lowas
     day.after.tomorrow 1PL-IRR-go 1PL-IRR-cut trees
     'the day after tomorrow we will (go) cut trees'
     (Conrad and Wogiga 1991: 3)

As in English *I am going to work*, there is some ambiguity between the deictic serialized construction and the emergent grammaticalized AVC. However, from an inflectional typology standpoint, it is clear that this belongs to the core serialization > doubled inflectional-AVC continuum. Slightly more grammaticalized in terms of functional semantics is the following Bukiyip AVC that likewise clearly derives from a core serialization formation.

(8) Bukiyip
     y-e-ne y-a-pwe
     1-RLS-do 1-RLS-be
     'I remained resting'
     (Conrad and Wogiga 1991: 55)

An example of double subject-and object-marking in an AVC is seen in Austronesian Wolio. Here the auxiliary preserves a trace of its original argument structure (a transitive verb meaning 'finish (sthg,)') in this original core-serialized formation grammaticalized as a perfective auxiliary.

(9) a. Wolio   b. Wolio
         a-pade-a a-ale-a   *a-pade-a a-kande-a*
         3-AUX-3 3-take-3   3-AUX-3 3-eat-3
         'he took it all'   'he ate them all up'
         (Anceaux [1952]: 45)

With portmanteau subject > object prefixes (and a possibly clitic or fused aspect marker), a split/doubled inflectional AVC may develop from this kind of serialized construction in such languages as Ndjébbana.

(10) Ndjébbana
      nga-lawáya nga-nó-ra
      1MIN>3MIN.MASC-know/think.about 1MIN(>3MIN.MASC)-AUX-CTP
      'I'm worrying about him'
      (McKay 2000: 287)

Doubly marked TAM forms deriving from core serialized constructions may also be seen. These mainly occur in Australian languages like Nyawaygi.

(11) Nyawaygi
      ɲaŋga wiriliɲa yuːɲa
      3SG.S asleep:UNM lie:UNM
      'he's lying down sleeping'
      (Dixon 1983: 498)

In its sister language, Djapu Yolngu, there is some ambiguity possible in these serialized-cum-doubly-marked AVC forms; that is, the element in question may have 'serialized' or 'auxiliary' functions or interpretations. This kind of semantic ambiguity is expected in emergent grammaticalized formations such as these.

(12) a. Djapu Yolngu
          mukthu-rr nhini
          be.quiet-POT sit/AUX.POT
          'keep quiet' or 'sit quietly'
          (Morphy 1983: 90)

    b. Djapu Yolngu
       naŋʔ-naŋdhu-n nhina bala dhukarr-kurr
       /Redpl/-run-UNM sit.UNM TLOC road-PERL
       '(it) ran and sat over there in the road (and then ran on again in
       fits and starts)'

or

       '(it) kept running away along the road' (Morphy 1983: 91)

As mentioned previously, in the case of the last Djapu Yolngu example, the second interpretation is probably the extra-contextually more normal interpretation, but not actually the one intended when this utterance was produced.

    Although the exact cross-linguistic criteria for distinguishing both between nuclear and core serialization on the one hand and SVCs and AVCs on the other is far from clear, it is possible to qualify sets of formally distinct monoclausal verb–verb concatenations within the structure of a given individual language. For example, nuclear (13) and core serialization formations (14) show distinct behaviour (and different possible developments into AVCs) in the Austronesian language Fehan Tetun, and these both differ from constructions that function as AVCs in this language. Regarding the distinction between nuclear and core serialization in Fehan Tetun, in the former construction only the first verb may have subject-marking, while both may in core-serialized forms (if (mor-pho)phonologically permissible), and further that the two verbal elements in a nuclear serialized form are inseparable (van Klinken 1999: 257).

(13) Fehan Tetun
      ha'u k-subar ha'i té ha'u k-foin mai
      I 1-hide neg because I 1-ONLY/JUST come
      'I didn't hide it because I have only just come'
      (van Klinken 1999: 219)

(14) a. Fehan Tetun
        lale ha'u k-o'i k-ola ó
        else I 1-NEG.DES 1-take you
        'otherwise I refuse to take you back'
        (Lumien van Klinken 1999: 215)

      b. Fehan Tetun
        sia at bá r-afaho r-akawak
        they IRR go 3-weed 3-assist.mutually
        'they were going to go and help each other weed'
        (Lumien van Klinken 1999: 221)

As for the AVC: SVC opposition in Fehan Tetun, it appears these two classes of constructions may be distinguished by the fact that postverbal modifiers follow a V₁ motion verb in a deictic SVC but follow the lexical verb in an AVC. Also, there is variation in inflectional patterns seen in the AVCs, specifically either doubled (<*core SVC) or in a presumably secondarily derived LEX-headed formation.

(15) a. Fehan Tetun
          ket saseni ha'u lai té ha'u sei k-akés
          DO.NOT hinder I first because I STILL 1-talk
          'don't interrupt me now because I am still talking'
          (Lumien van Klinken 1999: 219)

      b. Fehan Tetun
          ha'u k-sei dauk k-á tuan bót ida n-á uluk ti'an
          I 1-STILL NEG 1-eat important.man big one 3-eat go.first already
          '[when] I hadn't yet eaten, an important man had already eaten
              first'
          (Lumien van Klinken 1999: 220)

The majority of serial verb constructions show shared arguments between the components, and most typically shared subjects (this was in fact considered at one point to be required of serial verb constructions). In a nuclear serialized formation, where only one marker for subject may be encoded when V₂ is transitive, and V₁ is the verb specialized functionally into an auxiliary, one of the typical split-inflectional patterns seen in AVCs is formed, with the subject encoded on the auxiliary and the object on the lexical verb. Such forms are relatively common in Oceanic languages, e.g. Raga or Torau, where this development is reflected fairly straightforwardly.

(16) a. Raga (Oceanic; Vanuatu)   b. Raga
          ramuru ğita-ra   *ra-n ğita-ğo*
          3DL.CONT see-3PL   3PL-PRF see-2
          'they are looking at them'   'they saw you'
          (Crowley 2002a: 631–2)

(17) Torau
      pa-e alo-dia
      FUT-3 make-3PL.OBJ
      'he will make them'
      (Ross 1982b: 15)

In their sister language Simbo, the original V₁ in an SVC of this type, which became an auxiliary, has fused with the subject pronoun to yield the following relatively uncommon pattern of S:Aux V-OBJ.

(18) a. Simbo (Western Solomonic, Austronesian)
          poi sa teku-a p-ia na koburu
          then 3:AUX:RLS take-3OBJ ERG-she the child
          'then she took the child...'
          (Palmer 1996: 251)

      b. Simbo
          eyo gari ton-ia ria na rereko
          OK 3PL:AUX:RLS lead-3OBJ they the female
          'all the women would lead her...'
          (Palmer 1996: 252)

Other languages not belonging to the Austronesian phylum show similar formations. For example, in Eleme of Nigeria, it is likely that the split-inflectional pattern in certain AVCs historically reflects this kind of development from a nuclear serialized formation (19b), as the exact structure is found in the following serialized plus auxiliary formation.

(19) a. Eleme
          ὲbai   rɛ-do-do-rō̃   nɛ́-e   ńsā
          1PL   1PL-REDPL-be.PRES-PRTCL   give-3SG book
          'we are still giving him books'
          (Field Notes; Anderson and Bond 2004-MS)

      b. Eleme
          àbà   ba-bere   tʃú   ńsā   no   nɛ́-e
          3PL   3PL.DEF-PERF take   book DEM   give-3SG
          'they have picked up the book and given it to him'
          (Field Notes)

In second person plural forms, where a doubled inflectional pattern seems to be being generalized, a split/doubled pattern is yielded in SVCs of this type (indeed involving the same words).

(20) Eleme

òbàù tʃú-î	*ńsā*	*no*	*ne-i-e*	*àbà*	*tʃú-rī*	*ńsā*	*no*	*ne:*
2PL take-2PL	book	DEM	give-2PL-3SG	3PL	take-3PL	book	DEM	give.3SG

'you delivered the books to him'   'they delivered the books to him'
(Anderson and Bond 2004-MS)

As mentioned in Chapter 5, only the Daly language Kamor has this kind of split-inflectional structure among the languages of Australia.

(21)   Kamor
    pukunuŋ nuŋkur tat^y-nint^yi ka-wu-y
    soon you hit-2OBJ 1-AUX-FUT
    'I am going to hit you soon'
    (Tryon 1974f: 66)

Note that Kamor shows variation in the inflectional pattern attested, even with one and the same auxiliary in a given AVC. One alternate shows this split formation that may have derived from a nuclear serialization form, while the other has an AUX-headed structure, with the object moved to the auxiliary.

(22)   a.   Kamor   b.   Kamor
        t^yamaR kerer ler-ŋu pö-mö   *tal pö-mö-ŋu*
        dog leg bite-1OBJ 3M-AUX   spear 3M-AUX-1OBJ
        'the dog bit my leg'   'he speared me'
        (Tryon 1974f: 66)   (Tryon 1974f: 67)

The Adamawa language Doyayo demonstrates relatively clearly how split/doubled inflectional patterns might develop out of core-serialized constructions that consist of an intransitive V_1 that becomes an auxiliary and a V_2 lexical verb that is transitive. In fact, in the following, the first AVC derives from a deictic serialized construction, in which V_1 serves as host to a subject prefix, currently functioning as an auxiliary verb. The object is found on the transitive lexical verb, with the doubled subject pattern expected from a core-serialized structure, and one that appears to be relatively common in Doyayo.

(23)   a.   Doyayo
        be^1-re^3 be^1-tɔ^4-mɔ^1 gɔ ya^4
        1-AUX 1-devour-2 ANA Q
        'would I then (be so mean as to) eat you up'
        (Wiering and Wiering 1994: 217)

    b.   Doyayo
        hi^1-da^3 hi^1-taa^3-be^1
        3PL-POT 3PL-shoot-1
        'they might shoot me' or 'I might get shot'
        (Wiering and Wiering 1994: 222)

In the following example, the development of an SVC to split/doubled (object/subject) AVC is clear and the development is seen in multiple historical phases. The potential auxiliary verb derives from the lexical verb meaning 'come', which still functions in deictic serialized constructions. As an intransitive verb, it only bears a marker for subject, while the transitive lexical verb/V₂ in the construction bears markers of both subject and its subcategorized object. A complex split/doubled AVC-cum-deictic SVC is the result.

(24) Doyayo
      hi¹-za¹ hi¹-zaa¹³ hi¹-lɔ-mɔ
      3PL-POT 3PL-come 3PL-bite-2
      'they might come bite you'
      (Wiering and Wiering 1994: 221)

While most SVCs share subjects across the two (or more) component verbs, it is not always the case that the verbs in a serialized constructions show such a distribution. Such formations are known as 'switch-subject serialization' in the recent literature (Crowley 2002e, Bril 2004). In these formations, there is generally co-reference between the object of one verb and the subject of another, and thus one typically finds combinations of intransitive and transitive verbs in such formations.[3] Periphrastic causatives in numerous languages may be of this type, as in Warembori, with a serialized formation yielding a split/doubled pattern, and in Paamese, where there is a dummy third singular 'clausal' object and which yields a split-inflectional pattern.

(25) a. Warembori   b. Warembori
          e-vani y-ande-o   *w-or-i i-nan-do*
          1-make-3 3-laugh-IND   2-give-3 3-sleep-IND
          'I made her laugh'   'you put her to sleep'
          (Donohue 1999: 35)   (Donohue 1999: 36)

(26) Paamese
      ne-sakini{-e} ko-musau
      1SG:REAL-CAUS-3SG 2SG:REAL-sing
      'I made you sing'
      (Crowley 2002e: 81)

When no arguments are shared between the AV and the LV in a LEX-headed AVC, and the auxiliary expresses a kind of 'generalized state' and appear with a dummy 'clausal' subject marker, then the formation might reflect an 'ambient

---

[3] It is a paradox of studies on SVCs that it is taken as given that transitive verbs only rarely enter into serialization formations—but two of the most common verbs found in SVCs are 'take' and 'give' (cf. Crowley 2002e).

serialization' construction. This is probably the case in the development of certain LEX-headed AVCs in such languages as various members of the Nilotic family, e.g. Maasai or Turkana (27, 28) or in West Papuan Tobelo (29b).

(27) a. Maasai   b. Maasai
          ɛ-tɔn a-irrag   *ɛ-ɲɔr n-a-lɔ*
          3-AUX 1-lie.down   3-AUX CN-1-go
          'I am still lying down'   'I ought to go'
          (Tucker and Mpaayei 1955: 101; Hamaya 1993: 8)

(28) Turkana
      è-ìtem-o-kin-ò i-yoŋˋ i-los-ì-o tɔ̀kɔ̀naˋ
      3-AUX-EPIPAT-DAT-VB you 2-GO-ASP-VB now
      'you must go now'
      (Dimmendaal 1983: 162)

(29) a. Tobelo   b. Tobelo
          t-a-diai i-boto-oka   *i-boto ho-ma-kete-ade-ade*
          1-3-do 3-AUX-PRF   3-AUX 1IN-RFLXV-CONT-REDPL-tell.story
          'I have done it'   'we've finished telling stories'
          (Holton 2003: 63)

As is clear from example (29a), split/doubled patterns may derive from ambient or switch-subject serialized formations in languages such as Tobelo.[4]

It is not always the case that a given source construction for a particular AVC is clearly definable as a serialized construction, or one of the other source formations discussed below. In various languages, what appear to be functionally 'serialized' constructions, e.g. they express deictic serialized events, have the form of a clause-chained coordinate or quasi-subordinate formation. These may become grammaticalized as AUX-headed AVCs. Such is the case with the homophonous and/or identical 'habitual' nominalization found in AVCs and the corresponding 'agentive' nominalization in Ayacucho Quechua.

(30) a. Ayacucho Quechua b. Ayacucho Quechua
          miku-q ka-ni   *puklʸa-q ri-saq*
          eat-HAB.NOM AUX-1   play-AGT.NOM go-1.FUT
          'I used to eat (it)'   'I shall go and play'
          (Adelaar 2004: 223)   (Adelaar 2004: 227)

---

⁴ That is, it is not clear if an ambient or a switch-subject serialization structure underlies this Tobelo form historically.

A similar development is seen in the Papuan language Kaugel, only here the V_1 or lexical verb appears in a generalized dependent form. Thus one progressive formation in Kaugel bears an overt similarity to a 'serialized' formation in the language, while another progressive appears with a typical unmarked lexical verb component, both within an AUX-headed inflectional pattern.

(31) a. Kaugel   b. Kaugel
          no-kó-po mol-kó-ro   *mimi te-ké-ro*
          wait-PRES-DEP AUX-PRES-1   make AUX-PRES-1
          'I am waiting'   'I am making [something]'
          (Blowers and Blowers 1970: 52, 57)

Cf. SVC:

(32) Kaugel
      mebo o-kó-ro
      carry:DEP come-PRES-1
      'I am bringing'
      (Blowers and Blowers 1970: 51)

Note that with core serialized forms, it may in principle not be possible to distinguish these from paratactic coordination or subordination (with Ø complementizer/conjunctive marker) in a given language.

Finally, in Sye (Erromangan), there are a series of characteristic 'echo subject' forms which appear to represent a language-specific realization of the SVC > AVC development. These elements are also functionally akin to the same-subject or clause-sequencing formations discussed in 7.2.2 below, further underscoring the not necessarily discrete nature of all of the complex predicate types that may serve as source formations for AVCs.

(33) Erromangan (Austronesian; Vanuatu)
      yay-ahi me-ntorilki
      1SG.FUT-just.do>AUX SG:ES-return
      'I will just return'
      (Crowley 2002e: 193)

In a number of languages, former serial verbs end up, often via a stage of auxiliation, as inflectional or even derivational components of the verb morphology of a language. Such is the origin, for example, of some of the numerous applicatives or benefactive suffixes in various languages deriving from the verb 'give' (it may also take a nominal path of development > 'for' and ultimately end up in the verb as well). Instances of fused complexes where the relevant element ultimately came from a serial verb construction and seemingly passed through a stage of auxiliation is may be found, for example, in Kxoe.

(34) a. Kxoe   b. Kxoe
          ‖oàbà-ná-éi-yé-tè   kx'ó-ró-xu'-'è
          cover-JUNC-AUX-JUNC-TNS   eat.meat-JUNC-AUX-IMP
          'she covers it well'   'finish the meat!'
          (Heine and Reh 1984: 137; Köhler 1981: 503ff.)

      c. Kxoe
          djà(o)-rő-ma'-à-tè tí 'à
          work-JUNC-AUX-JUNC-TNS I ACC
          'he works for me'

In the Altai-Sayan Turkic languages, the auxiliary 'send' has been grammaticalized as a derivational perfective marker in Tuvan, Xakas, and Tofa, among other languages (Anderson 2004a).

(35) Xakas
      ol xïyïr-ïbïs-xan kniga-nï xayzï pol-da čat-ča
      s/he read-PRF-PST book-ACC which floor-LOC lie-PRES
      'he read the book that is lying on the floor'
      (Anderson 2004a: 105)

Note that in Hittite, unusually for Indo-European, there has been a development of deictic serial construction (with 'come') into a variety of subordinate or quasi-subordinate serialized-cum-auxiliary formations (van den Hout 2003).

TABLE 7.1. Some SVC > AVC developments

SVC > AVC type	Language
Nuclear > LEX-headed	Hatam
Nuclear > AUX-headed (Ø-for of lexical verb)	Yanuwa Kaugel
Nuclear > Split	Raga, Eleme
Core > Doubled	Yanuwa, Bukiyip, Wolio
Core > Split/Doubled line	Eleme, Doyayo
Switch Subject > Split/Doubled	Warembori, Paamese
Ambient > LEX-headed	Turkana
Ambient > Split/Doubled	Tobelo?

7.1.2 On nominal developments of SVCs

As is well known, the 'verbal' channel of development of serial verb constructions is not the only option available for functional development of SVCs, or
indeed the best-known one, or even necessarily the most common one.
Rather, what can be roughly characterized as the 'nominal' channel of development of serial verb constructions is also frequently attested. It is not the
purpose to outline all such developments in the world's languages that might
be construed as reflecting this nominal channel of SVCs. Rather I briefly
discuss just one such path, viz. the development of the serial verbs into
adpositions and case markers.

Adpositions and ultimately case forms frequently owe their origin to serial
verb formations. Note that as with all grammaticalized formations at least the
first stage of this development is to unbound but still grammaticalized
adpositional elements, which may themselves become bound case markers
in individual languages under appropriate morphophonological conditions.
It is these first unbound stages I briefly exemplify below.

Deictic serialized formations (ones involving the motion verbs 'go' and
'come') frequently develop into adpostional elements in the languages of the
world, as in the following forms from Thai, where one see 'fly come' > 'fly
from' and 'fly go/leave' > 'fly to'.

(36)   Thai
    thân cà bin càak krungthêep   *thân cà bin maa krungthêep*
    he FUT fly leave Bangkok   he FUT fly come Bangkok
    'he will fly to Bangkok'   'he will fly from Bangkok'
    (Blake 1994: 164)   (Blake 1994: 163)

As alluded to above, another common path of development of the verb 'give'
is into an adpositional element meaning 'for, on behalf of'. Such a process
occurred, for example, in Ewe.

(37)   Ewe
    me-wɔ dɔ' véví é ná dodókpɔ lá
    1-do work hard give exam DEF
    'I worked hard for the exam'
    (Blake 1994: 165)

That this is no longer just a serial construction in Ewe is seen by the fact
(among others) that the verb has lost some of its inflectional versatility (e.g.
does not assign case). However, such an element may retain some of its verbal

features in individual constructions, e.g. it accepts negation (although not independent negation) in the related Akan language.

(38)   Akan
       Kofi n-ye adwuma m-ma Amma
       Kofi NEG-do work NEG-give Amma
       'Kofi does not work for Amma'
       (Seuren 1990: 18; Schachter 1974: 266)

One last development that deserves mention is the specialization of the verb 'take' from an original serial construction into the function of an object (accusative) marker, seen, for example, in Mandarin Chinese.

(39)   Mandarin
       Tā bǎ fàntīng shōushi-gānjing le
       s/he OBJ dining.room tidy-clean PRF
       's/he tidied up the dining-room'
       (Blake 1994: 165)

A summary of some of the common developments of serial verb constructions into adpositional elements and then ultimately case elements is offered in Table 7.2.

7.2 Clause combining

In this section, I briefly discuss patterns of clause union, i.e., the development from a biclausal-structure verb–complement or clause-chaining structure to a monoclausal auxiliary verb construction. As was the case with the SVCs discussed in 7.1, a range of inflectional patterns of AVCs go back to various different verb complement structures, depending on factors such as the type of nominalization or degree of finiteness of the complement clause and the valence or argument structure of the source elements for the constructions. In 7.2.1, I discuss verb plus complement clause sequence in an original

TABLE 7.2. Common types of serial verb > adposition > case developments

Case target	Source	Case target	Source
ACC	'take', 'get'	COM	'take', 'follow'
DAT/BEN	'give'	LOC	'be at'
INS	'use', 'take' 'be'	PERL/PROL	'pass by'
ABL	'follow', 'come'		
ALL	'go', 'arrive', 'reach'		

subordination relation between a matrix clause and a complement clause (a so-called verb complement construction, or VCC), and in 7.2.2, I briefly present data on AVCs that derived from overtly conjoined, chained, or otherwise sequenced combinations of clauses.

Indeed, although discussed in separate sections in this chapter, and loosely defined as monoclausal and biclausal respectively, it is not always the case that one can tell that a given construction is always necessarily *a priori* a serialized formation or a verb–complement clause sequence. For example, the semantic connection between the verbal elements may be one of purpose or manner, with one verb representing the purpose or manner action, the other usually a motion verb logically preceding and performed specifically to manifest the purpose of the event, or accompanied by the manner of the event, embodied in the verb encoding that purpose/manner. This purpose-or manner-encoding verb may be marked by a morphological index that is also found in verb–complement structures. Auxiliary verb formations may exist in the language deriving from potentially either source, and it would not be possible to determine in these instances whether the AVC derived from an SVC or a VCC. Such is the case in the Misumalpan languages. As already mentioned above, there appears to be one formal construction that may be found in SVCs, VCCs, and AVCs.

(40) Miskitu
      usus pal-i bal-an
      buzzard fly-PROX come-PST:3
      'the buzzard came flying'
      (Hale 1991: 7)

(41) Ulwa
      kusma limd-i waa-da
      buzzard fly-PROX come-PST:3
      'the buzzard came flying'

(42) Miskitu
      naha w-a-tla mak-i ta alk-ri
      this house-CNSTR build-PROX end reach-PST:3
      'he finished building this house'
      (Hale 1991: 6)

(43) Ulwa
      aaka uu-ka yamt-i angka wat-ikda
      this house-CNSTR build-PROX end reach-PST:3
      'he finished building this house'
      (Hale 1991: 6)

(44) i. Ulwa
          bikiska isd-i bang-ka
          children play-PROX AUX-PL:3
          'the children are playing'
          (Hale 1991: 9)

ii. Ulwa
     yang bas-k-i kipt-i lau-yang
     I hair-CNSTR-1 comb-PROX AUX-1
     'I am combing my hair'

(45) i. Miskitu
          yang utla kum mak-i s-na
          I house one build-PROX AUX-1
          'I am building a house'
          (Hale 1991: 9)

ii. Miskitu
     yang utla kum mak-i kap-ri
     I house one build-PROX AUX-1:PST
     'I was building a house'

In fact, it is possible for a single language to use the same verb in a serialized formation and in a verb–complement sequence for the same functional AVC, i.e. to have its source in either a SVC or a VCC or, in other terms, a finite and a non-finite complement. Such is the case with the verb 'want' in the Kuliak language So and in Australian Dharumbal

(46) a. So (Kuliak; eastern Uganda)
          cám-ı(s)a gá-úg éù
          DES-1 go-INF home
          'I want to go home'
          (Heine and Reh 1984: 135)

b. So
    cám-ı(s)a mɔ-gá-sa éù
    DES-1 NAR-go-1 home
    'I want to go home'

(47) a. Dharumbal
          nhula wu-thayu yigi-nh
          he.NOM give-PURP want-NPST
          'he wants to give'
          (Terrill 2002: 41)

b. Dharumbal
    nhula yigi-nh yanggari-nh
    he.NOM want-NPST run-NPST
    'he wants to run'
    (Terrill 2002: 49)

7.2.1 Verb + complement clause sequences

Bolinger (1980: 297), among others, recognized the verb + complement clause (VCC) origin for AVCs: 'the moment a verb is given an infinitive complement, that verb starts down the road of auxiliariness.' Indeed, a number of different clause-combining strategies, not just those with infinitive complements, can yield auxiliary verb constructions among the languages of the world. The development of AVCs from subordinated verb–complement sequences—in which the reanalysis of a subordinate/nominalized lexical complement and an original finite verb which has undergone functional specialization to an auxiliary, resulting in a unified, mono-clausal structure—is one that has been frequently discussed in the theoretical literature on diachronic syntax in general, and in the study of the diachronic (morpho)syntax of auxiliaries in particular, especially those in English or West Germanic languages or Romance languages. There is far from one opinion or anything approximating a consensus about the processes involved, or how to represent the developments from the biclausal VCCs to the monoclausal AVCs. I do not labour this point here, as there are literally volumes devoted to the topic (cf. relevant chapters in e.g. Harris and Campbell (1995), Harris and Ramat (1987)).

A wide range of languages show auxiliary verb constructions where the auxiliary derives from a complement-taking verb appearing with a clausal or sentential complement that yields the 'lexical verb' component of the AVC. As mentioned in Chapter 2, a number of AUX-headed strategies possess lexical verbs with overtly nominalizing or adverbializing subordinate morphology. The residual biclausal nature of the construction may be preserved in just such morphology (infinitive forms, case-marking, etc.). An example of this is seen relatively clearly in the following forms from Leko, an isolate language of Bolivia.

(48) a. Leko
          chera du-kana-tean burua da-in-tean du-ch
          we speak-CAP-1PL Leko want-NEG-1PLspeak-INF
          'we can speak Leko, but we don't want to'
          (van der Kerke 2000: 26)

      b. Leko
          iya-iki o-sobon-di-ch da-no-to
          you-DAT2-visit-INCEP-INF want-PRS-1
          'I want to go to visit you'
          (van der Kerke 2000: 27)

      c. Leko
          Pedru Maria paus-mo-ch puidis-in-aya-te   ∼
          Pedro Maria forget-REC-INF AUX-NEG-PL-3
          'Pedro and Maria cannot forget each other'
          (van der Kerke 1998: 202)

      d. Leko
          P. M. paus-ich puidis-mo-in-aya-te
          P. M. forget-INF AUX-REC-NEG-PL-3
          'P. and M. cannot forget each other'
          (van der Kerke 1998: 202)

A range of source constructions with nominalized clausal complements of former matrix verbs yielding AUX-headed AVCs are found in the languages of the database, and I give but a small sample here. The range of the inflectional patterns exhibited by the resulting constructions which were grammaticalized as AVCs from verb–complement source constructions are best understood when viewing the range of such complements on a scale of finiteness. Some complements show distinctly nominal behaviour, and are most likely to yield particular ('nominal') subtypes of AUX-headed patterns. For example, a clausal complement may take the same case that a nominal complement of the same (original) matrix verb would, as in the following Kolyma Yukaghir form, which suggests that this is a verb + complement sequence rather than a serialized formation, as might be expected by the semantics.

(49)   Kolyma Yukaghir
        tami-l-ŋin qon-d'e
        help-ANR-DAT go-INTR:1SG
        'I went to help'
        (Maslova 2003b: 152)

A similar argument is likely to be made regarding the origin of new AVCs in such Bantu languages as Punu. Here the complement of the motion verb takes the same infinitive morphology common to so many AVCs in the Bantu languages.

(50)   Punu (Bantu, Niger-Congo; Gabon)
        bàɣé:tù bàkò[yê] mànû:ŋgì úvà:ɾə́
        PL:woman 3PL:go/AUX PL:plantation INF.cultivate
        'the woman are going to cultivate the plantations'
        (Hardermann 1996: 159)

In languages such as Nilo-Saharan Anywa, complements of former matrix verbs functioning as auxiliaries often appear in a so-called infinite complement form, speaking to their original biclausal structure.

(51)   a. Anywa
            ɔ́tɔ̄ y-áa gèɛr-ɔ̀
            house PRF:AUX-1 build-IFT
            'I have built a/the house'
            (Reh 1996: 267)

        b. Anywa
            ɔ́tɔ̄ pūut kàr-á gèɛr-ɔ̀
            house still AUX:NEG.PST-1 build-IFT
            'I have not yet built a/the house'

        c. Anywa
            wèelō d-áa góoró
            letter AUX:DEONT-1 write:IFT
            'I should write a letter'
            (Reh 1996: 267)

Other constructions in other languages may preserve some of their original verbal morphosyntax, and yield doubled or split formations of various types. Thus, although appearing in a 'nominalized' negative form, the lexical complement in the following form from Carib of Surinam appears with an object prefix yielding the attested split structure.

(52)   Carib of Surinam
       ayeekáápaane kïneixtan
       ay-eeka-xpa-:ne kï-n-weei-ta-n
       20-bite-NEG:NMZR-really EVID-3-AUX-FUT-EVID
       'it will not bite you'
       (Gildea 2003: 3)

In Nilotic Teso, lexical verb complements retain their original subject-marking, but this appears in the so-called subjunctive form, a modally dependent form of agreement used in complement and subordinate clauses.

(53)   a.   Teso   b.   Teso   c.   Teso
            a-bu ka-duk   *i-bu ko-duk*   *a-bu ko-duk*
            1-PST 1SBJ-build   2-PST 2SBJ-build   3-PST 3SBJ-build
            'I built'   'you built'   'he built'
            (Heine and Reh 1984: 185; Hilders and Lawrance 1956: 29–30)

The following Teso form derives from a structure of the type V S Complement > Aux S V—a common source for doubly inflected AVCs with the lexical verb in a dependent form.

(54)   Teso (aka Ateso)
       a-bu etelepat ko-lot ore bian
       3-AUX.PST boy 3SBJ-go home yesterday
       'the boy went home yesterday'
       (Heine and Reh 1984: 185; Hilders and Lawrance 1956)

Actual verb–complement sequences in individual languages may show a range of patterns, based on the degree of finiteness of the complement. Given a continuum of 'finiteness' and, accordingly, variation in the types of verbal morphology permitted in the former (lexical) complement clauses in such structures that serve as source formations, and also in the valence or argument structure of the former matrix verbs (and complement verbs), it should be relatively easy to see how verb–complement sequences would give rise to the full range of patterns of inflection attested in AVCs; but, much as was seen in the discussion of serial verb constructions above, there are observable tendencies that find certain target AVC inflectional patterns correlated with features of particular source verb–complement sequences.

Auxiliary verb constructions of the LEX-headed pattern, or at least one subtype of such a formation, may also derive from complement structures, in addition to the SVC sources of such constructions discussed above. For example, there are AVCs in which the lexical verb-bearing complement clause, which maintains its original subject marking, for example, are raised to subject of an auxiliary. This is one subtype of the 'clausal subject' formations that constitute a type of LEX-headed AVC as discussed in Chapter 3. For example, in various Nilotic languages, there are originally biclausal AVCs in which the the clause containing the subject-marked lexical verb functions as a third singular/default subject of a certain class of predicates that permit clausal complements. After a gradual process of grammaticalization and clausal union has taken place, the formation now functions as a LEX-headed AVC. Take the example of Acholi, a Western Nilotic language. One modal formation in Acholi is marked by a LEX-headed AVC using the auxiliary *omyero*. Historically, this is a third singular past form of a verb meaning 'be suitable', grammaticalized into this modal form.

(55)   Acholi (Nilo-Saharan, W. Nilotic; Uganda, Sudan)
     in   *omyero*   *i-cam*   *mot*
     you   [3:]AUX   2-eat   slowly
     'you should eat slowly'
     (Heine 1993: 41)
     [*omyero* < *o-myero*   3-be.suitable/fit.PAST]

As exemplified in Chapter 4, cross-linguistically the most common pattern in which the lexical verb bears some overtly dependent form but nevertheless bears doubled subject inflection belongs to the broad category of modal 'subordination' or modal dependency. Such a structure most likely derives from a verb–complement structure where the dependent lexical verb derives from a clause marked as unrealized, etc. Unsurprisingly, this is most common with forms indicating volition, desire, potentiality, etc. as well as future forms, which (as is well known) frequently derive from a grammaticalization of a volitional verb (Heine's 1993 'volitional' event schema).

In the Caddoan language Pawnee a 'quasi-auxiliary' verb–complement construction is found with doubled subject-marking and the second or 'lexical' verb in an infinitival subordinate form. This type of semi-finite complement construction is one common source for dependent marked lexical verbs in doubly inflected AVCs.

(56) Pawnee (Caddoan; USA)
      rawa taticka ratkura:ʔi:wa:ti
      rawa   ta-t-icka   ra-t-ku-ur-ra:-i:-wati-i
      now   IND-1-'AUX'   INF-1-INF-PREV-way-x-dig-SUBORD
      'now I want to talk about...'
      (Mithun 1999: 373; Parks 1976)

To be sure, 'quasi-auxiliary' constructions, i.e. forms that are somewhere on the SVC-or VCC-to-AVC continua, are found in languages across the world. Thus, for example, one finds constructions of this type with bound subject morphology in the South American language Toba.

(57) Toba
      sa-wotayke s-taqayapegeʔ namqom
      1-DES 1-talk.with Toba
      'I want to speak with a Toba'
      (Manelis Klein 2001: 42)

Split/doubled patterns can arise in AVCs derived from VCCs in which the complement appears with its own, or a predetermined set of, TAM marker[s], and the tense operator of the sentence as well as the subject encoded on the auxiliary. Such a situation appears to have occurred in the development of the following AVC in Limilngan.

(58) Limilngan
      i dak lambangi nga-n-a-yi nga-nami-ny
      yes town 1-FUT-go-FUT 1-AUX-PST.RLS.PRF
      'yes I wanted to go to town'
      (Harvey 2001: 7)

Another split/doubled pattern is found in the quasi-auxiliary verb–complement sequence in Arawakan Baure, offering an example of how one verb–verb sequence might get grammaticalized as a split/doubled AVC.

(59) Baure (Arawakan; Bolivia)
      ita- ro-kíʔinow ro-nikó-ni
      PROG-3M-want 3M-cut.with-1
      'he is wanting to eat me'
      (Baptista and Wallin 1967: 41)

Similar to the switch-subject serialized formation, complement structures may show inflectional patterning that is overtly similar to the split/doubled pattern seen with certain AVCs. Such a pattern is found in certain 'serialized' complement formations in Sye (aka Erromangan).

(60) a. Erromangam (Sye)
           yo-ch-oc kime-ntanis
           1:REC.PST-see-2 2:PRES-MR:dance
           'I saw you dancing'
           (Crowley 1998: 268)

      b. Erromangam (Sye)
           yac[a]m[e]-and[ə]g-or cum-naruvo
           1:PRES-MR:hear-3PL 3PL:PRES-MR:sing
           'I can hear them singing'
           (Crowley 1998: 268)

Verbs may take nominalized complements or actual nominal complements and be reanalysed as auxiliary verb + lexical verb complements as well. One such example has already been mentioned, viz. the dual role and thus ambiguous nature of forms like English *Mary is going to work*. Another is seen in the development of the perfect formations in various Indo-European languages, as discussed in the literature on diachronic syntax. Thus, auxiliaries in Latin have been often discussed both in the historical linguistic literature relating to Romance languages in particular and in the literature on historical syntax from a theoretical perspective. I will not labour these well-researched issues, for which the interested reader is referred to Vincent (1982), Bentley and Eythórsson (2004), Lightfoot (1979), and the relevant sections in Harris and Campbell (1995). Grossly oversimplifying for the sake of a cursory presentation here, it appears that there was a reanalysis of an original lexical verb + complex complement consisting of a noun modified by a participial phrase. This was reinterpreted as a combination of an auxiliary (the original lexical verb) and a participial form of a lexical verb and its accompanying nominal complement. This can be roughly schematized as follows:

(61) Latin
      [epistulam scriptam] [habeo] > >   *[epistulam] [scriptam habeo]*
      letter:F.ACC written:PP:F.ACC have:1   letter:F.ACC written:PP:F.ACC AUX:1
      'I have the letter (as) written'   'I have written the letter'
      (Bentley and Eythórsson 2004: 459)

7.2.2 Clause chaining and AVCs

In addition to complement sequences in which one verb (lexical verb) is a dependent of the other (auxiliary verb), actually often filling an argument role in the semantic frame of the verb, which have subsequently been reanalysed as an auxiliary verb and a lexical verb component in an AVC, there are also AVCs

TABLE 7.3. Some verb complement constructions > AVC developments

VCC > AVC type	Language
VCC > AUX-headed	Kolyma Yukaghir, Anywa, Leko
VCC > Split	Carib of Surinam[e]
VCC > Doubled	Teso, Toba, Pawnee
VCC > LEX-headed	Acholi
VCC > Split/Doubled	Limilngan, Baure

that appear to have derived from structures that had a coordinate or conjoined, clause-chained or clause-sequenced structure. This coordinative or conjunctive-type formation occurs in several guises: one in which the two elements were originally in a clause-sequencing formation, with a single, fully finite element, other forms showing only partial inflection or an additional marker of non-finalness/non-finiteness or sequencing. Depending on the language or tradition of analysis, such elements have been called converbs, same-subject/switch-reference markers, medial verb forms, etc.

One group of languages that utilize auxiliary verb constructions deriving from formations of this broad type includes various members of the Yuman language family. Here lexical verbs appear in a subject-marked form but bear a marker of shared or same-subject with the following finite auxiliary. Mojave shows a range of formations of this type.

(62)   Mojave (Yuman (Hokan); USA)
        hatcoq ʔ-kaʔa: -k ʔ-aʔwi:-m
        dog 1-kick-ss 1-AUX-REALIS
        'I kicked the dog'
        (Mithun 1999: 581; Langdon 1978; Langacker 1998: 41)

Various auxiliary verb constructions are found in its sister language Walapai, in which the lexical verb appears in a same-subject-marked/non-final form. These may occur in AUX-headed constructions in which the lexical verb bears only this same subject marker, or it may occur in forms with doubled subject inflection similar to the Mojave forms cited above. Note that these latter may also appear in univerbated complexes in Walapai.

(63)   a.   Walapai (Hualapai)
              nya-ch Hwalbay gwa:w-k spó-ʔ-wi
              I-SUBJ Hualapai speak-ss know-1-AUX
              'I can speak Walapai and that's why I am writing a grammar'
              (Watahomigie et al. 1982: 101)

b. Walapai (Hualapai)
nya-ch Hwalbay gwa:w-k spó-ʔ-yu
I-SUBJ Hualapai speak-SS know-1-AUX
'I can speak Walapai and that's the fact'

c. Walapai (Hualapai)   d. Walapai (Hualapai)
nya-ch ʔ-sma:-ʔ-yu   *ma-ch mi-sma:-ng-yu*   (∼-k-m-)
I-SUBJ 1-sleep-SS. 1-AUX   you-SUBJ 2-sleep-SS. 2-AUX
'I am sleeping'   'you are sleeping'
(Watahomigie et al. 1982: 84)

In another Yuman language, Jamul Tiipay, various constructions appear with a same-subject marked lexical verb, or an AVC in which the same subject suffix is lacking on the lexical verb. In any case, doubled subject inflection is found in all these Jamul Tiipay AVCs.

(64) a. Jamul Tiipay   b. Jamul Tiipay
          nyaach a'-shay '-aa   *shemally we-piitt-ch w-aa*
          I.SUBJ 1-be.fat 1-AUX   ears 3-be.closed+PL-SS 3-go
          'I'm getting fat'   'he is going deaf'
          (Miller 2001: 271)

      c. Jamul Tiipay
          puu-ch we-saaw-ch we-chaw
          that.one-SUBJ 3-eat-SS 3-AUX.COMPL
          'he finished eating'
          (Miller 2001: 315)

Similar to the same-subject marking in Yuman, converb forms in various Turkic languages serve similar clause-chaining functions, with all non-final verbs appearing in a coordinative-type converb form, and the last form bearing full inflection. As mentioned at various appropriate moments throughout the present volume, these are functionally very similar to the same-subject-marked forms in Yuman, although in Turkic the converb marked forms generally lack subject-markers (except in some Yakut constructions), and the resulting auxiliary formations derived from these sequenced constructions tend to be of the AUX-headed type. Given the functional overlap between converb sequencing and same-subject marking, perhaps it is not surprising to find in at least one Turkic language with an overt switch reference system, viz. Tofa, use of same subject morphology instead of the expected converb element, at least optionally, in certain AVCs.

(65) Tofa
    deʒaᵂɯtskɯs
    /*deʒip aɫɯvɯtɯksar bis*/
    say-REC-CV SUBJ.VERS-PRF-DES-P/F 1PL
    'we have already been talking about it'
    (ASLEP Field Notes)

(66) Tofa
    dilyi   oluk   barɨp   brææ yʃpyl   tùt-kaʃ al-ɣan.
    fox   right.away   go-CV   one hazel.grouse   catch-SS SUBJ.VERS-PST
    'right away the fox caught a hazel grouse'
    (Rassadin 1994: 198)

Note that the Tofa -*p* form may mark infinitive/purpose complements as well
with verbs in serialized-type same-subject functions.

(67) a. Tofa   b. Tofa
        pišek tɪle-p kel-dɪ-m   *če bar-aalɨ ihään aɲna-p*
        knife seek-CV come-REC.PST-1   well go-12 as.two hunt-CV
        'I came to seek a knife'   'let's the two of us go hunt'
        (Rassadin 1978: 199)   (Rassadin 1978: 199)

(68) a. Tofa   b. Tofa
        hartooʃqa pàʃta-p tʃi-ir   *bar-ɨp   kør-gen*
        ɔotato   cook.in.pot-CV eat-P/F go-CV (>SS)   see-PST
        '[you should] cook and eat potatoes' 'he went and saw'
        (ASLEP Field Notes)

In other languages, e.g. Papuan Nasioi, AVCs may derive from original
sequenced clauses in which one verb is marked by a simultaneous action
adverbializer very similar in function to certain converbs in Turkic languages.

(69) Nasioi
    oo-amp-id-i oʔno-di-n
    see-1-PL-WHILE/NEUTRAL AUX.1-PL-PST
    'we were watching it'
    (Hurd and Hurd 1970: 73)

A third formal type of construction that belongs to this broad structural type
of 'coordinated' or clause-sequenced constructions giving rise to auxiliary
verb constructions is the medial verb construction in Papuan languages.
These are non-final forms of chained or sequenced verbs which may encode,
depending on the language, not only arguments of its own clause but, in the

guise of the so-called 'anticipatory subject' forms, the subject of the following clause as well. Formations of these types have given rise in various individual Papuan languages to certain kinds of auxiliary verb constructions. In one such language, Umbungu Kaugel, either the auxiliary verb or the lexical verb in the resulting construction may be encoded for medial/dependent subject-marking, depending on which element comes first in these formations (variable relative order between auxiliary verbs and lexical verbs is attested globally speaking in this language, although the particular order is generally specific to individual constructions).

(70)   a.   Umbungu Kaugel
            akena nambe te-ko pu-nu-ye
            Hagen what AUX-2.DEP go-2[.PST]-Q
            'how did you go to Hagen?'
            (Head 1990: 105)

       b.   Umbungu Kaugel
            kako nambe te-pa te-ri-mu-ye
            belt what AUX-3.DEP make-DIST.PST-3.PST-Q
            'how did he make his belt?'

       c.   Umbungu Kaugel
            ulke molo-pa te-ke-mo
            house be-3.DEP AUX-PRES-3.PRES
            'she is probably in the house'
            (Head 1990: 106)

       d.   Umbungu Kaugel
            oleanga pu-ku te-ngi
            yesterday go-2.DEP AUX-2/3.PL[NR.PST]
            'they probably went yesterday'

On rare occasion, actual coordinating morphological elements may end up in the make-up of an AVC deriving from conjoined structures. Such is the case in the following form from Oceanic Manam. Subject is doubly marked but the lexical verb appears with an overt conjunctional clitic/suffix.

(71)   Manam
       i-ruʔuruʔu-be i-sóaʔi
       3-wash-and 3-AUX
       '(s)he is washing him-/herself'
       (Lichtenberk 1983: 565)

TABLE 7.4. Some 'conjunctive' clause construction > AVC developments

CCC > AVC type	Language
CCC > Split/Doubled	Mojave, Nasioi
CCC > Doubled	Walapai, Jamul Tiipay, Manam
CCC > AUX-Headed	Walapai, Tofa

The various interconnected and diverse range of developments from complex predicate source construction to target auxiliary verb construction may be described as follows. AVCs may arise from biclausal verb–complement formations and conjunctive–chained clause formations as well as from ostensibly monoclausal serial verb constructions of various types and nominal complement structures as well. Light verb constructions on the one hand, and possibly inflecting + co-verb constructions characteristic of Northern Australian languages, among others, are seen as particular verbal outcomes

TABLE 7.5. Verbal origins of auxiliary verb constructions

Bi-clausal

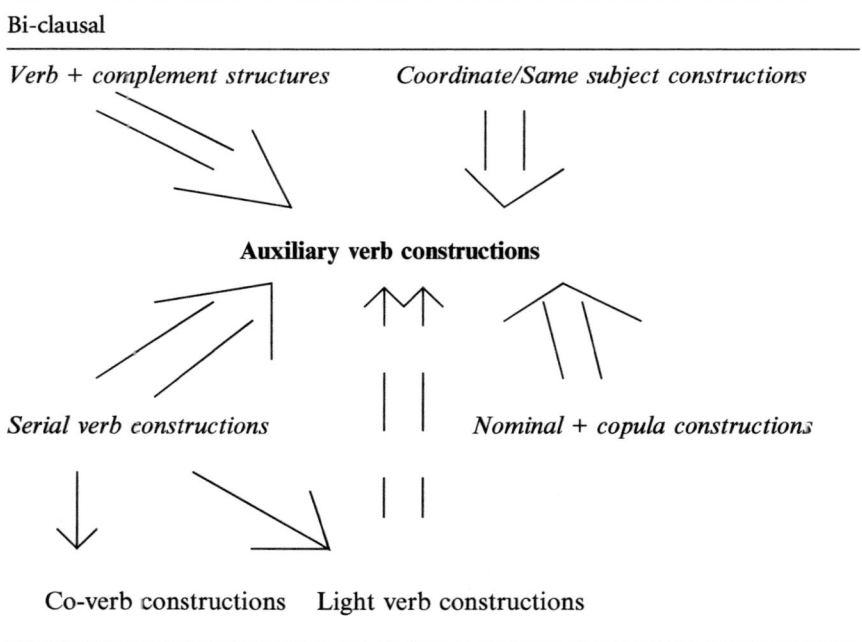

Verb + complement structures   *Coordinate/Same subject constructions*

Auxiliary verb constructions

Serial verb constructions   *Nominal + copula constructions*

Co-verb constructions   Light verb constructions

Mono-clausal

NB: Nominal outcomes of SVC (Adposition, Case) also possible.

of serialized constructions. However, it is clear that so-called light verb formations may be reanalysed or further semantically 'bleached', 'grammaticalized', or 'functionally generalized', and that they then begin to veer into the notional domain here described as 'auxiliary verb constructions'. This is represented as in Table 7.5.

Thus, the five inflectional macro-patterns of auxiliary verb constructions attested across the languages of the world are to be explained by their diverse heterogeneous constructional source pool, and the particular configurations of combinations of source verbs of differing valence and morphosyntactic properties yielding the diverse set of functional constructions embodied by AVCs. Specifically, complement clause structures of various sorts may give rise to all the macro-patterns of inflection discussed in this volume. With respect to serial constructions, core serialized forms give rise to doubled and split/doubled patterns; nuclear serialized formations, on the other hand, create LEX-headed, split, and occasionally AUX-headed patterns as well. Ambient serialized forms become either LEX-headed or split/doubled patterns, and switch-subject formations give rise to split/doubled, and split formations. Conjunctive structures likewise show restriction to AUX-headed, doubled, and split/doubled forms.

7.3 Semantic developments of AVCs: grammaticalization, event schema, etc.

I digress here briefly from the inflectional morphosyntax of auxiliary verb constructions to discuss their historical semantic developments. First, as mentioned above, from a metatheoretical perspective for many researchers, auxiliary verbs are basically limited to the expression of the functional categories of tense/aspect/mood. In fact, some even restrict their (at least 'original') functions to marking modal and aspectual categories alone, with temporal categories deriving from these along various well-known grammaticalization paths, e.g. ['want' >] desiderative > future (Heine's so-called 'volitional' or 'desire' schema), progressive > present or perfect[ive] > past; see also below. Indeed, even in Turkic languages where auxiliary verb constructions are highly varied and developed and which serve as the basis for the presentation below, the vast majority of Turkologists explicitly limit the functions of auxiliary verbs to marking these categories (Johanson 1971, 1990, 1991, 1992, 1995, 1998, 1999, Csató and Johanson 1993, Demir 1993, 1998). However, not only do a wide range of auxiliary verbs function within the grammar of the various Turkic languages, but an extensive array of categories or functions themselves are expressed. Thus, in addition to the tense, modal, and aspectual/Aktionsart functions, commonly attested throughout the world's languages associated with auxiliary verbs, one finds AVCs also marking such categories as verbal orientation (motion toward or away from the subject, topic, or discourse locus) and subject/object version. In certain cases, e.g. the orientation categories, the constructions seem to have derived from a functional specialization of a deictic serial verb construction, with non-final marking (or 'dependent' or 'converbal' marking) on the first verb. This kind of formal similarity between constructions that are functionally differentiated should come as no surprise, and is also seen between auxiliary verb constructions, verb + clausal complement constructions, and switch-subject or ambient serialization forms in Misumalpan languages.

From a historical syntactic/semantic perspective, whether deriving from coordinate or complement structures that are biclausal formations or a monoclausal serialized one, auxiliary verb constructions start out involving two verbs, one of which gradually becomes reinterpreted as contributing functional rather than content semantics, and ultimately loses some of its original syntactic and morphological properties (e.g. ability to assign case independently or even appear with independent non-subject arguments, ability to be independently negated, loss of original tonal or prosodic characteristics). These historical semantic and syntactic (and morphophonological) developments are commonly referred to as processes of 'grammaticalization' (originally from Kuryłowicz (1965) and now the standard term) in the linguistic literature. The complex processes of metaphorical extension, etc. which contribute to this (epi)phenomenon lie beyond the scope of the present volume, for which the reader is referred to such works as Sweetser (1988) or Kuteva (2001).

As is well known, the process conventionally known as 'grammaticalization' actually encompasses at least two (and probably more) logically unrelated scalar developments, one that is roughly characterizable as a shift from the lexical to the grammatical and the other from less grammatical to more grammatical.[5] While the shift from lexical to grammatical may well be straightforward or at least intuitive, the fact that the development of 'less' to 'more' grammatical is not is hardly worth mentioning. How does one

---

[5] Note that this is different from the fact that grammaticalization paths involve logically unrelated and not necessarily co-terminous clines of development, one involving semantic change and the other prosodic/phonological integration. Elements may be more 'grammaticalized', i.e. further along a line of development, for one parameter than for the other, e.g. unbound grammaticalized elements are high on the scale of semantic shift from lexical to functional but have not really begun to develop along the other. Lexical suffixes in languages such as those belonging to the Salish family show the opposite development—they are prosodically dependent but still (primarily) maintain content semantics.

actually measure degrees of grammaticalization in order to discuss meaning-
fully 'more' and 'less' grammatical (are different forms graded to some kind of
quantifiable scale of 'grammaticalizedness')? I will not labour this point here.
Suffice it to say that grammatical concepts are abstract, and defined by their
function in discourse; they also occupy a position, in both formal syntactic
analysis and functionally oriented perspectives of clause structure, that is
separate or somehow different from lexical content semantics. Broadly speaking, the semantics of grammatical elements move in the process of grammaticalization from the concrete to the abstract, i.e. from the lexical to the
functional.

As mentioned above, the 'traditional' grammaticalization path of auxiliary
verbs is as in (72). Remember that this grammaticalization path includes both
historical semantic and syntactic changes as well as historical phonological
processes of fusion and erosion.

(72)   lexical verb > auxiliary verb > affix > Ø

As the grammaticalization of auxiliary verbs moves from lexical to functional,
there is necessarily a period of imbalanced, and potentially ambiguous,
coexistence (see Harris and Campbell 1995), where lexical and functional
interpretations overlap within a syntactico-semantic set of hierarchies, and
bound and full forms of functional elements alternate along a prosodic–
phonological continuum. This can be indicated in the following simplified
chart (where stage II is ambiguous, variable, 'overlapping'):

(73)

Stage I	Stage II	Stage III
lexical >	ambiguous >	grammatical
going to town >	*going to work* >	*going to stay here*

Stage I	Stage II	Stage III
full	full/reduced	reduced
he will go	*he will go/ he'll go*	*he'll go*

While the grammaticalization path in (72) above is well known in the
literature, it should be explicitly stated here again that the principles of both
the semantic and syntactic characteristics of the development of auxiliary verb
constructions are logically independent of the phonological/prosodic ones.
Specifically, it is not always the case that a phonologically more fused construction is older or historically prior to a less phonologically fused one.
A single example of this, already discussed previously, should suffice to
demonstrate this fact.

In Xakas, there are two very common formations expressed by AVCs that are etymologically formally identical but functionally quite distinct. In both, the lexical verb appears in the common -*Ip* converb (or gerund) form followed by the auxiliary verb (as a strict SOV language of Eurasia, the auxiliary verb naturally follows the lexical verb in Xakas). One marks a (progressive) present and the other an evidential past formation. Thus, one finds the following developments:

(74) *-*Ip tur* 'stand' → evidential past and *-*Ip tur* 'stand' → progressive >

present

These are exemplified in (75) and (76) respectively.

(75)	Xakas		(76)	Xakas		
	ol	*oyna-ptïr*		*ol*	*oyna-p*	*tur*
	S/he	play-CV-EVID.PAST		S/he	play-CV	PRES.PROG
	'he played apparently'			'he is playing'		
	(Field Notes)			(Field Notes)		

The former auxiliary verb has been univerbated or fused, and therefore is bound phonologically in the current state of the language; the latter still remains a free-standing word. However, counter to the expectations of the well-known grammaticalization path given in (72), the latter is the older formation in the history of the Turkic languages. Specifically, the formation -*Ip tur* marking a progressive present is very common in many Altai-Sayan Turkic languages (77–79), and can probably be reconstructed for at least Common Turkic, while the evidential past formation is mainly restricted to a geographically definable subset of Altai-Sayan Turkic languages.[6]

(77)	a.	Tuvan		b.	Tuvan
		sen-i sakt-ïp tur men			*xal-ïp tur men*
		you-ACC remember-CV AUX 1			run-CV AUX 1
		'I remember you'			'I'm running'
		(Anderson and Harrison 1999: 65)			

(78)	a.	Altai-kiži	b.	Altai-kiži
		bala kïygïr-ïp tur-ï		*d'aygï kün d'e[r]-di izid-ip tur-u*
		child cry-CV AUX-3		summer(-DC) sun earth-ACC heat-CV AUX-3
		'the child is crying'		'the summer sun warms the earth'
		(Dyrenkova 1940: 236)		

---

[6] Possibly also found in the nearly contiguous Uighur language.

(79)   Tuba-kiži
    Men čanak yaza-ptï-m
    I ski make-[CV:]PRS-1
    'I am making skis'
    (Baskakov 1966: 73)

Many other non-Altai Sayan Turkic languages make use of the (progressive) present in **-Ip tur*. These include such genetically and geographically diverse members of the family as Turkmen, Uighur, and (Bashkir) Bašqort: see (80)–(82). See also Menges (1968) or Johanson (1971, 1976, 1999) for more on this construction.

(80)   a.   Turkmen
        Gün-lör xatar-xatar ɣeç-ip dur
        Day-PL over and over pass-CV PROG
        'the days are passing one after the other'
        (Hansar 1977: 98)

    b.   Turkmen
        Ol men-den utan-ip dur
        He I-ABLbe.ashamed-CV PROG/PRES
        'he is ashamed of me now'
        (Hansar 1977: 169)

(81)   Uighur   (82)   Bashkir (Bašqort)
    Jez-ip turu-sän   *El ör-öp tor-a*
    write-CV AUX.PRES-2   Wind blow-CV PROG-PRES
    'you are writing'   'the wind is blowing'
    (Nadžip 1971: 122)   (Juldašev et al. 1981: 217)

Note that the auxiliary alone is sufficient to mark present tense in Turkmen (as it was in the Tuvan examples above); but in Uighur and Bashqort (Bashkir) (as well as the other Altai-Sayan Turkic languages above), another marker of present is found.

    The evidential (or 'status') construction on the other hand, while common in the majority of Altai-Sayan Turkic languages (as well as Uighur), is basically restricted to these, and in fact is not found in all of them; for examples see (83–87).

(83)   a.   Shor   b.   Shor
        Oyna-ptïr-ziŋ   *oyna-baan-dïr-[b]ïm*
        Play-EVID.PST-2   play-NEG-EVID.PST-1
        'it seems you played'   'it seems I didn't play'
        (Babuškin and Donidze 1966: 475)

(84)   Tuba-kiži
    Kara-Küreŋ-di öltür-üp sal-tır
    Kara-Küreŋ-ACC kill-CV PRFV-EVID.PST
    'he killed Kara-Küreŋdi (it seems)'
    (Baskakov 1966: 82)

(85)   Quu-kiži
    it-ken it-iŋ karid-i-na ur-up ežik kiyn-i-na sal per-ten bo-ptir
    yellow dog-DAT dog-GEN bowl-3-DAT pour-CV door edge-3-DAT put
      OBJ.VERS-IMPERF AUX-EVID.PST
    'she poured out food for the yellow dog into the bowl and put it
      by the threshold'
    (Baskakov 1985: 91)

(86)   Teleut
    Suu-diŋ üst-i d'akši toŋ-golok bol-tır
    Water-GEN top-3 good freeze-UNACMPL AUX-EVID.PST
    'it seems the water surface hasn't frozen up yet'
    (Baskakov 1958: 90)

(87)   Chulym Turkic
    až-ip ukla-p pa:r-t'i-m
    There collapse-CV sleep-CV PRFV-EVID.PST-1
    'I apparently collapsed and passed out asleep there'
    (Dul'zon 1960: 120)

Strong evidence that the formation is a later innovation in the western Altai-Sayan Turkic languages comes from the fact that the evidential past formation in *-Ip tur* is found in Tuvan, but not the closely related Tofa. As mentioned above, it is also mainly lacking in non-Altai-Sayan Turkic languages.

(88)   a.   Tuvan
        söölgü üye-de öskelen-i ber-iptir sen
        last time-LOC change-CV INCH-EVID.PAST 2
        'it seems you changed recently'
        (Sat 1966: 395)

      b.   Tuvan
        men kör-üptür men
        I see-EVID.PAST 1
        'I saw (it would appear)'
        (Anderson and Harrison 1999: 50)

In the recent literature on auxiliary verbs, it is common to discuss the processes of grammaticalization in terms of cognitive 'event schema', i.e. complex discourse-pragmatically and semantically grounded constructions that serve as sources for the development of the various attested 'auxiliary' functions of verb formations. It turns out that the distribution of what the original semantics of an auxiliary verb are and what its grammaticalized functions are typically are non-random. In other words, certain kinds of content semantics lend themselves more readily to certain kinds of functional semantic reinterpretation. Given that one of the major cognitive processes in the development of functional semantics (out of recurrent constructions) is the metaphoric extension of the lexical semantics of the source construction, which operates in a non-random way, these semantic restrictions on paths of grammaticalization come as no surprise.

In this section I briefly outline the range of event schema that gave rise to the grammaticalization paths ultimately resulting in the auxiliary verb constructions and verbal affixes discussed in the preceding chapters. Heine (1993) discusses a wide range of these types. I exemplify these below using data mostly from AVCs found in the Altai-Sayan Turkic languages, supplemented with data taken from Heine (1993), Heine and Reh (1984), and Heine and Kuteva (2002) dealing mostly, though not exclusively, with African languages, as well as Eurasian, Papuan, Austronesian, Australian, and North, South, and Meso-American languages from the database. In this disparate areal grouping of Turkic languages, auxiliary verb constructions are extremely widely used (Anderson 2004a), constituting one of the core features of the verbal systems, and thus many phenomena found across unrelated languages around the world are attested in these languages. Furthermore, using data from several closely related languages underscores the need not to exclude data from such closely related languages when doing linguistic typology. A related fact relevant here is that despite the wide range of auxiliary verbs found in these languages, which generally show eighteen to twenty-five commonly used auxiliaries, certain constructions or event schemata enter the cycle of grammaticalization over and over and get codified in different functions across the languages of the region, and even within one and the same language itself. Also, as mentioned above, in addition to the commonly attested modal, aspectual, and Aktionsart categories typically found associated with auxiliary verb constructions cross-linguistically, Altai-Sayan Turkic languages also exhibit a range of less typical or uncommon functions of AVCs.

The notion of event schemata is based, as stated above, on the fact that the distribution of the functions of auxiliaries is non-random with respect to the original semantics of the elements involved. I summarize the typical event schema, which verbs are commonly associated with these (the 'source'), as well as which types of functional categories these characteristically yield (the 'target') in (89)–(91) below.

(89) Heine's event schema (following Langacker (1978))

Source	Meaning
LocationLocation	X is at Y.
Motion	X moves to/from Y.
Action	X does Y
Desire	X wants Y.
Change of state	X becomes Y
Equation	X is [like] Y.
Possession	X has Y
Manner	X stays in Y manner

(90)

Source	Typical auxiliary verbs
Location	be at, live at, remain at, stay at, etc.
Motion	go, come, move, etc.
Activity	do, take, continue, begin, finish, begin, finish, seize, put, keep, pull, throw, etc.
Desire	want, wish, etc.
Posture	sit, stand, lie
Relation	be like, be part of, be accompanied by, be with, etc.
Possession	have, get, own, etc.

(91)

Source	Typical grammaticalized target functions
Location	progressive, ingressive, continuous
Motion	ingressive, future, perfect, past
Action	progressive, continuous, ingressive, completive, perfect
Volition	ingressive, future
Change of state	ingressive, future
Equation	resultative, progressive, perfect, future
Accompaniment	progressive
Possession	resultative, perfect, future
Manner	progressive

Indeed, in one study (Kuteva (1991), cited in Heine (1993)), 117 AVCs were examined in eleven Indo-European, Finno-Ugric, and Sino-Tibetan languages and were found to have only twenty source verbs.

These lists are far from exhaustive, however, as such unusual formations as the development of 'spend the night' into a marker of unexpected action in various

TABLE 7.6. Common lexical sources for auxiliaries

'be'	'have'	'be on/at'
'come'	'go'	'walk'
'sit'	'stand'	'lie'
'begin'	'become'	'remain'
'finish'	'do'	'want'
'must'	'permit'	'take'
'see'	'hit'	'send'
'leave'	'put'	'give'

Altai-Sayan Turkic languages (e.g. Xakas, South Altai) or the development of 'pluck' (often in a univerbated form) into an intensive action construction in the North Munda (Austroasiatic) language Santali amply demonstrate.

(92)   Xakas
    ib-deŋ   *sïγara* *par-a* *xon-γa-m*
    house-ABL from   go-CV UNEXP -PAST -1
    'all of a sudden I left the house'
    (Pritsak 1959: 621)

(93)   South Altai
    Bir   *katap* *erten* *tura*   *kün* *čïg-ar-da,*   *ayïl-dïŋ*
    One   time   early morning sun go.out-PRTCPL-LOC yurt-GEN

    ežig-i   *ačïl-dï,*   *kïzïl* *tülkü* *kir-e*   *kon-dï*
    door-3 open-REC.PST red fox   enter-CV UNEXP-REC.PST

    'once at dawn the door of the yurt opened and the red fox darted in suddenly'
    (Tybykova 1966: 33)

(94)   Santali
    hɛc-gɔd-ɔk-me
    come-AUX-MDL-2
    'come quickly'
    (Bodding 1929)

Among these so-called 'simplex' event schema types found in Heine (1993), the following are found in the Altai-Sayan Turkic languages: the positional schema, the motion schema, the action schema, the change-of-state schema and finally the location schema. Each of these is presented briefly in turn below.

7.3.1 Positional/postural event schemata

The positional event schema gave rise to many of the fundamental auxiliary verb constructions in the Altai-Sayan Turkic languages (and elsewhere: see the articles in Newman (2002)). The verbs meaning 'sit', 'stand', and 'lie' all have been frequently used, and have repeatedly entered grammaticalization paths throughout these languages' history.

(95) *positional schema* → *stand, sit, lie*

i.	*stand, sit, lie*	>	*progressive*	(> *present*)
ii.	*stand*	>	*evidential (past)*	
iii.	*stand, sit, lie*	>	*imperfective*	
iv.	*stand*	>	*copula, expletive/dummy auxiliary*	
v.	*stand*	>	*habitual (present)*	

The most common and widespread, and probably oldest, formations are those used to mark progressive action, which, as is typically the case with such developments cross-linguistically, have been subsequently reanalysed as simple present tense formations in individual languages, e.g. Xakas (< 'lie'). Also, the verb 'stand' has been grammaticalized in a range of functions, in addition to progressive/present formations (see also below). These include copular functions, habitual (present) and evidential (past) functions as well.

stand, sit, lie > PROG (> PRES)

(96) Tofa
  men sana-p oli̇ri̇ men
  I read-CV AUX.PROG.III 1
  'I am reading'
  (Rassadin 1978: 133)

(97) Tofa
  men išten-ip turu men
  I work-CV AUX.PROG.I 1
  'I am working'

(98) Tofa
  i̇t mün či̇lʸya-p či̇ti̇ri
  dog soup eat-CV AUX.PROG.IV
  'the dog is eating soup'
  (Rassadin 1978: 378)

Progressive forms derived from the grammaticalization of the auxiliaries 'sit', 'stand', and 'lie' of the positional event schema are common among the world's languages. Such forms are found in languages like Panyjima and Ngambay-Moundou with 'stand', for example, and in numerous languages (e.g. Gunya, Tacana, Ono, Korowai, or Mamvu) with 'sit'.

stand > PROG

(99) a. Panyjima
    nyiya mama karri-ku jilya-yu thana-tharntu-ku palhama-lku
    this father AUX-PRES child-ACC 3SG.GEN-ACC paint-PRES
    'this father is painting his child'
    (Dench 1991: 185)

    b. Panyjima
    nhangu jampa-rla karri-rta wangka-nyayi-ku
    here moment-FOC AUX-FUTsay-COLL-PRES
    'they'll talk together for a moment here'
    (Dench 1991: 202)

(100) a. Ngambay-Moundou   b. Ngambay-Moundou
    m-ár m-úsā dā   *m-ár mbā k-ùsà dā*
    1-AUX 1-eat meat   1-AUX for NOM-eat meat
    'I am eating meat'
    (Heine and Reh 1984: 126; Vandame 1963: 94–6)

sit > PROG

(101) Gunya
    ŋaya una-nʸina-ni-ya
    I lie-CONT-PRES-1
    'I am lying down'
    (Breen 1981: 331)

(102) Ono
    koyaŋo ge met-ki ruo kere-ki
    rain-INST hit.SS AUX-3.DS night fall-3.DS
    'while it was raining, night fell...'
    (Phinnemore 1988: 117)

(103) a. Tacana   b. Tacana
    y-ani-ani   *e-pu-ani*
    INCOM-sit-AUX   INCOM-say-AUX
    'is sitting'   'says'
    (Ottaviano and Ottaviano 1967: 185–6)

    c. Tacana   d. Tacana
    e-neti-ani   *a-ta-i-tia*
    incom-stand-AUX   say-he-DUR-IMM:PST:AUX
    'is standing'   'he said to him'
    (Ottaviano and Ottaviano 1967: 188)   (Ottaviano and Ottaviano
                                         1967: 188)

(104) Korowai
    i-nè khami-ba-lè
    look-ss AUX-AUX-1PL:REAL
    'we are looking'
    (van Enk and de Vries 1997: 93)

(105) a. Mamvu   b. Mamvu
       ɔ́ɓɛ mu-taju   *mu-taju ɔ́ɓɛ*
       dance 1-AUX   1-AUX dance
       'I was dancing'   'I was dancing'
       (Heine and Reh 1984: 126; Vorbichler 1971: 248–50)

Related to progressive notions, the positional event schema may similarly be grammaticalized to encode durative action as well. Thus duratives are derived from the verb 'lie' in such languages as Manam, Alyawarra, or Beja and from 'sit' in Burushaski.

lie > DUR
(106) Alyawarra
    ayirn-iy-aynti-ka ilikithika
    ask-LIG-AUX-PST from.what
    'they kept asking what the matter was'
    (Yallop 1977: 64)

(107) Manam
    i-pile-lá-be i-éno
    3RLS-speak-LIM-and 3RLS-AUX
    'he kept talking'
    (Lichtenberk 1983: 98)

(108) Beja
    s'aa't tam-ee-tì baʔ-ání
    meat eat-PRTCPL AUX-1.AUX
    'I keep on eating meat'
    (Hudson 1976b: 105)

sit > DUR
(109) a. Burushaski
      in yágučume hurúṭumo
      s/he search:DUR:AP:GEN AUX:II.PST
      'she kept searching for him'
      (Berger 1998b: 172)

b. Burushaski
    harált diáaršume hurúṭimi
    rain *d*:precipitate:DUR:AP:GEN AUX:IV.PST
    'it kept raining'

Note that some original semantics of an auxiliary element may be preserved in its development from the positional event schema—a situation that is typical of emergent grammaticalized categories; cf. also the ambiguity typical of grammaticalization paths during their development mentioned above. Compare in this regard the following two forms with the original source semantics of 'stand' and 'sit' and resultant nuances associated with the progressive meaning in the targets in Tofa.

(110)   a. Tofa   b. Tofa
            neš ün-üp turu   *neš ün-üp oliri*
            tree grow-CV AUX.PROG.I   tree grow-CV AUX.PROG.III
            'a tall tree is growing'   'a planted/dwarf tree is growing'
            (Rassadin 1978: 151)

These same positional verbs have been grammaticalized as markers of imperfective aspect, seen in the following forms from Tofa and Xakas.

stand, sit, lie > *IMP(E)RF(V)*

(111)   a. Tofa
            kas-ördek ble káti ùh^j-up čerle-p čïtar sen
            goose-duck with together fly-CV live-CV PROG-FUT 2
            'you will live flying with the geese and ducks'
            (Rassadin 1990)

(112)   Xakas
        tasta-γla-p   tur-a   par-γan
        throw-ITER-CV IMPERF-CV INCH.III-PAST
        'she began to scatter (seeds)'
        (Pataeakova 1984: 98)

As briefly alluded to above, 'stand' has been grammaticalized as the copular or dummy verb stem in the Altai-Sayan Turkic language Tuvan.

stand > *COP, DUMMY AUX*

(113)   Tuvan
        bir eves bo bažïŋ-ni   tiv-al-gan tur-gan bol-z-um-za men amira-ar
        tur-gan men

if this house-ACC find-(SBEN)-PAST AUX-PAST(.I) AUX-CON-1-CON
I rejoice-P/F AUX-PAST.I 1
'if I had found this house I would have been happy'
(Anderson and Harrison 1999: 67)

Evidential semantics are associated with the AVC in *-*Ip tur* and fused forms resulting from these in various Altai-Sayan Turkic languages.

To recap, in Turkic (and generally speaking cross-linguistically), one canonically finds the following functions of AVCs resulting from the positional event schema.

(114) *positional schema* → PROGRESSIVE (>PRESENT)
                              IMPERFECTIVE {DURATIVE} {CONTINUATIVE}
                              COPULA
                              EVIDENTIAL
                              HABITUAL

In Zulu, habituals are marked by auxiliary formations derived from the positional event schema. Indeed such a formation is found with the positional verb 'stand' in Altai-Sayan Turkic languages as well. For example, habitual is marked by an AUX-headed AVC using an auxiliary originally meaning 'stand' in such languages as Xakas *kör-edɪr-bɪn* [see-HAB-1 < *-*A tur*] 'I usually see'.

(115) Zulu (Bantu; South Africa)
       'sit, stay'   >   habitual
       (Mkhatshwa 1991)

7.3.2 Motion event schemata

Another extremely common event schema crucial to the development of auxiliary verb constructions is the so-called 'motion' schema. Among the verbs commonly used in this event schema are 'walk', 'enter', 'go', 'come', 'leave', and 'fall'. While aspectual or Aktionsart categories are the most common functions associated with this event schema, including such categories as inchoative, perfective, and unexpected action, directional/orientational (or verbal deictic) functions may also be found with the auxiliary verbs 'go' and 'come'. In addition, the verb 'walk'/'move', like the positional schema mentioned above, has shown the development into first a progressive marker and subsequently a generalized present tense marker in a number of Altai-Sayan Turkic languages.

The typical functions associated with AVCs deriving from the motion event schema in the Altai-Sayan Turkic languages include the following:

(116)   *motion schema* → *walk/move, go, come, leave, fall, enter*

i.	*walk/move*	>	*progressive* (> *present*)
ii.	*enter*	>	*inchoative*
iii.	*go*	>	*inchoative*
iv.	*go*	>	*translocative (andative, itive)*
v.	*go*	>	*perfective*
vi.	*leave*	>	*inchoative*
vii.	*fall*	>	*unexpected action*
viii.	*come*	>	*cislocative (ventive)*

As alluded to above, in addition to the three common positional verbs grammaticalized to mark progressives and ultimately present tense forms, the verb 'walk' or 'move' has also been grammaticalized in these same functions. Examples include the following from the moribund language Tofa.

walk/move > PROG (> PRES)

(117)   a.   Tofa   b.   Tofa

      át ótta-p čoru   *oŋ aŋna-p čoru*

      horse graze-CV AUX.PROG.II   he hunt-CV AUX.PROG.II

      'the horse is grazing'   'he is hunting'

      (Rassadin 1978: 378)

Note that the same auxiliary marks an intentional mood in Xakas and Shor, with the lexical complement in the infinitive form, not a converb form. This appears to be a recent development in these two languages.

In Tofa, the verb 'enter' is one of several that have been grammaticalized within auxiliary verb constructions in the function of an inchoative or inceptive marker.

enter > INCH

(118)   a.   Tofa

      kel-ɪ sal-ɨ kil-ɪp kɪr-gen

      come-CV as.soon.as.AUX-CV do-CV INCH₂-PST

      'as soon as [he] came he began to do it'

      (Rassadin 1978: 153)

    b.   Tofa

      kar jaa-vɨt-kan soŋ aŋna-p kɪr-dɪ-m

      snow precipitate-PRFV-PST after hunt-CV INCH₂-REC.PST-1

      'as soon as it snowed, I started hunting'

In Xakas, both 'go' and 'leave' in various constructions have this function as well. Note that the lexical verb appears in the -*A* converb form with 'go' but the -*p* converb form with 'leave' in these AUX-headed AVCs in Xakas.

go > INCH

(119)a. Xakas

    tasta-ɣla-p   tur-a   par-ɣan

    throw-ITER-CV IMPERF-CV INCH-PAST

    'she began to scatter (seeds)'

    (Patačakova 1984: 98)

leave > INCH

b. Xakas

    ol   čooxta-p   six-xan

    s/he speak-CV INCH-PAST

    'he began to speak'

    (Pritsak 1959: 620)

The auxiliary 'come' has been grammaticalized in a construction marking inchoative action in Kathmandu Newar.

come > INCH

(120) a. Kathmandu Newar (Nepāl Bhāśā)

    pwa syan-a wɔl-ɔ

    stomach ache-NON.FIN AUX-PRF.DISJ

    '[my] stomach has begun to ache'

    (Hargreaves 2003: 380; Malla 1985: 76)

The motion event schema may be grammaticalized to mark perfectivity and even past tense ultimately. Thus, 'go' marks perfective in such languages as Xakas, Doyayo, and Yale of the Mek Stock, Papua New Guinea, while 'come', presumably via a stage of perfective marking, encodes past tense in Nilotic Teso.

go > PRF

(121) a. Doyayo (Adamawa-Eastern; Cameroon)

    be¹ re³ be¹ tɔ⁴mɔ¹ gɔ¹ ya⁴

    1 go 1 devour-2 ANA Q

    'would I then eat you up?'

    (Wiering and Wiering 1994: 217)

(122) Yale (Mek or isolate; Papua New Guinea)

    bunu-do ba-lam-ek

    swarm-INF AUX-DUR-3PL.REM.PST

    'they swarmed'

    (Heeschen 1998: 88)

come > PRF > PST

(123) Teso

    a-bu ke-ner

    1-AUX.PST 1SBJNCTV-say

    'I said'

    (Heine and Reh 1984: 104; Hilders and Lawrance 1956: 14)

Among the characteristic features of the auxiliary verb systems attested in the present-day Turkic languages of Siberia is the use of the verb originally meaning 'fall' in an AVC to mark sudden or unexpected action. Such a formation is found in languages across the region, including Tofa, Xakas, and, further off, in Yakut (Sakha) as well, and even Bashkir, spoken mainly across the Urals in the European part of Russia.

fall > UNEXP

(124)   Tofa
ög-e kɪr-e düš-tü-m
house-DAT enter-CV UNEXP-REC.PST-1
'I quickly entered the house'
(Rassadin 1978: 154)

(125)   Xakas

suɣ ɪn-zer	pray kir-gelek-t-ök	örke-nɪŋ paz-i	körɪn-e tüs-ken
water burrow-ALL	all enter-UNACMPL-LOC-EMPH	gopher-GEN head-3	appear-CV UNEXP-PAST

'even before all the water had gone into the burrow, the gopher's head suddenly appeared'
(Čeresmisina et al. 1984: 149)

(126)   Yakut (Sakha)
Makaar d'ik gin-a tüs-te
Makaar start/flinch AUX-CV UNEXP-PST
'Makar suddenly started/flinched'
(Korkina et al. 1982: 285)

(127)   Bashkir (Bašqort)
Sælmæn-deŋ asɪw-i ber až bašil-a töš-tö
Salman-GEN anger-3 a.little subside-CV UNEXP-PST
'Salman's anger (suddenly) subsided a little'
(Juldašev et al. 1981: 219)

Another characteristic use of the motion event schema in Turkic is the development of directionality or orientation formations marking cislocative and translocative action, i.e. action directed towards or away from the subject, topic, discourse locus, or deictic centre. Thus 'come' marks cislocative constructions and 'go' translocative in a range of these languages. Presumably these went through a stage of deictic serialization or some similar process before becoming the present-day AVCs, perhaps secondarily restructured to be formally similar to the auxiliary constructions.[7]

come > cislocative (venitive)
(128)   Tofa
     onson vjertaljo:t-tar uh^j-up kel-gen
     then helicopter-PL fly-CV CLOC-PST
     'then the helicopters flew in'
     (ASLEP Field Notes)

(129)   Tuvan
     čed-ip   *ke-er*   *men*
     come-CV CLOC.P/F 1
     'I'll come'
     (Anderson and Harrison 1999: 69)

(130)   Xakas
     učux   *kil-gen*
     fly   CLOC-PAST
     'flew here'
     (Pritsak 1959: 620)

go > translocative (andative, itive)
With regards to the translocative formation, the converb form of the lexical verb may vary considerably even in closely related languages. Thus, in Xakas it is the -*p* converb and in Tuvan the -*A/j* converb; in Tofa, the lexical verb may appear in either form.[8]

(131)   Tofa
     aj-da-a   *čil baγa* *ol*   *ool-nɨ*   *al-ɨp*   *bar-γan*   *aj-γa*
     moon-LOC-DC demon that boy-ACC take-CV TLOC-PST moon-DAT
     'the moon-demon took this boy up to the moon'
     (Rassadin 1971)

---

[7] In this light, perhaps the forms in Xakas (with Ø-form of the converb with consonant-final lexical stems and consonant-initial auxiliaries) are relics of a nuclear serialization stage with no 'dependent' morphology on the lexical, non-deictic/motion verb.

[8] A further complicating factor in Tofa is the collapse under way in the auxiliary verb system due to the advanced moribundity of the language. The translocative is increasingly being replaced by what appears to be emerging as the default auxiliary construction, which in this particular instance or function may also be in part phonologically motivated (*ber* is replacing *bar*), by the similarity between the original construction and the AVC being generalized; see also Anderson and Harrison (to appear) for details.

(132)   a.   Tuvan
         ol čoru-j bar-gan
         he go-CV TLOC-PAST.I
         'He's gone away'
         (Anderson and Harrison 1999: 69)

         b.   Tuvan
               àt maŋna-p čoru-j bar-gan
               horse run-CV AUX-CV TLOC-PAST.I
               'the horse ran away, went running away'
               (Babuškin 1966: 204)

(133)   Xakas
         učux   par-γan
         fly   TLOC-PAST
         'flew away'
         (Pritsak 1959: 620)

Developments from a motion schema into a tense marker can be found in numerous languages, e.g. various African languages. Especially common here is the development of 'come' to a future marker.

come > FUT

(134)   Lango
         dákô bínô nénô
         woman 3:AUX:HAB see:INF
         'the woman will see'
         (Noonan 1992: 126)

(135)   a.   Lotuko (Eastern Nilotic)   b.   Lotuko (Eastern Nilotic)
               a-ttu nɪ lɛtɛn   *a-lɔ nɪ coxuno*
               1-FUT I go:INF   1-FUT I return:INF
               'I'll leave immediately'   'I'll leave immediately'
               (Heine and Reh 1984: 132; Muratori 1938: 161ff.)

(136)   So (Kuliak; eastern Uganda)[9]
         ác-ìsa   >   ác-ísa gúg-ác
         come-1   FUT-1 transfer-VEN
         'I come'   'I shall buy'
         (Heine and Reh 1984: 39)

---

[9] Note that in this So form, the verb 'come' has been grammaticalized twice: once to mark FUT, once in a function more transparently related to its origin as an SVC marking the category VEN.

(137) Pare (G22)   (138) Luguru (G35)
       ni-za-et-a   *tu-tso-ɣul-a*
       1-FUT-bring-FV   1PL-FUT-buy-FV
       'I will bring (it)'   'we will buy'
       (Botne 1990: 191; Nurse 1979a, 1979b)

(139) a. Kinyarwanda   b. Kinyarwanda
           a-za gu-kora   *a-za-kora*
           1-FUT INF-work   1-FUT-work
           'he will work (later today)'   'he will work (after today)'
           (Botne 1990: 190; Hurel 1911)

(140) Zulu
       'come' > immediate future
       'go'   > remote future
       (Mkhatshwa 1991)

(141) Ewe
       ye-á-vá
       3-FUT-come
       'he will come'
       (Heine and Reh 1984: 38)

(142) Koyo (Kru, Niger-Congo; Côte d'Ivoire)
       Abi yi   du   mo
       Abi AUX town go
       'Abi will go to town'
       (Heine 1993: 34)

A potential construction is found using the auxiliary 'come' in Doyaɣo, an Adamawa language of Cameroon.

come > POT

(143) Doyayo (Adamawa; Cameroon)
       hi¹ za¹ hi¹ zaa¹³ hi¹ lɔ³mɔ¹
       3PL POT 3PL come 3PL bite-2
       'they might come bite you'
       (Wiering and Wiering 1994: 221)

A Partial list of common semantic developments of auxiliaries reflecting the motion event schema is offered in (144).

(144) *motion schema* → PROGRESSIVE (>PRESENT)
       PERFECTIVE (>PAST)
       INCHOATIVE
       UNEXPECTED

CISLOCATIVE

TRANSLOCATIVE

INTENTIONAL

POTENTIAL

FUTURE

7.3.3 Action event schemata

The action event schema is another extremely common and important source of auxiliary verb constructions. The most common verbs that have played a role in these developments include 'give', 'put', 'hit', 'send', 'see', and 'take'. An extensive range of categories is marked by AVCs expressed by forms reflecting the action event schema. These include various aspectual or Aktionsart categories (inchoative, immediate action, perfect(ive), etc.) as well as a range of modal categories. In addition, the verbs 'give' and 'take' have been grammaticalized in AVCs expressing various categories of version or voice in the Altai-Sayan Turkic languages, namely, benefactive action or object version ('give') and self-benefactive action or subject version ('take'). These fascinating and apparently archaic functions are discussed in Anderson (2001).

(145)   *action schema* → *give, take, hit, put, see, send*

i.	*give*	>	*inchoative*
ii.	*give*	>	*benefactive/object version*
iii.	*put*	>	*immediate*
iv.	*put*	>	*perfective*
v.	*hit*	>	*perfective*
vi.	*send*	>	*perfect[ive]*
vii.	*see*	>	*attemptive*
viii.	*take*	>	*capabilitive*
ix.	*take*	>	*self-benefactive/subject version*
x.	*take*	>	*perfective*

One of the most commonly used auxiliary verbs in Turkic is 'give', which has been grammaticalized into a range of functions via the action event schema. One common function found in this language family associated with auxiliary uses of 'give' is to mark inchoative or inceptive action. Tofa and Xakas provide examples of such a formation.

give > INCH

(146)   a.   Tofa

tùfa	*soot*	*ùttunu-ks-e*	*ber-di*	*tʃoyum*
Tofa	language	forget-DESID-GER	ASP-REC.PST	probably

'they probably wanted to forget the Tofa language'
[ASLEP Field Notes; P.B.]

b.   Tofa

am   nit-ter   kör-ʃ-i   ver-gen-ner
now   youth-PL   see-RCP-GER   ASP-PST-PL
'now the youths began seeing each other'
[ASLEP Field Notes; SDK]

(147)   Xakas
oyn-i pir-dɪ
play-CV INCH.II-PAST.II
'began to play'
(Pritsak 1959: 620)

Another common function is to mark benefactive action or object version, i.e. action performed to the benefit of, or otherwise primarily affecting, a non-subject. Such a construction is found in numerous Turkic languages.

give >BEN/OBJ.VERS
(148)   Tuvan
biž-ip   ber-di-m
write-CV BEN-PAST.II-1
'I wrote (it) for someone else'
(Field Notes)

(149)   a.   Tofa
men ögle-p ber-dɪ-m
I make.house-CV BEN-REC.PST-1
'I made him a house'
(Rassadin 1978: 154)

b.   Tofa
ìtɪk bɨhʲ-ip ber
boot cut-CV BEN
'cut me some boots'

(150)   Tatar
šu-nɨ tiz gěna tärǧěmä it-ěp bir-ěgěz
this-ACC speed POSTP translate AUX.TR-CV BEN-PL.IMP
'please translate this [for me] quickly'
(Schönig 1984: 91)

Another common auxiliary reflecting the action event schema is 'put'. This has at least two separate functions. In one, reflected in Tofa in an AVC in *-I sal*, it marks immediate action; in another, represented by Xakas, it marks a perfective construction in the form of an AUX-headed AVC in *(-p) sal*.

put > IMM

(151)   Tofa
    kör-ü sal-i ëëtir-di
    see-CV AUX-CV ask-REC.PST
    'as soon as he saw, he asked'
    (Rassadin 1978: 154)

put > PRF

(152)   Xakas
    oristi xaydar it saldar
    Russian-ACC to.where do PRF.IIA-PAST.II-2PL
    'where did you put the Russian?'
    (Anderson 1998a)

Another perfective AVC in Altai-Sayan Turkic reflecting the action event schema involves a verb originally meaning 'hit'. Tofa and the closely related Tuvan both use this construction.[10]

hit > PRF

(153)   Tofa
    tura kö-örde boriika-niŋ kuduru-un čü te oota deŋge
    morning see-DS wood-grouse-GEN tail-3.ACC what EMPH very level
    heyčila-p kaγ-an bol-γan òtir-a
    scissor-CV PRFV-PST AUX-PST cut.clean- CV
    'the next morning they looked: something had perfectly sheared off the wood-grouse's tail'
    (Rassadin 1971)

(154)   Tuvan
    ol   *kino-nu*   *kör-üp* *ka-an men*
    that   film-ACC   see-CV   AUX-PST 1
    'I've already seen that film'
    (Anderson and Harrison 1999: 64)

As mentioned in Chapter 6, among the most widespread of perfective constructions in Altai-Sayan Turkic languages reflecting the action event schema of grammaticalization involves a verb etymologically meaning 'send' (<*uið). In most, this synchronically functions as a stem-forming suffix, rather than an inflectional category as it once was.

---

[10] Note that fused AVCs with the auxiliary 'hit' occurs in Northern Yeniseic languages (Ket and Yugh[†]).

send > PRF

(155) Shor

apšak in-i-neŋ šïy-ïp tur-ïbïs-tï
bear den-3-ABL leave-CV stop-PRF-REC.PST
'the bear came out of its den and stopped'
(Nevskaja 1993: 36)

(156) Xakas

ol	*xïyïr-(ïb)ïs-xan*	*kniga-nï,*	*xayzï*	*pol-da*	*čat-ča*
s/he	read-PRF-PAST	book-ACC	which	floor-LOC	lie-PRES.I

'he read the book that is lying on the floor'
(Field Notes)

The action event schema has also been utilized to create modal functions in Turkic languages as well. For example, the verb stem originally meaning 'see' has been grammaticalized as a marker of attemptive mood.

see > ATT

(157) Tofa

bis ïnda aŋna-p kör-dü-vüs
we there hunt-CV ATT-REC.PST-1PL
'we tried to hunt here'
(Rassadin 1978: 169)

(158) Tuvan

bo xem-ge balïkta-p	*kör-dü-vüs*
this river-DAT fish-CV	ATT-PAST.II-1PL

'we tried to fish in this river'
(Anderson and Harrison 1999: 65; Shamina 1995: 35)

(159) a. Xakas

pu suy-nï kïč-ip kör
this river-ACC cross-CV ATT
'try to cross this river'
(Pristak 1959: 620)

b. Xakas

ol tïxta-p kör-gen
s/he fix-CV ATT-PAST
'he tried to fix it'

(160) Turkmen

otur-ïk gör-mek
sit-CV ATT-INF
'to try to sit'
(Hansar 1977: 168)

Another very common verb used as auxiliaries in the Turkic languages is the verb 'take'. This has entered into numerous different constructions across the languages of the family and has been grammaticalized to mark a range of different functional categories. One such category is capabilitive mood. This is marked by an AUX-headed AVC in *-A/-j al* in Tuvan (but in *-p al* in Xakas—see Chapter 1).

take > CAP

(161) Tuvan
    ol   biži-j   al-bas
    s/he write-CV CAP-NEG.FUT
    'she can't write'
    (Anderson and Harrison 1999: 62)

Another characteristic function of this element is to mark 'self-benefactive' action or subject version, i.e. action done for the benefit of, or otherwise primarily affecting, a subject. Such a formation is found across the languages of the Turkic family. The lexical verb in such constructions may appear in either converb form or, in the case of Tofa, optionally in a same-subject marked form as well.

take > SBEN/SUBJ.VERS

(162) Tofa
    dilʸi   oluk   bar-ɨp   bræœ   üšpül   tùt-kaš al-ɣan.
    fox   right.away go-CV one   hazel.grouse catch-SS SUBJ.VERS-PST
    'right away the fox caught himself a hazel grouse'
    (Rassadin 1994: 198)

(163) a. Tuvan   b. Tuvan
        am čed-ip aar men   *bižip aar men*
        now come-CV SUBJ.VERS:P/F 1   write-CV SUBJ.VERS:P/F1
        'I'll come now'   'I'll write it down'
        (Anderson and Harrison 1999: 62)

The construction has been univerbated in Uighur, and thus this AVC is farther along the prosodic/phonological integrity cline in this language than its cognates in most other Turkic languages.[11]

---

[11] As noted in Ch. 1, this element in modern Xakas appears to be fused in one verb stem, 'find', a lexical stem with which the original AVC was especially common.

(164) a. Uighur/Uyɣur
           adris-i-ni yez-iw-al-di-m
           address-3-ACC write-CV-SUBJ. VERS-PST-1
           'I wrote down her address (for my own benefit)'
           (Hahn 1991: 612)

       b. Uighur/Uyɣur
           qol-um-ni kes-iw-al-di-m
           hand-1-ACC cut-CV-SUBJ.VERS-PST-1
           'I got cut on my hand'

In Tucanoan Retuarã (165) the action schema through the auxiliary 'do' marks temporal/aspectual semantics close to an intentional future tense. A similar form is seen in Papuan Imonda (166), while in Agarabi (167), the function is rather that of a past tense form.

do > FUT
(165) a. Retuarã (Central Tucanoan; Colombia)
           karaka yi-baʔa-ẽrã baa-yu
           chicken 1-eat-PURP AUX-PRES
           'I am going to eat the chicken'
           (Strom 1992: 38)

       b. Retuarã
           bãharoka yi-oʔo-ẽrã baa-yu bãẽ
           story 1-write-PURP AUX-PRES now
           'I am going to write a story now'
           (Strom 1992: 72)

       c. Retuarã
           ki-re sa-yĩʔã -ẽrã baa-reʔka potohĩ
           3M-HMN.ARG 3M-capture-PURP AUX-PST when
           'when it was going to capture him'

(166) a. Imonda   b. Imonda
           ka uagl auaia fe-f-t   *ka maim uagl fe-f*
           I go no AUX-PRES-CNTRFACT   I anyway go AUX-PRES
           'I would not go'   'I will go anyway'
           (Seiler 1983/4: 165–166)

do > PST

(167)   Agarabi
        náh y-e-m-íh
        eat AUX-NEUT-IND-3
        'he ate'
        (Goddard 1980: 61)

The auxiliary 'do' grammaticalized via an action event schema into a habitual form is attested in Oksapmin, an isolate language ostensibly belonging to the Trans-New Guinea macro-phylum.

do > HAB

(168)   Oksapmin
        tima-m ha-t
        sleep-SUBORD AUX-AGT.VPT.C.MD.PST.SG
        'used to sleep'
        (Lawrence 1972: 56)

The action event schema involving the auxiliary 'do' can also give rise to progressive formations as well, in such languages as the Papuan Usarufa.

(169)   Usarufa (Papuan; Papua New Guinea)
        úbó-ubo kéiye
        dig-REDPL he's.doing
        'he is digging'
        (Heine 1993: 35; Bee 1973: 295)

Thus, the action schema is probably the most functionally diverse set. Constructions reflecting this path of development may mark Aktionsart or aspectual categories and modal functions, as well as version (primary affectedness) categories.

> action schema   →   PERFECTIVE
>   INCHOATIVE
>   CAPABILITIVE
>   SUBJECT VERSION/SELF-BENEFACTIVE
>   OBJECT-VERSION/BENEFACTIVE
>   ATTEMPTIVE
>   HABITUAL
>   PROGRESSIVE
>   TENSE (PST, FUT)

7.3.4 Change-of-state event schemata

The final common event schema that underlies important auxiliary verb constructions in the modern Altai-Sayan Turkic languages is the change-of-state schema. The two verbs that reflect this event schema are 'become' and 'grow'. The latter has a relatively restricted distribution and marks inchoative action, while the former is one of the most common and important auxiliary verbs throughout the languages of the world. The auxiliary verb 'be[come]' marks a range of modal categories, viz. capabilitive, possibilitive, and probabilitive. It is also used extensively in copular functions, as an expletive/dummy verb, and in the formation of many complex, periphrastic tense/mood/aspect forms.

(170)   *change-of-state schema* → *grow, become*

i.	*be[come]* >	*copula, expletive/dummy auxiliary*
ii.	*be[come]* >	*probabilitive*
iii.	*be[come]* >	*possibilitive*
iv.	*be[come]* >	*capabilitive*
v.	*be* >	*progressive* (*often* + LOC)
vi.	*grow* >	*inchoative*

The uses of 'be' or 'become' within auxiliary verb constructions in Altai-Sayan Turkic languages fall into two broad groups. One is copular, serving as an expletive or dummy inflectable stem for the purposes of creating a range of complex TAM forms.

be[come] > COP, AUX

(171)   a.   Tofa

boriika oyna-p kö-ör-de, men kuduru-un deŋge daar-ïp ka-ɣan bol-ïr men heyči ble

wood-grouse play-CV ATT-P/F-LOC I tail-3.ACC completely cut. off-CV PRFV-PST AUX-FUT 1 scissors with

'when the wood-grouse will try to play, I will have cut his tail clean off'

(Rassadin 1971)

b.   Tofa

üšpül tura-keǰe šeni čokka sïyïr-ip čit-ar bol-ɣan

hazel-grouse morning-and-night effortlessly whistle-CV PROG-FUT AUX-PST

'morning and night the hazel-grouse would whistle effortlessly'

(Rassadin 1971)

(172)   Xakas
    portnoy-ya   kip   tɪk-tɪr-gen   pol-ɣa-bɪs
    tailor-DAT   clothes   sew-CAUS-PAST   AUX-PAST-1PL
    'we had (had) a tailor sew (us) some clothes'
    (Baskakov et al. 1975: 354)

The other large set of categories encoded by the auxiliary verb could be defined as modal. The range of modal functions expressed by constructions involving an auxiliary verb reflecting the change-of-state event schema for grammaticalization includes probabilitive, capabilitive, and possibilitive.

As mentioned where relevant in various chapters above, the probabilitive in Altai-Sayan Turkic may be inflected as a split construction as in Xakas or as a LEX-headed one as in Shor.

be[come] > PROB
(173)   Tuvan
    čayaan-dös   oyna-p tur-gan boor iyin
    spirit   play-CV AUX-PAST.I PROB DISC
    '(by all appearances) the spirit(s) were playing about'
    (Letjagina 1989: 63)

(174)   a.   Xakas
        min nime-e   čobal-čatxan-ɪm-nɪ   sɪrer pɪl-če   polar-zar
        I   what-DAT   be.sad-PRS.PRTCPL-1-ACC   y'all know-PRS.I PROB-2PL
        'you probably know what I'm sad about'
        (Anderson 1998a: 60)

     b.   Xakas
        sin it-ken polar-zɪŋ
        you do-PAST.I PROB-2
        'you probably did it'

(175)   Tofa
    uhʲ-up kel-i čɪtarɪ-lar bol-ɪr, iŋʲa-l-sa ta bàhaj köstü-dürü
    fly-CV CLOC-CV AUX.PROG-PRS-PL PROB do.thus-PASS-CON EMPH bad
     appear-NARR
    'they were flying, it appeared, in bad shape however'
    (Rassadin 1994: 193)

The possibilitive and capabilitive formations are formally identical, and may well represent a single grammaticalization with subsequent semantic change rather than two separate grammaticalizations of formally identical sequences, as was the case with the capabilitive vs. subject version functions deriving from the sequence -*[I]p al* ('take').

be[come] > PSB

(176)   a.   Tofa
             sana-p bol-ir men
             read-CV PSB-FUT 1
             'I can, am able to, allowed
             to, may read'
             (Rassadin 1978: 167)

        b.   Tofa
             oŋ ùh^y-up bol-ir
             s/he fly-CV PSB-FUT
             's/he can/will be able to fly'
             (Rassadin 1978: 166)

be[come] > CAP

(177)   a.   Tuvan
             men oyna-p bol-ur men
             I play-CV CAP-P/F 1
             'I can play'
             (Anderson and Harrison 1999: 67)

        b.   Tuvan
             olar oyna-p bol-ur tur-gan
             they play-CV CAP-P/F AUX-PAST.I
             'they could have played'
             (Anderson and Harrison 1999: 67)

One of the common functions of AVCs grammaticalized out the copula/ auxiliary 'be' is a progressive. This is often, though by no means exclusively, found in tandem with some kind of (usually locational) adpositional complement. AVCs reflecting this event schema may be in a number of inflectional patterns, including doubled, AUX-headed, or LEX-headed.

be > PROG

(178)   Pipil
        ni-nemi ni-k-chiwa luchár
        1-AUX 1-do fight
        'I am fighting'
        (Campbell 1985: 137)

(179)   Nasioi
        oo-amp-aʔ oʔno-n
        see-1-NEG AUX.1-TEMP
        'I don't see it'
        (Hurd and Hurd 1970: 74)

(180) Remo   (181) Cabécar (Chibchan; Costa Rica)
       bəba ḍentiŋ   *yís tsóN muNlúNlbí suNwaN étaba*
       Rdpl-slap-PROG-NPAST-1   I AUX:NF:PRES deer see:NF one
       'I am slapping'   'I see (am seeing) a deer'
       (Fernandez 1968: 54)   (Young and Givón 1991: 226)

(182) a. Baluchi (Iranian; Pakistan, Iran, Afghanistan)
           mən svarəga koha ləgg-əg-a bin
           I lunch mountain climb-INF-DEF AUX:1
           'I shall be climbing the mountain at lunch(time)'
           (Bybee et al. 1994: 250–1; Barker and Mengal 1969: 233ff.)

       b. Baluchi
           če, təw ymšəpi van-əg-a bəy
           you tonight study AUX-INF-DEF AUX:2
           'will you be studying tonight?'

(183) Mamvu
       òro 'mà   <   **òro-ná ma*
       go:1 AUX   go-1 AUX
       'I am going, I want to go'
       (Heine and Reh 1984: 126; Vorbichler 1971: 248–50)

(184) a. Walapai (Hualapai)
           ha-ch sma:-k-yu
           he-SUBJ sleep-SS-AUX
           'he is sleeping'
           (Watahomigie et al. 1982: 78)

Lastly, the verb 'grow' has also been grammaticalized as a marker of inchoative action in the moribund Tofa language.

grow > INCH
(185) a. Tofa   b. Tofa
           aŋna-p ün-dü-m   *iš-ɪp ün-dü-büs*
           hunt-CV INCH-REC.PST-1   drink-CV INCH-REC.PST-1PL
           'I started hunting'   'we began to drink'
           (Rassadin 1978: 154)

Another common functional development from the change-of-state schema is a future tense formation. This is found in such languages as German.

(186)   German
   Hans wird kommen
   Hans FUT.3 come-INF
   'Hans will come'
   (Heine 1993: 35)

7.3.5 Location event schemata

The location event schema, while indeed attested, plays a relatively minor role in the system of auxiliary verb constructions in the Altai-Sayan Turkic languages. The two verbs most typically reflecting this event schema are 'stay' and 'spend the night'. Both are limited to particular subsets of languages and are used to mark certain aspectual/Aktionsart categories.

(187)   *location schema* → *stay, spend the night*
   i.   *stay*   >   *perfective, durative, progressive*
   ii. *spend night*   >   *unexpected action*

In such Turkic languages as Tofa, the verb originally meaning 'stay' has been grammaticalized as an auxiliary verb to mark perfective action.

stay > PRFV
(188)   i.   Tofa
         ol ašɲak onu gör-geš kis-tar-ni kiškir-ip hal-gan
         that man that.ACC see-ss girl-PL-ACC shout-CV PRFV-PST
         'the man saw this and podozval the girls'
         (Rassadin 1978: 155)

Although relatively uncommonly found in AVCs from a cross-linguistic perspective, the verb etymologically meaning 'spend the night, to overnight' has been grammaticalized in a function marking unexpected or sudden action in the Xakas and Altai-kizhi languages of south-central Siberia.

spend night > UNEXP
(189)   Xakas
         ib-deŋ   sïyara   par-a   xon-ɣa-m
         house-ABL   from   go-CV   UNEXP -PAST -1
         'all of a sudden I left the house'
         (Pritsak 1959: 621)

(190)   Altai-kizhi
         *Bir katap erten tura kün čig-ar-da, ayïl-dïŋ ežig-i ačil-dï, kizil tülkü
         kir-e kon-dï*

One time early morning sun go.out-PRTCPL-LOC yurt-GEN door-3
open-REC.PST red fox enter-CV UNEXP-REC.PST
'once at dawn the door of the yurt opened and the red fox darted in
suddently'
(Tybykova 1966: 33)

The location schema is frequently grammaticalized as either a durative or a progressive among the world's languages, as in the following examples from Huave, Siane, Kinnauri, and Tamang.

stay/remain > PROG, DUR

(191) Tamang
       ³mi ⁴pra-si-n ²ci-pa
       people walk-ING-INTENSIFIER AUX-IMPFV
       'people keep walking by'
       (Mazaudon 2003: 308)

(192) Kinnauri
       tuŋ-o nito-k
       drink-PRS.PRTCPL AUX-1
       'I shall be drinking'
       (Sharma 1988: 139)

(193) Huave (isolate; Mexico)   (194) Siane
       ᵑgiane al=ma-hlij Xwan   *númúná kŭ mínaiye*
       where DUR:AUX-he:SUBORD=be John   house build AUX:3:IND
       'where is John'   'he is building a house'
       (Suarez 1983b: 131)   (James 1983: 30)

The location schema is quite commonly found in a range of other languages marking other functional categories than those seen in the Turkic languages discussed above. Thus, for example, a very common development of the locational schema is a progressive. Such a process is seen, for example, in Diola Fogny, an Atlantic (Niger-Congo) language of Senegal and Gambia. Here the overt locational noun phrase in combination with the auxiliary marks progressive aspect. This 'locative origin of the progressive' has been widely discussed in the grammaticalization literature and will not be further discussed here.

(195) Diola Fogny (West Atlantic, Niger-Congo; Senegal, Gambia)
       burɔk n-ɛn di bɔ
       work 1-be in it
       'I'm working'
       (Heine 1993: 32)

(196) *location schema* → PERFECTIVE, UNEXPECTED, PROGRESSIVE, DURATIVE

7.3.6 Other simplex event schemata

Other event schemata may not be widely attested in Turkic but are nevertheless relatively frequently encountered in other languages. Such common
constructions include the development of a progressive (later developed
into a present tense) from the possession or accompaniment schema seen in
Swahili (102), the development of the volitional or desire schema into a future
found in English (103), and the so-called manner schema becoming a progressive in such languages as Italian (104). These are discussed in detail in
Heine (1993) and are not further discussed here.

(197) Swahili
  ni-na-soma
  1-PRES-read
  'I am reading'
  (Heine 1993: 33) cf. *ni-na* 'I have' < 'be with'

(198) English
  I will go

(199) Italian
  sto mangiando
  stay.1 eat-PRTCPL
  'I am eating'
  (Heine 1993: 36)

7.3.7 Complex event schemata

In addition to these so-called 'simplex' event schema, Heine also identifies a
small number of 'complex' event schemata, some of which are extremely
important in the development of certain inflectional patterns of AVCs discussed in the present work. Perhaps the most important of these comes from
the so-called serial schema. This appears to be a grammaticalization of a
particularly common type of serial verb construction (generally of the 'core'
serialization type) into an auxiliary verb construction. As mentioned above, it
is one of the primary sources of the 'doubled' inflectional pattern.

(200) Kirma (Gur; Niger-Congo)
mi	*ta*	*mi*	*wo*
1SG	AUX	1SG	eat
  'I am eating'
  (Heine 1993: 37, citing Prost 1964: 56–9; Blansitt 1975: 20)

(201)   Zulu (Bantu; Niger-Congo)   (202)   Venda (Bantu; Niger-Congo)
      ngi be   ngi tanda   *ndo-vha ndo-vhona*
      I AUX I love   1.PRF-AUX 1.PRF-see
      'I was loving'   'I had seen'
      (Heine 1993: 38)

Subsumed under the meta-template of the serial schema is a range of other constructions as well, each reflecting a subtype of the doubled inflectional pattern, for example, overtly conjoined verbs (203), or forms with overtly subordinate forms of the lexical verb (204).

(203)   Chamus (Maa, Eastern Nilotic, Nilo-Saharan)
      k-é-yyéu lcáni n-é-uróri
      k-3-want tree CONJ-3-fall
      'the tree almost fell'
      (Heine 1993: 39)

(204)   Venda
      vha=dzula vha=tshi=vhala
      3PL=CONT 3PL=SUBORD=read
      'they always/continuously read'
      (Heine 1993: 39)

Note, however, that as this Venda form is overtly marked as dependent it does not reflect a 'canonical' serialized form. Further, the serial schema, particularly when used with a third singular form, may give rise to a LEX-headed inflectional pattern as well. As discussed in Chapter 3, these derive from a stage with a different-subject construction, rather than a same-subject one; this is called the switch-subject serialization pattern (or possibly ambient serialization—either one is possible with this V$_2$) in the recent literature on serial verbs (Crowley 2002e, Bril 2004).

(205)   Ewe (Kwa; Niger-Congo)
      me ɖu i vɔ̀
      I eat it be.finished
      'I have eaten it up'
      (Heine 1993: 38)

Note that according to Heine (1993), auxiliary formations derived from the serial schema often show aspectual semantics functionally speaking, but do not invariably do so. Note the following Palaung forms in this regard, which are clearly modal in function.

(206)   Palaung (Austroasiatic, Palaung-Wa; Myanmar, South China)

yɛ:	*ka*	*bɛ:*	*yɛ:*	*r̆ɛ̆*
we	NEG	able	1PL	wait

'we could not wait'

(Milne 1921: 19)

Another complex schema enumerated by Heine (1993) is the so-called evaluative schema. These formations often are grammaticalized to express modal categories, usually deontic ones (requirement, obligation, permission). The lexical verb in such formations is not infrequently in a dependent complement/infinitive form.

(207)   Turkana (Eastern Nilotic, Nilo-Saharan)

ɛ-jɔ-ɪkína íyóŋ í-lósi-ó

3-be.good-DAT you 2-go-SBJ

'you'd better go'

(Heine 1993: 40)

Lastly, the possession/purpose schema is one that is quite well known in the grammaticalization literature because it is common in the development of various tense/mood/aspect forms in European languages. This takes the basic templatic shape of 'X has (Y) [in order] to Z'. Such a formation gave rise to (for example) the Romance future tense constructions.

(208)   Latin *cantare habeo*   > French *chanter-ai*

As is probably evident to the reader, the same event schemata can give rise to different functional categories, while conversely, different event schemata may yield the same functional categories. Two examples should suffice. There are at least two alternative future constructions in English, one historically prior to the other, and with different nuanced meanings or connotations for individual speakers. These have developed from the motion and volition event schema, respectively.

(209)   English

John *is going to* tell her   John *will* tell her

One the other hand, both the simplex location schema and complex serial schema have been grammaticalized into a past progressive or imperfect tense in Diola Fogny, with the auxiliary verb the same in both cases.

(210) a. Diola Fogny   b. Diola Fogny
           i-lakɔ   *fu-ri*   *i-lakɔ*   *i-ri*
           1-AUX   inf-eat   1-AUX   1-eat
           'I was eating'   'I was eating'
           (Heine 1993: 46)

According to Heine (1993: 46), this results from the grammaticalization of different 'event schema' in the same function in the process of auxiliation, with the doubly marked variant resulting from the serial schema and the infinitive form coming from the locational schema. Alternatively, it is possible that this synchronic variation is in part motivated by the general typological pressure to replace more marked structures (the doubled pattern) with less marked ones (the AUX-headed pattern) over time, with a period of imbalanced coexistence, i.e. the AUX-headed pattern derives directly from the doubled one (or possibly vice versa).

To summarize the common developments one sees semantically from content to functional semantics in the development of auxiliary verb constructions, examine Table 7.7, which is a summary based on evidence from Heine and Kuteva (2002), Anderson (2004a), and my database.

Examples of such correspondences between lexical source formations and target auxiliary functions which have undergone some kind of phonological 'reduction' or change include the following sets of data from Ewe (211).

(211) *Lexical source*   *Ewe form*   AUX *function*   *Ewe form*
       'stay, remain'   *nɔ*   habitual aspect   *-[n]a*
       'return'   *gbɔ*   repetitive aspect   *ga-*
       'come'   *vá*   future tense   *á-*
       (Heine 1993: 107)

In certain Oceanic languages of Vanuatu, various verbs show functions as both V$_1$ in a serialized formation and as an auxiliary in an auxiliary verb construction with the following functions.

(212) *Paamese*   *Erromangan*   SVC V$_1$ *AVC function*
       too   *ete*   'stay'   HAB, CONT
       saki viisi *tapmi*   'try'   ATTEMPTIVE
       (Crowley 2002e: 211)

Note that the source > target connections adduced above hold in the historical semantic development of AVCs regardless of whether these latter come from verb–complement (including nominal complement), clause-chained, or serialized formations. That is, the semantic paths of development remain the same, despite being embedded within syntactically different formations (e.g. biclausal complement or coordinate formations or monoclausal serialized ones).

TABLE 7.7. Some content > functional semantic shifts in AVCs

Source	Target	Languages
ABANDON	Terminative	Kxoe
ARRIVE	Ability	Koranko
	Succeed	Mandarin Chinese
BE	Progressive	Walapai, Mamvu, Nkonya, Somali, Nasioi, Remo, Pipil, Cabécar, Baluchi, Tsez
BECOME	Copula	Ngalakan, Djaru
	Future	German
	Present	Iquito
BEGIN	Inceptive	Lingala
BRING	Future	Nandi
	Transitive	Wunambul
COME	Consecutive	Kxoe, Godié, Negerhollands ['come and X']
	Future	Lotuko, Pare, Luguru, Kru lgs., Lango, So
	Progressive	Spanish, Tatar (+PRTCPL/GER)
	Venitive	Lahu, Aranda, Haitian Creole, Tok Pisin, Turkic
	Potential	Doyayo
	Perfect	Teso
	Habitual	Ndebele
	Inchoative	Kathmandu Newar
	Counterfactual	Tsanghla
	Passive	Maasai
COME.FROM	Near Past	Jiddu, Teso, Sotho, Klao, French, Malagasy
COME.TO	Proximative	Lahu, Tchien Krahn ['almost']
	Unaccomplished	Middle Chulym, Swahili
Copula	Avertive	Romanian, Finnish ['nearly']
	Conditional	Russian, Tofa, Chickasaw, Japanese (*Nara*)
	Future	Mongolian, Russian (+non-finite Lexical verb)
	Obligative	Mandarin Chinese
Copula + LOC	Progressive	Tyurama, Godié, Maninka, Lingala, Basque, Thai, Egyptian Arabic
DO/MAKE	Causative	Lendu, Moru, Tamil, Saramaccan, Amele
	Progressive	S. Barasano
	Future	Imonda, Retuarã
	Habitual	Tsanghla, Oksapmin
	Modal	Usarufa
	Past	Agarabi, Binandere
	Obligative	Punjabi, Korean
	Pro-Verb	Lahu, Hausa, Ket, Nisenan, Ngarinjin, Amanab, Tacana, Desano, Yale
EXIST	Continuous	Kongo, Yagaria
FAIL.TO	Negative	Somali

TABLE 7.7. (*Cont'd*)

Source	Target	Languages
FALL	Passive	Korean, Tamil, Tonga
	Unexpected	Altai-Sayan Turkic
FINISH	Already	Burmese, Tongan, Arawak, Vietnamese, Kugu Nganhcara, Hayu
	Consecutive	Khoe
	Completive	Mandarin Chinese, Engenni, Rama, Yabem, Siane, Dumi, Eastern Pomo, Cogste Gyarong, Mambila, Wolio, Tamang
GET	Ability	Burmese, Khmer, Réunion Creole French
	Change of state	Rodrigues Creole French
	Obligative	Mandarin Chinese
	Passive	Vietnamese, Welsh, Seychelles Creole French, Various Chinese varieties
	Perfect	Twi
	Past	Khmer
	Possibility	Chinese
GIVE	Applicative	Cahuilla, Usan, Efik, Thai, Tamil, Gahuku, Motu Fa d'Ambu Creole Portuguese, Eipo, Telefol, Kxoe, Tairora
	Causative	Luo, Vietnamese
	Perfect[ive]	Altai-Sayan Turkic
	Object version	Turkic, Buryat
	Andative	Tofa, Quu-kizhi
	Inceptive	Altai-Sayan Turkic
	Allow	Kham
	Deliberately	Gorum
GO	Andative	Gurenne, Man. Chinese, Negerhollands Creole Dutch, Maricopa, Camling
	Change of state	Tamil, Haitian Creole
	Progressive	Maricopa, Koasati, Aranda, Tok Pisin, Turkish, Xhosa, Ewe
	Durative	Amanab
	Habitual	Djinang, Diyari, Negerhollands Creole Dutch
	Past	Suena (for.long.time)
	Perfect	Yale, Doyayo, Ciyao
GO.TO	Future	Bari, Sotho, Ecuadorian Quechua, Tzotzil, Krio, Basque, Mochica, Lele, Tonga, Kru languages, Wapppo, Old Hurrian
HIT	Pro-Verb	Yugh, Ket
	Vigorously	Gorum

TABLE 7.7. (*Cont'd*)

Source	Target	Languages
KEEP	Continuative	Imonda, Waata Oromo
	Progressive	Standard Somali
	Present	Jiddu Somali
	Durative	Dabarro Somali, Mudung Somali
KNOW	Ability	Baluchi, Danish, Nung, Tayo Creole French, Nivkh
	Habitual	Moré, Papiamentu
LEAVE	Completive	Kxoe, Tamil, Nama, Altai-Sayan Turkic, Tairora
	Inchoative	Xakas
	Egressive	Portuguese, Lingala ['stop']
	Progressive	Kirma
LIE	Progressive	Yolngu, Cahuilla, Korean, Turkic, Panyjima, Choctaw, Tunica
	Durative	Alyawarra, Beja, Manam
LIVE/STAY	Progressive	Kisi, Aztec, Tok Pisin, Chadian Arabic, Kombai, Tsanghla, Kathmandu Newar
	Durative	Waskia, Lango, Gahuku, Önge, Usan, Tamang
	Habitual	Benin Ewe, Nkore-Kiga
	Perfect	Camling
PUT	Completive	Imonda, Yagaria, Altai-Sayan Turkic, Kham, Camling
REMAIN	Durative	Vietnamese, German, Kxoe, Huave
	Progressive	Kikongo, Siane, Kinnauri
	Habitual	Ewe
	Probable future	Oromo of Wellega (+NEG)
RETURN	Iterative	Sanuma, Sotho, Sardinian, Fa d'Amba Creole Portuguese
	Perfect	Jingpho
SAY	Future	Beja
	Tense/Aspect	Oksapmin
SEE	Attemptive	Siberian Turkic, Buryat
SEND	Perfect[ive]	Altai-Sayan Turkic
	Causative	Kham
SIT	Progressive	Diola Fogny, Mamvu, Kxoe, Korean, Kedah Malay, Turkic, Umbundu, Yandruwandha, Manam, Ono, Tacana, Gulf Arabic, Mbodomo, Korowai, (Maasai)
	Copula	Imonda, Sango, Arabana-Wangkangurru
	Durative	Alyawarra, Djapu Yolngu, Burushaski, (Maasai)
	Perfect	Gorum
	Habitual	Yankunytjatjara, Bulgarian, Kanakuru, Shona

TABLE 7.7. (*Cont'd*)

Source	Target	Languages
STAND	Progressive	Spanish, Kxoe, Diegueño, Imonda, Tariana, Turkic, Ngambay-Moundou, Panyjima, Mangarrayi
	Durative	Kewa[pi]
	Copula	Tuvan, Paathapathu Panyjima
TAKE	Causative	Twi
	Completive	Nupe
	Future	Sinto, Hungarian
	'Light verb'	Urdu, Mapudungu
	Subject Version	Turkic, Buryat
THROW	Perfect	Diyari, Camling, Gutob, Remo, Ollari Gadaba, Parji
WANT	Future	English, Kimbundu, Somali, Nandi

As briefly mentioned above, there is a range of further common historical developments of auxiliary verb constructions once they have been grammaticalized to express the functional categories typically associated with particular event schemata. Note that in the case of common target functional categories that may arise from the grammaticalization of more than one event schema such as progressives, these further developments are independent of which actual event schema the source derives from, e.g. whether from a positional verb like 'sit' or 'lie' or a motion verb like 'walk'. Perhaps it is these further developments that various researchers have in mind when discussing the development of 'less' grammaticalized to 'more' grammaticalized. A brief selection of these is given in (213).

(213)

> progressive >> [continuous/imperfective] >> present
> perfect >> [perfective] >> past
> past >> irrealis
> deontic modal >> future
> future >> epistemic modality

These shifts either move from aspect or mood to tense categories or from tense to mood. There are also continua of related functional notions that may be embodied by single or multiply grammaticalized formally identical AVCs or related sets of verbs (e.g. positional verbs). Such continua include imperfective/continuative/durative/progressive and perfective/completive/terminative/resultative.

In some instances, it appears that the auxiliary has lost all semantic function and has taken on a purely formal role, serving as a host to inflectional morphology required but otherwise unavailable for expression due to the particular morphophonological and morphosyntactic configurations of a given language. Long strings of such required 'dummy' auxiliaries can be found in the Amazonian language Jarawara. In the following example *ka-* attaches to a non-inflecting verb's auxiliary, which itself disallows a following grammatical suffix so the CONT affix must appear with its own auxiliary, which in turn requires that no following inflection is allowed, so a third AUX is necessary for other inflection in the clause.

(214) Jarawara
  jara owa haa:haa ka-na na-wi na-re-ka
  branco 1:OBJ laugh APPL-AUX$_a$ AUX$_d$-CONT AUX$_c$-IMM.PST.EYWTNS.
       M-DECL.M
  'the branco laughed at me for a considerable time'
  (Dixon 2002: 135)

7.4 Category encoding vs. category embodying

One further perhaps non-trivial characteristic of inflection with respect to auxiliary verb constructions is how or if one should distinguish between what might be called 'category encoding' and 'category embodying'. For example, an auxiliary verb may itself encode an obligatory function in the functional layer(s) of the clause (however conceived), such as tense, while further serving (in whole, part or no way) as the inflectional locus for other obligatory functional categories of the clause. An extreme example of this is seen in the fused subject-TAM-polarity forms discussed in 6.5 above. I separate its function *per se* from the fact that it has functional status in determining the inflectional pattern exhibited by a construction, which would otherwise render some patterns impossible: LEX-headed, which would be a special kind of split form, and doubled inflection, which then must be split/doubled. If any one prefers this analysis, they are welcome to this interpretation.

7.5 Monophrasis and univerbation (syntactic and prosodic headedness revisited)

As I have argued in this volume, there are (at least) two different trajectories that the grammaticalization of all constructions reflects, and in particular for my present concerns auxiliary verb constructions—that is, clines of shifts and developments in the semantics and phonology of the grammaticalized elements. Thus morphosemantic and prosodic hierarchies are interconnected but separate components of the grammaticalization macro-process or epiphenomenon, each one subject to its own concerns. That the auxiliary becomes fused to the lexical verb as a functional affix rather than the reverse most typically argues for a parallel path of development of the semantic and prosodic phrasal heads of the constructions, separate from both the syntactic/structural phrasal head and the inflectional head, or indeed, *in spite of* the fact that this latter type of head is the auxiliary verb in many instances.

To schematize this relation, one might project an architecture of grammar that articulates at least four (and actually more) separate functional/structural planes each with their own head-dependent relationships among their constituent elements. They are intersecting insofar as both logically connected and unrelated developments are exhibited by elements in each plane; all vie with each other and combine to determine the actual linguistic form produced. The inflectional head is determined by morphophonological and morphosyntactic hierarchies and often results from the type of syntactic construction serving as a source for the AVC. The structural or syntactic head occurs in the structural position licensed for the verb in verb phrases lacking auxiliaries. As I have shown amply throughout the preceding chapters, even in fused complex verb forms resulting from the univerbation of former AVCs, the auxiliary verb is often the syntactic or structural head in an AVC, regardless of the inflectional head, and thus may license a dependent form of the lexical verb. The semantic head is the lexical verb, as this determines the valence of the formations, assigns case to its arguments, etc. The prosodic head synchronically may be either the lexical verb or the auxiliary verb, but it tends to be the former, as this often attracts the latter, which in any event is often unstressed or clitic, giving rise to such constructions as the large clitic auxiliary chains seen in various Australian languages, or probably, for that matter (albeit differently), the development of verb-second position in the history of the Germanic or Kru languages.

A further point of note is that when viewed from a continuum-based perspective and pan-chronically, the distinctions between the monophrastic serialized or nominal origins of individual AVCs and those that derive from biclausal diphrastic verb–complement or clause-chained structures become blurred—a fact that is formally codified in grammaticalized systems in languages such as various members of the Turkic and Misumalpan families, where one element may encode sequences of predicates or predicate parts in conjoined, subordinate, and serialized constructions and may also mark lexical verbs in AVCs. Furthermore, the processes of clause union, juncture erasure, etc. or the univerbation of elements into phonological units are seen as separate but related processes of 'phrasal' or 'prosodic' integration in developments of AVCs from a pan-chronic perspective.

7.6 Synchronic variation and diachronic change in AVCs

As I have mentioned throughout the preceding chapters, a considerable degree of variation can be seen with respect to aspects of the patterns of inflection in AVCs both within a single language and in closely related languages/dialects. This includes variation between dependent and non-dependent forms, variation between types of dependent forms in functionally identical constructions, variation between the types of pattern exhibited, and variation in degree of fusion or phonological/prosodic integrity of the various components of an AVC. I also offer a small number of examples of grammaticalized variation, resulting in split-paradigms.

7.6.1 Variation between dependent and non-dependent forms

In various AVCs in a range of individual languages, there may be alternate forms expressing the same functional contrast, but with different formal realizations. In particular, lexical verb components of AVCs may appear in an optionally dependent or subordinate form. One such situation of this type is found in Kinyarwanda negative future progressive forms. Here the negative may appear in either a proclitic/prefixal form on the auxiliary or in a dependent negative form on the lexical verb, in either case with doubled subject inflection (although the subject form in the lexical verb appears in a phonologically dependent form) within a split/doubled inflectional configuration.

(215) a. Kinyarwanda
           abagabo nti-bá-záa-ba bâ-som-a
           men NEG-3PL-FUT-AUX 3PL-read-ASP
           'the men won't be reading'
           (Kimenyi 1980: 10)

       b. Kinyarwanda
           abagabo ba-zaa-ba bâ-da-som-a
           men 3PL-FUT-AUX 3PL-NEG.SUBORD-read-ASP
           'the men won't be reading'

In the isolate language Huave, lexical verbs may appear in either an independent or a subordinate form.

(216) a. Huave (isolate; Mexico)
           Maria ti·ts mamiaj a nine
           Maria PST:she:AUX she:SUBORD:sleep the child
           'Maria made the child sleep'
           (Suarez 1982: 130)

b.   Huave
   tⁱᵍgi=ahlɨj
   PST:CONT=he:walks:INDEP
   'he was walking'
   (Suarez 1982: 131)

In the Akuriyó progressive, there is variation between a doubled-subject inflectional pattern and one in which the lexical verb appears in an infinitive form in an AUX-headed formation. In both instances, the auxiliary appears in the guise of a fused subject/auxiliary form common in Cariban languages.

(217)   a.   Akuriyó (Cariban; Suriname)   b.   Akuriyó
            ə-w-ətʃena pə' manae   *ətʃena-nə pə' manae*
            2-Sa-cry OCCUPIED.WITH 2.AUX   cry-INF OCCUPIED.WITH 2.AUX
            'you're crying'   'you're crying'
            (Gildea 1998: 201)   (Gildea 1998: 202)

7.6.2   Variation between dependent forms

Variation between dependent forms of a lexical verb in functionally identical AVCs in a single language is also found with relative frequency. One such language exemplifying this kind of variation that has been mentioned at several points in the present study is the endangered Siberian Turkic language Tofa. In functionally similar AVCs in this language, a lexical verb might variably appear in one of two different converb forms (218), a same-subject form or a converb (219), or a participle form or a converb (220).

(218)   Tofa
         kilaʃta-p   *ba-ar bis*   *kàtte-j*   *bar-gan*
         go.on.foot-GER   TLOC-FUT 1PL pick.berry-GER TLOC-PST
         'we will set off on foot'   'died' (lit. 'went berry-picking')
         (ASLEP Field Notes)

(219)   a.   Tofa
            dilʸi   oluk   bar-ip   bræœ yʃpyl   tùt-kaʃ al-ɣan.
            fox   right.away   go-CV   one hazel.grouse catch-SS SUBJ.VERS-PST
            'right away the fox caught a hazel grouse'
            (Rassadin 1994: 198)

      b.   Tofa
            høørük kɨʃ-ka kusuk-tu orula-p al-ɣan

chipmunk winter-DAT pinecone-ACC gather/store.for.winter-CV
SUBJ.VERS-PST
'the chipmunk gathered pinecones to store for winter'
(Rassadin 1990: 51)

(220) a. Tofa   b. Tofa

sooda-p   *ber-di*   *sooda-dʒ-ir*   *be-er sen*

say-GER   OBJ.VERS-REC/PST   say-RCP-P/F   OBJ.VERS-PF 2

'(I) just said it (for you)'   'you say something (for me)'
(ASLEP Field Notes)

7.6.3 Variation between fused and unfused forms

A number of languages show variation between fused and synchronically
bipartite AVCs reflecting the full range of inflectional patterns. For example,
in the standardized register of Mari (Uralic), there is variation between a fused
and unfused form of an AUX-headed structure with the lexical verb in a
gerund form. In the fused form the auxiliary has been eroded to Ø.

(221) dialectal Mari   (222) literary Mari
nal-ân ul-na   *nal-ân-na*
take-GER AUX-1PL.PRES   take-GER-1PL.PRES
'we have taken'   'we have taken'
(Kangasmaa-Minn 1998: 238)

A similar situation is seen in Afar, except that the lexical verb is in a so-called
infinitive form and the auxiliary is only partially eroded.

(223) a. Afar   b. Afar
ha:'d-e-tto   ~   *ha:'d-e li'to*
fly-INF-AUX:2   fly-INF AUX:FUT:2
'you will fly'
(Bliese 1976: 147)

In Chamula Tzotzil, there appears to be a construction which shows variation
between a synchronic bipartite LEX-headed AVC and a fused formation
deriving from it.

(224) a. Chamula Tzotzil
muk ta x-kolta-oʃuk bal
NEG INCMPLTV 1-help-2PL going
'I will not help you go'
(Suarez 1983b: 120)

b.   Chamula Tzotzil
muk bu tʃ-a-x-max-ik
NEG RESTRCTV INCMPLTV-2-1-hit-2PL
'I will not hit you'

In Kinnauri, a split AVC with object on the lexical verb and subject encoded on the auxiliary may optionally appear in a fused form derived from this.

(225)   a.   Kinnauri   b.   Kinnauri
        khya-ci-du-k   *khya-ci du-k*
        see-2-AUX-1   see-2 AUX-1
        'I am seeing you'
        (Sharma 1988: 140)

Variation between fused and unfused versions of a single AVC in one language is also seen in Southeastern New Guinea languages. In Koiari, the progressive AVC is an AUX-headed formation with the lexical verb in a dependent form and variably univerbated.

(226)   a.   Koiari   b.   Koiari
        tatire da vima   ∼   *da tativima*
        laugh:DEP I AUX-PRS:1   I laugh:DEP:AUX:PRS:1
        'I'm laughing'
        (Dutton 1996: 30)

Daga also shows variation between a univerbated and a bi-partite formation of AVCs reflecting both the doubled and AUX-headed inflectional pattern (with a Ø-marked lexical verb).

(227)   a.   Daga   b.   Daga
        onam-iwanum   *onam wanum*
        come:3PL-3PL:CONT   come:3PL 3PL:CONT
        'they are coming'   'they are coming'
        (Murane 1974: 64)

        c.   Daga   d.   Daga
        wanig-iangin   ∼   *wanik angin*
        stay-1:PRES   stay 1:PRES
        'I stay'   'I stay'
        (Murane 1974: 65)

Verb–complement structures in quasi-auxiliary formations may also appear optionally fused in individual languages. Note in this regard the following alternate forms in Retuarã.

(228) Retuarã *(Central Tucanoan; Colombia)*
    a. *waʔia eʔe-ri-ka ko-yapa-yu*   b. *yi-kã-rĩ -rĩ-yapa-yu*
        fish get-DVBL-NEUT 3FEM-want-PRES   1-sleep-EP-DVBL-want-PRES
        'she wants to get fish'   'I want to sleep'
        (Strom 1992: 160)

Closely related speech varieties may show different degrees of fusion with respect to individual AVCs. For example, in Northern Tonga the future appears with a lexical verb in the infinitive form in a bipartite construction, while this has been fused in Southern Tonga.

(229)   Northern Tonga   (230)   Southern Tonga
         u-na ku-langa   *u-noo-langa*
         he-TNS INF-look   he-TNS:INF-look
         'he will look'   'he will look'
         (Lombard 1978: 327)

The Xhosa pluperfect offers another example of variation between a fused and unfused form within a single construction. This formation thus shows variation in the degree of univerbation (and erosion) in the AVC. The construction showed an original split/doubled pattern with subject doubly marked, tense on the auxiliary, and aspect on the lexical verb. This sometimes appears in a complex fused form with the original auxiliary eroded to zero.

(231)   a.   Xhosa (Bantu; South Africa)   b.   Xhosa
               nd-a-ye   *ndi-theth-ile*   *nd-a-ndi-theth-ile*
               1SG-PST-AUX   1SG-speak-PERF   1SG-PST-1SG-speak-PERF
               'I had spoken (long ago)'   'I had spoken (long ago)'
               (Heine 1993: 108)

Variation of a range of types is seen in cognate constructions in closely related languages. This relates to variation in pattern as well as variation in degree of fusing. To this latter type belong such formations as the following in Lango and Acholi, two closely related Western Nilotic languages (indeed, these are basically dialects of a single language). In Lango, the element is a synchronic bipartite AVC with a full form of the auxiliary identical to its lexical verb source. In Acholi, on the other hand, univerbation has occurred and the auxiliary has been reduced to its first syllable. In both instances the auxiliary itself encodes future tense, deriving from a motion lexical verb meaning 'go' or 'come' or both.

(232)   Lango   (233)   Acholi
        an a-bino cammo   *an a-bi-camo*
        I 1-FUT eat:INF   I 1-FUT-eat
        'I will eat'   'I will eat'
        (Heine and Reh 1984: 92)   (Bavin 1983: 151)

7.6.4 Variation between inflectional patterns

In addition to variation between dependent and independent forms, between specific types of dependent forms, and between forms exhibiting different degrees of fusion or phonological/prosodic integrity, there are also AVCs in individual languages that optionally display one or other of the major patterns of inflection discussed in this volume. For example, there may be variation between LEX-headed and (split/)doubled patterns, variation between AUX-headed and doubled patterns, and between split and AUX-headed patterns among others.

An example of a LEX-headed pattern alternating with a doubled pattern in the same functional construction is seen in the progressive in the Central Sudanic language Mbay. With first plural subjects, plural is marked only on the lexical verb, and a split/doubled pattern is created.

(234)   a.   Mbay (Central Sudanic; Chad)   b.   Mbay
             ndì m̄-sá yą́ą   or   *m̄-ndì m̄-sá yą́ą*
             AUX 1-eat food   1-AUX 1-eat food
             'I am/was eating'
             (Keegan 1997: 69)

        c.   Mbay   d.   Mbay
             ndì kə̀-sà-ñ yą́ą   or   *kə̀-ndì kə̀-sà-ñ yą́ą*
             AUX 1PL-eat-PL food   1PL-AUX 1PL-eat-PL food
             'we are/were eating'

In its sister language Ngambay-Moundou, on the other hand, the variation is between a doubled inflectional pattern and an AUX-headed one with a nominalized lexical verb (and one that is also a complement of a PP). According to Heine and Reh (1984), this variation is the result of two different grammaticalization paths involving the same auxiliary element—more accurately two related auxiliaries (originally meaning, as is commonly the case with elements acquiring progressive functional semantics, 'sit' and 'stand'), one reflecting a so-called 'serial periphrasis' path of development and the other one a path of 'PP-periphrasis'—one that is common in the development of progressives (referred to in chapters above as the 'nominal-' or 'locative origin' of the progressive).

(235) a. Ngambay-Moundou   b. Ngambay-Moundou
           m-îsî m-úsā dā   *m-ár m-úsā dā*
           1-AUX 1-eat meat   1-AUX 1-eat meat

       c. Ngambay-Moundou   d. Ngambay-Moundou
           m-îsî mbā k-ùsà dā   *m-ár mbā k-ùsà dā*
           1-AUX for NOM-eat meat   1-AUX for NOM-eat meat
           'I am eating meat'
           (Heine and Reh 1984: 126; Vandame 1963: 94–6)

The Kuliak language Ik exhibits variation between a fully inflected deictic (core-) serialized-type construction, and one which is overtly similar to an AUX-headed AVC, with a dependent marked lexical verb and no double marking. Note also the difference in case-marking on the accompanying lexical noun (object) complement.

(236) a. Ik (Kuliak; Uganda)
           ɗó-no saɓá-no loŋóta
           go-1PL.IMP kill-1PL.IMP enemies:OBL
           'let's go kill enemies'
           (König 2002: 313)

       b. Ik
           ɗó-no saɓ-ési loŋóta-i
           go-1PL.IMP kill-INF:OBL enemies-GEN

Bantu Shambala also shows variation between a doubled and an AUX-headed AVC in the future formation. Note that in Shambala, however, the lexical verb appears in an overtly dependent subjunctive form in the doubled pattern.

(237) a. Shambala   b. Shambala
           ni-ing-a ku-kund-a   *ni-ing-a ni-kund-e*
           1-FUT-IND INF-hope-FV/IND   1-FUT-IND 1-hope-SBJNTC
           'I will hope'   'I will hope'
           (Aksenova 1997: 34)

A slightly different variable situation is seen in Bantu Babole of Congo. In the negative future construction in Babole the subject is variably doubly or singly marked. In the latter construction, an AUX-headed formation, the lexical verb appears in a dependent marked form with the 'complementizer' prefix *mo-*.

(238)   a.   Babole (C-10; Congo)
             tò-èti tĕ tò-pá-hiet-á
             1PL-AUX:NEG that 1PL-FUT-escape-FIN
             'we will not escape (no possibility)'
             (Leitch 1994: 199)

        b.   Babole
             tò-èti mo-pá-híet-á
             1PL-AUX:NEG COMP-FUT-escape-FIN
             'we will not escape (neutral)'

Multiple variation in form in an AVC is seen in the Papuan language Waskia of the Madang-Adalbert Range family. In the past habitual construction, there are three possible variants. In the first form, there is a split-like inflectional pattern with a lexical verb marked in a habitual dependent form and a tense/subject marked auxiliary. The second example lacks the auxiliary (or has a Ø auxiliary) and appears in a habitual past form (in an AUX-headed 'fused/fused' formation). The last example has the dependent habitual form on the lexical verb and a habitual past form of the auxiliary in a quasi-split/doubled pattern.

(239)   a.   Waskia
             kadi pamu yu n-ala bager-am
             man this water drink-DEP:HAB AUX-PST.3
             'this man always used to drink water'
             (Ross and Natu Paol 1978: 45)

        b.   Waskia
             kadi pamu yu no-kiso
             man this water drink-PST.HAB.3
             'this man always used to drink water'

        c.   Waskia
             kadi pamu yu n-ala baga-kiso
             man this water drink-DEP.HAB AUX-PST.HAB.3
             'this man always used to drink water'

In the Oceanic language Western Mekeo, a clausal-subject construction with 'finish' is found in a LEX-headed configuration, while the functionally (and formally) cognate formation in Eastern Mekeo appears with doubled inflection. The Eastern Mekeo form appears to have derived from a core serialized structure and the Western Mekeo form from a switch subject (or ambient) serialized form.

(240) a. Eastern Mekeo   b. Western Mekeo
           la-iva la-fua   *a-oabi e-pua*
           1-speak 1-finish   1-speak 3-finish
           'I have finished speaking' 'I have spoken'
           (Jones 1998: 425)

Variation between a split inflectional pattern and an AUX-headed one may also be found in a small number of languages. These appear to have the AUX-headed pattern derived from the split one by attraction of the inflectional markers on the lexical verb to the auxiliary. Such is the case in Kamor and Tairora.

(241) a. Kamor   b. Kamor
           tʸamaR kerer ler-ŋu pö-mö   *tal pö-mö-ŋu*
           dog leg bite-1OBJ 3M-AUX   spear 3M-AUX-1OBJ
           'the dog bit my leg'   'he speared me'
           (Tryon 1974f: 66)

(242) a. Tairora   b. Tairora
           aru-e ke-ro   ~   *aru ke-ro-e*
           hit-Q AUX-he   hit AUX-he-Q
           'did he hit it?'
           (Vincent 1973: 363)

       c. Tairora   d. Tairora
           aiho bi bai-ro   *baite-ma bai-ro*
           air go AUX-3   sleep-IND AUX-3
           'the air is going'   'he is sleeping'
           (Vincent 1973: 581)

In Kuliak So, the desiderative element may appear with a lexical verb in the infinitive form reflecting an AUX-headed structure or a doubled formation with a dependent-marked lexical verb.

(243) a. So (Kuliak; eastern Uganda) b. So
           cám-ɪ(s)a gá-úg éù   *cám-ɪ(s)a mɔ-gá-sa éù*
           DES-1 go-INF home   DES-1 NAR-go-1 home
           'I want to go home'   'I want to go home'
           (Heine and Reh 1984: 135)

Nilo-Saharan Mursi shows similar variation in the quasi-auxiliary complement structure seen below. Thus, both serializing and complement taking formations offer variation for AVCs even at the source stage, so this variation in the target formations should hardly be surprising.

(244) a. Mursi   b. Mursi
           kì-hìnì wu-cen   *kì-hìnì ku-curo*
           1-want go-VN   1-want 1SBJ-wash
           'I want to go'   'I want to wash'
           (Turton and Bender 1976: 552)

In a particular Koiari formation, the desiderative appears in either a split inflectional construction with a dependent-marked lexical verb or in simplex formation with no auxiliary verb.

(245) a. Koiari
           Ela ota-riheni-ge no ra-va   ~
           Port Moresby go-DES-DEP:DES we AUX-PRS:PL
           'we want to go to Port Moresby'
           (Dutton 1996: 30)

       b. Koiari
           no Ela ota-riheni-va
           we P. M. go-DES-PL:PRES

7.6.5 Grammaticalized variation: split paradigms

In a small number of instances variation in the case of particular AVCs will become systematized, codified, or grammaticalized and result in split paradgms, one set of forms showing one pattern, another set a different pattern. One such case has already been discussed in Chapter 5—the split between AUX-headed and LEX-headed (and various split and split/doubled etc. configurations derived thence) in Eleme.

As mentioned there, one of the most characteristic and typologically unusual features of person inflection in Eleme AVCs is the curious split seen in a range of paradigms between second plural and third plural subjects. In

TABLE 7.8. Select variation in inflectional patterns in AVCs

LEX-headed ~ Doubled	Mbay
LEX-headed ~ Split/doubled	Mbay
AUX-headed ~ Doubled	Ngambay-Moundou
AUX-headed ~ Doubled (DEP)	Mursi, Shambala
AUX-headed ~ (Split) doubled	Babole
AUX-headed ~ Split	Kamor, Tairora
Split ~ AUX-headed (fused/fused) ~ split/doubled	Waskia
LEX-headed : doubled	Western Mekeo : Eastern Mekeo

these forms, one finds second plural suffixed to the lexical verb, but third plural to the auxiliary verb. Note that the subject prefix is found on the auxiliary verb in both instances. Some examples of sample partial and fuller paradigms are offered below.

(246)   a.   Eleme   b.   Eleme

          ɔ̀-ʔɔtɔ   *tʃá-î*   *ɛpɔ́*   *ɛ̀-ʔɔtɔ-rî*   *tʃá*   *ɛpɔ́*

          2-AUX   run-2PL   afraid   3-AUX-3PL   run   afraid

          'you became very afraid '   'they became very afraid '

          (Anderson and Bond 2004-MS: 246–8)

       c.   Eleme

          òbàù bere   *fɔ-á-î-ènu*

          2PL   PERF   plant-HAB-2PL-something

          'you used to plant something'

       d.   Eleme

          àbà bere-rî   *fɔ-ènu*

          3PL   PERF-3PL   plant-something

          'they used to plant something'

       e.   Eleme   f.   Eleme

          òbàù dosɛ dɛ́-î   *ńdʒa*   *àbà*   *dosɛ-ri*   *dɛ́*   *ńdʒa*

          2PL   must   eat-2PL   food   3PL   must-3PL   eat   food

          'you (PL) must eat food'   'they must eat food'

Fused forms of this inflectional sub-pattern of AVCs in Eleme can be seen in complex verb forms as well. Note the following paradigm, which reflects a fusing of an AVC where second plural was suffixed to the lexical verb, but third plural to the original auxiliary verb form.

(247)   a.   Eleme

          òbàù   *ka-kpã́nā-î*   *bɛ*   *dɛ*   *ènu*

          2PL   MOD-want-2PL   COP   eat   something

          'you want to/are about to eat something'

          (Anderson and Bond 2004-MS)

       b.   Eleme

          àbà   *ka-ra-kpã́nā*   *bɛ*   *dɛ*   *ènu*

          3PL   MOD-3PL-want   COP   eat   something

          'they want to/are about to eat something'

Other conjugations in Eleme show variation between the AUX-headed and the split/doubled inflectional pattern. In other words, third plural is marked on the auxiliary verb alone, while second plural is marked on both the lexical verb and the auxiliary verb.

(248) a. Eleme
    ò-bo-î-rú   e-ma:-î   àdádʒi ɔnɛnɛ
    2-AUX-2PL-PRTCL DEP-bring-2PL Adaji gift
    'you should bring Adaji a gift'
    (Anderson and Bond 2004-MS)

  b. Eleme
    è-bo-rî-rú   e-ma: àdádʒi ɔnɛnɛ
    3-AUX-3PL-PRTCL DEP-bring Adaji gift
    'they should bring Adaji a gift'
    (Anderson and Bond 2004-MS)

The origin of why the third plural marker appeared with the auxiliary but the second person marker with the lexical verb remains unclear. Perhaps it was originally dependent on the morphophonological nature of the markers themselves. Future research may resolve this issue.

 Another split paradigm comes from the Chibchan language Chimila of Colombia. In certain negative paradigms, second singular subjects appear on the negative element while third plural ones attach to the lexical verb. Possibly the cause of this split was also the original morphophonology of the subject-encoding elements (e.g. they may be different kinds of clitics historically).

(249) a. Chimila   b. Chimila
    dʼumma-ka dʼuŋŋa   dʼumma dʼuŋŋa-ne
    NEG-2 walk   NEG walk-3PL
    'you do not walk'   'they do not walk'
    (Trillos Amaya 1997: 163; Adelaar 2004: 78–9)

Different patterns can also be grammaticalized in different forms in single paradigms (or two related ones) in individual Kiranti languages. Take the following forms from Camling. The negative perfect appears in a synchronically bipartite split auxiliary verb construction also found in other Kiranti languages (although in those examples the lexical verb appears in a dependent gerund form, which this Camling form does not). The positive form is a fused auxiliary construction of the split/doubled pattern, with double-subject marking and tense on the former auxiliary.

(250) a. Camling   b. Camling
           mi-tim ŋas-i-e   *tip-i-ŋas-i-e*
           NEG-meet AUX-1PL-NPST   meet-1PL-AUX-1PL-NPST
           'we have not met'   'we have met'
           (Ebert 2003b: 541)

A further example of a language with a split paradigm may be seen in the treatment of first and second singular objects in Panare. The former are realized on the auxiliary and the latter on the lexical verb; in each case the lexical verb is marked (etymologically at least) as a dependent form via the nominalizer -*ñe*, synchronically also functioning in this construction as a non-specific tense/aspect marker.

(251) a. Panare
           Ø-pétyuma-ñe kë̈-yu mëj
           1-hit-NONSPEC.T AUX:ANIM:PROX-1SG:OBJ ANIM.VISIB
           'he/she/it is gonna hit me'
           (Gildea 1993: 49)

       b. Panare
           a-petyúma-ñe këj mëj
           2-hit-NONSPEC.T AUX:ANIM:PROX ANIM:VISIB
           'he/she/it is gonna hit you'

7.6.6 Macro-variation on a micro-scale: pattern variability in one language

A large number of fused AVCs are attested among the forms found in the verbal system of Tshangla, a Tibeto-Burman language of the Bodic group spoken mainly in Bhutan. Some verb forms seem to derive from AUX-headed patterns, while others rather appear to reflect LEX-headed or doubled inflectional patterns univerbated into large complexes. Note in this regard the following forms:

(252) a. Tshangla   b. Tshangla   c. Tshangla
           din-chho-wa   *din-chho-wa-uphe*   *din-chho-le*
           go-AUX-PST   go-AUX-PST-AUX   go-AUX-FUT
           'was going'   'will/would have been going' 'will be going'
           (Andvik 2003: 446)

       d. Tshangla   e. Tshangla
           di-wa-uphe   *din-chho-wa-chho-wa*
           go-PST-AUX   go-AUX-PST-AUX-PST
           'will have gone'   'had been going'

The auxiliary *-chho-* 'stay', appears fused in AUX-headed complexes or may itself appear doubled, each with its own tense marker. The tense form *-le* (FUT) may also be an auxiliary historically, requiring a lexical verb to be in a Ø-marked form; it is attested as a member of a complex fused in a LEX-headed or serialized construction. A similar pattern seems to have given rise to complexes with the fused auxiliary *-uphe* 'come', which likewise is fused into a larger complex, but which seems to have taken a tense-marked complement lexical verb in a fused LEX-headed formation. Note that the fused auxiliary element may occur in a synchronically bipartite AVC with a tense-marked lexical verb as well in Tshangla.

(253)   Tshangla
  di-le chho-wa
  go-FUT AUX-PST
  'was going to go' or 'would have gone'
  (Andvik 2003: 446)

Negative forms of former AVCs in Tshangla also reflect fusings of various patterns, specifically, whether the lexical verb or the auxiliary bore the negative prefix. Thus, complexes of this type may have either a prefix on the lexical stem or a synchronic infix, reflecting an earlier prefix on the auxiliary. Note that tense-marking also shows various split patterns in Tshangla, now on the lexical stem, now on the auxiliary, again reflecting the heterogeneous origin of these verb formations. Examples of negative formations in (former) AVCs in Tshangla include the following:

(254) a. Tshangla   b. Tshangla   c. Tshangla
     ma-din-chhi   *ma-di-la*   *ma-di-wa-chho-wa*
     NEG-go-AUX   NEG-go-FUT   NEG-go-PST-AUX-PST
     'did not go'   'will not go'   'had not gone'
     (Andvik 2003: 447)

   d. Tshangla   e. Tshangla   f. Tshangla
     ma-di-wa-uphe   *di-lu-man-chhi*   *din-ma-chho-la*
     NEG-go-PST-AUX   go-T/A-NEG-AUX   go-NEG-AUX-FUT
     'will/would not have gone' 'was not going'   'will not be going'

   g. Tshangla   h. Tshangla
     di-wa-man-chhi   *di-wa-man-(u)pha*
     go-PST-NEG-AUX   go-PST-NEG-AUX
     'had not been going'   'will/would not have been going'

That the order of the elements is determined by the function of the AVC, i.e. constructionally, and not necessarily by the elements themselves can be seen in the following pair of forms. In both cases the lexical verb bears the tense-marking. It is the position of the negative that is of concern presently.

(255)   a.   Tshangla   b.   Tshangla
             ma-di-le-uphe   vs.   *di-le-ma-(u)pha*
             NEG-go-FUT-AUX   go-FUT-NEG-AUX
             'will not be about to go'; 'may not go'   'should/ought not to go'
             (Andvik 2003: 447)

When the negative precedes the lexical verb, the meaning is either one of aspect or expressive of a notion of permissibility, while if the negative precedes the auxiliary verb, the meaning is rather one of obligation or properness. The ultimate cause of this may have been the original scope relations of the negative operator. Diachronically, the first example arose from a pure LEX-headed formation, while the latter was originally a split pattern, both synchronically fused into the attested complexes and well attested in other patterns of inflection in (former) AVCs in Tshangla. From the perspective of a pan-chronic analysis of AVCs, this comes as no surprise: formally different AVCs are generally speaking functionally different ones as well and would have been grammaticalized to express separate (sets of) functional operations.

Summary

Auxiliary verb constructions may derive from a range of verbal source constructions, both monoclausal and biclausal, including both nuclear and core serialized constructions, various kinds of verb + clausal complement structures, clause-chaining, and coordinate formations as well. This heterogeneous source pool for AVCs helps explain the extreme diversity of patterns of inflection attested in them across the languages of the world, i.e. the development of the morphosyntax and syntax of AVCs. The semantic-pragmatic paths of development of the specific sub-types of lexical classes of predicates into indexes of functional categories also follow particular and relatively straightforward shifts and specializations with respect to individual classes of auxiliaries in the process of their grammaticalization.

Appendix: Classification of Languages Used in Database for Study

Afroasiatic (44)
Berber	Tarifit Berber [Morocco]
Chadic	
Biu-Mandara	
A4	Hdi [Nigeria, Cameroon]
Western	
A1	Ader Hausa [Nigeria], Hausa [Nigeria, Niger]
A2	Karekare [Nigeria], Kwami [Nigeria], Lele [Chad], Pero [Nigeria]
A4	Daffo Ron [Nigeria]
B1	Ngizim [Nigeria]
B3	Sayanci [Nigeria]
Cushitic	
Central	Kemantney [Ethiopia]
Eastern	
Dullay	S'aamakko Dullay [Ethiopia]
Highland	Kambaata [Ethiopia]
	Burji [Ethiopia, Kenya]
	Sidamo [Ethiopia]
	Hadiyya [Ethiopia]
Omo-Tana	Dasenech [Kenya]
Oromo	Oromo of Wellegga [Ethiopia]
	Harar Oromo [Ethiopia]
Saho-Afar	Afar [Eritrea, Ethiopia, Djibouti]
Somali	Somali [Somalia+]
	Mudung Somali [Somalia]
	Dabarro Somali [Somalia]
	Jiddu Somali [Somalia]
Northern	Beja [Sudan, Eritrea]
Southern	Dahalo [Kenya]
Egyptian	Coptic [Egypt]
Omotic	
Northern	Dizi (Maji) [Ethiopia]
	Gimira (Benchnon) [Ethiopia]
	Gonga (Kefa/Kafa) [Ethiopia]
	Kullo [Ethiopia]
Southern	Aari [Ethiopia]
	Dime (Dim-Af) [Ethiopia]
	Hamer [Ethiopia]

Semitic	
Aramaic	Jilu Aramaic [Iraq]
Southern: Ethiopic	Amharic [Ethiopia]
	Chaha Gurage [Ethiopia]
	Tigrinya [Eritrea]
Western: Arabic	Egyptian Arabic [Egypt]
	Gulf Arabic [Iraq, UAE, Kuwait]
	Chadian Arabic [Chad]
	Standard Arabic [whole Arabic area]
Unclassified?	Ongota [Ethiopia]
Algonquian (1)	Fox (Meskwaki) [USA]
Andamanese (2)	
	Andamanese [India]
	Önge [India]
Araucanian (1)	
	Mapudungu(n) [Chile, Argentina]
	(Mapuche)
Arawakan (6)	
Maipuran	
Western	Amuesha [Peru]
Southern	Baure [Bolivia]
Northern	Guajiro [Colombia, Venezuela]
	Warekena [Venezuela, Brazil]
	Tariana [Brazil, Colombia]
Northern	
Caribbean	Lokono [Surinam, Guyana]
Aruán (2)	
	Paumarí [Brazil]
	Jarawara (Madi) [Brazil]
Athapaskan-Eyak-Tlingit (3)	
Athapaskan	
Hare-Chipewyan	Slave [Canada]
	Dogrib [Canada]
Oregon	Tututni [USA]
Australian (66)	
Non-Pama-Nyungan (35)	
Jaminjungan	Jaminjung [Australia]
W. Barkly	
Jingulic	Jingulu [Australia]
Wambayic	Gudanji [Australia]
	Wambaya [Australia]
Bunuban	Bunuba [Australia]
	Gungunma (Bunuba) [Australia]
Burarran	Djowanga Ndjébbana [Australia]
	Ndjébbana [Australia]
	Yirriddjanga Ndjébbana [Australia]
Daly	Ami [Australia]
	Kamor [Australia]
	Manda [Australia]
	Maramanandji [Australia]
	Maranungu [Australia]
	Marengar [Australia]

	Marithiel [Australia]
	Marityabin [Australia]
	Matngala [Australia]
	Mullukmulluk [Australia]
	Ngangkikurungkurr [Australia]
	Ngengomeri [Australia]
	Pungupungu [Australia]
	Tyeraity [Australia]
	Wadyiginy (Wogaity) [Australia]
	Yunggor [Australia]
Garawan	Garawa [Australia]
Gungwingguan	Jawoyn [Australia]
	Mangarayi [Australia]
	Ngalakan [Australia]
	Wardaman [Australia]
Laragian	Larrakia [Australia]
Wororan	Ngarinjin [Australia]
	Wunambul [Australia]
Pama-Nyungan (31)	
Arandic	Alywarra [Australia]
	Aranda [Australia]
Gumbaynggiric	Gumbaynggir [Australia]
Maric	Gunya/Bidjara [Australia]
	Yandruwandha [Australia]
Nyawaygic	Nyawaygi [Australia]
Paman	Gugadj [Australia]
	Kugu Nganhcara [Australia]
Southwestern	
Coastal Ngayarda	Martuthunira [Australia]
Inland Ngayarda	Panyjima [Australia]
Ngarga	Wa[r]lpiri [Australia]
Ngumbin	Djaru [Australia]
	Walmatjarri [Australia]
	Gurindji [Australia]
Kardu	Nhanda [Australia]
Baagandji	Bāgandji [Australia]
	Bārundji [Australia]
Dharumbal	Dharumbal [Australia]
Dyirbalic	Wargamay [Australia]
Karnic	Arabana-Wangkangurru [Australia]
	Diyari [Australia]
	Pitta-Pitta [Australia]
Tangic	Yukulta [Australia]
Wiradhuric	Yuwaalaraay [Australia]
	Ngiyambaa [Australia]
Yalandjic	Kuku-Yalanji [Australia]
Yanyuwan	Yanyuwa [Australia]
Yolngu	Djapu Yolngu [Australia]
Yorta-Yorta	Yorta-Yorta [Australia]
Yuin-Kuric	Dharawal [Australia]
	Dhurga [Australia]

Unclassified
Austroasiatic (18)
Aslian

Mon-Khmer
Khasic
Palaung-Wa
Munda
North Munda: Kherwarian

South Munda

Nicobarese
Austronesian (93)
Formosan
Paiwanic

Atayalic

Malayo-Polynesian
Western Malayo-Polynesian
Sulawesi: Muna-Buton

Sundic
Malayic
Acehnese-Cham
Moklen
Embaloh
Meso-Philippine: Kalamian
Northern Philippine: N. Luzon
Borneo: Dusunic
Sama-Bajaw: Sulu-Borneo
Central-Eastern Malayo-Polynesian
Central Malayo-Polynesian
Central Maluku: Eastern
Southeast Maluku: Kei-Aru

Timor-Flores
Central Timor
Leti-Moa
Eastern Malaycpolynesian Oceanic

Limilngan [Australia]

Temiar [Malaysia]

Khasi [India]
Palaung [Myanamar, China]

Asuri [India]
Bhumij [India]
Karmali [India]
Mundari [India]
Santali [India]
Turi [India]
Gorum [India]
Gta? [India]
Gutob [India]
Juang [India]
Juray [India]
Kharia [India]
Remo [India]
Sora [India]
Car [India]

Paiwan [Taiwan]
Siraya [Taiwan]
Atayal [Taiwan]
Seediq [Taiwan]

Muna [Sulawesi, Indonesia]
Wolio [Sulawesi, Indonesia]

Acehnese [Sumatra]
Indonesian [Indonesia]
Embaloh [Kalimantan, Indonesia]
Central Tagbanwa [Philippines]
Ilocano [Philippines]
Kimaragang [Malaysia]
Southern Sinama [Philippines]

Larike [Maluku, Indonesia]
Kola [Maluku, Indonesia]
Yamdena [Maluku, Indonesia]
Fehan Tetun [East Timor]
Tutukeian Leti [Maluku, Indonesia]

Admiralty Islands
Manus   Loniu [Papua New Guinea]
                                         Sisiva Titan [Papua New Guinea]
                                         Kele [Papua New Guinea]

Central Eastern
Remote Oceanic
Central Pacific: Rotuman-Fijian   Rotuman [Fiji]
Polynesian: Tongic   Niuean [Niue]
Eastern Outer Islands   Buma [Solomon Islands]
Loyalty Islands   Iaai [New Caledonia]
Micronesian   Ulithian [Federated States of Micronesia]
                                         Mokilese [Federated States of Micronesia]
                                         Puluwat [Federated States of Micronesia]

North/Central Vanuatu
Central Vanuatu   Nāti [Vanuatu]
Malekula   Vinmavis [Vanuatu]
Northeast Vanuatu–Banks Islands
                                         Raga [Vanuatu]
Central Vanuatu   Namakir [Vanuatu]
West Santo   Tamabo (Malo) [Vanuatu]
Epi   Lewo [Vanuatu]
East Vanuatu   Apma [Vanuatu]
                                         Araki [Vanuatu]
                                         Paamese [Vanuatu]
                                         SE Ambrym [Vanuatu]
Southern Vanuatu   Kwamera [Vanuatu]
                                         SW Tanna [Vanuatu]
                                         Anejom̃ [Vanuatu]
                                         Sye (Erromangan) [Vanuatu]
                                         Ura [Vanuatu]

Southeastern Solomons
Gela–Guadalcanal   Gela [Solomon Islands]
Malaita–San Cristobal   Kwaio [Solomon Islands]
South Halmahera–Western
    New Guinea   Taba [Makian, Indonesia]
Western
Meso-Melanesian
New Ireland
Lavongai-Nalik   Lavongai [Papua New Guinea]
                                         Nalik [Papua New Guinea]
                                         Tigak [Papua New Guinea]
Madak   Madak [Papua New Guinea]
Tabar   Tabar [Papua New Guinea]
Southern New Ireland/Northwest
    Solomonic
Bougainville
Northern/Eastern   Torau [Papua New Guinea]
                                         Nissan (Nehan) [Papua New Guinea]
                                         Petats [Papua New Guinea]
                                         Selau [Papua New Guinea]
                                         Solos [Papua New Guinea]
Western   Banoni [Papua New Guinea]

	Mono [Solomon Islands]
Nehan	Halia [Papua New Guinea]
	Hanahan [Papua New Guinea]
	Haku [Papua New Guinea]
	Taiof [Papua New Guinea]
Choiseul	Sisiqa (Sisingga) [Solomon Islands]
New Georgia: Western	Hoava [Solomon Islands]
	Simbo [Solomon Islands]
Santa Isabel: Central	Kokota [Solomon Islands]
Northern New Guinea	
Ngero-Vitiaz: Vitiaz	Kaulong [Papua New Guinea]
	Mangap-Mbula [Papua New Guinea]
	Kaliai-Kove [Papua New Guinea]
	Maleu [Papua New Guinea]
Huon Gulf: Markham	Mari [Papua New Guinea]
	Sarasira [Papua New Guinea]
	Sukurum [Papua New Guinea]
	Wampar [Papua New Guinea]
	Wampur [Papua New Guinea]
	Adzera [Papua New Guinea]
Huon Gulf: Numbami	Numbami [Papua New Guinea]
Huon Gulf: Southern	Iwal [Papua New Guinea]
Sarmi	Sobei [Papua, Indonesia]
Schouten: Kairiru-Manam	Manam [Papua New Guinea]
	Kairiru [Papua New Guinea]
Papuan Tip	
Peripheral: Central Papuan	
	Motu [Papua New Guinea]
	Sinaugoro [Papua New Guinea]
	Eastern Mekeo [Papua New Guinea]
	Mekeo [Papua New Guinea]
	Northern Mekeo [Papua New Guinea]
	Northwestern Mekeo [Papua New Guinea]
	Western Mekeo [Papua New Guinea]
Nuclear (Milne-Bay)	
Eastern	Sudest [Papua New Guinea]
Western	Tawala [Papua New Guinea]
	Kilivila [Papua New Guinea]
Aymaran (1)	
	Jaqaru [Peru]
Caddoan (1)	
	Pawnee [USA]
Cahuapanan (2)	
	Chayahuita [Peru]
	Jebero [Peru]
Cariban (14)	
Central	Apalaí [Brazil]
	Wayana [Surinam, French Guiana]
Guiana	Carijona [Colombia]
	Kaxuyana [Brazil]
	Tiriyó [Surinam, Brazil]
	Waiwai [Brazil, Guyana]

North Amazonian   Kapón[g] [Guyana, Brazil]
Makushi [Brazil, Guyana, Venezuela]
Pemón [Venezuela, Brazil. Guyana]

Northern
Galibi   Chayma[t] [Venezuela, Surinam]
Cumanagota[t] [Venezuela]
East–West Guiana   Akuriyó [Surinam]
Panare   Panare [Venezuela]
Central Khoisan (8)
Khoe   /Ani [South Africa]
Buga-/Anda [Botswana, Angola]
Khoe [Angola, Namibia, Botswana]
Khoekhoe   !Ora [South Africa]
Nama [Namibia, South Africa, Botswana]
Naro   Naro [Botswana]
Non-Khoe   Kua [Botswana, Zimbabwe]
Shua   Cara [Botswana]
Chapacuran (1)
Wari' (Pacaás Novos) [Brazil]

Chibchan (8)
Aruak   Chimila [Colombia]
Kogi [Colombia]
Ika [Colombia]
Chibcha   Muisca[t] (Chibcha) [Colombia]
Guaymi   Ngäbére (Guaymí) [Panama]
Paya   Pech (Paya) [Honduras]
Rama   Rama [Nicaragua]
Talamanca   Cabécar [Costa Rica]
Chocó (2)
Northern Embera [Colombia]
Epena Pedee [Colombia]

Chonan (1)
Selknam (Ona) [Chile, Argentina]

Chukotko-Kamchatkan (3)
Chukchi-Koryak   Chukchi [Russia (Siberia)]
Palana Koryak [Russia (Siberia)]
Itel'menic   Itel'men [Russia (Siberia)]
Chumashan (1)
Barbareño Chumash [USA]

Creole languages: (3)
Kituba [Democratic Republic of Congo]
Sango [Central African Republic]
Saramaccan Creole [Suriname]

Dravidian (13)
Central   Kolami [India]
Parji [India]
Northern   Brahui [Pakistan]
Kurukh [India, Bangladesh]
South-Central   Konda [India]
Gondi [India]
Old Telugu[t] [India]

	Pengo [India]
	Muria Gondi [India]
Southern	Old Tamil[†] [India]
	Tamil [India]
	Kannada [India]
	Betta Kurumba [India]
East Bird's Head (1)	
	Sougb [Papua, Indonesia]
East Papuan (8)	
Bougainville	Nasioi [Papua New Guinea]
	Motuna (Siwai) [Papua New Guinea]
Reef Islands-Santa Cruz	Ägiwo [Solomon Islands]
Yele-Solomons	Yele [Papua New Guinea]
Kuot	Kuot [Papua New Guinea]
Sulka	Sulka [Papua New Guinea]
Central Solomonic	Lavukaleve [Solomon Islands]
	Savosavo [Solomon Islands]
Eskimo-Aleut (1)	
Aleutic	Aleut [USA, Russia]
Geelvink Bay (1)	
Eastern Geelvink Bay	Bauzi [Papua, Indonesia]
Guahiban (1)	
	Cuiba-Wamonae [Colombia]
Hmong-Mien (1)	
	Hmong-Njua [Laos, etc.]
Huarpean (1)	
	Allentiac[†] [Argentina]
Hurro-Urartian (1)	
Hurrian	Old Hurrian[†] [Anatolia]
Indo-European (28)	
Albanian	Tosk Albanian [Albania]
Anatolian	Hittite[†] [Anatolia]
Armenian	West Armenian [Armenia, Turkey]
Baltic	Lithuanian [Lithuania]
Celtic	Breton [France]
	Manx[(†)] [Isle of Man]
	Middle Welsh[†] [Wales]
	North Welsh [Wales]
	Scots Gaelic [Scotland]
Germanic	Icelandic [Iceland]
	English [UK, USA, Australia, etc]
	German [Germany, Austria, Switzerland]
Greek	Modern Greek [Greece]
Iranian	Baluchi [Pakistan, Iran, etc.]
	Colloquial Persian [Iran]
Indo-Aryan	Hindi-Urdu [India]
	Kotgarhi Himachali [India]
	Maithili [India, Nepal]
Romance	French [France]
	Genzano [Italy]
	Italian [Italy]
	Latin [Italy, South and west Europe]

	Spanish [Spain, Latin America]
Slavic	Macedonian [Macedonia]
	Old Bulgarian[†] [Balkans]
	Old Macedonian[†] [Balkans]
	Bulgarian [Bulgaria]
	Russian [Russia, former USSR, etc.]
Isolates (36 in 41 varieties)	
Ainu	Ainu, Ishikari[†] [Japan]
	Ainu, Sakhalin[†] [Russia (Siberia)]
	Ainu, Saru[†] [Japan]
Basque	Basque [Spain, France]
	Eastern Basque [Spain]
Betoi	Betoi[†] [Venezuela]
Burushaski	Burushaski [Pakistan, India]
	Yasin Burushaski
	(Werchikwar) [Pakistan]
Candoshi	Candoshi [Peru]
Cayuvava	Cayuvava [Bolivia]
Cholon	Cholon[(†)] [Peru]
Coahuilteco	Coahuilteco[†] [USA]
Itonama	Itonama [Bolivia]
Kamsá	Kamsá [Colombia]
Kipeá Kariri[†]	Kipeá Kariri[†] [Brazil]
Kwaza	Kwaza [Brazil]
Leko	Leko [Bolivia]
Mochica	Mochica[†] [Peru]
Movima	Movima [Bolivia]
Nivkh (Gilyak)	Amur Nivkh [Russia (Siberia)]
	E. Sakhalin Nivkh [Russia (Siberia)]
Purépecha (Tarascan)	Purépecha (Tarascan) [Mexico]
Sumerian	Sumerian[†] [Iraq]
Timucua	Timucua[†] [USA]
Urarina	Urarina [Peru]
Waorani (Auca)	Waorani [Ecuador]
Warao	Warao [Venezuela]
Yaghan (Yamana)	Yaghan (Yamana) [Chile]
Yuchi (Euchee)	Yuchi (Euchee) [USA]
Yuracare	Yuracare [Bolivia]
Zuni	Zuni [USA]
[Huavean]	Huave [Mexico]
[Yuki-Wappo]	Wappo[†] [USA]
[Gulf]	Natchez[†] [USA]
	Tunica[†] [USA]
[Hokan]	Esselen[†] [USA]
	Tol (Jicaque) [Honduras]
	Washo [USA]
[Na-Dene]	Haida [USA, Canada]
[Altaic]	Japanese [Japan]
	Korean [North and South Korea, Russia]

Jivaroan (2)

Achuar [Peru, Ecuador]
Shuar [Ecuador]

Kartvelian (1)

Georgian [Georgia]

Katukinan (1)

Katukina [Brazil]

Kiowa-Tanoan (1)

Kiowa [USA]

Macro-Jê (3)
Ge-Kaingang: Ge: Northwest

Apinajé [Brazil]
Canela Timbirá [Brazil]
Canela-Krahô [Brazil]

Maiduan (⌐)

Central Hill Nisenan[†] [USA]
Konkow[†] [USA]
Maidu[†] [USA]
Nisenan[†] [USA]

Makú (1)   Dâw [Brazil, Colombia]
Mascoian (1)   Toba-Maskoy [Paraguay]
Mataco-Guaykuruan (1)   Toba [Argentina, Bolivia, Paraguay]
Mayan (9)
Mamean   Acatec [Guatemala]
                                      Mam [Guatemala]
Quichean   Tzutujil [Guatemala]
                                      K'ekchi [Guatemala]
Tzeltalan   Chamula Tzotzil [Mexico]
Yucatecan   Classical Yucatec[†] [Mexico]
                                      Yucatec [Mexico]
Kanjobalan   Jakaltek [Guatemala]
Chujean   Tojolabal [Mexico]
Misumalpan (3)

                                      Miskitu [Nicaragua, Honduras]
                                      North Sumu [Nicaragua, Honduras]
                                      Ulwa [Nicaragua]

Mixe-Zoquean (2)
Mixe   Sayula Popoluca [Mexico]
Zoquean   Sierra Popoluca [Mexico]
Mongolic (2)   Buryat [Russia]
                                      Khalkha Mongolian [Mongolia]
Mosetenan (1)   Mosetén [Bolivia]
Mura-Pirahã (1)   Pirahã [Brazil]
Muskogean (5)
Central   Apalachee [USA]
Eastern/Central   Koasati [USA]
                                      Mikasuki [USA]
Western   Chickasaw [USA]
                                      Choctaw [USA]

Nambiquaran (1)

                                      Nambiquara [Brazil]

Niger-Congo (121)
Atlantic–Congo
Atlantic
Northern   Diola-Fogny [Gambia, Senegal]
                                  Wolof [Senegal, Mauritania, Mali]
Southern   Kisi [Sierra Leone, Liberia]
Volta–Congo
Benue–Congo
Bantoid
Ekoid   Ejagham [Nigeria, Cameroon]
Mambiloid   Mambila [Nigeria, Cameroon]
Southern: unclassified   Ndendeule [Tanzania]
Bantu
Grassfields   Aghem [Cameroon]
                                  Babungo [Cameroon]

Narrow Bantu
A20   Duala [Cameroon]
A72   Ewondo [Cameroon]
B40   Punu [Congo]
C10   Babole [Congo]
C30   Akwa [Congo]
C40   Lingala [Democratic Republic of Congo, Congo]
D25   (Beya) Lega [Democratic Republic of Congo]
E10   Ekegusii [Kenya]
                                  Kuri(y)a [Tanzania, Kenya]
                                  Sonjo [Tanzania]
F21   Kimbu [Tanzania]
F24   Sukuma [Tanzania]
G10   Kaguru [Tanzania]
G20   Shambala [Tanzania]
G22   Pare [Tanzania]
G30   Dzalamo [Tanzania]
G35   Luguru [Tanzania]
G40   Swahili [Kenya, Tanzania+]
H10   Kikongo [Congo, Democratic Republic of Congo, Angola]
                                  Laadi [Democratic Republic of Congo, Congo]
                                  Ntandu [Democratic Republic of Congo]
J10   Luganda [Uganda, Tanzania]
                                  Nkore-Kiga [Uganda]
J20   Haya [Tanzania]
J30   Bukusu [Kenya]
                                  Tsotso [Kenya]
J60   Kinyarwanda [Rwanda]
                                  Kirundi [Burundi]
K40   Siluyana [Angola]
L23   Songye [Democratic Republic of Congo]
L30   Hemba [Democratic Republic of Congo]
M30   Nyakyusa [Tanzania, Malawi]
M50   Lamba [Zambia, Democratic Republic of Congo]
M60   N. Tonga [Zambia]
                                  S. Tonga [Zambia]
N21   Tumbuka [Tanzania, Malawi, Zambia]

N30	Chichewa [Malawi, Zambia]
P20	Ciyao [Malawi, Mozambique]
	Konde [Tanzania, Mozambique]
P25	Mabiha [Mozambique, Tanzania]
R10	Umbundu [Angola]
R20	Eunda [Namibia]
	Evale [Angola]
	Kafima [Angola]
	Kolonkadhi [Namibia]
	Kwambi [Namibia]
	Mbalanhu [Namibia]
	Mbandja [Angola, Namibia]
	Ngandjera [Namibia]
	Oshikwanyama [Namibia]
R30	Herero [Namibia]
S20	Venda [South Africa, Zimbabwe]
S30	N. Sotho [South Africa]
	Sesotho [Lesotho]
	Setswana [South Africa, Botswana]
S40	Siswati [Swaziland, South Africa]
	Xhosa [South Africa]
	Zulu [South Africa]
	Ndebele [Zimbabwe, South Africa]
S50	Tonga [South Africa, Mozambique]
Cross River	
Delta Cross	Ogbronuagom (Bukuma) [Nigeria]
	Ibibio [Nigeria]
Lower Cross: West	Obolo (Andoni) [Nigeria]
Ogonoid	Eleme [Nigeria]
	Gokana [Nigeria]
	Kana [Nigeria]
	Tai [Nigeria]
Defoid	
Yoruboid	Yoruba [Nigeria, Benin, Togo]
Edoid	
Delta	Engenni [Nigeria]
	Degema [Nigeria]
North Central	North Ibie [Nigeria]
Igboid	
	Izi [Nigeria]
Nupoid	
	Gade [Nigeria]
Platoid	
Jukunoid	Kuteb [Nigeria, Cameroon]
Dogon	Dogon [Mali, Burkina Faso]
Kru	
Eastern	Bété [Côte d'Ivoire]
	Godie [Côte d'Ivoire]
	Koyo [Côte d'Ivoire]
	Neyo [Côte d'Ivoire]
	Nyo [Liberia, Côte d'Ivoire]
	Vata [Côte d'Ivoire]

Kuwaa	Kuwaa [Liberia]
Western	Bassa [Liberia, Sierra Leone]
	Dewoin [Liberia]
	Gbaeson Krahn [Liberia]
	Grebo [Liberia, Côte d'Ivoire]
	Klao [Liberia, Sierra Leone]
	Tchien Krahn [Liberia]
	Wobé [Côte d'Ivoire]
	Borobo [Côte d'Ivoire]
	Sapo [Liberia]
	Tepo [Côte d'Ivoire]
Kwa	
Guang	Nawuri [Ghana]
	Nkonya [Ghana]
Gbe	Anexo-Ewe [Ghana]
	Ewe [Ghana, Togo]
Central	Twi [Ghana]
	Akan [Ghana]
Northern	
Adamawa-Ubangi	
Banda	Linda [Central African Republic]
Gbaya	Mbodomo [Cameroon]
Ubangi	Zande [Democratic Republic of Congo, Cameroon, Sudan]
Adamawa	Doyayo [Cameroon]
Gur	
	Dagaare [Ghana, Burkina Faso]
Central	Kirma [Burkina Faso, Côte d'Ivoire]
	Tyurama [Burkina Faso, Côte d'Ivoire]
Senufo	Supyire [Mali, Côte d'Ivoire]
Kordofanian	
Kadugli	Krongo [Sudan]
Mande	
Eastern	Bobo-Fing [Burkina Faso, Mali]
	Boko/Busa [Nigeria, Benin]
	Bokobaru [Nigeria, Benin]
Western	Maninka [Guinea, Mali, Sierra Leone]
	Mende [Sierra Leone, Liberia]
	Kpelle [Liberia]
Nilo-Saharan (35)	
Central Sudanic	
Bongo-Bagirmi	
	Mbay [Chad]
	Mödö [Sudan]
	Ngambay-Moundou [Chad]
East Central	
Lendu	Ngiti [Democratic Republic of Congo]
Mangbetu	Meje [Democratic Republic of Congo, Uganda]
Mangbutu-Efe	Mamvu [Democratic Republic of Congo+, Uganda]
Moru-Madi	Ma'di [Uganda, Sudan]

E. Sudanic
Nilotic
Eastern Nilotic

Maasai [Kenya, Tanzania]
Turkana [Kenya]
(A)Teso [Uganda, Kenya]
Bari [Sudan, Uganda, Democratic Republic of Congo]
Lotuko [Sudan]
Chamus [Kenya]

Southern Nilotic
Kalenjin   Nandi [Kenya]
Western Nilotic

Anywa [Sudan, Ethiopia]
Dinka [Sudan]
Dholuo [Kenya]
Acholi [Uganda, Sudan]
Lango [Uganda]
Dhó-Alúr̀ [Uganda, Democratic Republic of Congo]

East Jebel

Gaam [Sudan, Ethiopia]
Aka [Sudan]
Kelo [Sudan]
Molo [Sudan]

Eastern   Nera (Nara) [Eritrea]
Surmic

Mursi [Sudan, Ethiopia]
Koegu [Ethiopia]
Tennet [Sudan]
Baale [Ethiopia]
Majang [Ethiopia]

Kuliak

So [Kenya, Uganda]
Ik [Uganda]

Komuz
Gumuz   Sese Gumuz [Ethiopia, Sudan]
Kunama

Kunama [Eritrea, Sudan]

Songhay

Koyra Chiini [Mali]

Northeast Caucasian (7)
Daghestanian
Lezgic   Archi [Russia]
                                               Lezgian [Russia]
Avar-Andi-Tsez: Andi   Godoberi [Russia]
Avar-Andi-Tsez: Tsez   Hunzib [Russia]
                                               Tsez [Russia]
Lak-Dargwa: Dargwa   Megeb Dargwa [Russia]
Nakh   Ingush [Russia]
Northern Khoisan (1)

Ju/'hoan [Namibia, Angola]

Northwest Caucasian (2)
Abkhaz-Abazin   Abkhaz [Georgia]
Circassian   Kabardian [Russia]
Otomanguean (10)
Mazatecan   Huautla de Jimenez Mazatec [Mexico]
Chinantecan   Sochiapan Chinantec [Mexico]
Mixtecan   Diuxi Mixtec [Mexico]
                                 Yosondúa Mixtec [Mexico]
Otomian   Otomí de Toluca [Mexico]
                                 San Ildefonso Otomí [Mexico]
                                 Southwestern Otomí [Mexico]
Pamean   Jiliapan Pame [Mexico]
Zapotecan   Ayoquesco Zapotec [Mexico]
                                 Isthmus Zapotec [Mexico]

Paezan (4)
Barbacoan
                                 Awa-Kwaiker [Colombia, Ecuador]
                                 Tsafiki [Colombia]

Inter-Andine
                                 Nasa Yuwe (Páez) [Colombia]
                                 Guambiano [Colombia]

Panoan (4)
North Central   Capanawa [Peru]
                                 Isconawa [Peru]
Southern   Chacobo [Bolivia]
South Central   Amahuaca [Peru]
Peba-Yaguan (1)
                                 Yagua [Peru]

Pidgin languages (1)
                                 Kenyan Pidgin Swahili [Kenya]

Pomoan (1)
                                 Eastern Pomo [USA]

Puquinan (2)
                                 Callahuaya [Bolivia]
                                 Puquina† [Bolivia, Peru]

Quechuan (4)
Quechua A   Ecuadorian Quechua [Ecuador]
                                 Ayacucho Quechua [Peru]
Quechua B   Huallaga Quechua [Peru]
                                 Pacaroas Quechua [Peru]

Sahaptian (1)
                                 Nez Perce [USA]

Salish (8)
Bella Coola   Bella Coola [Canada]
Coast/Central   Halkomelem [Canada]
                                 Klallam [USA]
                                 Squamish [Canada]
Interior   Lillooet [Canada]
                                 Shuswap [Canada]
                                 Thompson [Canada]
Tillamook   Tillamook † [USA]

Sepik-Ramu (5)
Ndu   Iatmul [Papua New Guinea]
                                 Ambulas [Papua New Guinea]
Grass   Botin [Papua New Guinea]
Sepik Hill   Sanio-Hiowe [Papua New Guinea]
Yellow River   Namia [Papua New Guinea]
Serian (1)
                                 Seri [Mexico]
Sino-Tibetan (31)
Sinitic   Taixing Chinese [China]
                                 Mandarin [China]
Tibeto-Burman   Lepcha [Nepal, India, Bhutan]
Rung
Qiangic   Qiang [China]
Kiranti   Athpare [Nepal]
                                 Belhare [Nepal]
                                 Camling [Nepal]
                                 Chepang [Nepal]
                                 Dumi (Rai) [Nepal]
                                 Hayu [Nepal]
                                 Limbu [Nepal]
                                 Thulung [Nepal, India]
                                 Yakkha [Nepal, India]
Kham   Kham [Nepal]
Bodic
Tamangic   Chantyal [Nepal]
                                 Nar-Phu [Nepal]
                                 Tamang [Nepal]
Tsanghla   Tsanghla [Bhutan, India]
Tibetan   Lhasa Tibetan [China]
Bodish   Kinnauri [India]
Newari   Dolakha Newar [Nepal]
                                 Kathmandu Newar [Nepal]
Kuki-Chin-Naga   Impal Meithei [India]
                                 Hakha Lai [Myanmar, Bangladesh, India]
Gyalrongic   Cogste Gyarong [China]
Sal
Barish (Bodo)   Garo [India, Bangladesh]
Jinghpaw   Jinghpo [Myanmar, China, India]
Lolo-Burmese   Burmese [Myanmar]
Karenic   Bwe Karen [Myanmar, Thailand]
Tani   Bokar [China]
Siouan (4)
Southeastern   Biloxi[†] [USA]
Missouri Valley   Crow [USA]
Mississippi Valley   Lakhota [USA, Canada]
Mandan   Mandan [USA]
Sko (3)
                                 Barupu [Papua New Guinea]
                                 Skou [Papua, Indonesia]
                                 Vanimo [Papua New Guinea]

Subtiapa-Tlapanec (2)
Tlapanec   Malinaltepec Tlapanec [Mexico]
                                         Tlapanec [Mexico]
Tacanan (3)
Araona-Tacanan   Cavineña [Bolivia]
                                         Tacana [Bolivia]
Tiatinagua   Ese Ejja [Bolivia]
Tai-Kadai (2)
Kam-Sui   Northern Dong [China]
                                         Southern Dong [China]
Daic/Taic   Thai [Thailand]
Tequistlatecan (1)

                                         Tequistlatec
                                         (Chontal Oaxaca) [Mexico]

Trans-New Guinea (61)
Central/West
Angan   Baruya [Papua New Guinea]
                                         Menya [Papua New Guinea]
Dani-Kwerba: South   Dani [Papua, Indonesia]
Dani-Kwerba: North   Kwerba [Papua, Indonesia]
Houn–Finisterre
Finisterre   Wantoat [Papua New Guinea]
Huon: Eastern   Kâte [Papua New Guinea]
Huon: Western   Burum [Papua New Guinea]
                                         Ono [Papua New Guinea]
                                         Selepet [Papua New Guinea]
Sentani   Sentani [Papua, Indonesia]
Wissel Lakes   Ekari (Kapauku) [Papua, Indonesia]
Central/South: New Guinea
Awyu-Dumut: Awyu   Kombai [Papua, Indonesia]
Awyu-Dumut: unclassfied   Korowai [Papua, Indonesia]
Asmat-Komoro   Asmat [Papua, Indonesia]
Central/South: Ok: Mountain: Telefol [Papua New Guinea]

Eastern   Samo [Papua New Guinea]
Binanderean   Binandere [Papua New Guinea]
                                         Korafe [Papua New Guinea]
                                         Suena [Papua New Guinea]

East Central/Southeast
Dagan   Daga [Papua New Guinea]
Koiarian   Koiari [Papua New Guinea]
Koiarian: Baraic   Ömie [Papua New Guinea]
Yareban   Yareba [Papua New Guinea]
Eleman
Eastern   Toaripi [Papua New Guinea]
Western   Orokolo [Papua New Guinea]
Eastern New Guinea Highlands
Central: Chimbu: Hagen   Salt-Yui [Papua New Guinea]
                                         Umbungu Kaugel [Papua New Guinea]

Eastern: Tairora: Gadsup-Auyana- Awa Tairora [Papua New Guinea]

	Auyana [Papua New Guinea]
	Awa [Papua New Guinea]
	Gadsup [Papua New Guinea]
	Usarufa [Papua New Guinea]
	Agarabi [Papua New Guinea]
Eastern/Central: Gahuku-Benabena	Bena Bena [Papua New Guinea]
	Gahuku [Papua New Guinea]
	Upper Asaro [Papua New Guinea]
Kamono-Yagaria	Hua [Papua New Guinea]
	Yagaria [Papua New Guinea]
Siane	Siane [Papua New Guinea]
Kalam-Kobon	Kalam [Papua New Guinea]
	Kobon [Papua New Guinea]
Western/Central: Engan	Kewa[pi] [Papua New Guinea]
Isolate	Oksapmin [Papua New Guinea]
Madang/Adalbert Range	
Adalbert Range:	
Adalbert Range: Brahman	Tauya [Papua New Guinea]
Pihom-Isumrud-Mugil	Mugil [Papua New Guinea]
Adalbert Range: PIM: Isumrud	Waskia [Papua New Guinea]
Adalbert Range: PIM: Pihom	Usan [Papua New Guinea]
Madang: Gum	Amele [Papua New Guinea]
Mek: Western	Eipo [Papua, Indonesia]
	Una [Papua, Indonesia]
	Yale [Papua, Indonesia]
Northern	
Border: Waris	Amanab [Papua New Guinea]
	Imonda [Papua New Guinea]
Tor Lakes Plains	Orya [Papua, Indonesia]
Teberan	Daribi [Papua New Guinea]
	Polopa (Folopa) [Papua New Guinea]
Trans-Fly: Kiwaian	Island Kiwai [Papua New Guinea]
Torricelli (2)	
Kombio	Bukiyip [Papua New Guinea]
Monumbo	Monumbo [Papua New Guinea]
Totonacan (3)	
	Misantla Totonac [Mexico]
	San Marcos Atexquilapan [Mexico]
	Yecuatla [Mexico]
Tsimshianic (1)	
	Coast Tsimshian [USA, Canada]
Tucanoan (5)	
Central	Cubeo [Colombia]
Eastern	Desano [Colombia]
	South Barasano [Colombia]
	Tuyuca [Colombia, Brazil]
Western	Retuarã [Colombia]
Tungusic (5)	
Northern	Evenki [Russia (Siberia), China]
	Even [Russia (Siberia)]

Southern	Udihe [Russia (Siberia)]
	Orochi [Russia (Siberia)]
	Orok [Russia (Siberia)]
Tupi (5)	
Tupi	Cocama [Brazil, Colombia, Peru]
Monde	Gavião [Brazil]
Ramarama	Káro (Arará) [Brazil]
Oyampi	Urubu-Kaapor [Brazil]
Guaraní	Mbyá Guaraní [Paraguay]
Turkic (34)	
Chuvash	Chuvash [Russia]
Xalaj	Xalaj [Iran]
Yakut	Dolgan [Russia (Siberia)]
	Yakut (Sakha) [Russia (Siberia)]
'Altai-Sayan'	Tofa [Russia (Siberia)]
	Tuvan [Russia (Siberia)]
	Bel'tir [Russia (Siberia)]
	Sagai [Russia (Siberia)]
	Xaas [Russia (Siberia)]
	Xakas [Russia (Siberia)]
	Qumandy-Kizhi [Russia (Siberia)]
	Quu-Kizhi [Russia (Siberia)]
	Tuba-Kizhi [Russia (Siberia)]
	Shor [Russia (Siberia)]
	Xyzyl [Russia (Siberia)]
	Ös[Russia (Siberia)]
	Lower Chulym[†] [Russia (Siberia)]
	Altai [Russia (Siberia)]
	Telengit [Russia (Siberia)]
	Teleut [Russia (Siberia)]
Transitional	Kyrgyz [Kyrgyzstan]
Kypchak	Karakalpak [Uzbekistan]
	Nogay [Russia]
Volga–Ural	Bashkir [Russia]
	Tatar [Russia]
Oghuz	Turkish [Turkey+]
	Turkmen [Turkmenistan]
Karluk	Uighur [China]
	Uzbek [Uzbekistan, Afghanistan]
Caucasian	Karachay-Balkar [Russia]
'Old Turkic' (Hunnic)	Old Turkic[†] [Mongolia]
	Orkhon Turkic[†] [Mongolia]
	Yenisei Runic Turkic[†] [Russia]
Unattested reconstruction (4)	
	Proto-Kru
	Proto-Lavongai-Nalik
	Proto-New Ireland
	Pre-Swahili

Uralic (22)
Finno-Ugric
Finnic

	Estonian [Estonia]
	Finnish [Finland]
	Veps [Russia]
	Livonian [Latvia]
Saamic	North Saami [Norway, Finland]
Mordva	Erzya [Russia]
Mari	Literary Mari [Russia]
	Meadow Mari [Russia]
	Dialectal Mari [Russia]
	Western Mari [Russia]
Permic	Komi [Russia]
	Udmurt [Russia]

Ugric

Hungarian	Archaic Hungarian [Hungary]
	Hungarian [Hungary]
Ob-Ugric	Khanty [Russia (Siberia)]

Samoyedic

Northern	Nenets [Russia (Siberia)]
	Enets [Russia (Siberia)]
Nganasan/Northern	Nganasan [Russia (Siberia)]
Kamas/Sayan	Kamas† [Russia (Siberia)]
Mator/Sayan	Mator† [Russia (Siberia)]
Southern/Selkup	Selkup [Russia (Siberia)]

Uru-Chipaya (2)

Chipaya	Chipaya [Bolivia]
Uru	Uru [Bolivia]

Uto-Aztecan (10)

Aztecan	Classical Nahuatl† [Mexico]
	Pipil [El Salvador]
	Pochutla [Mexico]
Numic	Comanche [USA]
	Southern Paiute [USA]
Tepiman	Tohono 'O'odham [USA]
Takic	Cupeño [USA]
	Luiseño [USA]
	Serrano [USA]

Tübatulabal	Tübatulabal [USA]
Wakashan (1)	Makah [USA]

West Papuan (4)

Lower Mamberamo	Warembori [Papua, Indonesia]
Northern Halmahera	Tobelo [Maluku, Indonesia]
Bird's Head	Moi [Papua, Indonesia]
Barai-Hatam	Hatam [Papua, Indonesia]

Witotoan (2)

Andoque	Andoke [Colombia]
Boran	Bora [Peru]

Yanomam (2)

	Sanuma [Venezuela, Brazil]
	Yanomami [Venezuela, Brazil]

Yeniseic (2)
Northern

Ket [Russia (Siberia)]
Yugh[†] [Russia (Siberia)]

Yukaghiric (2)
Kolyma
Tundra

Kolyma Yukaghir [Russia (Siberia)]
Tundra Yukaghir [Russia (Siberia)]

Yuman (8)
Delta-Californian

Jamul Tiipay [USA, Mexico]
Mesa Grande 'Iipay [USA, Mexico]

River Yuman

Maricopa [USA]
Mojave [USA]

Pai: Upland Yuman

Walapai (Hualapai) [USA]
Tolkapaya (Yavapai) [USA]

Pai: Paipai
Kiliwa

Paipai [USA]
Kiliwa [Mexico]

Zamucoan (1)

Chamacoco [Paraguay]

Zaparoan (3)

Arabela [Peru]
Iquito [Peru]
Záparo [Ecuador]

References

AARON, UCHE (1999). *Tense and Aspect in Obolo Grammar and Discourse.* (Summer Institute of Linguistics and the University of Texas at Arlington Publications in Linguistics 128) Arlington: Summer Institute of Linguistics.

ABBOTT, MIRIAM (1991). 'Macushi', in Desmond D. Derbyshire and Geoffrey K. Pullum (eds.), *Handbook of Amazonian Languages, vol. iii.* Berlin: Mouton de Gruyter, 23–160.

ABONDOLO, DANIEL (1998a). 'Khanty', in D. Abondolo (ed.), *The Uralic Languages.* (Routledge Language Family series) London: Routledge, 358–86.

—— (1998b). 'Introduction', in D. Abondolo (ed.), *The Uralic Languages.* (Routledge Language Family series) London: Routledge, 1–42.

—— (1998c) 'Hungarian', in D. Abondolo (ed.), *The Uralic Languages.* (Routledge Language Family series) London: Routledge, 428–56.

ABRAHAM, WERNER (1974). *Terminologie zur Neuren Linguistik.* Tübingen: Niemeyer.

ADELAAR, K. ALEXANDER (1995). 'Problems of definiteness and ergativity in Embaloh', *Oceanic Linguistics* 34(2): 375–409.

—— (1997). 'Grammatical notes on Siraya, an extinct Formosan language', *Oceanic Linguistics* 36(2): 164–99.

ADELAAR, WILLEM F. H., with PIETER C. MUYSKEN (2004). *The Languages of the Andes.* Cambridge: Cambridge University Press.

AGESTHIALINGOM, S., and G. SRINIVASA VARMA (1980). *Auxiliaries in Dravidian.* Annamalainagar: Annamalai University.

AIKHENVALD, ALEXANDRA Y. (1998). 'Warekena', in Desmond D. Derbyshire and Geoffrey K. Pullum (eds.), *Handbook of Amazonian Languages, vol. iv.* Berlin: Mouton de Gruyter, 225–439.

—— (1999a). 'Areal diffusion and language contact in the Içana-Vaupés basin, northwest Amazonia', in R. M. W. Dixon and A. Aikhenvald (eds.), *The Amazonian Languages.* Cambridge: Cambridge University Press, 385–415.

—— (1999b). 'The Arawak language family', in R. M. W. Dixon and A. Y. Aikhenvald (eds.), *The Amazonian Languages.* Cambridge: Cambridge University Press, 65–106.

—— (1999c). Serial verb constructions and verb compounding: evidence from Tariana (North Arawak). *Studies in Language* 23: 479–508.

—— (2000). 'Transitivity in Tariana', in R. M. W. Dixon and Alexandra Y. Aikhenvald (eds.), *Changing Valency: Case Studies in Transitivity.* Cambridge: Cambridge University Press, 145–72.

—— and R. M. W. DIXON (1999). 'Other small families and isolates', in R. M. W. Dixon and A. Aikhenvald (eds.), *The Amazonian Languages.* Cambridge: Cambridge University Press, 341–83.

AISSEN, JUDITH (1987). *Tzotzil clause structure*. Dordrecht: Reidel.

AKAMINE, JUN (2003). *A Basic Grammar of Southern Sinama*. Kyoto: Nakanishi.

AKMAJIAN, ADRIAN, SUSAN M. STEELE, and THOMAS WASOW (1979). 'The category AUX in Universal Grammar', *Linguistic Inquiry* 10: 1–64.

AKSENOVA, I. S. (1997). *Kategorii vida, vremeni, i naklonenija v jazykax Bantu* [Categories of aspect, tense and mood in the Bantu language]. Moscow: Nauka.

ALLAN, EDWARD J. (1976a). 'Kullo', in M. L. Bender (ed.), *Non-Semitic Languages of Ethiopia*, East Lansing, Mich.: African Studies Center, 324–50.

—— (1976b). 'Dizi (Maji)', in M. L. Bender (ed.), *Non-Semitic Languages of Ethiopia*. East Lansing, Mich.: African Studies Center, 377–92.

ALLEN, ANDREW S. (1993). 'Ewe verbs in derivation and periphrastic constructions', in Salikoko S. Mufwene and Lioba Moshi (eds.), *Topics in African Linguistics*. Amsterdam: Benjamins, 35–43.

ALLEN, JERRY (1971). 'Tense/aspect and conjunctions in Halia discourse', *Oceanic Linguistics* 10(1): 63–77.

ALLETON, VIVIANE (1984). *Les auxiliaires de mode de chinois contemporain*. Paris: Maison des Sciences de l'Homme.

ALSINA, A., J. BRESNAN, and P. SELLS (eds.) (1997). *Complex Predicates*. Stanford, Calif.: Center for the Study of Language and Information.

ALVAREZ, JOSÉ (1994). *Estudios de lingüistica guajira*. Maracaibo: Gobernación del Estado Zulia, Secretaria de Cultura.

ANCEAUX, J. C. [1952] (1988). *The Wolio Language: Outline of Grammatical Description and Texts*, 2nd edn. (Verhandelingen van het koniklijk instituut voor taal-, land-en volkenkunde 11) Dordrecht: Foris.

ANDERSON, GREGORY D. S. (1993). 'Obligatory double-marking of morphosyntactic categories', in *Chicago Linguistic Society* 29. Chicago: CLS, 1–15.

—— (1995). 'Ditransitives, possessor-raising, copying-to-OBJ: animacy in morphosyntax', in *Chicago Linguistic Society* 31. Chicago: CLS, 1–17.

—— (1997). 'On "animacy maximization" in Fox (Mesquakie)', *International Journal of American Linguistics* 63(2): 227–47.

—— (1998a). *Xakas*. (Languages of the World/Materials 251) Munich: Lincom Europa.

—— (1998b). 'Discourse salience in Kalenjin inter-clausal syntax', in *Berkeley Linguistics Society* 23S: *Special Session on the Syntax/Semantics of African Languages*. Berkeley: BLS, 1–12.

—— (1999). 'A typology of inflection in auxiliary verb constructions: contributions of minor language data', in *Chicago Linguistic Society* 35: *Panel on Linguistic Diversity and Linguistic Theory*. Chicago: CLS, 1–15.

—— (2000). 'Split-inflection in auxiliary verb constructions', in Nancy Mae Antrim, Grant Goodall, Martha Schulte-Nafeh, and Vida Samiian (eds.), *Proceedings of the 28th Western Conference on Linguistics, 1999*. Fresno: California State University at Fresno.

—— (2001). 'Subject version and object version in Tofa auxiliary verb constructions', *Turkic Languages* 5(1): 240–69.

—— (2002). 'Case marked clausal subordination in Burushaski complex sentence structure', *Studies in Language* 26(3): 547–71.

—— (2003). 'Dravidian influence on Munda', *International Journal of Dravidian Linguistics* 32(1): 27–48.

—— (2004a). *Auxiliary verb constructions in Altai-Sayan Turkic.* Wiesbaden: Harrassowitz.

—— (2004b). 'The languages of central Siberia: introduction and overview', in E. Vajda (ed.), *Languages and Prehistory of Central Siberia.* (Current Issues in Linguistic Theory 262) Amsterdam: Benjamins, 1–122.

—— (to appear, a). 'Burushaski morphology', in Alan Kaye (ed.), *Morphologies of Asia and Africa.* Winona Lake, Ind.: Eisenbrauns.

—— (to appear, b). 'Auxiliary verb constructions in Old Turkic and Altai-Sayan Turkic', in Marcel Erdal (ed.), *Studies in Old Turkic Linguistics.* Wiesbaden: Harrassowitz.

—— (n.d.) 'Field notes on Xakas, Tuvan, Burushaski, Tofa, Eleme, Chulym, etc.'

—— and OLIVER BOND (2004-MS). 'Personal inflection in Eleme in areal-typological perspective'. Originally presented at World Congress of African Linguistics 4, New Brunswick, NJ, June 2003.

—— and RANDALL EGGERT (2001). 'A typology of verb agreement in Burushaski', *Linguistics of the Tibeto-Burman Area* 24(2): 235–54.

—— and K. DAVID HARRISON (1999). *Tyvan.* (Languages of the World/Materials 257) Munich: Lincom Europa.

—— —— (to appear). ' "Natural" and obsolescent change in Tofa', in Irina Nevskaja (ed.), *Studies in South Siberian Linguistics.* Wiesbaden: Harrassowitz.

—— —— (in preparation). *A Grammar of Tofa.*

ANDERSON, JOHN M. (1973). *An Essay Concerning Aspect: Some Considerations of a General Character Arising from Abbé Darrigol's Analysis of the Basque Verb.* (Janua Linguarum Seria Minor 167) The Hague: Mouton.

ANDERSON, MIKE, and MALCOLM ROSS (2002). 'Sudest', in Lynch et al. (2002: 322–46).

ANDREWS, HENRIETTA (1993). *The Function of Verb Prefixes in Southwestern Otomí.* (Summer Institute of Linguistics Publications in Linguistics 115) Arlington, Tex.: SIL.

ANDVIK, ERIK (2003). 'Tshangla', in Graham Thurgood and Randy J. LaPolla (eds.), *The Sino-Tibetan Languages.* New York: Routledge, 439–55.

ANNAMALAI, E. (1985). *Dynamics of Verbal Extensions in Tamil.* Trivandrum: Dravidian Linguistics Association of India.

ARON, ALBERT WILLIAM (1914). *Die 'progressive' Formen im Mittelhochdeutschen und Frühneuhochdeutschen.* Frankfurt: Baer.

ARONSON, HOWARD I. (1982). *Georgian: A Reading Grammar.* Columbus, Ohio. Slavica.

ASLEP Field Notes. Altai-Sayan Language and Ethnography Project. Supported by the Volkswagen Stiftung.

AUSTING, J., and J. AUSTING (1977). *Semantics of Ömie Discourse.* (Language Data, Asian Pacific Series 11) Hamilton Beach, Calif.: Summer Institute of Linguistics.

AVRORIN, V. A., and E. P. LEBEDEVA (1968). 'Oročskij jazyk' [The Oroch[i] language], in V. V. Vinogradov (ed.), *Jazyki narodov SSSR V.* Leningrad: Nauka, 191–209.

AZE, (F.) R. (1973). 'Clause patterns in Parengi-Gorum', in R. L. Trail (ed.), *Patterns in Clause, Sentence, Discourse in Selected Languages of India and Nepal* 1. Kathmandu: Tribuvan University Press, 235–312.

BABUŠKIN, G. F. (1966). *Morfologičeskaja struktura xakasskix dialektov v sravnenii s dialektami Altajo-Sajanskoj gruppy tjurkskix jazykov* [The morphological structure of Xakas dialects in comparison with dialects of the Altai-Sayan group of Turkic languages]. Unpublished MS. Abakan: XakNIIJaLI.

—— and G. I. DONIDZE (1966). 'Šorskij jazyk' [The Shor language], in Baskakov et al. (1966: 467–81).

BANERJEE, G. C. (1894). *Introduction to the Kharia Language.* Calcutta: Bengal Secretariat Press.

BAPTISTA, PRISCILLA, and RUTH WALLIN (1967). 'Baure', in Esther Matteson (ed.), *Bolivian Indian Grammars*: vol. i. Norman: Summer Institute of Linguistics/University of Oklahoma, 127–84.

BARKER, MUHAMMAD ABD-AL-RAHMAN, and AQIL KHAN MENGAL (1969). *A Course in Baluchi.* Montreal: McGill University, Institute of Islamic Studies.

BARNES, JANET (1994). 'Tuyuca', in Kahrel and van den Berg (1994: 325–42).

BASHIR, E. (1985). 'Towards a semantics of the Burushaski verb', in A. Zide et al. (eds.), *Proceeedings of the Conference on Participant Roles: South Asia and Adjacent Areas.* Bloomington: Indiana University Linguistics Club, 1–32.

BASKAKOV, N. A. (1958). *Altajskij jazyk* [The Altai language]. Moscow: AN ASSR.

—— (1966a). *Dialekt chernevyx tatar* [The dialect of the Black Forest Tatar]. Moscow: Nauka.

—— (1966b). 'Karakalpakskij jazyk' [Karakalpak language], in Baskakov et al. (1966: 301–19).

—— (1966c). 'Nogajskij jazyk' [Nogai language], in Baskakov et al. (1966: 280–300).

—— (1972). *Dialekt kumandintsev* [The dialect of the Kumandy]. Moscow: Nauka.

—— (1985). *Dialekt lebedinskix tatar* [The dialect of the Swan Tatar]. Moscow: Nauka.

—— et al. (eds.) (1966). *Jazyki SSSR, ii: Tjurkskie jazyki* [Languages of the USSR, ii: Turkic languages]. Moscow: AN SSSR.

—— et al. (1975). *Grammatika xakasskogo jazyka* [A grammar of Xakas]. Moscow: Nauka.

BASSET, LOUIS (1979). *Les Emplois périphrastiques du verbe grec mellein: étude de linguistique grecque et essai de linguistique générale.* Lyon: Maison de l'Orient.

BATALOVA, R. M. (1993). 'Komi-permjatskij jazyk' [The Komi-Permyak language], in K. E. Majtinskaja et al. (eds.), *Jazyki mira: Ural'skie jazyki.* Moscow: Indrik, 229–39.

BAUCOM, KENNETH L. (1972). 'The Wambo Languages of South West Africa and Angola', *Journal of African Languages* 11(2): 45–73.

BAVIN, EDITH L. (1983). 'Morphological and syntactic divergence in Lango and Acholi', in Rainer Voßen and Marianne Bechhaus-Gerst (eds.), *Nilotic Studies: Proceedings of the International Symposium on Languages and History of Nilotic Peoples, Cologne*

January 4–6, 1982, Part 1. (Kölner Beiträge zur Afrikanistik 10.1) Berlin: Reimer, 147–68.

BEAUMONT, CLIVE H. (1989). 'The verb phrase in Tigak, Lavongai (Tungag) and Kara of New Ireland', in Ray Harlow and Robin Hooper (eds.), *VICAL 1: Oceanic Languages. Papers from the Fifth International Conference on Austronesian Linguistics.* Auckland: Linguistic Society of New Zealand.

BEE, DARLENE (1973). 'Usarufa: a descriptive grammar', in McKaughan (1973a): 225–323.

BELL, ALAN (1978). 'Language samples', in Joseph H. Greenberg et al. (eds.), *Universals of Human Language*, vol. iv. Stanford, Calif.: Stanford University Press, 123–56.

BENDER, JORIGINE, and AKIRA Y. YAMAMOTO (1992). 'Hualapai verbs of being, doing, and saying: transitivity and auxiliaries', *Anthropological Linguistics* 34(1–4): 293–310.

BENDER, M. LIONEL (1989). 'The Eastern Jebel languages', in M. Lionel Bender (ed.), *Topics in Nilo-Saharan Linguistics.* (Nilo-Saharan Linguistic Analyses and Documentation 3) Hamburg: Buske, 151–80.

—— (1996). *Kunama.* (Languages of the World/Materials 59) Munich: Lincom Europa.

BENDOR-SAMUEL, JOHN T. (1961). *The Verbal Piece in Jebero.* Supplement to *Word* 17, monograph 4.

—— (1968). 'Verb clusters in Izi', *Journal of African Languages* 5(2): 119–28.

BENJAMIN, GEOFFREY (1976). 'An outline of Temiar grammar', in Philip N. Jenner, Laurence C. Thompson, and Stanley Starosta (eds.), *Austroasiatic Studies*, pt. i. (Oceanic Linguistics Special Publications) Honolulu: University of Hawai'i Press, 129–88.

BENNIE, W. G. (1953). *A Grammar of Xhosa for the Xhosa Speaking.* Cape Province, South Africa: Lovedale Press.

BENTLEY, DELIA, and THÓRHALLUR EYTHÓRSSON (2004). 'Auxiliary selection and the semantics of unaccusativity', *Lingua* 114: 447–71.

BENTLEY, MAYRENE, and ANDREW KULEMEKA (2001). *Chichewa.* (Languages of the World/Materials 345) Munich: Lincom Europa.

VAN DEN BERG, HELMA (1995). *A Grammar of Hunzib (with Texts and Lexicon).* (Lincom Studies in Caucasian Linguistics 1) Munich: Lincom Europa.

VAN DEN BERG, RENÉ (1989). *A Grammar of the Muna Language.* Dordrecht: Foris.

BERGEL'SON, M. A., and A. A. KIBRIK (1987a). Sistema perekluchenija referentsii v tuvinskom jazyke [The system of switch reference in Tuvan]. *Sovetskaja Tjurkologija* 2: 16–32.

—— —— (1987b). Sistema perekluchenija referentsii v tuvinskom jazyke [The system of switch reference in Tuvan]. *Sovetskaja Tjurkologija* 4: 30–45.

BERGER, H. (1974). *Das Yasin-Burushaski (Werchikwar).* Wiesbaden: Harrassowitz.

—— (1998). *Die Burushaski-Sprache von Hunza und Nager.* 3 vols. Wiesbaden: Harrassowitz.

BERGSLAND, K. (1997). *Aleut Grammar: Unangam Tunuganaan Achixaasix̂.* Fairbanks: Alaska Native Language Center.

BERINSTEIN, AVA (1998). 'Antipassive and 2–3 Retreat in K'ekchi Mayan: two constructions with the same verbal reflex', in Leanne Hinton and Pamela Munro (eds.), *Studies in American Indian Languages: Description and Theory*. Berkeley: University of California Press, 212–22.

BICKEL, BALTHASAR (2003). 'Belhare', in Thurgood and La Polla (2003: 546–69).

BILIGIRI, H. S. (1965). *Kharia: Phonology, Grammar, Vocabulary*. Poona: Deccan College.

BISANG, WALTER (1995). 'Verb serialization and converbs: differences and similarities', in Ekkehard König and Martin Haspelmath (eds.), *Converbs in Cross-linguistic Perspective*. Berlin: Mouton de Gruyter, 137–88.

—— (2001). 'Finite vs. non-finite languages', in Martin Haspelmath et al. (eds.), *Language Typology and Language Universals: An International Handbook, vol. ii.* Berlin: de Gruyter, 1400–1413.

BLACKINGS, MAIRI, and NIGEL FABB (2003). *A Grammar of Ma'di*. (Mouton Grammar Library 32) Berlin: Mouton de Gruyter.

BLAKE, BARRY J. (1979). 'Pitta-Pitta', in Dixon and Blake (1979: 183–242).

BLAKE, BARRY J. (1994). *Case*. Cambridge: Cambridge University Press.

—— (2001). 'Global trends in language', *Linguistics* 39(5): 1009–28.

—— and R. M. W. Dixon (1979). 'Introduction', in Dixon and Blake (1979: 1–25).

BLANSITT, EDWARD L. (1975). 'Progressive aspect', *Stanford Working Papers on Language Universals* 18: 1–34.

BLEVINS, JULIETTE (2001). *Nhanda: An Aboriginal Language of Western Australia*. (Oceanic Linguistics Special Publications 30) Honolulu: University of Hawai'i Press.

BLIESE, LOREN (1976). 'Afar', in M. L. Bender (ed.), *Non-Semitic Languages of Ethiopia*. East Lansing, Mich.: African Studies Center, 133–65.

BLOOMFIELD, LEONARD (1933). *Language*. Chicago: University of Chicago Press.

BLOWERS, BRUCE L., and RUTH BLOWERS (1970). 'Kaugel verb morphology', in *Papers in New Guinea Linguistics* 12: 37–60. (Pacific Linguistics A-25) Canberra: Australian National University.

BOBALJIK, JONATHAN, and SUSI WURMBRAND (2001). 'Seven prefix–suffix asymmetries in Itelmen'. Paper presented at Chicago Linguistic Society 37, Apr. 2001.

BODDING, P. O. (1929). *Materials for a Santal Grammar, mostly morphological*. Dumka: Santal Mission of Northern Churches.

BODOMO, ADAMS (1997). *The Structure of Dagaare*. Stanford, Calif.: CSLI.

BOLINGER, D. (1980). 'Wanna and the gradience of auxiliaries', in G. Brettschneider and C. Lehmann (eds.), *Wege zur Universalienforschung: Sprachwissenschaftliche Beiträge zum 60 Geburtstag von Hansjakob Seiler*. (Tübingen Beiträge zur Linguistik 145) Tübingen: Narr, 292–9.

BOND, OLIVER (2006). 'Eleme verb morphology'. University of Manchester Ph.D. dissertation.

—— and GREGORY D. S. ANDERSON (2005). 'Divergent structure in Ogonoid languages'. *Berkeley Linguistics Society* 31.

BORGMAN, D. M. (1990). 'Sanuma', in Desmond D. Derbyshire and Geoffrey K. Pullum (ed.), *Handbook of American Languages, vol. ii.* Berlin: Mouton de Gruyter, 17–248.

BOTNE, ROBERT (1986). 'The temporal role of Eastern Bantu −ba and −li', *Studies in African Linguistics* 17(3): 303–17.

—— (1990). 'The origins of the remote future formatives in Kinyarwanda, Kirundi and Giha (J61)', *Studies in African Linguistics* 21(2): 189–210.

—— (1999). 'Future and distal—ka-'s: Proto-Bantu or nascent form(s)?', in Jean-Marie Hombert and Larry M. Hyman (eds.), *Bantu Historical Linguistics: Theoretical and Empirical Perspectives.* Stanford, Calif.: CSLI, 473–515.

—— (2003). 'Lega (Beya dialect)', in D. Nurse and G. Phillipson (eds.), *The Bantu Languages.* London: Routledge, 422–49.

BOUMA, LOWELL. (1973). *Semantics of Modal Auxiliaries in Contemporary German.* The Hague: Monton.

BOWDEN, JOHN. (2001). *Taba: Description of a South Halmahera Language.* (Pacific Linguistics 521) Canberra: Australian National University.

BOWE, HEATHER, and STEPHEN MOREY (1999). *The Yorta Yorta (Bangerang) Language of the Murray Gouldburn including Yabula Yabula.* (Pacific Linguistics C-154) Canberra: Australian National University.

BOWERN, CLAIRE (2002). 'Grammatical reanalysis and verb serialization: the unusual case of Sisiva Titan', in *Proceedings of Austronesian Formal Linguistics Association 8: MIT Working Papers in Linguistics 44.* Cambridge, Mass.: MIT Press, 47–60.

BOYD, GINGER (2003). 'Tense and aspect in Mbodomo narrative discourse', *Studies in African Linguistics* 29(1): 43–74.

BOYNTON, SYLVIA. (1982). 'Mikasuki grammar in outline'. University of Florida Ph.D. dissertation.

BRADSHAW, JOEL (1993). 'Subject relationships within serial verb constructions in Numbami and Jabêm', *Oceanic Linguistics* 32(1): 133–61.

—— (2001). 'Iwal grammar essentials, with comparative notes', in Andrew Pawley et al. (eds.), *The Boy from Bundaberg: Studies in Melanesian Linguistics in honour of Tom Dutton.* Canberra: Australian National University, 51–74.

BRAINE, JEAN CRITCHFIELD (1970). 'Nicobarese grammar (Car dialect)'. University of California at Berkeley Ph.D. dissertation.

BREEN, J. G. (1981). 'Margany and Gunya', in R. M. W. Dixon and Barry J. Blake (eds.), *Handbook of Australian Languages, vol. ii.* Canberra: Australian National University, 275–395.

BREEZE, MARY J. (1990). 'A sketch of the phonology and grammar of Gimira (Benchnon)', in Richard J. Hayward (ed.), *Omotic Language Studies.* London: School of Oriental and African Studies, 1–67.

BRIL, ISABELLE (2004). 'Complex nuclei in Oceanic languages: contribution to an areal typology', in Bril and Ozanne-Rivierre (2004: 1–48).

—— and FRANÇOISE OZANNE-RIVIERRE (eds.) (2004). *Complex Predicates in Oceanic Languages.* Berlin: Mouton de Gruyter.

BRILEY, DAVID (1997). 'Four grammatical marking systems in Bauzi', in Karl J. Franklin (ed.), *Papers in Papuan Linguistics* No. 2. (Pacific Linguistics A-85) Canberra: Australian National University, 1–131.

BRINTON, L. (1988). *The Development of English Aspectual Systems: Aspectualizers and Post-Verbal Particles.* Cambridge: Cambridge University Press.

BRODERICK, GEORGE (1993). 'Manx', in Martin J. Ball and James Fife (eds.), *The Celtic Languages.* (Routledge Language Family Series) London: Routledge, 228–85.

BROWN, H. A. (1974). 'The Eleman language family', in Karl Franklin (ed.), *The Linguistic Situation in the Gulf District and Adjacent Areas, Papua New Guinea.* (Pacific Linguistics C-26) Canberra: Australian National University, 279–376.

BUECHEL, EUGENE (1939). *A Grammar of Lakota.* St. Francis, S. Dak.: St. Francis Mission.

BUGENHAGEN, ROBERT D. (1995). *A Grammar of Mangap-Mbula: An Austronesian Language of Papua New Guinea.* (Pacific Linguistics C-101) Canberra: Australian National University.

BULATOVA, N. J., and L. GRENOBLE (1999). *Evenki.* (Languages of the World/Materials 141) Munich: Lincom Europa.

BURLING, ROBINS (2003). 'Garo', in Thurgood and La Polla (2003: 387–400).

BURUSPHAT, SAMSONYE (1998). *Discourse Functions of Auxiliaries in the Bouyei Origin Myth.* Salaya: Institute of Language, Culture and Rural Development, Mahidol University.

BUßMANN, HADUMOD (1990). *Lexikon der Sprachwissenschaft,* 2nd rev. edn. Stuttgart: Kröner.

—— (2002). *Lexicon der Sprachwissenschaft,* 3rd edn. Stuttgart: Kröner.

BUTLER, JAMES H., and JUDY GARLAND BUTLER (1977). *Tzutujil Verbs.* Guatemala City: Summer Institute of Linguistics.

BUTT, MIRIAM, and WILHELM GEUDER (2001). 'On the (Semi)lexical status of light verbs', in Norbert Corver and Henk van Riemsdijk (eds.), *Semi-lexical Categories: On the Content of Function Words and the Function of Content Words.* Berlin: Mouton de Gruyter, 323–70.

—— (2003). 'Light verbs in Urdu and grammaticalization', in Regine Eckardt, Klaus von Heusinger, and Christoph Schwarze (eds.), *Words in Time: Diachronic Semantics from Different Points of View.* Berlin: Mouton de Gruyter, 295–349.

BYBEE, J., R. PERKINS, and W. PAGLIUCA (1994). *The Evolution of Grammar: Tense, Aspect, and Modality in the Languages of the World.* Chicago: University of Chicago Press.

BYBEE, J. L., and Ö. DAHL (1989). 'The creation of tense and aspect systems in the languages of the world', *Studies in Language* 13(1): 51–103.

—— WILLIAM PAGLIUCA, and REVERE D. PERKINS (1991). 'On the asymmetries in the affixation of grammatical material', in W. Croft, K. Denning, and S. Kemmer (eds.), *Studies in Typology and Diachrony for Joseph H. Greenberg.* (Typological Studies in Language 20) Amsterdam: Benjamins, 1–42.

CAMP, ELIZABETH L. (1985). 'Split ergativity in Cavineña', *International Journal of American Linguistics* 51(1): 38–58.

CAMP (B.), ELIZABETH, and MILLICENT LICCARDI (O.) (1965). 'Itonama', in Gramaticas Estructurales de lenguas Bolivianas, ii. Riberalta, Beni, Bolivia: Instituto Lingüístico de Verano, 223–383.

CAMPBELL, LYLE (1985). The Pipil Language of El Salvador. Berlin: Mouton de Gruyter.

—— (1987). 'Syntactic change in Pipil', International Journal of American Linguistics 53(3): 253–80.

CAPELL, ARTHUR (1940/41). 'Notes on the Wunambal language', Oceania 11: 295–308.

—— (1969). 'Structure of the Binandere verb', in Papers in New Guinea Linguistics 9. (Pacific Linguistics A-18) Canberra: Australian National University, 1–32.

CARLSON, ROBERT (1994). A Grammar of Supyire. Berlin: Mouton de Gruyter.

CARON, BERNARD (1989). 'The verbal system of Ader Hausa', in Zygmunt Frajzyngier (ed.), Current Progress in Chadic Linguistics. (Amsterdam Studies in the Theory and History of Linguistic Science 62) Amsterdam: J Benjamins, 131–69.

CASALI, ROBERT (1995). 'An overview of the Nawuri verbal system', Journal of West African Languages 15 (1): 63–86.

CASTARÉDE, J. (1962). A Complete Treatise on the Conjugation of French Verbs. London: Hachette.

CAUGHLEY, ROSS CHARLES (1982). The Syntax and Morphology of the Verb in Chepang. (Pacific Linguistics B-84) Canberra: Australian National University.

ČEREMISINA, M. N. et al. (1984). Predikativnoe sklonenie pričastij v altajskix jazykax [Predicative declension of participles in Altaic languages]. Novosibirsk: Nauka.

CHAMEREAU, CLAUDINE (2000). Grammaire du Purépecha parlé sur des îles du lac de Patzcuaro. Munich: Lincom Europa.

CHAPHOLE, SOLOMON RAMPASANE (1988). 'A study of the auxiliary verbs in Sesotho.' University of Cape Town Ph.D. dissertation.

CHAPMAN, SHIRLEY, and DESMOND DERBYSHIRE (1991). 'Paumarí', in Desmond C. Derbyshire and Geoffrey K. Pullum (eds.), Handbook of Amazonian Languages, vol. iii. Berlin: Mouton de Gruyter, 161–354.

CHARNEY, JEAN ORMSBEE (1994). A Grammar of Comanche. Lincoln: University of Nebraska Press.

CHELLIAH, SHOBHANA L. (2003). 'Meithei', in Thurgood and La Polla (2003: 427–38).

CHILDS, G. TUCKER (1995). A Grammar of Kisi. Berlin: Mouton de Gruyter.

CHIRIKBA, VYACHESLAV A. (2003). Abkhaz. (Languages of the World/Materials 119) Munich: Lincom Europa.

CHRISTALLER, J. G. (1875). A Grammar of the Asante and Fante Language called Tshi (Chwee, Twi) Based on the Akuapem Dialect with Reference to the Other (Akan and Fante) Dialects. Basel: Basel Evangelical Missionary Society.

CHRISTIE, P. (1991). 'Modality in Jamaican Creole', in W. Edwards and D. Winford (eds.), Verb Phrase Patterns in Black English and Creoles. Detroit: Wayne State University Press, 217–33.

CHUNG, CHUL-HWA, and KYUNG-JA CHUNG (1996). 'Kuot grammar essentials', in John Clifton (ed.), Two Non-Austronesian Grammars from the Islands. (Data Papers on Papua New Guinea Languages 42) Ukarumpa, Papua New Guinea: Summer Institute of Linguistics, 1–75.

CHUNG, JAY J. (1979). A lexicalist study of Korean auxiliary expressions. University of North Carolina Ph.D. dissertation.

CLAUDI, ULRIKE (1988). 'The development of tense/aspect marking in Kru languages'. review article, *Journal of African Languages and Linguistics* 10: 53–77.

CLAUSON, GERARD (1972). *An Etymological Dictionary of pre-Thirteenth Century-Turkish*. Oxford: Oxford University Press.

COATE, H. H. J., and LYNETTE OATES (1970). *A Grammar of Ngarinjin*. (Australian Aboriginal Studies 25) Canberra: Australian Institute of Aboriginal Studies.

COATES, DAVID R. (1969). *A Grammar of Kaliai-Kove*. (Oceanic Linguistics Special Publications 6) Honolulu: University of Hawai'i Press.

COELHO, GAIL (2003). 'Non-finite verb markers in Betta Kurumba'. Presented at South Asian Linguistic Analysis 23, Austin, Tex., Oct. 2003.

COLARUSSO, JOHN (1992). *A Grammar of the Kabardian Language*. Alberta: University of Calgary Press.

COLE, DESMOND T. (1955). *An Introduction to Tswana Grammar*, 6th edn. London: Longmans, Green.

COLLINS, WESLEY M. (1994). 'Maya-Mam', in Kahrel and van den Berg (1994: 365–81).

COMRIE, BERNARD (2000). 'Valency-changing derivations in Tsez', in R. M. W. Dixon and Alexandra Y. Aikhenvald (eds.), *Changing Valency: Case Studies in Transitivity*. Cambridge: Cambridge University Press, 360–74.

—— (1985). 'Causative verb formation and other verb-deriving morphology', in T. Shopen (ed.), *Language Typology and Syntactic Description, vol. iii: Grammatical Categories and the Lexicon*. Cambridge: Cambridge University Press, 309–48.

CONRAD, ROBERT J., and KEPAS WOGIGA (1991). *An Outline of Bukiyip Grammar*. (Pacific Linguistics C-113) Canberra: Australian National University.

CONRAD, RUDI (ed.) (1988). *Lexikon sprachwissentschaftilcher Termini*. Leipzig: VEB Bibliographisches Institut.

CORBETT, GREVILLE G. (1991). *Gender*. New York: Cambridge University Press.

COURO, TED, and MARGARET LANGDON (1975). *Let's Talk 'Iipay Aa*. Banning: Malki Museum Press.

COWAN, H. K. J. (1965). *Grammar of the Sentani Language, with Specimen Texts and Vocabulary*. (Verhandelingen van het Koninklijk Instituut voor taal-, land-, en volkekunde 47) The Hague: Nijhoff.

COWPER, ELIZABETH A. (1992). *A Concise Introduction to Syntactic Theory: The Government and Binding Approach*. Chicago: University of Chicago Press.

CRAIG, C. (1977). *The Structure of Jacaltec*. Austin: University of Texas Press.

CREIDER, CHET (1989). *Syntax of the Nilotic Languages: Themes and Variations*. Berlin: Reimer.

—— and JANE TAPSUBEI CREIDER (1989). *A Grammar of Nandi*. Hamburg: Buske.

CROFT, WILLIAM (2000). 'Parts of speech as language universals and as language-particular categories', in P. Vogel and B. Comrie (eds.), *Approaches to the Typology of Word Classes*. Berlin: Mouton de Gruyter, 63–102.

—— (2001). *Radical Construction Grammar*. Oxford: Oxford University Press.

—— (2002). *Typology and Universals*, 2nd edn. Cambridge: Cambridge University Press.

CROWLEY, TERRY (1987). 'Serial verbs in Paamese', *Studies in Language* 11: 35–84.

—— (1991). 'Parallel development and shared innovation: some developments from Central Vanuatu inflectional morphology', *Oceanic Linguistics* 30(2): 179–222.

—— (1998). *An Erromangan (Sye) Grammar.* (Oceanic Linguistics Special Publications 27) Honolulu: University of Hawai'i Press.

—— (1999). *Ura: A Disappearing Language of Southern Vanuatu.* (Pacific Linguistics C-156) Canberra: Australian National University.

—— (2002a). 'Raga', in Lynch et al. (2002: 626–37).

—— (2002b). 'Gela', in Lynch et al. (2002: 525–37).

—— (2002c). 'Vinmavis', in Lynch et al. (2002: 638–49).

—— (2002d). 'Southeast Ambrym', in Lynch et al. (2002: 660–70).

—— (2002e). *Serial Verbs in Oceanic.* Oxford: Oxford University Press.

CRYSTAL, DAVID (1980). *A First Dictionary of Linguistics and Phonetics.* London: Deutsch.

CSATÓ, ÉVA ÁGNES, and LARS JOHANSON (1993). 'On gerundial syntax in Turkic', *Acta Orientalia Academiae Hungaricae* 46(2/3): 133–41.

CSÚCS, SÁNDOR (1998). 'Udmurt', in Daniel Abondolo (ed.), *The Uralic Languages.* (Routledge Language Family series) London: Routledge, 276–304.

CUNHA DE OLIVEIRA, CHRISTINE (2003). 'Lexical categories and the status of descriptives in Apinajé', *International Journal of American Linguistics* 69(3): 243–74.

CURIEUX, TULIO ROJAS, ROCÍO NIEVES OVIEDO, and MARCOS YULE YATACUE (1991). *Estudios gramaticales de la lengua paez (nasa yuwe).* (Lenguas aborigenes de Colombia Descripciones 7) Bogotá: Universidad de los Andes.

DAS GUPTA, D., and S. R. SHARMA (1982). *A Handbook of the Önge Language.* Calcutta: Anthropological Survey of India.

DAVIES, JOHN (1981). *Kobon.* (Lingua Descriptive series 3) Amsterdam: North-Holland.

DAVIS, DONALD (1964). 'Wantoat verb stems: classes and affixation', in *Studies in Five New Guinea Languages.* Norman, Okla.: Summer Institute of Linguistics, 131–82.

DAVIS, KAREN (2003). *A Grammar of the Hoava Language, Western Solomons.* (Pacific Linguistics 535) Canberra: Australian National University.

DEIBLER, ELLIS W. (1976). *Semantic Relationships of Gahuku Verbs.* Norman, Okla.: Summer Institute of Linguistics.

DELANCEY, SCOTT (1991). 'The origins of verb serialization in Modern Tibetan', *Studies in Language* 15: 1–23.

—— (2003). 'Lhasa Tibetan', in Thurgood and La Polla (2003: 270–88).

DEMIR, NURETTIN (1993). *Postverbien in Türkeitürkischen.* (Turcologica 17) Wiesbaden: Harrassowitz.

—— (1998). 'On the status of a Turkish postverb', in Lars Johanson, Éva Ágnes Csató, Vanessa Locke, Astrid Menz, and Dorothea Winterling (eds.), *The Mainz Meeting: Proceedings of the Seventh International Conference on Turkish Linguistics.* (Turcologica 32) Wiesbaden: Harrassowitz, 224–33.

DENCH, ALAN (1991). 'Panyjima', in R. M. W. Dixon and Barry J. Blake (eds.), *Handbook of Australian Languages, vol. iv.* Oxford: Oxford University Press, 125–243.

—— (1995). *Martuthunira: A Language of the Pilbara Region of Western Australia.* Canberra: Australian National University.

DICKINSON, CONNIE (2002). 'Complex predicates in Tsafiki'. University of Oregon Ph.D. dissertation.

DIMMENDAAL, G. J. (1983). *The Turkana Language.* Dordrecht: Foris.

—— (1998). 'A syntactic typology of the Surmic language family from an areal and historical-comparative point of view', in Gerrit J. Dimmendaal and Marco Last (eds.), *Surmic Languages and Cultures.* (Nilo-Saharan Linguistic Analyses and Documentation 13) Cologne: Köppe, 35–82.

DIXON, R. M. W. (1980). *The Languages of Australia.* Cambridge: Cambridge University Press.

—— (1981). 'Wargamay', in R. M. W. Dixon and Barry J. Blake (eds.), *Handbook of Australian Languages,* vol. ii. Canberra: Australian National University, 1–144.

—— (1983). 'Nyawaygi', in R. M. W. Dixon and Barry J. Blake (eds.), *Handbook of Australian Languages, vol. iii.* Canberra: Australian National University, 431–525.

—— (2000). 'A typology of causative: form, syntax and meaning', in R. M. W. Dixon and Alexandra Y. Aikhenvald (eds.), *Changing Valency: Case Studies in Transitivity.* Cambridge: Cambridge University Press, 30–83.

—— (2002). 'The eclectic morphology of Jarawara, and the status of word', in R. M. W. Dixon and Alexandra Y. Aikhenvald (eds.), *Word: A Cross-linguistic Typology.* Cambridge: Cambridge University Press, 125–52.

—— and BARRY J. BLAKE (eds.) (1979). *Handbook of Australian Languages, vol. i.* Canberra: Australian National University.

DOBLE, MARION (1987). 'A description of some features of Ekari language structure', *Oceanic Linguistics* 26(1–2): 55–113.

DOERFER, G. (1988). *Das Chorasantürkische.* Wiesbaden: Harrassowitz.

DOKE, CLEMENT (1938). *Textbook of Lamba Grammar.* Johannesburg: Witwatersrand University Press.

DOKE, C. M. (1947). *Textbook of Zulu Grammar,* 3rd edn. London: Longmans, Green.

DOMOŽAKOV N. G. (1948). *Opisanie kyzylskogo dialekta xakasskogo jazyka.* [A description of the Kyzyl dialect of Xakas] MS. Abakan: XakNIIJaLI.

DONNER, KAI (1944). *Kamassisches Wörterbuch.* Helsinki: Soumalais-ugrilainen seura.

DONOHUE, MARK (1999). *Warembori.* (Languages of the World/Materials 341). Munich: Lincom Europa.

—— (2003a). 'Morphological templates, headedness and applicatives in Barupu', *Oceanic Linguistics* 42(1): 111–43.

—— (2003b). 'Agreement in the Skou language: a historical account', *Oceanic Linguistics* 42(2): 479–98.

DOOLEY, R. A. (1990). 'The positioning of non-pronominal clitics and particles in lowland South American languages', in D. L. Payne (ed.), *Amazonian Linguistics:*

Studies in Lowland South American Languages. Austin: University of Texas Press, 457–93.

VAN DRIEM, GEORG (1987). *A Grammar of Limbu*. Berlin: Mouton de Gruyter.

—— (1993). *A Grammar of Dumi*. (Mouton Grammar Library 10) Berlin: Mouton de Gruyter.

DRINKA, BRIDGET (2003). 'Areal factors in the development of the European periphrastic perfect', *Word* 54(1): 1–38.

DRYER, MATTHEW S. (1986). 'Primary objects, secondary objects, and antidative', *Language* 62(4): 808–45.

—— (1989). 'Large linguistic areas and language sampling', *Studies in Language* 13: 257–92.

—— (1992). 'The Greenbergian word order correlations', *Language* 68(1): 81–138.

—— (2003). 'Word order in Sino-Tibetan from a typological and geographical perspective', in Thurgood and La Polla (2003: 43–55).

DUL'ZON, A. P. (1960). 'Lično-vremennye formy čulymsko-tjurkskogo glagola' [Personal-temporal (finite) forms of the Chulym Turkic verb], *Učenye zapiski* 8: 101–45. Abakan: XakNIIJaLI.

—— (1966). 'Čulymsko-tjurkskij jazyk' [The Chulym Turkic language], in Baskakov et al. (1966: 446–66).

DUNN, JOHN A. (1979). 'Prononimal concord in Coast Tsimshian', *International Journal of American Linguistics* 45(3): 224–31.

DUNN, MICHAEL JOHN (1999). 'A Grammar of Chukchi'. Australian National University Ph D. dissertation.

DURIE, MARK (1985). *A Grammar of Acehnese on the Basis of a Dialect of North Aceh*. Dordrecht: Foris.

—— (1988). 'Verb serialization and "verbal-prepositions" in Oceanic languages', *Oceanic Linguistics* 27(1–2): 1–23.

—— (1997). 'Grammatical structures in verb serialization', in A. Alsina J. Bresnan, and P. Sells (eds.), *Complex Predicates*. Stanford, Calif: Centre for the Study of Language and Information, 289–354.

DUTKIN, X. I. (1995). *Allajxovskij govor evenov Jakutii*. [The Allajxov speech variety of the Even of Yakutia] St Petersburg: Nauka.

DUTTON, TOM E. (1996). *Koiari*. (Languages of the World/Materials 10) Munich: Lincom Europa.

DYRENKOVA, N. P. (1940). *Grammatika ojrotskogo jazyka* [Grammar of Oirot]. Moscow and Leningrad.

—— (1941). *Grammatika šorskogo jazyka* [Grammar of Shor]. Moscow/Leningrad.

EADES, DIANA KELLOWAY (1976). *The Dharawal and Dhurga Languages of the New South Wales South Coast*. (Australian Aboriginal Studies Regional Research Studies 8) Canberra: Australian Institute of Aboriginal Studies.

—— (1979). 'Gumbaynggir', in Dixon and Blake (1979: 245–361).

EARLY, ROBERT (1993). 'Nuclear layer serialization in Lewo', *Oceanic Linguistics* 32(1): 65–93.

EASTMAN, ROBERT, and ELIZABETH EASTMAN (1963). 'Iquito', in Benjamin F. Elson (ed.), *Studies in Peruvian Indian Languages*, vol. i. (Summer Institute of Linguistics Publications in Linguistics and Related Fields 9) Norman, Okla.: SIL. 145–92.

EATOUGH, ANDREW (1999). *Central Hill Nisenan Texts with Grammatical Sketch*. (University of California Publications in Linguistics 132) Berkeley: University of California Press.

EBERT, KAREN (2003a). 'Kiranti languages: an overview', in Thurgood and La Polla (2003: 505–17).

—— (2003b). 'Camling', in Thurgood and La Polla (2003: 533–45).

EDEL'MAN, D. A. (1997). 'The Burushaski language', in A. P. Volodin et al. (eds.), *Jazyki mira: paleoaziatskie jazyki*. Moscow: Indrik, 204–20.

EGESDAL, STEPHEN, and M. TERRY THOMPSON (1998). 'A fresh look at Tillamook (Hutyéyu) inflectional morphology', in Ewa Czaykowska-Higgins and M. Dale Kinkade (eds.), *Salish Languages and Linguistics: Theoretical and Descriptive Perspectives*. Berlin: Mouton de Gruyter, 235–73.

EGGENSPERGER, KLAUS (1995). *Modale Nebenverben im Jiddischen: eine korpusgestützte Untersuchung zu 'soln' und 'wolt'*. Osnabrück: Rasch.

EGGERT, RANDALL (2002). 'Dis-concordance: the syntax, semantics and pragmatics of "or"-agreement'. University of Chicago Ph.D. dissertation.

EGLI, HANS (1990). *Paiwangrammatik*. Wiesbaden: Harrassowitz.

VAN EIJK, JAN (1997). *The Lillooet Language*. Vancouver: UBC Press.

EINAUDI, PAULA FERRIS (1976). *A Grammar of Biloxi*. New York: Garland.

ELLESGÅRD, A. (1953). *The Auxiliary 'Do': Its Development and Use in English*. Stockholm: Almqrist & Wiksell.

ELSON, BENJAMIN F. (1967). 'Sierra Popoluca', in Norman A. McQuown (ed.), *Handbook of Middle American Indians, Vol. v: Linguistics*. Austin: University of Texas Press, 269–90.

EMENANJO, E. NOLUE (1985). *Auxiliaries in Igbo Syntax: A Comparative Study*. Bloomington: Indiana University Linguistics Club.

EMONDS, J. (1976). *A Transformational Approach to English Syntax*. New York: Academic Press.

ENDEMANN, K. (1876). *Versuch einer Grammatik des Sotho*. Berlin. Repr. 1964, Farnborough: Gregg Press.

VAN ENGELENHOVEN, AONE T. P. G. (1995). *A Grammar of Leti as Spoken in Tutukei*. Ridderkerk: Offsetdrukkerij Ridderprint.

—— (2004). *Leti: A Language of Southwest Maluku*. Leiden: KITLV Press.

VAN ENK, GERRIT J., and LOURENS DE VRIES (1997). *The Korowai of Irian Jaya: Their Language in its Cultural Context*. (Oxford Studies in Anthropological Linguistics 9) Oxford: Oxford University Press.

ENRICO, JOHN (1983). 'Tense in the Haida relative clause', *International Journal of American Linguistics* 49(2): 134–66.

ESPINAL I FARRÉ, MARIA TERESA (1998). *Els verbs auxiliars em català*. Bellaterra: Escola Universitària de Traductors i Intèrprets Universitat Autònoma de Barcelona.

ESSIEN, OXON E. (1987). 'The aspectual system of Ibibio', in David Odden (ed.), *Current Approaches to African Linguistics, vol. iv.* Dordrecht: Foris, 151–65.

ETXEBARRIA, L., JOXE M. (2002). *El verbo auxiliar vasco: formas unificadas y dialectales.* Munich: Lincom Europa.

EYTHÓRSSON, THÓRHALLUR, and NIGEL VINCENT (2003). 'Internal vs external factors in the development and spread of the periphrastic perfect'. Paper presented at International Conference on Historical Linguistics 16, Copenhagen, Aug. 2003.

EZARD, BRYAN (1997). *A Grammar of Tawala: An Austronesian Language of the Milne Bay Area, Papua New Guinea.* (Pacific Linguistics C-137). Canberra: Australian National University.

FABRE, ALAIN (2002). 'Algunos rasgos tipologicos del Kamsá (Valle de Sibundoy, Alto Putomayo sudoeste de Colombia) vistos desde una perspectiva areal', in Mily Crevels, Simon van der Kerke, Sérgio Meira, and Hein van der Voort (eds.), *Current Studies on South American Languages.* Leiden: Leiden University CNWS, 159–98.

FARR, CYNTHIA J. M. (1999). *The Interface between Syntax and Discourse in Korafe, a Papuan Language of Papua New Guinea.* (Pacific Linguistics C-148) Canberra: Australian National University.

FARRIS, EDWIN R. (1992). 'A syntactic sketch of Yosondúa Mixtec', in C. Henry Bradley and Barbara E. Hollenbach (eds.), *Studies in the Syntax of Mixtecan Languages, vol. iv.* (Summer Institute of Linguistics Publications in Linguistics 111) Arlington, Tex.: SIL, 1–171.

FARROKHPEY, MAHMOUD (1979). 'A syntactic and semantic study of auxiliaries and modals in modern Persian'. University of Colorado Ph.D. dissertation.

FAST, GERHARD, and RUBY FAST (1981). *Introduccion al idioma Achuar.* Yarinacocha, Pucallpa, Peru: Centro Amazonico de Lenguas Autoctonas Peruanas Hugo Pesce, Instituto de Lingüístico de Verano.

FAUST, NORMA (1971). 'Cocama clause types', in David Bendor-Samuel (ed.), *Tupi Studies, vol. i.* Norman, Okla.: Summer Institute of Linguistics Publications, 73–105.

FEHDERAU, HAROLD WERNER (1966). *The Origin and Development of Kituba (Lingua Franca Kikongo).* Ann Arbor, Mich. University Microfilms.

FELDPAUSCH, TOM, and BECKY FELDPAUSCH (1992). 'Namia grammar essentials', in John R. Roberts (ed.), *Namia and Amanab Grammar Essentials.* (Data Papers on Papua New Guinea Languages 39). Ukarumpa, Papua New Guinea: Summer Institute of Linguistics, 1–103.

FEOKTISOV, A. P. (1966). 'Erzjanskij jazyk' [The Erzja language], in V. V. Vinogradov (ed.), *Jazyki narodov SSSR III.* Moscow: Nauka, 177–98.

FERNANDEZ, FRANK (1968). 'A grammatical sketch of Remo: a Munda language'. University of North Carolina Ph.D. dissertation.

—— (1983). 'The morphology of the Remo (Bonda) verb', *International Journal of Dravidian Linguistics* 12(1): 15–45.

FIELDS, PHILIP C. (1997). 'Pivot and nominalization in Orya', in Karl J. Franklin (ed.), *Papers in Papuan Linguistics, vol. ii.* (Pacific Linguistics A-85), Canberra: Australian National University, 237–69.

FLEMING, HAROLD C. (1976). 'Gonga (Kefa)', in M. L. Bender (ed.), *Non-Semitic Languages of Ethiopia*. East Lansing, Michi.: African Studies Center, 351–76.

—— (1990). 'A grammatical sketch of Dime (Dim-Af) of the Lower Omo', in Richard J. Hayward (ed.), *Omotic Language Studies*. London: School of Oriental and African Studies, 494–583.

—— AKLILU YILMA, AYYALEW MIKITU, RICHARD HAYWARD, YUKIO MIYAKAWI, PAVEL MIKESH, and J. MICHAEL SEELIG (1992). 'Ongota or Birale: a moribund language of Gemu-Gofa (Ethiopia)', *Journal of Afroasiatic Linguistics* 3(3): 181–225.

FOLEY, W. A. (1986). *The Papuan Languages of New Guinea*. Cambridge: Cambridge University Press.

—— and M. OLSON (1985). 'Clausehood and verb serialization', in J. Nichols and A. C. Wooodbury (eds.), *Grammar Inside and Outside the Clause: Some New Approaches to Theory from the Field*. Cambridge: Cambridge University Press, 17–60.

FORD, CAROLYN M. (1991). 'Notes on the phonology and grammar of Chaha-Gurage', *Journal of Afroasiatic Linguistics* 2(3): 231–96.

FORIS, DAVID PAUL (2000). *A Grammar of Sochiapan Chinantec*. (Studies in Chinantec Languages 6); Summer Institute of Linguistics Publications in Linguistics 135) Arlington, Tex.: SIL.

FORTESCUE, MICHAEL (2003). 'The origin and further development of transitive auxiliary verbs in Chukotko-Kamchatkan'. Paper presented at ICHL 16, Copenhagen, Aug. 2003.

FORTUNE, G. (1955). *An analytical grammar of Shona*. London: Longmans Green.

FOURIE, DAVID J. (1993). *Mbalanhu*. (Languages of the World/Materials 3). Munich: Lincom Europa.

FOX, SAMUEL ETHAN (1991). 'The phonology and morphology of the Jilu dialect of Neo-Aramaic', *Journal of Afroasiatic Linguistics* 3(1): 35–57.

FRAJZYNGIER, ZYGMUNT. (1989). *A Grammar of Pero*. Berlin: Reimer.

—— (2001). *A Grammar of Lele*. (Stanford Monographs in African Languages) Stanford, Calif.: Center for the Study of Language and Information.

—— and ERIN SHAY (2002). *A Grammar of Hdi*. Berlin: Mouton de Gruyter.

FRANÇOIS, ALEXANDRE (2002). *Araki: A Disappearing Language of Vanuatu*. (Pacific Linguistics 522) Canberra: Australian National University.

FRANK, PAUL (1990). *Ika Syntax*. (Studies in the Languages of Colombia 1; Summer Institute of Linguistics Publication 93). Arlington, Texas: SIL.

FRANKLIN, KARL J. (1964). 'Kewa verb morphology', in *Verb Studies in Five New Guinea Languages*. Norman, Okla.: Summer Institute of Linguistics, 100–130.

FRANTZ, CHESTER, and HOWARD McKAUGHAN (1964). 'Gadsup independent verb affixes', in *Verb Studies in Five New Guinea Languages*. Norman, Okla.: Summer Institute of Linguistics, 84–99.

FREED, A. F. (1979). *The Semantics of English Aspectual Complementation*. Dordrecht: Reidel.

FURBEE-LOSEE, LOUANNA (1976). *The Correct Language: Tojolabal: A Grammar with Ethnographic Notes*. New York: Garland.

FURBY, CHRISTINE E. (1972). 'The pronominal system of Garawa', *Oceanic Linguistics* 11: 1–32.

VON GABAIN, A. [1941] (1974). *Alttürkische Grammatik.* Wiesbaden: Harrassowitz.

GABAS, NILSON (1999). 'A Grammar of Karo (Tupi, Brazil)'. University of California, Santa Barbara Ph.D. dissertation.

GENETTI, CAROL (1986). 'The syntax of the Newari non-final construction'. University of Oregon MA thesis.

—— (1990). 'A descriptive and historical account of the Dolakha Newari dialect'. University of Oregon Ph.D. dissertation.

—— (2003). 'Dolakhā Newār', in Thurgood and La Polla (2003: 353–70).

GENSLER, ORIN, and TOM GÜLDEMANN (2003). 'S-AUX-O-V-OTHER in Africa: typological and areal perspective'. Paper presented at World Congress of African Linguistics 4, Rutgers University, June 2003.

GERÖ, EVA-CARIN, and ARNIM VON STACHOW (2003). 'Tense in time: the Greek perfect', in Regine Eckardt, Klaus von Heusinger, and Christoph Schwarze (eds.), *Words in Time: Diachronic Semantics from Different Points of View.* Berlin: Mouton de Gruyter, 251–93.

GHOMESHI, JILA (1999). 'An alternative to spec-head agreement'. Paper presented at Western Conference on Linguistics, El Paso, Texas.

GHOSH, A. (1994). *Santali: A Look into Santali Morphology.* New Delhi: Gyan.

GILDEA, SPIKE (1993). 'The rigid VS order of Panare (Cariban): a historical explanation', *International Journal of American Linguistics* 59(1): 44–63.

—— (1998). *On Reconstructing Grammar: Comparative Cariban Morphosyntax.* New York: Oxford University Press.

—— (2003). 'Givonian text counts: the interface between theory and method'. Paper presented at University of Oregon, Nov. 2003.

GILLIES, WILLIAM (1993). 'Scottish Gaelic', in Martin J. Ball and James Fife (eds.), *The Celtic Languages.* (Routledge Language Family Series) London: Routledge, 145–227.

GIRAULT, LOUIS (1989). *Kallawaya: el idioma secreto de los Incas: Diccionario.* La Paz: Unicef, OPS, OMS.

GIVÓN, TALMY (1971). 'On the verbal origin of the Bantu verb suffixes', *Studies in African Linguistics* 2(2): 145–62.

—— (1973). 'The time-axis phenomenon', *Language* 48: 890–925.

—— (1991a). 'Serial verbs and the mental reality of "event": grammatical vs. cognitive packaging', in E. Traugott and B. Heine (eds.), *Approaches to Grammaticalization*, vol. ii. Amsterdam: Benjamins, 91–127.

—— (1991b). 'Some substantive issues concerning verb serialization', in Lefebvre (1991: 137–84).

GLOCK, NAOMI (1972). 'Clause and sentence in Saramaccan', *Journal of African Languages* 11(1): 45–61.

GODDARD, JEAN (1967). 'Agarabi narrative and commentary', in *Papers in New Guinea Linguistics* 7. (Pacific Linguistics A-13) Canberra: Australian National University, 1–25.

GODDARD, JEAN (1980). 'Notes on Agarabi grammar', in *Papers in New Guinea Linguistics* 20. (Pacific Linguistics A-56) Canberra: Australian National University, 35–76.

GOLBERT DE GOODBAR, PERLA (1977). 'Yagán I: las partes de la oración', in *VICUS Cuadernos Lingüistica* 1. Amsterdam: Benjamins, 87–101.

GOLLA, VICTOR (1976). 'Tututni (Oregon Athapaskan)', *International Journal of American Linguistics* 42(3): 217–26.

GONZÁLEZ DE PÉREZ, MARIA STELLA (1987). *Diccionario y gramática chibcha*. Bogota: Instituto Caro y Cuervo.

GRACZYK, R. (1991). 'Incorporation and cliticization in Crow morphosyntax'. University of Chicago Ph.D. dissertation.

GRAGG, GENE (1976). 'Oromo of Wellega', in M. L. Bender (ed.), *Non-Semitic Languages of Ethiopia*. East Lansing, Mich.: African Studies Center, 166–95.

GRANBERRY, J. (1993). *A Grammar and Dictionary of the Timucua Language*. Tuscaloosa: University of Alabama Press.

GRANITES, ROBIN JAPANANGKA, and MARY LAUGHREN (2001). 'Semantic contrasts in Warlpiri verbal morphology: a Walpiri's world view', in J. Simpson et al. (eds.), *40 Years On: Ken Hale and Australian Languages*. Canberra: Australian National University, 151–9.

GREEN, J. N. (1982). 'The status of the Romance auxiliaries of voice', in N. Vincent and M. Harris (eds.), *Studies in the Romance Verb*. London: Croom Helm, 97–138.

GREEN, M. M., and G. E. IGWE (1963). *A Descriptive Grammar of Igbo*. Berlin: Akademic.

GRIERSON, G. A. (1906). *Linguistic Survey of India, vol. iv: Munda and Dravidian*. Calcutta: Office of the Superintendant of Government Printing.

GRUZDEVA, E. (1998). *Nivkh*. Munich: Lincom Europa.

GÜLDEMANN, TOM (2003). 'Present progressive vis-à-vis predication focus in Bantu: a verbal category between semantics and pragmatics', *Studies in Language* 27(2): 323–60.

—— and RAINER VOSSEN (2000). 'Khoisan', in B. Heine and D. Nurse (eds.) *African Languages: An Introduction*. Cambridge: Cambridge University Press, 99–122.

HAAS, MARY R. (1941). 'Tunica', in *Handbook of American Indian Languages, vol. iv*. New York: Augustin.

—— (1977). 'From auxiliary verb phrase to inflectional suffix', in Charles N. Li (ed.), *Mechanisms of Syntactic Change*. Austin: University of Texas Press, 525–37.

—— (1979). 'The auxiliary verb in Natchez', *Berkeley Linguistic Society* 5: 94–105.

HACKER, PAUL (1958). *Zur Funktion einiger Hilfsverben im modernen Hindi*. Mainz: Akademie der Wissenschaften und der Literatur.

HAHN, R., with IBRAHIM ABLAHAT (1991). *Spoken Uyghur*. Seattle: University of Washington Press.

HAIMAN, JOHN (1980). *Hua: A Papuan Language of the Eastern Highlands of New Guinea*. (Studies in Language Companion Series 5) Amsterdam: Benjamins.

HAJI-ABDOLHOSSEINI, M. D. MASSAM, and K. ODA (2002). 'The number of events: verbal reduplication in Niuean', *Oceanic Linguistics* 41(2): 475–92.

HALE, KENNETH (1991). 'Misumalpan verb sequencing constructions', in Lefebvre (1991: 1–35).

—— (1997). 'The Misumalpan causative construction', in J. Bybee, J. Haiman, and S. A. Thompson (eds.), *Essays on Language Type and Language Function, Dedicated to T. Givón*. Amsterdam: Benjamins, 199–216.

HÄMÄLÄINEN, A. (1966). 'Okinukke Inkerin vuotuisjuhlissa', *Kalevalaseuran Vuosikirja* 56: 276–93.

HAMAYA, MITSUYO (1993). 'Maasai auxiliaries and infinitival constructions'. University of Oregon MA thesis.

HAMEL, PATRICIA J. (1994). *A Grammar of Loniu, Papua New Guinea*. (Pacific Linguistics C-103). Canberra: Australian National University.

HANGIN, JOHN G. (1968). *Basic Course in Mongolian*. (Uralic and Altaic Series 73) Bloomington: Indiana University Press.

HANSAR, OSKAR (1977). *Turkmen Manual: Descriptive Grammar of Contemporary Literary Turkmen, Texts, Glossary*. (Beihefte zür Wiener Zeitschrift für die Kunde des Morgenlandes) Vienna: Verlag des Verbandes der wissenschaftlichen Gesellschafter Österreichs.

HARDEMANN, PASCALE (1996). 'Grammaticalisation de la structure *Infinitif* +Verbe_{conjugu} dans quelques langues bantoues', *Studies in African Linguistics* 25(2): 155–69.

HARDMAN, M. J. (2000). *Jaqaru*. (Languages of the World/Materials 183) Munich: Lincom Europa.

HARDY, HEATHER J. (1998). 'Demonstratives and verbal suffixes in Tolkapaya: an outline', in Leanne Hinton and Pamela Munro (eds.), *Studies in American Indian Languages: Description and Theory*. Berkeley: University of California Press, 16–22.

HARGREAVES, DAVID (2003). 'Kathmandu Newar (Nepāl Bhāṣā)', in Thurgood and La Polla (2003: 371–84).

HARMS, ROBERT (1994). *Epena Pedee Syntax*. (Studies in the Languages of Colombia) Arlington, Tex.: Summer Institute of Linguistics.

HARRIEHAUSEN, BETTINA (1990). *Hmong Njua: Syntaktische Analyse einer gesprochenen Sprache mithilfe datenverarbeitungstechnischer Mittel und sprachvergleichende Beschreibung des südostasiatischen Sprachraumes*. Tübingen: Niemeyer.

HARRIES, LYNDON (1940). 'An outline of Mawiha grammar', *African Studies* 14: 91–146; 410–33.

HARRIS, ALICE C. (2002). 'The word in Georgian', in R M. W. Dixon and Alexandra Y. Aikhenvald (eds.), *Word: A Cross-Linguistic Typology*. Cambridge: Cambridge University Press, 227–42.

—— and LYLE CAMPBELL (1995). *Historical Syntax in Crosslinguistic Perspective*. Cambridge: Cambridge University Press.

HARRIS, MARTIN, and PAOLO RAMAT (eds.) (1987). *Historical Development of Auxiliaries*. Berlin: Mouton de Gruyter.

HARRISON, K. DAVID, and GREGORY D. S. ANDERSON (2003). 'Middle Chulym: theoretical aspects, recent fieldwork and current state', *Turkic Languages* 7(2): 245–56.

HARVEY, MARK (2001). *A Grammar of Limilngan, a Language of the Mary River Region, Northern Territory, Australia.* (Pacific Linguistics 516) Canberra: Australian National University.

HASPELMATH, MARTIN (1993). *A Grammar of Lezgian.* (Mouton Grammar Library 9) Berlin: Mouton de Gruyter.

—— (1994). 'Functional categories, X-bar category, and grammaticalization theory', *Sprachtypologie und Universalienforschung* 47(1): 3–15.

—— (1999). 'Why is grammaticalization irreversible?', *Linguistics* 37(6): 1043–68.

HATTORI, S. (1967). 'Personal affixes in the Sakhalin dialect of Ainu', *Linguistics* 29: 58–79.

HAUSENBERG, ANU-REET (1998). 'Komi', in D. Abondolo (ed.), *The Uralic Languages.* (Routledge Language Family series) London: Routledge, 305–26.

HAWKINS, ROBERT E. (1998). 'Wai Wai', in Desmond D. Derbyshire and Geoffrey K. Pullum (eds.), *Handbook of Amazonian Languages*, vol. iv. Berlin: Mouton de Gruyter.

HAYWARD, RICHARD (1990). 'Notes on the Aari Language', in Richard J. Hayward (ed.), *Omotic Language Studies.* London: School of Oriental and African Studies, 425–93.

HAYWARD, RICHARD J. (1989). 'Comparative notes on the language of the S'aamakko', *Journal of Afroasiatic Linguistics* 2(1): 1–53.

HAYWOOD, GRAHAM (1996). 'A Maleu grammar outline and text', in M. Ross (ed.), *Studies in Languages of New Britain and New Ireland.* (Pacific Linguistics C-135) Canberra: Australian National University, 145–95.

HEAD, JUNE (1990). 'Two verbal constructions in Kaugel', *Languages and Linguistics in Melanesia* 21: 99–121.

—— (1993). 'Observations on verb suffixes in Umbu-Ungu', *Languages and Linguistics in Melanesia* 24: 63–72.

HEATH, JEFFREY (1999). *A Grammar of Koyra Chiini: The Songhay of Timbuktu.* Berlin: Mouton de Gruyter.

HEESCHEN, VOLKER (1998). *An Ethnographic Grammar of the Eipo language.* Berlin: Reimer.

HEINE, BERND (1973). *Pidgin-Sprachen im Bantu-Bereich.* (Kölner Beiträge zur Afrikanistik 3) Berlin: Reimer.

—— (1986). 'Bemerkungen zur Entwicklung der Verbaljunkturen im Kxoe und anderen Zentralkhoisan-Sprachen', in R. Vossen and K. Keuthmann (eds.), *Contemporary Studies on Khoisan.* Hamburg: Buske, 9–21.

—— (1993). *Auxiliaries: Cognitive Forces and Grammaticalization.* New York: Oxford University Press.

—— ULRIKE CLAUDI, and FREDERIEKE HÜNNEMEYER (1991). *Grammaticalization: A Conceptual Framework.* Chicago: University of Chicago Press.

—— and TANIA KUTEVA (2002). *World Lexicon of Grammaticalization.* Cambridge: Cambridge University Press.

—— and MECHTHILD REH (1984). *Grammaticalization and Reanalysis in African Languages.* Hamburg: buske.

HELD, WARREN H., WILLIAM R. SCHMALSTEIG, and JANET E. GERTZ (1988). *Beginning Hittite*. Columbus, Ohio: Slavica.

HELIMSKI, EUGENE (1998a). 'Sel'kup', in D. Abondolo (ed.), *The Uralic Languages*. (Rontledge Language Family series) London: Routledge, 548–79.

—— (1998b). 'Nganasan', in D. Abondolo (ed.), *The Uralic Languages*. (Routledge Language Family series) London: Routledge, 480–515.

HENDERSON, EUGÉNIE J. A. (1997). *Bwe Karen Dictionary with Texts and English–Karen word list*. London: School of Oriental and African Studies.

HENDERSON, JAMES (1995). *The Phonology and Grammar of Yele, Papua New Guinea*. (Pacific Linguistics B-112) Canberra: Australian National University.

HENDRIKSEN, HANS (1990). 'Sentence position of the verb in Himachali', *Acta Linguistica Hafniensia* 22: 159–71.

HERCUS, LOUISE A. (1982). *The Bāgandji Language*. (Pacific Linguistics B-67) Canberra: Australian National University.

—— (1994). *A Grammar of the Arabana-Wangkangurru Language, Lake Eyre Basin, South Australia*. (Pacific Linguistics C-128) Canberra: Australian National University.

HIEDA, OSAMU (1991). 'Word order and word order change in Western Nilotic', in Franz Rottland and Lucia A. Omondi (eds.), *Proceedings of the Third Nilo-Saharan Linguistics Colloquium Kisumu, Kenya August 4–9, 1986*. (Nilo-Saharan Linguistic Analyses and Documentation 6) Hamburg: Buske, 97–122.

—— (1998). 'A sketch of Koegu grammar: towards reconstructing Proto-Southeastern Surmic', in Gerrit J. Dimmendaal and Marco Last (eds.), *Surmic Languages and Cultures*. (Nilo-Saharan Linguistic Analyses and Documentation 13) Cologne: Köppe, 345–73.

HILDERS, J. H., and J. C. D. LAWRANCE (1956). *An Introduction to the Teso Language*. Kampala: Eagle Press.

HODDINOTT, W. G., and F. M. KOFOD (1988). *The Ngankikurungkurr language, Daly River Area, Northern Territory*. (Pacific Linguistics D-77) Canberra: Australian National University.

HOLES, CLIVE (1990). *Gulf Arabic*. London: Croom Helm.

HOLMER, ARTHUR J. (1996). *A Parametric Grammar of Seediq*. Lund: Lund University Press.

HOLT, DENNIS (1999a). *Tol (Jicaque)*. (Languages of the World/Materials 170) Munich: Lincom Europa.

—— (1999b). *Pech (Paya)*. (Languages of the World/Materials 366) Munich: Lincom Europa.

HOLTON, GARY (2003). *Tobelo*. (Languages of the World/Materials 328) Munich: Lincom Europa.

HOLZKNECHT, SUSANNE (1989). *The Markham Languages of Papua New Guinea*. (Pacific Linguistics C-115) Canberra: Australian National University.

HOOK, P. E. (1991). 'The compound verb in Munda: an areal overview', *Language Sciences* 13(2): 181–95.

HOPPER, PAUL, and ELIZABETH CLOSS TRAUGOTT (1993). *Grammaticalization*. Cambridge: Cambridge University Press.

HORTON, A. E. (1949). *A Grammar of Luvale*. Johannesburg: Witwatersrand University.

VAN DEN HOUT, THEO (2003). 'Studies in the Hittite phraseological construction I: Its syntactic and semantic properties', in G. Beckman et al. (eds.), *Hittite Studies in Honor of Harry A. Hoffner, Jr. on the Occasion of His 65th Birthday*. Winona Lake, Ind.: Eisenbrauns, 177–203.

HOVDHAUGEN, EVEN (2004). *Mochica*. (Languages of the World/Materials 433) Munich: Lincom Europa.

HOWARD, LINDA (1977). 'Esquema de los tipos de párrafo en camsá', in L. Howard and M. Schöttelndreyer (eds.), *Estudios en camsá y catío*. Lomalinda: Instituto Lingüístico de Verano, 1–67.

HUALDE, JOSE IGNACIO, and JON ORTIZ de URBINA (2003). *A Grammar of Basque*. (Mouton Grammar Library 26) Berlin: Mouton de Gruyter.

HUANG, LILLIAN (1994). 'Ergativity in Atayal', *Oceanic Linguistics* 33(1): 129–43.

HUDDLESTON, R. (1984). *Introduction to the Grammar of English*. Cambridge: Cambridge University Press.

HUDSON, GROVER (1976a). 'Highland East Cushitic', in M. L. Bender (ed.), *Non-Semitic Languages of Ethiopia*. East Lansing, Mich.: African Studies Center, 232–77.

—— (1976b). 'Beja', in M. L. Bender (ed.), *Non-Semitic Languages of Ethiopia*. East Lansing, Mich.: African Studies Center, 96–132.

HUDSON, JOYCE (1978). *The Core of Walmatjarri Grammar*. Canberra: Australian Institute of Aboriginal Studies.

HUDSON, RICHARD (1987). 'Zwicky on heads', *Journal of Linguistics* 23: 109–32.

HURD, CONRAD, and PHYLLIS HURD (1970). 'Nasioi verbs', *Oceanic Linguistics* 9(1): 37–78.

HUREL, EUGÈNE (1911). 'Manuel de langue kinyarwanda', *Mitteilungen des Seminars für Orientalische Sprachen* 14: 1–159.

HYMAN, LARRY M. (1985). 'Dependency relations in syntax: the mysterious case of the empty determiner in Aghem', *Studies in African Linguistics*, supplement 9: 151–6.

IKORO, SUANU (1996). 'The Kana language'. Leiden University Ph.D. dissertation.

INNES, GORDON (1969). *A Mende–English Dictionary*. London: Cambridge University Press.

IRWIN, BARRY (1974). *Salt-Yui Grammar*. (Pacific Linguistics B-35) Canberra: Australian National University.

ITTMANN, JOHANNES, with CARL MEINHOF (1939). *Grammatik des Duala (Kamerun)*. (*Zeitschrift für Eingeborenen-Sprachen* 20) Berlin: Reimer/Hamburg: Friederichsen, de Gruyter.

JACOBSEN, WILLIAM H. Jr. (1964). 'A grammar of the Washo language'. University of California at Berkeley Ph.D. dissertation.

JAMES, DOROTHY (1983). 'Verb serialization in Siane', *Languages and Linguistics in Melanesia* 14: 24–73.

JARRETT, K. A. (1981). 'The development of the Kanuri aspect system within Western Saharan', in Thilo C. Shadeberg and M. Lionel Bender (eds.), *Nilo-Saharan: Pro-*

ceedings of the First Nilo-Saharan Linguistics Colloquium, Leiden, September 8–10, 1980. Dordrecht: Foris, 201–15.

JAUNCEY, DOROTHY (2002). 'Tamabo', in Lynch et al. (2002: 608–25).

JELINEK, ELOISE (1983). 'Person-subject marking in AUX in Egyptian Arabic', in F. Heny and B. Richards (eds.), *Linguistic Categories: Auxiliaries and Related Puzzles, vol. i: Categories*. Dordrecht: Reidel, 21–46.

JOHANSON, LARS (1971). *Aspekt im Türkischen: Vorstudien zu einer Beschreibung des Türkeitürkischen Aspeksystems*. (Studia Turcica Uppsaliensia 1) Lund: Berlingska Boktryckeriet.

—— (1976). 'Zum Präsens der nordwestlichen und mittelasiatischen Türksprachen', *Acta Orientalia* 37: 57–74.

—— (1990). 'Zur Postterminalität türkischer syndetischer Gerundien', *Ural-Altaische Jahrbücher* n.s. 9: 137–51.

—— (1991). 'Zur Typologie türkischer Gerundialsegmente', *Türk Dilleri Arastirmalari*, 98–110.

—— (1992). *Strukturelle Faktoren in Türkischen Sprachkontakten*. Stuttgart: Steiner.

—— (1995). 'Mehrdeutigkeit in der türkischen Verbalkomposition', in M. Erdal and S. Tezcan (eds.), *Beläk Bitig: Sprachstudien für Gerhard Doerfer zum 75. Geburtstag*. (Turcologica 23) Wiesbaden: Harrassowitz, 81–101.

—— (1998). 'History of Turkic', in Lars Johanson and Eva A. Csató (eds.), *The Turkic Languages*. London: Routledge, 81–125.

—— (1999). 'Typological notes on aspect and actionality in Kipchak Turkic', in Werner Abraham and Leonid Kulikov (eds.), *Tense-Aspect, Transitivity, and Causativity: Essays in Honor of Vladimir Nedjalkov*. Amsterdam: Benjamins, 171–84.

JOHNSON, RICHARD (1972). 'The application of matrix analysis to the Kâte verb system', in A. Capell (ed.), *Oceania Linguistic Monographs* 15. Sydney: University of Sydney Press, 132–43.

JONES, A. A. (1998). *Towards a Lexicogrammar of Mekeo (an Austronesian Language of Western Central Papua)*. (Pacific Linguistics C-138) Canberra: Australian National University.

JONES, ROSS MCCALLUM (1998). *The Boko/Busa Language Cluster*. (Lincom Studies in African Linguistics 30) Munich: Lincom Europa.

JOSEPH, BRIAN, and ARNOLD ZWICKY (eds.) (1990). *When Verbs Collide*. Columbus: Ohio State University Press.

JUDY, H. ROBERTO, and JUDIT EMERIC de JUDY (1965). 'Movima', in *Gramaticas estructurales de lenguas bolivianas, vol. ii*. Riberalta, Beni, Bolivia: Instituto Lingüístico de Verano, 131–222.

JULDAŠEV, A. A. (1966). 'Baškirskij jazyk' [The Bashkir language], in Baskakov et al. (1966: 173–93).

—— et al. (1981). *Grammatika sovremennogo bashkirskogo literaturnogo jazyka*. Moscow: Nauka.

JUNG, INGRID (1989). 'Grammatik des Paez: ein Abriss'. University of Osnabrück Ph.D. dissertation.

JUNUSALIEV, B. M. (1966). 'Kirgizskij jazyk' [Kyrgyz language], in Baskakov et al. (1966: 482–505).

KACHRU, YAMUNA (1990). 'Hindi', in Bernard Comrie (ed.), *The World's Major Languages.* Oxford: Oxford University Press, 470–89.

KAHREL, PETER, and RENÉ VAN DEN BERG (eds.) (1994). *Typological Studies in Negation.* Amsterdam: Benjamins.

KAKAMASU, JAMES (1986). 'Urubu-Kaapor', in Desmond D. Derbyshire and Geoffrey K. Pullum (eds.), *Handbook of Amazonian Languages, vol. i.* Berlin: Mouton de Gruyter, 326–403.

KANGASMAA-MINN, EEVA (1998). 'Mari', in Daniel Abondolo (ed.), *The Uralic Languages.* (Routledge Language Family series) London: Routledge, 219–48.

KAPLAN, RONALD M, and JOAN BRESNAN (1995). 'Lexical functional grammar: a formal system for grammatical representation', in Mary Dalrymple, Ronald M. Kaplan, John T. Maxwell III, and Annie Zaenen (eds.), *Formal Issues in Lexical Functional Grammar.* Stanford, Calif.: Center for the Study of Language and Information, 29–130.

KARI, ETHELBERT E. (1997). *Degema.* (Languages of the World/Materials 180) Munich: Lincom Europa.

—— (2000). *Ogbronuagum (The Bukuma Language).* (Languages of the World/Materials 329). Munich: Lincom Europa.

KARSTEN, RAFAEL (1935). *The Head-Hunters of Western Amazonas: The Life and Culture of the Jibaro Indians of Eastern Ecuador and Peru.* Helsingfors: Akademiska Bokhandeln.

KEEGAN, JOHN (1997). *A Reference Grammar of Mbay.* Munich: Lincom Europa.

KEEN, SANDRA (1983). 'Yukulta', in R. M. W. Dixon and Barry J. Blake (eds.), *Handbook of Australian Languages, vol. iii.* Canberra: Australian National University, 191–304.

KEESING, ROGER M. (1985). *Kwaio Grammar.* (Pacific Linguistics B-88) Canberra: Australian National University.

KELLOGG, K. (1990). 'The use of auxiliary verbs in Jamul Diegueño', in *Papers from the 1990 Hokan-Penutian Languages Workshop.* Carbondale: Southern Illinois University Press, 32–42.

KENETHLOW, GWAS (2002). *Cornish Grammar for Beginners and the auxiliary verbs.* Hayle: Kesva an Taves Kernewek.

VAN DER KERKE, SIMON (1998). 'Verb formation in Leko: causative, reflexive, reciprocal', in Leonid Kulikov and Heinz Vater (eds.), *Typology of Verbal Categories: Papers Presented to Vladimir Nedjalkov on the Occasion of his 70th birthday.* Tübingen: Niemeyer, 195–203.

—— (2000). 'Case marking in Leko', in Hein van der Voort and Simon van der Kerke (eds.), *Indigenous Languages of Lowland South America.* Leiden: Leiden University CNWS, 25–37.

KERR, ISABEL J. (1995). *Gramática pedagógica del cuiba-wamonae: lengua indígena de la familia lingüística guahiba de los llanos orientales.* Santafé de Bogotá: Asociación Instituto Lingüístico de Verano.

KEY, HAROLD (1967). *Morphology of Cayuvava.* The Hague: Mouton.

KIAGAWA, CHISATO, and ATSUO IGUCHI (1988). *Jodoshi.* Tokyo: Aratake Shuppan.

KIBRIK, ALEXANDR E., with SERGEJ G. TATEVOSOV and ALEXANDER EULENBERG (1996). *Godoberi.* (Lincom Studies in Caucasian Linguistics 2) Munich: Lincom Europa.

KIHM, ALAIN (2003). 'Inflectional categories in creole languages', in Ingo Plag (ed.), *Phonology and Morphology of Creole Languages.* Tübingen: Niemeyer, 333–63.

KIMBALL, GEOFFREY (1987). 'A grammatical sketch of Apalachee', *International Journal of American Linguistics* 53(2): 136–74.

—— (1991). *Koasati Grammar.* Lincoln: University of Nebraska Press.

KIMENYI, ALEXANDRE (1979). 'Double negation and negative shift in Kinyarwanda', *Studies in African Linguistics* 10(2): 179–96.

—— (1980). *A Relational Grammar of Kinyarwanda.* (University of California Publications in Linguistics 91) Berkeley: University of California Press.

KIRTON, JEAN F., and BELLA CHARLIE (1996). *Further Aspects of the Grammar of Yanyuwa, Northern Australia.* (Pacific Linguistics C-131) Canberra: Australian National University.

KLEIN, PHILIP W. (1981) [1968]. 'Modal auxiliaries in Spanish'. University of Washington MA thesis.

KLIMOV, G. A., and D. I. EDEL'MAN (1970). *Jazyk burušaski* [The Burushaski language]. Moscow: Nauka.

VAN KLINKEN, CATARINA LUMIEN (1999). *A Grammar of the Fehan Dialect of Tetun.* Pacific Linguistics C-155. Canberra: Australian National University.

KNAPPERT, J. (1963). 'The verb in Dhó-Alúr', *Journal of African Languages* 2(2): 103–27.

KÖHLER, OSWIN (1981). 'La langue Kxoe', in Jean Perrot (ed.), *Les Langues dans le monde ancien et moderne, vol. i: Les Langues de l'Afrique subsaharienne.* Paris: Centre National de la Recherche Scientifique, 483–555.

KÖNIG, CHRISTA (2002). *Kasus im Ik.* (Nilo-Saharan Linguistic Analyses and Documentation 17) Cologne: Köppe.

KOOPS, ROBERT, and JOHN T. BENDOR-SAMUEL (1974). 'The recapitulating pronouns in Kuteb', *Journal of West African Languages* 9(1): 5–16.

KORKINA, E. I. et al. (1982). *Grammatika sovremennogo jakutskogo literaturnogo jazyka* [A grammar of modern literary Yakut]. Moscow: Nauka.

KOVEDJAEVA, E. I. (1966). 'Lugovo-vostočnyj Marijskij jazyk' [The Meadow-East Mari language], in V. V. Vinogradov (ed.), *Jazyki narodov SSSR,* vol. iii. Moscow: Nauka, 221–40.

KRISHNAMURTI, BHADRIRAJU (2003). *The Dravidian Languages.* Cambridge: Cambridge University Press.

KROEBER, PAUL D. (1999). *The Salish Language Family.* Lincoln: University of Nebraska Press.

KROEGER, PAUL R. (1988). 'Verbal focus in Kimaragang', in *Papers in Western Austronesian Linguistics 3.* (Pacific Linguistics A-78) Canberra: Australian National University, 217–40.

KUIPER, ALBERTHA, and WILLIAM R. MERRIFIELD (1975). 'Diuxi Mixtec verbs of motion and arrival', *International Journal of American Linguistics* 41(1): 32–45.

KUIPERS, AERT (1967). *The Squamish Language: Grammar, Texts, Dictionary.* The Hague: Mouton.

—— (1974). *The Shuswap Language: Grammar, Texts, Dictionary.* The Hague: Mouton.

KÜNNAP, AGO (1999a). *Enets.* (Languages of the World/Materials 186) Munich: Lincom Europa.

—— (1999b). *Kamass.* (Languages of the World/Materials 185) Munich: Lincom Europa.

KURYŁOWICZ, J. (1965). 'The evolution of grammatical categories', *Diogenes* 51: 55–71.

KUTEVA, TANIA A. (1991). 'The auxiliarization constraint and reference'. Unpublished MS.

—— (2001). *Auxiliation.* Oxford: Oxford University Press.

KUTSCH LOJENGA, CONSTANCE (1994). *Ngiti: A Central-Sudanic Language of Zaire.* (Nilo-Saharan Linguistic Analyses and Documentation 9) Cologne: Köppe.

LAANEST, A. (1975). 'Pribaltyskie-Finnskie jazyki' [Balto-Finnic Languages], in V. I. Lytkin, K. E. Majtinksaja, and K. Redei (eds.), *Osnovy finno-ugorskogo jazykoznanija: Pribaltyjskie, Saamskie, i Mordovskie jazyki.* Moscow: Nauka, 5–122.

LA FAUCI, NUNZIO (1979). *Construzioni con verbo operatore in testi italiani antichi: esplorazioni sintattiche.* Pisa: Giardini.

LAIDIG, WYN D., and CAROL J. LAIDIG (1991). *Tarus Sou Rikedu. Tata Bahasa Larike. Larike Grammar.* Ambon, Maluku, Indonesia: Summer Institute of Linguistics and Pattimura University.

LAMERE, SILVINUS, and TONI METTLER (1994). *Tnyangkwar. Mengenal Bahasa Yamdena-Indonesia-Inggeris. Let's Talk Yamdena.* Ambon, Maluku, Indonesia: Summer Institute of Linguistics.

LANDABURU, JON (1979). *La langue des Andoke (Amazonie colombienne): grammaire.* (Langues et civilisations à tradition orale 36) Paris: Centre National de la Recherche Scientifique.

—— (1994). 'Deux types de prédication, avec ou sans sujet: quelques illustrations colombiennes', in J. Landaburu (ed.), *Estructuras sintácticas de la predicación: lenguas amerindias de Colombia. Bulletin de L'Institut Français d'Études Andines* 23(3): 639–63.

—— (2000). 'La lengua Ika', in M. S. Gozález de Pérez and M. L. Rodríguez de Montes (eds.), *Lenguas indigenas de Colombia.* Bogota: Instituto Caro y Cuervo, 733–48.

LANGACKER, RONALD W. (1977). *Studies in Uto-Aztecan Grammar, vol. i: An Overview of Uto-Aztecan Grammar.* Arlington, Tex.: Summer Institute of Linguistics/University of Texas at Arlington.

—— (1978). 'On the form and meaning of the English auxiliary', *Language* 54(4): 853–84.

—— (1991). *Foundations of Cognitive Grammar, vol. ii: Descriptive Application.* Stanford, Calif.: Stanford University Press.

—— (1998). 'Cognitive grammar meets the Yuman auxiliary', in Leanne Hinton and Pamela Munro (eds.), *Studies in American Indian Languages: Description and Theory.* Berkeley: University of California Press, 41–8.

LANGDON, MARGARET. (1970). *A Grammar of Diegueño: The Mesa Grande Dialect.* (UCPIL 66) Berkeley: University of California Press.

—— (1978). 'Auxiliary verb constructions in Yuman', *Journal of California Anthropology Papers in Linguistics.* Banning, Calif.: Malki Museum, 93–130.

LA POLLA, RANDY (2003). 'Qiang', in Thurgood and La Polla (2003: 573–87).

LASTRA, YOLANDA (1992). *El Otomi de Toluca.* Mexico: Instituto de Investigaciones Antropologicas, Universidad Nacional Autónoma de Mexico.

LAWES, REVD W. G. [1896] (1979). *Grammar and Vocabulary of the Motu Tribe.* Sydney: Charles Potter Government Printer. Repr. Canberra: Australian National University.

LAWRENCE, MARSHALL (1972). 'Structure and function of Oksapmin verbs', *Oceanic Linguistics* 11(1): 47–66.

LAYTON, BENTLEY (2000). *A Coptic Grammar.* Wiesbaden: Harrassowitz.

LEE, ROBERT (1989). 'The Madak verb phrase', *Language and Linguistics in Melanesia* 20: 65–114.

LEFEBVRE, CLAIRE (ed.) (1991). *Serial Verbs: Grammatical, Comparative and Cognitive Approaches.* Amsterdam: Benjamins.

LEGER, RUDOLF (1994). *Eine Grammatik der Kwami-Sprache (Nordostnigeria).* (Westafrikanische Studien. Frankfürter Beiträge zur Sprach-und Kulturgeschichte Band 8) Cologne: Köppe.

LEHMANN, CHRISTIAN (1990). 'Yukatekisch', *Zeitschrift für Sprachwissenschaft* 9: 28–51.

LEITCH, MILES (1994). 'Babole', in Kahrel and van den Berg (1994: 190–210).

LEONT'EV, A. A. (1974). *Papuasskie jayki* [Papuan languages]. Moscow: Nauka.

LESLAU, WCLF (1968). 'The expression of the future in the Ethiopian languages', *Journal of African Languages* 7(1): 68–72.

LETJAGINA, N. I. (1989). 'Vyraženie količestvennyx otnošennij v tuvinskom jazyke (vzaimodejstvie jazykovyx sredstv raznyx urovnej)' [The expression of quantitative relations in Tuvan (the interaction of multiple linguistic levels)], in *Grammatičeskie issledovanija po otdel'nym altajskim jazykam.* Leningrad: Nauka, 59–92.

LEWIS, S. C. (1972). 'Sanio-Hiowe verb phrases', in *Papers in New Guinea Linguistics* 15. (Pacific Linguistics A-31) Canberra: Australian National University, 11–22.

LEYEW, ZELEALEM (2003). *The Kemantney Language: A Sociolinguistic and Grammatical Study of Language Replacement.* (Cushitic Language Studies 20) Cologne: Köppe.

LI, YAFEI (1991). 'On deriving serial verb constructions', in Lefebvre (1991: 103–35).

LICHTENBERK, FRANTISEK (1983). *A Grammar of Manam.* (Oceanic Linguistics Special Publications 18) Honolulu: University of Hawai'i Press.

—— (1985). 'Syntactic-category change in Oceanic languages', *Oceanic Linguistics* 24(1–2): 1–84.

LIGHTFOOT, DAVID (1979). *Principles of Diachronic Syntax.* Cambridge: Cambridge University Press.

LINDSTRÖM, EVA (2002). 'Topics in the grammar of Kuot: a non-Austronesian language of New Ireland, Papua New Guinea'. University of Stockholm Ph.D. dissertation.

LINDSTROM, LAMONT, and JOHN LYNCH (1992). *Kwamera.* (Languages of the World/ Materials 2) Munich: Lincom Europa.

LINN, MARY SARAH (2001). A grammar of Euchee (Yuchi). University of Kansas Ph.D. dissertation.

LLOYD, J. A. (1997). 'Contrastive and grammatically defined tone in Baruya', in Karl J. Franklin (ed.), *Papers in Papuan Linguistics* 2. (Pacific Linguistics A-85) Canberra: Australian National University, 283–361.

LOMBARD, DAAN (1978). 'A diachronic-tonological analysis of certain rank-shifted verbal structures in Northern Sotho', *Studies in African Linguistics* 9(3): 319–28.

LONG, YAOHONG, and ZHENG GUOQIAO (1998). *The Dong Language in Guizhou Province, China*, trans. by D. Norman Geary. Arlington, Tex.: Summer Institute of Linguistics.

LOOS, EUGENE E. (1999). 'Pano', in R. M. W. Dixon and A. Y. Aikhenvald, (eds.), *The Amazonian Languages*. Cambridge: Cambridge University Press, 227–50.

LORD, CAROL (1993). *Historical Change in Serial Verb Constructions*. (Typological Studies in Language 26) Amsterdam: J Benjamins.

LORIMER, D. A. (1935–8). *The Burushaski Language*. 3 vols. Oslo: Aschenhoug.

LOUBSER, JACQUES EMIL (1961). *Die saamgestelde verbale vorm van Nederlands na Afrikaans*. Groningen: Wolters.

LOUW, J. A. (1963). 'n Vergelykende Studie van die Defisiënte Verbum in die Ngunitale'. University of Stellenbosch D.Litt. thesis.

—— et al. (1967). *A Handbook of the Zulu Language*. Pretoria: Van Schaik.

LOUWERSE, JOHN (1988). *The Morphosyntax of Una in Relation to Discourse: A Descriptive Analysis*. (Pacific Linguistics B-100) Canberra: Australian National University.

LOVING, RICHARD and HOWARD MCKAUGHAN (1964a). 'Awa verbs, part i: Inflectional structure of independent verbs', in Alan R. Pence (ed.), *Verb Studies in Five New Guinea Languages*. Norman, Okla.: Summer Institute of Linguistics, 1–30.

—— —— (1964b). 'Awa verbs, part ii: Inflectional structure of dependent verbs', in Alan R. Pence (ed.), *Verb Studies in Five New Guinea Languages*. Norman, Okla.: Summer Institute of Linguistics, 31–44.

LOWE, IVAN (1999). 'Nambiquara', in R. M. W. Dixon and A. Y. Aikhenvald (eds.), *The Amazonian Languages*. Cambridge: Cambridge University Press, 269–92.

LYDALL, JEAN (1976). 'Hamer', in M. L. Bender (ed.), *Non-Semitic languages of Ethiopia*. East Lansing, Mich.: African Studies Center, 393–438.

LYNCH, JOHN (2000). *A Grammar of Anejom̃*. (Pacific Linguistics 507) Canberra: Australian National University.

—— (2002a). 'Anejom̃', in Lynch et al.(2002: 723–52).

—— (2002b). 'Iaai', in Lynch et al. (2002: 776–91).

—— (2002c). 'Ulithian', in Lynch et al. (2002: 797–803).

—— MALCOLM ROSS, and TERRY CROWLEY (eds.) (2002). *The Oceanic Languages*. London: Curzon.

MACAULAY, M. (1996). *A Grammar of Chalcatongo Mixtec*. (UCPIL 127) Berkeley: University of California Press.

MACDONALD, GEORGE E. (1974). 'The Teberan language family', in Karl Franklin (ed.), *The Linguistic Situation in the Gulf District and Adjacent Areas, Papua New Guinea*. (Pacific Linguistics C-26) Canberra: Australian National University, 111–48.

MacDonald, Lorna (1990). *A Grammar of Tauya*. (Mouton Grammar Library 6) Berlin: Mouton de Gruyter.

MacKay, Carolyn J. (1999). *A Grammar of Misantla Totonac*. (Studies in Indigenous Languages of the Americas) Salt Lake City: University of Utah Press.

MacLaury, Robert E. (1989). 'Zapotec body-part locatives: prototypes and metaphoric extensions', *International Journal of American Linguistics* 55(2): 119–54.

Magomedov, A. A. (1982). *Megebskij dialekt darginskogo jazyka*. Tbilisi: Mecniereba.

Mahapatra, K., with Dobek Pujari and P. K. Panda (1989). *Ḍiḍayi*. Bhubaneshwar: Academy of Tribal Dialects and Culture, Government of Orissa.

Mahapatra, K. P., and N. H. Zide (n.d.). *Gtaʔ Texts*. Unpublished MS.

Malhotra, V. (1982). 'The structure of Kharia: a study in linguistic typology and change'. Jawaharlal Nehru University Ph.D. dissertation.

Malla, K. P. (1985). *The Newari Language*. (Momunenta Serindica 14, Institute for the Study of Languages and Cultures of Asia and Africa) Tokyo: Tokyo University of Foreign Studies.

Manelis Klein, H. (2001). *Toba*. Munich: Lincom Europa.

Manohoran, S. (1989). *A Descriptive and Comparative Study of Andamanese Language*. Calcutta: Anthropological Survey of India.

Manrique C., Leonardo. (1967). 'Jiliapan Pame', in Norman A. McQuown (ed.), *Handbook of Middle American Indians, vol. v: Linguistics*. Austin: University of Texas Press, 331–48.

Marchese, Lynell (1982). 'Basic aspectual categories in Proto-Kru', *Journal of West African Languages* 12(1): 3–23.

—— (1986). *Tense/Aspect and the Development of Auxiliaries in Kru Languages*. (Summer Institute of Linguistics Publication 78) Arlington, Tex.: SIL.

Marlett, Stephen A. (1986). 'Syntactic levels and multiattachment in Sierra Popoluca', *International Journal of American Linguistics* 52(4): 359–88.

—— (1990). 'Person and number inflection in Seri', *International Journal of American Linguistics* 56(4): 503–41.

—— and Velma B. Pickett (1987). 'The syllable structure and aspect morphology of Isthmus Zapotec', *International Journal of American Linguistics* 53(4): 398–422.

Maslova, Elena (2003a). *Tundra Yukaghir*. (Languages of the World/Materials 372) Munich: Lincom, Europa.

—— (2003b). *Kolyma Yukaghir*. (Mouton Grammar Library 27) Berlin: Mouton de Gruyter.

Matseke, A. K. (1968). *Setswana sa ka Metlha*. Johannesburg: Better Books.

Matson, D. (1964). 'A grammatical sketch of Juang'. University of Wisconsin Ph.D. dissertation.

Mayorga, Susana Yang (1979). 'A study of auxiliary verbs in Mandarin Chinese: a proposal for instruction and materials preparation'. Florida State University, thesis.

Mazaudon, Martine (2003). 'Tamang', in Thurgood and La Polla (2003: 291–314).

McClelland, Clive W. III (2000). *The Interrelations of Syntax, Narrative Structure, and Prosody in a Berber Language*. Lewiston, NY: Mellen.

McClendon, Sally (1996). 'Sketch of Eastern Pomo, a Pomoan Language', in Ives Goddard (ed.), *Handbook of North American Indians*, xvii: *Languages*. Washington, DC: Smithsonian Institution, 507–50.

McConvell, Patrick, and Eva Schultze-Berndt (2001). 'Complex verb convergence and bilingual interaction in the Victoria River District, Australia'. Paper presented at the Symposium on Linguistic Perspectives on Endangered Languages, Helsinki, Aug. 2001.

McElhanon, K. A. (1967). 'Preliminary observations on Huon Peninsula languages', *Oceanic Linguistics* 6(1): 1–45.

—— (1970). 'Selepet verb morphology', in *Papers in New Guinea Linguistics* 12. (Pacific Linguistics A-25) Canberra: Australian National University, 19–35.

McGregor, William (2001). 'Structural changes in language obsolescence: a Kimberley (Australia) perspective'. Paper presented at the Symposium on Linguistic Perspectives on Endangered Languages, Helsinki, Aug. 2001.

—— (2002). *Verb Classification in Australian Languages*. Berlin: Mouton de Gruyter.

McKaughan, Howard (ed.) (1973a). *The Languages of the Eastern Family of the East New Guinea Highlands Stock*, vol. i. Anthropological Studies in the Eastern Highlands of New Guinea) Seattle: University of Washington Press.

—— (1973b). 'Auyana texts', in McKaughan (1973a: 324–89).

McKay, Graham (2000). 'Ndjébbana', in R. M. W. Dixon and Barry J. Blake (eds.), *Handbook of Australian Languages*, vol. v. Oxford: Oxford University Press, 155–354.

McKee, Robert G. (1991). ' "Here", "there" "Yonder", and beyond with Meje aspect', in Franz Rottland and Lucia A. Omondi (eds.), *Proceedings of the Third Nilo-Saharan Linguistics Colloquium Kisumu, Kenya August 4–9, 1986*. (Nilo-Saharan Linguistic Analyses and Documentation 6) Hamburg: Buske, 165–80.

McQuown, Norman A. (1967). 'Classical Yucatec (Maya)', in Norman A. McQuown (ed.), *Handbook of Middle American Indians, vol. v: Linguistics*. Austin: University of Texas Press, 201–47.

Meinhof, Carl (1948). *Grundzüge einer vergleichenden Grammatik der Bantusprachen. Zweite Völlig Umgearbeitete Auflage*. Hamburg: Eckardt & Messtorff.

Menges, Karl H. (1968). *The Turkic Languages and Peoples: An Introduction to Turkic Studies*. (Veröffentlichungen des Societas Uralo-Altaica 42) Wiesbaden: Harrassowitz (2nd edn. 1995).

Menick, Raymond (1995). 'Moi: A language of the West Papuan phylum: a preview', in Connie Baak, Mary Bakker, and Dick van der Meij (eds.), *Tales From a Concave World: Liber Amicorum Bert Voorhoeve*. Leiden: Leiden University Press, 55–73.

Merlan, Francesca C. (1979). 'On the prehistory of some Australian verbs', *Oceanic Linguistics* 18(1): 33–79.

—— (1982). *Mangarayi*. (Lingua Descriptive Studies 4) Amsterdam: North-Holland.

—— (1994). *A Grammar of Wardaman: A Language of the Northern Territory of Australia*. (Mouton Grammar Library 11) New York: Mouton de Gruyter.

—— (2001). 'Form and context in Jawoyn placenames', in J. Simpson et al. (eds.), *40 Years On: Ken Hale and Australian Languages*. Canberra: Australian National University, 367–83.

MFUMBWA BESHA, RUTH (1989). *A Study of Tense and Aspect in Shambala.* (Language and Dialect Studies in East Africa 10) Berlin: Reimer.

MICHAILOVSKY, BOYD (2003). 'Hayu', in Thurgood and La Polla (2003: 518–32).

MIGEOD, F. W. H. (1908). *The Mende Language.* London: Kegan Paul, Trench, Trübner.

MILLER, AMY (2001). *A Grammar of Jamul Tiipay.* Berlin: Mouton de Gruyter.

MILLER, MARION (1999). *Desano Grammar.* (Studies in the Languages of Colombia 6: Summer Institute of Linguistics Publication 132) Arlington, Tex.: SIL.

MILNE, Mrs L. (1921). *Palaung Grammar.* Oxford: Clarendon Press.

MINCH, ANDY (1992). 'Amanab grammar essentials', in John R. Roberts (ed.), *Namia and Amanab Grammar Essentials.* (Data Papers on Papua New Guinea Languages 39) Ukarumpa: Summer Institute of Linguistics, Papua New Guinea 105–73.

MITHUN, MARIANNE (1999). *The Languages of Native North America.* Cambridge: Cambridge University Press.

MIXCO, MAURICIO (1997). *Mandan* (Languages of the World/Materials 159) Munich: Lincom Europa.

MIXCO, MAURICIO J. (1985). 'The Kiliwa resumptive aspect and nondistinct arguments', *International Journal of American Linguistics* 51(4): 508–10.

MKHATSHWA, SIMON NYANA LEON (1991). 'Metaphorical extensions as a basis for grammaticalization. With special reference to Zulu auxiliary verbs'. University of South Africa, Pretoria, MA thesis.

MONTLER, TIMOTHY (2003). 'Auxiliaries and other categories in Straits Salishan', *International Journal of American Linguistics* 69(2): 103–34.

MOORE, DENNY (1994). 'A few aspects of comparative Tupí syntax', *Revista Latinoamericana de Estudios Etnolingüísticos* 8: 151–62.

MOOSALLY, MICHELLE (1998). 'Noun phrase coordination: Ndebele agreement patterns and cross-linguistic variation'. University of Texas Ph. D. dissertation.

MORPHY, FRANCES (1983). 'Djapu, a Yolngu dialect', in R. M. W. Dixon and Barry J. Blake (eds.), *Handbook of Australian Languages, vol. iii.* Canberra: Australian National University, 1–188.

MORSE, NANCY L., and MICHAEL B. MAXWELL (1999). *Cubeo Grammar.* (Studies in the Languages of Colombia 5; Summer Institute of Linguistics Publication 130) Arlington, Tex.: SIL.

MORTENSEN, CHARLES A. (1999). *Northern Embera Languages.* (Studies in the Languages of Colombia 7; Summer Institute of Linguistics Publication 134) Arlington, Tex.: SIL.

MOSER, MARY B. (1978). 'Switch reference in Seri', *International Journal of American Linguistics* 44(2): 113–20.

MUFWENE, SALIKOKO S. (1978). 'A reconsideration of Lingala temporal inflections', *Studies in African Linguistics* 9(1): 91–105.

—— (1991). 'On the status of auxiliary verbs in Gullah'. Paper presented at Linguistic Society of America/Society for Pidgin and Creole Languages meeting, Chicago.

MÜLLER, REIMAR and MARGA REIS (2001). *Modalität und Modalverben im Deutschen.* Hamburg: Buske.

MUNDHENK, NORMAN ARTHUR (1967). *Auxiliary Verbs in Myang of Northern Thailand.* Hartford, Conn.: Hartford Theological Seminary.

MUNRO, PAMELA (1976a). *Mojave Syntax.* New York: Garland.

—— (1976b). 'Subject copying, auxiliarization, and predicate raising: the Mojave evidence', *International Journal of American Linguistics* 42(2): 99–112.

—— (2003). 'The clausal status of zero-marked complements in Chickasaw'. Paper presented at Society for the Study of the Indigenous Languages of the Americas, Atlanta, Georgia, Jan. 2003.

MURANE, ELIZABETH (1974). *Daga Grammar.* Norman, Okla.: Summer Institute of Linguistics.

MURATORI, P. CARLO (1938). *Gramatica Lotuxo.* Verona: Missioni Africane.

MUYSKEN, PIETER (1977). *Syntactic Developments in the Verb Phrase of Ecuadorian Quechua.* Lisse: Ridder.

MYHILL, J. (1988). 'The grammaticalization of auxiliaries: Spanish clitic climbing', *Berkeley Linguistics Society* 14: 352–63.

NADŽIP, E. N. (1971). *Modern Uigur.* Moscow: Nauka.

NAÏT-ZERRAD, K. (1996). *Grammaire de berbiri contemporain, vol. ii: Syntaxe.* Algiers: Entreprise Nationale des Arts Graphiques.

NAJLIS, ELENA (1973). *Lengua selknam.* Buenos Aires: Universidad del Salvador.

NAKANO, YASUHIKO (2003). 'Cogste Gyarong', in Thurgood and La Polla (2003: 467–89).

NEBEL, P. A. (1948). *Dinka Grammar (Rek-Malual Dialect) with Texts and Vocabulary.* (Museum Combonianum) Verona: Missioni Africane.

NEVSKAJA, IRINA A. (1993). *Formy deepričastnogo tipa v šorskom jazyke* [Forms of the 'gerund' type in Shor]. Novosibirsk: NGU.

—— (2000). 'Shor–Russian contact features', in Dicky Gilbers et al. (eds.), *Languages in Contact.* (Studies in Slavic and General Linguistics 28) Amsterdam: Rodopi, 283–98.

NEWMAN, JOHN (ed.) (2002). *The Linguistics of Sitting, Standing, Lying.* Amsterdam: Benjamins.

NEWMAN, STANLEY (1967). 'Classical Nahuatl', in Norman A. McQuown (ed.), *Handbook of Middle American Indians, vol. v: Linguistics.* Austin: University of Texas Press, 179–99.

—— (1996). 'Sketch of the Zuni Language', in Ives Goddard (ed.), *Handbook of North American Indians, vol. xvii: Languages.* Washington, DC: Smithsonian Institution, 483–506.

NICHOLS, JOHANNA (1986). 'Head-marking and dependent-marking grammar', *Language* 62: 56–119.

NIKOLAEVA, IRINA (1999). *Ostyak.* (Languages of the World Munich: Lincon Europa. Materials 305).

—— and MARIA TOLSKAJA (2001). *A Grammar of Udihe.* (Mouton Grammar Library 22) Berlin: Mouton de Gruyter.

NOONAN, MICHAEL (1992). *A Grammar of Lango.* Berlin: Mouton de Gruyter.

—— (2003a). 'Chantyal', in Thurgood and La Polla (2003: 315–35).

—— (2003b). 'Nar-Phu', in Thurgood and La Polla (2003: 336–52).

NORDLINGER, RACHEL (1998). *A Grammar of Wambaya, Northern Territory (Australia)*. (Pacific Linguistics C-140) Canberra: Australian National University.

NURSE, DEREK (1979a). *Classification of the Chaga Dialects*. Hamburg: Buske.

—— (1979b). 'Description of sample Bantu languages of Tanzania', *African Languages (Langues Africaines)* 5: 1–150.

—— (2003). 'Aspect and tense in Bantu languages', in D. Nurse and G. Phillipson (eds.), *The Bantu Languages*. London: Routledge, 90–102.

—— and ROTTLAND, FRANZ (1994). 'Sonjo: description, classification, history', *Sprache und Geschichte in Afrika* 12/13 1991/1992: 171–290.

OBANDO ORDÓÑEZ, PEDRO VICENTE (1992). 'Awa-Kwaiker: an outline grammar of a Colombian/Ecuadorian language, with a cultural sketch'. University of Texas at Austin Ph.D. dissertation.

OBILADE, TONY (1977). 'On the logical structure of the serial verb construction in Yoruba', *Berkeley Linguistics Society* 3: 386–93.

ÖHLSCHLÄGER, GÜNTHER (1989). *Zur Syntax und Semantik der Modalverben des Deutschen*. Tübingen: Niemeyer.

OLAWSKY, KNUT J. (2002). *Urarina Texts*. (Languages of the World/Text Collections 17) Munich: Lincom Europa.

O'NEIL, J. (1935). *A Shona Grammar*. London: Longmans, Green.

ONISHI, MASAYUKI, with DORA LESLIE and THERESE MINITONG KEMELFIELD (2003). *Motuna Texts*. Kyoto: Nakanishi.

ONO, TSUYOSHI (1996). 'Information flow and grammatical structure in Barbareño Chumash'. University of California at Santa Barbara Ph.D. dissertation.

ORTIZ RICAURTE, C. (1994). 'Clases y tipos de predicados en la lengua kogui', in J. Landaburu (ed.), *Estructuras sintácticas de la predicación: lenguas amerindias de Colombia. Bulletin de L'Institut Français d'Études Andines* 23(3): 377–99.

ORWIN, MARTIN (1995). *Colloquial Somali: A Complete Language Course*. London: Routledge.

OSADA, TOSHIKI (1992). *A Reference Grammar of Mundari*. Tokyo: Institute for the Study of Languages and Cultures of Asia and Africa.

OTTAVIANO, JOHN C., and IDA OTTAVIANO (1967). 'Tacana', in Ester Matteson (ed.), *Bolivian Indian Grammars, vol. i*: Summer Institute of Linguistics Publications in Linguistics and Related Fields 16. Norman, Okla.: SIL, 139–207.

OWENS, JONATHAN (1985). *A Grammar of Harar Oromo*. Hamburg: Buske.

OZAWA, SHIGEO (1965). *Auxiliary Verbs in a- and bü-in Middle Mongolian: A Study in the Difference between their Sememes*. Tokyo: Tokyo Gaikokugo Daigaku.

PALANCAR, ENRIQUE (2004). 'Middle voice in Otomi', *International Journal of American Linguistics* 70(1): 52–85.

PALMER, BILL (1996). 'Notes on mood and aspect in Simbo [Mandeghusu, Solomon Islands]', in John Lynch and Fa'afo Pat (eds.), *Oceanic Studies: Proceedings of the First International Conference on Oceanic Linguistics*. (Pacific Linguistics C-133) Canberra: Australian National University, 249–70.

PALMER, BILL (2002). 'Kokota', in Lynch et al. (2002: 498–524).

PALMER, F. R. (1974). *The English Verb*. London: Longman.

—— (1979). 'Why auxiliaries are not main verbs', *Lingua* 47: 1–25.

PARAMASIVAM, K., and J. LINDHOLM (1980). *A Basic Tamil Reader and Grammar*. Evanston, Ill.: Tamil Language Study Association.

PARK, INSUN (1994). 'Grammaticalization of verbs in three Tibeto-Burman languages'. University of Oregon Ph.D. dissertation.

PARKS, DOUGLAS (1976). *A Grammar of Pawnee*. New York: Garland.

PAROZ, R. A. (1946). *Elements of S. Sotho*. Basutoland: Morija Sesuto Book Depot.

PATAČAKOVA, D. F. (ed.) (1973). *Xakas tılınıŋ dialekterı: Dialekty xakasskogo jazyka* [Dialects of Xakas]. Abakan: XakNIIJaLI.

—— (1984). 'Deepričastnye formy v xakasskom jazyke' [Gerund forms in Xakas], in M. I. Borgojakov et al. (eds.), *Voprosy xakasskogo literaturnogo jazyka*. Abakan: XakNIIJaLI, 89–113.

PATZ, ELISAZBETH (2002). *A Grammar of the Kuku Yalanji language of North Queensland*. (Pacific Linguistics 527) Canberra: Australian National University.

PAYNE, DORIS L., and THOMAS E. PAYNE (1990). 'Yagua', in Desmond D. Derbyshire and G. Pullum (eds.), *Handbook of Amazonian Languages, vol. ii*. Berlin: Mouton de Gruyter, 249–467.

PAYNE, JOHN R. (1985). 'Negation', in T. Shopen (ed.), *Language Typology and Syntactic Description, vol. i: Clause Structure*. Cambridge: Cambridge University Press, 197–242.

PEEKE, [M.] CATHERINE (1962). 'Structural summary of Záparo', in B. F. Elson (ed.), *Studies in Ecuadorian Indian Languages, vol. i*. Norman, Okla.: Summer Institute of Linguistics, 125–216.

—— (1994). 'Waorani', in Kahrel and van den Berg (1994: 267–90).

PEÑALOSA, FERNANDO (1987). 'Major syntactic structures of Acatec (dialect of San Miguel Acatán)', *International Journal of American Linguistics* 53(3): 281–310.

PENSALFINI, ROBERT (2003). *A Grammar of Jingulu, an Aboriginal Language of the Northern Territory*. (Pacific Linguistics 536) Canberra: Australian National University.

PERKINS, REVERE D. (2001). 'Sampling procedures and statistical methods', in Martin Haspelmath, Ekkehard König, Wulf Oesterreicher, and Wolfgang Raible (eds.), *Language Typology and Linguistic Universals: An International Handbook, vol. i*. Berlin: de Gruyter, 419–34.

PERSSON, ANDREW M., and JANET R. PERSSON (1991). *Mödö–English Dictionary with Grammar*. (Bilingual Dictionaries of Sudan 1) Nairobi: Summer Institute of Linguistics-Sudan.

PETERSON, D. A. (1999). 'The morphosyntactic status of dative subjects in Ingush'. Paper presented at the 1st Biennial Chicago Conference on Caucasia, May 1999.

PETERSON, DAVID (2003). 'Hakha Lai', in Thurgood and La Polla (2003: 409–26).

PETERSON, JOHN (to appear). 'Kharia', in Gregory D. S. Anderson (ed.), *The Munda Languages*. London: Routledge.

PETROVA, T. I. (1967). *Jazyk orokov (ul'ta)* [The language of the Orok (ul'ta]]. Leningrad: Nauka.

—— (1968). 'Orokskij jazyk' [The Orok language], in V. V. Vinogradov (ed.), *Jazyki narodov SSSR V.* Leningrad: Nauka, 172–90.

PHINNEMORE, PENNY (1988). 'Coordination in Ono', *Languages and Linguistics of Melanesia* 19(1–2): 97–123.

PHINNEY, ARCHIE (1934). *Nez Perce texts.* (Columbia University Contributions to Anthropology 25) New York: Columbia University Press.

PIKE, EUNICE V. (1967). 'Huautla de Jiménez Mazatec'. In Norman A. McQuown (ed.), *Handbook of Middle American Indians*, vol. v: *Linguistics.* Austin: University of Texas Press, 311–30.

PINNOW, H. J. (1960). *Beiträge zur Kenntnis der Juang-Sprache.* Unpublished MS.

PLAISIER, HELENE (2003). 'Lepcha', in Thurgood and La Polla (2003: 705–16).

PLUNGIAN, VLADIMIR. (1995). *Dogon.* Munich: Lincom Europa.

PODLESSKAJA, VERA (2001). 'Conditional constructions', in Martin Haspelmath et al. (eds.), *Language Typology and Language Universals: An International Handbook*, vol. ii. Berlin: de Gruyter, 998–1010.

POLINSKY, MARIA (1995). 'Agreement in Tsez: the trivial and the unusual'. Paper presented at NSL 9, Chicago, May 1995.

POLLOCK, JEAN-YVES (1989). 'Verb movement, Universal Grammar, and the structure of the clause', *Linguistic Inquiry* 20: 365–424.

PONTES, EUNICE (1973). *Verbos auxiliares em portugues.* Petrópolis: Vozes.

POPJES, JACK, and JO POPJES (1986). 'Canela-Krahô', in Desmond C. Derbyshire and Geoffrey K. Pullum (eds.), *Handbook of Amazonian Languages, vol. i.* Berlin: Mouton de Gruyter, 128–99.

PRESS, IAN (1986). *A Grammar of Breton.* Berlin: Mouton de Gruyter.

PRITSAK, OMELJAN (1959). 'Das Abakan-türkische (Chakassische)', in Jean Deny, Kaare Grønbeck, Helmuth Scheel, and Seki Velidi Togan (eds.), *Philologiae turcicae fundamenta*, vol. i. Aquis Mattiacis: Steiner, 598–622.

PROST, ANDRÉ (1964). *Contribution à l'étude des langues voltaïques.* (Mémoires de l'Institut Français d'Afrique Noire 70) Dakar: IFAN.

PROST, GILBERT R. (1967). 'Chacobo', in Ester Matteson (ed.), *Bolivian Indian Grammars, vol. i:* Summer Institute of Linguistics Publications in Linguistics and Related Fields 16. Norman, Okla.: SIL, 285–359.

PRYOR, BONITA, and CINDI FARR (1989). 'Botin deictics: go and come', *Languages and Linguistics in Melanesia* 20: 115–45.

PRYOR, J. (1990). 'Deixis and participant tracking in Botin', *Languages and Linguistics in Melanesia* 21: 1–29.

PULLUM, GEOFFREY, and DEIRDRE WILSON (1977). 'Autonomous syntax and the analysis of auxilaries', *Language* 53: 741–88.

QINGXIA, DAI, and LON DIEHL (2003). 'Jinghpo', in Thurgood and La Polla (2003: 401–8).

QUEIXALOS, FRANCESCO (2002). 'Sobre um sujeito Katukina e um objeto Sikuani', in Ana Cabral and Suelly Arruda Câmara (eds.), *Línguas indígenas brasileiras: fonolo-*

gia, gramática e história. Atas do I Encuentro Internacional do Grupo de Trabalho sobre Línguas Indígenas da ANPOLL, vol. ii. Belém-Pará: Editoria Universitaria UFPA, 260–70.

RADFORD, ANDREW (1997). *Syntax: A Minimalist Introduction.* Cambridge: Cambridge University Press.

RADIN, PAUL (1929). *A Grammar of the Wappo Language.* (University of California Publications in American Archaeology and Ethnology 27) Berkeley: University of California Press.

RAJASEKHARAN NAIR, N. (1990). *Auxiliary Verbs in Malayalam.* Annamalainagar: Annamalai University.

RAMAMURTI, G. V. (1931). *A Manual of the So:ra: (or Savara) Language.* Madras: Govt. Press.

RAMAT, PAOLO (1987). 'Introductory paper', in M. Harris and P. Ramat (eds.), *Historical Developments of Auxiliaries.* Berlin: Mouton de Gruyter, 3–19.

RANDAL, SCOTT (1998). 'A grammatical sketch of Tennet', in Gerrit J. Dimmendaal and Marco Last (eds.), *Surmic Languages and Cultures.* (Nilo-Saharan Linguistic Analyses and Documentation 13) Cologne: Köppe, 219–72.

RANKIN, ROBERT, JOHN BOYLE, RANDOLPH GRACZYK, and JOHN KOONTZ (2002). 'Synchronic and diachronic perspectives on "word" in Siouan', in R. M. W. Dixon and Alexandra Y. Aikhenvald (eds.), *Word: A Cross-Linguistic Typology.* Cambridge: Cambridge University Press, 180–204.

RASSADIN, V. I. (1971). *Fonetika i leksika tofalarskogo jazyka* [Phonetics and lexicon of Tofalar]. Ulan-Ude: BurjatsKoe Knizhnoe izdatel'stvo.

—— (1978). *Morfologija tofalarskogo jazyka v sravnitel'noj osveščenii* [The morphology of Tofalar in a comparative light]. Moscow: Nauka.

—— (1990). *Syltyschyk* [Little Star]. Irkutsk: Vostochno-sibirskoe knizhnoe izdatel'stvo.

—— (1994). *Töræœn soot* [Native Word]. Irkutsk: Vostochno-sibirskoe knizhnoe izdatel'stvo.

—— (1997). 'Tofalarskij jazyk' [The Tofa language], in E. R. Tenišev et al. (eds.), *Jazyki Mira: Tjurkskie jazyki.* Moscow: Indrik, 371–82.

REDDEN, JAMES E. (1979). *A Descriptive Grammar of Ewondo.* (Occasional Papers in Linguistics 4). Carbondale: Department of Linguistics, Southern Illinois University.

REESINK, GER (1994). 'Domain-creating constructions in Papuan languages', in Ger Reesink (ed.), *Topics in Descriptive Papuan Linguistics*, Semaian 10. Leiden: Vakgroep Talen en Culturen van Zuidoost-Azië en Oceanië, 98–121.

REESINK, GER P. (1999). *A Grammar of Hatam: Bird's Head Peninsula, Irian Jaya.* (Pacific Linguistics C-146) Canberra: Australian National University.

—— (2002). 'A grammar sketch of Sougb', in Ger P. Reesink (ed.), *Languages of the eastern Bird's Head.* (Pacific Linguistics 524) Canberra: Australian National University, 181–275.

REH, MECHTHILD (1996). *Anywa Language: Description and Internal Reconstructions.* (Nilo-Saharan Linguistic Analyses and Documentation 11) Cologne: Köppe.

REINEKE, BRIGITTE (1972). *The Structure of the Nkonya Language.* Leipzig: VEB Verlag Enzyklopädie.

RENCK, G. L. (1975). *A Grammar of Yagaria.* (Pacific Linguistics B-40) Canberra: Australian National University.

RENKER, ANN M. (1987). 'Rethinking noun and verb: an investigation of "AUX" in a Southern Wakashan language'. American University Ph.D. dissertation.

RICE, KEREN (1989). *A Grammar of Slave.* Berlin: Mouton de Gruyter.

—— (2000). 'Voice and valency in the Athapaskan family', in R. M. W. Dixon and Alexandra Y. Aikhnevald (eds.), *Changing Valency: Case Studies in Transitivity.* Cambridge: Cambridge University Press, 173–235.

RICH, R. (1999). *Diccionario Arabela-Castellano.* (Serie Lingüística Peruana 49) Lima: Instituto Lingüístico de Verano.

RIESE, TIMOTHY (1998). 'Permian', in Daniel Abondolo (ed.), *The Uralic Languages.* (Routledge Language Family series) London: Routledge: 249–75.

RIJKHOFF, JAN et al. (1993). 'A method of language sampling', *Studies in Language* 17: 169–203.

—— and DIK BAKKER (1998). 'Language sampling', *Linguistic Typology* 2(2–3): 263–314.

ROBERTS, H. [1891] (1995). *A Grammar of the Khasi Language.* New Delhi: Mittal.

ROBERTS, IAN (1985). 'Serial verbs and Government Binding theory', *Studies in African Linguistics*, Supplement 9: 262–8.

ROBERTS, JOHN (1997). 'Switch reference in Papua New Guinea', in Andrew Pawley (ed.), *Papers in Papuan Linguistics*, vol. iii. (Pacific Linguistics A-87) Canberra: Australian National University, 101–241.

RODRIGUES, ARYON D. (1999a). 'Tupí', in R. M. W. Dixon and A. Y. Aikhenvald (eds.), *The Amazonian Languages.* Cambridge: Cambridge University Press, 107–24.

—— (1999b). 'Macro-Jê', in R. M. W. Dixon and A. Y. Aikhenvald (eds.), *The Amazonian Languages.* Cambridge: Cambridge University Press, 165–206.

ROJAS CURIEUX, T. (1994). 'Expresión de la categoría de tiempo gramatical en el predicado nasa yuwe (lengua páez)', in J. Landaburu (ed.), *Estructuras sintácticas de la predicación: lenguas amerindias de Colombia. Bulletin de L'Institut Français d'Études Andines* 23(3): 567–600.

ROMERO-FIGEROA, ANDRÉS (1997). *A Reference Grammar of Warao.* (Lincom Studies in Native American Linguistics 6) Munich: Lincom Europa.

DE ROP, A. (1963). *Introduction à la linguistique bantoue congolaise.* Brussels: Mimosa.

ROSCH E. (1978). 'Principles of categorization', in E. Rosch and B. B. Lloyd (eds.), *Cognition and Categorization.* Hillsdale, NJ: Erlbaum, 27–48.

ROSS, J. R. (1969). 'Auxiliaries as main verbs', in W. Todd (ed.), *Studies in Philosophical Linguistics*, series I. Evanston, Ill.: Great Expectations, 77–102.

ROSS, MALCOLM (1980). 'Some elements of Vanimo: a New Guinea tone language', *Papers in New Guinea Linguistics* 20. (Pacific Linguistics A-56) Canberra: Australian National University, 77–109.

Ross, Malcolm D. (1982a). 'Aspect-marking in New Ireland: towards a historical reconstruction', in *Gava': Studies in Austronesian Languages and Cultures dedicated to Hans Kähler.* Berlin: Reimer, 173–96.

—— (1982b). 'The development of the verb phrase in the Oceanic languages of the Bougainville region', in Amran Halim, Lois Carrington, and S. A. Wurm (eds.), *Papers from the Third International Conference on Austronesian Linguistics, vol. i: Currents in Oceanic.* (Pacific Linguistics C-74) Canberra: Australian National University, 1–57.

—— (2002a). 'Kele', in Lynch et al. (2002: 123–47).

—— (2002b). 'Kaulong' in Lynch et al. (2002: 387–409).

—— with John Natu Paol (1978). *A Waskia Grammar Sketch with Vocabulary.* (Pacific Linguistics B-56) Canberra: Australian National University.

Rubino, Carl R. G. (1997). 'A reference grammar of Ilocano'. University of California Santa Barbara Ph.D. dissertation.

Rude, Noel (1985). 'Studies in Nez Perce grammar and discourse'. University of Oregon Ph.D. dissertation.

—— (1986). 'Topicality, transitivity, and the direct object in Nez Perce', *International Journal of American Linguistics* 52(2): 124–53.

Rudin, Catherine (1983). '*Da* and the category AUX in Bulgarian', in Frank Heny and Barry Richards (eds.), *Linguistic Categories: Auxiliaries and Related Puzzles, vol. i: Categories.* Dordrecht: Reidel, 3–20.

Rumsey, Alan (2000). 'Bunuba', in R. M. W. Dixon and Barry J. Blake (eds.), *Handbook of Australian Languages, vol. v.* Oxford: Oxford University Press, 35–152.

Sadock, Jerrold M. (1998). 'Grammatical tension', *CLS* 34: *The Panels.* Chicago: Chicago Linguistics Society, 179–98.

Sag, Ivan A., and Carl Pollard (1989). 'Subcategorization and head-driven phrase structure', in Mark R. Baltin and Anthony S. Kroch (eds.), *Alternative Concepts of Phrase Structure.* Chicago: University of Chicago Press, 139–81.

Sakel, Jeanette (2003). 'A Grammar of Mosetén'. Nijmegen University Ph.D. dissertation.

Salone, Sukari (1979). 'Typology of conditionals and conditionals in Haya', *Studies in African Linguistics* 10(1): 65–80.

Saltarelli, Mario (1988). *Basque.* London: Croom Helm.

Samarin, William J. (1967). *A Grammar of Sango.* (Janua Linguarum, Series Practica 38) The Hague: Mouton.

Sarma, Taranatha (1980). 'The auxiliary in Nepali'. University of Wisconsin Ph.D. dissertation.

Sasse, Heinz-Jürgen (1976). 'Dasenech', in M. L. Bender (ed.), *Non-Semitic Languages of Ethiopia.* East Lansing, Mich.: African Studies Center, 196–221.

Sat, S. C. (1966). 'Tuvinskij jazyk' [The Tuvan language], in Baskakov et al. (1966: 387–402).

Saunders, Ross, and Philip W. Davis (1982). 'The control system of Bella Coola', *International Journal of American Linguistics* 48(1): 1–15.

SAWADA, HARUMI (1995). *Studies in English and Japanese Auxiliaries: A Multi-stratal Approach.* Tokyo: Hitsuji Shobo.

SCEBOLD, ROBERT A. (2003). *Central Tagbanwa: A Philippine Language on the Brink of Extinction. Sociolinguistics, Grammar and Lexicon.* Manila: Linguistic Society of the Philippines.

SCHACHTER, PAUL (1974). 'A non-transformational account of serial verbs', *Studies in African Linguistics,* supplement 5: 253–70.

—— (1985). 'Parts-of-speech systems', in T. Shopen (ed.), *Language Typology and Syntactic Description, vol. i: Clause Structure.* Cambridge: Cambridge University Press, 3–61.

SCHAEFER, RONALD P., and RICHARD MASAGBOR (1984). 'The forms of negation in North Ibie and their functions', *Journal of West African Languages* 14(2): 27–42.

SCHAUB, WILLI (1985). *Babungo.* London: Croom Helm.

SCHILLER, ERIC (1990). 'On the definition and distribution of serial verb constructions', in B. Joseph and A. Zwicky (eds.), *When Verbs Collide.* Columbus: Ohio State University Press, 34–64.

SCHMIDT, HANS (2002). 'Rotuman', in Lynch et al. (2002: 815–32).

SCHNEEBERG, NAN (1971). 'Sayanci verb tonology', *Journal of African Languages* 10(1): 87–100.

SCHÖNIG, CLAUS (1984). *Hilfsverben im Tatarischen.* Wiesbaden: Steiner.

SCHUH, RUSSELL G. (1976). 'The Chadic verbal system and its Afroasiatic nature', *Journal of Afroasiatic Linguistics* 3(1): 1–14.

SCHULTZE-BERNDT, EVA (2000). 'Simple and complex verbs in Jaminjung: a study of event categorisation in an Australian language'. Katholieke Universiteit Nijmegen Ph.D. thesis.

SEBBA, MARK (1987). *The Syntax of Serial Verbs.* Amsterdam: Benjamins.

SEILER, WALTER (1983/4). 'Topic marking in the Papuan language of Imonda', *Oceanic Linguistics* 22/3(1–2): 151–74.

—— (1985). *Imonda, a Papuan Language.* (Pacific Linguistics B-93) Canberra: Australian National University.

SENFT, GUNTHER (1986). *Kilivila.* Berlin: Mouton de Gruyter.

—— (2004). 'What do we really know about serial verb constructions in Austronesian and Papuan languages?', in Bril and Ozanne-Rivierre (2004: 49–64).

SETSHEDI, JACOB EDIASEFAGWA (1974). 'The auxiliary verbs and the deficient verbs in Tswana'. University of the North, Pietersburg, MA thesis.

SEUREN, PIETER (1990). 'Serial verb constructions', in B. Joseph and A. Zwicky (eds.), *When Verbs Collide.* Columbus: Ohio State University Press, 14–33.

SEV, GÜLSEL (2001). *Etmek fiiliyle yapilan birleski fiiller ve tamlayicilarla kullanilisi. The use of determinatives and compound verb forms with etmek.* Ankara: TDK.

SHAKYA, DAYA R. (1992). 'Nominal and verbal morphology in six dialects of Newari'. University of Oregon MA thesis.

SHAMINA, L. A. (1995). 'Analitičeskie konstrukcii modal'no-infinitivnogo tipa v tuvinskom jazyke' [Analytic constructions of the modal-infinitive type in Tuvan], in M. N. Čeremisina (ed.), *Jazyki korennyx narodov Sibiri.* Novosibirsk: RAN, 52–67.

SHANIDZE, A. (1976). *Dzveli kartuli enis gramat'ik'a* [Grammar of the Old Georgian language]. Tbilisi: Tbilisi University Press.

SHARMA, D. D. (1988). *A Descriptive Grammar of Kinnauri.* (Studies in Tibeto-Himalayan Languages 1). Delhi: Mittal.

SHARPE M. R. L. (1980). *Everyday Sesotho Grammar.* Morija, Lesotho: Morija Sesuto Book Depot.

SHAUL, DAVID (1995). 'The Huelel (Esselen) language', *International Journal of American Linguistics* 61: 191–239.

SHAW, KAREN (1974). 'Grammatical notes on Samo', in Karl Franklin (ed.), *The Linguistic Situation in the Gulf District and Adjacent Areas, Papua New Guinea.* (Pacific Linguistics C-26) Canberra: Australian National University, 214–16.

SHCHERBAKOVA, A. M. (1954). 'Formy otritsanija v nenetskom jazyke' [Negative forms in Nenets], *Učenye zapiski Leningradskogo gospedinstituta imeni Gertsena* 101: 181–231.

SHIBATANI, M. (1990). *The Languages of Japan.* Cambridge: Cambridge University Press.

SHOEMAKER, JACK S., and NOLA K. SHOEMAKER (1967). 'Essejja', in Ester Matteson (eds.), *Bolivian Indian Grammars*, vol. i.: Summer Institute of Linguistics Publications in Linguistics and Related Fields 16. Norman, Okla.: SIL, 209–83.

SIMONCSICS, PÉTER (1998). 'Kamassian', in Daniel Abondolo (ed.), *The Uralic Languages.* (Routledge Language Family Series) London: Routledge, 580–601.

SKORIK, P. J. (1986). 'Kategorii imeni sushchestvitel'nogo v chukotsko-kamchatskix jazykax' [Categories of the noun in Chukotko-Kamchatkan languages], in P. J. Skorik (ed.), *Paleoaziatskie jazyki.* Novosibirsk: Akademija Nauk SSSR, 76–111.

SKRIBNIK, ELENA (2003). 'Buryat', in Juha Janhunen (ed.), *The Mongolic Languages.* (Routledge Language Family series) London: Routledge, 102–28.

SKVORCOV, M. I. (1999). *Chavashla-vyralsa tata vyrasla-chavashla slovar'.* [Chuvash—Russian and Russian–Chuvash dictionary] Cheboksary: Chuvknizdat.

SLATTERY, H. (1981). *Auxiliary verbs in Zulu.* (Communication 10) Department of African Languages, Rhodes University, Grahamstown, South Africa.

SMEETS, CATHARINA J. M. A. (1989). 'A Mapuche grammar'. Leiden University Ph.D. dissertation.

SMITH, IAN, and STEVE JOHNSON (2000). 'Kugu Nganhcara', in R. M. W. Dixon and Barry J. Blake (eds.), *Handbook of Australian Languages*, vol. v. Oxford: Oxford University Press, 355–489.

SONG, JAE JUNG (2001). *Linguistic Typology: Morphology and Syntax.* (Longmans Linguistics Library) Harlow: Pearson.

SOOKGASEM, PRAPA (1990). 'Morphology, syntax and semantics of auxiliaries in Thai'. University of Arizona Ph.D. dissertation.

SPAGNOLO, L. M. (1933). *Bari Grammar.* Verona: Missioni Africane.

SPARING-CHÁVEZ, MARGARETHE W. (1998). 'Amahuaca (Panoan)', in Desmond C. Derbyshire and Geoffrey K. Pullum (eds.), *Handbook of Amazonian Languages, vol. iv.* Berlin: Mouton de Gruyter, 441–85.

SPERLICH, WOLGANG B. (1993). 'Serial verb constructions in Namakir of Central Vanuatu', *Oceanic Linguistics* 32(1): 97–110.

STAPPERS, LEO (1964). *Morfologie van het Songye*. (Annales Linguistiques 51) Tervuren: Musée Royal de l'Afrique Centrale.

STEELE, S. (1978). 'The category AUX as a language universal', in J. Greenberg (ed.), *Universals of Human Language*, vol. iii. Stanford, Calif.: Stanford University Press, 7–45.

STEELE, S. M., A. AKMAJIAN, R. DEMERS, E. JELINEK, C. KITAGAWA, R, OEHRLE, and T. WASOW (1981). *An Encyclopedia of AUX: A Study in Cross-Linguistic Equivalence.* (Linguistic Inquiry Monographs 5) Cambridge, Mass.: MIT Press.

STEELE, SUSAN. (1977). 'Clisis and diachrony', in Charles N. Li (ed.), *Mechanisms of Syntactic Change*. Austin: University of Texas Press, 539–79.

—— (1994). 'Auxiliary verbs', in R. E. Asher and J. M. Y. Simpson (eds.), *Encyclopedia of Language and Linguistics*. Oxford, Pergamon Press: 284–90.

STEEVER, SANFORD (1988). *The Serial Verb Formation in the Dravidian Languages*. Delhi: Motilal Banarsidass.

—— (1997). Gondi in S. Steever (ed.), *The Dravidian Languages*. London: Routledge, 270–97.

STERK, JAN P. (1994). *Gade–English Dictionary including English–Gade Reference Dictionary and Summary of Gade Grammar*. (Sprache und Oralität in Afrika 15) Berlin: Reimer.

STERNER, JOYCE, and MALCOLM ROSS (2002). 'Sobei', in John Lynch, Malcolm Ross, and Terry Crowley (eds.), *The Oceanic Languages*. London: Curzon, 167–85.

STOLZ, T., and C. STOLZ (2001). 'Mesoamerica as a linguistic area', in Martin Haspelmath et al. (eds.), *Language Typology and Language Universals: An International Handbook*, vol. ii. Berlin: de Gruyter, 1539–54.

STRANGE, DAVID (1973). 'Indicative and subjunctive in Upper Asaro', *Linguistics* 110: 82–97.

STREHLOW, T. G. H. (1943–4). 'Aranda grammar', *Oceania* 13: 71–103, 177–200, 310–61 and Oceania 14: 68–90, 159–81, 250–6.

STROM, CLAY (1992). *Retuarã Syntax*. (Studies in the Languages of Colombia 3); Summer Institute of Linguistics Publication 112 Arlington, Tex.: SIL.

SUAREZ, JORGE A. (1983a). *La lengua tlapaneca de Malinaltepec*. Mexico: Universidad Nacional Autónoma de Mexico.

—— (1983b). *The Mesoamerican Indian Languages*. Cambridge: Cambridge University Press.

SUH, YOUNGHWAN (2000). 'A study of the auxiliary verb constructions and verb serialization in Korean'. University of Washington Ph.D. dissertation.

SUN, JACKSON T. S. (2003). 'Tani languages', in Thurgood and La Polla (2003: 456–66).

SUSNIK, BRANISLAVA (1977). *Lengua-Maskoy. Su Hablar. Su Pensar. Su Vivencia*. (Lenguas Chaqueñas 6) Asuncion del Paraguay: Museo Etnografico Andres Barbero.

SUSNIK, BRANKA J. (1957). *Estructura de la lengua Chamacoco-Ebitqso*. (Boletin de la Sociedad Cientifica del Paraguay Volumen 1. Etnolinguistica I) Asuncíon: Museum Andres Barbero Etnografico e Historico Natural.

SWEETSER, EVE E. (1988). 'Grammaticalization and semantic bleaching', *Berkeley Linguistics Society* 14: 389–405.

TAKATA, MASAHIRO, and YUKO TAKATA (1991). *Dahlang dal Kola relih. Percakapan dalam bahasa Kola. Kola Conversations.* Ambon, Maluku, Indonesia: Summer Institute of Linguistics and Pattimura University.

TAUBERSCHMIDT, GERHARD (1999). *A Grammar of Sinaugoro: An Austronesian Language of the Central Province of Papua New Guinea.* (Pacific Linguistics C-143) Canberra: Australian National University.

TAYLOR, CHARLES (1985). *Nkore-Kiga.* London: Croom Helm.

TERRILL, ANGELA (2002). *Dharumbal: The Language of Rockhampton, Australia.* (Pacific Linguistics 525) Canberra: Australian National University.

—— (2003). *A Grammar of Lavukaleve.* (Mouton Grammar Library 30) Berlin: Mouton de Gruyter.

THARP, DOUG (1996). 'Sulka grammar essentials', in John Clifton (ed.), *Two Non-Austronesian Grammars from the Islands.* (Data Papers on Papua New Guinea Languages 42) Ukarumpa, Papua New Guinea: Summer Institute of Linguistics, 77–179.

THIESEN, W. (1996). *Gramática del idioma Bora.* (Serie Lingüística Peruana 38) Yarinacocha, Pucallpa: Instituto Lingüístico de Verano.

THOMAS, E. (1978). *A Grammatical Description of the Engenni Language.* Arlington, Tex.: Summer Institute of Linguistics.

THOMPSON, CHAD (1993) 'The areal prefix *hʉ* in Koyukon Athapaskan', *International Journal of American Linguistics* 59(3): 315–41.

THOMPSON, E. DAVID (1976). 'Nera', in M. L. Bender (ed.), *Non-Semitic Languages of Ethiopia.* East Lansing, Mich.: African Studies Center, 484–94.

THOMPSON, LAURENCE, and M. TERRY THOMPSON (1992). *The Thompson Language.* (University of Montana Occasional Papers in Linguistics 8) Missoula: University of Montana Press.

THOMSEN, M. L. (1984). *The Sumerian Language: An Introduction to Its History and Grammatical Structure.* Copenhagen: Akademisk (2nd edn. 2001).

THURGOOD, GRAHAM, and RANDY LA POLLA (eds.) (2003). *Sino-Tibetan Languages.* (Routledge Language Family series) London: Routledge.

TIFFOU, E., and Y.-C. MORIN (1982). 'A note on split ergativity in Burushaski', *Bulletin of the School of Oriental and African Studies* 45: 88–94.

TODD, EVELYN, S. A. WURM, and LOIS CARRINGTON (eds.) (1982). *Second International Conference on Austronesian Linguistics: Proceedings,* Fascicle ii: *Eastern Austronesian.* (Pacific Linguistics C-61) Canberra: Australian National University, 1181–1206.

TOMIĆ, OLGA MIŠESKA (2004). 'The syntax of the Balkan Slavic Future tenses', *Lingua* 114: 517–42.

TORREND, J. (1891). *A Comparative Grammar of the South African Bantu Languages. Comprising Those of Zanzibar, Mozambique, The Zambezi, Kafirland, Benguela, Angola, The Congo, The Ogowe, The Cameroons, The Lake Region, etc.* London: Kegan, Paul, Trench, Trübner.

TOSCO, MAURO (1991). *A Grammatical Sketch of Dahalo.* (Cushitic Language Studies 8) Hamburg: Buske.

TRASK, R. L. (1999). *Key Concepts in Language and Linguistics.* London: Routledge.

TRAUGOTT, ELIZABETH C., and BERND HEINE (eds.) (1991). *Approaches to Grammaticalization.* (2 vols.) Amsterdam: Benjamins.

TRILLOS AMAYA, MARIA (1997). *Categorias gramaticales del ette taara: lengua de los chimilas.* Bogota: Universidad de los Andes, Centro Colombiano de Estudios de Lenguas Aborigenes.

TROIKE, RUDOLPH (1996). 'Coahuilteco (Pajalate)', in I. Goddard (ed.), *Handbook of North American Indians, vol. xvii: Languages.* Washington, DC: Smithsonian Institution, 644–65.

TRYON, DARREL (2002). 'Buma', in Lynch et al. (2002: 573–86).

TRYON, D. T. (1974a). *Daly Family Languages, Australia.* (Pacific Linguistics C-32) Canberra: Australian National University.

—— (1974b). 'Mullukmulluk', in Tryon (1974a: 1–23).

—— (1974c). 'Tyeraity', in Tryon (1974a: 24–41).

—— (1974d). 'Matngala', in Tryon (1974a: 42–55).

—— (1974e). 'Yunggor', in Tryon (1974a: 56–61).

—— (1974f). 'Kamor', in Tryon (1974a: 62–9).

—— (1974g). 'Marithiel', in Tryon (1974a: 70–93).

—— (1974h). 'Marityabin', in Tryon (1974a: 94–100).

—— (1974i). 'Maramanandji', in Tryon (1974a: 104–19).

—— (1974j). 'Marengar', in Tryon (1974a: 120–37).

—— (1974k). 'Maranunggu', in Tryon (1974a: 138–57).

—— (1974l). 'Ami', in Tryon (1974a: 159–73).

—— (1974m). 'Manda', in Tryon (1974a: 174–86).

—— (1974n). 'Pungupungu', in Tryon (1974a: 187–205).

—— (1974o). 'Wadyiginy', in Tryon (1974a: 206–27).

—— (1974p). 'Ngengomeri', in Tryon (1974a: 251–64).

TSUNODA, TASAKU (1981). *The Djaru Language of Kimberley, Western Australia.* (Pacific Linguistics B-78) Canberra: Australian National University.

TUCKER, A. N. (1994). *A Grammar of Kenya Luo (Dholuo),* ed. Chet A. Creider. (Nilo-Saharan Linguistic Analyses and Documentation 8) Cologne: Köppe.

TUCKER, A. N., and J. T. OLE MPAAYEI (1955). *A Maasai Grammar with Vocabulary.* London: Longmans.

TUCKER, ARCHIBALD N., with P. E. HACKETT (1959). *Le Groupe linguistique Zande.* (Annales du Musée Royale du Congo Belge 8.22), Tervuren: MRCB.

TUGGY, S. (1982). 'Las secuencias temporales y lógicas en candoshi', in M. Wise and H. Boonstra (eds.), *Conjunciones y otros nexos en tres idiomas Amazónicos.* (Serie Lingüística Peruana 19) Pucallpa: Instituto Lingüístico de Verano, 37–75.

TURTON, D. J., and M. L. BENDER (1976). 'Mursi', in M. L. Bender (ed.), *Non-Semitic Languages of Ethiopia.* East Lansing, Mich.: African Studies Center, 533–61.

TWADDELL, W. F. (1963). *The English Verb Auxiliaries*. Providence, RI: Brown University Press.

TYBYKOVA, A. T. (1966). *Slozhnye glagoly v altajskom jazyke* [Complex verbs in Altai]. Gorno-Altajsk: Altknizdat.

UBRJATOVA, E. I. (1985). *Jazyk noril'skix dolgan* [The language of the Norilsk Dolgan]. Novosibirsk: Nauka.

UNSETH, PETE (1989). 'Sketch of Majang syntax', in M. Lionel Bender (ed.), *Topics in Nilo-Saharan Linguistics*. (Nilo-Saharan Linguistic Analyses and Documentation 3) Hamburg: Buske, 97–128.

—— (1991). 'Reduplication in Majang', in Franz Rottland and Lucia A. Omondi (eds.), *Proceedings of Third Nilo-Saharan Linguistics Colloquium Kisumu, Kenya August 4–9, 1986*. (Nilo-Saharan Linguistic Analyses and Documentation 6). Hamburg: Buske, 239–62.

UZAR, HENNING (1989). 'Studies in Gumuz: Sese phonology and TMA system', in M. Lionel Bender (ed.), *Topics in Nilo-Saharan Linguistics*. (Nilo-Saharan Linguistic Analyses and Documentation 3) Hamburg: Buske, 347–83.

VÄÄRI, E. E. (1966). 'Livskij jazyk' [Livonian language], in V. V. Vinogradov (ed.), *Jazyki narodov SSSR III*. Moscow: Nauka, 138–54.

VAJDA, EDWARD J. (2000). 'Aktantnye sprjazhenija v ketskom jazyke' [Actant conjugations in Ket], *Voprosy jazykoznanija* 67(3): 21–41.

—— (2001). 'The role of position class in Ket verb morphophonology', *Word* 52(3): 369–436.

—— (2003). 'Ket verb structure in typological perspective', in Edward J. Vajda and Gregory D. S. Anderson (eds.), *Studia Yeniseica*, special issue of *Sprachtypologie und Universalienforschung* 56(2): 55–92.

VALENTE, JOSE FRANCISCO (1964). *Gramática umbundu*. Lisbon: Junta de Investigações do Ultamar.

VANDAME, CHARLES (1963). *Le Ngambay-Moundou: phonologie, grammaire et textes*. (Mémoires de l'Institut Français d'Afrique Noire 69) Dakar: IFAN.

VÁSQUEZ DE RUIZ, BEATRIZ (1988). *La predicación en guambiano*. Bogota: Universidad de los Andes, Centro Colombiano de Estudios de Lenguas Aborigenes.

—— (1994). 'La oración compuesta en guambiano', in J. Landaburu (ed.), *Estructuras sintácticas de la predicación: lenguas amerindias de Colombia*. *Bulletin de L'Institut Français d'Études Andines* 23(3): 619–37.

VELLARD, JEHAN A. (1967). *Contribución al estudio de la lengua Uru*. Buenos Aires: Universidad de Buenos Aires Facultad de Filosofia y letras Centro de Estudios Lingüísticos.

VERHAAR, J. (1988). 'Syntactic ergativity in contemporary Indonesian', in Richard McGinn (ed.), *Studies in Austronesian Linguistics*. (Monographs in International Studies Southeast Asia) Athens: Ohio University, 347–84.

VERNER, G. K. (1997). 'Ketskij jazyk' [The Ket language], in A. P. Volodin et al. (eds.), *Jazyki Mira: Paleoaziatskie jazyki*. Moscow: Indrik, 177–87.

VIITSO, TIIT-REIN (1998). 'Estonian', in Daniel Abondolo (ed.), *The Uralic Languages*. (Routledge Language Family series) London: Routledge, 115–48.

VINCENT, ALEX (1973). 'Tairora verb structure', in McKaughan (1973a: 561–87).

VINCENT, NIGEL (1982). 'The development of the auxiliaries *habere* and *esse* in Romance', in Nigel Vincent and Martin Harris (eds.), *Studies in the Romance Verb*. London: Croom Helm, 71–96.

VOEGELIN, CHARLES F. (1935). 'Tübatulabal grammar'. *University of California Publications in American Archaeology and Ethnology* 34: 55–190. Berkeley: University of California Press.

VOELTZ, F. K. ERHARD (1980). 'The etymology of the Bantu perfect', in Luc Bouquiaux (ed.), *L'expansion bantoue, Viviers (France), 4–16 avril 1977*, vol. ii. Paris: Société d'Études Linguistiques et Anthropologiques de France, 487–92.

VOLKER, CRAIG A. (1998). *The Nalik Language of New Ireland, Papua New Guinea*. New York: Lang.

VOORHOEVE, C. L. (1965). *The Flamingo Bay Dialect of the Asmat Language*. The Hague: s-Gravenhage: Nijhoff.

VAN DER VOORT, HEIN (2004). *A Grammar of Kwaza*. Berlin: Mouton de Gruyter.

VORBICHLER, ANTON (1971). *Die Sprache der Mamvu*. (Afrikanistiche Forschungen 5) Glückstadt: Augustin.

VORMANN, FRANZ, and W. SCHARFENBERGER (1914). *Die Monumbo-Sprache: Grammatik und Wörterverzeichnis*. (Anthropos 1). Vienna: Mechitharisten Buchdruckerei.

VOSSEN, RAINER (1997). *Die Khoe-Sprachen: Ein Beiträg zur Erforschung der Sprachgeschichte Afrikas*. (Quellen zur Khoisan-Forschung 12) Cologne: Köppe.

DE VRIES, JAMES A., and SANDRA A. DE VRIES (1997). 'An overview of Kwerba verb morphology', in A. Pawley (ed.), *Papers in Papuan Linguistics*, iii. (Pacific Linguistics A-87) Canberra: Australian National University, 1–35.

DE VRIES, LOURENS (1993). *Forms and Functions in Kombai, an Awyu Language of Irian Jaya*. (Pacific Linguistics B-108) Canberra: Australian National University.

—— (1993). *Forms and Functions in Kombai, an Awyu language of Irian Jaya*. Canberra: Australian National University Press.

WAGNER, DONNA (1985). 'Objects in Gokana', *Studies in African Linguistics* supplement 9: 304–8.

WARNER, A. (1993). *English Auxiliaries: Structure and History*. Cambridge: Cambridge University Press.

WATAHOMIGIE, LUCILLE J., JOROGINE BENDER, AKIRA Y. YAMAMOTO et al. (1982). *Hualapai Reference Grammar*. Los Angeles, Calif.: American Indian Studies Center, University of California Los Angeles.

WATERHOUSE, VIOLA (1967). 'Huamelultec Chontal', in Norman A. McQuown (ed.), *Handbook of Middle American Indians, vol. v: Linguistics*. Austin: University of Texas Press.

WATKINS, LAUREL (1984). *A Grammar of Kiowa*. Lincoln: University of Nebraska Press.

—— (1976). 'Position in grammar: sit, stand, lie', *Kansas Workpapers in Linguistics* 1: 16–41.

WATKINS, T. ARWYN (1993). 'Welsh', in Martin J. Ball and James Fife (eds.), *The Celtic Languages*. (Routledge Language Family descriptions) London: Routledge, 289–348.

WATTERS, DAVID E. (2002). *A Grammar of Kham*. Cambridge: Cambridge University Press.

—— (2003). 'Kham', in Thurgood and La Polla (2003: 683–704).

WATTERS, JOHN R. (2000). 'Syntax', in B. Heine and D. Nurse (eds.), *African Languages: An Introduction*. Cambridge: Cambridge University Press, 194–230.

WEBER, D. J. (1989). *A Grammar of Huallaga (Huánaco) Quechua*. (UCPIL 112) Berkeley: University of California Press.

WECHSLER, STEPHEN (1999). 'Gender resolution in coordinate structures', in C. Smith (ed.), *Proceedings of the Workshop on the Structure of Spoken and Written Texts*. Austin: University of Texas Press, 1–22.

WEGNER, ILSE (2000). *Hurritisch: Eine Einführung*. Wiesbaden: Harrassowitz.

WEIMER, HARRY (1972). 'Yareba verb morphology', *Te Reo* 15: 58–70.

WELMERS, WILLIAM E. (1973). *African Language Structures*. Berkeley: University of California Press.

WERNER, HEINRICH (1997a). *Das Jugische (Sym-Ketische)*. Wiesbaden: Harrassowitz.

—— (1997b). *Die ketische Sprache*. (Tunguso-Sibirica 3) Wiesbaden: Harrassowitz.

WESTERMANN, DIEDRICH (1907). *Grammatik der Ewe-Sprachen*. Berlin: Reimer.

WHEATLEY, JULIAN K. (2003). 'Burmese', in Thurgood and La Polla (2003: 195–207).

WHITEHEAD, CARL R. (1991). 'Tense, aspect, mood and modality: verbal morphology in Menya', in Tom Dutton (ed.), *Papers in Papuan linguistics* 1. (Pacific Linguistics A-73) Canberra: Australian National University, 245–311.

WHITELEY, W. H. (1966). *A Study of Yao Sentences*. Oxford: Clarendon Press.

WICHMANN, SØREN (2003). 'The grammaticalization and reanalysis of a paradigm of auxiliaries in Texistepec Popoluca: a case study in diachronic adaptation', *SKY Journal of Linguistics* 16: 161–83.

—— (to appear). 'Tlapanec cases', in *Proceedings from the Conference on Otomanguean and other Oaxacan languages*. Survey of California and Other Indian Languages.

WIEMER, BJÖRN (1998). 'Pragmatical inferences at the threshold to grammaticalization: the case of Lithuanian predicative participles and their functions', *Linguistica Baltica* 7: 229–43.

WIERING, ELISABETH, and MARINUS WIERING (1994). *The Doyayo Language: Selected Studies*. Arlington, Tex.: Summer Institute of Linguistics.

WILLIAMS, CORINNE J. (1980). *A Grammar of Yuwaalaraay*. (Pacific Linguistics B-74) Canberra: Australian National University.

WILSON, DARRYL (1974). *Suena Grammar*. (Workpapers in Papua New Guinea Linguistics 8) Ukarumpa, Papua New Guinea: Summer Institute of Linguistics.

WILSON, PATRICIA R. (1980). *Ambulas Grammar*. (Workpapers in Papua New Guinea Linguistics 26) Ukarumpa, Papua New Guinea: Summer Institute of Linguistics.

WISE, MARY RUTH (1986). 'Grammatical characteristics of preAndine Arawakan languages of Peru', in Desmond C. Derbyshire and Geoffrey K. Pullum (eds.), *Handbook of Amazonian Languages, vol. i*. Berlin: Mouton de Gruyter, 567–642.

—— (1999). 'Small language families and isolates in Peru', in R. M. W. Dixon and A. Aikhenvald (eds.), *The Amazonian Languages*. Cambridge: Cambridge University Press, 307–40.

WIVELL, RICHARD (1981). 'Kairiru grammar'. University of Auckland Ph.D. thesis.

WURM, S. A. (1972). *Papuan Languages of Oceania*. Tübingen: Narr.

—— (1974). 'The Kiwaian language family', in Karl Franklin (ed.), *The Linguistic Situation in the Gulf District and Adjacent Areas, Papua New Guinea*. (Pacific Linguistics C-26). Canberra: Australian National University, 217–60.

—— and LOUISE A. HERCUS (1976). 'Tense-marking in Guu pronouns', in J. F. Kirton et al. (eds.), *Papers in Australian Linguistics* 10. (Pacific Linguistics A-47) Canberra: Australian National University, 33–5.

XELIMSKIJ, E. A. (1993). 'Matorsko-Tajgijsko-Karagasskij jazyk', [The Mator-Taigi-Karagas language], in J. S. Eliseev et al. (eds.), *Jazyki mira: Ural'skie jazyki*. Moscow: Indrik, 372–9.

XOŽIEV, A. (1966). *Uzbek tilida kumakči fe"llar* [Auxiliary verbs in Uzbek]. Tashkent: Fan.

YADAV, RAMAWATAR (1996). *A Reference Grammar of Maithili*. (Trends in Linguistics: Documentation 11) Berlin: Mouton de Gruyter.

YALLOP, COLIN (1977). *Alyawarra: An Aboriginal Language of Central Australia*. (Australian Aboriginal Studies Research and Regional Studies 10) Canberra: Australian Institute of Aboriginal Studies.

YARAPEA, APOI (1993). 'Kewapi verbal morphology and semantics', *Languages and Linguistics in Melanesia* 24: 95–110.

YIGEZU, MOGES, and GERRIT J. DIMMENDAAL (1998). 'Notes on Baale', in Gerrit J. Dimmendaal and Marco Last (eds.), *Surmic Languages and Cultures*. (Nilo-Saharan Linguistic Analyses and Documentation 13) Cologne: Köppe, 273–317.

YOUNG, PHILIP D., and TALMY GIVÓN (1991). 'The puzzle of Ngäbére auxiliaries: grammatical reconstruction in Chibchan and Misumalpan', in W. Croft, K. Denning, and S. Kemmer (eds.), *Studies in Typology and Diachrony for Joseph H. Greenberg*. (Typological Studies in Language 20) Amsterdam: Benjamins 209–43.

YOUNG, ROBERT A. (1964). 'The primary verb in Bena-Bena', in *Verb Studies in Five New Guinea Languages*. Norman, Okla.: Summer Institute of Linguistics, 45–83.

YRIZAR, PEDRO DE (1991). *Morfología del verbo auxiliar guipuzcoano: estudio dialectológico*. Kutxa (Bilbao): Euskaltzaindia.

—— (1992). *Morfología del verbo auxiliar vizcaino: estudio dialectológico*. Kutxa (Bilbao): Euskaltzaindia.

YUE, ANNE O. (2003). 'Chinese dialects: grammar', in Thurgood and La Polla (2003: 84–125).

ZAMPONI, RAOUL (2003). *Betoi*. (Languages of the World/Materials) Munich: Lincom Europa.

ZEPEDA, OFELIA (1983). *A Papago Grammar*. Tucson: University of Arizona Press.

Z'GRAGGEN, J. A. (1971). *Classificatory and Typological Studies in Languages of the Madang District*. (Pacific Linguistics C-19) Canberra: Australian National University.

ZIDE, A. (1983). 'The story of two girls (excerpt from a Juray text)', *International Journal of Dravidian Linguistics* 12(1): 109–11.

—— (1997). 'Gutob pronominal clitics and related phenomena elsewhere in Gutob-Remo-Gta?', in A. Abbi (ed.), *Languages of Tribal and Indigenous Peoples of India*. Delhi: Motilal Banarsidass, 307–34.

ZIDE, N. H. (n.d.) *Gutob Texts*. Unpublished MS.

ZIERVOGEL, D. (1952). *A Grammar of Swazi*. Johannesburg: Witwatersrand University.

—— (1959). *A Grammar of Northern Transvaal Ndebele*. Pretoria: Van Schaik.

—— and R. S. DAU (1961). *Handbook of the Venda Language*. Pretoria: University of South Africa.

—— and E. J. MABUZA (1976). *A Grammar of the Swati Language (Siswati)*. Pretoria: van Schaik.

ZIMMERMANN, WOLFGANG, and PAAVO HASHEELA (1998). *Oshikwanyama Grammar*. Windhoek: Gamsberg Macmillan.

ZUÑIGA, FERNANDO (2000). *Mapudungun*. (Languages of the World/Materials 376) Munich: Lincom Europa.

ŽUKOVA, A. N. (1980). *Jazyk palanskix korjakov*. Leningrad: Nauka.

ZWICKY, ARNOLD (1985). 'Heads', *Journal of Linguistics* 21: 1–30.

—— (1990). 'What are we talking about when we talk about serial verbs?', in Brian Joseph and Arnold Zwicky (eds.), *When Verbs Collide*. Columbus: Ohio State University Press, 1–13.

—— (1993). 'Heads, bases, and functors', in Greville Corbett, Norman M. Fraser, and Scott McGlashan (eds.), *Heads in Grammatical Theory*. Cambridge: Cambridge University Press, 292–315.

Subject Index

Language Index

Languages cited in Text

Other Languages in database

Abkhaz

Acehnese

Achuar

Ader Hausa

Aghem

Ägiwo

Ainu Saru

Amele

Amur Nivkh

Andoke

Apinajé

Arabana-Wangkangurru

Araki

Archaic Hungarian

Awa

Awa-Kwaiker

Banoni

Baraba Tatar

Bari

Bassa

Bauzi

Bella Coola

Bel'tir

Bété

Bhumij

Bora

Borobo

Botin

Burmese

Bwe Karen

Callahuaya

Car

Central Tagbanwa

Chaha Gurage

Chamacoco

Chayahuita

Chipaya